T0156079

Pivotal Certified Professional Core Spring 5 Developer Exam

A Study Guide Using Spring Framework 5

Second Edition

Iuliana Cosmina

Apress®

Pivotal Certified Professional Core Spring 5 Developer Exam: A Study Guide Using Spring Framework 5

Iuliana Cosmina
Iasi, Sibiu, Romania

ISBN-13 (pbk): 978-1-4842-5135-5
https://doi.org/10.1007/978-1-4842-5136-2

ISBN-13 (electronic): 978-1-4842-5136-2

Managing Director, Apress Media LLC: Welmoed Spahr
Acquisitions Editor: Steve Anglin
Development Editor: Matthew Moodie
Coordinating Editor: Mark Powers

Cover designed by eStudioCalamar

Cover image designed by Raw Pixel (www.rawpixel.com)

Distributed to the book trade worldwide by Springer Science+Business Media New York, 233 Spring Street, 6th Floor, New York, NY 10013. Phone 1-800-SPRINGER, fax (201) 348-4505, e-mail orders-ny@springer-sbm.com, or visit www.springeronline.com. Apress Media, LLC is a California LLC and the sole member (owner) is Springer Science + Business Media Finance Inc (SSBM Finance Inc). SSBM Finance Inc is a **Delaware** corporation.

For information on translations, please e-mail editorial@apress.com; for reprint, paperback, or audio rights, please email bookpermissions@springernature.com.

Apress titles may be purchased in bulk for academic, corporate, or promotional use. eBook versions and licenses are also available for most titles. For more information, reference our Print and eBook Bulk Sales web page at http://www.apress.com/bulk-sales.

Any source code or other supplementary material referenced by the author in this book is available to readers on GitHub via the book's product page, located at www.apress.com/9781484251355. For more detailed information, please visit http://www.apress.com/source-code.

Printed on acid-free paper

To Marian Lopatnic, my oldest friend, my best friend, my rock. Thank you for always lifting me up and for believing in me when I don't.

Table of Contents

vi

About the Author

 **Iuliana Cosmina** is currently a software engineer for Cloudsoft Edinburgh. She has been writing Java code since 2002. She has contributed to various types of applications, including experimental search engines, ERPs, track and trace, and banking. During her career, she has been a teacher, a team leader, a software architect, a DevOps professional, and a software manager. She is a Spring-certified Professional, as defined by Pivotal, the makers of Spring Framework, Boot, and other tools, and considers Spring the best Java framework to work with. When she is not programming, she spends her time reading, blogging, learning to play piano, traveling, hiking, or biking.

You can find some of her personal work on her GitHub account: `https://github.com/iuliana`.

You can find her complete CV on her LinkedIn account: `https://www.linkedin.com/in/iulianacosmina/`.

You can contact her at: `Iuliana.Cosmina@gmail.com`.

About the Technical Reviewer

Manuel Jordan Elera is an autodidactic developer and researcher who enjoys learning new technologies for his own experiments and creating new integrations. Manuel won the Springy Award – Community Champion and Spring Champion 2013. In his free time, he reads the Bible and composes music on his guitar. Manuel is known as dr_pompeii. He has tech reviewed numerous books for Apress, including *Pro Spring Boot 2* (2019), *Rapid Java Persistence and Microservices* (2019), *Java Language Features* (2018), *Spring Boot 2 Recipes* (2018), and *Java APIs, Extensions and Librarie*s (2018). You can read his 13 detailed tutorials about Spring technologies, or contact him, through his blog at www.manueljordanelera.blogspot.com, and follow him on his Twitter account, @dr_pompeii.

Acknowledgments

I cannot believe this book has gotten a second edition! Writing this book has been a challenging experience, because of all the changes the Java world is going through and I couldn't have made this happen without the support of my long time Apress collaborators Mark Powers ans Manuel Jordan. Mark has been very supportive, sharing with me his experience in book writing and making sure everything I needed was in place to finish this book at the established deadline.

Manuel is a great reviewer, I love our exchanges of technical ideas and working together we've both grown professionally and personally.

Many thanks to the team that helped turn my technical verbiage into human-readable literature.

Most of all, I want to thank Steve Anglin for trusting me to get this book done as well.

Apress has published many of the books I have read and used to improve myself professionally during my studies and beyond. It is is a great honour for me to collaborate with one of the most renown technical publishers in the world, and it gives me enormous satisfaction to be able to contribute to the education of the next generation of developers.

I am grateful to all of my friends who had the patience to listen to me complain about sleep loss, having too much work to do, and writer's block. Thank you all for being supportive and making sure I still had some fun while writing this book.

A special thank you to all those that bought the previous edition of this book and contributed with their own corrections and recommendations: Vittorio Marino, Gautham Kurup, Farid Guliyev, Patrick Dobner, Tibor Kalman, Marco Pelucchi and Edward Whiting.

Introduction

More than five years have passed since I wrote my first Spring project, and since then, the Spring Framework has turned into a full-blown technology that provides everything needed to build complex and reliable Java Enterprise applications.

Five major versions of Spring have been released so far, and the sixth is right around the corner. When the first edition of this book conceived, except for the official study guide required for passing the certification exam, there was no additional resource like this. And although Spring has grown in popularity and the internet is full of resources you could choose to learn Spring from, I am very thankful to you for choosing this book.

This study guide provides a complete overview of all the technologies involved in creating a Spring core application from scratch. It guides you, step by step, into the Spring world, covering Spring 5 fundamental building blocks. More advanced topics, such as Reactive programming and microservices, are covered in detail as they have taken over the software industry and might stay for quite a while.

There is a multi-module project called Criminal Evidence Management System, or CEMS, associated with this book; it covers every example presented in the book. As this book was written, Oracle has released Java version 11 and 12, new minor versions of Spring 5 were released, a new version of IntelliJ IDEA was released, and new versions of Gradle were released as well. I upgraded to the new versions in order to provide the most recent information and keep this book synchronized with the official documentation. Some projects in this book use Java Modules, and the sources were tested with Java 12 as well. A group of reviewers has gone over the book, but if you notice any inconsistencies, please send an email to editorial@apress.com, and corrections will be made.

The example source code for this book can be found on GitHub via the **Download Source Code** button on the book's product page, located at `www.apress.com/9781484251355`. It will be maintained, synchronized with new versions of the technologies, and enriched based on the recommendations of the developers using it to learn Spring. The code for the CEMS project will likewise be made available on a public GitHub repository.

An appendix with answers to the questions at the end of every chapter and additional information related to development tools that can be used to develop and run the code samples of the book is now available as part of the book.

I truly hope you will enjoy using this book to learn Spring as much as I enjoyed writing it.

CHAPTER 1

Book Overview

Programming is designing a list of instructions—also known as an *algorithm*—for a computer to execute. Computers are a wonder of technology, but at the present time, they cannot do much without a human mind behind them. Even the most competent AIs have been developed by humans; computers do a lot of things, but thinking is not one of them. There are a lot of programming languages out there, but if you are reading this book, you have already chosen Java. This book will provide you the means to use the most renowned technology: Spring.

Spring continues to be one of the most influential and rapidly growing Java frameworks; it is very practical for building anything, really. Every time a new startup idea is born, if the development language is Java, Spring is the first framework taken into consideration. Spring turned 17 years old on October 1, 2019,[1] and with the support provided by Pivotal and a huge open source community, it will continue to grow over the coming years.

This book covers much of the core functionality from multiple Spring projects, but the emphasis is on the topics for the ones required to pass the Spring Professional certification exam.[2] The topics that are required for the official certification exam are covered in depth, and all the extras are covered succinctly enough to give you a taste and make you curious to learn more.

---

[1]According to Wikipedia, the first version was written by Rod Johnson, who released the framework with the publication of his book *Expert One-on-One J2EE Design and Development* in October 2002: `https://en.wikipedia.org/wiki/Spring_Framework`, but apparently the official birthday of Spring is considered the release date of version 1.0, which is 25th of March 2003: `https://spring.io/blog/ 2019/03/26/this-week-in-spring-happy-15th-birthday-spring-march-26-2019`. So, officially Spring is 15 years old, but in this book, the unofficial and real age of the framework is considered to emphasize its importance in the Java world.

[2]This is the certification page: `https://pivotal.io/training/certification/ spring-professional-certification`

© Iuliana Cosmina 2020
I. Cosmina, *Pivotal Certified Professional Core Spring 5 Developer Exam*,
https://doi.org/10.1007/978-1-4842-5136-2_1

What Is Spring, and Why Should You Be Interested in It?

When a project is built using Java, a great deal of functionality needs to be constructed from scratch. Yet many useful functionalities have already been built and are freely available because of the open source world that we are living in. A long time ago, when the Java world was still quite small, when you were using open source code in a project developed by somebody else and shipped as a *∗ jar*, you would say that you were using a **library**.

The Apache Commons Lang Library,[3] for example, is a single *jar* that provides a host of helper utilities for the java.lang API. When you add this library as a dependency, all classes in it become accessible for use. Even if all you need is a single class, you cannot simply import that into your application; you have to import them all.

As more code is written, a jar can get quite complex and bloated; it becomes cumbersome and inefficient. The people working with it may not need everything it contains. So the contents of a jar can be split and organized into separate *jars*—each with a functionality focused on a certain topic. A collection of jars, more or less decoupled with different purposes, can create a more complex application called a *framework*. From this point of view, *Spring* is definitely a framework, because depending on the type of application you are building, you can choose related collections of jars to declare as dependencies of your application, as you will see further in the book.

There is a lot of hype online over the differences between a library and a framework. There are many valid points, and it's not my place to define a universal truth about it. For me, it is all related to complexity. I consider a library a single jar with classes with clear and simple responsibilities, and no transitive dependencies. I consider a framework to be a family of libraries (more or less related) that can be combined in more than one way, depending on the type of application that you are building. So a framework is complex, but also flexible and more powerful, because some interactions between the components are predefined and supported by the dependency relationships between them.

As frameworks grew, the tools to build projects and add frameworks as dependencies evolved. One of the most widely used tools to build projects is Maven, but new build

---

[3]Apache Commons Lang is used in project attached to the book, mostly because it provides a *NotImplementedException* class. Official site: `https://commons.apache.org/proper/commons-lang/`

tools are now stealing the scene. One of these new-age build tools is used to build the projects in this book. It will be introduced later.

The Spring Framework was released a long time ago as an open source framework and the inversion of a control container developed using Java. As Java evolved, so did Spring. Spring version 5.1.x, the one covered in this book, is supposed to be fully compatible with Java 11, as announced at the SpringOne Platform conference in September 2018; but considering the size of the Spring Framework, chances are that while writing the code for this book, I might have stumbled across some incompatibility bugs.

Spring comes with a great deal of default behavior already implemented. Components called *infrastructure beans* have a default configuration that can be easily customized to fit a project's requirements. Having been built to respect the "convention over configuration" principle, it reduces the number of decisions that a developer has to make when writing code, since the infrastructure beans can create functional basic applications with little or no customization required.

Spring is open source, which means that many talented developers have contributed to it, but the last word on analyzing the quality of the components being developed belongs to the Pivotal Spring Development team, previously known as the SpringSource team, before Pivotal and VMware merged. The full code of the Spring Framework is available to the public on GitHub,[4] and any developer that uses Spring can fork the repositories and propose changes.

A Java application is essentially composed of objects talking to each other. The reason why Spring has gained so much praise in Java application development is because it makes connecting and disconnecting objects easy by providing comprehensive infrastructure support for assembling objects. Using Spring to develop a Java application is like building a lightly connected Lego castle; each object is a Lego piece that you can easily remove and replace with a different one. Spring is currently the VIP of Java frameworks, and if all you have read so far has not managed to make you at least a bit interested in it, then I am doing a really bad job at writing this book, and you should write an email and tell me so.

This is the second edition of this book, and there are considerable differences between Spring 4.x and Spring 5.x. These differences extend to the entire collection of Spring projects. The IT world is changing with incredible speed, and with the full

---

[4]GitHub Spring Framework sources: `https://github.com/spring-projects/spring-framework`.

support of Pivotal, Spring has changed a lot too. So much has changed in these two years that if you bought my previous book because you were interested in Spring, and bought this one just to support me as an author, you will still be able to benefit a lot. Because while preparing the skeleton of the book and going over what was added to and removed from Spring 5 compared to the previous versions, I was mind-blown about the amount of work needed to upgrade this book to Spring 5. Before going any further about this book, let's look at how the Spring project collection has changed over two years.[5]

Figure 1-1 depicts all the Spring projects.

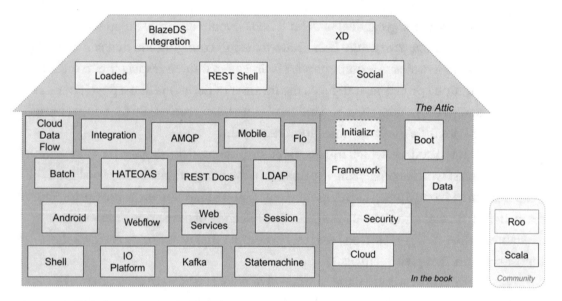

Figure 1-1. *The Spring stack*

At the beginning of 2019, there were twenty-two main projects, two community projects, and five projects "in the attic," so to speak, because they are going to be dropped in the future. Funny enough, three of them were in the same situation when the previous edition of this book was written, which can only mean that "the attic" may not be the place where Spring projects go to die, but where Spring projects end up staying until somebody decides to pick them up and give them a facelift.

I added Spring Initializr as a project because it is practical enough to be covered in this book, but it is not actually a Spring project. It is a Spring utility accessible at `https://start.spring.io/`.

---

[5]The previous edition of this book was released two years ago.

What Is the Focus of This Book?

The topics covered in this book are mostly Spring components for the back-end tier, which are all part of the Spring Framework package. This book aims to provide a natural path in the development of a complete Spring application. With each chapter, the application will become more complex, until its final form is reached. It will have a security setup (a simple web application) and support REST requests. Topics like cloud microservices and Webflux will only be covered lightly because they are not topics for the certification exam.

This book is focused on helping developers understand how Spring's infrastructure was designed and how to write Spring applications in a few easy steps using the maximum of Spring's potential. Its objectives are to provide enough knowledge for a developer to be able to

- use Spring to develop applications

- use Spring Security to secure resources

- use Spring Test and other test frameworks(JUnit, jMock) to test applications

- create Spring applications using Gradle[6]

- create Reactive Spring applications

Who Should Read This Book?

This book was written to provide clear insight into creating applications using Spring core components. It can also be a big help to a developer who wants to become a **Certified Spring Professional**. That is why every topic that is found in the official Pivotal Spring Core study guide is given the attention that it deserves.

---

[6]Gradle is an automated build tool that is easy to configure and use for any type of application. Its build files are written using Groovy, but they can be written in Kotlin as well. Gradle combines the power and flexibility of Ant with the dependency management and conventions of Maven into a more effective way to build. Read more about it at `https://www.gradle.org/`.

You only need a minimal knowledge of Java to make good use of this book, but online documentation for Java[7] and Spring[8] should be consulted every time something is not fully covered in the book.

In a nutshell, this book was written to be used by the following audiences.

- Java developers who want a taste of Spring (You can even be a beginner in Java; this book was made to teach you a little bit about programming and design patterns as well.)

- Spring developers who are interested in learning how to use Spring proficiently, but are not interested in official certification

- Spring and Java developers who want to become certified and want all the help they can get

- Spring developers who want to renew their knowledge or want a crash course in what's new in Spring 5

About the Certification Exam

If you are interested in becoming a **Certified Spring Professional**, the first step is to go to the official Pivotal learning site at `http://pivotal.io/training` and search for the Spring Certification section. There you will find all the information that you need on official training, if you are interested and can afford it, including when and where they take place. The training sessions last four days. But because all Spring official reference documentation is publicly available, and numerous other resources are more affordable (such as this book), two years ago, Pivotal decided that developers should be able to take the exam without taking an official course. The exam voucher cost $225 when this book was written. The required topics are listed on the official site.[9]

---

[7]JSE 11 official reference: `https://docs.oracle.com/en/java/javase/11/`; JEE 8 official documentation: `https://www.oracle.com/technetwork/java/javaee/overview/index.html`.

[8]Spring official Javadoc: `https://docs.spring.io/spring-framework/docs/current/javadoc-api/`; Spring Reference: `https://docs.spring.io/spring-framework/docs/current/spring-framework-reference/`.

[9]Spring Professional Certification official page: `https://pivotal.io/training/certification/spring-professional-certification`

! The exam duration is **90 minutes** and consists of **50 questions**. There are both single- and multiple-answer questions. You are told which is single answer and which is not.

The questions cover the following topics.

- Container (20%)
- AOP (8%)
- JDBC (4%)
- Transactions (8%)
- MVC (8%)
- Security (6%)
- REST (6%)
- JPA Spring Data (4%)
- Testing (4%)
- Boot Into (8%)
- Boot Autoconfig (8%)
- Boot Actuator (8%)
- Boot Testing (8%)

The passing score for the exam is **76%**. This means that **38** correct answers are needed in order to pass. Most of the questions present a piece of Java code or a configuration and ask you what it does, so make sure that you understand the code attached to this book and write your own beans and configurations so that you understand the framework better. If you decide to go to an official training, the good news is that the code samples cover all the topics. If you don't go to a training, this book will be quite handy as well.

Other questions present you with assertions about Spring and require you to select the correct or the invalid statement.

If you read this book, understand all the examples, solve the practice exercises (and/or attend the official training), my recommendation is that you take the certification exam as soon as possible. Do not allow too much time to pass between finishing the book (or taking the training course) and taking the exam, because information can be forgotten. Also, **the certification voucher is valid for only 90 days**. If you fail the exam, you need to buy another voucher.

How to Use This Book as a Study Guide

This book is a step-by-step guide through the wonderful technology that is Spring. It follows the same learning curve as the official training course and focuses on the same topics that are required for the certification exam, which are the most needed in real production applications. The topics that are not needed for the certification exam are marked, so you know that you can skip them; although if you are truly interested in Spring, you will definitely not do that. The official course contains topics like Spring Cloud and Spring Webflux, which are not currently part of the exam, but we can rightly assume that these will be in the future (Spring Boot was an additional topic a few years ago). Aside from the official Spring topics, this book comes with bonuses as well, including a section about Spring using Kotlin, Spring Boot application monitoring, and Spring Data MongoDB.

The main differences are in the tools used for the practical examples, which are covered shortly.

How Is This Book Structured?

This book has 12 chapters and an appendix. The appendix contains answers to quizzes and technical information about the structure and configuration of the project attached to the book. The contents of the book are aligned with the official Pivotal study guide.[10]

The list of chapters and a short description of each are presented in Table 1-1.

---

[10]Just in case things change, you can bookmark this URL `https://pivotal.io/training/certification/spring-professional-certification` and access it from time to time.

Table 1-1. *List of Topics by Chapter*

Chapter	Topic	Description
1	Book overview	Introduction to Spring history, technologies, and tools used for practice
2	Spring LifeCycle and configuration	Fundamental Spring core concepts, components, and configuration and introduction to Spring Boot
3	Testing Spring applications	How Spring applications can be tested, the most-used testing libraries and test principles, testing Spring Boot applications
4	Aspect-oriented programming	AOP concepts, the problems that it solves, and how it is supported in Spring
5	Spring Data access	Advanced Spring Data access using JDBC, Hibernate, Spring Data JPA, and Spring Boot JPA applications and Spring Data MongoDB
6	Spring MVC and the web layer	Basic introduction of Spring MVC, writing a web application using Spring Boot
7	Spring REST	REST with MVC, REST with Boot
8	Spring Security	Authentication, authorization, security filter chain, securing Spring Boot applications
9	Monitoring Spring applications	Monitoring with Spring Boot Actuator and Pivotal tc Server
10	Spring and Kotlin	Nothing more to say here, a union of genius
11	Spring Microservices with Spring Cloud	Introduction to Spring Microservices and what they can be used for
12	Reactive applications using Spring	Webflux: Flux, Mono, WebClient
A	Appendix	Extra technical details, two mock exams, answers to review questions, and other comments

How Each Chapter Is Structured

This introductory chapter covers the basics of Spring that every developer using this book should know: what Spring is, how it has evolved, the official Spring projects, the technologies used to build and run the practical exercises, how you can register for the exam to become a Certified Spring Professional, and so on. This chapter is the exception. It is structured differently from the others, because it was designed to prepare you for what it is coming next.

The remaining chapters are designed to cover several related Spring modules and associated technologies that will help you build a specific type of Spring application. Each chapter is split into a few sections, but most of them follow the same template.

- Basics

- Configuration

- Components

- Summary

- Quick quiz

- Practical exercise

The longer chapters deviate from this structure, introducing small practice exercises after key sections, since solving these exercises will help you to check your understanding and solidify your knowledge of the presented components.

Code that is irrelevant to Spring understanding will not always be quoted in this book, but it is available to you in the book's practice project.

Conventions

The following are some of this book's conventions.

> ! This symbol appears in front of paragraphs to which you should pay particular attention.

> ** This symbol appears in front of a paragraph that is an observation, a metaphor, a fun fact, or an execution step that you can skip.

> ? This symbol appears in front of a question for the user.

... This symbol represents missing code that is not relevant to the example.

CC This symbol appears in front of a paragraph that describes a **convention over configuration** practice in Spring, a default behavior that helps the developer reduce his or her work.

[random text here] Text between square brackets should be replaced with a context-related notion.

Downloading the Code

This book has code examples and practical exercises associated with it. There will be missing pieces of code that you will have to fill in to make applications work and to test your understanding of Spring. I recommend that you go over the code samples and do the exercises, since similar pieces of code and configurations will appear in the certification exam.

There are three ways to get the sources for the book.

- Download the zipped package directly from GitHub.

- Clone the repository on a terminal (or Git Bash Shell in Windows) using the following command.

  ```
  git clone git@github.com:Apress/pivotal-certified-pro-
  spring-dev-exam-02.git
  ```

- Clone the project using IntelliJ IDEA. For this and cloning from the command line, you need a GitHub user.

Contacting the Author

More information about Iuliana Cosmina is at `https://www.linkedin.com/in/iulianacosmina/`. She can be reached at `iuliana.cosmina@gmail.com`.

Follow her personal coding activity at `https://github.com/iuliana`.

Recommended Development Environment

If you decide to take the official course, you will notice that the development environment recommended in this book differs considerably from the one used in the course. A different editor, a different application server, and even a different build tool are recommended. The reason for this is to improve and expand your experience as a developer and to offer a practical development infrastructure. The motivation behind each choice is mentioned in the corresponding sections.

Recommended JVM

Java 11 is the official JVM provided by Oracle. Download the JDK matching your operating system from www.oracle.com and install it.

! I recommend that you set the JAVA_HOME environment variable to point to the directory where Java was installed (the directory in which the JDK was unpacked) and add %JAVA_HOME%\bin for Windows and $JAVA_HOME/bin for Unix-based operating systems to the general path of the system. The reason behind this is to ensure that other development applications written in Java will use this version of Java and prevent strange incompatibility errors during development.

Verify that the version of Java the operating system sees is the one that you just installed by opening a terminal (Command Prompt in Windows, or any type of terminal you have installed on macOS and Linux) and typing the following:

```
java -version
```

You should see something similar to this:

```
java version "11.0.3" 2019-04-16 LTS
Java(TM) SE Runtime Environment 18.9 (build 11.0.3+12-LTS)
Java HotSpot(TM) 64-Bit Server VM 18.9 (build 11.0.3+12-LTS,
mixed mode)
```

Recommended Project Build Tool

Gradle **Grade 5.x** ∗∗ The sources attached to this book can be compiled and executed using the Gradle wrapper, which is a batch script on Windows and a shell script for other operating systems. When you start a Gradle build via the wrapper, Gradle is automatically downloaded and used to run the build; thus, you do not need to install Gradle as stated previously. Instructions on how to do this are at `www.gradle.org/docs/current/userguide/gradle_wrapper.html`.

A good practice is to keep code and build tools separately, which is why this study guide recommends that you have Gradle installed on your system. You can download the Gradle binaries only (or if you are curious, you can download the full package, which contains binaries, sources, and documentation) from their official site (`www.gradle.org`), unpack them, and copy the contents somewhere on the hard drive. Create a `GRADLE_HOME` environment variable and point it to the location where you have unpacked Gradle. Also add `%GRADLE_HOME%\bin` for Windows, or `$GRADLE_HOME/bin` for Unix-based operating systems, to the general path of the system.

Gradle was chosen as a build tool for the sources of this book because of the easy setup, small configuration files, flexibility in defining execution tasks, and the fact that the Pivotal Spring team currently uses it to build Spring projects.

!   Verify that the version of Gradle the operating system sees is the one that you just installed. Open a terminal (Command Prompt in Windows, and any type of terminal you have installed on macOS and Linux) and type

```
gradle -version
```

You should see something similar to this:

```
-------------------------------------------------------------
Gradle 5.5-20190414000043+0000
-------------------------------------------------------------
Build time:   2019-04-14 00:00:43 UTC
Revision:     cd2bc0f4d27b09a9a0df96f46ebdf5ef1d2b95e6
Kotlin:       1.3.21
Groovy:       2.5.4
```

```
Ant:            Apache Ant(TM) version 1.9.13 compiled on
                July 10 2018
JVM:            11.0.3 (Oracle Corporation 11.0.3+12-LTS)
OS:             -- whatever operating system you have --
```

The text displayed is confirmation that Gradle commands can be executed in your terminal; thus, Gradle was installed successfully.

Gradle was used to build the projects in this book because of its simplicity. Gradle is a modern, open source, polyglot, build automation system with configuration files that can be written in Groovy or Kotlin in a very compact way. Compared to the XML Maven configuration files that respect a rigid XML structure, the Gradle configuration files have a flexible structure that is limited only by the knowledge and creativity of the developer.

Recommended IDE

The recommended IDE to use in this study guide is IntelliJ IDEA. The reason for this is that it is the most intelligent Java IDE. IntelliJ IDEA offers outstanding framework-specific coding assistance and productivity-boosting features for Java EE and Spring, and includes support for Maven and Gradle. It is the perfect choice to help you focus on learning Spring; not how to learn to use an IDE. It can be downloaded from the JetBrains official site at www.jetbrains.com/idea/. It is also light on your operating system and quite easy to use.

Since Spring Boot is used to run the web applications in the project attached to the book, you can use the Community Edition to build and solve the TODOs in the project. But if you are looking for a professional experience in development with Java and Spring, you can try working with the Ultimate Edition, which has a trial period of 30 days. The figures with code, launchers, and other IDE-related information were made using the IntelliJ IDEA Ultimate version.

I believe that an IDE should be easy to use and intuitive, so that you can focus on what really matters: the solution you are implementing. But if you are already familiar with a different Java editor, you can use it as long as it supports Gradle.

The Project Sample

The project attached to this book is called the **Criminal Evidence Management System**. It is an application used to manage police criminal evidence for various cases. It is a proof-of-concept application inspired by the CSI series, so it cannot be used as a real application. The example is just complex enough to use a lot of what Spring has to offer, and simple enough for somebody with medium programming knowledge to easily understand and be able to extend the code. The following describes what this little project provides.

- A user should have a secured account to access the application. The following are the types of accounts.

    - VIEWER: The user can query the evidence database to retrieve information.

    - DETECTIVE: The user that can submit evidence, retrieve it for analysis, or return it to the evidence locker.

    - ADMIN: An account with special privileges that can manage other users' activities on the evidence system.

- Evidence has to be linked to a case.

- A case usually has multiple evidence items linked to it.

- Every time a piece of evidence is submitted, retrieved for analysis or returned, a track entry is created that contains the detective accessing the evidence and the reason for him/her to do so.

- A detective can be a lead on a case investigation, but can also be an investigator for another case. Thus, a detective can work on multiple cases at once.

- A detective can have different ranks.

    - TRAINEE: No access to the evidence system

    - JUNIOR: Read access to the evidence system

    - SENIOR: Write access to the evidence system.

- INSPECTOR: Write access to the evidence system and read access to personnel system.

- CHIEF_INSPECTOR: Write access to the evidence system and personnel system.

- Cases can be classified based on their severity as follows.

  - INFRACTION: The smallest of crimes, punishable with community service and/or a fine.

  - MISDEMEANOR: A crime punishable with incarceration for one year or less.

  - FELONY: The most serious crimes.

- Cases can be classified by the investigation status as follows.

  - SUBMITTED: Recently introduced into the system.

  - UNDER_INVESTIGATION: The evidence is being collected; the investigation is in process.

  - IN_COURT: All evidence is submitted, conclusions have been drawn, people have been arrested, and now the lawyers are doing their thing in court.

  - CLOSED: All evidence is archived, the case has been solved; people have been sentenced.

  - DISMISSED: An invalid case that required no investigation.

  - COLD: A case that was in UNDER_INVESTIGATION state for more than 10 years.

- When a case is closed, all evidence is archived.

- Evidence is stored in different storage locations.

The IntelliJ IDEA Ultimate edition can generate a diagram with the relationship between the classes, but also JPA specific relations between entity classes. The core classes of the application and the relationship between them are depicted in Figure 1-2.

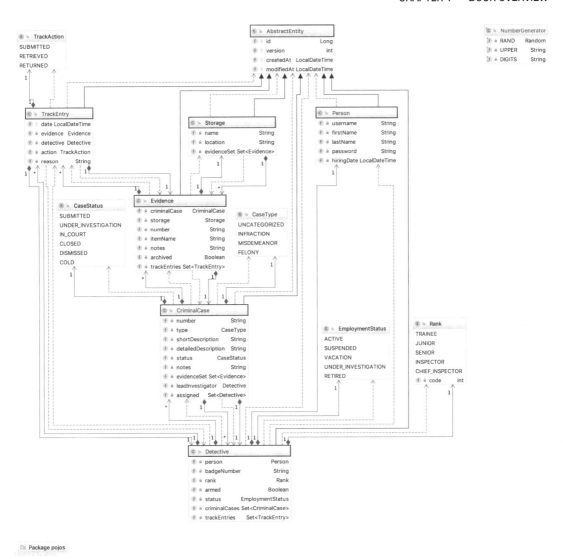

Figure 1-2. *Core classes for the Criminal Evidence Management System*

The classes that are wrapped in dark rectangles in Figure 1-2 are the entity classes and they map to tables in the database. The entities have common fields used by hibernate to identify uniquely each entity instance (`id`) and fields used to audit each entity instance (`createdAt` and `modifiedAt`) and keep track of how many times an entity was modified (`version`). These fields have been grouped in the `AbstractEntity` class to avoid having duplicated code. Other classes are enumerations used to define different types of objects and other utility classes (for conversion and serialization).

The database structure and the foreign keys are depicted in Figure 1-3.

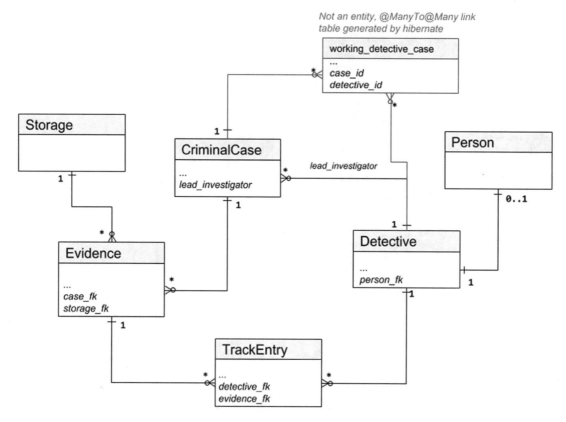

Figure 1-3. *Database structure for the Criminal Evidence Management System*

Figure 1-4 depicts the structure of the **Criminal Evidence Management System** project as it is viewed in IntelliJ IDEA.

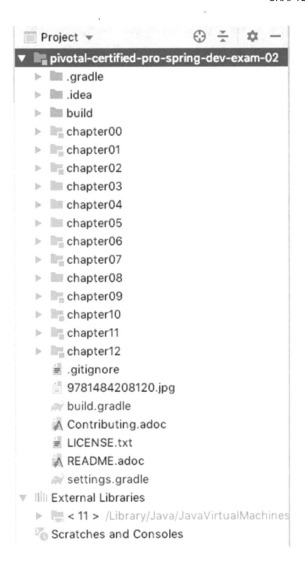

Figure 1-4. *Criminal Evidence Management System project structure*

The project is a hierarchical Gradle multimodule project. Each module name is named as the chapter the sources are meant to be used with. The chapter modules have submodules which match specific sections of the chapter in case this is needed. The projects suffixed with `practice` are missing pieces of code and configuration and are the ones that need to be solved by you to test your understanding of the Spring Framework. The projects without the suffix are a proposed resolution for the tasks. Some projects are suffixed with `sample` to tell you that they contain a sample of code or configuration that you are to analyze and pay special attention to.

The **chapter00** project contains the entity classes that map in database tables, enumerations, and other utility classes that are referenced from other modules. This is the core project; the base tier. The other projects are implementation of service tiers that are built upon it.

The **Criminal Evidence Management System** was designed with the multitier architecture in mind. The abstract internal layer structure is depicted in Figure 1-5.

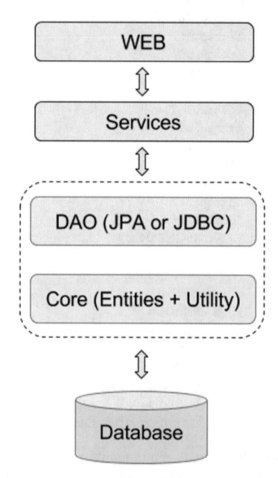

Figure 1-5. *Criminal Evidence Management System application layers*

The UML diagram in Figure 1-6 describes the general functionality of the application. The *Request Dispatcher* and *Controller* are part of the web tier and are included here because some subprojects also have a simple web tier in place, and basic notions of Spring Web are part of the certification exam.

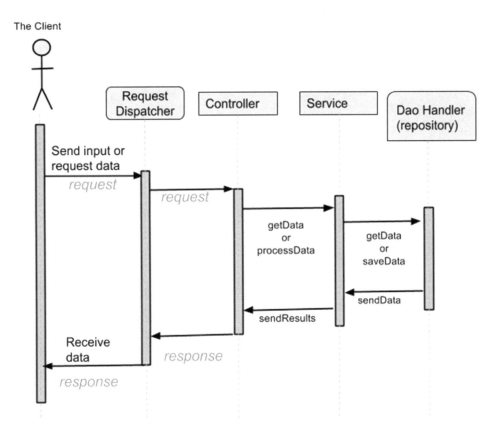

Figure 1-6. *UML diagram describing the general behavior of the Criminal Evidence Management System project*

This chapter does not have any practice and sample code attached to it, so more information regarding the setup of the project and the way that it is built and executed is provided in the upcoming chapters.

CHAPTER 2

Spring Bean Lifecycle and Configuration

The Spring Framework provides an easy way to create, initialize, and connect software components into practical, decoupled, easy-to-test, enterprise-ready applications. Every software application consists of software components that interact, collaborate, and depend on other components to successfully execute a set of tasks. The relationships between components are established during the design phase, and linking dependents with their dependencies is called *dependency injection*. Spring provides a very simplistic way to define the connections between them to create an application.

Before Spring entered the picture, defining connections between classes and composing them required development to be done by following different design patterns, including *Factory, Abstract Factory, Singleton, Builder, Decorator, Proxy, Service Locator,* and Reflection[1] (which is not an option in Java 9+ unless the module is configured to support it).

Spring was built to make dependency injection easy. This software design pattern implies that dependent components delegate the dependency resolution to an external service that will take care of injecting the dependencies. The dependent component is not allowed to call the injector service and has very little to say when it comes to the dependencies that will be injected. This is why the behavior is also known as the *"Don't call us, we'll call you!"* principle, and it is technically known as *inversion of control (IoC)*. If you do a quick Google search, you will find a lot of conflicting opinions about dependency injection and inversion of control. You will find programming articles calling them programming techniques, programming principles, and design patterns.

---

[1] If you are interested in more books about Java Design Patterns, you can check out this book from Apress: https://www.apress.com/gp/book/9781484240779.

23

© Iuliana Cosmina 2020
I. Cosmina, *Pivotal Certified Professional Core Spring 5 Developer Exam*,
https://doi.org/10.1007/978-1-4842-5136-2_2

I recommend an article by Martin Fowler (see `https://martinfowler.com/articles/injection.html#InversionOfControl`), which is recognized in the Java world as the highest authority when it comes to design patterns. If you do not have the time to read it, here is a summary: *Inversion of control is a common characteristic of frameworks that facilitate injection of dependencies. And the basic idea of the dependency injection pattern is to have a separate object that injects dependencies with the required* **behavior***, based on an interface contract.*

The software components that Spring uses to build applications are called *beans*, which are *Plain Old Java Objects* (POJOs) that are created, assembled (dependencies are injected), initialized, and managed by the Spring *IoC* container and located in the Spring application context. The order of these operations and the relationships between objects are provided to the Spring IoC container using XML configuration files prior to Spring version 2.5. Starting with 2.5, a small set of annotations was added for configuring beans, and with Spring 3, Java configuration was introduced, and a Spring application could be configured without any XML needed at all. In Spring 4, even more configuration annotations were introduced, most of them specialized for an application type (e.g., JPA, WEB), as if the intention was to remove the need for XML configuration completely, which eventually happened in Spring 5.

This chapter covers everything a developer needs to know to configure a basic Spring application using Java configuration. A few code samples using XML configuration are covered just to give you an idea of the evolution of the Spring configuration style. From now on, each chapter contains a section that covers how to configure a project with Spring Boot. Spring Boot is a project that makes it very practical to create stand-alone, production-grade, Spring-based applications that you can "just run," reducing a developer's effort when configuring an application.

When configuring Spring applications, there are typical groups of infrastructure beans that have to be configured in a certain way, depending on the application we are building. After years of Spring applications being built, a pattern of configuration has emerged. When the same configuration is used in 90% of the applications written, this makes a good case for favoring *convention over configuration*. This is a software design paradigm used by software frameworks; it attempts to decrease the number of decisions that a developer using the framework is required to make without necessarily losing flexibility. **Spring Boot is the epitome of convention over configuration**.

Old-Style Application Development

In the most competent development style, a Java application should be composed of POJOs—simple Java objects, each with a single responsibility. In the previous chapter, the entity classes that will be used throughout the book were introduced along with the relationships between them. To manage this type of object at the lowest level, the *DAO (repository) layer* of the application—classes called *repositories*, will be used. The purpose of these classes is to retrieve, update, create, and delete entities from the storage support, which usually is some type of database.

In the code for this book, the names of the *repositories* are created by concatenating a short denomination for the type of entity management, the name of the entity object being managed, and the *Repo* postfix. For example, a class managing Person entities should be named PersonRepo. Each class implements a simple interface that defines the methods to be implemented to provide the desired behavior for that entity type. All interfaces extend a common interface declaring the common methods that should be implemented for any type of entity. For example, saving, searching by ID, and deleting should be supported for every type of entity. This method of development is used because Java is a very object-oriented programming language, and in this case, the inheritance principle is very well respected. Also, generic types make possible such a level of inheritance.

In Figure 2-1, the *AbstractRepo* interface and the child interfaces for each entity type are depicted. You can see how the *AbstractRepo* interface defines typical method skeletons for every entity type, and the child interface defines the method skeletons designed to work with only a specific type of entity.

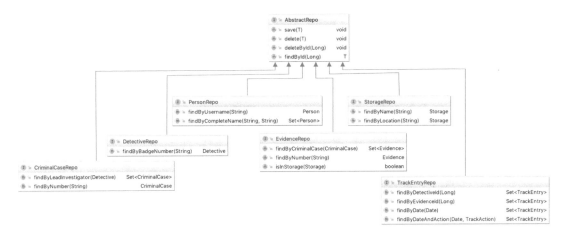

Figure 2-1. *Repository interfaces hierarchy*

At the end of this section, you can take a break from reading to get comfortable with this implementation. The project is named pojos-practice, and you can find it under chapter02. It contains stub[2] implementations for the repository classes, which can be found in the test sources under the com.apress.cems.pojos.repos.stub package. In Figure 2-2, the stub classes are depicted. Again, inheritance was used to reduce the amount of code and avoid writing duplicate code.

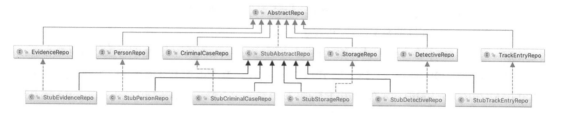

Figure 2-2. *Repository stub implementations*

The stub repositories store all the data created by the user in a map data structure named records. The unique ID for each record is generated based on the size of this map. The implementation is in the StubAbstractRepo class, which is depicted as follows with all the basic repository operations.

```
package com.apress.cems.pojos.repos.stub;

import com.apress.cems.dao.AbstractEntity;
import com.apress.cems.pojos.repos.AbstractRepo;

import java.util.HashMap;
import java.util.Map;

public abstract class StubAbstractRepo <T extends AbstractEntity>
        implements AbstractRepo<T> {

    protected Map<Long, T> records = new HashMap<>();

    @Override
    public void save(T entity) {
        if (entity.getId() == null) {
```

---

[2]In software development a stub is a piece of code used to stand in for actual functionality to help test another desired functionality in isolation.

```java
        Long id = (long) records.size() + 1;
        entity.setId(id);
    }
    records.put(entity.getId(), entity);
}

@Override
public void delete(T entity) {
    records.remove(entity.getId());
}

@Override
public void deleteById(Long entityId) {
    records.remove(entityId);
}

@Override
public T findById(Long entityId) {
    return records.get(entityId);
}
}
```

The next layer after the DAO (repository) layer is the *service layer*. This layer is composed of classes doing modifications to the entity objects before being passed on to the repositories for persisting the changes to the storage support (database). The service layer is the bridge between the web layer and the DAO layer and will be the main focus of the book. It is composed of specialized classes that work together to implement behavior that is not specific to web or data access. It is also called *the business layer*, because most of the application business logic is implemented here. Each service class implements an interface that defines the methods that it must implement to provide the desired behavior. Each service class uses one or more repository fields to manage entity objects. Typically, for each entity type, a service class also exists, but more complex services can be defined that can use multiple entity types to perform complex tasks. In the code for this book, a complex service class is the SimpleOperationsService, which contains methods useful for executing common operations such as create a CriminalCase record, assign a lead investigator to it, link the evidence, and solve the case.

In Figure 2-3, all the service classes and interfaces are depicted.

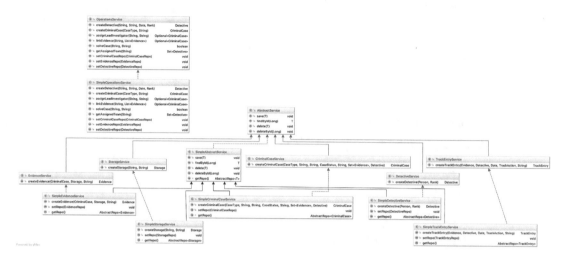

Figure 2-3. *Service interfaces and implementations*

All the classes presented here are parts that will be assembled to create an application that will manage criminal cases data. In a production environment, a service class needs to be instantiated, and a repository instance must be set for it so data can be managed properly. Applications running in production support complex operations such as transactions, security, messaging, remote access, and caching. To test them, pieces of them have to be isolated, and some of them that are not the object of testing are replaced with simplified implementations. In a test environment, stub or mock[3] implementations can replace implementations that are not meant to be covered by the testing process. In Figure 2-4, you can see a service class and a dependency needed for it in a production and test environment side by side.

---

[3]In object-oriented programming, mock objects are simulated objects that mimic the behavior of real objects in controlled ways.

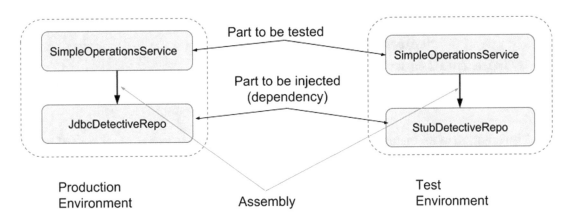

Figure 2-4. *Service class and its dependency in different running environments*

Both JdbcDetectiveRepo and StubDetectiveRepo classes implement the same interface, named DetectiveRepo.

This is practical because the interface type can be used when declaring references so that concrete implementations can be easily swapped one with another. The code snippet relevant to the previous image is depicted as follows, which is a piece of the SimpleOperationsService class definition.

```
package com.apress.cems.pojos.services.impl;

import com.apress.cems.pojos.repos.DetectiveRepo;

public class SimpleOperationsService
    implements OperationsService {

    private DetectiveRepo detectiveRepo;
    ...

    public void setDetectiveRepo(DetectiveRepo detectiveRepo) {
        detectiveRepo = detectiveRepo;
    }
}
```

The dependency is defined using the interface type, DetectiveRepo interface, so any implementation is a suitable dependency. So in a production environment, an instance of type JdbcDetectiveRepo will be provided, and that type will be defined to implement the DetectiveRepo interface.

```
public class JdbcDetectiveRepo extends JdbcAbstractRepo<Detective>
                implements DetectiveRepo {
    //implementation not relevant at this point
...
}
```

The creation of an instance of type `SimpleOperationsService` requires the following steps.

1. Instantiate and initialize the repository instance.

    ```
    DetectiveRepo detectiveRepo = new JdbcDetectiveRepo(...);
    ```

2. Instantiate the service class.

    ```
    OperationsService service = new SimpleOperationsService();
    ```

3. Inject the dependency.

    ```
    service.setDetectiveRepo(detectiveRepo);
    ```

In a test environment, a mock or a stub will do, as long as it implements the same interface.

```
public class StubDetectiveRepo extends StubAbstractRepo<Detective>
            implements DetectiveRepo {
    //implementation not relevant at this point
...
}
```

For the test environment, the assembly steps are the same.

```
1.    DetectiveRepo detectiveRepo = new StubDetectiveRepo(...);
2.    OperationsService service = new SimpleOperationsService();
3.    service.setDetectiveRepo(detectiveRepo);
```

Spring makes assembling the components a very pleasant job. Swapping them (depending on the environment) is also possible in a practical manner, which is supported by the fact that the two types are linked together by implementing the same interface. Because connecting components is so easy, writing tests becomes a breeze also, since each part can be isolated from the others and tested without any unknown influence. Spring provides support for writing tests via the spring-test.jar library, but that will be the topic of Chapter 3.

And now that you know what Spring can help you with, you are invited to have a taste of how things are done without it. Take a look at the pojo-practice project. In the SimpleOperationsService class, there is a method named createResponse that needs an implementation. The following are the steps to create a CriminalCase instance.

1. Retrieve the Detective instance using detectiveRepo.

2. Save the Evidence instance collection using evidenceRepo and retrieve Storage instances using storageRepo.

3. Instantiate a CriminalCase instance.

4. Populate the CriminalCase instance.

   a. Set the shortDescription property.

   b. Set the caseType property.

   c. Set the leadInvestigator property to the detective instance.

   d. Save the CriminalCase instance using the criminalCaseRepo.

   e. Add all Evidence instances to the CriminalCase instance.

   f. Save all Evidence instances using the evidenceRepo.

Figure 2-5 depicts the sequence of operations.

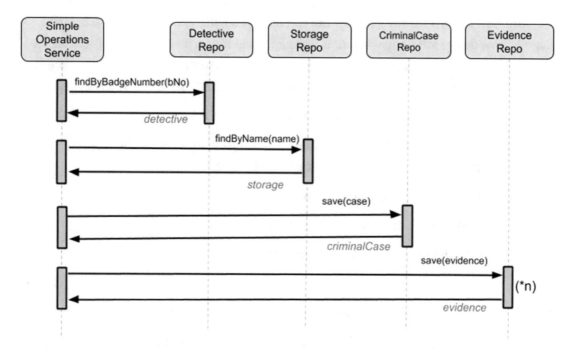

Figure 2-5. *SimpleOperationsService create criminal case abstract functional diagram. The (∗n) stands for multiple calls of a method*

! In this example, because we are assuming pure Java implementation with no frameworks, there is no dependency to handle persistency to the database, so the Evidence instances must be saved explicitly. In a real, complex implementation a persistency framework, such as Hibernate will propagate the save operation from the CriminalCase instance to the Evidence instances linked to it.

Because Java 11 is used, Optional has been declared as a wrapper class for results returned by repository implementations to avoid NullPointerException. You can create a CriminalCase without a lead investigator, because this is a position that can be filled later, so take that into consideration when writing your implementation.

To run the implementation, search for the class com.apress.cems.pojos.services. SimpleOperationsServiceTest under the test directory of the pojo-practice project. Inside this class there is a method annotated with @Test. This is a JUnit annotation. More information about testing tools is covered in Chapter 3. To run a unit test in IntelliJ IDEA,

just right-click the method name, and a menu like the one in Figure 2-6 is displayed.
Select the Run option to run the test. Select Debug if you want to run the test in debug
mode and check field values.

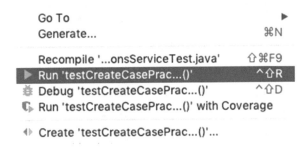

Figure 2-6. *JUnit test contextual menu in IntelliJ IDEA*

If the implementation is not correct, the test will fail, and in the IntelliJ IDEA console
you should see something similar to what is depicted in Figure 2-7. And yes, a lot of
messages written in red is a clear sign that the test failed.

Figure 2-7. *JUnit test failure in IntelliJ IDEA*

If the implementation is correct, the test will pass, and there will not be much red in
the IntelliJ IDEA console, exactly as depicted in Figure 2-8.

Figure 2-8. *JUnit test passed in IntelliJ IDEA*

You can check the solution by comparing it with the proposed code from the chapter02/pojos project.

Spring IoC Container and Dependency Injection

The Spring Framework IoC component is the nucleus of the framework. It uses dependency injection to assemble Spring-provided (also called infrastructure components) and development-provided components to rapidly wrap up an application. Figure 2-9 depicts where the Spring IoC container fits in the application development process; the option of providing configurations using XML is kept because it is still supported.

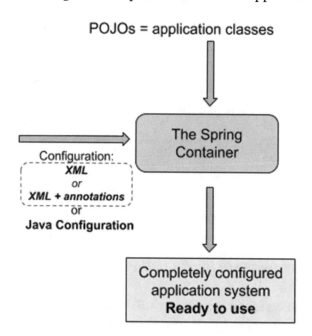

Figure 2-9. Spring IoC Container purpose

So, the Spring IoC container is tasked with the responsibility of connecting beans together to build a working application and it does so by reading a configuration provided by the developer. The Spring IoC container is thus an external authority that passes a dependency to a dependent object that will use it. Providing dependencies, a process called *injection*, happens at runtime, when the application is being put together after being compiled, and this allows a lot of flexibility, because the functionality of an application can be extended by modifying an external configuration without a full recompile of the application.

> **!**   For example, some parameter values can be declared into files with the
> `*.properties` extension, which are not packaged into the application, but their
> location can be provided when the application starts. This allows those files to be
> modified, and reloaded while the application is running. If those values happen to
> specify concrete types to be injected, they will require an application context restart.

Having an external responsible for injecting dependencies allows very loosely coupled applications to be built. And since low coupling often correlates with high cohesion, Spring applications are very easy to navigate through, very easy to test and maintain.

The application being developed over the course of this book includes service classes that are built using repository instances. For example, this is how a `DetectiveService` implementation can be defined.

```
public class SimpleDetectiveService extends SimpleAbstractService<Detective>
               implements DetectiveService {
    private DetectiveRepo repo;

    public SimpleDetecitveService(DetectiveRepo detectiveRepo) {
        this.repo = detectiveRepo;
    }
    ...
}
```

As you can see, the dependency is injected using a constructor, so creating the service instance requires a repository instance to be provided as a parameter. The repository instance is needed to retrieve and persist `Detective` objects in the database. The repository can be defined like the following.

```
import javax.sql.DataSource;

public class JdbcDetectiveRepo extends JdbcAbstractRepo<Detective>
      implements DetectiveRepo  {

    public JdbcDetectiveRepo(DataSource dataSource) {
        super(dataSource);
    }
    ...
}
```

```
//JdbcAbstractRepo.java contains common
//implementation for all repository classes
import javax.sql.DataSource;

public class JdbcAbstractRepo<T extends AbstractEntity>
      implements AbstractRepo<T> {
    protected DataSource dataSource;

    public JdbcAbstractRepo(DataSource dataSource) {
        this.dataSource = dataSource;
    }

    @Override
    public void save(T entity) {...}

    @Override
    public void delete(T entity) {... }

    @Override
    public void deleteById(Long entityId) {...}

    @Override
    public T findById(Long entityId) {...}
}
```

A repository instance requires a DataSource instance to be injected into it, which is used to connect to the database.

The Spring IoC container decides how to create these objects and how to link them together based on the configuration.

Although XML is no longer a topic for the Spring certification exam, the next section will cover a basic Spring XML configuration file, just to give you an idea of how things used to be done before Spring 5.

Providing Configuration via XML Files

The configuration in Figure 2-10 depicts the contents and template of an XML Spring Configuration file used to define the components that will make up the application. The beans that are being injected into other beans and their locations are made obvious by the dotted red arrows.[4]

```xml
<?xml version="1.0" encoding="UTF-8"?>
<beans xmlns="http://www.springframework.org/schema/beans"
      xmlns:xsi="http://www.w3.org/2001/XMLSchema-instance"
      xsi:schemaLocation="http://www.springframework.org/schema/beans
       http://www.springframework.org/schema/beans/spring-beans.xsd">

    <bean id="simpleDetectiveService"
            class="com.apress.cems.pojos.services.impl.SimpleDetectiveService">
        <property name="repo" ref="detectiveRepo"/>
    </bean>

    <bean id="detectiveRepo" class="com.apress.cems.xml.repos.impl.JdbcDetectiveRepo">
        <property name="dataSource" ref="dataSource"/>
    </bean>

    <bean id="dataSource" class="oracle.jdbc.pool.OracleDataSource">
        <property name="URL" value="jdbc:oracle:thin:@localhost:1521:xe"/>
        <property name="user" value="prod"/>
        <property name="password" value="prod"/>
        <property name="loginTimeout" value="300"/>
    </bean>
</beans>
```

Figure 2-10. *Application context and the beans managed by it*

The XML file is usually placed in the project directory under `src/main/resources/spring`. The name is not mandatory, and you can use any name you wish, or no directory at all, Spring configuration can be located directly under the `resources` directory if you so desire. The `spring` directory tells you that files under it are Spring configuration files, because an application can have more XML configuration files for other purposes

---

[4]Oracle was used for data storage in this example because most production applications use Oracle for storage, and this book aims to provide real configurations such as you will probably encounter and need while working in software development. If you want to try this configuration, you can do so for a better understanding of Spring. A README file is provided in the project to instruct how to install Docker and use Oracle in a Docker container to avoid installing Oracle on your machine, because we all know how much of a pain that is.

(configuring other infrastructure components like Hibernate, configuring caching with Ehcache, logging, etc.). All the beans declared in the previous configuration will be used to create an application context.

In the previous example, a lot of information is new for you if you are looking into Spring for the first time. Unfortunately, it is also deprecated (sort of) as the preferred way to configure Spring applications starting with Spring 5 is using Java configuration. But before getting into that, it is important to explain the XML configuration a little. XML configuration is still supported for Spring 5, but the elements available for creating a configuration are specific to Spring 4, no new XML elements (like `<bean ../>`), nor namespaces were added in Spring 5. When writing a Spring XML configuration file, the elements you are allowed to use are defined by special namespaces each containing element definitions grouped by purpose.

The following is a list with the namespaces that you are most likely to find in Spring applications written to use XML configuration files. In Spring 5, everything can be configured using specialized annotations and Java configuration.[5]

- beans: Also known as the core namespace, this is the only configuration needed to create a basic Spring application configuration. All the versions of this namespace are publicly available at `www.springframework.org/schema/beans/`. The most recent is Spring version 4.3. This namespace is the only one used in the previous example, because the configuration is quite simple and does not require anything else.

- context: Defines the configuration elements for the Spring Framework's application context support, basically extends the beans namespace with elements that make configuration more practical to write. All the versions of this namespace are publicly available at `www.springframework.org/schema/context/`.

- util: Provides the developer utility elements, such as elements for declaring beans of `Collection` types, accessing static fields, and so forth. All the versions of this namespace are publicly available at `www.springframework.org/schema/util/`.

---

[5]You can see the full list of namespaces available by accessing this url: `http://www.springframework.org/schema/`

- aop: Provides the elements for declaring aspects. All the versions of this namespace are publicly available at www.springframework.org/schema/aop/.

- jdbc: Provides the elements for declaring embedded databases useful for testing without a full-blown database. All the versions of this namespace are publicly available at www.springframework.org/schema/jdbc/.

- tx: Provides the elements for declaring transactional behavior. All the versions of this namespace are publicly available at www.springframework.org/schema/tx/.

- jee: Provides the elements useful when writing an application that uses JEE components such as EJBs. All the versions of this namespace are publicly available at www.springframework.org/schema/jee/.

- jms: Provides the elements to configure message driven beans. All the versions of this namespace are publicly available at www.springframework.org/schema/jms/.

- mvc: Provides the elements to configure Spring web applications (controllers, interceptors, and view components). All the versions of this namespace are publicly available at www.springframework.org/schema/mvc/.

- security: Provides the elements to configure Secured Spring applications. All the versions of this namespace are publicly available at www.springframework.org/schema/security/.

When writing XML configuration files, it is a recommended practice not to use the version of the namespace in its schemaLocation, so that the version of the namespace will be picked up automatically based on the Spring version on the classpath. In the configuration provided as an example in the chapter02/xml project, the version picked up is declared within the spring-beans.jar found in the classpath. And if you open that jar and look into the spring-beans.xsd file, you will see that the version in the file is Spring 4.3.

An application context is an instance of any type implementing org.springframework.context.ApplicationContext, which is the central interface for providing configuration for a Spring application. The application context will manage all objects instantiated and initialized by the Spring IoC container, which from now on, I will refer to it as beans to get you accustomed to the Spring terminology. The relationship among these objects and the application context is depicted in Figure 2-11 along with their unique identifier.

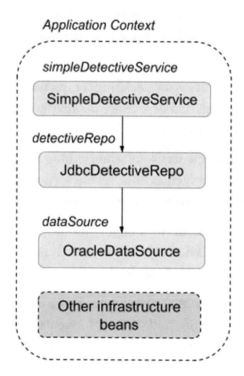

Figure 2-11. *Application context and the beans managed by it*

There are more implementations for the application context provided by Spring, and the one to use depends on the location and the resources containing the configuration. For XML, the class `org.springframework.context.support.ClassPathXmlApplicationContext` is used.

```
//creating the context
(1)ApplicationContext context = new ClassPathXmlApplicationContext
                ("classpath:spring/application-cfg-prod.xml");

// Get the bean to use to invoke the service
(2)DetectiveService detectiveService =
    (DetectiveService)context.get("simpleDetectiveService");
```

```
// create user entity
(3)Detective detective = new Detective();
// populate detective

// invoking the save method of the bean
(4)detectiveService.save(detective);
```

classpath is a common prefix used in Spring applications configured using XML files; it tells the Spring IoC container where the configuration is located. Any path declared with the classpath: prefix is relative to the src/main/resources/ directory. The bean unique identifier in the application context, the bean id was evidentiated by underlining its value to give you a hint as to how the identification of a certain instance is done. More on this topic is covered in the following sections.

Using Java Configuration

The beans definitions that make up a Spring application are provided using XML files, annotations, Java-based Configuration, or all of them together. When Spring 1.0 was released in 2004, it supported only XML as a method of configuration. The annotation concept was not even invented yet.

I remember that the first time I had contact with Spring was in 2006. To a young coder eager to learn to write Java code, writing applications using XML did not seem appealing. As soon as the idea of annotations emerged, Spring adopted it and rapidly provided its own annotations (the stereotypical annotations: @Component and its specializations, @Service and @Repository, etc.) to make configuring Spring applications more practical. This happened in 2007, when Spring 2.5 was released. In this version, XML was still needed. Starting with Spring 3.0 in 2009 and the introduction of Java configuration (annotations @Configuration and @Bean), a configuration method based on annotations placed inside the Java code, XML became expendable. The stereotype annotations and the Java configuration annotations complement each other to provide a practical, non-XML way to define the configuration for a Spring application. XML configuration is still supported because of legacy code and because XML might still be suitable for certain application configurations. Indeed, there are programmers who still prefer to completely decouple all configurations from the code. Small XML configuration snippets can still be found in the official Spring Reference Documentation, and if you have any questions unanswered by this book, you can look for the answers there.[6]

---

[6]Official Spring Reference Documentation here: https://docs.spring.io/spring/docs/ current/spring-framework-reference/

In this section, all aspects of configuration and dependency injection types will be covered, so get yourself a big cup of coffee (or tea) and start reading.

For developer bean definitions to be discovered and created by the Spring IoC container, many Spring-provided beans (the infrastructure beans) must be created too. That is why a few core Spring modules must be added as dependencies to your project.

- `spring-core`: The fundamental parts of the Spring Framework, basic utility classes, interfaces, and enums that all other Spring libraries depend on.

- `spring-beans`: Together with `spring-core` provide the core components of the framework, including the Spring IoC container and dependency Injection features.

- `spring-context`: Expands the functionality of the previous two, and it contains components that help build and use an application context. The `ApplicationContext` interface is part of this module, being the interface that every application context class implements.

- `spring-context-support`: Provides support for integration with third-party libraries; for example, Quartz, FreeMarker, and a few more.

- `spring-expressions`: Provides a powerful expression language (Spring Expression Language, also known as SpEL) used for querying and manipulating objects at runtime; for example, properties can be read from external sources decided at runtime and used to initialize beans. But this language is quite powerful, since it also supports logical and mathematical operations, accessing arrays, and manipulating collections.

But you do not need to bother that much with the libraries required in your classpath, as everything has been taken care of for you. The project attached to this book is a Gradle multimodule project with configuration files that are very easy to read and easy to customize to your personal projects. Also, since we are using Java 11, each module of the project has its own `module-info.java` configuration files, containing all required module configurations. Mentions of specific module configurations appear in the book, so you might want to take a look at the module configuration files, even if they are not a topic for the exam.

Let's start with an overview of the annotations used in this book and in the code attached to it.

The Annotations

The core annotation in Spring is the `@Component` from the `org.springframework.stereotype` package. This annotation marks a class from which a bean will be created. Such classes are automatically picked up using annotation-based configuration (classes annotated with `@Configuration`) and classpath scanning (enabled by annotating a configuration class with `@ComponentScan`). In Figure 2-12, the most important annotations used in this book are depicted and are grouped by their purpose. (Spring Boot annotations are not part of this diagram).

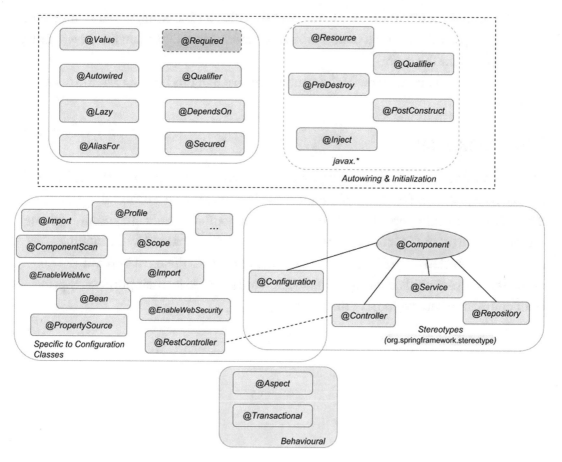

Figure 2-12. *Most important annotations used in this book*

- Stereotype annotations are used to mark classes according to their purpose.

  - @Component: template for any Spring-managed component(bean).

  - @Repository: template for a component used to provide data access, specialization of the @Component annotation for the DAO layer.

  - @Service: template for a component that provides service execution, specialization of the @Component annotation for the Service layer.

- @Controller: template for a web component, specialization of the @Component annotation for the web layer.[7]

- @Configuration: configuration class containing bean definitions (methods annotated with @Bean).[8]

- Autowiring and initialization annotations are used to define which dependency is injected and what the bean looks like. For example.

  - @Autowired: core annotation for this group; is used on dependencies to instruct the Spring IoC to take care of injecting them. Can be used on fields, constructors, setters and even methods mentioned in the **Injection Types** section. Use with @Qualifier from Spring to specify name of the bean to inject.

  - @Inject: equivalent annotation to @Autowired from javax.inject package. Use with @Qualifier from javax.inject to specify name of the bean to inject.

  - @Resource: equivalent annotation to @Autowired from javax.annotation package. Provides a name attribute to specify name of the bean to inject.

  - @Required: Spring annotation that marks a dependency as mandatory. It can be used on setter methods, but since Spring 5.1 was deprecated as of in favor of using constructor injection for required settings.

  - @Lazy: dependency will be injected the first time it is used. Although this annotation exists, avoid using it if possible. When a Spring application is started ApplicationContext implementations

---

[7]The *@Component, @Repository, @Service,* and *@Controller* are part of the *org.springframework. stereotype* package and are the core annotations for creating beans. You will find them referred in official documentation and in this book as *the stereotype annotations*.

[8]There is quite a controversy regarding if the *@Configuration* annotation is a stereotype annotation or not. According to the Spring Reference Documentation we could consider that *@Configuration* is a marker for any class that fulfils the role or stereotype of a configuration class. *@ComponentScan* is able to detect it according a technical perspective because it has *@Component*, but semantically would have no sense, because a bean of type configuration will rarely be used for anything else than bean declaration. Also, because it is not part of the Spring stereotype package, we could conclude that this annotation is not a stereotype annotation.

eagerly create and configure all singleton beans as part of the
initialization process, this is useful because configuration errors in
the configuration or supporting environment (e.g., database) can
be spotted fast. When @Lazy is being used spotting these errors
might be delayed.

- Annotations that appear only in (and on) classes annotated
  with @Configuration are infrastructure specific; they define the
  configuration resources, the components, and their scope.

- Behavioral annotations are annotations that define behavior of a
  bean. They might as well be named proxy annotations, because they
  involve proxies being created to intercept requests to the beans being
  configured with them.

JSR 250 annotations contained in JDK, package javax.annotations are supported.
Also in Spring 3, support for JSR 330[9] was added, and some Spring annotations
analogous of some annotations in JSR 330. A complete list of the annotations in
each package is depicted in Figure 2-13, and on the right, you can see a few Spring
annotations connected using red lines to the analogous annotations in JSR 330. Most of
the annotations in the JSRs are Java annotations that provide a minimum behavior of the
Spring annotations.

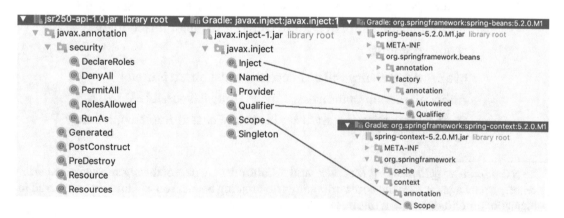

Figure 2-13. *JSR 250 and JSR 330 annotations supported by Spring*

Now that the stars of the book have been introduced, let the show begin!

---

[9]Extension of the Java dependency injection API at https://jcp.org/en/jsr/detail?id=330.

Spring Configuration Classes and the Application Context

The most important annotation when creating Java configuration classes for Spring applications is the @Configuration annotation. Classes annotated with this annotation either contain bean declarations(@Bean) or can be further configured by adding extra annotations (e.g., @Profile, @Scope) to tell the Spring IoC container how the bean declarations can be found.

Any Spring application has at its core one or more configuration classes. These classes either contain bean declarations or are configured to tell the Spring IoC container where to look for bean declarations. Configuration classes can be combined with XML configuration files. These classes can be bootstrapped[10] in many ways, depending on the configuration setup.

The simplest Spring configuration class is just an empty Java class annotated with the @Configuration.

```
package com.apress.cems.beans.simple;
import org.springframework.context.annotation.Configuration;

@Configuration
public class SimpleConfig {
}
```

This class can create the Spring application by creating an application context based on it.

---

[10]Bootstrapping in Spring means loading an application context.

! But before starting Spring applications, we have to enable more detailed logging so we can see what Spring is doing under the hood, because there is no better way to learn and understand Spring than looking at it in action. All applications in the book use Logback as the logging library and in every `resource` directory there is a configuration file named `logback.xml` with the logging configuration for the application. For test modules, which is where all our test classes reside, the configuration file is named `logback-test.xml`. If you open any of these files you might notice the next configuration lines.

```
<logger name="com.apress.cems" level="debug"/>
<logger name="org.springframework" level="trace"/>
```

The first line configures the level of logging for the package where the book sources are. The second line configures the log level for the Spring packages. Logback offers seven levels of logging: OFF, ERROR, WARN, INFO, DEBUG, TRACE, and ALL, which are represented by numeric values in the `ch.qos.logback.classic.Level` enum. ALL, which is the most granular, is associated with `Integer.MIN_VALUE` and enables logging messages of any level. At the other end of the interval is the OFF value, which is associated with `Integer.MAX_VALUE` and disables writing logs. The other values enable writing logs at their specific level. So if you want to add your own code to the project and need to silence the Spring Framework, just change the log setting in the second line to OFF or INFO.

The easiest way to create an application context is to directly initialize it.

```
package com.apress.cems.simple;

import com.apress.cems.config.RepositoryConfig;
import com.apress.cems.config.TestDataSourceConfig;
import org.junit.jupiter.api.Test;
import org.slf4j.Logger;
import org.slf4j.LoggerFactory;
import org.springframework.context.ApplicationContext;
```

```
import org.springframework.context.annotation.
AnnotationConfigApplicationContext;

public class OneSimpleConfigTest {
    private Logger logger = LoggerFactory.getLogger(OneSimpleConfigTest.
    class);

    @Test
    void testSimpleConfiguration() {
        ApplicationContext ctx =
                new AnnotationConfigApplicationContext(SimpleConfig.class);

        for (String beanName : ctx.getBeanDefinitionNames()) {
            logger.info("Bean " + beanName);
        }
    }
}
```

The `org.springframework.context.ApplicationContext` is the interface implemented by classes that provide the configuration for an application. This interface is an extension of the interface `org.springframework.beans.factory.BeanFactory`, which is the root interface for accessing a Spring Bean container. Implementations of `ApplicationContext` manage a number of bean definitions uniquely identified by their name. Multiple Spring application context implementations exist, each one specific to development needs. For example, if the configuration for an application is provided using an XML file the implementation to use to read the bean declarations is `XmlWebApplicationContext` or any of its extensions. You will be introduced to the most important of them in this book. An `ApplicationContext` implementation provides the following.

- Access to beans using bean factory methods

- The ability to load file resources using relative or absolute paths or URLs

- The ability to publish events to registered listeners

- The ability to resolve messages and support internationalization (most used in international web applications)

An application context is created by the Spring IoC container and initialized with a configuration provided by a resource that can be an XML file (or more) or a configuration class (or more) or both. When the resource is provided as a `String` value, the Spring container tries to load the resource based on the prefix of that string value. When instantiating an application context, different classes are used, based on the prefix (see Table 2-1).

Table 2-1. *Prefixes and Corresponding Paths*

Prefix	Location	Comment
no prefix	In root directory where the class creating the context is executed	In the `main` or `test` directory. The resource being loaded has a type that depends on the ApplicationContext instance being used. (A detailed example is presented after the table.)
`classpath:`	The resource should be obtained from the class-path	In the `resources` directory and the resource will be of type ClassPathResource. If the resource is used to create an application context, the `ClassPathXmlApplicationContext` class is suitable.
`file:`	In the absolute location following the prefix	Resource is loaded as a URL, from the filesystem and the resource will be of type UrlResource. If the resource is used to create an application context, the `FileSystemXmlApplicationContext` class is suitable.
`http:`	In the web location following the prefix	Resource is loaded as a URL and the resource will be of type UrlResource. If the resource is used to create an application context, the `WebApplicationContext` class is suitable.

To provide the functionality for loading resources, an application context must implement the `org.springframework.core.io.ResourceLoader` interface. Here is an example of resource loading without using a prefix.

```
Resource template = ctx.getResource("application-config.xml");
```

Depending on the context class used, the resource loaded can have one of the following types.

- If ctx is a ClassPathXmlApplicationContext instance resource type will be ClassPathResource

- If ctx is a FileSystemXmlApplicationContext instance resource type will be FileSystemResource

- If ctx is a WebApplicationContext instance resource type will be ServletContextResource

And this is where prefixes come in. If we want to force the resource type, no matter what context type is used, the resource must be specified using the desired prefix.

An application context can be created based on a configuration class using a corresponding type of implementation of the ApplicationContext interface: the org.springframework.context.annotation.AnnotationConfigApplicationContext class, and exactly this was done in the OneSimpleConfigTest class. The method in that class is not really a test method, we are using it more like a practical way to start up an application. When the testSimpleConfiguration test method is run, a Spring application is started, meaning an application context is created that contains beans declared by the SimpleConfig class. The class is empty in this case, so in the log, you only see a minimal list of infrastructure beans that the Spring IoC container needs to build a Spring application.

```
INFO  c.a.c.s.OneSimpleConfigTest - Bean
  org.springframework.context.annotation.internalConfigurationAnnotationProcessor
INFO  c.a.c.s.OneSimpleConfigTest - Bean
  org.springframework.context.annotation.internalAutowiredAnnotationProcessor
INFO  c.a.c.s.OneSimpleConfigTest - Bean
  org.springframework.context.annotation.internalCommonAnnotationProcessor
INFO  c.a.c.s.OneSimpleConfigTest - Bean
  org.springframework.context.event.internalEventListenerProcessor
INFO  c.a.c.s.OneSimpleConfigTest - Bean
  org.springframework.context.event.internalEventListenerFactory
INFO  c.a.c.s.OneSimpleConfigTest - Bean simpleConfig
```

The @Configuration annotation is a specialization of the @Component annotation, which is the core annotation for creating beans. This means that the configuration class itself is a declaration for a bean, which is why in the previous log, a bean of type SimpleConfig is listed and the name of that bean is the same with the class name with the first letter in lower case.

The configuration classes can have beans declarations inside them. A bean declaration inside a configuration class is any method annotated with @Bean that returns an instance of a class.

```
package com.apress.cems.simple;

import com.apress.cems.beans.ci.SimpleBean;
import com.apress.cems.beans.ci.SimpleBeanImpl;
import org.springframework.context.annotation.Bean;
import org.springframework.context.annotation.Configuration;

@Configuration
public class OneBeanConfig {

    @Bean
    SimpleBean simpleBean(){
        return new SimpleBeanImpl();
    }
}
```

The following is the SimpleBean and SimpleBeanImpl code.

```
// SimpleBean.java
package com.apress.cems.beans.ci;

public interface SimpleBean {
}

// SimpleBeanImpl.java
package com.apress.cems.beans.ci;
import org.slf4j.Logger;
import org.slf4j.LoggerFactory;
import org.springframework.stereotype.Component;
```

```
@Component
public class SimpleBeanImpl implements SimpleBean {

    private Logger logger = LoggerFactory.getLogger(SimpleBeanImpl.class);

    public SimpleBeanImpl() {
        logger.info("[SimpleBeanImpl instantiation]");
    }

    @Override
    public String toString() {
        return "SimpleBeanImpl{ code: " + hashCode() + "}";
    }
}
```

Although inside the simpleBean() method a constructor is called, annotating it with @Bean ensures that once an instance of type SimpleBeanImpl has been created, calling the simpleBean method will always return the same instance. This is because every bean declared in a Spring application is a singleton by default, unless explicitly configured otherwise. This method is being called by the Spring IoC container when the application context is initially created. This is quite easy to test; we just modify the preceding test class, and we use the context instance to access the declared bean.

```
package com.apress.cems.simple;

import com.apress.cems.beans.ci.SimpleBean;
import org.junit.jupiter.api.Assertions;
import org.junit.jupiter.api.Test;
import org.slf4j.Logger;
import org.slf4j.LoggerFactory;
import org.springframework.context.ApplicationContext;
import org.springframework.context.annotation.
AnnotationConfigApplicationContext;
```

```java
public class OneSimpleConfigTest {

    @Test
    void testOneBeanConfiguration() {
        ApplicationContext ctx =
                new AnnotationConfigApplicationContext(OneBeanConfig.class);

        SimpleBean simpleBeanOne = ctx.getBean(SimpleBean.class);
        SimpleBean simpleBeanTwo = ctx.getBean(SimpleBean.class);
        Assertions.assertEquals(simpleBeanTwo, simpleBeanOne);
    }
}
```

In the previous code snippet, the getBean(..) method is called on the context twice and we assume that the two beans that were returned are one and the same.

Beans that depend on simpleBean can be declared in two ways: using the @Autowired annotation (covered later in the chapter) and using the @Bean annotation. The one that is interesting here is when a bean is declared with the @Bean annotation. Let's declare a new bean type named DependentBeanImpl and its interface named DependentBean.

```java
// DependentBean.java
package com.apress.cems.beans.db;

public interface DependentBean {
}
```

```java
// DependentBeanImpl.java
package com.apress.cems.beans.db;

import com.apress.cems.beans.ci.SimpleBean;

public class DependentBeanImpl implements DependentBean {
    private SimpleBean simpleBean;

    public DependentBeanImpl(SimpleBean simpleBean) {
        this.simpleBean = simpleBean;
    }
}
```

To declare a bean of this type in a configuration class, a method named dependentBean() is declared.

```
package com.apress.cems.beans.db;

import com.apress.cems.beans.ci.SimpleBean;
import com.apress.cems.beans.ci.SimpleBeanImpl;
import org.slf4j.Logger;
import org.slf4j.LoggerFactory;
import org.springframework.context.annotation.Bean;
import org.springframework.context.annotation.Configuration;

@Configuration
public class SimpleDependentCfg {
    private Logger logger = LoggerFactory.getLogger(SimpleDependentCfg.
    class);

    @Bean
    SimpleBean simpleBean(){
        logger.info("---> Creating 'simpleBean' ");
        return new SimpleBeanImpl();
    }

    @Bean
    DependentBean dependentBean(){
      return new DependentBeanImpl(simpleBean());
    }
}
```

As you can see, it is annotated with @Bean and it looks like it is calling the simpleBean(). When the application context is created, the Spring IoC intercepts that call. And instead of creating a new instance of SimpleBeanImpl, it returns the one already created. This is done using a mechanism called *proxying*, which you will learn more about in Chapter 4. Without getting too deep into how this is done *under the hood*, the easiest way to test that the simpleBean() is called only once is to add a statement to write a log message when the method is called. To test that the method is called only once, a test method can be written, which even retrieves the simpleDependentCfg() configuration bean and calls the simpleBean() on it.

```
package com.apress.cems.beans.db;

import com.apress.cems.beans.ci.SimpleBean;
import org.junit.jupiter.api.Test;
import org.springframework.context.ConfigurableApplicationContext;
import org.springframework.context.annotation.
AnnotationConfigApplicationContext;

import static org.junit.jupiter.api.Assertions.*;

public class SimpleDependentCfgTest {

    @Test
    void testSimpleBeans() {
        ConfigurableApplicationContext ctx =
            new AnnotationConfigApplicationContext(SimpleDependentCfg.
            class);
        ctx.registerShutdownHook();

        SimpleDependentCfg simpleDependentCfg =
            ctx.getBean(SimpleDependentCfg.class);
        assertNotNull(simpleDependentCfg);

        SimpleBean simpleBean = simpleDependentCfg.simpleBean();
        assertNotNull(simpleBean);
    }
}
```

If logging is turned off for the Spring Framework, the only log messages we expect to see in the console are the one printed by the SimpleBeanImpl constructor and the one printed by the simpleBean() method.

```
14:35:00.785 [main] INFO  c.a.c.b.d.SimpleDependentCfg - ---> Creating
'simpleBean'
14:35:00.788 [main] INFO  c.a.c.b.c.SimpleBeanImpl - [SimpleBeanImpl
instantiation]
```

The beans declarations that are not part of the configuration class are identified using a process named component scanning that is enabled by annotating the configuration class with the @ComponentScan annotation. When used with no attributes, it activates various annotations to be detected in the bean classes in the current package and all subpackages: Spring's @Required and @Autowired, JSR 250's @PostConstruct, @PreDestroy, and @Resource and all stereotype annotations: @Component, @Service, @Repository, @Controller, and @Configuration. Using the @ComponentScan naked (without arguments) is not recommended, because of performance concerns; in a project there will be packages with classes are not configured as bean declarations, so there is no use scanning them. The @ComponentScan annotation can be used with a various list of attributes for filtering and reducing scope of scanning, in the next example, scanning for bean annotations was enabled only for package com.apress.cems.simple.

```
package com.apress.cems.beans.ci;
import org.springframework.context.annotation.Configuration;

@ComponentScan(basePackages =  {"com.apress.cems.simple"})
@Configuration
public class SimpleConfig {
}
```

Let's play with configuration classes a little more. The DataSourceConfig depicted next is a typical Java configuration class, which contains two bean definitions and some properties that are injected from a properties file using the @PropertySource annotation. This annotation provides a convenient and declarative mechanism for adding an org.springframework.core.env.PropertySource instance to the Spring environment. Placeholders like these ${..} present in a class annotated with @PropertySource will be resolved against the set of property sources registered against the environment. In the following code snippet, the @PropertySource annotation receives as argument the location where the properties can be loaded.

```
package com.apress.cems.config;

import org.springframework.beans.factory.annotation.Value;
import org.springframework.context.annotation.Bean;
import org.springframework.context.annotation.Configuration;
import org.springframework.context.annotation.PropertySource;
import org.springframework.context.support.
PropertySourcesPlaceholderConfigurer;
import org.springframework.jdbc.datasource.DriverManagerDataSource;
```

```java
import javax.sql.DataSource;
import java.sql.SQLException;

@Configuration
@PropertySource("classpath:db/test-datasource.properties")
public class TestDataSourceConfig {

    @Value("${db.driverClassName}")
    private String driverClassName;
    @Value("${db.url}")
    private String url;
    @Value("${db.username}")
    private String username;
    @Value("${db.password}")
    private String password;

    @Bean
    public static PropertySourcesPlaceholderConfigurer
        propertySourcesPlaceholderConfigurer() {
        return new PropertySourcesPlaceholderConfigurer();
    }

    @Bean
    public DataSource dataSource() throws SQLException {
        DriverManagerDataSource ds = new DriverManagerDataSource();
        ds.setDriverClassName(driverClassName);
        ds.setUrl(url);
        ds.setUsername(username);
        ds.setPassword(password);
        return ds;
    }
}
```

!   The `propertySourcesPlaceholderConfigurer` bean declaration is done using a static method. The reason for this is so that the bean declaration is picked up when the context is created, earlier than the configuration class annotated with `@Configuration`, and so the property values are added to the Spring environment and become available for injection in the said configuration class, before this class is initialized.

The `@Bean` annotation tells Spring that the result of the annotated method will be a bean that has to be managed by it. The `@Bean` annotation together with the method are treated as a bean definition, and the method name becomes the bean id, so be careful with the method naming. There are more ways to change names, but this topic is covered later in the chapter.

The `@PropertySource` annotation adds a bean of type `PropertySource` to Spring's environment that will be used to read property values from a property file set as argument. The configuration also requires a bean of type `PropertySourcesPlaceholderConfigurer` to replace the placeholders set as arguments for the `@Value` annotated properties.

Spring applications provide a way to access the environment in which the current application is running using a bean of type `org.springframework.core.env.Environment`. This bean models two key aspects of an application environment: *properties* (which will be covered now) and *profiles* (which is covered later). Properties play an important role in all applications because pair of keys and values enable or disable certain capabilities and customize application behavior, most times without the need to recompile the application. Properties may originate from a variety of sources: property files (which have already been introduced), JVM system properties, system environment properties, JNDI, `Properties` instances, `Map` instances, and so forth. The role of the `Environment` bean is to provide a convenient way to declare property sources and inject property values from them where required. In the previous example, the `Environment` bean is not used directly, but resolves the placeholders in the `@Value` annotations under the hood. The same class can be used by injecting the `Environment` infrastructure bean and using it to read the properties from it.

```
package com.apress.cems.config;
...
import org.springframework.core.env.Environment;

@Configuration
@PropertySource("classpath:db/test-datasource.properties")
public class EnvTestDataSourceConfig {

    @Autowired
    Environment environment;

    @Bean
    public static PropertySourcesPlaceholderConfigurer
        propertySourcesPlaceholderConfigurer() {
        return new PropertySourcesPlaceholderConfigurer();
    }

    @Bean
        public DataSource dataSource() {
        DriverManagerDataSource ds = new DriverManagerDataSource();
        ds.setDriverClassName(environment.getProperty("db.
        driverClassName"));
        ds.setUrl(environment.getProperty("db.url"));
        ds.setUsername(environment.getProperty("db.username"));
        ds.setPassword(environment.getProperty("db.password"));
        return ds;
    }
}
```

We've crossed over to bean declarations, and since we are already here, let's introduce the types of dependency injection Spring supports. Beans can be declared in various ways—depending on the way the dependencies are injected. We'll come back to the configuration later in this chapter.

Injection Types

In the preceding configuration, we defined a bean with the `simpleBeanImpl` ID of type `com.apress.cems.beans.ci.SimpleBeanImpl` that has no dependencies. To define a bean with dependencies, we have to decide how those dependencies are injected. Spring supports three types of dependency injection.

- **constructor injection**: The Spring IoC container injects the dependency by providing it as an argument for the constructor

- **setter injection**: The Spring IoC container injects the dependency as an argument for a setter

- **field injection**: The Spring IoC container injects the dependency directly as a value for the field (via reflection and this requires the open directive in the `module-info.java` file)

The central annotation used to declare dependencies in Spring is the `@Autowired` annotation and can be used on fields, constructors, setters, and even methods.[11]

The term `autowire` is the short version for automatic dependency injection. This is possible only in Spring applications using component scanning and stereotype annotations to create beans. The `@Autowire` annotation indicates that Spring should take care of injecting that dependency. This raises an interesting question: how does Spring know what to inject?

Every bean in the application context has a unique identifier. It is the developer's responsibility to name beans accordingly if needed. In XML, this can be done using the `id` or `name` attributes, but when using annotations, the line between the ID and the name is blurred, so in this book, only the name will be referred to as a unique bean identifier. To declare beans, we must annotate classes with stereotype annotations: `@Component` and its specializations: `@Service`, `@Repository`, and `@Controller`.

```
package com.apress.cems.beans.ci;

import org.slf4j.Logger;
import org.slf4j.LoggerFactory;
import org.springframework.stereotype.Component;
```

---

[11]You will see an example of this in Chapter 8.

```
@Component
public class SimpleBeanImpl implements SimpleBean {

    private Logger logger = LoggerFactory.getLogger(SimpleBean.class);

    public SimpleBeanImpl() {
        logger.info("[SimpleBeanImpl instantiation]");
    }

    @Override
    public String toString() {
        return "SimpleBeanImpl{ code: " + hashCode() + "}";
    }
}
```

CC When stereotype annotations are used without any arguments, the responsibility of naming the beans is passed to the Spring container and this guy likes to keep things simple; when doing component scanning and finding classes with stereotype annotations, it creates the beans and just down-cases the first letter of the class names and sets them as the bean names.

That is why in the previous example, the bean name was simpleBeanImpl, because the class name was SimpleBeanImpl.

If you want to rename it, all you have to do is give the name to the @Component annotation (or any of the stereotype annotations) as argument.

```
package com.apress.cems.beans.ci;
```

```
@Component("simple")
public class SimpleBeanImpl implements SimpleBean {
...
}
```

To test that the bean is really named simpleBeanImpl, we can write a test class that creates an application context containing the previous bean, and we use the context reference to call its getBean(..) method to obtain a reference to the bean. This method has more than one version; the version that we are interested now is the one that receives as arguments the bean name and the assumed bean type. The configuration class is named SimpleAppCfg.

```java
package com.apress.cems.beans.ci;

import org.junit.jupiter.api.Test;
import org.springframework.context.ConfigurableApplicationContext;
import org.springframework.context.annotation.
AnnotationConfigApplicationContext;

import static org.junit.jupiter.api.Assertions.*;

class SimpleAppCfgTest {
    @Test
    void testBeanNames() {
        ConfigurableApplicationContext ctx =
            new AnnotationConfigApplicationContext(SimpleAppCfg.class);

        SimpleBean simpleBean = ctx.getBean("simpleBeanImpl", SimpleBean.
        class);
        assertNotNull(simpleBean);
        assertTrue(simpleBean instanceof SimpleBeanImpl);
    }
}
```

If the previous test executes successfully, it means that a bean named
simpleBeanImpl was found in the context and has the expected type. If you want to
see the name that the container assigns to this bean, all you have to do is to print all
the bean names in the context, and look for yours and this can be done by calling
getBeanDefinitionNames() provided by the application context and iterating the
returned results.

```java
ApplicationContext ctx =
    new AnnotationConfigApplicationContext(SimpleAppCfg.class);
for (String beanName : ctx.getBeanDefinitionNames()) {
        logger.info("Bean " + beanName + " of type "
            + ctx.getBean(beanName).getClass().getSimpleName());
 }
```

Aside from other infrastructure beans, here is what we can see in the console.

```
DEBUG AnnotationConfigApplicationContext - Refreshing
..AnnotationConfigApplicationContext
...
INFO   SimpleAppCfgTest - [Bean simpleBeanImpl of type SimpleBeanImpl]
DEBUG AnnotationConfigApplicationContext - Closing
..AnnotationConfigApplicationContext
```

But what if we want a different name for the bean? Not a problem, stereotype annotations can receive a name as argument.

```
package com.apress.cems.beans.ci;
...
@Component("simple")
public class SimpleBeanImpl implements SimpleBean {
...
}
```

By annotating the class `SimpleBeanImpl` with `@Component("simple")` the bean being created is now is named `simple`. But what if, for some reason we need to give multiple names to a bean? Aliases cannot be defined using stereotype annotations, but a request has been made to provide such a feature in 2010 and it is still open, so there is still hope.[12]

It is possible to have multiple names for a bean, but one of them will be the unique identifier and all the other names are just aliases. Declaring aliases using stereotype annotations is not supported at the moment, but it is possible using the @Bean annotation. The caveat of declaring aliases using the @Bean annotation is that the method name will no longer be used as a bean name, only the names declared as values for the `name` attribute in the annotation will be used.

```
package com.apress.cems.beans.naming;
...
@Configuration
public class AliasesCfg {
```

---

[12]If you are interested in this feature, you can follow the evolution of the issue here:
`https://github.com/spring-projects/spring-framework/issues/11402`.

```
    @Bean(name= {"beanOne", "beanTwo"})
    SimpleBean simpleBean(){
        return new SimpleBeanImpl();
    }
}
```

Let's test the assumptions made so far, shall we?

```
package com.apress.cems.beans.naming;
...
public class AliasesCfgTest {

    private Logger logger = LoggerFactory.getLogger(AliasesCfg.class);

    @Test
    void testSimpleBeans() {
        ConfigurableApplicationContext ctx =
            new AnnotationConfigApplicationContext(AliasesCfg.class);

        SimpleBean simpleBean = ctx.getBean("beanOne", SimpleBean.class);
        assertNotNull(simpleBean);
        assertTrue(simpleBean instanceof SimpleBeanImpl);

        SimpleBean simpleBean2 = ctx.getBean("beanTwo", SimpleBean.class);
        assertEquals(simpleBean2, simpleBean);

        // no bean named 'simpleBean'
        assertThrows(NoSuchBeanDefinitionException.class, () -> {
            ctx.getBean("simpleBean", SimpleBean.class);
        });

        ctx.close();
    }
}
```

The previous test, if it passes, proves that there is a bean of type SimpleBeanImpl that can be referred by two names, beanOne and beanTwo, and cannot be referred by simpleBean.

Related to bean naming is the @Description annotation, which was added in Spring 4.x. This annotation adds a description to a bean, which is quite useful when beans are exposed for monitoring pupuses. It can be used with @Bean and

@Component (and its specializations). An example of its usage is depicted in the following code listing.

```
package com.apress.cems.scopes;
import org.springframework.context.annotation.Description;
 ...
@Description("Salary for an employee might change,
      so this is a suitable example for a prototype scoped bean")
@Component
public class Salary {
...
}

// or
package com.apress.cems.beans.db;
 ...
public class SimpleDependentCfg {

    @Description("This bean depends on 'simpleBean'")
    @Bean
    DependentBean dependentBean(){
      return new DependentBeanImpl(simpleBean());
    }
    ...
}
```

!   The Spring convention is to use the standard Java convention for instance field names when naming beans. This means that bean names start with a lowercase letter and are camel-cased from then on. The purpose of good bean naming is to make the configuration quick to read and understand. Also, when using more advance features like AOP, it is useful to apply advice to a set of beans related by name. But if you want to define your own naming configurations, just know that anything goes; special characters are accepted as part of a bean name. Whatever you decide, just keep it consistent in the context of an application.

CC Out of the box, Spring will try to **autowire by type**, because rarely in an application more than one bean of a type is needed. Spring inspects the type of dependency necessary and will inject the bean with that exact type.

So let's start slow and cover each type of injection type, before going deeper into how Spring does it under the hood.

Constructor Injection

Constructor injection is a mechanism of providing dependencies through constructor arguments if the bean definition looks like the following.

```
package com.apress.cems.beans.ci;

import org.springframework.beans.factory.annotation.Autowired;
import org.springframework.stereotype.Component;

@Component
public class ComposedBeanImpl implements ComposedBean {

    private SimpleBean simpleBean;

    @Autowired
    public ComposedBeanImpl(SimpleBean simpleBean) {
        this.simpleBean = simpleBean;
    }
}
```

!   Starting with Spring 4.3 using @Autowired if the class has a single constructor is no longer necessary. Even if redundant, the annotation was used in the previous example for teaching purposes to show @Autowired being used on a constructor.

The ComposedBeanImpl class has a field of type SimpleBean defined, which is initialized when the constructor is called with the value passed as argument. Because of the @Autowired annotation, the Spring IoC container knows that before creating the composedBeanImpl, it first has to create a bean of type SimpleBean and inject it as an argument. The preceding code and configuration snippets provide all the necessary information so that the Spring IoC container can create a bean of type `SimpleBean` named `simpleBeanImpl` and then inject it into a bean of type `ComposedBean` named `composedBeanImpl`. The following is done behind the scenes.

```
SimpleBean simpleBean = new SimpleBeanImpl();
ComposedBean composedBean = new ComposedBeanImpl(simpleBean);
```

Spring creates the beans in the order they are needed. The dependencies are first created and then injected into the beans that need them.

CC By default, if Spring cannot decide which bean to autowire based on type (because there are more beans of the same type in the application), it first searches for any type of bean declared with a `@Qualifier` annotation on it. If nothing is found, then it defaults to autowiring by name. The name considered as the criterion for searching the proper dependency is the name of the field being autowired.

In the previous case, if Spring cannot decide what to autowire based on type, it looks for a bean declared with a `@Qualifier` annotation. And if nothing is found, it looks for a bean with the required type, which is named `simpleBean`. If nothing is found, then an exception of type `org.springframework.beans.factory.NoSuchBeanDefinitionException` occurs.

The configuration class used to register the bean declaration listed previously and its dependencies can be seen in the next code listing.

```
package com.apress.cems.beans.ci;
import org.springframework.context.annotation.ComponentScan;
import org.springframework.context.annotation.Configuration;

@Configuration
@ComponentScan(basePackages = {"com.apress.cems.beans.ci"} )
public class SimpleAppCfg {
}
```

The class is empty because it exists only to be annotated with the configuration annotations necessary to enable bean discovery and to provide a basis to create an application context. Component scanning enables for classes annotated with stereotype annotations to auto-detected using classpath scanning, and a bean to be created for each one of them within the application context. Creating an application context based on that class is easy, just instantiate an `AnnotationConfigApplicationContext`. The full class to test the bean is depicted in the next code listing.

```
package com.apress.cems.beans.ci;

...
import org.springframework.context.ConfigurableApplicationContext;
import org.springframework.context.annotation.
AnnotationConfigApplicationContext;

import static org.junit.jupiter.api.Assertions.*;

class SimpleAppCfgTest {

    private Logger logger =
        LoggerFactory.getLogger(SimpleAppCfgTest.class);

    @Test
    void testSimpleBeans() {
        ConfigurableApplicationContext ctx =
            new AnnotationConfigApplicationContext(SimpleAppCfg.class);

        ComposedBean composedBean = ctx.getBean(ComposedBean.class);
        assertNotNull(composedBean);
        ctx.close();
    }
```

If we check the log, it will become obvious which type of autowiring was used.

```
...
DEBUG o.s.b.f.s.DefaultListableBeanFactory - Creating shared instance of
singleton
    bean 'simpleBeanImpl'
DEBUG o.s.b.f.s.DefaultListableBeanFactory - Creating shared instance of
singleton
    bean 'composedBeanImpl'
...
DEBUG o.s.b.f.s.DefaultListableBeanFactory - Autowiring by type from bean
name
    'composedBeanImpl' via constructor to bean named 'simpleBeanImpl'
TRACE o.s.b.f.s.DefaultListableBeanFactory - Finished creating instance of
    bean 'composedBeanImpl'
```

If we were to declare another bean of type `SimpleBean` when starting up the Spring application, the results might become unpredictable. But, how do we create another bean of type `SimpleBean`? We either create another class that implements that interface and annotate it with `@Component`, or we chose an easier way and we develop the configuration class a little bit more.

```
package com.apress.cems.beans.ci;
import org.springframework.context.annotation.Bean;
import org.springframework.context.annotation.ComponentScan;
import org.springframework.context.annotation.Configuration;

@Configuration
@ComponentScan(basePackages = {"com.apress.cems.beans.ci"} )
public class SimpleAppCfg {
    @Bean
    SimpleBean anotherSimpleBean(){
        return new SimpleBeanImpl();
    }
}
```

In the previous code snippet, a bean is declared explicitly using the `@Bean` annotation. This annotation is used at the method level to indicate that the method produces a bean managed by the Spring IoC container. Typically, `@Bean` methods are declared within `@Configuration` classes and they are detected by the Spring IoC container without the need for classpath scanning. If we run the previous test class with the new configuration class, the console log will display the cause why the application context could not be created.

```
...
DEBUG o.s.b.f.s.DefaultListableBeanFactory - Creating shared instance of
singleton
    bean 'anotherSimpleBean'
DEBUG o.s.b.f.s.DefaultListableBeanFactory - Creating shared instance of
singleton
    bean 'simpleBeanImpl'
...
```

```
org.springframework.beans.factory.UnsatisfiedDependencyException: Error
creating
    bean with name 'composedBeanImpl' defined in file [..ComposedBeanImpl.
    class]:
    Unsatisfied dependency expressed through constructor parameter 0;
    nested exception 0
    is org.springframework.beans.factory.the
    NoUniqueBeanDefinitionException:
    No qualifying bean of type 'com.apress.cems.beans.ci.SimpleBean'
    available:
    expected single matching bean but found 2: simpleBeanImpl,another
    SimpleBean
```

In this case, we have two beans with the same SimpleBean type; neither is annotated with @Qualifier to make it a candidate for injection. And because neither of them is named simpleBean, Spring does not know which dependency to inject, so it unable to create a proper application context. This is a conflict that cannot be resolved without additional configuration changes. In this case, we have quite a few choices.

- Specify a name for the bean to be created by annotating SimpleBeanImpl and, in our case, to remove any ambiguity, we annotate the class with @Component("simpleBean").

- Specify a name for the bean created in the configuration class; in our case, we annotate the method to @Bean("simpleBean").

- Specify a name for the bean created in the configuration class by modifying the method name from anotherSimpleBean to simpleBean.

- Specify the name of the bean to inject in the ComposedBeanImpl class using the @Qualifer annotation on the constructor parameter.

    ```
    package com.apress.cems.beans.ci;
    import org.springframework.beans.factory.annotation.Autowired;
    import org.springframework.beans.factory.annotation.Qualifier;
    ...
    ```

```
@Component
public class ComposedBeanImpl implements ComposedBean {

    private SimpleBean simpleBean;

    @Autowired
    public ComposedBeanImpl(@Qualifier("anotherSimpleBean")) {
        this.simpleBean = simpleBean;
    }
    ...
}
```

The @Autowire annotation can be used on constructors to tell Spring to use autowiring to provide arguments for that constructor. The way Spring will identify the autowiring candidate is by using the same logic presented before: it will try to find a unique bean of the parameter type. If it finds more than one, the one annotated with @Qualifier will be considered, if there is no such bean, the one named as the parameter will be injected. In using @Autowired on constructors, it makes no sense to have more than one constructor annotated with it, and Spring will complain about it because it will not know what constructor to use to instantiate the bean.

Everything that was mentioned about the capabilities of @Autowired and @Qualifier and how to use them to control bean autowiring applies to setter injection. It applies to instance variables too, even if field injection is not recommended, because of performance costs caused by the use of reflection.

Everything that was mentioned about the capabilities of @Autowired and @Qualifier and how to use them to control bean autowiring applies to the JSR-330 @Inject and @Named as well.

All of this is fine, but what if my dependency is a String or some other simple type of object, or a primitive that should be read from a properties file? For that, the @Value annotation was introduced. So, let's make our ComposedBean more complicated by adding two more fields one of type String and one of type boolean and add them to the constructor to see the power of Spring IoC container. And since reading from properties files requires extra infrastructure beans to be created, we'll keep it simple for now and just declare the values to be injected on the spot.

```java
package com.apress.cems.beans.ci;
import org.springframework.beans.factory.annotation.Autowired;
import org.springframework.beans.factory.annotation.Value;
import org.springframework.stereotype.Component;

@Component
public class ComposedBeanImpl implements ComposedBean {

    private SimpleBean simpleBean;
    private String code;
    private boolean complicated;

    @Autowired
    public ComposedBeanImpl(SimpleBean simpleBean,
            @Value("AB123") String code, @Value("true") boolean complicated) {
        this.simpleBean = simpleBean;
        this.code = code;
        this.complicated = complicated;
    }

    public SimpleBean getSimpleBean() {
        return simpleBean;
    }

    public String getCode() {
        return code;
    }

    public boolean isComplicated() {
        return complicated;
    }
}
```

The @Value annotation is used when the value to inject is a scalar.[13] Text values, numbers, and booleans can be used as arguments for the constructor using the @Value attribute. So what happens here is equivalent to the following.

```
ComposedBean composedBean = new ComposedBeanImpl(simpleBean, "AB123", true);
```

Developers choose to use constructor injection when it is mandatory for the dependencies to be provided, since the bean depending on them cannot be used without them. Constructor injection enforces this restriction since the dependent bean cannot even be created if the dependencies are not provided.

!   The @Autowired annotation provides an attribute named `required` which, when it is set to `false` declares the annotated dependency as not being required. When @Autowired is used on a constructor, this argument can never be used with a value of `false`, because it breaks the configuration. It's logical if you think about it, you cannot make optional the only means you have to create a bean, right? We'll come back to this topic when we talk about setter injection.

If the Spring IoC container cannot find a bean to inject into when creating a bean declared to use constructor injection, an exception of type `org.springframework.beans.factory.UnsatisfiedDependencyException` will be thrown and the application will fail to start. You can cause such an issue yourself in the `chapter02/beans` project by commenting the @Component annotation in class `SimpleBeanImpl` and then running the `SimpleAppCfgTest` test class.

Dependency injection also is suitable when a bean needs to be immutable by assigning the dependencies to final fields. The most common reason to use constructor injection is that sometimes third-party dependencies are used in a project, and their classes were designed to support only this type of dependency injection. In creating a bean, there are two steps that need to be executed one after the other. The bean first needs to be **instantiated**, and then the bean must be **initialized**. The constructor

---

[13]The term *"scalar"* comes from linear algebra, where it differentiates a number from a vector or matrix. In computing, the term has a similar meaning. It distinguishes a single value such as an integer or float from a data structure like an array. In Spring, *scalar* refers to any value that is not a bean and cannot be treated as such.

injection combines two steps into one, because injecting a dependency using a constructor means basically instantiating and initializing the object at the same time.

Enough reading; it's time to write some code. In the chapter02/beans-practice project, the Item interface and the Book class implementing it have been declared. This class has a single field of type String that has to be injected with a value of your choosing when the bean is created. There is also a Human interface and a Person class implementing it, which has a single field of type Item. Your assignment is to declare define two beans, one of type Person, one of type Book, make sure the book bean is injected into the person bean.

To test your implementation run the class com.apress.cems.beans. HumanAppCfgTest class that contains a few test statements making sure everything was configured correctly. If you get stuck, you can take a look at the proposed beans configurations in the chapter02/beans project.

This section has introduced the simplest way to create beans using constructor injection. There are other things that can be done when creating a bean—all configurable, but since they are more related to customization than creation, they will be covered in future sections.

The equivalent XML configuration for the previously declared bean is depicted in the following code snippet.

```xml
<?xml version="1.0" encoding="UTF-8"?>
<beans xmlns="http://www.springframework.org/schema/beans"
       xmlns:xsi="http://www.w3.org/2001/XMLSchema-instance"
       xsi:schemaLocation="http://www.springframework.org/schema/beans
        http://www.springframework.org/schema/beans/spring-beans.xsd">

    <bean name="simpleBeanImpl"
        class="com.apress.cems.beans.ci.SimpleBeanImpl" />

    <bean name="composedBeanImpl"
        class="com.apress.cems.beans.ci.ComposedBeanImpl">
        <constructor-arg index="0" ref="simpleBeanImpl"/>
        <constructor-arg index="1" value="AB123" />
        <constructor-arg index="2" value="true" />
    </bean>

</beans>
```

An important thing to point out about XML configuration: the ref attribute is used to specify bean dependencies, and the value attribute is used to specify scalar dependencies.

In XML, arguments can be specified using indexes defined by the order of the parameters in the constructor by setting the index attribute to specify the argument where each value is injected. If the next code snippet, you can see the declaration of the ComposedBeanImpl(..) constructor.

```
package com.apress.cems.beans.ci;

@Component
public class ComposedBeanImpl implements ComposedBean {

    private SimpleBean simpleBean;
    private String code;
    private Boolean complicated;

    @Autowired
    public ComposedBeanImpl(
                /* index = "0" */  SimpleBean simpleBean,
                /* index = "1" */  String code,
                /* index = "2" */  Boolean complicated
        ) {
        this.simpleBean = simpleBean;
        this.code = code;
        this.complicated = complicated;
    }
}
```

In the XML, the names of the beans are explicitly configured, so the configuration will perfectly match the one created using annotations. The XML configuration can be simplified using the **c-namespace**, a special namespace, without a schema location that exists with the sole purpose of simplifying XML configuration. A sample of the previous configuration using this namespace is depicted in the following configuration listing.

```
<?xml version="1.0" encoding="UTF-8"?>
<beans xmlns="http://www.springframework.org/schema/beans"
       xmlns:xsi="http://www.w3.org/2001/XMLSchema-instance"
       xmlns:c="http://www.springframework.org/schema/c"
```

```
        xsi:schemaLocation="http://www.springframework.org/schema/beans
          http://www.springframework.org/schema/beans/spring-beans.xsd">

    <bean name="simpleBeanImpl"
        class="com.apress.cems.beans.ci.SimpleBeanImpl" />

    <bean name="composedBeanImpl"
        class="com.apress.cems.beans.ci.ComposedBeanImpl"
        c:_0-ref="simpleBeanImpl" c:_1="AB123" c:_2="true"/>

</beans>
```

XML arguments can also be specified using the names of the parameters in the constructor. The following snippet shows how to created beans using constructor argument names with the **c-namespace** and without.

```
<?xml version="1.0" encoding="UTF-8"?>
<beans ...>

    <bean name="simpleBeanImpl"
        class="com.apress.cems.beans.ci.SimpleBeanImpl" />

     <bean name="composedBeanImpl"
          class="com.apress.cems.beans.ci.ComposedBeanImpl">
        <constructor-arg name="simpleBean" ref="simpleBeanImpl"/>
        <constructor-arg name="code" value="AB123" />
        <constructor-arg name="complicated" value="true" />
     </bean>
```

And if the preceding declaration looks a little too verbose, there is always the **c-namespace** syntax.

```
<?xml version="1.0" encoding="UTF-8"?>
<beans ...>

 <bean name="composedBeanImpl"
     class="com.apress.cems.beans.ci.ComposedBeanImpl"
     c:simpleBean-ref="simpleBeanImpl" c:code="AB123"
c:complicated="true"/>

</beans>
```

Although XML is not required for the certification exam, samples are presented in the book for comparison, so that you have a complete understanding of how Spring applications are configured and to cover things that require a typical Java configuration.

Setter Injection

To use the setter injection, the class type of the bean must have setter methods used to set the dependencies. A constructor is not mandatory. If no constructor is declared, Spring will use the default no argument constructor, which every class automatically inherits from the Java Object class to instantiate the object and the setter methods to inject dependencies. If a no argument constructor is explicitly defined, Spring will use it to instantiate the bean. If a constructor with parameters is defined, the dependencies declared in this way will be injected using constructor injection, and the ones defined using setters will be injected via setter injection.

In conclusion, when creating a bean using setter injection, the bean is first instantiated by calling the constructor. If there are any dependencies declared as arguments for the constructor these will be obviously initialized first. When the constructor does not require arguments, the bean is then initialized by injecting the dependencies using setters, so in this case, instantiation and initialization are two different steps.[14] So if your bean definition looks like the following.

```
package com.apress.cems.beans.si;

import com.apress.cems.beans.ci.SimpleBean;
import org.springframework.beans.factory.annotation.Autowired;
import org.springframework.stereotype.Component;

@Component
public class AnotherComposedBeanImpl implements AnotherComposedBean {

    private SimpleBean simpleBean;

    @Autowired
    public void setSimpleBean(SimpleBean simpleBean) {
        this.simpleBean = simpleBean;
    }
}
```

---

[14]Later in this chapter, you will learn that initialization can be split into two steps as well: setting dependencies and calling a special initialization method that makes use of those dependencies.

```
    public SimpleBean getSimpleBean() {
        return simpleBean;
    }
}
```

The preceding code and configuration snippet provide all the necessary information so that the Spring container can create a bean of type `AnotherComposedBeanImpl` and then inject into it a bean of `SimpleBean` type. The `SimpleBean` interface that was introduced in the previous section is used as a type for the dependency. This allows a bean of any type extending this interface to be injected as a dependency. The dependency is injected after the bean is instantiated by calling the `setSimpleBean` setter method and providing the bean of `SimpleBeanImpl` type as argument. Assuming that there is a class named `AnotherSimpleBeanImpl` that implements the `SimpleBean` interface, the following is done behind the scenes.

```
SimpleBean simpleBean = new AnotherSimpleBeanImpl();
AnotherComposedBeanImpl complexBean = new AnotherComposedBeanImpl();
complexBean.setSimpleBean(simpleBean);
```

What is obvious for setter injection in Spring is that the `@Autowired` annotation must be present on setter methods to tell the Spring IoC container where the dependency must be injected. If a dependency is not mandatory you can always annotate the setter with `@Autowired(required = false)`, but in this case, you have to carefully design your code so that `NullPointerExceptions` will be avoided. The next code sample contains the declaration of a class named `BadBeanImpl` that can be used to create a bean with an optional dependency of `MissingBean` type.

```
 package com.apress.cems.beans.aw;

import org.springframework.beans.factory.annotation.Autowired;
import org.springframework.stereotype.Component;

@Component
public class BadBeanImpl implements BadBean {
    private MissingBean missingBean;
    private BeanTwo beanTwo;
```

```
    public MissingBean getMissingBean() {
        return missingBean;
    }

    @Autowired(required = false)
    public void setMissingBean(MissingBean missingBean) {
        this.missingBean = missingBean;
    }

    public BeanTwo getBeanTwo() {
        return beanTwo;
    }

    @Autowired
    public void setBeanTwo(BeanTwo beanTwo) {
        this.beanTwo = beanTwo;
    }
}
```

Interfaces and implementations for MissingBean and BeanTwo are empty and irrelevant for this example. Assuming we have a configuration class named NotRequiredBeanCfg that is used to create an application context containing the bean declared previously, testing that the missingBean dependency is not provided is quite easy.

```
package com.apress.cems.beans.cw;
...
public class NotRequiredBeanCfgTest {

    @Test
    void testAutowire(){
        ConfigurableApplicationContext ctx =
            new AnnotationConfigApplicationContext(NotRequiredBeanCfg.class);
        assertNotNull(ctx);

        BadBean badBean = ctx.getBean(BadBean.class);
        assertNotNull(badBean.getBeanTwo());
        assertNull(badBean.getMissingBean());
    }
}
```

By declaring the dependency optional, if there is no bean of `MissingBean` type found in the application context, the bean `BadBean` type can be created without it, a null value will be used instead and no exception of `NoSuchBeanDefinitionException` type will be thrown. But beware of using this, and be careful with your design, because it opens up the possibility for errors.

And this is all that can be said about the setter injection for now. Choosing between setter and constructor injection depends only on the needs of the application; the code that is already written and cannot be changed (legacy code) and third-party libraries. In Spring, constructor injection is preferred as it allows beans to be immutable and dependencies not `null` which will ensure that beans will always be completely initialized and fully functional. When deciding on which type of injection to configure, just make the decisions based on the existing code and best coding practices (e.g., do not define a constructors with more than six arguments, because this is considered a bad practice named *code smell*).

There are three main reasons for using setter injection.

- It allows reconfiguration of the dependent bean, as the setter can be called explicitly later in the code, and a new bean can be provided as a dependency (this obviously means that a bean created using setter injection is not immutable)

- Preferably, it is used for bean dependencies that can be set with default values inside the bean class

- Third-party code only supports setter injections.

A constructor and setter injection can create the same bean. We can modify the `AnotherComposedBeanImpl` class to add a constructor too. Since we just introduced optional dependencies, let's make use of them.

```
package com.apress.cems.beans.si;

import com.apress.cems.beans.ci.SimpleBean;
import org.springframework.beans.factory.annotation.Autowired;
import org.springframework.beans.factory.annotation.Value;
import org.springframework.stereotype.Component;
```

```java
@Component
public class AnotherComposedBeanImpl implements AnotherComposedBean {

    private SimpleBean simpleBean;

    private boolean complex;

    @Autowired
    public AnotherComposedBeanImpl(@Value("true") boolean complex) {
        this.complex = complex;
    }

    @Autowired(required = false)
    public void setSimpleBean(SimpleBean simpleBean) {
        this.simpleBean = simpleBean;
    }

    public SimpleBean getSimpleBean() {
        return simpleBean;
    }

    public boolean isComplex() {
        return complex;
    }
}
```

The previous bean can be configured using an XML file with the following contents.

```xml
<?xml version="1.0" encoding="UTF-8"?>
<beans xmlns="http://www.springframework.org/schema/beans"
      xmlns:xsi="http://www.w3.org/2001/XMLSchema-instance"
      xmlns:c="http://www.springframework.org/schema/c"
      xmlns:p="http://www.springframework.org/schema/p"
      xsi:schemaLocation="http://www.springframework.org/schema/beans
        http://www.springframework.org/schema/beans/spring-beans.xsd">

    <bean name="anotherSimpleBeanImpl"
        class="com.apress.cems.beans.si.AnotherSimpleBeanImpl" />
```

```
<bean name="anotherComposedBeanImpl"
    class="com.apress.cems.beans.si.AnotherComposedBeanImpl"
    c:complex="true">
    <property name="simpleBean" ref="anotherSimpleBeanImpl" />
</bean>
```

The following code snippet depicts the simplified version of the same configuration using the **p-namespace**, which simplifies the XML even more. In a similar way, the **c-namespace** simplifies bean configuration when using constructors.

```
<?xml version="1.0" encoding="UTF-8"?>
<beans ../>
    <!-- using the p-namespace -->
    <bean name="anotherComposedBeanImpl"
            class="com.apress.cems.beans.si.AnotherComposedBeanImpl"
            c:complex="true"
            p:simpleBean-ref="anotherSimpleBeanImpl"/>

</beans>
```

When XML configuration is used bean declarations using setter dependency injection allows dependencies to be optional. In the com.apress.cems.xml. ApplicationContextTest from the chapter02/xml project, there is a test case named method testJdbcRepo() using a configuration file named application-opt-prod.xml that contains a bean declaration with a dependency that could be injected using a setter, but the configuration to do so was commented out.

```
<?xml version="1.0" encoding="UTF-8"?>
<beans ...>
    <!-- Missing dependency -->
    <bean id="detectiveRepo"
        class="com.apress.cems.xml.repos.impl.JdbcDetectiveRepo">
        <!-- <property name="dataSource" ref="dataSource"/> -->
    </bean>
</beans>
```

If you run that method, you will see that the test passes and that the method contains this line: `assertThrows(NullPointerException.class, () -> detectiveRepo.findById(1L));`. This calls a repository method making use of the `dataSource` dependency. It does not expect the dependency to be there, and a `NullPointerException` is thrown.

All other examples can be found in the `chapter02/beans` project. The package containing all beans and configurations for trying setter injection is named `com.apress.cems.beans.si`.

Field Injection

Another type of injection supported in Spring is *field-based injection*. In this case, the `@Autowired` annotation is placed directly on a class field and the Spring IoC Container is in charge of injecting a bean as value to the field when the application is started. So, another way of writing a composed bean that makes use of field injection is depicted in the following code snippet.

```
package com.apress.cems.beans.fi;

import com.apress.cems.beans.ci.ComposedBean;
import com.apress.cems.beans.ci.SimpleBean;
import org.springframework.beans.factory.annotation.Autowired;
import org.springframework.beans.factory.annotation.Value;
import org.springframework.stereotype.Component;

@Component
public class BadComposedBean implements ComposedBean {

    @Autowired
    private SimpleBean simpleBean;

    private String code;
    private boolean complicated;

    public BadComposedBean(@Value("AB123") String code,
            @Value("true") boolean complicated) {
        this.code = code;
        this.complicated = complicated;
    }
```

```
    @Override
    public SimpleBean getSimpleBean() {
        return simpleBean;
    }

    @Override
    public String getCode() {
        return code;
    }

    @Override
    public boolean isComplicated() {
        return complicated();
    }
}
```

The `com.apress.cems.beans.ci.ComposedBean` interface was implemented and a constructor that initializes the fields that are not injected with beans was added. The configuration class for this example is named `FiAppCfg` and is an empty configuration class annotated with `@Configuration` and `@ComponentScan`. The test class that test the proper creation of this bean is called `FiAppCfgTest` and contains the following code.

```
package com.apress.cems.beans.fi;

import com.apress.cems.beans.ci.ComposedBean;

import org.junit.jupiter.api.Test;
import org.springframework.context.ConfigurableApplicationContext;
import org.springframework.context.annotation.
AnnotationConfigApplicationContext;

import static org.junit.jupiter.api.Assertions.*;

public class FiAppCfgTest {
    @Test
    void testSimpleBeans() {
        ConfigurableApplicationContext ctx =
            new AnnotationConfigApplicationContext(FiAppCfg.class);
```

```
    ComposedBean composedBean = ctx.getBean(ComposedBean.class);
    assertNotNull(composedBean);
    assertNotNull(composedBean.getSimpleBean());
    assertEquals("AB123", composedBean.getCode());
    assertTrue(composedBean.isComplicated());
    ctx.close();
  }
}
```

The code that is underlined is the line that verifies that a bean of type `SimpleBean` was injected into the `simpleBean` field.

! Although it seems practical to use field injection, because the need for writing setters disappears, and the classes become more readable, using field injection hides the dependencies of a class. As a developer you would not know the dependencies of a class without looking at the source code. This practice had led to people referring to Spring as "magic," and dependencies being wired "automagically" in Spring applications. So the fields defining the state of an object should be publicly available to avoid objects being created with an inconsistent state and the risk of `NullPointerExceptions` being thrown.

Another reason why I personally do not like field injection is because it makes my classes more difficult to test (especially when writing unit tests). A class designed for field-injection is harder to use outside of a Spring context. So if I want to test a small functionality in my class, and the injected field is declared private and there is no setter for it, I would not be able to inject a stub or a mock implementation. Sure, there is always reflection, and testing libraries like Mockito provide utility methods to avoid the typical reflection boilerplate, but that should not even be considered for many reasons (performance and security), but also because starting with Java 9, it become trickier as hell.

Also, if the previous arguments did not convince you, constructor and setter injection is done using autowiring, which involves proxying. That is why these two types of dependency injection types are recommended. Field injection is done using reflection, because this is the only way to access a private field in Java, which can lead to a slow performance so, avoid using it unless you really have no other choice.

I recommend using field injection only in the following contexts.

- `@Configuration` classes: Bean A is declared in configuration class A1, and bean B declared in configuration class B1, depends on bean A.

- `@Configuration` classes: To inject infrastructure beans that are created by the Spring IoC container and need to be customized. (Be careful when doing this because it ties your implementation to Spring.)

- Test classes: The tested bean should be injected using field injection as it keeps things readable.

Bean Scopes

The word *singleton* was used a little bit so far in the book in relation to beans, and you've definitely noticed it in the logs. I never really explained why, because there is a time for everything. A *bean scope* is a term that describes how long a bean's lifespan is. Spring refers to the beans as singletons, because that is the default scope.[15] A singleton bean is created when the application is bootstrapped, and is managed by the Spring IoC container until the application is shutdown or the context is closed. If you've executed some of the sources, you've probably noticed an important piece of the log in the console.

```
DEBUG o.s.b.f.s.DefaultListableBeanFactory - Destroying singletons in
org.springframework.beans.factory.support.DefaultListableBeanFactory@10e92f8f:
defining beans simpleBean1,simpleBean2,complexBean,
o.s.c.a.internalConfigurationAnnotationProcessor...
```

When the Spring IoC instantiates beans, it creates a single instance for each bean, which is destroyed when the application context is shut down. The scope of a bean can be changed by using a special Spring annotation. This annotation is @Scope, and the default scope for a bean is `singleton`. The scopes are defined in Table 2-2.

---

[15]The Singleton design pattern is therefore used heavily in Spring.

Table 2-2. *Bean Scopes*

Scope	Annotation	Description
singleton	none, @Scope("singleton"), @Scope(ConfigurableBean Factory.SCOPE_SINGLETON)	The Spring IoC creates a single instance of this bean, and any request for beans with a name (or aliases) matching this bean definition results in this instance being returned.
prototype	@Scope("prototype"), @Scope(ConfigurableBean Factory.SCOPE_PROTOTYPE)	Every time a request is made for this specific bean, the Spring IoC creates a new instance.
request	@Scope("request"), @RequestScope, @Scope(WebApplication Context.SCOPE_REQUEST)	The Spring IoC creates a bean instance for each HTTP request. Only valid in the context of a web-aware Spring ApplicationContext.
session	@Scope("session"), @SessionScope, @Scope(WebApplication Context.SCOPE_SESSION)	The Spring IoC creates a bean instance for each HTTP session. Only valid in the context of a web-aware Spring ApplicationContext.
application	@Scope("application"), @ApplicationScope, @Scope(WebApplication Context.SCOPE_APPLICATION)	The Spring IoC creates a bean instance for the global application context. Only valid in the context of a web-aware Spring ApplicationContext.
websocket	@Scope("websocket")	The Spring IoC creates a bean instance for the scope of a WebSocket. Only valid in the context of a web-aware Spring ApplicationContext.
thread	@Scope("thread")	Introduced in Spring 3.0, it is available, but not registered by default, so the developer must explicitly register it in the same way as if a custom scope would be defined.

The SCOPE_REQUEST, SCOPE_SESSION and SCOPE_APPLICATION scope variables are declared in the org.springframework.web.context.WebApplicationContext interface, because they are specific to web applications.

So when a bean is created in the simplest way just by annotating a class with a stereotype annotation (@Component or any of its specializations), like we've done until now.

```
@Component
public class DepBean {
...
}
```

The default scope is singleton. The scope of a bean can be changed by annotating the class with @Scope.

```
 import org.springframework.context.annotation.Scope;
 ...
@Scope("prototype")
@Component
public class DepBean {
}
```

The preceding declaration is the same as the following one.

```
import org.springframework.beans.factory.config.ConfigurableBeanFactory;
import org.springframework.context.annotation.Scope;
 ...
@Scope(ConfigurableBeanFactory.SCOPE_PROTOTYPE)
@Component
public class DepBean {
}
```

There are constants matching the scope types, which are listed in Table 2-3. They are declared in various interfaces based on their domain. For example, the ones for basic configuration like *singleton* and prototype are declared in the org.springframework.beans.factory.config.ConfigurableBeanFactory:

```
package org.springframework.beans.factory.config;
 ...
public interface ConfigurableBeanFactory extends
      HierarchicalBeanFactory, SingletonBeanRegistry {
         String SCOPE_SINGLETON = "singleton";
         String SCOPE_PROTOTYPE = "prototype";
         ....
}
```

Now that we know that more beans scopes are available, how do we solve dependencies between beans with different scopes? When we have a `prototype` bean depending on a `singleton`, there is no problem. Every time the prototype bean is requested from the context, a new instance is created, and the singleton bean is injected into it. But the other way around, things get a little complicated.

The domain that is most sensitive when it comes to dependencies among beans with different scopes is the web applications domain. There are three main bean scopes designed to be used in web applications: `request`, `session`, and `application`. Let's assume that we have a service bean called `ThemeManager` that manages updates on an object of type `UserSettings` containing the settings that a `User` has for an interface in a web application. This means that the `ThemeManager` bean has to work with a different `UserSettings` bean for each HTTP session. Obviously, this means that the `UserSettings` bean should have the scope session.

```
import org.springframework.web.context.WebApplicationContext;
import org.springframework.context.annotation.Scope;
...

@Component
@Scope(value = WebApplicationContext.SCOPE_SESSION)
public class UserSettings {...}

\\ ThemeManager.java contents
@Component
public class ThemeManager {
    private UserSettings userSettings;
```

```
    @Autowired
    public void setUserSettings(UserSettings userSettings) {
        this.userSettings = userSettings;
    }
}
```

But how can the problem with single instantiation be solved? On different HTTP sessions, methods like themeManager.saveSettings(userSettings) should be called with the userSettings bean specific to that session. But the preceding configuration does not allow for this to happen. The preceding configuration just sets the scope for the bean, but does nothing about it. The ThemeManager bean is created, it requires an instance of type UserSettings as dependency, the dependency is injected, and that's it. Since the setter method is not called explicitly with a different instance, how can Spring refresh that dependency? Well, something extra has to be added to the @Scope annotation.

```
import org.springframework.web.context.WebApplicationContext;
import org.springframework.context.annotation.Scope;
import org.springframework.context.annotation.ScopedProxyMode;
...
@Component
@Scope(value = WebApplicationContext.SCOPE_SESSION,
        proxyMode = ScopedProxyMode.INTERFACES)
public class UserSettings implements BasicUserSettings {...}

\\ ThemeManager.java contents
@Component
public class ThemeManager {
    private UserSettings userSettings;

    @Autowired
    public void setUserSettings(UserSettings userSettings) {
        this.userSettings = userSettings;
    }
}
```

The ScopedProxyMode enum is part spring-context module and contains a list of values for scoped-proxy options. To customize a bean based on its annotations Spring makes use of the Proxy pattern[16]. A proxy is an implementation that wraps around the target implementation and provides extra behavior in a transparent manner. The proxy implements the same interface(s) the target implementation does, so the same API is available. When the target type is not an interface, but a class, the proxy will be a class extending the target class. This was supported in previous versions of Spring by adding a library like CGLIB on the classpath. This is no longer needed in Spring 5 because CGLIB was repackaged and is now part of Spring AOP.[17] By annotating the UserSettings class with @Scope, we can tell the Spring IoC container how we want our proxy to behave. The WebApplicationContext.SCOPE_SESSION means that the proxy should reinstantiate the target every time a new HTTP Session is created. The ScopedProxyMode.INTERFACES means that the proxy that will be wrapped around our target (of type UserSettings) will implement the BasicUserSettings interface. The TeamManager bean will not be injected with a simple UserSettings bean, but with a proxy that is wrapped around a bean of type UserSettings to provide the behavior of refreshing its state based on the HTTP Session.

If the proxy type used is ScopedProxyMode.TARGET_CLASS, then this scope configuration annotation.

```
@Scope(value = WebApplicationContext.SCOPE_SESSION, proxyMode =
ScopedProxyMode.TARGET_CLASS)
```

It can be replaced with the @SessionScope annotation from package org. springframework.web.context.annotation, which is a specialization of the @Scope annotation that fixes the proxy type to class-based proxies. The Spring Web MVC module provides specializations for most common used scopes in web applications.

The AOP framework was introduced here because it was important to show how beans with different scopes can be used correctly. The AOP framework complements the Spring IoC container. The Spring container can be used without AOP in small applications (teaching applications mostly) that do not require the use of security or

---

[16]More info here https://en.wikipedia.org/wiki/Proxy_pattern

[17]AOP is an acronym for aspect-oriented programming, which is a programming paradigm aiming to increase modularity by allowing the separation of cross-cutting concerns. This is done by defining something called "pointcut," which represents a point in the code where new behavior will be injected. You can read more about it in Chapter 4.

transactions, because these are the key crosscutting concerns for enterprise applications. But keep in mind that even if you do not use any AOP components in your application, Spring uses AOP a lot under the hood. The Spring AOP framework has the entire fourth chapter of this book dedicated to it.

And since the previous code sample is web specific and difficult to play with, let's build an example that makes use of a prototype bean that can be tested easily. Let's consider an employee that constantly lies when asked about his salary. So each time employee.getSalary() is called a different salary is returned. The implementation consists of a Salary class that contains a declaration of a prototype bean, which is declared as having a field of type Integer that is initialized with a random value when the constructor is called.

```
package com.apress.cems.scopes;

...
import org.springframework.context.annotation.Scope;
import org.springframework.stereotype.Component;
import org.springframework.beans.factory.config.ConfigurableBeanFactory;

import java.util.Random;

@Component
@Scope(value = ConfigurableBeanFactory.SCOPE_PROTOTYPE)
public class Salary {
    private Logger logger = LoggerFactory.getLogger(Salary.class);

    private Integer amount;

    public Salary() {
        logger.info(" -> Creating new Salary bean");
        Random rand = new Random();
        this.amount = rand.nextInt(10_000) +  50_000;
    }

    public Integer getAmount() {
        return amount;
    }
}
```

> **!** Fun fact: Using @Scope(value = ConfigurableBeanFactory.SCOPE_
> PROTOTYPE) does nothing. Because the Spring IoC container is not being told
> what kind of proxy to wrap the bean in, instead of throwing an error, just creates
> a singleton. So if you really want to customize scope proxyMode attribute must
> be set.

Which value should be used for the proxyMode in the previous implementation to make sure that it always gets a fresh new instance when the bean is accessed? If you really want to delegate that decision to Spring, you can use proxyMode = ScopedProxyMode.DEFAULT and the container will play it safe and create a CGLIB-based class proxy by default. But if you want to make the decision, just look at the class code. If the class implements an interface, then proxyMode = ScopedProxyMode.INTERFACES can be used. But if the class does not implement an interface, the only possible option is proxyMode = ScopedProxyMode.TARGET_CLASS.

So, to fix the preceding bean declaration, we should annotate the class properly.

```
package com.apress.cems.scopes;
...
import org.springframework.context.annotation.ScopedProxyMode;
import org.springframework.stereotype.Component;

import java.util.Random;

@Component
@Scope(value = ConfigurableBeanFactory.SCOPE_PROTOTYPE,
        , proxyMode = ScopedProxyMode.TARGET_CLASS)
public class Salary {
    private Logger logger = LoggerFactory.getLogger(Salary.class);

    private Integer amount;

    public Salary() {
        logger.info(" -> Creating new Salary bean");
        Random rand = new Random();
        this.amount = rand.nextInt(10_000) +  50_000;
    }
```

```
    public Integer getAmount() {
        return amount;
    }
}
```

And now that we have the proper annotation for Salary, to make this bean a prototype, we can declare the Employee class, the type for our singleton bean that depends on the prototype bean declared previously.

```
package com.apress.cems.scopes;

import org.springframework.beans.factory.annotation.Autowired;
import org.springframework.stereotype.Component;

@Component
public class Employee {
    private Salary salary;

    public Employee(Salary salary) {
        this.salary = salary;
    }

    @Autowired
    public void setSalary(Salary salary) {
        this.salary = salary;
    }

    public Salary getSalary() {
        return salary;
    }
}
```

We're all set. How do we test that this works as intended? The simplest way is to just get a reference to the salary bean and call employee.getSalary().getAmount() a few times and if we get a different value, this means it works.

```java
package com.apress.cems.scopes;

import org.junit.jupiter.api.Test;
import org.slf4j.Logger;
import org.slf4j.LoggerFactory;
import org.springframework.context.ConfigurableApplicationContext;
import org.springframework.context.annotation.
AnnotationConfigApplicationContext;

import static org.junit.jupiter.api.Assertions.assertNotNull;

public class AppConfigTest {
    private Logger logger = LoggerFactory.getLogger(AppConfigTest.class);

    @Test
    void testBeanLifecycle() {
        ConfigurableApplicationContext ctx =
            new AnnotationConfigApplicationContext(AppConfig.class);
        ctx.registerShutdownHook();

        Employee employee = ctx.getBean(Employee.class);
        assertNotNull(employee);

        Salary salary = employee.getSalary();
        assertNotNull(salary);
        logger.info("Salary bean actual type: {}", salary.getClass().
        toString());

        logger.info("Salary: {}", salary.getAmount());
        logger.info("Salary: {}", salary.getAmount());
        logger.info("Salary: {}", salary.getAmount());
    }
}
```

The configuration class for this example is named AppConfig and is just an empty configuration class annotated with @Configuration and @ComponentScan and not really relevant for the topic in this section so it won't be depicted here, but you can find it in the source code for this book.

When I ran the example, I saw the following in the log.

```
DEBUG o.s.b.f.s.DefaultListableBeanFactory - Creating shared instance of
    singleton bean 'employee'
...
TRACE o.s.b.f.s.DefaultListableBeanFactory - Creating instance of bean
'scopedTarget.salary'
INFO  c.a.c.s.Salary -  -> Creating new Salary bean
INFO  c.a.c.s.AppConfigTest - Salary: 59521
TRACE o.s.b.f.s.DefaultListableBeanFactory - Creating instance of bean
'scopedTarget.salary'
INFO  c.a.c.s.Salary -  -> Creating new Salary bean
INFO  c.a.c.s.AppConfigTest - Salary: 52210
TRACE o.s.b.f.s.DefaultListableBeanFactory - Creating instance of bean
'scopedTarget.salary'
INFO  c.a.c.s.Salary -  -> Creating new Salary bean
INFO  c.a.c.s.AppConfigTest - Salary: 54566
...
```

In the preceding log, you can see that our proxy works, every time we access the salary bean to retrieve the amount property, the salary bean is accessed by calling getAmount() and a new amount is returned. But what exactly is happening *under the hood*? If we look in the console log and scroll up a little, we find something that looks very weird.

```
...
DEBUG o.s.b.f.s.DefaultListableBeanFactory -
        Creating shared instance of singleton bean 'employee'
TRACE o.s.b.f.s.DefaultListableBeanFactory - Creating instance of bean
'employee'
DEBUG o.s.b.f.s.DefaultListableBeanFactory -
        Creating shared instance of singleton bean 'salary'
...
TRACE o.s.a.f.CglibAopProxy - Creating CGLIB proxy: SimpleBeanTargetSource
for target
        bean 'scopedTarget.salary' of type [com.apress.cems.scopes.Salary]
```

```
TRACE o.s.b.f.s.DefaultListableBeanFactory - Finished creating instance of
bean 'salary'
DEBUG o.s.b.f.s.DefaultListableBeanFactory - Autowiring by type from bean
name
  'employee' via constructor to bean named 'salary'
...
```

The first underlined line in the previous snippet says *Creating shared instance of singleton bean 'salary'*.

?   Wait, what??? What the actual...? What is the Spring IoC container doing? Wasn't the salary bean supposed to be a prototype? Why are the logs saying it is a singleton?

Remember how I mentioned that a proxy bean wraps around the intended bean, and the proxy is injected into the dependent bean? Well, the bean named salary is that proxy, and that bean is a singleton. It can easily be proven. We can modify the test class and add the following two lines.

```
Salary salary = employee.getSalary();
logger.info("Salary bean actual type: {}", salary.getClass().toString());
```

The two previous lines, print the type of the instance. If we run the test class again, we can see the following in the log.

```
...
INFO  c.a.c.s.AppConfigTest - Salary bean actual type: class
  com.apress.cems.scopes.Salary$$EnhancerBySpringCGLIB$$474c423f]
...
```

So, when the employee bean is created, it requires a dependency of type Salary. Since it's not practical to call the setter repeatedly to inject a new instance of type Salary, because that defeats the purpose of agnostic dependency injection, the salary bean that was injected is a proxy bean. This bean is of a type generated internally that is a subclass of Salary (because of the proxyMode = ScopedProxyMode.TARGET_CLASS). This means that the same methods can be called on it as on a Salary bean, but because it is a different type of bean, the methods do something else. In our case, calling getAmount()

on the proxy bean causes it to create a new instance of Salary, call getAmount() on it and returns the result. This behavior is depicted visually in Figure 2-14.

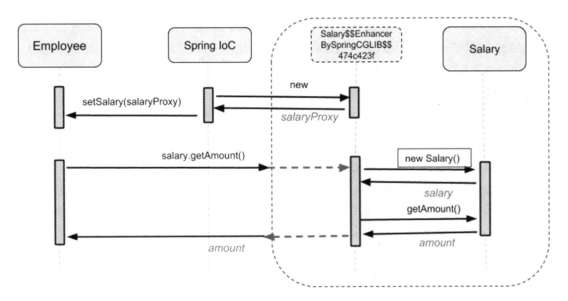

Figure 2-14. *Proxy bean behavior for scope prototype*

The employee bean calls the getAmount() on the proxy bean and gets the result, which is agnostic to how that result is obtained. The proxy bean ensures the prototype behavior by creating a new instance every time it is being accessed. The instances being created internally are referred to in the log as scopedTarget.salary.

Proxies created with proxyMode = ScopedProxyMode.TARGET_CLASS are referred to as a *CGLIB-based class proxy*, because they are created at runtime by subclassing the target type. To do this, additional libraries are necessary; in this case, CGLIB, which fortunately was included in Spring so that you won't need to declare it as a dependency in your project configuration. The disadvantage of these proxies is that they can only intercept public methods, since non-public methods cannot be overridden. Also, if for some reason, you would need to declare your class or methods final, using this type of proxying is not possible.

Proxies created with the proxyMode = ScopedProxyMode.INTERFACES are referred to as *JDK interface-based proxies*, because they are created at runtime by implementing the same interface as the target class and do not require additional libraries in the classpath. This unfortunately means that the class must implement at least one interface. The advantage here is that interfaces definitely do not have non-public methods that might escape proxying.☺

> **!** Starting with Java 8, interfaces can be declared to contain *private* and *default* methods. For obvious reasons, related to their access modifier, private methods are not proxied. Default methods are methods that are declared in the interface, so that classes implementing the interface don't have to. They are inherited by the classes, so they are proxied just like any normal method, with the specific behavior being executed before the call being forwarded to the target object.

Proxy beans are quite powerful. Spring uses proxy beans to add behavior to developers created beans, behavior which implemented explicitly would lead to a lot of redundancy (e.g., adding transactional behavior), but depending on the type of behavior we need added it can lead to performance issues. In our example, because we need a new salary every time we call getAmount() multiple beans are created and discarded, imagine what would happen if the Salary class would define some big object to be stored in memory or that the application is running on a system with little memory (memory issues might be unavoidable). The discussion about proxies will stop here because it continues in Chapter 4.

The @Scope annotation can annotate @Bean declarations as well. The bean declaration in the Salary class is identical to the following.

```
package com.apress.cems.scopes;

import org.springframework.context.annotation.*;

@Configuration
@ComponentScan(basePackages = {"com.apress.cems.scopes"} )
public class AppConfig {

    @Bean
    @Scope(value = "prototype",
        proxyMode = ScopedProxyMode.TARGET_CLASS)
    Salary salary(){
        return new Salary();
    }
}
```

We can even create a specialization of the @Scope annotation specific to Salary instances.

```
package com.apress.cems.scopes;

import org.springframework.beans.factory.config.ConfigurableBeanFactory;
import org.springframework.context.annotation.Scope;
import org.springframework.context.annotation.ScopedProxyMode;
import org.springframework.core.annotation.AliasFor;

import java.lang.annotation.*;

@Target({ElementType.TYPE, ElementType.METHOD})
@Retention(RetentionPolicy.RUNTIME)
@Documented
@Scope(ConfigurableBeanFactory.SCOPE_PROTOTYPE)
public @interface SalaryScope  {

    /**
     * Alias for {@link Scope#proxyMode}.
     * <p>Defaults to {@link ScopedProxyMode#TARGET_CLASS}.
     */
    @AliasFor(annotation = Scope.class)
    ScopedProxyMode proxyMode() default ScopedProxyMode.TARGET_CLASS;
}
```

** The list of annotations applied to the @SalaryScope annotation are the same ones that annotate the @Scope annotation and have the following purpose.

- @Target indicates the contexts in which an annotation type is applicable; in our case, the annotation is applicable at class and method levels.

- @Retention indicates how long annotations with the annotated type are to be retained; in our case, they are recoded at compile time and they are retained by the VM at runtime.

- @Documented indicates to a tool like Javadoc that annotations like these must be displayed in its output.

So, the previous bean declaration can be simplified to the following.

```
package com.apress.cems.scopes;

import org.springframework.context.annotation.*;

@Configuration
@ComponentScan(basePackages = {"com.apress.cems.scopes"} )
public class AppConfig {

    @Bean
    @SalaryScope
    Salary salary(){
        return new Salary();
    }
}
```

This is all that can be said about bean scopes, and it is more than enough information for you to pass the exam.☺

! Since this is quite an interesting section, some practice is in order. In project chapter02/config-practice look in the com.apress.cems. scopes package. It contains classes Employee and Salary. The Salary class is used to declare a bean of scope prototype. TODO 14 requires you to modify the implementation to make use of JDK-based interface proxying. TODO 15 requires you to create a specialization of the @Scope annotation equivalent to the configuration used on your bean.

Use the com.apress.cems.scopes.AppConfigTest class to test your implementation.

A proposed solution can be found in the chapter02/config project in the com.apress.cems.scopes package.

@AliasFor

In Spring 4.2, the @AliasFor annotation was added. This annotation is set on annotation attributes to declare aliases for them. And since I've just recently mentioned the @Scope annotation, let's take a look at its source code.[18]

```
package org.springframework.context.annotation;
...
@Target({ElementType.TYPE, ElementType.METHOD})
@Retention(RetentionPolicy.RUNTIME)
@Documented
public @interface Scope {
        @AliasFor("scopeName")
        String value() default "";

        @AliasFor("value")
        String scopeName() default "";

        ScopedProxyMode proxyMode() default ScopedProxyMode.DEFAULT;
}
```

As you can see, attributes value and scopeName are used as aliases for each other, so they are interchangeable. Thus, the following three @Scope annotation usages are equivalent.

```
@Scope(ConfigurableBeanFactory.SCOPE_SINGLETON)
@Scope(value = ConfigurableBeanFactory.SCOPE_SINGLETON)
@Scope(scopeName = ConfigurableBeanFactory.SCOPE_SINGLETON)
```

And even more can be done with it. Aliases for meta-annotation attributes can be declared. In this case, the attribute annotated with @AliasFor is an alias for an attribute in another annotation. The best example here is for the @Component and @Repository annotations. The @Component is a meta-annotation, because it can annotate other

---

[18]You can inspect it on GitHub here: https://github.com/spring-projects/spring-framework/blob/master/spring-context/src/main/java/org/springframework/context/annotation/Scope.java or just click <Ctrl> + left-click or <Command> + left-click, and if you have an Internet connection, IntelliJ IDEA will download the code for you.

annotations; this is a fact that is indicated by the @Target(ElementType.TYPE),[19] which is declared as follows.

```
package org.springframework.stereotype;
...
@Target(ElementType.TYPE)
@Retention(RetentionPolicy.RUNTIME)
@Documented
@Indexed
public @interface Component {
...
        String value() default "";
}
```

The @Repository, which is its specialization for declaring data access objects called *repositories|*, declares an attribute named value that is declared as an alias for the value attribute of the @Component annotation.

```
package org.springframework.stereotype;
...
@Target({ElementType.TYPE})
@Retention(RetentionPolicy.RUNTIME)
@Documented
@Component
public @interface Repository {

...

        @AliasFor(annotation = Component.class)
        String value() default "";
}
```

The @AliasFor on the value attribute ensures that using @Repository("myRepo") on a bean, the bean will be named myRepo. Since the @Component annotation has an attribute named *value*, the @AliasFor annotation does not even have to reference the

---

[19]*java.lang.annotation.ElementType.TYPE* includes: class, interface (including annotation type), or enum declaration

attribute name, because it matches the attribute name in the @Repository annotation. So @AliasFor(annotation = Component.class) is equivalent to @AliasFor(annotation = Component.class, attribute = "value").

Bean Lifecycle Under the Hood

In the previous section, we could not mention bean scope unless we made a connection with the bean lifespan. This section covers the steps that are executed when a Spring application is run. The bean starts up as a class that is annotated with a stereotype annotation or is instantiated in a method annotated with @Bean from a configuration class. In all the previous sections, the focus was on the technical details of a configuration and what an application context is; the references to bean creation steps were scarce. So we need to fix that.

A Spring application has a lifecycle of three phases.

- **Initialization**: In this phase, bean definitions are read, beans are created, dependencies are injected, and resources are allocated, also known as the bootstrap phase. After this phase is complete, the application can be used.

- **Use**: In this phase, the application is up and running. It is used by clients, and beans are retrieved and used to provide responses for their requests. This is the main phase of the lifecycle and covers 99% of it.

- **Destruction**: The context is being shut down, resources are released, and beans are handed over to the garbage collector.

These three phases are common to every type of application, whether it is a JUnit System test, a Spring or JEE web, or an enterprise application. Look at the following code snippet (the sources can be found in the /chapter-02/config project); it was modified to make it obvious where each phase ends.

```
package com.apress.cems.lc;
import org.springframework.context.ConfigurableApplicationContext;
...
public class ApplicationContextTest {
    private Logger logger = LoggerFactory.getLogger(ApplicationContextTest.
    class);
```

```java
    @Test
    void testSimpleBeans() {
        ConfigurableApplicationContext ctx =
            new AnnotationConfigApplicationContext(DataSourceCfg.class);
        ctx.registerShutdownHook();
        logger.info(" >> init done.");

        DataSource dataSource = ctx.getBean(DataSource.class);
        assertNotNull(dataSource);

        logger.info(" >> usage done.");
    }
}
// DataSourceCfg.java contents
@Configuration
@PropertySource("classpath:db/prod-datasource.properties")
public class DataSourceCfg {
    @Value("${driverClassName}")
    private String driverClassName;
    @Value("${url}")
    private String url;
    @Value("${username}")
    private String username;
    @Value("${password}")
    private String password;

    @Bean
    public static PropertySourcesPlaceholderConfigurer
        propertySourcesPlaceholderConfigurer() {
        return new PropertySourcesPlaceholderConfigurer();
    }

    @Bean
    public DataSource dataSource() {
        DriverManagerDataSource ds = new DriverManagerDataSource();
        ds.setDriverClassName(driverClassName);
        ds.setUrl(url);
        ds.setUsername(username);
```

```
        ds.setPassword(password);
        return ds;
    }
}
```

The initialization phase of a Spring application ends when the application context initialization process ends. If the logger for the Spring Framework is set to TRACE before the *init done* message is printed, a lot of log entries show what the Spring IoC container is doing. The following is a simplified sample.

```
TRACE o.s.c.a.AnnotationConfigApplicationContext - Refreshing
 <<1>> ..AnnotationConfigApplicationContext@fa36558, started on ...
DEBUG o.s.b.f.s.DefaultListableBeanFactory - Creating shared instance of
singleton bean
'org.springframework.context.annotation.
internalConfigurationAnnotationProcessor'
...
TRACE o.s.c.a.ConfigurationClassBeanDefinitionReader - Registering bean
definition
<<2>> for @Bean method ..DataSourceCfg.
propertySourcesPlaceholderConfigurer()
TRACE o.s.c.a.ConfigurationClassBeanDefinitionReader - Registering bean
definition
    for @Bean method ..DataSourceCfg.dataSource()
...
DEBUG o.s.b.f.s.DefaultListableBeanFactory - Creating shared instance of
singleton bean
<<3>>  'propertySourcesPlaceholderConfigurer'
DEBUG o.s.b.f.s.DefaultListableBeanFactory - Creating shared instance of
singleton bean
    'org.springframework.context.annotation.internalAutowiredAnnotation
    Processor'
DEBUG o.s.b.f.s.DefaultListableBeanFactory - Creating shared instance of
singleton bean
    'org.springframework.context.annotation.internalCommonAnnotationProcessor'
...
```

```
TRACE o.s.b.f.s.DefaultListableBeanFactory - Pre-instantiating singletons in
..DefaultListableBeanFactory@7d3e8655: defining beans
[..internalConfigurationAnnotationProcessor,
..internalAutowiredAnnotationProcessor,
..internalCommonAnnotationProcessor,... dataSourceCfg,propertySources
PlaceholderConfigurer,
   dataSource]; root of factory hierarchy
...
TRACE o.s.b.f.s.DefaultListableBeanFactory - Creating instance of bean
'dataSourceCfg'
TRACE o.s.b.f.a.InjectionMetadata - Registered injected element on class
   [com.apress.cems.lc.DataSourceCfg$$EnhancerBySpringCGLIB$$8f107e20]:
   AutowiredFieldElement for private java.lang.String
   ..DataSourceCfg.driverClassName
TRACE o.s.b.f.a.InjectionMetadata - Registered injected element on class
   [com.apress.cems.lc.DataSourceCfg$$EnhancerBySpringCGLIB$$8f107e20]:
   AutowiredFieldElement for private java.lang.String ..DataSourceCfg.
   username
...
DEBUG o.s.c.e.PropertySourcesPropertyResolver - Found key 'driverClassName'
   in PropertySource 'class path resource [db/prod-datasource.properties]'
   with value of type String
TRACE o.s.u.PropertyPlaceholderHelper - Resolved placeholder
'driverClassName'
TRACE o.s.c.e.PropertySourcesPropertyResolver - Searching for key
'username'
   in PropertySource 'class path resource [db/prod-datasource.properties]'
TRACE o.s.u.PropertyPlaceholderHelper - Resolved placeholder 'username'
...
DEBUG o.s.b.f.s.DefaultListableBeanFactory - Creating shared instance of
   singleton bean 'dataSourceCfg'
<<4>>  DEBUG o.s.b.f.s.DefaultListableBeanFactory - Creating shared
instance of
   singleton bean 'dataSource'
DEBUG o.s.j.d.DriverManagerDataSource - Loaded JDBC driver: oracle.jdbc.
OracleDriver
```

```
TRACE o.s.b.f.s.DefaultListableBeanFactory - Finished creating instance of
bean 'dataSource'
INFO  c.a.c.l.ApplicationContextTest -  >> init done.
TRACE o.s.b.f.s.DefaultListableBeanFactory - Returning cached instance of
   singleton bean 'dataSource'
INFO  c.a.c.l.ApplicationContextTest -  >> usage done.
DEBUG o.s.c.a.AnnotationConfigApplicationContext - Closing
 ..AnnotationConfigApplicationContext@fa36558, started on ...
<<7>>   TRACE o.s.b.f.s.DefaultListableBeanFactory - Returning cached
instance of
  singleton bean 'lifecycleProcessor'
<<9>>TRACE o.s.b.f.s.DefaultListableBeanFactory - Destroying singletons in
 ..DefaultListableBeanFactory@7d3e8655: defining beans
 [..internalConfigurationAnnotationProcessor,..
internalAutowiredAnnotationProcessor,
 ..internalCommonAnnotationProcessor,dataSourceCfg,
 propertySourcesPlaceholderConfigurer,dataSource]; root of factory hierarchy
```

Although the log is incomplete, all the important details were marked (either by numbers in <<*>> or by underlining). To make things easier, the following steps were marked in the log with the corresponding step number.

1. The application context is initialized.

2. The bean definitions are loaded (from the class DataSourceCfg in this case).

3. The bean definitions are processed (in our case a bean of type PropertySourcesPlaceholderConfigurer is created and used to read the properties from prod-datasource.properties, which are then added to the dataSource bean definition).

4. Beans are instantiated.

5. Dependencies are injected (not visible from the log, since the dataSource bean does not require any dependencies).

6. Beans are processed (also not visible from the log, since the dataSource does not have any processing defined).

7. Beans are used.

8. The context starts the destruction process. (This is not visible in the log.)

9. Beans are destroyed.

Figure 2-15 depicts the whole application context lifecycle and the bean lifecycle.

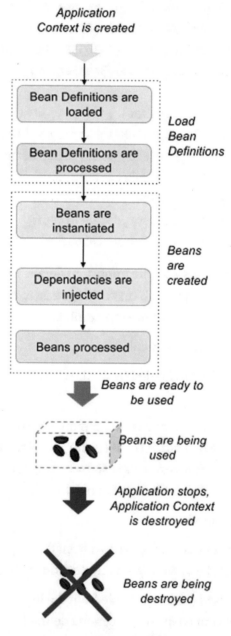

Figure 2-15. *Application context and bean lifecycle*

In the **Load Bean Definition** step, the Configuration classes are parsed, Java classes are scanned for configuration annotations and bean definitions are loaded into the application context, indexed by names. The bean definitions are then processed by beans called *bean factory post processors* that are automatically picked up by the application context, created, and applied before any other beans are created. These bean types implement the `org.springframework.beans.factory.config.BeanFactoryPostProcessor` interface, which is how the application context recognizes them. In the previous example, the `PropertySourcesPlaceholderConfigurer` type was mentioned. This class is a type of bean factory post processor implementation that resolves placeholders like `${propName}` within bean declarations by injecting property values read from the Spring environment and its set of property sources, declared using the `@PropertySource`.

! The `propertySourcesPlaceholderConfigurer` bean declaration needs to be a static method picked up when the context is created, earlier than the configuration class annotated with `@Configuration`, so the property values are added to the Spring Environment and become available for injection in the said configuration class, before this class is initialized.

Since the `propertySourcesPlaceholderConfigurer` modifies the declaration of a configuration class, this obviously means that these classes are proxied by Spring IoC container, and this obviously means that these classes cannot be final. The infrastructure bean responsible for bootstrapping the processing of `@Configuration` annotated classes is the bean named `internalConfigurationAnnotationProcessor` and is of type `org.springframework.context.annotation.ConfigurationClassPostProcessor` which is an implementation of `BeanFactoryPostProcessor`.

The `BeanFactoryPostProcessor` interface contains a single method definition (annotated with `@FunctionalInterface` so that it can be used in lambda expressions) that must be implemented: `postProcessBeanFactory(ConfigurableListableBeanFactory)`. The parameter with which this method will be called is the factory bean used by the application context to create the beans. Developers can create their own bean factory post processors and define a bean of this type in their configuration, and the application context will make sure to invoke them.

Figure 2-16 depicts the effect of a `PropertySourcesPlaceholderConfigurer` bean used on the `dataSourceCfg` configuration bean definition.

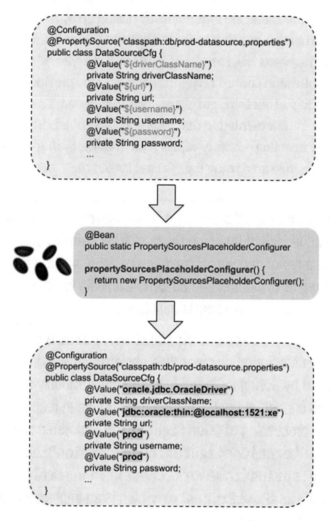

Figure 2-16. *Effect of a PropertySourcesPlaceholderConfigurer on a bean definition using placeholders*

These types of beans are useful, because they can process bean definitions at runtime and change them based on resources that are outside the application, so the application does not need to be recompiled to change a bean definition. It is also useful in development too, because configuration values can be swapped easily, without a recompile being needed, and this is especially useful when applications get bigger.

In the preceding example, if the property values used to configure the `dataSourceCfg` bean are hard-coded in the configuration class, when the database connection details change, the configuration class has to be changed, and the application has to be recompiled and restarted. Not that practical, right?

The **bean creation** process can be split into a small number of stages.

1. In the first stage, **the beans are instantiated**. This basically means that the bean factory is calling the constructor of each bean. If the bean is created using constructor dependency injection, the dependency bean is created first and then injected where needed. For beans that are defined in this way, the instantiation stage coincides with **the dependency injection** stage.

2. In the second stage, **dependencies are injected**. For beans that are defined having dependencies injected via setter, this stage is separate from the instantiation stage. The same goes for dependencies inject using field injection.

3. The next stage is the one in which **bean post process beans are invoked before initialization**.[20]

4. In this stage, **beans are initialized**.

5. The next stage is the one in which **bean post process beans are invoked after initialization**.

As you can see, there are two stages that involve the bean post process beans being called. What is the difference between them? The stage between them, the initialization stage, splits them into bean post processors that are invoked before it and after it. Since the bean post processor subject is quite large, the initialization stage will be covered first.

Long story short, a bean can be defined so that a certain method is called right after the bean is created and dependencies are injected to execute code. This method is called an *initialization method*. When using Java configuration, this method is set by annotating it with the `@PostConstruct` annotation. The method must return void. The must have no arguments defined, and can have any access rights since Spring uses

---

[20]Unfortunately, there is no other way to formulate this. We are talking about beans that have the ability to post process other beans. And they are called, confusingly: **bean post process beans.**

reflection to find and call it (just make sure you add the proper configuration in your module-info.java if needed).

Some developers recommend that you make it private so that it cannot be called from outside the bean, to make sure that Spring has total control over it, and so that it calls it only one time during the bean lifecycle. In the following code snippet, you can see the configuration of such a method for a bean of type ComplexBean. The bean is a very simple one with two dependencies: one is provided using a setter and one is set with an instance created within the initialization method. This means that the object created within the method is not a bean; it is not managed by Spring.

```java
package com.apress.cems.lc;
...
@Component
public class ComplexBean {
    private Logger logger = LoggerFactory.getLogger(ComplexBean.class);

    private SimpleBean simpleBean;

    private AnotherSimpleBean anotherSimpleBean;

    public ComplexBean() {
        logger.info("Stage 1: Calling the constructor.");
    }

    @Autowired
    public void setSimpleBean(SimpleBean simpleBean) {
        logger.info("Stage 2: Calling the setter.");
        this.simpleBean = simpleBean;
    }

    /**
      * The initialization method.
      * Just for fun: it instantiates the anotherSimpleBean only
      * if the current time is even.
      */
```

```
    @PostConstruct
    private void initMethod() {
        logger.info("Stage 3: Calling the initMethod.");
        long ct = System.currentTimeMillis();
        if (ct % 2 == 0) {
            anotherSimpleBean = new AnotherSimpleBean();
        }
    }
}
```

When initializing an application context based on the preceding configuration, the following is what is seen in the log.

```
 ...
TRACE o.s.b.f.s.DefaultListableBeanFactory -
     Creating instance of bean 'anotherSimpleBean'
TRACE o.s.b.f.s.DefaultListableBeanFactory - Creating instance of bean
'complexBean'
INFO  c.a.c.l.ComplexBean - Stage 1: Calling the constructor.
TRACE o.s.c.a.CommonAnnotationBeanPostProcessor -
        Found init method on class com.apress.cems.lc.ComplexBean:
                private void com.apress.cems.lc.ComplexBean.initMethod()
TRACE o.s.c.a.CommonAnnotationBeanPostProcessor -
   Registered init method on class [com.apress.cems.lc.ComplexBean]:
   o.s.b.f.a.InitDestroyAnnotationBeanPostProcessor$LifecycleElement@21c6920f
 ...
TRACE o.s.b.f.a.AutowiredAnnotationBeanPostProcessor - Autowiring by type
    from bean name 'complexBean' to bean named 'simpleBean'
INFO  c.a.c.l.ComplexBean - Stage 2: Calling the setter.
TRACE o.s.c.a.CommonAnnotationBeanPostProcessor - Invoking init method
   on bean 'complexBean': private void com.apress.cems.lc.ComplexBean.
   initMethod()
INFO  c.a.c.l.ComplexBean - Stage 3: Calling the initMethod.
TRACE o.s.b.f.s.DefaultListableBeanFactory -
     Finished creating instance of bean 'complexBean'
 ...
```

As you can see, the bean is created, dependencies are injected, and then the initMethod is called. Annotations support was introduced in Spring 2.5 for a small set of annotations. Since then, Spring has evolved, and currently with Spring 5.0, an application can be configured using only annotations (stereotypes and the complete set of Java configuration).

The @PostConstruct annotation is part of the JSR 250[21] and is used on a method that needs to be executed after dependency injection is done to perform initialization. The annotated method must be invoked before the bean is used, and, like any other initialization method chosen, may be called **only once** during a bean lifecycle. If there are no dependencies to be injected, the annotated method will be called after the bean is instantiated. Only one method should be annotated with @PostConstruct. To use this annotation, the jsr250 library must be in the classpath and dependency of the jsr250. api module must be configured in the module-info.java file. The method annotated with @PostConstruct is picked up by enabling component scanning (annotating configuration classes with @ComponentScanning) and called by a pre-init bean named org.springframework.context.annotation.internalCommonAnnotationProcessor[22] of a type that implements the org.springframework.beans.factory.config. BeanPostProcessor interface named CommonAnnotationBeanPostProcessor. Classes implementing this interface are factory hooks that allow for modifications of bean instances. The application context autodetects these types of beans and instantiates them before any other beans in the container, since after their instantiation they are used to manipulate other beans managed by the IoC container.

The BeanPostProcessor interface declares two methods to be implemented, which have been declared as default interface methods so that the developer can freely implement only the one that presents interest. The methods are named postProcessBeforeInitialization and postProcessAfterInitialization. In Figure 2-17, the two pink rectangles depict when the bean post processor is invoking methods on the bean.

---

[21]Java Request Specification 250 https://jcp.org/en/jsr/detail?id=250.

[22]The name of this bean and its purpose and a few others are part of the *org.springframework. context.annotation.AnnotationConfigUtils* class. You can see the code here https://github. com/spring-projects/spring-framework/blob/3a0f309e2c9fdbbf7fb2d348be8615281 77f8555/spring-context/src/main/java/org/springframework/context/annotation/ AnnotationConfigUtils.java

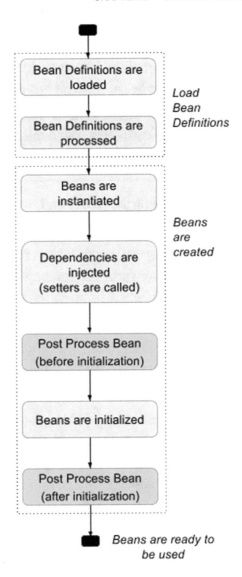

Figure 2-17. *Bean lifecycle expanded*

Typically, post processors that populate bean properties pick up methods annotated with @PostConstruct implement postProcessBeforeInitialization, while post processors that wrap beans with proxies will normally implement postProcessAfterInitialization.

!   From the behavior described so far, you've probably realized that invocation of the @PostConstruct annotated method is specific to the third stage of bean creation when bean post process beans are invoked **before initialization**, but because there is no other actual initialization method defined, the line is kinda fuzzy here as well. So the annotated method is called the initialization method because it is the only method with this purpose declared for this bean.

If an init method is not specified using the @PostConstruct annotation, there are other two ways of initializing a bean available in Spring. The following is the complete list.[23]

- Implementing the org.springframework.beans.factory. InitializingBean interface and providing an implementation for the method afterPropertiesSet (most times, this is not recommended since it couples the application code with Spring infrastructure).

- Annotating with @PostConstruct the method that is called right after the bean is instantiated and dependencies injected.

- Using Java configuration by annotating an initialization method with @Bean(initMethod="..."). This method of initialization is very useful when the code comes from a third-party library or a dependency and cannot be edited.

!   Fun fact: all these three initialization methods can be configured together for the same bean, although technically I cannot see a valid reason for doing that.

The InitializingBean interface is implemented by beans that need to react once all their dependencies have been injected by the BeanFactory. It defines a single method that is named accordingly, afterPropertiesSet(), which is called by the factory creating the bean. And, because this method is not the responsibility of a bean post processor, its execution corresponds to the initialization stage of a bean. In the following code snippet, the ComplexBean class is modified to implement this interface.

---

[23]The XML way of initialization configuration is not taken into consideration here.

```
package com.apress.cems.ib;

import org.springframework.beans.factory.InitializingBean;
  ...
@Component
public class ComplexBean implements InitializingBean {
    private Logger logger = LoggerFactory.getLogger(ComplexBean.class);

    private SimpleBean simpleBean;

    private AnotherSimpleBean anotherSimpleBean;

    public ComplexBean() {
        logger.info("Stage 1: Calling the constructor.");
    }

    @Autowired
    public void setSimpleBean(SimpleBean simpleBean) {
        logger.info("Stage 2: Calling the setter.");
        this.simpleBean = simpleBean;
    }

    @Override
    public void  afterPropertiesSet() throws Exception {
        logger.info("Stage 3: Calling the afterPropertiesSet.");
        long ct = System.currentTimeMillis();
        if (ct % 2 == 0) {
            anotherSimpleBean = new AnotherSimpleBean();
        }
    }
}
```

If an application context is created using the previous configuration, the following is seen in the log.

...

```
TRACE o.s.b.f.s.DefaultListableBeanFactory - Creating instance of bean
'complexBean'
INFO  c.a.c.l.ComplexBean - Stage 1: Calling the constructor.
TRACE o.s.b.f.s.DefaultListableBeanFactory - Eagerly caching bean
'complexBean'
     to allow for resolving potential circular references
TRACE o.s.b.f.a.AutowiredAnnotationBeanPostProcessor - Autowiring by type
from
     bean name 'complexBean' to bean named 'simpleBean'
INFO  c.a.c.l.ComplexBean - Stage 2: Calling the setter.
TRACE o.s.b.f.s.DefaultListableBeanFactory - Invoking afterPropertiesSet() on
     bean with name 'complexBean'
INFO  c.a.c.l.ComplexBean - Stage 3: Calling the afterPropertiesSet.
TRACE o.s.b.f.s.DefaultListableBeanFactory - Finished creating instance of
bean 'complexBean'
```

...

Calling the afterProperties method is a responsibility of the same factory bean that creates the complexBean; in this case, the factory bean is an infrastructure bean of type DefaultListableBeanFactory.

?   If the previous bean class would be modified to add an initialization method annotated with @PostConstruct when creating the bean, which method do you think will be executed first?

The third type of bean initialization is done by declaring beans using the @Bean annotation and by setting the value for the initMethod to the initialization method name. So, let's write a class named AnotherComplexBean that can configure a bean by using the @Bean(initMethod = "...") annotation.

```
package com.apress.cems.im;
   ...

 public class AnotherComplexBean {
   private Logger logger = LoggerFactory.getLogger(AnotherComplexBean.class);
```

```java
    private SimpleBean simpleBean;

    private AnotherSimpleBean anotherSimpleBean;

    public AnotherComplexBean() {
        logger.info("Stage 1: Calling the constructor.");
    }

    @Autowired
    public void setSimpleBean(SimpleBean simpleBean) {
        logger.info("Stage 2: Calling the setter.");
        this.simpleBean = simpleBean;
    }

    /**
     * The initialization method.
     * Just for fun: it instantiates the anotherSimpleBean only
     * if the current time is even.
     */
    public void  beanInitMethod() {
        logger.info("Stage 3: Calling the beanInitMethod.");
        long ct = System.currentTimeMillis();
        if (ct % 2 == 0) {
            anotherSimpleBean = new AnotherSimpleBean();
        }
    }
}
```

The configuration of the bean is quite simple.

```java
package com.apress.cems.im;
import org.springframework.context.annotation.Bean;
...

@Configuration
@ComponentScan(basePackages = {"com.apress.cems.im"} )
public class AcbConfig {
```

```
@Bean(initMethod = "beanInitMethod")
AnotherComplexBean anotherComplexBean(){
    return new AnotherComplexBean();
}
}
```

When executing a test class and creating an application context containing a bean of type AnotherComplexBean, if we look in the console, we can see the three stages of creating this bean in the printed log messages.

```
...
INFO  c.a.c.i.AnotherComplexBean - Stage 1: Calling the constructor
TRACE o.s.b.f.s.DefaultListableBeanFactory - Creating instance of bean
'simpleBean'
TRACE o.s.b.f.a.AutowiredAnnotationBeanPostProcessor - Autowiring by type
from bean
    name 'anotherComplexBean' to bean named 'simpleBean'
INFO  c.a.c.i.AnotherComplexBean - Stage 2: Calling the setter.
TRACE o.s.b.f.s.DefaultListableBeanFactory - Invoking init
method 'beanInitMethod' on
  bean with name 'anotherComplexBean'
INFO  c.a.c.i.AnotherComplexBean - Stage 3: Calling the beanInitMethod.
TRACE o.s.b.f.s.DefaultListableBeanFactory - Finished creating instance of
    bean 'anotherComplexBean'
...
```

When configuring a bean initialization method using @Bean(initMethod = "..."), the responsible for calling the method is the same bean factory responsible with the instantiation of the bean as well: DefaultListableBeanFactory. So the execution of the method matches the initialization stage of a bean.

We are at the end of the section, so now we have to cover what happens to beans after they have been used and are no longer needed and the application shuts down, or only the context managing them.[24] When a context is closed, it destroys all the beans; that is obvious. But some beans (singletons) work with resources that might refuse to

---

[24]Complex Spring applications can have multiple application contexts and they can be closed independently.

release them if they are not notified before destruction. In Spring, this can be done in two ways: [25]

- Modify the bean to implement the org.springframework.beans. factory.DisposableBean interface and provide an implementation for the destroy() method (not recommended, since it couples the application code with Spring infrastructure).

- Annotate a method with @PreDestroy, which is also part of JSR 250 and one of the first supported annotations in Spring.

- Configure a bean using @Bean(destroyMethod="...").

The destroy method of a bean has the same purpose as the finalize method for POJOs. The ComplexBean was modified to make use of the destroy method.

```
package com.apress.cems.lc;
...
import javax.annotation.PreDestroy;

@Component
public class ComplexBean {
    private SimpleBean simpleBean;
    private AnotherSimpleBean anotherSimpleBean;

    public ComplexBean() {
        logger.info("Stage 1: Calling the constructor.");
    }

    @Autowired
    public void setSimpleBean(SimpleBean simpleBean) {
        logger.info("Stage 2: Calling the setter.");
        this.simpleBean = simpleBean;
    }
```

---

[25]If XML configuration is considered, there are three ways.

```
@PostConstruct
  private void initMethod() {
      logger.info("Stage 3: Calling the initMethod.");
      long ct = System.currentTimeMillis();
      if (ct % 2 == 0) {
          anotherSimpleBean = new AnotherSimpleBean();
      }
  }

  @PreDestroy
  private void destroy(){
      logger.info("Stage 4: Calling the destroy method.");
  }
}
```

To view something useful in the log, we need to close the application context gracefully, and this can be done by calling the close() or the registerShutdownHook() method.

```
@Test
public void testBeanCreation() {
      ConfigurableApplicationContext ctx =
          new AnnotationConfigApplicationContext(SimpleConfig.class);
      ctx.registerShutdownHook();

      ComplexBean complexBean = ctx.getBean(ComplexBean.class);
      assertNotNull(complexBean);
}
```

And *voila*. (Only the last part of the log is depicted, where the invocation of the destroy method is logged.)

```
...
TRACE o.s.b.f.s.DefaultListableBeanFactory - Creating instance of bean
'complexBean'
INFO  c.a.c.l.ComplexBean - Stage 1: Calling the constructor.
...
```

```
TRACE o.s.c.a.CommonAnnotationBeanPostProcessor - Registered destroy method
    on class [com.apress.cems.lc.ComplexBean]: org.springframework.beans.
    factory.annotation.
    InitDestroyAnnotationBeanPostProcessor$LifecycleElement@4748d4bc
...
INFO  c.a.c.l.ComplexBean - Stage 2: Calling the setter.
TRACE o.s.c.a.CommonAnnotationBeanPostProcessor - Invoking init method on
bean
    'complexBean': private void com.apress.cems.lc.ComplexBean.initMethod()
INFO  c.a.c.l.ComplexBean - Stage 3: Calling the initMethod.
TRACE o.s.b.f.s.DefaultListableBeanFactory - Finished creating instance of
    bean 'complexBean'
...
DEBUG o.s.c.a.AnnotationConfigApplicationContext -
  Closing o.s.c.a.AnnotationConfigApplicationContext@fa36558, started on ...
TRACE o.s.b.f.s.DefaultListableBeanFactory - Destroying singletons in
    ..DefaultListableBeanFactory@14dd7b39: defining beans
    (...,simpleConfig,anotherSimpleBean,complexBean,
    dataSourceCfg,simpleBean,...; root of factory hierarchy
TRACE o.s.c.a.CommonAnnotationBeanPostProcessor - Invoking destroy method on
    bean 'complexBean': private void com.apress.cems.lc.ComplexBean.destroy()
INFO  c.a.c.l.ComplexBean - Stage 4: Calling the destroy method.
```

As you can see, the destroy() method is registered and invoked by the CommonAnnotationBeanPostProcessor bean.

! For the destroy method, the same rules and recommendations regarding signature and accessors apply as for the init method.

The destroy method may be called **only once** during the bean lifecycle.

The destroy method can have any accessor; some developers even recommend to make it private, so that only Spring can call it via reflection.

The destroy method must not have any parameters.

The destroy method must return void.

And in case it was not obvious by now (and from the log), since only singleton beans get to live until the application context is shutdown, all of these rules apply only to singleton beans.

As you probably suspect by now, there is a matching interface for `InitializingBean` named `DisposableBean` that provides a method to be implemented for bean destruction, and it is named (obviously) `destroy()`. If the `ComplexBean` implements `DisposableBean`, the dirty work is delegated to a bean of type `org.springframework.beans.factory. support.DisposableBeanAdapter`.[26]

```
package com.apress.cems.ib;
import org.springframework.beans.factory.DisposableBean;

public class ComplexBean implements implements InitializingBean,
    DisposableBean {
    private Logger logger = LoggerFactory.getLogger(ComplexBean.class);

    private SimpleBean simpleBean;

    private AnotherSimpleBean anotherSimpleBean;

    public ComplexBean() {
        logger.info("Stage 1: Calling the constructor.");
    }

    @Autowired
    public void setSimpleBean(SimpleBean simpleBean) {
        logger.info("Stage 2: Calling the setter.");
        this.simpleBean = simpleBean;
    }
```

---

[26]*DisposableBeanAdapter* is an internal infrastructure bean type that performs various destruction steps on a given bean instance. Its code is available here: https://github.com/ spring-projects/spring-framework/blob/master/spring-beans/src/main/java/org/ springframework/beans/factory/support/DisposableBeanAdapter.java.

```
    @Override
    public void afterPropertiesSet() throws Exception {
        logger.info("Stage 3: Calling the afterPropertiesSet.");
        long ct = System.currentTimeMillis();
        if (ct % 2 == 0) {
            anotherSimpleBean = new AnotherSimpleBean();
        }
    }

    @Override
    public void destroy() throws Exception {
        logger.info("Stage 4: Calling the destroy method.");
    }
}
```

The difference between the destroy() method being declared with @PreDestroy
and by implementing the DisposableBean can be seen in the console log.

```
INFO  c.a.c.i.ComplexBean - Stage 1: Calling the constructor.
TRACE o.s.b.f.a.AutowiredAnnotationBeanPostProcessor - Autowiring by type
from bean
   name 'complexBean' to bean named 'simpleBean'
...
INFO  c.a.c.i.ComplexBean - Stage 2: Calling the setter.
TRACE o.s.b.f.s.DefaultListableBeanFactory - Invoking afterPropertiesSet on
bean
    with name 'complexBean'
INFO  c.a.c.i.ComplexBean - Stage 3: Calling the afterPropertiesSet.
...
TRACE o.s.b.f.s.DefaultListableBeanFactory - Destroying singletons in
    ..DefaultListableBeanFactory@14dd7b39: defining beans
[...,complexBean,simpleBean,
    anotherSimpleBean]; root of factory hierarchy
TRACE o.s.b.f.s.DisposableBeanAdapter - Invoking destroy on bean with
   name 'complexBean'
INFO  c.a.c.i.ComplexBean - Stage 4: Calling the destroy method.
```

Also, if declaring a destroy method with the @PreDestroy annotation is not an option, there is the analogous attribute of the @Bean annotation used for configuring a destroy method, named destroyMethod.

```
package com.apress.cems.im;
import org.springframework.context.annotation.Bean;
...
@Configuration
@ComponentScan(basePackages = {"com.apress.cems.im"} )
public class AcbConfig {

    @Bean(initMethod = "beanInitMethod", destroyMethod = "beanDestroyMethod")
    AnotherComplexBean anotherComplexBean(){
        return new AnotherComplexBean();
    }

    @Bean
    SimpleBean simpleBean(){
        return new SimpleBean();
    }
}
```

When a context is created with the bean declared as in the previous code snippet, in the log, you see that the job of calling the destroy() method is delegated to the DisposableBeanAdapter as in the case where the method is declared by annotating it with @PreDestroy.

```
INFO  c.a.c.i.AnotherComplexBean - Stage 1: Calling the constructor.
TRACE o.s.b.f.a.AutowiredAnnotationBeanPostProcessor - Autowiring by type
from bean
   name 'anotherComplexBean' to bean named 'simpleBean'
...
INFO  c.a.c.i.AnotherComplexBean - Stage 2: Calling the setter.
...
TRACE o.s.b.f.s.DefaultListableBeanFactory - Destroying singletons in
   ..DefaultListableBeanFactory@14dd7b39: defining beans [...,another
   ComplexBean,simpleBean,
    anotherSimpleBean]; root of factory hierarchy
```

```
TRACE o.s.b.f.s.DisposableBeanAdapter - Invoking destroy method
       'beanDestroyMethod' on bean with name 'anotherComplexBean'
INFO  c.a.c.i.AnotherComplexBean - Stage 4: Calling the beanDestroyMethod.
```

! Since this is the end of a big section, there is an exercise for you. In `chapter02/config-practice`, there is a class named FunBean that has a comment TODO 12 on it. Complete this class by adding a method annotated with `@PostConstruct`, one with `@PreDestroy`, then implement `InitializingBean` and `DisposableBean` and add an initialization and a destroy method do be configured with the @Bean annotation.

In the FunBeanConfig class, there is TODO 13, which requires you to declare a bean of type FunBean using the @Bean annotation and declare an initialization and a destroy method.

Add logging messages with numbers to each method to reflect the order of the execution for the methods based on the information provided to you so far.

Use the FunBeanConfigPracticeTest class to test your configuration.

A proposed solution is provided in the `chapter02/config` project.

Bean Declaration Inheritance

Since classes are templates for creating objects and they can be extended, the same is true for classes that are used to declare beans. A hierarchy of classes can create different beans, and injected values can be inherited or overwritten depending on the needs. Also, subclasses can declare their own fields that can be initialized separately from the parent bean declaration. Using abstract types is a recommended practice in Spring applications, but declaring different beans using classes in the same hierarchy requires for these classes to be instantiated, so we cannot have an abstract class on top of the hierarchy. This is why the following code snippet declares a superclass named ParentBean that has two String properties named familyName and surname which are both annotated with @Value, only one property value is initialized using the constructor, and one via a constructor.

```
package com.apress.cems.beans.inheritance;

import org.springframework.beans.factory.annotation.Value;
import org.springframework.stereotype.Component;

@Component
public class ParentBean {

    @Value("Smith")
    protected String familyName;

    protected String surname;

    public ParentBean(@Value("John")String surname) {
        this.surname = surname;
    }
    ...
}
```

A class named ChildBean extends this class. It is annotated with @Component and declares its own constructor that initializes the property inherited from the parent and its property named adult (which is set to false because a child is obviously not an adult).

```
package com.apress.cems.beans.inheritance;

import org.springframework.beans.factory.annotation.Value;
import org.springframework.stereotype.Component;

@Component
public class ChildBean extends ParentBean {

    private Boolean adult;

    public ChildBean(@Value("Lil' John") String surname,
            @Value("false")Boolean adult) {
        super(surname);
        this.adult = adult;
    }
...
}
```

The two bean declarations will be picked up by the Spring container and two beans will be created within the application context. Both beans will have the value of the familyName field equal to *Smith* the value injected in the ParentBean class. The bean of type ChildBean will have the value of its surname field set to *Lil' John*, as declared in the ChildBean class. This value overwrites the value of *John* declared in the ParenBean constructor. To test that the beans were initialized as we intended, a test class can be created that tests the equality of their fields, but that also prints all the fields of every bean.

The configuration class for this example is named FamilyAppConfig and is just an empty configuration class annotated with @Configuration and @ComponentScan.

```
package com.apress.cems.beans.inheritance;

...

import static org.junit.jupiter.api.Assertions.*;

public class FamilyAppConfigTest {

    private Logger logger =
        LoggerFactory.getLogger(FamilyAppConfigTest.class);

    @Test
    void testSimpleBeans() {
        ConfigurableApplicationContext ctx =
                new AnnotationConfigApplicationContext(FamilyAppConfig.
                class);

        ParentBean parentBean = ctx.getBean("parentBean",ParentBean.class);
        assertNotNull(parentBean);

        ChildBean childBean = ctx.getBean("childBean", ChildBean.class);
        assertNotNull(childBean);

        assertEquals(parentBean.getFamilyName(),
                childBean.getFamilyName());
        assertNotEquals(parentBean.getSurname(),
                childBean.getSurname());
```

```
        logger.info(parentBean.toString());
        logger.info(childBean.toString());
        ctx.close();
    }
}
```

The fact that this class test executes correctly is all the proof we need that the beans were created exactly as we intended, but if we really want to make sure we can also check the logs.

```
DEBUG Refreshing ..AnnotationConfigApplicationContext
...
DEBUG Creating shared instance of singleton bean 'familyAppConfig'
DEBUG Creating shared instance of singleton bean 'childBean'
DEBUG Creating shared instance of singleton bean 'parentBean'
DEBUG FamilyAppConfigTest - ParentBean{ familyName='Smith', surname='John'}
DEBUG FamilyAppConfigTest - ChildBean{ familyName='Smith', surname='Lil' John'
    , isAdult=false}
DEBUG Closing ..AnnotationConfigApplicationContext
```

Bean declaration inheritance is not really such a big thing when configuration is done using annotations, because to share commons parts, the classes must be related. In XML, the classes do not really have to be in a hierarchy, they just have to share field names and configuration values can be inherited. Also, in XML if beans have the same type, the only bean that has to declare the type is the parent bean, and any bean that inherits from it can override it.

Another advantage of using XML is that abstract classes can provide a template for beans of types that extend the abstract class to be created. Let's assume that the CEMS[27] application must run in production on a cluster of three servers. Each server has its own database, and the configuration must mention them all. All of them are Oracle databases, so by using XML, the configuration file for connecting to the database would look like the following.

---

[27]Criminal Evidence Management System - the name is too long, using the acronym from now on 😊

```
<beans ...>
    <bean id="abstractDataSource" class="oracle.jdbc.pool.OracleDataSource"
                abstract="true">
        <property name="user" value="admin"/>
        <property name="loginTimeout" value="300"/>
    </bean>

      <bean id="dataSource-1" parent="abstractDataSource">
        <property name="URL" value="jdbc:oracle:thin:@192.168.1.164:1521:
        PET"/>
    </bean>

    <bean id="dataSource-2" parent="abstractDataSource">
        <property name="URL" value="jdbc:oracle:thin:@192.168.1.164:1521:
        PET"/>
    </bean>

    <bean id="dataSource-3" parent="abstractDataSource"
                    class="com.apress.CustomizedOracleDataSource">
        <property name="URL" value="jdbc:oracle:thin:@192.168.1.164:1521:
        PET"/>
        <property name="loginTimeout" value="100"/>
    </bean>
</beans>
```

By declaring a `<bean ../>` element with the attribute `abstract` set to `true`, we tell the Spring IoC container that this bean is not meant to be instantiated itself, but it is just serving as parent for concrete child bean definitions. And since this bean is not meant to be instantiated, the `class` attribute can even be set to an abstract class.

Writing all that configuration using Java would be a pain, so although XML is not a topic for the certification exam, there are cases when it would be more suitable to use XML configuration files.

Injecting Dependencies That Are Not Beans

Dependency injection with Spring is a vast subject, and this book was written with the intention of covering all the cases you might need in enterprise development. It was mentioned previously in the book that `scalar` values can be injected into bean configurations, which opens the discussion about type conversion. In the previous examples, we injected boolean, String, and Integer values, and the Spring container knew to take the text value from the configuration file and convert it to the property type defined in the bean type definition. The Spring container knows how to do this for all primitive types and their reference wrapper types. String values, Booleans, and numeric types are supported by default. Just keep in mind that for Booleans and decimal types, however, the syntax typical for these types must be respected[28]; otherwise, the default Spring conversion will not work.

Spring also knows to automatically convert Date values before injection if the syntax matches any date pattern with "/" separators (e.g., dd/MM/yyyy, yyyy/MM/dd, and dd/yyyy/MM). Take care, because even invalid numerical combinations are accepted and converted (e.g., 25/2433/23), which leads to unexpected results.

To support any other type, the Spring container must be told how to convert the value of the attribute to the type that the constructor, setter, or instance variable requires. The most common method until Spring 3 was to use a property editor. In Spring 3 a core. convert package was introduced that provides a general type conversion system that defines an SPI [29] that you have to implement to provide the desired conversion behavior. The interface is named Converter<S,T> and its code is depicted in the following snippet.[30]

```
package org.springframework.core.convert.converter;

public interface Converter<S, T> {
    T convert(S source);
}
```

This is a Spring concept that describes a component used to handle the transformation between any two types of objects. To make such a conversion possible, you have to define an implementation for the org.springframework.core.convert. converter.Converter interface and register it in the Spring context. Out of the box, Spring provides a number of Converter implementations for commonly used types, in the core.convert.support package.

---

[28]For example, values "0" and "1" cannot be used as values for a boolean field.

[29]An application programming interface (API) describes what a class/method does; a Service Provider Interface (SPI) describes what you need to extend and implement.

[30]Full code and copyright notices on GitHub: https://github.com/spring-projects/spring-framework/blob/master/spring-core/src/main/java/org/springframework/core/convert/converter/Converter.java

Let's assume we want to define a Person bean as follows.

```
package com.apress.cems.beans.scalars;

import org.springframework.beans.factory.annotation.Autowired;
import org.springframework.beans.factory.annotation.Value;
import org.springframework.stereotype.Component;

import java.time.LocalDate;

@Component
public class PersonBean implements Creature {

    private LocalDate birthDate;
    private String name;

    @Autowired
    public PersonBean(@Value("1977-10-16") LocalDate birthDate,
        @Value("John Mayer") String name) {
        this.birthDate = birthDate;
        this.name = name;
    }

    @Override
    public LocalDate getBirthDate() {
        return birthDate;
    }

    @Override
    public void setBirthDate(LocalDate birthDate) {
        this.birthDate = birthDate;
    }

    public String getName() {
        return name;
    }

    public void setName(String name) {
        this.name = name;
    }
}
```

Spring provides more than one way to tell the Spring IoC container how the value 1977-10-16 can be converted to a LocalDate. An implementation of the JDK java.beans. PropertyEditor provided out of the box by Spring, the org.springframework.beans. propertyeditors.CustomDateEditor was used in the previous edition of this book, when the java.util.Date was used for the birthDate field. This is how you use this class: you create an instance of CustomDateEditor and provide as a parameter a SimpleDateFormat instance, register the CustomDateEditor instance with a PropertyEditorRegistrar that is then used to create a bean of type CustomEditorConfigurer.[31]

But since the Converter SPI was mentioned, and our type is the new and improved JDK LocalDate, an implementation is required.

In order for our converter to be used at runtime the following things must be done.

- Define a class that implements the org.springframework.core. convert.converter.Converter and implement the convert method to provide a way to convert String values to LocalDate values.

```
package com.apress.cems.beans.scalars;

import org.springframework.core.convert.converter.Converter;
import org.springframework.stereotype.Component;

import java.time.LocalDate;
import java.time.format.DateTimeFormatter;

@Component
public class StringToLocalDate implements Converter<String,
LocalDate> {

    private DateTimeFormatter formatter =
            DateTimeFormatter.ofPattern("yyyy-MM-dd");

    @Override
    public LocalDate convert(String source) {
        return LocalDate.parse(source, formatter);
    }
}
```

---

[31]If you are curious about this implementation just clone this GitHub repository https://github.com/Apress/pivotal-certified-pro-spring-dev-exam and take a look at the '02-ps-container-01-solution' project.

- Add a bean declaration of type `org.springframework.core.convert.ConversionService`, named `conversionService`. The name is mandatory, as this is an infrastructure bean, and add the `StringToLocalDate` converter to its list of supported converters. When using XML, the configuration is pretty straightforward, even if to create the bean a factory bean is used. Spring supports instantiating beans using factory beans as well.

```
<bean id="conversionService"
    class="org.springframework.context.support.
    ConversionServiceFactoryBean">
    <property name="converters">
        <set>
            <bean class="com.apress.cems.beans.scalars.
            StringToLocalDate"/>
        </set>
    </property>
</bean>
```

When using Java configuration, the bean declaration looks a little different from what you've seen so far in the chapter. The `configurationService` bean is not directly instantiated, but created by a factory bean of type `ConversionServiceFactoryBean`. The `getObject()` method is called explicitly to obtain an instance of type `org.springframework.core.convert.ConversionService`.

```
package com.apress.cems.beans.scalars;

import org.springframework.beans.factory.annotation.Autowired;
import org.springframework.context.annotation.Bean;
import org.springframework.context.annotation.ComponentScan;
import org.springframework.context.annotation.Configuration;
import org.springframework.context.support.ConversionServiceFactoryBean;
import org.springframework.core.convert.ConversionService;
```

```java
import java.util.Set;

@Configuration
@ComponentScan(basePackages = {"com.apress.cems.beans.scalars"} )
public class AppCfg {

    @Autowired
    StringToLocalDate stringToLocalDateConverter;

    @Bean
    ConversionService conversionService(
            ConversionServiceFactoryBean factory){
        return factory.getObject();
    }

    @Bean
    ConversionServiceFactoryBean conversionServiceFactoryBean() {
        ConversionServiceFactoryBean factory = new
        ConversionServiceFactoryBean();
        factory.setConverters(Set.of(stringToLocalDateConverter,
        stringToDate));
        return factory;
    }
}
```

Because of its syntax and its definition, @Autowired cannot be used to autowire primitive values, which is quite logical, considering that there is an annotation named @Value that specializes in this exactly. The @Value annotation can insert scalar values or used with placeholders and SpEL[32] to provide flexibility in configuring a bean.

SpEL is the Spring Expression language. It is quite powerful, since it supports querying and manipulating an object graph at runtime. This means the language supports getting and setting property values, method invocation, and usage of arithmetic and logic operators and bean retrieval from the Spring IoC container. The SpEL is

---

[32]Spring Expression Language

inspired from WebFlow EL,[33] a superset of Unified EL,[34] and it provides considerable functionality, such as

- method invocation

- access to properties, indexed collections

- collection filtering

- Boolean and relational operators

and many more.[35]

There are several extensions of SpEL (OGNL, MVEL, and JBoss EL), but the best part is that it is not directly tied to Spring and can be used independently.

! An example bean with fields of various types was provided in `chapter02/beans`. The class is called `com.apress.cems.beans.scalars.MultipleTypesBean`, and it can be tested by running the test class called `com.apress.cems.beans.scalars.AppConvertersCfgTest`. The configuration class for this example is named `AppConvertersCfg` and is just an empty configuration class annotated with `@Configuration` and `@ComponentScan`.

```
package com.apress.cems.beans.scalars;

import org.springframework.beans.factory.annotation.Autowired;
import org.springframework.beans.factory.annotation.Value;
import org.springframework.stereotype.Component;

import java.util.Date;
```

---

[33]An expression language used to configure web flows: `http://docs.spring.io/spring-webflow/docs/current/reference/html/el.html`.

[34]Unified EL is the Java expression language used to add logic in JSP pages: `https://docs.oracle.com/javaee/6/tutorial/doc/bnahq.html`.

[35]The full list of capabilities is not in the scope of this book. If you are interested in SpEL, the official documentation is the best resource: `http://docs.spring.io/spring/docs/current/spring-framework-reference/html/expressions.html`.

```java
@Component
public class MultipleTypesBean {
    private int noOne;
    private Integer noTwo;

    private long longOne;
    private Long longTwo;

    private float floatOne;
    private Float floatTwo;

    private double doubleOne;
    private Double doubleTwo;

    private boolean boolOne;
    private Boolean boolTwo;

    private char charOne;
    private Character charTwo;

    private Date date;

    @Autowired void setNoOne(@Value("1") int noOne) {
        this.noOne = noOne;
    }

    @Autowired void setNoTwo(@Value("2")Integer noTwo) {
        this.noTwo = noTwo;
    }

    @Autowired void setFloatOne(@Value("5.0")float floatOne) {
        this.floatOne = floatOne;
    }

    @Autowired void setFloatTwo(@Value("6.0")Float floatTwo) {
        this.floatTwo = floatTwo;
    }

    @Autowired void setDoubleOne(@Value("7.0")double doubleOne) {
        this.doubleOne = doubleOne;
    }
```

```java
    @Autowired void setDoubleTwo(@Value("8.0")Double doubleTwo) {
        this.doubleTwo = doubleTwo;
    }

    @Autowired void setLongOne(@Value("3")long longOne) {
        this.longOne = longOne;
    }

    @Autowired void setLongTwo(@Value("4")Long longTwo) {
        this.longTwo = longTwo;
    }

    @Autowired void setBoolOne(@Value("true")boolean boolOne) {
        this.boolOne = boolOne;
    }

    @Autowired void setBoolTwo(@Value("false")Boolean boolTwo) {
        this.boolTwo = boolTwo;
    }

    @Autowired void setCharOne(@Value("1")char charOne) {
        this.charOne = charOne;
    }

    @Autowired void setCharTwo(@Value("A")Character charTwo) {
        this.charTwo = charTwo;
    }

    @Autowired void setDate(@Value("1977-10-16") Date date) {
        this.date = date;
    }
...
}
```

Run the test in debug mode, as depicted in Figure 2-18, and set a breakpoint on line 55, right after the mtb bean is returned by the application context. In the Debug console (visible at the bottom of the figure), you can see the values for all the fields of the mtBean.

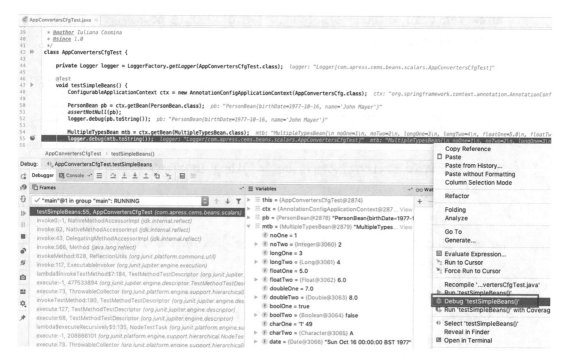

Figure 2-18. *Running a test in debug mode to inspect the fields of a bean of type MultipleTypesBean*

The fields with names postfixed with One are primitives, because Spring knows out of the box how to convert String values to primitives, when the text represent valid values; the others are objects. Notice how they were all initialized correctly, and the values in the bean definition were converted to the appropriate types.

Collections are a type of object often used. To make using them with beans easier, the Spring development team created the util namespace. But since the focus of this book is not on XML configuration, let's see how we can use collections as beans using Java configuration. Consider the CollectionHolder class defined in the following code snippet.

```
package com.apress.cems.beans.scalars;

import com.apress.cems.beans.ci.SimpleBean;
import org.springframework.beans.factory.annotation.Autowired;
import org.springframework.stereotype.Component;
```

```java
import java.util.List;
import java.util.Map;
import java.util.Set;

public class EmptyCollectionHolder {

    private List<SimpleBean> simpleBeanList;
    private Set<SimpleBean> simpleBeanSet;
    private Map<String, SimpleBean> simpleBeanMap;

    public void setSimpleBeanList(List<SimpleBean> simpleBeanList) {
        this.simpleBeanList = simpleBeanList;
    }

    public void setSimpleBeanSet(Set<SimpleBean> simpleBeanSet) {
        this.simpleBeanSet = simpleBeanSet;
    }

    public void setSimpleBeanMap(Map<String, SimpleBean> simpleBeanMap) {
        this.simpleBeanMap = simpleBeanMap;
    }

     /**
      * This method was implemented just to verify the collections injected
      *  into this bean
      */
    @Override
    public String toString() {
        return "CollectionHolder{" +
                "simpleBeanList=" + simpleBeanList.size() +
                ", simpleBeanSet=" + simpleBeanSet.size()  +
                ", simpleBeanMap=" + simpleBeanMap.size()  +
                '}';
    }
}
```

The state of the collectionHolder bean will be tested using the AppConvertersCfgTest:

```
package com.apress.cems.beans.scalars;

import org.junit.jupiter.api.Test;
import org.springframework.context.ConfigurableApplicationContext;
import org.springframework.context.annotation.
AnnotationConfigApplicationContext;

import static org.junit.jupiter.api.Assertions.assertNotNull;
import org.slf4j.Logger;
import org.slf4j.LoggerFactory;

class AppConvertersCfgTest {

    private Logger logger = LoggerFactory.getLogger(AppConvertersCfgTest.
    class);

    @Test
    void testSimpleBeans() {
        ConfigurableApplicationContext ctx =
        new AnnotationConfigApplicationContext(AppConvertersCfg.class);

        EmptyCollectionHolder collectionHolder =
                    ctx.getBean(EmptyCollectionHolder.class);
        (*) logger.debug(collectionHolder.toString());

        ctx.close();
    }
}
```

The collections to be injected can be created just like normal beans by annotating methods in configuration classes with @Bean. This will result in beans of collection types being created and injected where necessary. Next, you can see a few examples of collection beans being declared.

- inject empty collections

  ```
  package com.apress.cems.beans.scalars;

  import com.apress.cems.beans.ci.SimpleBean;
  import org.springframework.context.annotation.Bean;
  import org.springframework.context.annotation.Configuration;
  ```

```java
import java.util.*;

@Configuration
public class AppConvertersCfg {

    ...

    @Bean
    List<SimpleBean> simpleBeanList(){
        return new ArrayList<>();
    }

    @Bean
    Set<SimpleBean> simpleBeanSet(){
        return new HashSet<>();
    }

    @Bean
    Map<String, SimpleBean> simpleBeanMap(){
        return new HashMap<>();
    }
}
```

If you run the AppConvertersCfgTest class aside from the test passing, the logger.debug(..) statement in the line marked with (*) in the test class will print the following: CollectionHolder{simpleBeanList=0, simpleBeanSet=0, simpleBeanMap=0}

We injected empty collections here because their content is not really important at the moment. In XML configuration injecting empty collections is even easier and readable.

```xml
 <?xml version="1.0" encoding="UTF-8"?>
<beans xmlns="http://www.springframework.org/schema/beans"
       xmlns:xsi="http://www.w3.org/2001/XMLSchema-instance"
       xsi:schemaLocation="http://www.springframework.org/schema/
       beans
        http://www.springframework.org/schema/beans/spring-beans.
        xsd">
```

```
    <bean id="collectionHolder"
          class="com.ps.beans.others.EmptyCollectionHolder">
        <property name="simpleBeanList">
            <list/>
        </property>

        <property name="simpleBeanSet">
            <set/>
        </property>

        <property name="simpleBeanMap">
            <map/>
        </property>
    </bean>
</beans>
```

If you are wondering why the util namespace is not used in the
previous example, this is because the collections are declared as
values for the properties of the collectionHolder bean and this can
be done by using configuration elements like the ones underlined
which are declared in the beans namespace.

- inject a property of type List with SimpleBean elements. Using Java
  configuration, the only thing that changes is the declaration of the
  collection beans, instead of creating an empty collection, we just
  have to make sure to add some instances in it. We can even add null,
  although best practices say that you should avoid using null objects
  as much as possible.

```
 package com.apress.cems.beans.scalars;

import com.apress.cems.beans.ci.SimpleBean;
import com.apress.cems.beans.ci.SimpleBeanImpl;
import java.util.*;
...

@Configuration
public class AppConvertersCfg {
    ...
```

```java
@Bean
  SimpleBean simpleBean(){
      return new SimpleBeanImpl();
  }

  @Bean
  List<SimpleBean>  simpleBeanList(){
    return List.of(simpleBean());
  }

  @Bean
  Set<SimpleBean>  simpleBeanSet(){
      return Set.of(simpleBean());
  }

  @Bean
  Map<String, SimpleBean> simpleBeanMap(){
      return Map.of("simpleBean", simpleBean());
  }
}
```

We can either add existing beans as in the previous example, or create them on the spot, in the simpleBeanList. Or both, it really does not matter. Everything mentioned can be done in XML too, and working code can be found in the repository for the previous edition of the book. If you do not want to scan the previous GitHub repo, the following is an XML configuration sample in which the list to be injected in the collectionHolder bean is populated with an existing bean named simpleBean, an instance of SimpleBeanImpl created on the spot, and a null element, configured using a <null /> element. Pretty intuitive, right?

```xml
<bean id="simpleBean" class="com.apress.cems.beans.ci.SimpleBeanImpl"/>

<bean id="collectionHolder"
    class="com.apress.cems.beans.scalars.CollectionHolder">
      <property name="simpleBeanList">
          <list>
              <ref bean="simpleBean"/>
              <bean class="com.apress.cems.beans.ci.SimpleBeanImpl"/>
```

```
            <null/>
         </list>
      </property>
</bean>
```

The `logger.debug(..)` statement in the line marked with (*) in the test class will print something similar to the following sample.

```
CollectionHolder{simpleBeanList=3, ... }
```

And since I mentioned SpEL, the `@Value` annotation can also be used to inject values from other beans by making use of the SpEL language in the following case of a `Properties` object.

```
@Configuration
public class DataSourceConfig1 {

    @Bean
    public Properties dbProps(){
        Properties p = new Properties();
        p.setProperty("driverClassName", "org.h2.Driver");
        p.setProperty("url", "jdbc:h2:~/sample");
        p.setProperty("username", "sample");
        p.setProperty("password", "sample");
        return p;
    }

    @Bean
    public DataSource dataSource(
            @Value("#{dbProps.driverClassName}")String driverClassName,
            @Value("#{dbProps.url}")String url,
            @Value("#{dbProps.username}")String username,
            @Value("#{dbProps.password}")String password) throws
            SQLException {
        DriverManagerDataSource ds = new DriverManagerDataSource();
        ds.setDriverClassName(driverClassName);
        ds.setUrl(url);
```

```
        ds.setUsername(username);
        ds.setPassword(password);
        return ds;
    }
}
```

The dbProps is an object that was instantiated and initialized, and it is treated as a bean in the application because of the @Bean annotation. There is no equivalent for @Value in any JSR.

Using Bean Factories

In the previous section, when we created a bean of type ConversionService we did so by using a bean of type ConversionServiceFactoryBean. This is an approach that makes use of the *Factory Pattern*. A pattern in the software world is a list of steps, an algorithm, or a model for a solution that solves a class of problems.[36] Alongside Singleton, the *Factory pattern*[37] is one of the most used patterns for writing Java applications. The Factory pattern is a creation pattern that provides a practical way to create objects of various types that implement the same interface by hiding the creation logic and exposing only a minimal API. It comes in two flavors: the *Factory Method pattern* and the *Abstract Factory pattern*. Spring supports creating beans using implementations following both patterns by using the @Bean annotation. The same annotation can be used when creating a bean of a singleton class (a class that can only be instantiated once). Before the introduction of this annotation, different attributes were required in XML to create beans.

Let's create a simple singleton class[38] and use the @Bean annotation to declare a bean of its type. We'll call the class SimpleSingleton to really make it obvious what we're doing.

---

[36]In the Java world there is a book considered the bible of patterns named *Design Patterns: Elements of Reusable Object-Oriented Software* written by four authors known as the *Gang of Four*; it describes various development techniques and covers 23 object-oriented java patterns.

[37]More information about this pattern can easily be found on the Internet using a simple search on Google, but here is a quick good source: https://en.wikipedia.org/wiki/Factory_method_pattern.

[38]The overview of the Singleton pattern

```
package com.apress.cems.beans.misc;

import org.slf4j.Logger;
import org.slf4j.LoggerFactory;

public class SimpleSingleton {
    private Logger logger = LoggerFactory.getLogger(SimpleSingleton.class);

    private static SimpleSingleton instance = new SimpleSingleton();

    private SimpleSingleton() {
        logger.info(">> Creating single instance.");
    }

    public static synchronized SimpleSingleton getInstance(){
        return instance;
    }
}
```

The use of synchronized is the worst approach to apply the Singleton pattern, indicate that for academic or simplicity purposes you are using this approach.

! In the previous example, the keyword `synchronized` is used on the `getInstance()` method. This is to respect the Singleton design pattern, which requires to ensure that even in a multithreaded environment a single instance is created. This causes a bottleneck in accessing this instance, but is a drawback it can be lived with. But in a Spring environment for using the `SimpleSingleton` class as a template for a bean factory synchronization is not necessary.

This class is not annotated with @Component because we want more control over the creation of the bean. The class declares a private static field of the class type that is instantiated on the spot, and it is returned by the getInstance() method.

The @Bean annotation is used on a method creating and returning a bean that is declared inside a configuration class annotated with @Configuration. The class and bean declaration are depicted in the next code snippet and you can see that the bean is created by calling the getInstance() method.

```
package com.apress.cems.beans.misc;

import org.springframework.context.annotation.Bean;
import org.springframework.context.annotation.Configuration;

@Configuration
public class MiscAppCfg {

    @Bean
    SimpleSingleton simpleSingleton(){
        return SimpleSingleton.getInstance();
    }
}
```

And this is all there is. And if you want to test that only one bean is created, you can run the com.apress.cems.beans.misc.MiscAppCfgTest class. This class retrieves two beans of type SimpleSingleton using two different methods and testing that the instances retrieved are equal.

```
package com.apress.cems.beans.misc;

import org.junit.jupiter.api.Test;
import org.slf4j.Logger;
import org.slf4j.LoggerFactory;
import org.springframework.context.ConfigurableApplicationContext;
import org.springframework.context.annotation.
AnnotationConfigApplicationContext;

import static org.junit.jupiter.api.Assertions.assertEquals;
import static org.junit.jupiter.api.Assertions.assertNotNull;

public class MiscAppCfgTest {
    private Logger logger = LoggerFactory.getLogger(MiscAppCfgTest.class);

    @Test
    void testSimpleBeans() {
        ConfigurableApplicationContext ctx =
            new AnnotationConfigApplicationContext(MiscAppCfg.class);

        SimpleSingleton simpleSingleton = ctx.getBean(SimpleSingleton.class);
        assertNotNull(simpleSingleton);
```

```java
    SimpleSingleton simpleSingleton2 =
        ctx.getBean("simpleSingleton", SimpleSingleton.class);
    assertNotNull(simpleSingleton2);

    assertEquals(simpleSingleton, simpleSingleton2);
    ctx.close();
    }
}
```

Now that this is covered, let's jump to the next one. Let's implement a class that uses a factory method to create a few types of beans. To show you how the factory method is used, let's create a method that depending of a text value, will return an instance of a class implementing the interface com.apress.cems.beans.misc.TaxFormula that groups together a hierarchy of classes that can calculate taxes. The hierarchy and the class containing the factory method are depicted in Figure 2-19.

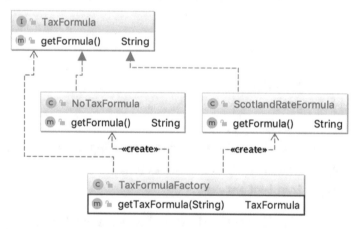

Figure 2-19. *Class hierarchy making use of the Factory Method pattern*

The implementations are naive, and the TaxFormula interface and the TaxFormulaFactory class are the only one relevant for this example.

```java
// TaxFormula.java
package com.apress.cems.beans.misc;

public interface TaxFormula {
    String getFormula();
}
```

```java
// TaxFormulaFactory.java
package com.apress.cems.beans.misc;

public class TaxFormulaFactory {

    public TaxFormula getTaxFormula(final String taxPlanCode){
        if(taxPlanCode == null){
            return null;
        }

        switch (taxPlanCode) {
            case "S":
                return new ScotlandRateFormula();
            case "NT":
                return new NoTaxFormula();
        }
        return null;
    }
}
```

The getTaxFormula()method creates beans of either a ScotlandRateFormula or NoTaxFormula type. To use it, we have to first instantiate the TaxFormulaFactory. The declaration of a bean using an instance of the previous class is depicted in the following code snippet.

```java
 package com.apress.cems.beans.misc;

import org.springframework.context.annotation.Bean;
import org.springframework.context.annotation.Configuration;

@Configuration
public class MiscAppCfg {

    @Bean
    SimpleSingleton simpleSingleton(){
        return SimpleSingleton.getInstance();
    }
```

```
@Bean
TaxFormula taxScotlandFormula(){
    return new TaxFormulaFactory().getTaxFormula("S");
}
}
```

In the previous code snippet you might have noticed that the bean type is declared to be TaxFormula. This allows future modifications to the body of the taxScotlandFormula() method and return a different implementation, without causing compile time errors in the code using the created beans. Interfaces are contracts, a description of a set of methods and classes implementing them should provide a concrete behavior for them. Using interface types for references is practical for larger systems, because no matter how much the system evolves as long as the interface contract is respected, dependencies can be swapped at runtime without fear of the system malfunctioning. The previous example is quite succinct, and the factory class is instantiated in place inside the method declaring the bean.

Another version of implementing this is to declare the factory bean and use it whenever necessary. Although it seems somewhat redundant, creating beans in this way might be useful when one is using third-party libraries that only allow creating objects using a factory class. And this method connects existing components to provide a certain behavior, such as helping Spring to convert String values to Date objects (remember how the conversionService bean was created) using a format pattern different from the default one.

When writing your own bean factories, you might want to follow the guideline provided by Spring and implementing the org.springframework.beans.factory. FactoryBean<T> interface. This interface is used by many Spring implementations to simplify configuration, including the ConversionServiceFactoryBean used earlier in the chapter. Even if implementing your factories this way ties your code to Spring components (which is usually not recommended), this method is practical when XML configuration is needed because it simplifies it a lot. The class named TaxFormulaFactoryBean creates a singleton bean of type TaxFormula and implements the Spring interface. The class name follows the recommended Spring name template: [ClassName]FactoryBean.

```java
 package com.apress.cems.beans.xml.misc;

import com.apress.cems.beans.misc.ScotlandRateFormula;
import com.apress.cems.beans.misc.TaxFormula;
import org.slf4j.Logger;
import org.slf4j.LoggerFactory;
import org.springframework.beans.factory.FactoryBean;

public class TaxFormulaFactoryBean implements FactoryBean<TaxFormula> {

    private Logger logger = LoggerFactory.getLogger(TaxFormulaFactoryBean.
    class);
    private TaxFormula taxFormula = new ScotlandRateFormula();

    public TaxFormulaFactoryBean() {
        logger.info(">> Look ma, no definition!");
    }

    @Override getObject() throws Exception {
        return this.taxFormula;
    }

    @Override
    public Class<?> getObjectType() {
        return ScotlandRateFormula.class;
    }

    @Override
    public boolean isSingleton() {
        return true;
    }
}
```

If the previous class did not implement the FactoryBean<T> interface, but just had a method named getObject() that returns the instance being created, the XML declaration would look like the following.

```xml
    <bean id="taxFormulaFactoryBean"
          class="com.apress.cems.beans.xml.misc.TaxFormulaFactoryBean" />
    <bean id="taxScotlandFormula" factory-bean="taxFormulaFactoryBean" />
```

Yes, as you probably suspected, the method name is important, and it can be recognized by Spring as a factory method even if it is not part of class implementing FactoryBean. If the method is named differently, let's say getInstance(), then the XML configuration has to be adjusted to tell Spring the name of the factory method. And this can be done by adding the factory-method attribute and set the method name as its value.

```
<bean id="taxFormulaFactoryBean"
      class="com.apress.cems.beans.xml.misc.TaxFormulaFactoryBean" />
<bean id="taxScotlandFormula" factory-bean="taxFormulaFactoryBean"
    factory-method="getInstance" />
```

But because a Spring interface is used, the configuration can be reduced to the following.

```
<bean id="scotlandTaxFactory" class="com.apress.cems.beans.xml.misc.
TaxFormulaFactoryBean" />
```

And although the class attribute value is com.apress.cems.beans.xml.misc. TaxFormulaFactoryBean<T>, the bean instance named scotlandTaxFactory will be of type com.apress.cems.beans.misc.ScotlandRateFormula.

If you are curious about the Spring classes that implement org.springframework. beans.factory.FactoryBean, IntelliJ IDEA can help you there. The class depicted in the previous code snippet is part of 02-ps-container-01-practice. Just open that class, click the interface name, and press CTRL (Command in macOS)+ALT+B, and a list of classes implementing it will be displayed, as depicted in Figure 2-20.

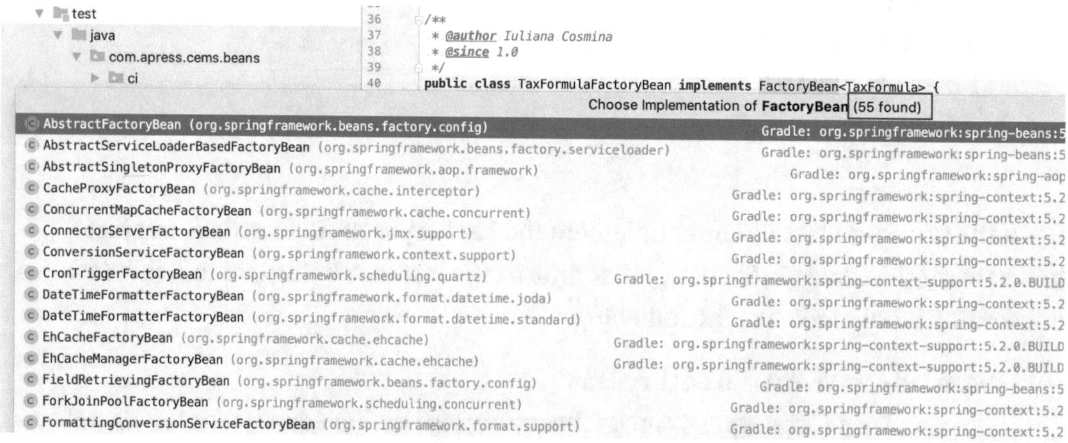

Figure 2-20. *Classes implementing the FactoryBean interface*

Spring factory bean classes provide assistance for configuring data access using Hibernate and JPA, for handling transactions, for configuring caching with EhCache, and so on. A few of them will be used in the code samples for this book, so you will have occasion to see them in action.

More About Autowiring

The @Autowired annotation is equivalent to JSR 330's @Inject. The infrastructure bean that is responsible for detecting and processing these annotations is named org.springframework.context.annotation.internalAutowiredAnnotationProcessor of type AutowiredAnnotationBeanPostProcessor[39] and implements the org. springframework.beans.factory.config.BeanPostProcessor interface, which means this type of bean modifies bean instances, which should be obvious since this annotation declares the dependencies to be injected.

The @Autowired annotation requires the dependency to be mandatory, but this behavior can be changed by setting the required attribute to false.

```
@Autowired(required=false)
public void setDataSource(DataSource dataSource) {
    this.dataSource = dataSource;
}
```

In the previous case, if a bean of type DataSource is not found within the context the value that is injected is null. The @Autowired annotation works on methods. If Spring can identify the proper bean, it will autowire it. This is useful for development of special Spring configuration classes that have methods that are called by Spring directly and have parameters that have to be configured. The most common example is the setting method global security using classes annotated with @EnableGlobalMethodSecurity:

---

[39]The name of this bean and its purpose and a few others are part of the *org.springframework. context.annotation.AnnotationConfigUtils* class. You can see the code here https://github. com/spring-projects/spring-framework/blob/3a0f309e2c9fdbbf7fb2d348be8615281 77f8555/spring-context/src/main/java/org/springframework/context/annotation/ AnnotationConfigUtils.java

```
@Configuration
@EnableGlobalMethodSecurity
public class MethodSecurityConfig {

// method called by Spring
  @Autowired
  public void registerGlobal(AuthenticationManagerBuilder auth)
      throws Exception {
    auth
        .inMemoryAuthentication()
          .withUser("john").password("test").roles("USER").and()
          .withUser("admin").password("admin").roles("USER", "ADMIN");
    }

  @Bean
  public MethodSecurityService methodSecurityService() {
    return new MethodSecurityServiceImpl()
  }
}
```

A more detailed version of this code snippet is explained in the "Spring Security" section in Chapter 6.

A strong feature for @Autowired added in Spring 4.x is the possibility to use generic types as qualifiers. This is useful when you have classes that are organized in a hierarchy and they all inherit a certain class that is generic, like the repositories in the project attached to the book, all of which extend JdbcAbstractRepo<T>. Let's see how this feature can be used.

```
// repository classes extending JdbcAbstractRepo
@Component
public class JdbcCriminalCaseextends JdbcAbstractRepo<CriminalCase>
  implements CriminalCaseRepo {...}

@Component
public class JdbcDetectiveRepo extends JdbcAbstractRepo<Detective>
   implements DetectiveRepo {...}
```

```
@Configuration
@ComponentScan(basePackages = {"com.apress.cems.repos"})
public class RepositoryConfig {

        ...

}
 // Test class
@RunWith(SpringJUnit4ClassRunner.class)
@ContextConfiguration(classes = {RepositoryConfig})
public class GenericQualifierTest {

    @Autowired
    JdbcAbstractRepo<CriminalCase> criminalCaseRepo;

    @Autowired
    JdbcAbstractRepo<Detective> detectiveRepo;

....
}
```

This helps a lot, because in related classes, the Qualifier annotation is no longer needed to name different beans of related types to make sure that Spring does not get confused. However, if Spring cannot use generic types as qualifiers because this type is the same for two related implementations, the use of @Qualifer is necessary; otherwise, the application context cannot be created.

```
// repository classes extending JdbcAbstractRepo<CriminalCase>
@Component
public class JdbcCriminalCaseRepo extends JdbcAbstractRepo<CriminalCase>
  implements CriminalCaseRepo {...}

@Component
public class JPACriminalCaseRepo extends JdbcAbstractRepo<CriminalCase>
   implements CriminalCaseRepo {...}

@Configuration
@ComponentScan(basePackages = {"com.apress.cems.repos"})
public class RepositoryConfig {

        ...

}
```

```
// Test class
@ExtendWith(SpringExtension.class)
@ContextConfiguration(classes = {RepoConfig.class})
public class TestRepoCfg {

    @Qualifier("jdbcCriminalCaseRepo")
    @Autowired
    CriminalCaseRepo jdbcRepo;

    @Qualifier("JPACriminalCaseRepo")
    @Autowired
    CriminalCaseRepo jpaRepo;

    @Test
    void allGoodTest(){
        assertNotEquals(jdbcRepo,jpaRepo);
    }
}
```

In this example, we specified in the test class exactly which bean we want autowired by annotating the fields with @Qualifier and providing the bean name as an argument for it. Without this annotation, Spring cannot figure out which bean we want to inject, since both available bean types are subtypes of CriminalCaseRepo.

The JSR 250 and JSR 330 annotations are supported and can be used alongside Spring annotations, but they have quite a few common functionalities. In Table 2-3, you can see the correspondences and the differences between them.

Table 2-3. *Autowiring Annotations*

Spring	JSR	Comment
@Component	@Named	@Named can be used instead of all stereotype annotations except @Configuration
@Qualifier	@Qualifier	JSR Qualifier is a marker annotation used to identify qualifier annotations, like @Named, for example
@Autowired	@Inject	@Inject may apply to static as well as instance members
@Autowired + @Qualifier	@Resource(name= "beanName")	@Resource is useful because replaces two annotations.

Another interesting annotation is @Lazy, which starting with Spring 4.x can be used on injection points (wherever @Autowired is used) too. This annotation postpones the creation of a bean until it is first accessed by adding this annotation to the bean definition. So yes, as with @Scope, @Lazy can be used with a @Component or @Bean annotation. This is useful when the dependency is a huge object, and you do not want to keep the memory occupied with this object until it is really needed, but since it allows creating an application context without the full dependency tree being created when the application starts, it leaves room for configuration errors, so use it wisely.

```
@Component
@Lazy
public class SimpleBean { ... }

// or on a @Bean
@Configuration
public class RequestRepoConfig {

    @Lazy
    @Bean
    public RequestRepo anotherRepo(){
        return new JdbcRequestRepo();
    }
}
```

```
// on injection point
@Repository
public class JdbcPetRepo  extends  JdbcAbstractRepo<Pet>
implements PetRepo {
    ...
    @Lazy
    @Autowired(required=false)
    public void setDataSource(DataSource dataSource) {
        this.dataSource = dataSource;
    }
}
```

In the previous example, you can see @Lazy used with Autowired(required = false). This is the only correct usage that allows the dependency to be lazily initialized. Without Autowired(required = false), the Spring IoC container will do its normal job and inject dependencies when the bean is created and ignoring the presence of @Lazy.

Aside from all the annotations discussed so far, developers can write their own annotations. You've already seen an example of a @Scope specialization earlier in the chapter. Many of the annotations provided by Spring can be used as meta-annotations in your own code. You can view a meta-annotation as a super class. A meta-annotation can annotate another annotation. All stereotype specializations are annotated with @Component, for example. Meta-annotations can be composed to obtain other annotations. For example, let's create a @CustomTx annotation that will be used to mark service beans that will use a different transaction.

```
import java.lang.annotation.ElementType;
import java.lang.annotation.Retention;
import java.lang.annotation.RetentionPolicy;
import java.lang.annotation.Target;

import org.springframework.transaction.annotation.Transactional;

@Target({ElementType.METHOD, ElementType.TYPE})
@Retention(RetentionPolicy.RUNTIME)
@Transactional("customTransactionManager", timeout="90")
public @interface CustomTx {
    boolean readOnly() default false;
}
```

Spring configuration using annotations is really powerful and flexible. In this book, Java configuration and annotations are covered together, because this is the way they are commonly used in practice. There definitely are old-style developers who still prefer XML and more grounded developers who like to *mix and match*. Configuration using annotations is practical, because it can help you reduce the number of resource files in the project, but the downside is that it is scattered all over the code. But being linked to the code, refactoring is a process that becomes possible without the torture of searching bean definitions in XML files, although smart editors help a lot with that these days. The annotations configuration is more appropriate for beans that are frequently changing: custom business beans such as services, repositories, and controllers. Imagine adding a new parameter for a constructor and then going hunting beans in the XML files, so the definition can be updated. Java configuration annotations should be used to configure infrastructure beans (data sources, persistence units, etc.).

There are advantages to using XML too. The main advantage is that the configuration is centralized in a few XML files and is decoupled from the code. You could just modify the XML configuration files and repackage the application without a full rebuild being necessary. But Java configuration can be done in a smart way too; nothing stops you from declaring all the configuration in a set of packages that can be wrapped together in a configuration library. When you change configuration details, you only need to rebuild those packages, not the full project. Then, XML is widely supported and known, and there are more than a few legacy applications out there. Ultimately, it is only the context that decides the most appropriate solution. If you are a Spring expert starting to work on your own startup application, you will probably go with Java configuration and annotations. And probably Spring Boot, which will make your work much easier by providing super-meta-annotations to configure much of the infrastructure needed for the project. If you are working on a big project with legacy code, you will probably have to deal with some XML configuration here and there. Whatever the case, respect good practices and read the manual, and you should be fine.

Using Multiple Configuration Classes

In a Spring test environment, the spring-test module provides the @ContextConfiguration to bootstrap a test environment using one or multiple configuration resources. This is an alternative to creating an application context by directly instantiating a specific context class. The following code depicts this scenario, and it provides a different way to test spring applications by delegating the responsibility of creating the application context to the Spring Test Framework. (Chapter 3 is fully dedicated to testing Spring applications.)

```java
package com.apress.cems.config;

import org.junit.Test;
import org.junit.runner.RunWith;
import org.springframework.beans.factory.annotation.Autowired;
import org.springframework.test.context.ContextConfiguration;
import org.springframework.test.context.junit4.SpringRunner;

import javax.sql.DataSource;

import static org.junit.jupiter.api.Assertions.assertNotNull;

@RunWith(SpringRunner.class)
@ContextConfiguration(classes = {TestDataSourceConfig.class})
public class BootstrapDatasourceTest {

    @Autowired
    DataSource dataSource;

    @Test
    public void testBoot() {
        assertNotNull(dataSource);
    }
}
```

Let's declare another configuration class that will pick up bean declarations of repositories using the dataSource bean referred previously.

```java
package com.apress.cems.config;

import com.apress.cems.pojos.repos.DetectiveRepo;
import com.apress.cems.repos.JdbcDetectiveRepo;
import org.springframework.beans.factory.annotation.Autowired;
import org.springframework.context.annotation.Bean;
import org.springframework.context.annotation.ComponentScan;
import org.springframework.context.annotation.Configuration;
import org.springframework.context.annotation.Import;
```

```
import javax.sql.DataSource;

@Configuration
@ComponentScan(basePackages = {"com.apress.cems.repos"})
@Import(TestDataSourceConfig.class)
public class RepositoryConfig {

    @Autowired
    DataSource dataSource;

    @Bean
    DetectiveRepo detectiveRepo(){
        return new JdbcDetectiveRepo(dataSource);
    }
}
```

The repository implementations are not really important, but what is important is the fact that the JdbcDetectiveRepo class was not configured as a bean. A bean of type JdbcDetectiveRepo is declared using the @Bean annotation in the RepositoryConfig configuration class. This style of configuration gives me the opportunity to show you how to declare beans that depend on this bean in a different configuration class.

The @Import annotation imports the configuration from another class into the class annotated with it.

The repository classes identified using component scanning by the RepositoryConfig class in the previous example, have been declared as beans by annotating them with @Repository which is a specialization of @Component. This decision was made to make the purpose of these bean obvious. As example, this is the JdbcEvidenceRepo class and annotations that configure it as a bean declaration.

```
package com.apress.cems.repos;

...
import com.apress.cems.pojos.repos.EvidenceRepo;
import org.springframework.beans.factory.annotation.Autowired;
import org.springframework.stereotype.Repository;
```

```
@Repository
public class JdbcEvidenceRepo extends
        JdbcAbstractRepo<Evidence> implements EvidenceRepo {

    public JdbcEvidenceRepo(){
    }

    @Autowired
    public JdbcEvidenceRepo(DataSource dataSource) {
        super(dataSource);
    }

    ...
}
```

The previous configuration can be tested by writing a typical Spring test class that runs in a test context based on the RepositoryConfig configuration class.

```
package com.apress.cems.config;

import com.apress.cems.pojos.repos.DetectiveRepo;
import com.apress.cems.pojos.repos.EvidenceRepo;
import org.junit.Test;
import org.junit.runner.RunWith;
import org.springframework.beans.factory.annotation.Autowired;
import org.springframework.test.context.ContextConfiguration;
import org.springframework.test.context.junit4.SpringRunner;

import static org.junit.Assert.assertNotNull;

@RunWith(SpringRunner.class)
@ContextConfiguration(classes = {RepositoryConfig.class})
public class MultipleResourcesTest {

    @Autowired
    EvidenceRepo evidenceRepo;

    @Autowired
    DetectiveRepo detectiveRepo;
```

```
    @Test
    public void testInjectedBeans(){
        assertNotNull(evidenceRepo);
        assertNotNull(detectiveRepo);
    }
}
```

When run, the previous test passes, because both evidenceRepo and detectiveRepo beans are created and were injected correctly in the test context. This works fine, because the @Import(TestDataSourceConfig.class) annotation was used to decorate the RepositoryConfig class. Without this annotation on the TestDataSourceConfig, both classes have to be used as arguments for the classes attribute in the @ContextConfiguration annotation.

The following test class configuration depicts exactly this scenario, when @Import| is not used on TestDataSourceConfig.

```
package com.apress.cems.config;

import com.apress.cems.pojos.repos.DetectiveRepo;
import com.apress.cems.pojos.repos.EvidenceRepo;
import org.junit.Test;
import org.junit.runner.RunWith;
import org.springframework.beans.factory.annotation.Autowired;
import org.springframework.test.context.ContextConfiguration;
import org.springframework.test.context.junit4.SpringRunner;

import static org.junit.Assert.assertNotNull;

@RunWith(SpringRunner.class)
@ContextConfiguration(classes =
        {RepositoryConfig.class, TestDataSourceConfig.class})
public class MultipleResourcesTest {
    ...
}
```

Also, if you want to write a test class that creates a context without using the @ContextConfiguration annotation, the AnnotationConfigApplicationContext class can be used with multiple arguments as well.

```
package com.apress.cems.config;
...
class DataSourceConfigTest {

    @Test
    void testMultipleCfgSource() {
        ApplicationContext ctx =
                new AnnotationConfigApplicationContext(TestDataSource
                Config.class,
                    RepositoryConfig.class);

        EvidenceRepo evidenceRepo = ctx.getBean(JdbcEvidenceRepo.class);
        DetectiveRepo detectiveRepo = ctx.getBean(JdbcDetectiveRepo.class);

        assertNotNull(evidenceRepo);
        assertNotNull(detectiveRepo);
    }
}
```

In the configuration examples we've done so far, we have declared bean definitions (infrastructure and business) by methods annotated with @Bean, which are always found under a class annotated with @Configuration. For large applications, you can imagine that this is quite impractical, which is why beans configurations should be done using stereotype annotations. The simplest way to define a bean in Spring is to annotate the bean class with @Component (or any of the stereotype annotations that apply) and enable component scanning. Of course, this is applicable only to classes that are part of the project. For classes that are defined in third-party libs like the DataSource in the examples presented so far, declaring beans using @Bean is the only solution.

Having multiple configuration classes is useful to separate beans based on their purpose; for example, to separate infrastructure beans from application beans, because infrastructure change between environments.[40]

```
ApplicationContext ctx =
                new AnnotationConfigApplicationContext(
                    TestDataSourceConfig.class,
                    RepositoryConfig.class);
```

---

[40]Most companies use three types of environments: development, testing, and production.

In the preceding example, the configuration for the storage layer is decoupled from the rest of the application configuration in `TestDataSourceConfig` configuration class. This makes the database configuration easily replaceable depending on the environment. The contents of the `TestDataSourceConfig` configuration class contain a dataSource bean definition that uses an in-memory H2 database; this type of database is often used in test environments. The configuration file containing the connection information and credentials for the in-memory database are contained in the `test-datasource.properties` file.

```
db.driverClassName=org.h2.Driver
db.url=jdbc:h2:~/sample
db.username=sample
db.password=sample
```

The production configuration is (usually) more complex than a test configuration (as it usually involves transaction management and connection pooling), and requires a different implementation of the `javax.sql.DataSource`. For this example, let's assume that the database used in production is Oracle. The connection information and credentials are contained in a `prod-datasource.properties` file and the class using that file to create a production configuration using an Oracle datasource is named `ProdDataSourceConfig`. Both are depicted in the next code listing.

```
 // prod-datasource.properties
driverClassName=oracle.jdbc.OracleDriver
url=jdbc:oracle:thin:@localhost:1521:xe
username=prod
password=prod
```

```java
// ProdDataSourceConfig.java
package com.apress.cems.config;

import com.apress.cems.ex.ConfigurationException;
import oracle.jdbc.pool.OracleDataSource;
import org.springframework.context.annotation.Bean;
import org.springframework.context.annotation.Configuration;
import org.springframework.core.io.ClassPathResource;
import org.springframework.core.io.support.PropertiesLoaderUtils;
```

```java
import javax.sql.DataSource;
import java.io.IOException;
import java.sql.SQLException;
import java.util.Properties;

@Configuration
public class ProdDataSourceConfig {

    @Bean("connectionProperties")
    Properties connectionProperties(){
        try {
            return PropertiesLoaderUtils.loadProperties(
                    new ClassPathResource("db/prod-datasource.properties"));
        } catch (IOException e) {
            throw new ConfigurationException(
                    "Could not retrieve connection properties!", e);
        }
    }

    @Bean
    public DataSource dataSource() {
        try {
            OracleDataSource ds = new OracleDataSource();
            ds.setConnectionProperties(connectionProperties());
            return ds;
        } catch (SQLException e) {
            throw new ConfigurationException(
                    "Could not configure Oracle database!", e);
        }
    }
}
```

The org.springframework.core.io.support.PropertiesLoaderUtils provides a set of convenient utility methods for loading of java.util.Properties, performing standard handling of input streams. It was used here because the OracleDataSource class can be instantiated using a Properties object containing a specific set of properties. It also makes a simple configuration class, don't you think?

Based on the following information, a test context should be created by calling.

```
ApplicationContext ctx =
    new AnnotationConfigApplicationContext(TestDataSourceConfig.class,
        RepositoryConfig.class);
```

A production context should be created by calling the following.

```
ApplicationContext ctx =
    new AnnotationConfigApplicationContext(ProdDataSourceConfig.class,
        RepositoryConfig.class);
```

The differences between the two environments are only represented here by the bean of the DataSource type being injected into the repository classes. And because we have control of both environments, we can modify a test class to use the ProdDataSourceConfig class as a part of the configuration, and use debugging to inspect the dataSource bean. You can see the differences between the two environments in Figure 2-21.

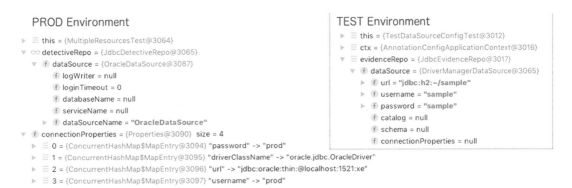

Figure 2-21. *Test and Production environments different configurations*

!   Since this is the end of an important section, there is a task for you. In project chapter02/config-practice there is a configuration class that has gotten a little too big:

com.apress.cems.config.FullConfig. Split this file into one or more configuration files, and modify the test class com.apress.cems.config. FullConfigTest to use those files to load the context. The test must execute successfully to validate your configuration. In project chapter02/config you have an implementation which is quite closer to how your solution should look like.

Also, do not forget that after you have modified a class, you might want to build your project using `gradle build` in the command line or run the `compileJava` task from the IntelliJ IDEA interface to make sure you are running your test with the most recent sources. In Figure 2-22, the location of the `compileJava` task is evidentiated for you.

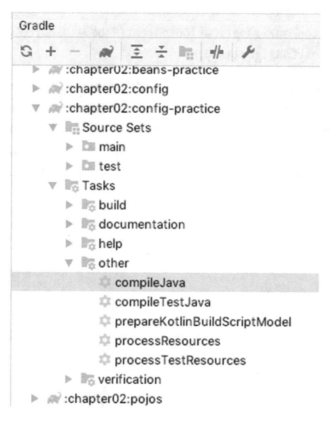

Figure 2-22. *The Gradle view in IntelliJ IDEA*

The `Environment` bean models two key aspects of an application environment: *properties* and *profiles*. We've already covered properties; it is only fair that *profiles* be covered as well. A profile is a logical group of bean definitions that is registered within the Spring IoC container when the profile is active. Similarly, profiles can group property files or property values that are supposed to be active only when the profile is. Using profiles within a Spring application is practical because it becomes easier to activate configuration for one environment or another. For the previous example we had the following configuration classes: `TestDatasourceConfig`, `ProdDatasourceConfig`, and `RepositoryConfig`. And to bootstrap one environment or the other, we would couple the specific environment configuration class `TestDatasourceConfig` with the class declaring beans specific to both environments (e.g., `RepositoryConfig`). Using profiles, we can bootstrap an application that is configured using all the classes, but that is specific only to environment activated by the profile, because when using profiles Spring analyses the configuration classes available and creates all beans that are not annotated with `@Profile` and only the beans annotated with `@Profile` and specific to the activated profile. For this to work, fist we have to annotate each of the data source configuration classes with the `@Profile` annotation to make them specific to a profile.

```
 ...
 import org.springframework.context.annotation.Profile;

@Configuration
@PropertySource("classpath:db/test-datasource.properties")
@Profile("test")
public class TestProfileDataSourceConfig {
 ...
}

@Configuration
@Profile("prod")
public class ProdDataSourceConfig {
 ...
}
```

After doing this, we just have to bootstrap an application using a class annotated with `@ContextConfiguration`, adding all configuration classes as arguments and activating the profile by annotating it with `@ActiveProfiles`.

```
 package com.apress.cems.config;

import org.junit.Test;
import org.junit.runner.RunWith;
import org.springframework.beans.factory.annotation.Autowired;
import org.springframework.jdbc.datasource.DriverManagerDataSource;
import org.springframework.test.context.ActiveProfiles;
```

```
import org.springframework.test.context.ContextConfiguration;
import org.springframework.test.context.junit4.SpringRunner;

import javax.sql.DataSource;

import static org.junit.Assert.assertNotNull;

@RunWith(SpringRunner.class)
@ActiveProfiles("test")
@ContextConfiguration(classes = {ProdDataSourceConfig.class,
      TestProfileDataSourceConfig, RepositoryConfig.class})
public class ProfilesTest {

    @Autowired
    DataSource dataSource;

    @Test
    public void testInjectedBeans(){
        assertNotNull(dataSource instanceof DriverManagerDataSource);
    }
}
```

The previous class activated the test profile which means the application context
will be created only using configuration classes that are either annotated with
@Profile("test") and classes that are not annotated with @Profile.

The line assertNotNull(dataSource instanceof DriverManagerDataSource) tests
that the dataSource bean is of the type declared in the TestProfileDataSourceConfig
class, the one specific to the test profile.

Spring Boot

Spring Boot is a set of preconfigured set of frameworks/technologies designed to reduce
boilerplate configuration (infrastructure) and provide a quick way to have a Spring
application up and running. Its goal is to allow developers to focus on implementation of
the actual required functionality instead of how to configure an application by providing
ready-to-use infrastructure beans. On the official Spring Boot page[41] a REST application

---

[41]Spring Boot official page: http://projects.spring.io/spring-boot/

is given as an example and almost 20 lines of code are needed to have a runnable application. Impressive, right? And this is only one of the advantages of using Spring Boot.

Spring Boot is built on top of the Spring Framework and is represented by a collection of libraries named *starters* which, when used as dependencies of a project provide a collection of preconfigured dependencies that allow starting an application with one click. Spring Boot might seem like one of those tools that seem to function *auto-magically* but really, under the hood provides the configuration of your application, so you don't have to because it is easier to change something that exists and customize it to match your needs than building it from scratch.

One thing that can be said about Spring Boot is that it is *opinionated.* It serves you with a configuration that a team of people from Pivotal thought it is suitable to what you are trying to build; so they basically turned their opinion into a configuration, they packed it up and decided to offer it to developers as a dependency.

For example, if you are trying to build a Spring web application that saves data into a database, no matter what form that data has you will most likely need the following dependencies: Spring MVC for the web layer; Spring Data JPA for the data access layer; and Spring Security if you want to restrict access to the data. You might need Spring Test to test it, and a database driver. To create a configuration like this, you first need to specify the dependencies in a build tool like Gradle and make sure that the versions are compatible. Then you have to declare configuration classes with the infrastructure beans that you need. Seems like a lot of work and very prone to errors. But since most applications of this type require almost the same dependencies and almost the same infrastructure beans, a template can be determined and provided out of the box.

Spring Boot makes it easier for developers to build stand-alone, production-level applications that are just ready to run. Spring Boot can create applications that are packed as a `jar` can be run with `java -jar` or typical `war`-packed projects that can be deployed on an application server. The new thing is that web archives (`.war` files) can be executed with `java -jar` as well.

Spring Boot focuses on the following.

- Setting up the infrastructure for a Spring project in a really short time.

- Providing a default, common infrastructure configuration, while allowing easy divergence from the default as the application grows (so any default configuration can easily be overridden).

175

- Providing a range of non-functional[42] features common to a wide range of projects (embedded servers, security, metrics, health checks, externalized configuration, etc.).

- Removing the need for XML and code configuration.

The stable version of Spring Boot when this book was written was 2.1.4.RELEASE, which works with JDK 11. In the book source, version 2.2.0-M2 was used. By the time this book is released, this version will have changed, since the sources are updated to work with the most recent versions of Spring and Java.

Configuration

Spring Boot can be used as any Java library. It can be added to a project as a dependency, because it does not require any special integration tools, and it can be used in any IDE. Spring Boot provides "starter" POMs to simplify the Maven configuration of a project. When using Maven, the project must have `spring-boot-starter-parent` so that the useful Maven defaults are provided. Since the sources attached to this book use Gradle, it is very suitable that Gradle is supported too. For Gradle there is no need to specify a parent, because the Spring Boot Gradle plugin makes sure that the dependencies specific to a certain type of application are provided. There are different starter dependencies, depending on the type of application; in the following sample, only a few are declared.[43] To reuse configuration declarations from the parent project, all Spring Boot components and versions will be declared in the `pivotal-certified-pro-spring-dev-exam-02/build.gradle` file.

```
//pivotal-certified-pro-spring-dev-exam-02/build.gradle configuration file
snippet
allprojects {
    group 'com.apress.cems'
    version '1.0-SNAPSHOT'
}

...
```

---

[42]The *non-functional* term means they are not critical for the functionality of the project (e.g., a project can function without metrics).

[43]The full list is available in the Spring Boot Reference documentation http://docs.spring.io/ spring-boot/docs/current/reference/htmlsingle/#using-boot-starter

```
ext {
    springBootVersion = '2.2.0-M2'
...

    boot = [
    springBootPlugin:
        "org.springframework.boot:spring-boot-gradle-
        plugin:$springBootVersion",
    starterWeb       :
        "org.springframework.boot:spring-boot-starter-
        web:$springBootVersion",
    starterSecurity :
        "org.springframework.boot:spring-boot-starter-
        security:$springBootVersion",
    starterJpa       :
        "org.springframework.boot:spring-boot-starter-data-
        jpa:$springBootVersion",
    starterTest      :
        "org.springframework.boot:spring-boot-starter-
        test:$springBootVersion",
    actuator         :
        "org.springframework.boot:spring-boot-starter-
        actuator:$springBootVersion",
    starterWs        :
        "org.springframework.boot:spring-boot-starter-
        ws:$springBootVersion",
    devtools         :
        "org.springframework.boot:spring-boot-devtools:$springBootVersion"
    ]
        ...
}
```

In the Gradle configuration file of the parent project `pivotal-certified-pro-spring-dev-exam-02`, versions for main libraries or family of libraries are declared, as well as repositories where dependencies are downloaded from and version of Java used for compiling and running the project. The `chapter02/boot` is a subproject of the `pivotal-certified-pro-spring-dev-exam-02` project with its separate dependencies managed by the Spring Boot Gradle plugin. The `chapter02/boot/build.gradle` configuration file only contains the dependencies needed, without versions, because these are inherited from the parent configuration.

```
//pivotal-certified-pro-spring-dev-exam-02/chapter02/boot/build.gradle
buildscript {
    repositories {
        ...
    }

    dependencies {
     /* 1 */ classpath boot.springBootPlugin
    }
}

apply plugin: 'java-library'
/* 2 */ apply plugin: 'org.springframework.boot'

group 'com.apress.cems'
/* 3 */ext.moduleName = 'com.apress.cems.boot'

apply plugin: 'java'
apply plugin: 'idea'

dependencies {
    compile boot.starterWeb
    /* 4 */ testImplementation boot.starterTest
}
...
}
```

The marked lines have the following purposes within the configuration.

1. The `springBootPlugin` artifact is declared as a classpath dependency, because it is needed to build the Spring Boot dependency tree.

2. The Spring Boot Gradle Plugin is applied to the project to extend the project's capabilities, which is referred to by its name, `org.springframework.boot`.

3. Since we are using Java 11, the project uses modules; this line just tells Gradle what the module name of this project is.

4. This project is configured to use a very smart Gradle plugin named java-library[44] to manage dependencies that allows special types of dependencies, the testImplementation type means this dependency will be used to test the application, and that this dependency is internal to this project.

Each release of Spring Boot provides a curated list of dependencies it supports. The versions of the necessary libraries are selected so the API matches perfectly and this is handled by Spring Boot. The collection of libraries that end up in the application classpath is curated to the extreme so there is no API mismatch between versions. Therefore, the manual configuration of dependencies versions is not necessary. Upgrading Spring Boot ensures that those dependencies are upgraded as well. This can easily be proven by looking at the transitive dependencies of the spring-boot-starter-web in IntelliJ IDEA Gradle view, as depicted in Figure 2-23.

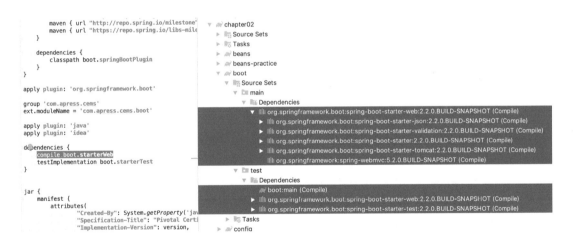

Figure 2-23. *chapter-2/boot: spring-boot-starter-web transitive dependencies in IntelliJ IDEA Gradle view*

The version for Spring Boot and project version is inherited from the pivotal-certified-pro-spring-dev-exam-02 project. To have this project built and running, all we need is one class annotated with @SpringBootApplication.

---

[44]More info about it here: https://docs.gradle.org/current/userguide/java_library_plugin.html

This annotation is a top-level annotation designed to use only at the class level. It a convenience annotation that is equivalent to declaring the following three annotations on the same class.

- @SpringBootConfiguration, which is a specialization of @Configuration because the class is a configuration class and can declare beans with @Bean. Can be used as an alternative to the Spring's standard @Configuration annotation so that configuration can be found automatically.

- @EnableAutoConfiguration this is a specific Spring Boot annotation from package org.springframework.boot.autoconfigure that has the purpose to enable auto-configuration of the Spring ApplicationContext, attempting to guess and configure the beans that you are likely to need based on the specified dependencies and libraries found in the classpath.

  ! @EnableAutoConfiguration works well with Spring provided starter dependencies, but it is not directly tied to them, so other dependencies outside the starters can be used. For example, if there is a specific embedded server on the classpath this will be used unless there is another one configured for in the project (e.g., an external Tomcat server).

- @ComponentScan, because the developer will declare classes annotated with stereotype annotations that will become beans of some kind. By default, the base packages and its subpackages will be scanned. The attribute used to list the packages to scan with @SpringBootApplication is scanBasePackages. There are other attributes declared, such as scanBasePackageClasses, which allow you to specify a configuration class as a filter. The package containing it is scanned, thus providing a type-safe alternative scanning argument, because you might happen to write a package name wrong, but when specifying a class, the editor makes sure that you do not refer to a class that does not exist.

If no attribute is set relating to component scanning by default, the package where the class annotated with @SpringBootApplication and its subpackages will be scanned for bean annotations.

```
package com.apress.cems.boot;

import org.springframework.boot.SpringApplication;
import org.springframework.boot.autoconfigure.SpringBootApplication;

@SpringBootApplication
public class Application {

    public static void main(String[] args) {Teiubesc!2
        SpringApplication.run(Application.class, args);
    }
}
```

The main method is the entry point of the application and follows the Java convention for an application entry point. This method calls the static run method from the org.springframework.boot.SpringApplication class that bootstraps the application and start the Spring IoC container, which starts the default embedded web server. Because we are creating a Spring Boot web application and we did not specify in the configuration the type of embedded server to use, the default is used, which is Tomcat. So, if you run this class in IntelliJ IDEA, or compile and build the application and execute the jar, the result will be the same: a Spring application will be started with a lot of infrastructure beans already configured with the default common configurations.

Now that we have a Spring application context, let's do something with it, like inspect all the beans. The easiest way to do this is to add a controller class that will display all of those beans. But declaring a controller means views also have to be resolved, so the simplest way is to use a REST controller. A REST controller is a controller class annotated with @RestController. This annotation is a combination of @Controller, the typical stereotype annotation marking a bean as a web component and @ResponseBody an annotation that basically tells spring that the result returned by methods in this class do not need to be stored in a model and displayed in a view. The CtxController depicted in the following code snippet contains one method that returns a simple HTML code containing a list of all beans in the application context.

```java
package com.apress.cems.boot;

import org.springframework.beans.factory.annotation.Autowired;
import org.springframework.context.ApplicationContext;
import org.springframework.web.bind.annotation.GetMapping;
import org.springframework.web.bind.annotation.RestController;

import java.util.Arrays;

@RestController
public class CtxController {

    @Autowired
    ApplicationContext ctx;

    @GetMapping("/")
    public String index() {
        StringBuilder sb = new StringBuilder("<html><body>");

        sb.append("Hello there dear developer,
            here are the beans you were looking for: </br>");

        //method that returns all the bean names in the context of the
        application
        Arrays.stream(ctx.getBeanDefinitionNames()).sorted().forEach(
                beanName ->  sb.append("</br>").append(beanName)
        );
        sb.append("</body></htm>");
        return sb.toString();
    }
}
```

!   The same thing that was done by the previous code is done more professionally by a Spring Boot Monitoring module named Spring Boot actuator. When this module is added as a dependency of a Spring Boot application, a number of endpoints are enabled for access under the path /actuator. The /actuator/ beans must be activated explicitly by adding the following property to the application.yml file.

```
management:
endpoints:
  web:
    exposure:
      include: 'beans'
```

The Spring Boot Actuator is configured for the application corresponding to this chapter, and when opening `http://localhost:8081/boot/actuator/beans` in your browser, a complete list of all the Spring beans in this application and a few of their properties are displayed in JSON format. You can find out more about Spring Boot monitoring, including the actuator, in Chapter 9.

But, since we know how powerful the @SpringBootApplication annotation is, we can write the code in such a way that the functionality depicted previously is part of the ApplicationThree class. We know that this class is a configuration class that is treated as a bean by the Spring IoC container, so we can add the @RestController annotation on it, right? Yes, that is correct. We add the contents with a few modifications to this class, and we reduce our application to a single class.

```
package com.apress.cems.boot3;

import org.springframework.beans.factory.annotation.Autowired;
import org.springframework.boot.SpringApplication;
import org.springframework.boot.autoconfigure.SpringBootApplication;
import org.springframework.context.ApplicationContext;
import org.springframework.web.bind.annotation.GetMapping;
import org.springframework.web.bind.annotation.RestController;

import java.util.Arrays;
import java.util.function.Function;

@RestController
@SpringBootApplication
public class ApplicationThree.class {

    public static void main(String[] args) {
        SpringApplication.run(ApplicationThree.class, args);
    }
```

```
@Autowired
ApplicationContext ctx;

@GetMapping("/")
public String index() {
   return ctxController.apply(ctx);
}

Function<ApplicationContext, String> ctxController = ctx -> {
    StringBuilder sb = new StringBuilder("<html><body>");

    sb.append("Hello there dear developer,
        here are the beans you were looking for: </br>");

    //method that returns all the bean names in the context of the
    application
    Arrays.stream(ctx.getBeanDefinitionNames()).sorted().forEach(
            beanName -> sb.append("</br>").append(beanName)
    );
    sb.append("</body></htm>");
    return sb.toString();
};
```

If the application is made only from what it was listed up to this point, when running the main method and accessing http://localhost:8080 the list of all the beans in the application context will be depicted like in Figure 2-24.

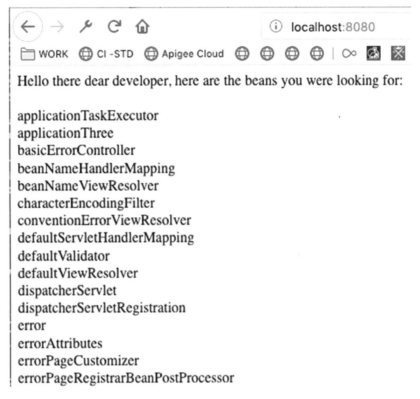

Figure 2-24. *Infrastructure beans of an application context created by Spring Boot*

To test the implementation, you can run the ApplicationThree class in the IDE, or you can run the application in the console. The Spring Boot Gradle Plugin provides a Gradle task named bootJar that packages the Spring Boot application as a runnable jar, just go to the chapter02/boot directory an execute the following command.

```
gradle clean build bootJar
```

The resulting jar is a web application that can be run by executing the following.

```
java -jar boot-1.0-SNAPSHOT.jar
```

If there are no exceptions thrown in the console, http://localhost:8080 should return the expected output, exactly as before.

The application will run on an embedded Tomcat container that can be customized easily to use a different port and context for the application. There are multiple ways, but the easiest way is by adding a file named application.properties or application.yml (Spring Boot supports them out of the box) in your resources directory and setting some Spring Boot properties that are declared for these purposes with customized values.

```
# application.properties
server.port=8081
server.servlet.context-path=/boot
```

```
# application.yml
server:
  port: 8081
  servlet:
    context-path: /boot
```

Spring Boot property files could be filled with Spring Boot properties with customized values, but developer can add their own properties in there and injecting their values wherever needed. A list with all the properties that Spring Boot recognizes is found at `https://docs.spring.io/spring-boot/docs/current/reference/html/common-application-properties.html`.

By using the preceding configuration, the web page with all the bean names within the context can be accessed now at `http://localhost:8081/boot/`, just make sure to rebuild the application and restart it, before accessing that URL.

To provide configuration for a Spring Boot application, you can use properties files, YAML files, environment variables, and command-line arguments. The mechanism of reading properties for Spring Boot involves the use of a very special `PropertySource` implementation that is designed to allow the overriding of values in a specific order. So, when running a Spring Boot application, the properties are considered in the following order.

- If you are running your application in development mode (boot-devtools library is on the classpath), properties from your home directory `~/.spring-boot-devtools.properties` are read first.

- If a `@TestPropertySource` annotation is found on your test classes, properties will be picked up from there.

- `properties` attribute on test classes on classes annotated with the @SpringBootTest annotation and the test annotations for testing a particular slice of your application.

- Properties and values can be provided using command-line arguments.

- Properties can also be provided in JSON format referred to by the `SPRING_APPLICATION_JSON` environment variable per system property

- `ServletConfig` init parameters.

- `ServletContext` init parameters.

- JNDI attributes from `java:comp/env`.

- Java System properties: accessible by calling `System.getProperties()`.

- Operating System environment variables.

- A `RandomValuePropertySource` that has properties only in `random.*`.

- Profile-specific application properties outside of your packaged jar (`application-{profile}.properties` or `application-{profile}.yml`).

- Profile-specific application properties packaged inside your jar (`application-{profile}.properties` or `application-{profile}.yml`).

- Application properties outside of your packaged jar (`application.properties` or `application.yml`)

- Application properties packaged inside your jar (`application.properties` and `application.yml`).

- `@PropertySource` annotations on `@Configuration` classes.

- Default properties (specified by calling `SpringApplication.setDefaultProperties`).

This list is ordered by precedence. The properties defined in the upper positions override the ones in lower positions. The `application.properties` file is provided when executing the application from the command line by using the `spring.config.location` argument.

```
java -jar ps-boot.jar --spring.config.location=
        /Users/iuliana.cosmina/temp/application.properties
```

The file name can be changed by using the `spring.config.name` in the command line.

```
java -jar sample-boot.jar --spring.config.name=my-boot.properties
```

There is more to be said about Spring Boot, but since each chapter contains a Spring Boot section that covers how to build one type of application, information is spread throughout the book for easier association with a topic and for learning that is more efficient.

And now let's have a little bit of fun customizing our Spring Boot application. While running the `ApplicationThree.class` when the application starts, the Spring Boot banner is depicted in the console. This can be replaced by creating a file named `banner.txt` under `src/main/resources` that contains the desired banner in ASCII format. The original Spring Boot banner and the Apress banner are depicted side by side in Figure 2-25.[45]

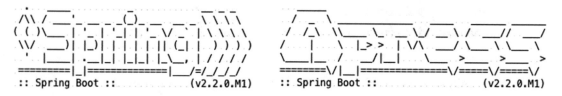

Figure 2-25. *Spring Boot Apress banner*

Logging

Spring Boot uses Logback by default, but leaves the underlying implementation open. Log4j2 and Java Util Logging are also supported. The application attached to this book makes used of the default: Logback. The starters use Logback by default. It is preconfigured to use the console as output, but it can be configured via the `logback.xml` file, which is located under `/src/main/resources`.

By default, ERROR, WARN, and INFO –level messages are logged. To modify this behavior and enable the writing of DEBUG messages for a category of core loggers (embedded container, Hibernate, and Spring Boot), the `application.properties` file must be edited and the `debug=true` property must be added.

Logging is initialized before the application context, so it is not possible to control logging from using @PropertySources in @Configuration classes. System properties and conventional Spring Boot external configuration files should be used. Depending on

---

[45]You can create your own ASCII banner using this site: `http://patorjk.com`

the logging system, Spring Boot looks for the specific configuration files in the following order.

- `logback-spring.xml`, `logback-spring.groovy`, `logback.xml`, `logback.groovy` for Logback

- `log4j2-spring.xml`, `log4j2.xml` for Log4j2

- `logging.properties` for Java Util Logging

The logfile name to use by Spring Boot is configured by using the `logging.file` Spring environment variable. There are other Spring environment variables that configure Spring Boot logging; the full list and purpose is available in the Spring Boot official reference documentation.[46]

Using file names postfixed with `-spring` is recommended because Spring cannot completely control log initialization when using standard configuration locations.

For now, this is all that can be said about Spring Boot. But no worries, there is a lot more to come. For this to make sense and to be easily assimilated, more knowledge about Spring is a prerequisite.

Spring Initializr

And since you've been introduced to Spring Boot that helps you build an application context with everything necessary in it in the most practical way. There is something that can make building a Spring application even quicker: **Spring Initializr**. This is a web application accessible at `https://start.spring.io/`. This application can help you start building a String application. On the web site, you can enter the desired configuration for your application, and it is generated for you with the build tool of your choice and using the language of your choice, because Spring applications can be written in Groovy and Kotlin. Let's take the site for a small run and enter the information for generating a Spring web application that makes use of JPA to save records into a H2 database and uses Spring Boot version 2.2.0-M2 and Java version 11.

In Figure 2-26, you can see a snapshot of the information entered into the Spring Initializr form.

---

[46]Spring Environment logging variables: `http://docs.spring.io/spring-boot/docs/current/reference/htmlsingle/#boot-features-custom-log-configuration`

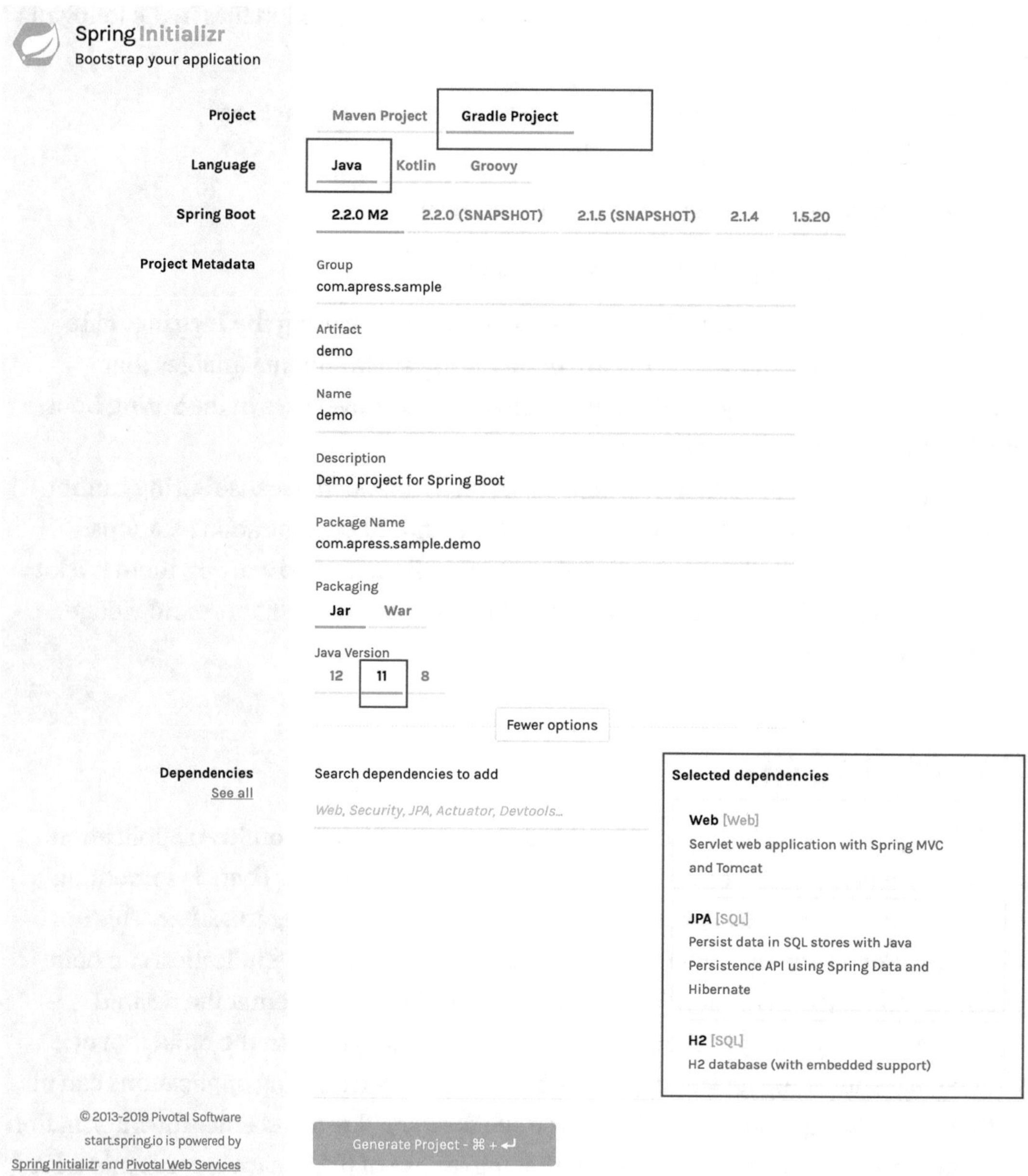

Spring Initializr
Bootstrap your application

Project	Maven Project	**Gradle Project**			

Language	**Java**	Kotlin	Groovy		

Spring Boot	**2.2.0 M2**	2.2.0 (SNAPSHOT)	2.1.5 (SNAPSHOT)	2.1.4	1.5.20

Project Metadata

Group
com.apress.sample

Artifact
demo

Name
demo

Description
Demo project for Spring Boot

Package Name
com.apress.sample.demo

Packaging
Jar   War

Java Version
12   **11**   8

Fewer options

Dependencies
See all

Search dependencies to add

Web, Security, JPA, Actuator, Devtools...

Selected dependencies

Web [Web]
Servlet web application with Spring MVC
and Tomcat

JPA [SQL]
Persist data in SQL stores with Java
Persistence API using Spring Data and
Hibernate

H2 [SQL]
H2 database (with embedded support)

© 2013-2019 Pivotal Software
start.spring.io is powered by
Spring Initializr and Pivotal Web Services

Generate Project - ⌘ + ↵

Figure 2-26. *The Spring Initializr interface with information to generate a Spring application*

When the Generate Project button is pressed, a browser pop-up window should appear asking you to save a file archived as **zip**. Save it and unpack it to inspect its contents. You should see something similar to the following output.

```
Downloads/app -  $ tree
.
|------ HELP.md
|------ build.gradle
|------ gradle
|        |------ wrapper
|                  |------ gradle-wrapper.jar
|                  |------ gradle-wrapper.properties
|------ gradlew
|------ gradlew.bat
|------ settings.gradle
|------ src
        |------ main
        |        |------ java
        |        |        |--- com
        |        |              |--- apress
        |        |                    |--- sample
        |        |                          |--- app
        |        |                                |--- AppApplication.java
        |        |------ resources
        |                  |--- application.properties
        |                  |--- static
        |                  |--- templates
        |------ test
                |------ java
                        |--- com
                              |--- apress
                                    |--- sample
                                          |--- app
                                                |--- AppApplicationTests.java
18 directories, 10 files
```

The contents match the internal structure of a typical Gradle project. The build.
gradle file is the Gradle configuration file generated by Spring Initializr and contains
a compact and working Gradle single-module configuration for a Spring Boot web
application.

```
plugins {
        id 'org.springframework.boot' version '2.2.0.M2'
        id 'java'
}

apply plugin: 'io.spring.dependency-management'

group = 'com.apress.sample'
version = '0.0.1-SNAPSHOT'
sourceCompatibility = '11'

repositories {
        mavenCentral()
        maven { url 'https://repo.spring.io/snapshot' }
        maven { url 'https://repo.spring.io/milestone' }
}

dependencies {
        implementation 'org.springframework.boot:spring-boot-starter-data-jpa'
        implementation 'org.springframework.boot:spring-boot-starter-web'
        runtimeOnly 'com.h2database:h2'
        testImplementation 'org.springframework.boot:spring-boot-starter-test'
}
```

You can use any type of terminal to build the project by executing

```
gradle clean build
```

Or if you do not have Gradle installed on your system, you can use the Gradle wrapper script that was generated for you.

```
./gradlew clean build
```

In your console, you should see an output looking quite similar to the following log listing.

```
 Downloads/app -  $ ./gradlew clean build
Downloading https://services.gradle.org/distributions/gradle-5.5-bin.zip
....................................................................
```

Welcome to Gradle 5.5!

Here are the highlights of this release:
 - Define sets of dependencies that work together with Java Platform plugin
 - New C++ plugins with dependency management built-in
 - New C++ project types for gradle init
 - Service injection into plugins and project extensions

For more details see https://docs.gradle.org/5.5/release-notes.html

Starting a Gradle Daemon (subsequent builds will be faster)

> Task :test
2019-03-24 10:42:52.940 INFO 10244 --- [Thread-4] o.s.s.concurrent.
ThreadPoolTaskExecutor   :
   Shutting down ExecutorService 'applicationTaskExecutor'
2019-03-24 10:42:52.940 INFO 10244 --- [Thread-4] j.LocalContainerEntity
ManagerFactoryBean :
  Closing JPA EntityManagerFactory for persistence unit 'default'
2019-03-24 10:42:52.941 INFO 10244 --- [Thread-4] .SchemaDropperImpl$Delay
edDropActionImpl :
  HHH000477: Starting delayed evictData of schema as part of SessionFactory
  shut-down'
2019-03-24 10:42:52.942 INFO 10244 --- [Thread-4] com.zaxxer.hikari.
HikariDataSource   :
  HikariPool-1 - Shutdown initiated...
2019-03-24 10:42:52.946 INFO 10244 --- [Thread-4] com.zaxxer.hikari.
HikariDataSource   :
  HikariPool-1 - Shutdown completed.

BUILD SUCCESSFUL in 50s
6 actionable tasks: 6 executed
```
```

The chances are slim that you would ever get a build failure, and most likely the cause would be local, like restricted rights on your computer; for example, sometimes a freshly installed Windows or macOS might not allow Java applications to be executed or ports being blocked by other applications. (Skype is known to use port 8080, the default port for a Spring Boot application.) If that ever happens, feel free to reach out and let me know, and I'll try to help.

The next step is to open this project using IntelliJ IDEA. Use either the Import Project from the initial pop-up window when opening IntelliJ IDEA without any project already loaded or the Open option from the File menu when you already have a project opened and choose the app directory. IntelliJ IDEA will guide you through the process of selecting the Gradle version and JDK for your project. After the project is loaded, you might need to select the project JDK manually in IntelliJ IDEA, because if you have multiple versions installed (as I do), version 8 might be selected by default. Just go to the File menu and select Project Structure and make sure the appropriate JDK is selected.

After that just run the AppApplicationTests class, if that passes you have a working application. Let's test that the application is really a web application by adding an index. html in the src/main/resources/static directory. The file can be as simple as the following.

```
<!DOCTYPE html>
<html lang="en">
<head>
    <meta charset="UTF-8">
    <title>Index </title>
</head>
<body>

<h3>Sample App</h3>
</body>
</html>
```

After doing this, just run the AppApplication class and try to access http://localhost:8080/. It should be a simple web page with the *Sample App* text on it. This works because Tomcat looks for an index.html file to display.

At this point, you might be really enthusiastic. You have a web application, and all you did was add an HTML page to make sure the application works as intended. How did this all happened? The simplest answer is **convention over configuration**. The web application that Spring Initializr generated is a typical Spring web application. It needs a web context that contains a typical set of infrastructure beans. By default, it uses Logback to write logs and an internal embedded Tomcat server that is started on port 8080. Any of these details can be changed by modifying the contents of the `application.properties`, which initially is empty, and by adding your own beans for that purpose.

Spring Initializr generated a fully working Gradle configuration file with dependencies on Spring Boot and the necessary plugins already configured, so you can start developing your beans right away. The configuration is quite succinct, specific to a single module project and it does not use Java modules either. That job is left to you because these configurations are quite peculiar and depend a lot on the developers' project design. But you must admit, it is nice and practical to have as a starting point when working on something new, a full working environment configuration.

There is not much that can be said about the Spring Initializr project. It is so easy to use and intuitive that the only thing that is important for a developer to know is that it can be accessed by using your browser at `https://start.spring.io/`.

Summary

After reading this chapter, you should possess enough knowledge to configure a Spring application using Java configurations and to harness the power of beans to develop small Spring applications.

Here is a little summary for you.

- Spring is built for dependency injection and provides a container for *IoC*, which takes care of injecting the dependencies according to the configuration.

- There are two flavors of configuration for Spring applications and they can also be mixed: XML-based when beans declarations are decoupled from code and Java configuration when bean declarations are in the code.

- Spring promotes the use of interfaces, so beans of types implementing the same interface can be easily interchanged.

- The Spring way of configuration promotes testability. Since beans can be interchanged, it is easy to use stubs and mocks to isolate components.

- The bean lifecycle can be controlled; behavior can be added at specific points during the bean lifecycle.

- Spring provides many ways to simplify configuration by respecting the convention over configuration principle. Bean names are precisely inferred in bean declarations that do not specifically specify one, beans are autowired by type, and there are a lot of specialized annotations available so you do not have to write your own for the most used cases.

- Bean definition sources can be coupled by importing them one into another, or by composing them to create an application context.

- Resources used to build an application context are selectable based on profiles.

- Spring Boot is the epitome of convention over configuration

- There are three terms that are specific to Spring Boot: auto-configuration, stand-alone, and opinionated.

- Spring Initializr is a Pivotal project that can generate complex Maven and Gradle Spring projects configuration.

Quiz

Question 1. What are the advantages of an application that is built making use of dependency injection? (Choose one.)

    A. low coupling

    B. high cohesion

    C. high readability

    D. easiness of testing

    E. all of the above

Question 2. When should constructor injection be used? (Choose two.)

    A.   when the dependent bean can be created without its dependencies

    B.   when creating an immutable bean that depends on another bean

    C.   when the type of bean being created does not support other types of injection (e.g., legacy or third-party code)

Question 3. What is an application context? (Choose two.)

    A.   any instance of a class implementing interface ApplicationContext

    B.   the software representation of the Spring IoC Container

    C.   the means to provide configuration information for a Spring application

Question 4. Which of the following affirmations about component scanning is true? (Choose two.)

    A.   to enable component scanning a configuration class should be annotated with `@ComponentScan`

    B.   component scanning is enabled by the `@Configuration` annotation

    C.   `@ComponentScan` without arguments tells the Spring IoC container to scan the current package and all of its subpackages.

Question 5. We have the following bean declaration. What is the created bean's ID? (Choose one.)

```
@Bean
DataSource prodDataSource() {
    return new DriverManagerDataSource();
}
```

    A.   `dataSource`

    B.   `driverManagerDataSource`

    C.   `prodDataSource`

Question 6. What is the complete definition of a bean? (Choose one.)

A. a Plain Old Java Object

B. an instance of a class

C. an object that is instantiated, assembled, and managed by a
Spring IoC Container

Question 7. What are the types of dependency injection supported by Spring IoC Container? (Choose all that apply.)

A. setter injection

B. constructor injection

C. interface-based injection

D. field-based injection

Question 8. The Spring IoC container by default tries to identify beans to autowire by type; if multiple beans are found, it chooses for autowiring the one with the name matching the @Qualifier value.

A. true

B. false

Question 9. What is the correct way to import bean definitions from a configuration class into another configuration class? (Choose one.)

A. @Import(DataSourceConfig.class)

B. @Resource(DataSourceConfig.class)

C. @ImportResource(DataSourceConfig.class)

Question 10. Spring Boot Question. @SpringBootConfiguration is a specialization of @Configuration? (Choose one.)

A. True

B. False

Question 11. Spring Boot Question. Which of the following annotations are used as meta annotations to declare the @SpringBootApplication annotation? (Choose three.)

    A. @ComponentScan

    B. @Repository

    C. @Import

    D. @ContextConfiguration

    E. @EnableAutoConfiguration

    F. @SpringBootConfiguration

The answers are in the appendix.

CHAPTER 3

Testing Spring Applications

Before an application is delivered to the client, it must be tested and validated by a team of professionals called *testers*. As you can imagine, testing an application after development is complete is a little too late, because perhaps specifications were not understood correctly, or were not complete. Also, the behavior of an application in an isolated development system differs considerably from the behavior in a production system. This is why there are multiple testing steps that have to be taken—some of them before development. (Before development, a project must be designed; the design can be tested as well). And there is the human factor. Since no one is perfect, mistakes are made, and testing helps find those mistakes and fix them before the application reaches the end user, thus ensuring the quality of the software. The purpose of software testing is to verify that an application satisfies the functional (application provides the expected functions) and nonfunctional (application provides the expected functions as fast as expected and does not require more memory than is available on the system) requirements and to detect errors, and all activities of planning, preparation, evaluation, and validation are part of it.

There are specific courses and certifications for testers that are designed to train them in functional and software testing processes that they can use to test an application, and the ISTQB[1] is the organization that provides the infrastructure for training and examination.

---

[1]International Software Testing Qualification Board: `http://www.istqb.org/`.

© Iuliana Cosmina 2020
I. Cosmina, *Pivotal Certified Professional Core Spring 5 Developer Exam*,
https://doi.org/10.1007/978-1-4842-5136-2_3

A Few Types of Testing

There are multiple types of testing classified by the development step in which they are executed, or by their implementation, but it is not the object of this book to cover them all. Only those that imply writing actual code using testing libraries and frameworks will be covered.

Test-Driven Development

Quality starts at the beginning of a project. Requirements and specifications are decided and validated, and based on them a process called **Test-Driven Development** can be executed. This process implies creation of tests before development of code. The tests will initially fail, but will start to pass one by one as the code is developed. The tests decide how the application will behave, and thus this type of testing is called test-driven development. This type of testing ensures that the specifications were understood and implemented correctly. The tests for this process are designed by business analysts and implemented by developers. This approach puts the design under question: if tests are difficult to write, the design should be reconsidered. It is more suitable to JavaScript applications (because there is no compilation of the code), but it can be used in Java applications too when the development is done using interfaces.

In Figure 3-1, the test-driven development process is described for exactly one test case.

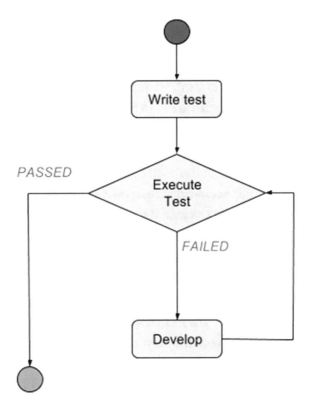

Figure 3-1. *Test-driven development logical schema*

This testing technique is good for finding problems early in the development process. And considering that the effort to solve a problem grows exponentially in proportion to the time it takes to find it, no project should ever be developed without it. Also, the tests should be run automatically using a continuous integration tool like Jenkins, Hudson, or Bamboo. Test-driven development can produce applications of high quality in less time than is possible with older methods, but it has its limitations. Sometimes tests might be incorrectly conceived or applied. This may result in units that do not perform as expected in the real world. Even if all the units work perfectly in isolation and in all anticipated scenarios, end users may encounter situations not imagined by the developers and testers. And since testing units was mentioned, this section will end here to cover the next one.

Unit and Integration Testing

Unit testing implies testing the smallest testable parts of an application individually and independently, and isolated from any other units that might affect their behavior in an unpredictable way. The dependencies are kept to a minimum, and most of them will be replaced with pseudo-units reproducing the expected behavior. This means that the unit of functionality is taken out of context. The unit tests are written by developers and are run using automated tools, although they can be run manually too in case of need.

A unit test exercises a single scenario with a provided input and compares the expected results for that input with the actual results. If they match, the test passes; if they don't, the test fails. This method of testing is fast and is often used in many projects. The tests are written by developers, and the recommended practice is to cover every method in a class with positive and negative tests. *Positive tests* are the ones that test valid inputs for the unit, while *negative tests* test invalid inputs for the unit. These are tests that cover a failure of the unit. They are considered to have failed if the unit does not actually fail when tested. The core framework helping developers to easily write and execute unit tests in Java since 2000 is JUnit. The current version when this chapter is being written is 4.13-beta-2, but probably this will be the last version since JUnit Jupiter is already at version 5.5.0-M1.

There are not many JUnit extensions, because there is little that this framework is missing; but there is a framework called Hamcrest that the Spring team is quite fond of, which is interesting because it provides a set of matchers that can be combined to create flexible expressions of intent. It originated as a framework based on JUnit, and it was used for writing tests in Java, but managed to break the language barrier, and currently it is provided for most currently used languages such as Python and Swift. Learn more about it on the official site at http://hamcrest.org/.

Also, a small open source library named AssertJ[2] is gaining ground because of its simplistic and intuitive syntax.

Running a suite of unit tests together in a context with all their real dependencies provided is called *integration testing*. As the name of this technique implies, the infrastructure needed to connect objects being tested is also a part of the context in which tests are executed. In Figure 3-2, is a simple diagram for comparing unit and integration testing concepts.

---

[2]More information is on the official site: http://joel-costigliola.github.io/assertj/

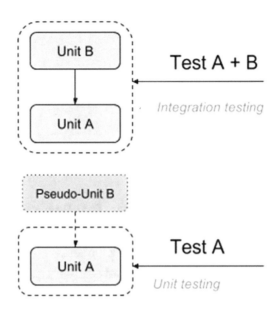

Figure 3-2. *Unit and integration testing concepts*

For functional units to be tested in isolation, dependencies must be replaced with pseudo-dependencies, fake objects with simple implementation that mimics the behavior of the real dependency as far as the dependent is concerned. The pseudo-dependencies can be *stubs* or *mocks*. Both perform the same function—to replace a real dependency, but the way that they are created is what sets them apart.

Testing with Stubs

Stubs are created by the developer; they do not require extra dependencies. A stub is a concrete class implementing the same interface as the original dependency of the unit being tested, so its methods produce dummy results of the correct types. They should be designed to exhibit a small part or the whole behavior of the actual dependency. If this approach seems familiar is because the book started with a similar example that was relevant for old style, pre-Spring Java development.

For example, let's try to test one of the service classes that were introduced in the previous chapter, the `SimpleCriminalCaseService`.

```java
 package com.apress.cems.pojos.services.impl;
...

public class SimpleCriminalCaseService
     extends SimpleAbstractService<CriminalCase>
     implements CriminalCaseService {

    private CriminalCaseRepo repo;

    @Override
    public CriminalCase createCriminalCase(CaseType type,
            String shortDescription, String detailedDescription,
            CaseStatus caseStatus, String notes,
            Set<Evidence> evidenceSet, Detective leadInvestigator) {
        CriminalCase criminalCase = new CriminalCase();
        // call setters
        ...

        repo.save(criminalCase);
        return criminalCase;
    }

    @Override
    public Set<CriminalCase> findByLeadInvestigator(Detective detective) {
        return repo.findByLeadInvestigator(detective);
    }

    @Override
    public Optional<CriminalCase> findByNumber(String caseNumber) {
        return Optional.empty();
    }

    @Override
    public Set<CriminalCase> findByStatus(CaseStatus status) {
        return repo.findByStatus(status);
    }
```

```java
    @Override
    public Set<CaseType> findByType(CaseType type) {
        return repo.findByType(type);
    }

    public void setRepo(CriminalCaseRepo repo) {
        this.repo = repo;
    }

    @Override
     AbstractRepo<CriminalCase> getRepo() {
        return repo;
    }
}

//abstract class containing concrete general implementations
public abstract class SimpleAbstractService<T extends AbstractEntity>
    implements AbstractService<T> {

    public void save(T entity) {
        getRepo().save(entity);
    }

    public T findById(Long entityId){
        return getRepo().findById(entityId);
    }

    @Override
    public void delete(T entity) {
        getRepo().delete(entity);
    }

    @Override
    public void deleteById(Long entityId) {
        getRepo().deleteById(entityId);
    }

    abstract AbstractRepo<T> getRepo();
}
```

```
// the interface defining the specific CriminalCase behavior
public interface CriminalCaseService extends
            AbstractService<CriminalCase> {
    CriminalCase createCriminalCase(CaseType type,
          String shortDescription, String detailedDescription,
          CaseStatus caseStatus, String notes,
          Set<Evidence> evidenceSet,
          Detective leadInvestigator);
}

// the interface defining the general service behavior
public interface AbstractService<T> {
    void save(T entity);

    T findById(Long entityId);

    void delete(T entity);

    void deleteById(Long entityId);
}
```

Although the number of tests varies depending on developer experience and what the code actually does, also related in a funny short story by Alberto Savoia, posted on the Google official blog,[3] my recommendation is to start unit testing by trying to write at least two tests for each method: one positive and one negative, for methods that can be tested in this way. There are four methods in `SimpleCriminalCaseService`, besides the getter and setter for the repository, so the test class should have approximately eight tests. When testing the service class, the concern is that the class should interact correctly with the repository class. The behavior of the repository class is assumed known, tested, and immutable. The stub class will implement the typical repository behavior but without a database connection needed, because interaction with a database introduces an undesired lag in test execution. The implementation presented here will use a `java.util.Map` to simulate a database. Like the application, there are more repository classes extending `SimpleAbstractService<T>`. The stubs will follow the same inheritance design, so the abstract class will be stubbed as well.

---

[3]Here it is, in case you are curious: `http://googletesting.blogspot.ro/2010/07/ code-coverage-goal-80-and-no-less.html`.

```java
package com.apress.cems.stub.repo;
...
public abstract class StubAbstractRepo
     <T extends AbstractEntity> implements AbstractRepo<T> {

    protected Map<Long, T> records = new HashMap<>();

    @Override
    public void save(T entity) {
        if (entity.getId() == null) {
            Long id = (long) records.size() + 1;
            entity.setId(id);
        }
        records.put(entity.getId(), entity);
    }

    @Override
    public void delete(T entity) throws NotFoundException {
        records.remove(findById(entity.getId()).getId());
    }

    @Override
    public void deleteById(Long entityId) throws NotFoundException {
        records.remove(findById(entityId).getId());
    }

    @Override
    public T findById(Long entityId) {
        if(records.containsKey(entityId)) {
            return records.get(entityId);
        } else {
            throw new NotFoundException("Entity with id "
+ entityId + " could not be processed because it does not exist.");
        }
    }
}
```

The StubCriminalCaseRepo class extends the previous stub class, adding its specific behavior. And since Map contains <Detective,Set<CriminalCase>> pairs, neither of the specific CriminalCaseRepo methods can be stubbed, so a new map is needed.

```
package com.apress.cems.stub.repo;
...
public class StubCriminalCaseRepo extends
      StubAbstractRepo<CriminalCase> implements CriminalCaseRepo {

    protected Map<Detective, Set<CriminalCase>> records2 = new HashMap<>();

    public void init(){
        // create a few entries to play with
        final Detective detective = buildDetective
              ("Sherlock", "Holmes", Rank.INSPECTOR);
        this.save(buildCase(detective,
            CaseType.FELONY, CaseStatus.UNDER_INVESTIGATION));
        this.save(buildCase(detective,
            CaseType.MISDEMEANOR, CaseStatus.SUBMITTED));
    }

    @Override
    public void save(CriminalCase criminalCase) {
        super.save(criminalCase);
        addWithLeadInvestigator(criminalCase);
    }

    private void addWithLeadInvestigator(CriminalCase criminalCase){
        if (criminalCase.getLeadInvestigator()!= null) {
            Detective lead = criminalCase.getLeadInvestigator();
            if (records2.containsKey(lead)) {
                records2.get(lead).add(criminalCase);
            } else {
                Set<CriminalCase> ccSet = new HashSet<>();
                ccSet.add(criminalCase);
                records2.put(lead, ccSet);
            }
        }
    }
}
```

```
@Override
public Set<CriminalCase> findByLeadInvestigator(Detective detective) {
    return records2.get(detective);
}

@Override
public Optional<CriminalCase> findByNumber(String caseNumber) {

    final CriminalCase[] result = new CriminalCase[1];

    records2.values().forEach(set -> set.stream()
            .filter(c -> c.getNumber().equalsIgnoreCase(caseNumber))

                .findFirst().ifPresent(c -> result[0] = c)
    );
    return Optional.of(result[0]);

}

...
}
```

Now that we have the stubs, they have to be used.

Unit Testing Using JUnit

To write multiple unit tests and execute them together as a suite, a dependency is needed to make the implementation run more easily. This dependency is JUnit,[4] a Java framework to write repeatable unit tests. It provides annotations to prepare and run unit test suites.

The recommended practice is to create a class named the same as the class to be tested but postfixed with Test, so the test class in this case is named SimpleCriminalCaseServiceTest. Only a few test examples will be depicted here. For more, look in the code attached to the book for this chapter, project chapter03/junit-tests. The full structure of the project is depicted in Figure 3-3; the location of the SimpleCriminalCaseServiceTest is obvious.

---

[4]JUnit official site: http://junit.org/junit4/.

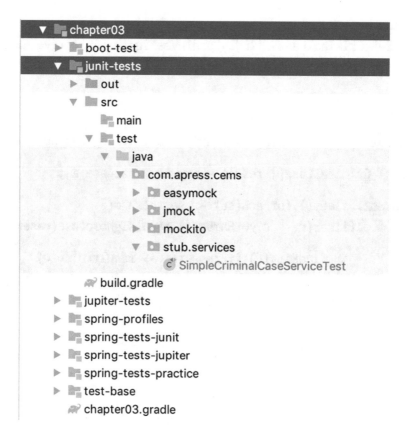

Figure 3-3. *Chapter 3 testing projects*

```
package com.apress.cems.stub.services;

import org.junit.Before;
import org.junit.BeforeClass;
import org.junit.Test;
import static org.junit.Assert.assertEquals;
import static org.junit.Assert.assertNotNull;
import static org.junit.Assert.assertNull;
...

public class SimpleCriminalCaseServiceTest {

    static final Long CASE_ID = 1L;
    final Detective detective = buildDetective("Sherlock",
            "Holmes", Rank.INSPECTOR, "TS1234");
```

```
StubCriminalCaseRepo repo = new StubCriminalCaseRepo();

// object to be tested
 SimpleCriminalCaseService service = new SimpleCriminalCaseService();

@Before
public void setUp(){
    repo.init();

    //create object to be tested
    service = new SimpleCriminalCaseService();
    service.setRepo(repo);
}

  //positive test, we know that a Case with ID=1 exists
@Test
public void findByIdPositive() {
    CriminalCase criminalCase = service.findById(CASE_ID);
    assertNotNull(criminalCase);
}

//negative test, we know that a Case with ID=99 does not exist
@Test(expected = NotFoundException.class)
public void findByIdNegative() {
    CriminalCase criminalCase = service.findById(99L);
    assertNull(criminalCase);
}

  //negative test, we know that cases for this detective do not exist
@Test
 void findByLeadNegative() {
    Detective detective = buildDetective("Jake", "Peralta", Rank.
    JUNIOR, "TS1122");
    Set<CriminalCase> result =  service.findByLeadInvestigator(detective);
   assertNull(result);
}
```

```java
//positive test, we know that cases for this detective exist and how
many
@Test
public void findByLeadPositive() {
    Set<CriminalCase> result =  service.findByLeadInvestigator(detective);
    assertEquals(result.size(), 2);
}

//positive case, deleting existing case record
@Test
public void deleteByIdPositive() {
    service.deleteById(CASE_ID);

    try {
        CriminalCase criminalCase = service.findById(CASE_ID);
        assertNull(criminalCase);
    } catch (NotFoundException nfe){
      assertTrue(nfe.getMessage().contains(
         "Entity with id 1 could not be processed because it does not
         exist"));
    }
}

//negative case, attempt to delete non-existing case
@Test(expected = NotFoundException.class)
public void deleteByIdNegative() {
    service.deleteById(99L);
}

@After
public void tearDown(){
    repo.clear();
}
}
```

There are special methods like the `findByIdNegative()` test method which is a negative test that expects for a type of exception to be thrown, not for a result to be returned that can be used in an assertion. Since this behavior is known, the test methods are written using the `expected` attribute of the `@Test` annotation and the type of exception is provided as argument.

In the preceding code snippet, the following JUnit components were used.

- The `@Before` annotation is used on methods that should be executed before executing each test method. These prepare the context for that test to execute in. All objects used in the test methods should be created and initialized in this method. Methods annotated with `@Before` are executed before every method annotated with `@Test`.

- The `@Test` annotation is the annotation that tells JUnit that the code in this method should be run as a test case. In JUnit 4, methods annotated with `@Test` should always be public and return void. It can also be used to treat expected exceptions.

- The `org.junit.jupiter.api.Assertions.*` static methods are defined in the `org.junit.Assert` class and can simplify the code of a test method. Without them, the user would have to write the code that specifies when the test should pass or fail.

- The `@After` annotation is used on methods that should be executed after executing each test method. These methods clean up the context after the test was executed. All objects initialized in the method `@Before` should be destroyed in the method annotated with `After`, because tests might modify them and cause unpredictable results when running the tests.

All the annotations and utilities are declared in this case under package `org.junit`.

After a quick analysis of the code, one thing should be obvious: testing code with stubs is time-consuming, and writing stubs seems to take as much time as development itself. Indeed, testing using stubs is applicable only for really simple applications and scenarios. The worst thing about testing with stubs, though, is that if the interface changes, the stub implementation must change too. So, not only do you have to adapt the tests, but the stubs too. Since we are using Java 11, there is the option of using default methods in interfaces, but this might lead to your tests not being accurate. The second-worst thing is that all methods have to be implemented when stubs are used, even those that are not used by a test scenario. For example,

```
@Override
 public Set<CriminalCase> findByType(CaseType type) {
        throw new NotImplementedException("Not needed for this stub.");
 }
```

This method was not involved in any test scenario, and to avoid providing an implementation, the decision was made to throw a NotImplementedException. The third-worst thing about stubs is that if we have a hierarchy of stubs, refactoring the one at the base of the hierarchy means refactoring all the stubs based on them, or else tests will fail. And this is the case in our example as well, since all stubs are based on StubAbstractRepo.

Unit Testing Using JUnit 5

JUnit 5 is also known as JUnit Jupiter, and compared to previous versions of JUnit, it is composed of several different modules from three different subprojects.

- **JUnit Platform**: A foundation for launching testing frameworks on the JVM.

- **JUnit Jupiter**: The new library for writing JUnit 5 tests.

- **JUnit Vintage**: A library providing engines that support execution of JUnit 3 and JUnit 4 tests.

The previous section covered how to write unit tests using stubs and JUnit 4. This section will cover how the same tests can be written using JUnit 5. Before discussing everything let's introduce the JUnit 5 version of SimpleCriminalCaseServiceTest.

```
package com.apress.cems.jupiter.services;

import org.junit.jupiter.api.AfterEach;
import org.junit.jupiter.api.BeforeEach;
import org.junit.jupiter.api.Test;
import static org.junit.jupiter.api.Assertions.*;

...
```

```java
public class SimpleCriminalCaseServiceTest {
    static final Long CASE_ID = 1L;
    final Detective detective = buildDetective("Sherlock", "Holmes", Rank.
    INSPECTOR,
        "TS1234");

    StubCriminalCaseRepo repo = new StubCriminalCaseRepo();

    SimpleCriminalCaseService service = new SimpleCriminalCaseService();

    @BeforeEach
    public void setUp(){
        repo.init();

        //create object to be tested
        service = new SimpleCriminalCaseService();
        service.setRepo(repo);
    }

    //positive test, we know that a Case with ID=1 exists
    @Test
    public void findByIdPositive() {
        CriminalCase criminalCase = service.findById(CASE_ID);
        assertNotNull(criminalCase);
    }

    //negative test, we know that a Case with ID=99 does not exist
    @Test
    public void findByIdNegative() {
        assertThrows( NotFoundException.class, () ->
                service.findById(99L), "No such case exists");
    }

    ... // other test methods available on GitHub repository

    @AfterEach
    public void tearDown(){
        repo.clear();
    }
```

There are a few differences, but overall the logic is the same: there must be a method that is executed before every test method (in this case, annotated with @BeforeEach), and there must be a method to be executed after a test method (in this case, annotated with @AfterEach).

A difference that can be easily observed is the way the negative test was written using JUnit 5. The assertThrows(..) method allows developers to test assumptions about the exceptions being thrown when a certain method is executed. The method receives as a parameter the type of exception that is expected to be thrown. An instance of type org.junit.jupiter.api.function.Executable, which is an interface annotated with @FunctionalInterface, can be used within a lambda expression that simplifies the code to be written. There is an assertThrows(..) in JUnit 4 as well that was used in version 4.13; it receives a ThrowingRunnable instance instead of an executable. So in JUnit 4, you have more than one way of testing an assumption that involves exceptions.

All the annotations and utilities are declared in this case under package org.junit.jupiter.api. Actually, a comparison table would be better, right?

In Table 3-1, you can see a small set of components used for the same purpose in JUnit 4 and JUnit 5.

Table 3-1. *JUnit 4 Compare to JUnit 5 Equivalences*

JUnit 4	JUnit 5	Description
org.junit	org.junit.jupiter.ap	iBase package.
@Test	@Test	Annotation that marks test methods. Test methods must not be private or static and must not return a value. In JUnit 5, the test methods can also have *package* access.
@Test(expected = Exception.class)	@Test plus assertThrows(..)	Annotation that marks test methods containing assumptions about exceptions being thrown.
@BeforeClass	@BeforeAll	Used on static public (also *package* in JUnit 5) methods, mark them for execution before all test methods in the class, to create a mutable context for tests to be executed in.

(continued)

Table 3-1. (*continued*)

JUnit 4	JUnit 5	Description
`@Before`	`@BeforeEach`	Annotation that marks methods to be execute before every test method in a class. These methods must not be private or static and must not return a value. In JUnit 5, the test methods can also have *package* access.
`@AfterClass`	`@AfterAll`	Used on static public methods, mark them for execution after all test methods in the class, to destroy the mutable context the tests were executed in. In JUnit 5, the test methods can also have *package* access.
`@After`	`@AfterEach`	Annotation that marks methods to be execute after every test method in a class. These methods must not be private or static and must not return a value.

`org.junit.Assert.`
`assertNotNull`
	`org.junit.jupiter.`
	`api.Assertions.`
	`assertNotNull`
		Static method used to test the assumption that the tested snippet of code does not return a `null` value.

`@Ignore`	`@Disabled`	Annotations to be used on a class or method that will cause for the test method(s) not to be executed.

JUnit 5 has more annotations than JUnit 4; the same goes for assertion/assumption methods. Some of them are used later in this book, when the context requires it. Explanations are provided on the spot, and since the focus of the book is on Spring testing, this section will end here.

> !   Executing JUnit 4 or JUnit 5 tests require different dependencies on the class-path of the application, and the configuration for this is all taken care of by Gradle. The sources attached to the book provide a working configuration for both. That is why, there are two projects one for each version: `chapter03/junit-tests` for tests written using JUnit 4 and `chapter03/jupiter-tests` for tests written using JUnit 5.

Conclusion: Stubs make testing seem like a tedious job, so let's see what *mocks* can do to improve the situation.

Testing with Mocks

A mock object is also a pseudo object, replacing the dependency we are not interested in testing and helping to isolate the object in which we are interested. Mock code does not have to be written, because there are a few libraries and frameworks that can generate mock objects. The mock object will implement the dependent interface on the fly. Before a mock object is generated, the developer can configure its behavior: what methods will be called and what will they return. The mock object can be used after that, and then expectations can be checked to decide the test result.

There are other libraries and frameworks for mock generation written in Java applications. The one that you use is up to you.

- **EasyMock** is a framework that provides an easy way to replace collaborators of the unit under test. Learn more about it on their official site at `http://easymock.org/`. This library is very popular and was used extensively in Spring development until version 3.1 made the switch to Mockito.[5]

- **jMock** is a small library, and the team that created it brags about making it quick and easy to define mock objects. The API is very nice and is suitable for complex stateful logic. See the official site at `www.jmock.org`.

---

[5]More information on the Spring IO Official blog: `https://spring.io/blog/2012/11/07/spring-framework-3-2-rc1-new-testing-features`

- **Mockito** is a mocking framework that provides a really clean and simple API for writing tests. The interesting thing about it is that it provides the possibility of partial mocking; real methods are invoked but still can be verified and stubbed. More about it on their official site at http://mockito.org.

- **PowerMock** is a framework that extends other mock libraries such as EasyMock with more powerful capabilities. It was created to provide a way of testing code considered untestable. It uses a custom classloader and bytecode manipulation to enable mocking of static methods, constructors, final classes and methods, private methods, removal of static initializers, and more. You can read more about it at https://github.com/jayway/powermock.

Each of these mocking tools will be covered in this chapter. All of them also provide annotations when used in a Spring context, when doing integration testing. But until Spring testing is covered, we will stick to simple unit testing.

EasyMock

The class to test with mocks generated by EasyMock is SimpleDetectiveService. This class inherits all methods from SimpleAbstractService<T> and provides its own for detective-specific behavior.

```
package com.apress.cems.services.impl;
...

import java.util.Optional;
import java.util.Set;

public class SimpleDetectiveService extends
    SimpleAbstractService<Detective> implements DetectiveService {

    private DetectiveRepo repo;

    @Override
    public Detective createDetective(Person person, Rank rank) {
        Detective detective = new Detective();
        //set properties
```

```
        repo.save(detective);
        return detective;
    }

    @Override
    public Optional<Detective> findByBadgeNumber(String badgeNumber) {
        return repo.findByBadgeNumber(badgeNumber);
    }

    @Override
    public Set<Detective> findByRank(Rank rank) {
        return repo.findbyRank(rank);
    }

    public void setRepo(DetectiveRepo repo) {
        this.repo = repo;
    }

    @Override AbstractRepo<Detective> getRepo() {
        return repo;
    }
}

// interface for Detective specific behavior
public interface DetectiveService extends AbstractService<Detective> {

    Detective createDetective(Person person, Rank rank);

    Optional<Detective> findByBadgeNumber(String badgeNumber);

    Set<Detective> findByRank(Rank rank);
}
```

To perform a test using mocks generated with EasyMock, the following steps have to be completed:

1. Declare the mock.

2. Create the mock.

3. Inject the mock.

4. Record what the mock is supposed to do.

5. Tell the mock the actual testing that is being done.

6. Test.

7. Make sure that the methods were called on the mock.

8. Validate the execution.

The following test class is named `SimpleDetectiveServiceTest`. In the following test snippet, the `findById()` method is tested, and the preceding steps are underlined.

```
package com.apress.cems.easymock;

import org.junit.jupiter.api.BeforeEach;
import org.junit.jupiter.api.Test;
...
import static org.easymock.EasyMock.*;
import static org.easymock.EasyMock.verify;
import static org.junit.jupiter.api.Assertions.*;

public class SimpleDetectiveServiceTest {
    static final Long DETECTIVE_ID = 1L;

    (1)private DetectiveRepo mockRepo;
    private SimpleDetectiveService service;

    @BeforeEach
    public void setUp() {
    (2)mockRepo = createMock(DetectiveRepo.class);

     //create object to be tested
     service = new SimpleDetectiveService();

     (3) service.setRepo(mockRepo);
    }

    @Test
    public void findByNamePositive() {
        //record what we want the mock to do
      Detective simpleDetective = buildDetective("Sherlock", "Holmes",
          Rank.INSPECTOR, "TS1234");
        simpleDetective.setId(DETECTIVE_ID);
```

```
(4)expect(mockRepo.findById(DETECTIVE_ID)).
andReturn(simpleDetective);
(5)replay(mockRepo);

(6)Detective detective = service.findById(DETECTIVE_ID);
(7)verify(mockRepo);
(8)assertAll(
        () -> assertNotNull(detective),
        () -> assertEquals(detective.getId(), simpleDetective.getId()),
        () -> assertEquals(detective.getBadgeNumber(),
                                    simpleDetective.getBadgeNumber())
    );
  }
}
```

The EasyMock framework provides static methods to process the mock. When multiple mocks are needed, the `replay` and `verify` methods are replaced with `replyAll` and `verifyAll`, and the mocks are picked up and processed without direct reference to any of them. The main advantage of using mocks is that there is no need to maintain any extra classes, because when using mocks, the behavior needed from the dependency is defined on the spot, inside the test method body, and the generating framework takes care of mimicking the behavior. Inexperienced developers might have difficulty understanding how mocking works, but if you are a mentor, just ask them to create stubs first and then switch them to mocks. They will understand more easily and will be enchanted by the possibility of not needing to write too much extra code to test an object.

EasyMock can be used with JUnit 4 and JUnit 5, but the syntax differs accordingly.

Another thing about the previous example is the `assertAll(..)` method, which was introduced in JUnit 5 and receives as argument an array of `Executable` instances. Executable is a functional interface that can be used in lambda expressions. The advantage of using `assertAll(..)` is that all assertions provided as arguments will be executed, even if one of more fails. In JUnit 4, there is no such grouping method, which means that if more than one assertion is used within the same test method, the execution stops at the first failure.

Let's test that, shall we? Try modifying the `assertAll(..)` as follows.

```
assertAll(
        () -> assertNotNull(detective),
        () -> assertEquals(detective.getId(), 2L),
        () -> assertEquals(detective.getBadgeNumber(), "SH2211")
);
```

If you are not familiar with lambda expressions, you might be asking yourself right about now: *Heeeey, where are those Executable instances that were mentioned earlier?* Well, the previous code listing depicts the collapsed version of the `assertAll(..)` call. Each line in its body represents an `Executable` instance. If we expand the code, and not use lambdas, we get the following.

```
import org.junit.jupiter.api.function.Executable;
...

        assertAll(
                new Executable() {
                    @Override
                    public void execute() throws Throwable {
                        assertNotNull(detective);
                    }
                },
                new Executable() {
                    @Override
                    public void execute() throws Throwable {
                        assertEquals(detective.getId(), 2L);
                    }
                },
                new Executable() {
                    @Override
                    public void execute() throws Throwable {
                        assertEquals(detective.getBadgeNumber(), "SH2211");
                    }
                }
        );
```

Not so simple and easy to read anymore, right?

Anyway, if the previous code snippet is run (collapsed form or not), the following is seen in the console.

```
expected: <1> but was: <2>
Comparison Failure:
Expected :1
Actual   :2
<Click to see difference>

expected: <TS1234> but was: <SH2211>
Comparison Failure:
Expected :TS1234
Actual   :aaa
<Click to see difference>

org.opentest4j.MultipleFailuresError: Multiple Failures (2 failures)
        expected: <1> but was: <2>
        expected: <TS1234> but was: <SH2211>
```

Quite practical, right?

jMock

The class to test with mocks generated by jMock is SimpleEvidenceService. This class inherits all methods from SimpleAbstractService<T> and provides its own for requesting specific behavior.

```
package com.apress.cems.services.impl;
 ...
public class SimpleEvidenceService extends
    SimpleAbstractService<Evidence> implements EvidenceService {
    private EvidenceRepo repo;

    public SimpleEvidenceService() {
    }
```

```java
public SimpleEvidenceService(EvidenceRepo repo) {
    this.repo = repo;
}

@Override
public Evidence createEvidence(CriminalCase criminalCase,
    Storage storage, String itemName) {
    Evidence evidence = new Evidence();
    evidence.setCriminalCase(criminalCase);
    evidence.setNumber(NumberGenerator.getEvidenceNumber());
    evidence.setItemName(itemName);
    evidence.setStorage(storage);
    repo.save(evidence);
    return evidence;
}

@Override
public Set<Evidence> findByCriminalCase(CriminalCase criminalCase) {
    return repo.findByCriminalCase(criminalCase);
}

@Override
public Optional<Evidence> findByNumber(String evidenceNumber) {
    return repo.findByNumber(evidenceNumber);
}

public void setRepo(EvidenceRepo repo) {
    this.repo = repo;
}

@Override
AbstractRepo<Evidence> getRepo() {
    return repo;
}
}
```

```
// interface for Request specific behavior
public interface EvidenceService extends AbstractService<Evidence> {
    Evidence createEvidence(CriminalCase criminalCase, Storage storage,
                String itemName);

    Set<Evidence> findByCriminalCase(CriminalCase criminalCase);

    Optional<Evidence> findByNumber(String evidenceNumber);
}
```

To perform a test using mocks generated with jMock, the following steps have to be completed.

1. Declare the mock.

2. Declare and define the context of the object under test, an instance of the org.jmock.Mockery class.

3. Create the mock.

4. Inject the mock.

5. Define the expectations we have from the mock.

6. Test.

7. Check that the mock was used.

8. Validate the execution.

The test class is named SimpleEvidenceServiceTest, and in the following test snippet, the creation of anEvidence instance is tested and the preceding steps are underlined.

```
package com.ps.repo.services;

import org.jmock.Expectations;
import org.jmock.Mockery;
...

public class SimpleEvidenceServiceTest  {

    (1)private EvidenceRepo mockRepo;

    (2)private Mockery mockery = new JUnit5Mockery();
```

```
    private SimpleEvidenceService service;

    @BeforeEach
    public void setUp() {
        (3)mockRepo = mockery.mock(EvidenceRepo.class);

        service = new SimpleEvidenceService();
        (4)service.setRepo(mockRepo);
    }

    @Test
    public void testCreateEvidence() {
        Detective detective = buildDetective("Sherlock", "Holmes",
            Rank.INSPECTOR, "TS1234");
        CriminalCase criminalCase = buildCase(detective, CaseType.FELONY,
            CaseStatus.UNDER_INVESTIGATION);
        Evidence evidence = new Evidence();
        evidence.setNumber("123445464");
        evidence.setItemName("Red Bloody Knife");
        evidence.setId(EVIDENCE_ID);
        evidence.setCriminalCase(criminalCase);

        (5)mockery.checking(new Expectations() {{
            allowing(mockRepo).findById(EVIDENCE_ID);
            will(returnValue(evidence));
        }});

        (6)Evidence result = service.findById(EVIDENCE_ID);
        (7)mockery.assertIsSatisfied();
        (8)assertAll(
            () -> Assertions.assertNotNull(result),
            () -> Assertions.assertEquals(result.getId(), evidence.
                getId()),
            () -> Assertions.assertEquals(result.getNumber(), evidence.
                getNumber())
        );
    }
}
```

When multiple mocks are used, or multiple operations are executed by the same mock, defining the expectations can become a bit cumbersome. Still, it is easier than defining stubs.

There are two jMock libraries: jmock-junit4 for JUnit 4 and jmock-junit5 for JUnit 5. As you can see, the central class to create mocks with jMock is the Mockery class. Each version of the jMock library provides a particular implementation, JUnit5Mockery and JUnit4Mockery.

Mockito

Mockito has the advantage of mocking behavior by writing code that is readable and very intuitive. The collection of methods provided was designed so well that even somebody without extensive programming knowledge can understand what is happening in that code, if that person also understands English. The class that will be tested with Mockito is SimpleStorageService. This class inherits all methods from SimpleAbstractService<T> and provides its own for request specific behavior.

```
package com.apress.cems.services.impl;
...

public class SimpleStorageService extends
    SimpleAbstractService<Storage> implements StorageService {
    private StorageRepo repo;

    @Override
    public Storage createStorage(String name, String location) {
        Storage storage = new Storage();
        storage.setName(name);
        storage.setLocation(location);
        repo.save(storage);
        return storage;
    }

    @Override
    public Optional<Storage> findByName(String name) {
        return repo.findByName(name);
    }
```

```
    @Override
    public Optional<Storage> findByLocation(String location) {
        return repo.findByLocation(location);
    }

    public void setRepo(StorageRepo repo) {
        this.repo = repo;
    }

    @Override
    AbstractRepo<Storage> getRepo() {
        return repo;
    }
}

// interface for Service specific behavior
public interface StorageService extends AbstractService<Storage> {

    Storage createStorage(String name, String location);

    Optional<Storage> findByName(String name);

    Optional<Storage> findByLocation(String location);
}
```

To perform a test using mocks generated with Mockito, the following steps have to be completed:

1. Declare and create the mock

2. Inject the mock

3. Define the behavior of the mock

4. Test

5. Validate the execution

The test class will be named SimpleStorageServiceTest3, and in the following test snippet, the findById method is tested and the preceding steps are underlined.

```
package com.apress.cems.mockito;

import org.junit.jupiter.api.Test;
import org.junit.jupiter.api.extension.ExtendWith;
import org.mockito.InjectMocks;
import org.mockito.Mock;

import static org.junit.jupiter.api.Assertions.*;
import org.mockito.junit.jupiter.MockitoExtension;
import static org.mockito.ArgumentMatchers.any;
import static org.mockito.Mockito.when;
...

@ExtendWith(MockitoExtension.class)
public class SimpleStorageServiceTest3 {
    public static final Long STORAGE_ID = 1L;

    @Mock //Creates mock instance of the field it annotates
    (1)private StorageRepo mockRepo;

     (2)@InjectMocks
    private SimpleStorageService storageService;

    @Test
    public void findByIdPositive() {
        Storage storage = new Storage();
        storage.setId(STORAGE_ID);
        (3) when(mockRepo.findById(any(Long.class))).thenReturn(storage);

        (4) Storage result = storageService.findById(STORAGE_ID);
        (5) assertAll(
                () -> assertNotNull(result),
                () -> assertEquals(storage.getId(), result.getId())
        );
    }
}
```

The org.mockito.junit.jupiter.MockitoExtension class initializes mocks and handles strict stubbings. It is used with the @ExtendWith JUnit 5 annotation so that Junit 5 annotations are recognized within a Mockito context.

Defining the behavior of the mock is so intuitive that looking at the line marked with (3), you can directly figure out how the mock works: when the findById method is called on it with any Long argument, it will return the storage object declared previously. When multiple mocks are used or multiple methods of the same mock are called, then more when statements must be written.

The @InjectMocks has a behavior similar to the Spring IoC, because its role is to instantiate testing object instances and to try to inject fields annotated with @Mock or @Spy into private fields of the testing object.

Also, Mockito provides matchers that can replace any variables needed for mocking environment preparation. These matchers are static methods in the org.mockito. ArgumentMatchers class and can be called to replace any argument with a pseudo-value of the required type. For common types, the method names are prefixed with any, (anyString(), anyLong(), and others), while for every other object type, any(Class<T>) can be used. So the line

```
Mockito.when(criminalCaseRepo.findByLeadInvestigator(detective))
    .thenReturn(sample);
```

can be written using a matcher, and no *detective* variable is needed.

```
Mockito.when(criminalCaseRepo.findByLeadInvestigator(any(Detective.class)))
    .thenReturn(sample);
```

When a mock method is being called multiple times, Mockito also has the possibility to check how many times the method was called with a certain argument using a combination of verify and times methods. So a check for the number of calls can be added to the assertions block.

```
when(mockRepo.findById(any(Long.class))).thenReturn(storage);

Storage result = storageService.findById(STORAGE_ID);

verify(mockRepo, times(1)).findById(any(Long.class));
```

Quite practical, right? Probably this is the reason why the Spring team switched from EasyMock to Mockito. Of course, there is more than one way to test using Mockito mocks and those are depicted in the code attached to this book in classes SimpleStorageServiceTest and SimpleStorageServiceTest2. Make sure that you do not mix and match with your classpath, because if mockito-all and mockito-junit-jupiter are both used as dependencies, you will get an ugly exception as they both contain classes with the same name in packages with the same name. Because of some confusion when configuring my projects, I initially got the exception, and you can see the error message in the following snippet.

```
java.lang.NoSuchMethodError: org.mockito.Mockito.mockitoSession()
    Lorg/mockito/session/MockitoSessionBuilder;
  at org.mockito.junit.jupiter.MockitoExtension.
  beforeEach(MockitoExtension.java:112)
  at org.junit.jupiter.engine.descriptor.TestMethodTestDescriptor.lambda
    $invokeBeforeEachCallbacks$0(TestMethodTestDescriptor.java:129)
  at org.junit.jupiter.engine.execution.ThrowableCollector.execute(
    ThrowableCollector.java:40)
  at org.junit.jupiter.engine.descriptor.TestMethodTestDescriptor
    .invokeBeforeMethodsOrCallbacksUntilExceptionOccurs(
    TestMethodTestDescriptor.java:155)
```

PowerMock

PowerMock was born because sometimes code is not testable, perhaps because of bad design or because of some necessity. The following is a list of untestable elements.

- static methods

- classes with static initializers

- final classes and final methods; sometimes there is need for an insurance that the code will not be misused or to make sure that an object is constructed correctly

- private methods and fields

PowerMock is not that useful in a Spring application, since you will rarely find static elements there, but there is always legacy code and third-party libraries/frameworks that might require mocking, so it is only suitable to know that it is possible to do so and the tool to use for this. If you want to know more, go to their official site at `https://github.com/jayway/powermock`.

When it comes to testing applications, the technique and tools to use are defined by the complexity of the application, the experience of the developer, and ultimately legal limitations, because there are companies that are restricted to using software under a certain license. During a development career, you will probably get to use all the techniques and libraries/frameworks mentioned in this book. Favor mocks for nontrivial dependencies and nontrivial interfaces. Favor stubs when the interfaces are simple with repetitive behavior, but also because stubs can log and record their usage.

That said, you can switch over to the next section, which shows you how to use these things to test a Spring application.

Testing with Spring

Spring provides a module called `spring-test` that contains Spring JUnit 4 and JUnit 5 test support classes that can make testing Spring applications a manageable operation. The next two sections will cover how to test a Spring application using both JUnit versions.

Testing with Spring and JUnit 4

The core class of the `spring-test` for working with JUnit 4 is `org.springframework.test.context.junit4.SpringJUnit4ClassRunner` (lately known as its alias `SpringRunner`), which caches an `ApplicationContext` across JUnit 4 test methods. All the tests are run in the same context, using the same dependencies; thus, this is integration testing.

To define a test class for running in a Spring context, the following steps have to be done.

1. Annotate the test class with `@RunWith(SpringJUnit4ClassRunner.class)` or `@RunWith(SpringRunner.class)`.

2. Annotate the class with `@ContextConfiguration` to tell the runner class where the bean definitions come from

```
// bean definitions are provided by class ReposConfig
@ContextConfiguration(classes = {ReposConfig.class})
public class RepositoryTest {...}
// bean definitions are loaded from file all-config.xml
@ContextConfiguration(locations = {"classpath:spring/all-config.xml"})
public class RepositoryTest {...}
```

CC If @ContextConfiguration is used without any attributes defined, the default behavior of Spring is to search for a file named {testClassName}-context.xml in the same location as the test class and load bean definitions from there if found. So, not only this annotation can be used with XML configuration files, but it is specific to JUnit 4, in case it was not obvious.

The easiest way to previous affirmations is by writing a very simple test. Take a look at the following test class.

```
package com.apress.cems;
...
@RunWith(SpringRunner.class)
@ContextConfiguration
public class ContextLoadingTest {

    @Autowired
    ApplicationContext ctx;

    @Test
    public void testContext() {
      assertNotNull(ctx);
    }
}
```

The ContextLoadingTest has a single test method declared that checks if a Spring application context is created. Since the @ContextConfiguration annotation does not specify where that configuration is coming from, when the method is executed, the test fails and the console output is as follows.

```
DEBUG o.s.t.c.j.SpringJUnit4ClassRunner -
SpringJUnit4ClassRunner constructor
        called with [class com.apress.cems.
        ContextLoadingTest]
...
DEBUG o.s.t.c.s.AbstractContextLoader - Did not detect
default resource location for
    test class [com.apress.cems.ContextLoadingTest]: class
    path resource
[com/apress/cems/ContextLoadingTest-context.xml] does not
exist
INFO  o.s.t.c.s.AbstractContextLoader - Could not detect
default resource locations
    for test class [com.apress.cems.ContextLoadingTest]:
        no resource found for suffixes {-context.xml}.
...
INFO  o.s.t.c.s.AnnotationConfigContextLoaderUtils - Could
not detect default
    configuration classes for test class [com.apress.cems.
    ContextLoadingTest]:
    ContextLoadingTest does not declare any static, non-
    private, non-final,
    nested classes annotated with @Configuration.
...
```

The log clearly shows that a Spring test context cannot be created because there is no configuration, of any kind provided for the Spring Container to do so.

---

3.   Use @Autowired to inject beans to be tested.

This method of testing was introduced to test Java configuration-based applications in the previous chapter; but in this chapter, you will find out how you can manipulate the configuration so that tests can be run in a test context. The following code snippet tests the class JdbcPersonRepo in a Spring context defined by two Spring configuration classes. The test uses an H2 in-memory database; a bean of type DataSource is declared as a bean and injected in `JdbcPersonRepo` indirectly by first being injected in a bean of type `JdbcTemplate`. In Figure 3-4, the classes and files involved in defining the test context and running the test are depicted.

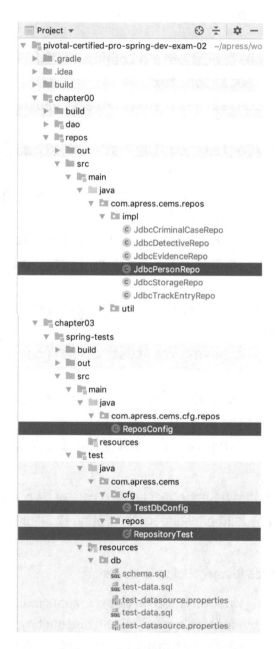

Figure 3-4. *Spring test context for testing JdbcPersonRepo*

The ReposConfig is a configuration class for all the repository beans declared in the com.apress.cems.repos.

```
package com.apress.cems.cfg.repos;

import org.springframework.beans.factory.annotation.Autowired;
import org.springframework.context.annotation.Bean;
import org.springframework.context.annotation.ComponentScan;
import org.springframework.context.annotation.Configuration;
import org.springframework.jdbc.core.JdbcTemplate;

import javax.sql.DataSource;

@Configuration
@ComponentScan(basePackages = {"com.apress.cems.repos"})
public class ReposConfig {

    @Autowired
    DataSource dataSource;

    @Bean
    public JdbcTemplate userJdbcTemplate() {
        return new JdbcTemplate(dataSource);
    }

}
```

The configuration decouples the database from the rest of the application, because a bean of this type is injected into this configuration using @Autowired. This means that a bean of this type is provided in a different configuration class, depending on the execution context. In this case, we are using a test context, and the dependency for executing this test is provided by the class TestDbConfig.

```
package com.apress.cems.cfg;

import org.springframework.beans.factory.annotation.Autowired;
import org.springframework.beans.factory.annotation.Value;
import org.springframework.context.annotation.Bean;
import org.springframework.context.annotation.PropertySource;
```

```java
import org.springframework.context.support.
PropertySourcesPlaceholderConfigurer;
import org.springframework.core.env.Environment;
import org.springframework.jdbc.datasource.DriverManagerDataSource;
import org.springframework.jdbc.datasource.init.DatabasePopulator;
import org.springframework.jdbc.datasource.init.DatabasePopulatorUtils;
import org.springframework.jdbc.datasource.init.ResourceDatabasePopulator;

import org.springframework.core.io.Resource;
import javax.sql.DataSource;

@PropertySource("classpath:db/test-datasource.properties")
public class TestDbConfig {

    @Autowired
    Environment environment;

    @Bean
    public static PropertySourcesPlaceholderConfigurer
        propertySourcesPlaceholderConfigurer() {
        return new PropertySourcesPlaceholderConfigurer();
    }

    @Bean
    public DataSource dataSource() {
        DriverManagerDataSource ds = new DriverManagerDataSource();
        ds.setDriverClassName(environment.getProperty("db.
        driverClassName"));
        ds.setUrl(environment.getProperty("db.url"));
        ds.setUsername(environment.getProperty("db.username"));
        ds.setPassword(environment.getProperty("db.password"));
        DatabasePopulatorUtils.execute(databasePopulator(), ds);
        return ds;
    }
```

```
@Value("classpath:db/schema.sql")
private Resource schemaScript;

@Value("classpath:db/test-data.sql")
private Resource dataScript;

private DatabasePopulator databasePopulator() {
    ResourceDatabasePopulator populator = new
    ResourceDatabasePopulator();
    populator.addScript(schemaScript);
    populator.addScript(dataScript);
    return populator;
}
```

}

The schema.sql contains the SQL DDL script to create the PERSON table. The test-data.sql contains a DML script to insert two records in the Person table. A bean of type PersonRepo can manipulate entries in this table.

All the test methods will run in the same Spring test context. The object to be tested and its dependencies are created only once, when the application context is created, and they are used by all methods. The object to be tested is a bean, and it is injected in the class testing it using @Autowired. The following test methods test integration between the declared datasource and a bean of type JdbcPersonRepo.

```
package com.apress.cems.repos;

import com.apress.cems.cfg.TestDbConfig;
import com.apress.cems.cfg.repos.ReposConfig;
import com.apress.cems.dao.Person;
import org.junit.Before;
import org.junit.Test;
import org.junit.runner.RunWith;
import org.springframework.beans.factory.annotation.Autowired;
import org.springframework.test.context.ContextConfiguration;
import org.springframework.test.context.junit4.SpringRunner;
```

```java
import java.util.Set;

import static org.junit.Assert.assertEquals;
import static org.junit.Assert.assertNotNull;

@RunWith(SpringJUnit4ClassRunner.class)
@ContextConfiguration(classes = {TestDbConfig.class, ReposConfig.class})
public class RepositoryTest{

    public static final Long PERSON_ID = 1L;;

    @Autowired
    PersonRepo personRepo;

    //positive test, we know that a Person with ID=1 exists
    @Test
    public void findByIdPositive() {
        Person person = personRepo.findById(PERSON_ID);
        assertNotNull(person);
        assertEquals("Sherlock", person.getFirstName());
    }

    //positive test, we know that a person matching the criteria exists
     @Test
    public void testFindByComplete(){
        Set<Person> personSet = personRepo.findByCompleteName("Sherlock",
        "Holmes");
        assertNotNull(personSet);
        assertEquals(1, personSet.size());
    }
}
```

The Spring test context is created using the two configuration classes, which will make sure the test DataSource dependency is the only one available to be injected into the jdbcPersonRepo bean. As you can see, a method annotated with @Before is not really necessary, because there is nothing else needed to have a context for the tests to execute in. Also, there is no longer any need to manipulate the jdbcPersonRepo object, since it is created, initialized, and injected by Spring. So all that is left for the developer to do is to inject the bean being tested and jump right to writing tests.

In Spring 3.1, the org.springframework.test.context.support.
AnnotationConfigContextLoader class was introduced. This class loads bean
definitions from static nested annotated classes. So a configuration class specific to
a test scenario can be created in the body test class to create the beans needed to
complete the test context. The class must be internal to the test class and static, and the
AnnotationConfigContextLoader class must be used as a value for the loader attribute
of the @ContextConfiguration annotation.

Please look at the following code snippet.

```java
package com.ps.integration;
import
  org.springframework.test.context.support.AnnotationConfigContextLoader;
import org.springframework.jdbc.datasource.embedded.EmbeddedDatabase;
import org.springframework.jdbc.datasource.embedded.
EmbeddedDatabaseBuilder;
import org.springframework.jdbc.datasource.embedded.EmbeddedDatabaseType;
 ...
@RunWith(SpringJUnit4ClassRunner.class)
@ContextConfiguration(loader=AnnotationConfigContextLoader.class)
public class RepositoryTest2 {

    public static final Long PET_ID = 1L;

    @Configuration
    static class TestCtxConfig {

      @Bean
        PersonRepo jdbcPersonRepo() {
            return new JdbcPersonRepo(jdbcTemplate());
        }

      @Bean
        JdbcTemplate jdbcTemplate() {
            return new JdbcTemplate(dataSource());
        }
```

```java
    @Bean
    public DataSource dataSource() {
        EmbeddedDatabaseBuilder builder = new
        EmbeddedDatabaseBuilder();
        EmbeddedDatabase db = builder
                    .setType(EmbeddedDatabaseType.H2)
                    .addScript("db/schema.sql")
                    .addScript("db/test-data.sql")
                    .build();
        return db;
    }
}

 @Autowired
PersonRepo personRepo;

@Before
public void setUp() {
    assertNotNull(personRepo);
}

@Test
public void testFindByIdPositive() {
    Person person = personRepo.findById(PERSON_ID);
    assertNotNull(person);
    assertEquals("Sherlock", person.getFirstName());
}

@Test
public void testFindByComplete() {
    Set<Person> personSet = personRepo.findByCompleteName("Sherlock",
    "Holmes");
    assertNotNull(personSet);
    assertEquals(1, personSet.size());
}
}
```

As you can see, the `dataSource` bean is an embedded database that is created under the hood by Spring. This bean can be easily replaced by a stub or a mock if necessary.

To cover this specific scenario, concrete implementations for the repository classes must be used. Since their implementation is irrelevant to this chapter and is covered in Chapter 5, the full code will not be presented here. To manage `Person` objects, a repository class is needed. The most basic way to provide access to a database in Spring applications is to use a bean of type `org.springframework.jdbc.core.JdbcTemplate`, so repository classes will be created with a dependency of that type. The methods querying the database from this bean require an object that can map database records to entities, which is why each repository class should define an internal class (or external) implementing the Spring-specific mapping interface `org.springframework.jdbc.core.RowMapper<T>`.

```
//abstract repository base class
 package com.ps.repos.impl;
 import org.springframework.jdbc.core.JdbcTemplate;
 ...
public class JdbcAbstractRepo<T extends AbstractEntity>
     implements AbstractRepo<T> {

   protected JdbcTemplate jdbcTemplate;

   public JdbcAbstractRepo(JdbcTemplate jdbcTemplate) {
       this.jdbcTemplate = jdbcTemplate;
   }
 ...
 }

@Repository
public class JdbcPersonRepo extends
    JdbcAbstractRepo<Person> implements PersonRepo {
    private RowMapper<Person> rowMapper
        = new PersonRowMapper();

    @Autowired
    public JdbcPersonRepo(JdbcTemplate jdbcTemplate) {
        super(jdbcTemplate);
    }
 ...
```

```java
    @Override
    public Person findById(Long id) {
        String sql = "select id, username, firstname, lastname,
            password, hiringdate from person where id= ?";
        return jdbcTemplate.queryForObject(sql, rowMapper, id);
    }
...
    // the DB record to entity mapper class
    class PersonRowMapper implements RowMapper<Person> {
    @Override
    public Person mapRow(ResultSet rs, int rowNum) throws SQLException {
        Long id = rs.getLong("ID");
        String username = rs.getString("USERNAME");
        String firstname = rs.getString("FIRSTNAME");
        String lastname = rs.getString("LASTNAME");
        String password = rs.getString("PASSWORD");
        String hiringDate = rs.getString("HIRINGDATE");

        Person person = new Person();
        person.setId(id);
        person.setUsername(username);
        person.setFirstName(firstname);
        person.setLastName(lastname);
        person.setPassword(password);
        person.setHiringDate(toDate(hiringDate));
        return person;
    }
  }
}
```

A configuration class that provides a mock that replaces the jdbcTemplate could be used, thus this will allow unit testing within a Spring context. The mock is created by a static method in the org.mockito.Mockito class called mock(Class<T>). In the following example, the jdbcPersonRepo bean is tested in isolation within a Spring Context created using the MockCtxConfig nested class.

```java
package com.apress.cems.mock;

import com.apress.cems.dao.Person;
import com.apress.cems.repos.PersonRepo;
import com.apress.cems.repos.impl.JdbcPersonRepo;
import com.apress.cems.repos.util.PersonRowMapper;
import org.junit.ClassRule;
import org.junit.Rule;
import org.junit.Test;
import org.junit.runner.RunWith;
import org.mockito.Mockito;
import org.mockito.runners.MockitoJUnitRunner;
import org.springframework.beans.factory.annotation.Autowired;
import org.springframework.context.annotation.Bean;
import org.springframework.context.annotation.Configuration;
import org.springframework.jdbc.core.JdbcTemplate;
import org.springframework.test.context.ContextConfiguration;
import org.springframework.test.context.junit4.rules.SpringClassRule;
import org.springframework.test.context.junit4.rules.SpringMethodRule;
import org.springframework.test.context.support.
AnnotationConfigContextLoader;

import static org.junit.Assert.assertNotNull;
import static org.mockito.Matchers.*;
import static org.mockito.Mockito.mock;
...
@RunWith(MockitoJUnitRunner.class)
@ContextConfiguration(loader = AnnotationConfigContextLoader.class)
public class SpringUnitTest {
    public static final Long PERSON_ID = 1L;

    @ClassRule
    public static final SpringClassRule SPRING_CLASS_RULE = new
    SpringClassRule();

    @Rule
    public final SpringMethodRule springMethodRule = new
    SpringMethodRule();
```

```
@Autowired
PersonRepo personRepo;

// mocking the database
@Autowired
JdbcTemplate jdbcTemplate;

@Test
public void testFindByIdPositive() {
    Mockito.when(jdbcTemplate.queryForObject(was
        any(PersonRowMapper.class), anyLong())).thenReturn(new Person());

    Person person = personRepo.findById(PERSON_ID);
    assertNotNull(person);
}

@Configuration
static class MockCtxConfig {
    @Bean
    JdbcTemplate jdbcTemplate() {
        return mock(JdbcTemplate.class);
    }

    @Bean
    PersonRepo jdbcPersonRepo() {
        return new JdbcPersonRepo(jdbcTemplate());
    }

}
}
```

To be executed correctly, the test class must respect the following two rules.

- It must be executed with MockitoJUnitRunner runner class.

- Two Spring-specific components must be added to the test class so
  the context can be loaded.

```
@ClassRule
public static final SpringClassRule SPRING_CLASS_RULE = new
SpringClassRule();
```

```
@Rule
public final SpringMethodRule springMethodRule = new
SpringMethodRule();
```

`org.springframework.test.context.junit4.rules.`
`SpringClassRule` is an implementation of JUnit `org.junit.rules.`
TestRule that supports class-level features of the Spring TestContext
Framework. The `@ClassRule` annotation is used on fields that
reference rules or methods that return them. Fields must be public,
static and a subtype of `org.junit.rules.TestRule`. Methods must
be public, static and return an implementation of `TestRule`.

The `org.springframework.test.context.junit4.rules.`
`SpringMethodRule` is an implementation of JUnit `org.junit.rules.`
MethodRule that supports instance-level and method-level features
of the Spring TestContext Framework. The `@Rule` annotation is used
on fields that reference rules or methods that return them. Fields
must be public and not static and an implementation of `TestRule`
or `MethodRule`; methods must be public and not static and return an
implementation of `TestRule` or `MethodRule`.

If you haven't figured out yet what happens in the previous example, I'll explain.
A test context was created containing all the beans in the `MockCtxConfig` configuration
class. One of the beans is the `jdbcTemplate`. It is a mock defined as a bean and is injected
automatically by Spring where needed (in the repository bean).

Testing with Spring and JUnit 5

After the launch of JUnit 5, a new package was added to the `spring-test` library: `org.`
`springframework.test.context.junit.jupiter`. This package contains a set of special
classes and annotation that write JUnit 5 tests that run in a Spring context.

`@RunWith(SpringRunner.class)` must be dropped since the annotation and the
runner class are specific to JUnit 4. So to migrate our tests to JUnit 5, they have to be
replaced with their JUnit 5 equivalents which are: `@ExtendWith(SpringExtension.`
`class)`. The `SpringExtension` class integrates the Spring test context into the Junit 5 test
context.

@ContextConfiguration is Spring-test specific, so it will work with JUnit 5 as well. All that is left is to replace the annotations inside the class. So the RepositoryTest for execution with JUnit 5 will look like the following.

```
package com.apress.cems.repos;

import org.junit.jupiter.api.BeforeEach;
import org.junit.jupiter.api.Test;
import org.junit.jupiter.api.extension.ExtendWith;
import org.springframework.test.context.ContextConfiguration;
import org.springframework.test.context.junit.jupiter.SpringExtension;
import static org.junit.jupiter.api.Assertions.assertEquals;
import static org.junit.jupiter.api.Assertions.assertNotNull;
...

@ExtendWith(SpringExtension.class)
@ContextConfiguration(classes = {TestDbConfig.class, ReposConfig.class})
public class RepositoryTest {

    public static final Long PERSON_ID = 1L;

    @Autowired
    PersonRepo personRepo;

    @BeforeEach
    public void setUp(){
        assertNotNull(personRepo);
    }

    @Test
    public void testFindByIdPositive(){
        Person person = personRepo.findById(PERSON_ID);
        assertNotNull(person);
        assertEquals("Sherlock", person.getFirstName());
    }
}
```

If you want something simpler, you can use the @SpringJUnitConfig[6] annotation, which is a composed annotation that combines @ExtendWith(SpringExtension.class) and @ContextConfiguration.

```
package com.apress.cems.repos;

import org.springframework.test.context.junit.jupiter.SpringJUnitConfig;
...

@SpringJUnitConfig(classes = {TestDbConfig.class, ReposConfig.class})
public class RepositoryTest {

    public static final Long PERSON_ID = 1L;

    @Autowired
    PersonRepo personRepo;

    @BeforeEach
    public void setUp(){
        assertNotNull(personRepo);
    }

    @Test
    public void testFindByIdPositive(){
        Person person = personRepo.findById(PERSON_ID);
        assertNotNull(person);
        assertEquals("Sherlock", person.getFirstName());
    }
}
```

The same goes for Spring test classes where mocks are used, for Mockito there is an extension that can be used. If @RunWith(MockitoJUnitRunner.class) is replaced with @ExtendWith(MockitoExtension.class), the specific test annotations are migrated to JUnit 5. If the proper JUnit 5 dependencies are added in the classpath, then the SpringUnitTest class is executed as intended, but on a Jupiter test engine. (Test samples are provided for you in the GitHub repository for this book.)

---

[6]The code of SpringJUnitConfig annotation is available at https://github.com/spring-projects/spring-framework/blob/master/spring-test/src/main/java/org/springframework/test/context/junit/jupiter/SpringJUnitConfig.java

This is all that there is. The most important thing that there is to know here is how to create a Spring shared context for your tests to run in. How complex the tests are and how they are executed really depends on your knowledge and understanding of the additional testing libraries introduced so far. But that is not a topic for this book, so let's continue with Spring-related testing details, shall we?

A Few Other Useful Spring Test Annotations

So far in our tests, all the test data was declared in a single file named test-data.sql. But what if we need to execute tests on different data sets, and we do not want to lose time initializing the database all at once before executing the tests? Well, there are a couple of Spring useful annotations that can come in handy: the @Sql family: @Sql, @SqlConfig, and @SqlGroup. Let's see how they can be used.

```java
package com.apress.cems.testrepos;

 import org.springframework.test.context.jdbc.Sql;
 import org.springframework.test.context.jdbc.SqlConfig;
 ...

@SpringJUnitConfig(classes = RepositoryTest3.TestCtxConfig.class)
public class RepositoryTest3 {
 public static final Long PERSON_ID = 1L;

    @Autowired
    PersonRepo personRepo;

    @BeforeEach
    public void setUp() {
        assertNotNull(personRepo);
    }

    @Test
    @Sql(
            scripts = "classpath:db/test-data-one.sql",
            config = @SqlConfig(commentPrefix = "`", separator = "@@")
    )
```

```java
public void testFindByIdPositive() {
    Person person = personRepo.findById(PERSON_ID);
    assertNotNull(person);
    assertEquals("Sherlock", person.getFirstName());
}

@Test
@Sql({"classpath:db/test-data-two.sql"})
public void testFindByComplete() {
    Set<Person> personSet = personRepo.findByCompleteName("Irene",
    "Adler");
    assertNotNull(personSet);
    assertEquals(1, personSet.size());
}

@Configuration
static class TestCtxConfig {
    @Bean
    PersonRepo jdbcPersonRepo() {
        return new JdbcPersonRepo(jdbcTemplate());
    }

    @Bean
    JdbcTemplate jdbcTemplate() {
        return new JdbcTemplate(dataSource());
    }

    @Bean
    public DataSource dataSource() {
        EmbeddedDatabaseBuilder builder = new
        EmbeddedDatabaseBuilder();
        EmbeddedDatabase db = builder
                .setType(EmbeddedDatabaseType.H2)
                .generateUniqueName(true)
                .addScript("db/schema.sql")
                .build();
```

```
            return db;
        }
    }

}
```

The @Sql annotation is used on methods annotated with @Test, which will cause the script or statement referred by it to be executed in the test database before the test is executed because it is the default setting.

The @Sql annotation provides an attribute named executionPhase that specify when a script or statement should be executed. Its default value is set to Sql.ExecutionPhase. BEFORE_TEST_METHOD (a member of the ExecutionPhase declared in the body of the @Sql annotation), so the script or statement is executed before the test method is executed, but it can be changed to be executed after it by setting its value to Sql.ExecutionPhase. AFTER_TEST_METHOD.

In the previous example, the @Sql was used to refer to files on the classpath containing SQL statements, but statements can be specified as arguments for the annotation directly. For example, @Sql({"classpath:db/test-data-two.sql"}) is equivalent to

```
@Sql(statements = {"INSERT INTO PERSON(ID, USERNAME, FIRSTNAME,
      LASTNAME, PASSWORD, HIRINGDATE, VERSION, CREATED_AT,
      MODIFIED_AT)
    VALUES (2, 'irene.adler', 'Irene', 'Adler', 'id123ds', '1990-08-18', 1,
          '1990-07-18', '1998-01-18');"})
```

The @Sql annotation can also be used at the class level, and in this case, the script is executed before each test method (actually, before the method annotated with @BeforeEach if such method exists), so you might need another script to clean up the database after each test method. This can be done easily with @Sql, because executions of SQL scripts can be linked to test execution phases using the executionPhase attribute. Take a look at the following example.

```
package com.apress.cems.testrepos;
...
import org.springframework.test.context.jdbc.Sql;
import org.springframework.test.context.jdbc.SqlConfig;
...
```

```java
@Sql(
        scripts = "classpath:db/test-data.sql",
        config = @SqlConfig(commentPrefix = "`", separator = "@@")
)
@Sql(statements = "DELETE FROM PERSON",
        executionPhase = Sql.ExecutionPhase.AFTER_TEST_METHOD)
@SpringJUnitConfig(classes = RepositoryTest5.TestCtxConfig.class)
public class RepositoryTest5 {
    static final Long PERSON_ID = 1L;

    @Autowired
    PersonRepo personRepo;

    @BeforeEach
    void setUp() {
        assertNotNull(personRepo);
    }

    @Test
    void testFindByIdPositive() {
        Person person = personRepo.findById(PERSON_ID);
        assertNotNull(person);
        assertEquals("Sherlock", person.getFirstName());
    }

    @Test
    void testFindAll(){
        Set<Person> all = personRepo.findAll();
        assertAll(
                () -> assertNotNull(all),
                () -> assertEquals(2, all.size())
        );
    }

    @Configuration
    static class TestCtxConfig {
    ... //same as the previous code listing
    }

}
```

When the previous code is executed, both tests pass because both are executed on a database that is initialized with the content declared in the `test-data.sql` file and cleaned right after the test execution method ends. And, we can do something even smarter: we can use the class level Sql annotation to create the database structure, or only the table that is required in the test context.

In the next code sample, we annotate the RepositoryTest5 class with an Sql annotation that is declared to be executed before each test method.

```
package com.apress.cems.testrepos;
...
import org.springframework.test.context.jdbc.Sql;
import org.springframework.test.context.jdbc.SqlConfig;
...
@Sql(
        scripts = {"classpath:db/person-schema.sql",
            "classpath:db/test-data.sql"},
        executionPhase = Sql.ExecutionPhase.BEFORE_TEST_METHOD
)
@SpringJUnitConfig(classes = RepositoryTest5.TestCtxConfig.class)
public class RepositoryTest5 {
    ... // same code as in previous code listing
}
```

If we run this class, the test methods will pass as before, because the `person-schema.sql` script starts with a declaration to drop the PERSON table if it exists. So each test method is executed on a new version of the table.

The @SqlConfig annotation provides extra information about the syntax used in the SQL script file provided as argument to an @Sql annotation.

The SqlGroup groups multiple Sql annotations, which use different scripts/statements. You can use it on test classes or methods. The syntax should be similar to the one in the next code snippet.

```
@SqlGroup({
    @Sql(scripts = "classpath:db/test-data-one.sql",
            config = @SqlConfig(commentPrefix = "`")),
    @Sql({"classpath:db/test-data-two.sql"})
})
```

When the application is more complex and transactions are in place, integration testing might require test methods to be executed within a transactional context. This means test methods will be annotated with @Transactional (from package org. springframework.transaction.annotation). And because controlling the context matters in a test environment, Spring Test provides annotations to use to mark methods for executing before (@BeforeTransaction) and after a transaction is closed (@AfterTransaction).

There is also an annotation used to require a rollback (@Rollback) of the last transaction. After a test has been executed, it is quite useful to preserve the state of the test database so that other tests are executed on the same set of data. This is the reason why rolling back a transaction after the execution of a test method is the default behavior. But in some integration tests, you might need a "dirty" database, and in those cases, you can annotate your test methods with @Rollback("false"). There is also the case when you might need a transactional test method to be committed after the test method has completed; the @Commit annotation is suitable in that case.

All of these annotations are used in Chapter 5, when integration tests using persistence context is created.

Using Profiles

In the previous chapter, out of necessity, using profiles for customizing an application behavior was introduced. In Spring version 3.1, the @Profile annotation became available. With this annotation, classes become eligible for registration when one or more profiles are activated at runtime. Spring profiles have the same purpose as Maven profiles, but they are much easier to configure and are not linked to an application's builder tool. Different environments require different configurations, and much care should be used during development so that components are decoupled enough, and they can be swapped depending on the context in which processes are executed.

Spring profiles help considerably in this case. For example, during development, tests are run on development machines, and a database is not really needed; or if one is needed, an in-memory simple and fast implementation should be used. This can be set up by creating a test datasource configuration file that is used only when the development profile is active. The datasource classes for production and test environments are depicted in the following code snippet.

```java
//production dataSource
 package com.ps.config;
 import org.springframework.context.annotation.Profile;
 ...
@Configuration
@PropertySource("classpath:db/datasource.properties")
@Profile("prod")
public class ProdDbConfig {

    @Bean("connectionProperties")
    Properties connectionProperties(){
        try {
            return PropertiesLoaderUtils.loadProperties(
                    new ClassPathResource("db/prod-datasource.
                    properties"));
        } catch (IOException e) {
   throw new ConfigurationException("Could not retrieve connection
   properties!", e);
        }
    }

    @Bean
    public DataSource dataSource() {
        try {
            OracleDataSource ds = new OracleDataSource();
            ds.setConnectionProperties(connectionProperties());
            return ds;
        } catch (SQLException e) {
   throw new ConfigurationException("Could not configure Oracle
   database!", e);
        }
    }
}

// development dataSource
@Configuration
@Profile("dev")
```

```java
public class TestDbConfig {

    @Bean
    public DataSource dataSource() {
        EmbeddedDatabaseBuilder builder = new EmbeddedDatabaseBuilder();
        EmbeddedDatabase db = builder
                .setType(EmbeddedDatabaseType.H2)
                .generateUniqueName(true)
                .addScript("db/schema.sql")
                .addScript("db/test-data.sql")
                .build();
        return db;
    }
}
```

In the preceding sample, we have two configuration classes, each declaring a bean named dataSource, each bean specific to a different environment. The profiles are named simply *prod*, for the production environment, and *dev*, for the development environment. In the test class, we can activate the development profile by annotating the test class with @ActiveProfiles annotation and giving the profile name as argument. Thus, in the following test context, only the beans defined in classes annotated with @ Profile("dev") will be created and injected.

The test class is depicted in the following code snippet.

```java
import org.springframework.test.context.ActiveProfiles;
  ...
@ExtendWith(SpringExtension.class)
@ContextConfiguration(classes = {TestDbConfig.class,
    ProdDbConfig, ReposConfig.class})
@ActiveProfiles("dev")
public class RepositoryTest {

    public static final Long PERSON_ID = 1L;

    @Autowired
    PersonRepo personRepo;

    //positive test, we know that a Person with ID=1 exists
```

```
@Test
    public void testFindByIdPositive(){
        Person person = personRepo.findById(PERSON_ID);
        assertNotNull(person);
        assertEquals("Sherlock", person.getFirstName());
    }
}
```

The ProdDbConfig looks out of place in the previous example, but it is there to prove that only beans specific to the dev profile are created.

The advantage of using profiles become obvious when the beans within the application context must be replaced in the test context, but the configuration does not allow that because it is not decoupled enough. In the previous code sample, the datasource is configured in its own file. But what if the datasource is declared in a configuration class named AllConfig that declares all other application beans as well, either by using @Bean annotation or by using component scanning? If the configuration is not decoupled, how do we override the bean declarations we are interested in within a test context? Well, easy really, the @Profile annotation can be used directly on bean declarations as well. We have to make sure that the dataSource bean is declared as specific to the prod profile by annotating it with @Profile("prod"). Yes, the @Profile annotation can be used both at the class level and at the method level.

```
package com.apress.cems.cfg;
 import org.springframework.context.annotation.Profile
 ....

@Configuration
@ComponentScan(basePackages = {"com.apress.cems.repos"})
public class AllConfig {

    @Bean
    public JdbcTemplate userJdbcTemplate() {
        return new JdbcTemplate(dataSource());
    }
```

```
@Bean("connectionProperties")
Properties connectionProperties(){
    try {
        return PropertiesLoaderUtils.loadProperties(
                new ClassPathResource("db/prod-datasource.
                properties"));
    } catch (IOException e) {
        throw new ConfigurationException(
            "Could not retrieve connection properties!", e);
    }
}

@Profile("prod")
@Bean
public DataSource dataSource() {
    try {
        OracleDataSource ds = new OracleDataSource();
        ds.setConnectionProperties(connectionProperties());
        return ds;
    } catch (SQLException e) {
        throw new ConfigurationException("Could not configure Oracle
        database!", e);
    }
}
}
```

After this is done, we can create a test context using this class and the configuration class containing the dataSource bean specific to the dev environment, the TestDbConfig class and activate the dev profile.

```
@ContextConfiguration(classes = {TestDbConfig.class, AllConfig.class})
@ActiveProfiles("dev")
public class RepositoryTest {
...
}
```

By annotating the test class @ActiveProfiles("dev"), the development profile is activated, so when the context is created, bean definitions are picked up from the configuration class (or files) specified by the @ContextConfiguration annotation and all the configuration classes annotated with @Profile("dev"). Thus, when running the test, the in-memory database will be used, making the execution fast and practical.

Any bean that is not specific to a profile is created and added to the application context, regardless if there is an active profile at runtime or not. There is a test class named SampleProfileConfigTest in the chapter03/spring-profiles project. It contains an internal Spring configuration class, which declares a few beans, some of them specific to profiles. You can play with it; activate and deactivate profiles to check the beans created in each scenario.

In conclusion, using the Spring-provided test classes to test a Spring application is definitely easier than not doing it, since no external container is needed to define the context in which the tests run. If the configuration is decoupled enough, pieces of it can be shared between the test and production environment. For basic unit testing, Spring is not needed, but to implement proper integration testing, the ability to set up a test context in record time is surely useful.

Spring Boot Testing

Spring Boot was introduced in the previous chapter. Just in case you skipped that one, let me remind you that Spring Boot is a preconfigured set of frameworks/technologies designed to reduce boilerplate configuration (infrastructure) and provide a quick way to have a Spring web application up and running. As expected, Spring Boot includes a library that makes testing of Spring Boot Application super easy.

Adding the library spring-boot-starter-test as a dependency adds multiple testing libraries to the classpath: JUnit 4 and 5, Hamcrest, Mockito, AssertJ. In this chapter, a small but complete Spring Boot application is created to manage Person instances. We have an Oracle database, a special JPA management interface named PersonRepo to manipulate Person instances, and a class named PersonServiceImpl (that implements interface PersonService). A bean of type PersonService uses a bean of type PersonRepo to persist changes to the database. There is also a bean of type PersonController that receives web requests and forwards specific actions to a bean of type PersonService. The connection between these beans makes for a perfect application to write unit and integration tests for.

Not all classes are depicted in Figure 3-5, because some of them contain implementations specific to other chapters. Figure 3-5 depicts all the classes of interest for the application.

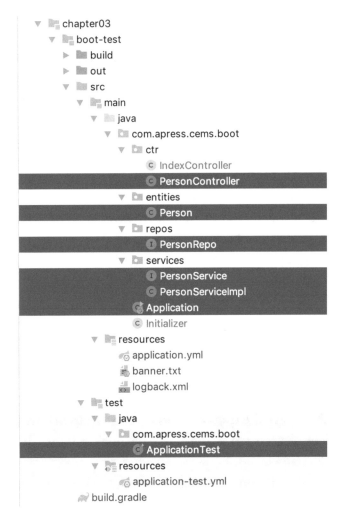

Figure 3-5. *Test-driven development logical schema*

The Spring Boot application class annotated with @SpringBootApplication also enables component scanning on package com.apress.cems.boot and its subpackages, so all the bean declarations will be discovered and all beans will be created.

```
package com.apress.cems.boot;

import org.slf4j.Logger;
import org.slf4j.LoggerFactory;
import org.springframework.boot.SpringApplication;
import org.springframework.boot.autoconfigure.SpringBootApplication;
import org.springframework.context.ConfigurableApplicationContext;

@SpringBootApplication
public class Application {

    private static Logger logger = LoggerFactory.getLogger(Application.class);

    public static void main(String... args) {
        ConfigurableApplicationContext ctx =
            SpringApplication.run(Application.class, args);
        ctx.registerShutdownHook();
        logger.info("Application Started ...");
    }
}
```

When executing this class, (if you have Oracle Database installed locally, or in a Docker container[7] and a database user as specified in the properties file) if no exception appears in the console, it means that the context was initialized correctly. You can confirm that the application is up and running by accessing http://localhost:8080/ in your browser. You should see the text *This works!*.[8] The details of how everything works under the hood will be clear to you by the end of the book. For now, let's focus on testing this application.

To test this application, we need to create a Spring Boot context based on the Application class. By default, any test class annotated with @SpringBootTest in the package com.apress.cems.boot and subpackages looks for an application class annotated with @SpringBootApplication to use for bootstrapping a test context. The test context can be customized either by specific annotations configurations of the

---

[7]Instructions for installing Docker and setting up a Docker container with an Oracle database are provided together with the sources associated to the chapter.

[8]This text is returned by a method of a web specialized bean of type *IndexController*.

boot test class, or by properties declared in specific test properties files (like `src/test/resources/application.yml` or `src/test/resources/application.properties`).

The awesome part is that Spring Boot has embraced JUnit 5, because if we were to look into the `@SpringBootTest` code, we see that this annotation is meta-annotated with `@ExtendWith(SpringExtension.class)`. This means that tests annotated with `@SpringBootTest` are automatically picked up and executed by the JUnit 5 Jupiter engine. Let's quickly write a simple test to check that the `PersonService` class is implemented properly.

```
package com.apress.cems.boot;

import com.apress.cems.boot.entities.Person;
import com.apress.cems.boot.services.PersonService;
import org.junit.jupiter.api.Assertions;
import org.junit.jupiter.api.Test;
import org.springframework.beans.factory.annotation.Autowired;
import org.springframework.boot.test.context.SpringBootTest;

@SpringBootTest(webEnvironment =
    SpringBootTest.WebEnvironment.NONE)
public class ApplicationTest {

    @Autowired
    private PersonService personService;

    @Test
    public void testSavePerson(){
        Person person = new Person();
        person.setFirstName("Irene");
        person.setLastName("Adler");
        personService.save(person);

        Assertions.assertEquals(personService.count(), 2);
    }
}
```

The previous class tests the ability of the `personService` bean to create an instance of type `Person`. The reason that we expect two entries is because one of them was created by a class named `Initializer`, which is declared within the application.

The personService bean, calls methods of the personRepo bean which makes use of an H2 data base. The first to beans are production specific beans, the database is declared in the test configuration file. This is an integration test that covers the application's service and DAO layers. As you can see, we do not need a full web environment booted up to run our test, which is why the SpringBootTest.WebEnvironment.NONE argument is used.

Earlier, the @Transactional and @Rollback annotations were mentioned. Since we now have a transactional service, we can actually make use of them. Let's modify the previous test class to roll back all changes done by the testSavePerson() and add another test that counts the entries in the test database to make sure their number is unchanged. Sure, the @Rollback annotation is redundant since the default test behavior is to rollback anyway, but for teaching purposes, it will be used anyway. Examples that are more relevant are in Chapter 4.

```
package com.apress.cems.boot;

import com.apress.cems.boot.entities.Person;
import com.apress.cems.boot.services.PersonService;
import org.junit.jupiter.api.Test;
import org.springframework.beans.factory.annotation.Autowired;
import org.springframework.boot.test.context.SpringBootTest;
import import org.springframework.transaction.annotation.Transactional;
import org.springframework.test.annotation.Rollback;

import static org.junit.jupiter.api.Assertions.assertEquals;

@SpringBootTest(webEnvironment =
            SpringBootTest.WebEnvironment.NONE)
public class ApplicationTest {

    @Autowired
    private PersonService personService;

    @Rollback    @Transactional
    @Test
    public void testSavePerson(){
        Person person = new Person();
        person.setFirstName("Irene");
```

```
        person.setLastName("Adler");
        personService.save(person);

        assertEquals(2, personService.count());
    }

    @Test
    void testCount(){
        //get all persons, list should only have one
        assertEquals( 1, personService.count());
    }
}
```

So, the @SpringBootTest is basically a @ContextConfiguration on steroids. Under the hood, when no loader is specified (like in the @ContextConfiguration(loader = AnnotationConfigContextLoader.class) examples from previous sections, a SpringBootContextLoader loads a Spring Boot configuration from a class annotated with @SpringBootConfiguration or any specialization of it, like @SpringBootApplication. It looks for properties on the test classpath to be injected in the Environment and registers a TestRestTemplate and WebTestClient beans, can be used to test web applications. You will become familiar with this in Chapter 6.

Tests that cover integration with the web layer can be written as well. And there are specific classes for simulating a web request and matcher to test the contents of the response that do not requiring starting up the web server. The MockMvcBuilders class is part of the spring-test module and provides a series of builder instances that simulate a call to web specialized beans called *controllers*. The standaloneSetup(..) method returns a builder of type StandaloneMockMvcBuilder to register one or more controller beans and configure the Spring MVC infrastructure programmatically. Other relevant examples are covered in Chapter 6.

```
package com.apress.cems.boot;

import com.apress.cems.boot.ctr.PersonController;
import org.junit.jupiter.api.BeforeEach;
import org.junit.jupiter.api.Test;
import org.springframework.beans.factory.annotation.Autowired;
import org.springframework.boot.test.context.SpringBootTest;
import org.springframework.http.MediaType;
```

```java
import org.springframework.test.web.servlet.MockMvc;
import org.springframework.test.web.servlet.setup.MockMvcBuilders;

import static org.hamcrest.Matchers.*;
import static org.springframework.test.web.servlet.request.
MockMvcRequestBuilders.get;
import static org.springframework.test.web.servlet.result.
MockMvcResultMatchers.*;

@SpringBootTest(webEnvironment =
      SpringBootTest.WebEnvironment.NONE)
public class ApplicationWebTest {

    @Autowired
    PersonController personController;

    private MockMvc mockMvc;

    @BeforeEach
    public void setup() {
        this.mockMvc = MockMvcBuilders.
            standaloneSetup(this.personController).build();
    }

    @Test
    public void testfindAll() throws Exception {

        mockMvc.perform(get(String.format("/person/all")))
                .andExpect(status().isOk())
                .andExpect(content().contentTypeCompatibleWith
                    (MediaType.APPLICATION_JSON))
                .andExpect(jsonPath("$", hasSize(1)))
                .andExpect(jsonPath("$..firstName",
                hasItem(is("Sherlock"))));

    }
}
```

In the previous test, we use an instance of type `MockMvc`, created by the `StandaloneMockMvcBuilder` instance to simulate a GET request to `http://localhost/person/all`. There is no need for a port in the test context because the `mockMvc` bean is automatically configured by Spring. Pretty neat, right?

MockMvc is designed very well, and the method making the request can be chained with the methods testing the contents of the response. In the previous test a bunch of matcher methods form the Hamcrest library are used too, for testing assumptions made regarding the number of items in the response and the value of the properties.

The `jsonPath(..)` method is a static method from the `MockMvcResultMatchers` class that can navigate the structure of a JSON text to extract values to test assumptions on. The two dots in the previous example are called *deep scan operators* [9] and are used to access the first JSON element in a JSON array.

The value returned by `personController` is `[{"firstName":"Sherlock","last Name":"Holmes","id":1}]` and since the test passes, the `jsonPath(..)` call works as expected.

Once a test class is annotated with `@SpringBootTest` a test context is set up and available, so the tests that can be written can make use of any library at your disposal. You will probably hear that if it is difficult to test an application, the test environment setup is too complex. This is a clear sign that the application's design is bad. The fact that testing Spring Boot applications is so easy is clearly a sign that Spring Boot promotes good design.

Summary

After reading this chapter you should possess enough knowledge to test a Spring application using unit and integration testing and you should be able to answer to the following questions.

- What is unit testing, and which frameworks are useful for writing unit tests in Java?

- What is a stub?

- What is a mock?

---

[9]If you are interested in more information about *jsonPath(..)*, check out the official repository: `https://github.com/ json-path/JsonPath`

- What is integration testing?

- How does one set up a Spring Test Context?

- What is the purpose of the @SpringBootTest annotation?

Quick Quiz

Question 1. Given the following test class declaration,

```
@RunWith(SpringRunner.class)
@ContextConfiguration
public class SimpleTest {
 //test methods here
}
```

Which of the following affirmations is true? (Choose one.)

A.   The tests will be executed on a JUnit 4 engine.

B.   The tests will be executed on a JUnit 5 engine.

C.   The tests will be executed on a JUnit engine found in the class
     path.

Question 2. Given the following unit test, what is missing from the class definition that prevents the test from being executed correctly? (Choose all that apply.)

```
import org.junit.jupiter.api.Test;
import static org.junit.jupiter.api.Assertions.*;

...

public class SimplePersonServiceTest {

  @InjectMocks
  SimplePersonService personService;

  @Mock
  PersonRepo personRepo;
```

```
@Test
public void findById() {
    Mockito.when(petRepo.findById(1L)).thenReturn(new Pet());
    Pet pet = personService.findById(1L);
    assertNotNull(pet);
}
}
```

A. The `@ExtendWith(MockitoExtension.class)` annotation.

B. Nothing. The test will be executed correctly, and it will pass.

C. A `setUp` method is missing with the following content.

`MockitoAnnotations.initMocks(this);`

Question 3. The `SpringJUnit4ClassRunner` class enhances a JUnit 4 test class with Spring context.

A. true

B. false

Question 4. What is the `@ContextConfiguration` used for? (Choose one.)

A. to load and configure a TestApplicationContext instance

B. to load and configure an ApplicationContext for integration testing

C. to inject beans used in unit testing

Question 5. What library is mandatory for writing unit tests for a Spring application? (Choose one.)

A. JUnit

B. spring-test

C. any mock generating library such as jMock, Mockito, or EasyMock

Question 6. Which of the affirmations describes unit testing best? (Choose one.)

A. Unit testing is a software practice of replacing dependencies with small units of mock code during application testing.

B. Unit testing is a software practice of testing how small individual units of code work together in the same context.

C. Unit testing is a software practice of testing small individual units of code in isolation.

Practical Exercise

The project to use to test your understanding of testing is chapter03/spring-tests-practice. This project contains part of the implementation depicted in the code snippets. The missing parts are marked with a TODO task and are visible in IntelliJ IDEA in the TODO view. There are six tasks for you to solve to test your acquired knowledge of testing, and they are focused on Mockito usage and Spring testing.

Tasks TODO 15 and 16 require you to complete two unit tests that test a com.apress.cems.stub.SimpleCriminalCaseServiceTest object using a stub. Task TODO 17 requires you to place the missing annotations in the MockPersonServiceTest.

Tasks TODO 18 require you to complete the test class definitions so that the test cases can execute correctly. To run a test case, just click anywhere on the class content or on the class name in the project view and select the Run '{TestClassName'} option. If you want to run a single test, right-click, and from the menu select Run '{TestMethodName}'. The options are depicted in Figure 3-6 for a test class and a test method in the project. You can even run the tests using debug in case, you are interested in stopping the execution at specific times.

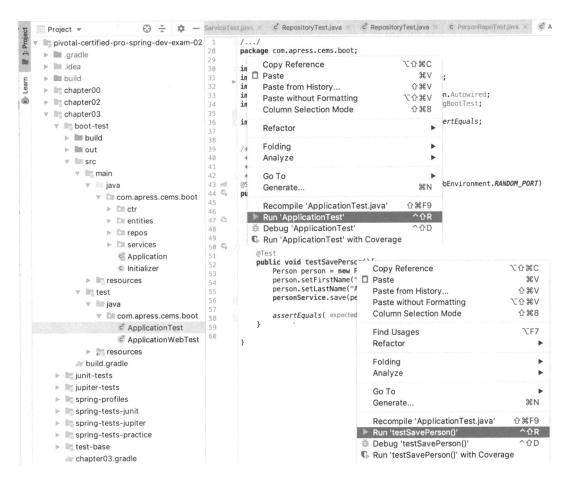

Figure 3-6. *How to run tests in IntelliJ IDEA*

After implementing all the solutions, you can run the Gradle `test` task to run all your tests. You should see a green check next to the test results, similar to what is depicted in Figure 3-7.

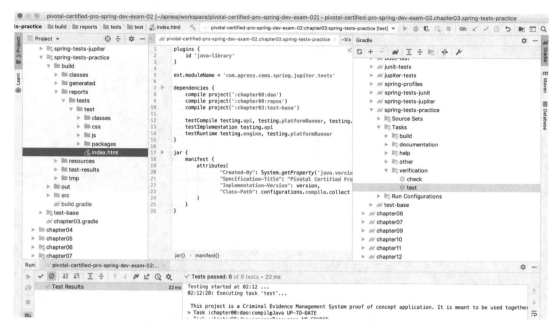

Figure 3-7. *Running all tests for a module in IntelliJ IDEA, using the Gradle test task*

In Figure 3-7, the Gradle task appears on the right in the Gradle view selected in gray. For any module it can be found under `Sub-ProjectName/Tasks/verification`.

On the left, the `index.html` file generated when Gradle tests are run is selected. You can open that file in the browser when writing the test to check percentages of the tests passing and detailed logs telling you why tests fail. If all is well at the end, you should see a page looking like the one depicted in Figure 3-8.

Figure 3-8. *Gradle web report after all tests have passed*

All other projects under chapter03 contain code samples presented in this chapter including proposed solutions for the TODOS. Please compare yours with the provided ones to make sure all was implemented according to the specifications.

Also, because the project has grown, you can try doing a Gradle build scan using the gradle clean build --scan command and analyze its stability and execution time. Also, to build modules in parallel, you can add the -Dorg.gradle.parallel=true option.

```
gradle clean build --scan -Dorg.gradle.parallel=true
```

Tests in *-practice projects are either annotated with @Disabled or are missing annotations that would allow them being picked up from execution until you provide a solution and enable for them to be picked up. After agreeing with the Gradle terms, the build will end with a link that opens in your browser to a web page with the result analysis of the build. In Figure 3-9, you can see the result of my current build scan. If there are build failures, they will appear in the build scan. Feel free to click around to inspect the details of the build.

Figure 3-9. *Official Gradle report about the CEMS project build*

CHAPTER 4

Aspect-Oriented Programming with Spring

AOP is the acronym for **a**spect-**o**riented **p**rogramming, which refers to a type of programming that aims to increase modularity by allowing the separation of cross-cutting concerns. A cross-cutting concern is a functionality that is tangled with business code, which usually cannot be separated from the business logic. Auditing, security, and transaction management are good examples of cross-cutting concerns. They are mingled with the business code and heavily coupled with functionalities that might be affected if they fail. They are good candidates for separation using *aspects*, because there is no design pattern that allows writing code in such a way that it is separated from the business logic. This means that additional behavior is added to existing behavior when the application is compiled.

Transaction management, security logic, and auditing can be developed separately and mingled with functionality at compile time. This is done by defining an *advice* containing code that will be executed in a location named *join point* specified by a *pointcut*. This approach allows code that implements behavior that is not related to business logic to be separated from functional code; the result is a more modular, less coupled, and less cluttered application.

The business or base code is not actually changed, you can imagine aspects as plugins. They modify the behavior, not the actual implementation.

> *AOP is a type of programming that aims to help with separation of cross-cutting concerns to increase modularity; it implies declaring an aspect class that will alter the behavior of base code by applying advices to specific join points specified by pointcuts.*

© Iuliana Cosmina 2020
I. Cosmina, *Pivotal Certified Professional Core Spring 5 Developer Exam*,
https://doi.org/10.1007/978-1-4842-5136-2_4

AOP is a complement of OOP (**o**bject-**o**riented **p**rogramming). AOP and OOP can be used together to write powerful applications, because both provide different ways of structuring your code. OOP is focused on making everything an object, while AOP introduces the *aspect,* which is a special type of object that injects and wraps its behavior to complement the behavior of other objects. The following are other features that might be implemented as cross-cutting concerns.

- Logging

- Data validation

- Caching

- Internationalization[1]

- Error detection and correction

- Memory management

- Performance monitoring

- Synchronization

Problems Solved by AOP

When databases store data, a connection to the database interacts with the application. The connection to the database needs to be opened before the communication and closed afterward to successfully complete communication with the database. Every database implementation will allow a limited number of connections simultaneously, thus connections that are no longer used need to be closed, so that others can be opened. A JDBC repository method that looks for a person based on ID looks similar to the implementation shown in Figure 4-1.

---

[1]When a *MessageSource* instance is called directly to replace texts based on a Locale instance.

```java
public Person findById(Long id) {
        String sql = "select p.ID as ID, p.USERNAME as USERNAME," +
                " p.FIRSTNAME as FIRSTNAME, p.LASTNAME as LASTNAME" +
                " from PERSON p where p.ID = ?";
        Connection conn = null;
        PreparedStatement ps = null;
        ResultSet rs = null;
        try {
                conn = dataSource.getConnection();
                ps = conn.prepareStatement(sql);
                ps.setLong(1, id);
                rs = ps.executeQuery();
                Set<Person> persons = mapPersons(rs);
                if (!persons.isEmpty()) {
                        return persons.iterator().next();
                }
        } catch (SQLException e) {
                throw new RuntimeException("User not found!", e);
        } finally {
                if (rs != null) {
                        try {
                                rs.close();
                        } catch (SQLException ex) {}
                }
                if (ps != null) {
                        try {
                                ps.close();
                        } catch (SQLException ex) {}
                }
                if (conn != null) {
                        try {
                                conn.close();
                        } catch (SQLException ex) {}
                }
        }
        return null;
}
```

Figure 4-1. *Method using JDBC to search for a person based on its ID in a database, with cross-cutting concern-specific code highlighted*

The code implementing the opening and closing of the connection is enclosed in red rectangles. Whenever access to the database is required, almost identical code must be written. This code was specifically chosen to underline a cross-cutting concern that tangles in the base code, which leads to code scattering. It is not a clean solution, and it is not a stable one either. In a big project, database communication methods are written by different programmers, which is enough for one to make a mistake that leads to connections to the database not being closed correctly. The application could end up unable to communicate with the database because a new connection cannot be opened.

The preceding example is archaic, and the call diagram for that method is depicted in Figure 4-2.

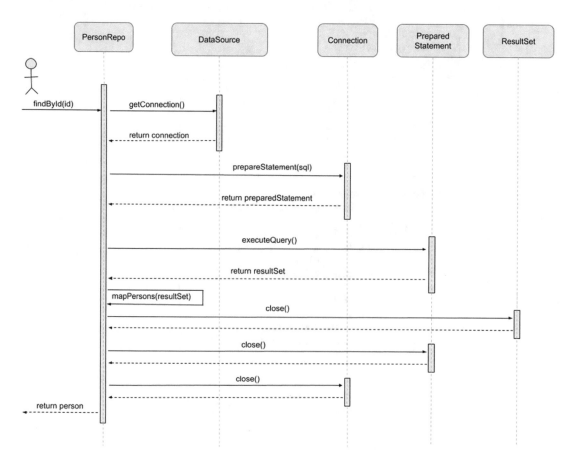

Figure 4-2. *UML call diagram for the JDBC method extracting a person by its ID*

Complicated, right? AOP can help decouple the connection management code from the business code. Using AOP, the previous diagram should be reduced to something like what is depicted in Figure 4-3.

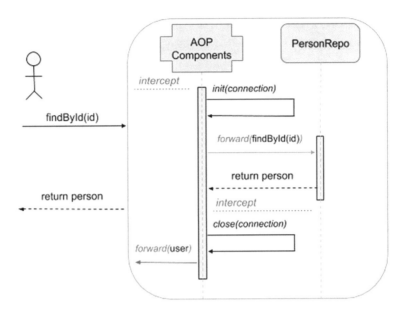

Figure 4-3. *Conceptual schema for the findById() method with AOP*

The schema in Figure 4-3 is a conceptual one, and it depicts the basic idea. AOP components intercept calls to certain objects and inject their own functionality, without being strongly connected to the initial target, and they do so in a transparent way.

There are not many applications left that use JDBC components directly. Currently there are frameworks that provide classes to manage the connections for you, so you do not have to write all that code. For example, in Spring, the class org.springframework. jdbc.core.JdbcTemplate does that for you, and it will be covered in Chapter 5. Repository components can be created based on JdbcTemplate instances, and database connections are managed by connection pool components.

Connection pooling is a technique of reusing connections: when a connection is closed, it can reside in memory to be reused the next time a connection is required, eliminating the cost of creating a new connection. But using connections directly is cumbersome, because application crashes can lead to inconsistent data. Aside from connections, applications use transactions to group database operations in units of work. When all operations have completed successfully, the transaction is committed, and the changes are persisted into the database. If one operation fails, the transaction is rolled back, leaving the database untouched.

In this case, transactions become a cross-cutting concern because a method that is supposed to be called into a transaction has to obtain a transaction, open it, perform its actions, and then commit the transaction.

Usually, an application uses more than one cross-cutting concern. The most common grouping is security + logging (or auditing) + transactions. So, service classes that provide and regulate access to data end up looking like what's shown in Figure 4-4.

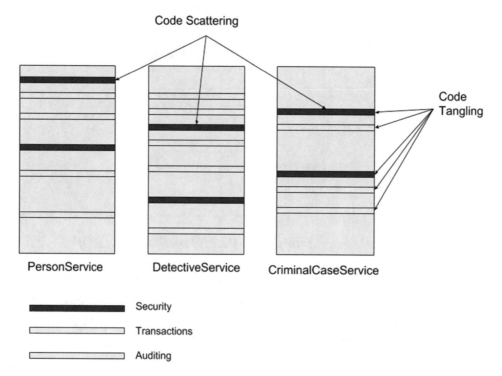

Figure 4-4. *Code tangling and scattering in service classes without AOP*

Code tangling and code scattering are two issues that come together when base code needs to be executed under certain conditions. *Code tangling* is a term used to describe mixing cross-cutting concerns and business logic, which leads to tight coupling. *Code scattering* is caused by identical code put in every module. The resulting solution is difficult to extend and to maintain, harder to understand, and a pain to debug. Using AOP, a developer can focus on the core implementation, and define aspect components to cover the cross-cutting concerns. AOP provides even more modularization than OOP does.

Spring AOP

The original library that provided components for creating aspects is named **AspectJ**. It was developed by the Xerox PARC company and released in 1995. It defined a standard for AOP because of its simplicity and usability. The language syntax used to define aspects was similar to Java and allowed developers to define special constructs called aspects. The aspects developed in AspectJ are processed at compile time, so they directly affect the generated bytecode.

The Spring AOP framework is a complement to the current version of AspectJ and contains many annotations that can develop and configure aspects using Java code, but the Spring development team knows and recognizes its limitations. For example, it cannot advise fine-grained objects such as domain objects. Spring AOP functionality is based on AspectJ which is why when Spring AOP libraries are used, `aspectjweaver` and `aspectjrt` must be added to the application classpath.

Spring AOP cannot advise objects that are not managed by the Spring container. AspectJ does that. Spring AOP uses dynamic proxies for aspect weaving, so the bytecode of the target object is not affected in any way. This is a specific of the Java language; once a class has been compiled, its code can no longer be changed. The target object is effectively wrapped at runtime into a generated object that either implements the same interfaces that the target object class does, or extends the class of the target object.

Spring AOP is also non-invasive; it was developed to keep AOP components decoupled from application components.

In earlier versions, XML was used to define aspects. The purpose of this chapter is to help you modularize your code so that tangling and scattering are eliminated (or at least reduced to a minimum) using everything Spring has to offer.

The Spring Framework is composed of a few libraries.[2]

- **spring-aop** provides AOP alliance API compliant components that can define method interceptors and pointcuts so that code with different responsibilities can be cleanly decoupled.

- **spring-aspects** provides integration with AspectJ.

- **spring-instrument** provides class instrumentation support and classloader implementations that can be used on application servers.

---

[2]The *spring-instrument-tomcat* module contains Spring's instrumentation agent for Tomcat. It was dropped from Spring 5, but it is still being maintained form Spring 4.

Spring IoC can write software applications. For business applications that require the use of cross-cutting concerns, Spring AOP is a must. Before digging into it, let's discuss AOP concepts and how they are declared in Spring.

AOP Terminology

A few AOP terms were mentioned earlier in this chapter, but more detailed descriptions are required.

- **Aspect**: A class containing code specific to a cross-cutting concern. A class declaration is recognized in Spring as an aspect if it is annotated with the @Aspect annotation.

- **Weaving**: A synonym for this word is *interlacing*, but in software the synonym is *linking* and it refers to aspects being combined with other types of objects to create an advised object.

- **Join point**: A point during the execution of a program. In Spring AOP, a join point is always a method execution. Basically, the join point marks the execution point where aspect behavior and target behavior join.

- **Target object**: An object to which the aspect applies.

- **Target method**: the advised method.

- **Advice**: The action taken by an aspect at a join point. In Spring AOP, there are multiple advice types.

  - **Before advice**: Methods annotated with @Before that will execute before the join point. These methods do not prevent the execution of the target method unless they throw an exception.

  - **After returning advice**: Methods annotated with @AfterReturning that will execute after a join point completes normally, meaning that the target method returns normally without throwing an exception.

  - **After throwing advice**: Methods annotated with @AfterThrowing that will execute after a join point execution ends by throwing an exception.

  - **After (finally) advice**: Methods annotated with @After that will execute after a join point execution, no matter how the execution ended.

- **Around advice**: Methods annotated with @Around intercept the target
  method and surround the join point. This is the most powerful type of
  advice since can perform custom behavior before and after the invocation.
  It has the responsibility of choosing to perform the invocation or return its
  own value, and it provides the option of stopping the propagation of an
  exception.

- **Pointcut**: A predicate used to identify join points. Advice definitions
  are associated with a pointcut expression and the advice will execute
  on any join point matching the pointcut expression. Pointcut
  expressions are defined using AspectJ Pointcut Expression Language[3]
  Pointcut expressions can be defined as arguments for Advice
  annotations or as arguments for the @Pointcut annotation.

- **Introduction**: Declaring additional methods, fields, interfaces being
  implemented, and annotations on behalf of another type. Spring AOP
  allows this using a suite of AspectJ @Declare* annotations that are
  part of the aspectjrt library.[4]

- **AOP proxy**: The object created by AOP to implement the aspect
  contracts. In Spring proxy objects can be JDK dynamic proxies or
  CGLIB proxies. By default, the proxy objects are JDK dynamic proxies,
  and the object being proxied must implement an interface that is also
  implemented by the proxy object. But a library like CGLIB can create
  proxies by subclassing, so an interface is not needed.

Quick Start

To quickly introduce most of the Spring AOP terms, let's consider a very simple example.
Let's consider a JdbcPersonRepo bean with a few simple methods used to query for or
modify Person instances.

---

[3]Complete reference here: https://eclipse.org/aspectj/doc/next/progguide/language.html
[4]If you want to know more you might find this url interesting https://www.eclipse.org/
aspectj/doc/next/adk15notebook/annotations-declare.html

```java
package com.apress.cems.repos.impl;
...
@Repository
public class JdbcPersonRepo extends JdbcAbstractRepo<Person>
        implements PersonRepo {
    private RowMapper<Person> rowMapper = new PersonRowMapper();

    public JdbcPersonRepo(JdbcTemplate jdbcTemplate) {
        super(jdbcTemplate);
    }

    @Override
    public Optional<Person> findById(Long id) {
        String sql = "select id, username, firstname, lastname, password,
                hiringdate from person where id= ?";
        return Optional.of(jdbcTemplate.queryForObject(sql, rowMapper, id));
    }

    @Override
    public Optional<Person> findByUsername(String username) {
        String sql = "select id, username, firstname, lastname, password,
                hiringdate from person where username= ?";
        return Optional.of(jdbcTemplate.queryForObject(sql, rowMapper,
        username));
    }

    @Override
    public Optional<Person> findByCompleteName(String firstName, String
    lastName) {
        String sql = "select id, username, firstname, lastname, password,
                hiringdate from person where firstname= ? and lastname= ?";
        return Optional.of(jdbcTemplate.queryForObject(sql,
                new Object[]{firstName, lastName}, rowMapper));
    }
```

```java
    @Override
    public void save(Person person) {
        jdbcTemplate.update(
                "insert into person(id, username, firstname, lastname,
                password,
                    hiringdate) values(?,?,?,?,?,?)",
                person.getId(), person.getUsername(), person.getFirstName(),
                    person.getPassword(), person.getHiringDate()
        );
    }

    @Override
    public Set<Person> findAll() {
        String sql = "select id, username, firstname, lastname, password,
            hiringdate from person";
        return new HashSet<>(jdbcTemplate.query(sql, rowMapper));
    }
}

// Maps a row returned from a query executed on the PERSON table to a
Person object.
//implementation not relevant for this chapter
package com.apress.cems.repos.util;
...
public class PersonRowMapper implements RowMapper<Person>  {

        ...
}
```

The PersonRowMapper implementation is not relevant for this chapter, but in case you are curious, this class implements the Spring RowMapper<T> interface and it is used by JdbcTemplate instances to transform database records into domain objects to be used by the application. Objects of this type are typically stateless and reusable. They are covered in Chapter 5.

An aspect can be created to monitor the execution of the methods of this bean. The following code snippet depicts an aspect class definition that contains a single advice that prints a message every time the findById method is called.

```java
package com.apress.cems.aop;

import org.springframework.stereotype.Component;
import org.aspectj.lang.JoinPoint;]
import org.aspectj.lang.annotation.Aspect;
import org.aspectj.lang.annotation.Before;
import org.slf4j.Logger;
import org.slf4j.LoggerFactory;

@Aspect
@Component
public class PersonMonitor {
    private static final Logger logger =
        LoggerFactory.getLogger(PersonRepoMonitor.class);

    @Before
        ("execution(public * com.apress.cems.repos.*.JdbcPersonRepo+.
        findById(..))")
    public void beforeFindById(JoinPoint joinPoint) {
        String methodName = joinPoint.getSignature().getName();
        logger.info(" ---> Method " + methodName + " is about to be called");
    }
}
```

The class containing the aspect definition must be declared as a bean. This can be done using any of the three ways covered in Chapter 2[5] In the preceding example, the declaration is done by annotating the class with @Component. The @Before annotation is used with a parameter that is called a *pointcut expression*, which is used to identify the method to advise. This identifies the method execution on which the behavior will be applied.

To test the following code, we need a configuration class and a test class. The configuration for the datasource is decoupled in the class com.ps.config. TestDataConfig that is not relevant for this chapter, but you can find it in the sources attached to this chapter in project chapter04/aop. The application configuration will be provided by the AopConfig class. To enable aspect support, the configuration class must be annotated with @EnableAspectJAutoProxy.

---

[5]Using XML configuration *<bean/>* elements, using *@Bean* or *@Component* and specializations annotations

```
package com.apress.cems.aop.config;

import org.springframework.context.annotation.ComponentScan;
import org.springframework.context.annotation.Configuration;
import org.springframework.context.annotation.EnableAspectJAutoProxy;

@Configuration
@ComponentScan(basePackages = {"com.apress.cems.aop"})
@EnableAspectJAutoProxy
public class AopConfig {
}
```

To add behavior to existing objects, Spring uses a method called *proxying*, which implies creating an object that wraps around the target object. By default, Spring creates JDK dynamic proxies, which are proxy objects implementing the same interface the target object does. The @EnableAspectJAutoProxy annotation can also be used to modify the type of proxies created. By default, JDK dynamic proxies (interface-based proxies) are created, but CGLIB proxies can be requested by specifying the proxyTargetClass attribute and setting its value to true. The CGLIB proxies are called *subclass proxies* because they extend the type of the target object. But before getting deeper into this topic, let's do some testing.

```
 package com.apress.cems.aop;
 ... // imports here

@ExtendWith(SpringExtension.class)
@ContextConfiguration(classes = {AopConfig.class, TestDbConfig.class})
public class PersonMonitorTest {

    @Autowired
    PersonRepo personRepo;

    @Test
    public void testFindById() {
        Person person = personRepo.findById(1L);
        assertEquals("sherlock.holmes", person.getUsername());
    }
}
```

! Because the PersonRepoMonitor aspect class only prints messages, to clearly see the advice in action, all the logs will be set to OFF; except the one for the aspect class. This is done by editing the chapter04/aop/src/test/resources/logback-test.xml and setting all logs for other packages to OFF and the log level for the com.ps.aspects on INFO, as the following code snippet shows.

```xml
<?xml version="1.0" encoding="UTF-8"?>
<configuration>

    <contextListener class="ch.qos.logback.classic.jul.
    LevelChangePropagator">
        <resetJUL>true</resetJUL>
    </contextListener>

    <appender name="console" class="ch.qos.logback.core.
    ConsoleAppender">
        <encoder>
            <pattern>%d{HH:mm:ss.SSS} [%thread] %-5level
            %logger{5} - %msg%n</pattern>
        </encoder>
    </appender>

    <logger name="org.springframework" level="off"/>
    <logger name="org.h2" level="off"/>
    <logger name="com.apress.cems.aop" level="info"/>

    <root level="info">
        <appender-ref ref="console" />
    </root>
</configuration>
```

When the testFindById method is executed, a single line is printed in the log.

```
INFO  c.a.c.a.PersonMonitor -  ---> Method findById is about to be called.
```

The Before advice was executed since the expected text was printed by beforeFindById in the PersonMonitor aspect class. But how does it actually work? Spring IoC creates the jdbcPersonRepo bean. Then the aspect definition with an advice that has to be executed before the findById method tells Spring that this bean has to be wrapped in a proxy object that adds additional behavior. This object is injected (instead of the original) everywhere it is needed. And because we are using JDK dynamic proxies, the proxy will implement the PersonRepo interface. Figure 4-5 depicts this situation.

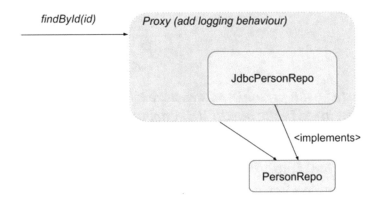

Figure 4-5. *The personRepo proxy bean*

The bean that is injected into the test bean can be inspected by placing a breakpoint inside the testFindById method and starting the test in debug mode. In the debugger view the personRepo can be expanded and its contents inspected. Figure 4-6 is a side-by-side view of the structure of a personRepo bean when aspects are used and when they aren't.[6]

---

[6]You can disable aspects support in your application by commenting the *@EnableAspectJAutoProxy* annotation and Spring will just ignore the *@Aspect* annotation, leaving the *PersonMonitor* as a simple bean declaration.

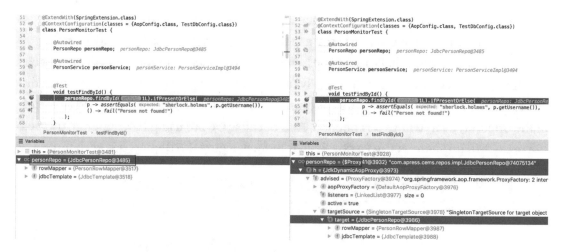

Figure 4-6. *Injected bean personRepo structure when aspects are used and when they are not as displayed in the IntelliJ IDEA debugger view. On the right, you see the type of the injected bean: JdkDynamicAopProxy*

In this case, the type of proxy created is the default JDK dynamic proxy, which is useful when the target class implements one or more interfaces. Spring creates a proxy that implements all of them. The JDK proxies are created at runtime using JDK Reflection API and reflection is known to affect performance.

If CGLIB proxies are needed, Spring must be told that we want subclass-based proxies by modifying the aspect enabling annotation to @EnableAspectJAutoProxy(proxyTargetClass = true). This approach is suitable when the target class does not implement any interface, so Spring will create a new class on the fly that is a subclass of the target class. CGLIB is suitable for that because it is a bytecode generation library. The proxies generated with CGLIB are called subclass-based and one of their advantages is that they can override methods optionally. They use specialized interceptors to call methods, which can actually improve performance.

In Figure 4-7, you can see the structure of the personRepo bean when CGLIB creates proxies.

```
     C  PersonMonitorTest.java  ×

     51       @ExtendWith(SpringExtension.class)
     52       @ContextConfiguration(classes = {AopConfig.class, TestDbConfig.class})
     53       class PersonMonitorTest {
     54
     55           @Autowired
     56           PersonRepo personRepo;    personRepo: "com.apress.cems.repos.impl.JdbcPersonRepo@740
     57
     58           @Autowired
     59           PersonService personService;   personService: "com.apress.cems.aop.service.PersonSe
     60
     61
     62           @Test
     63           void testFindById() {
     64               personRepo.findById( entityId: 1L).ifPresentOrElse(   personRepo: "com.apress.cems
     65                   p -> assertEquals( expected: "sherlock.holmes", p.getUsername()),
     66                   () -> fail("Person not found!")
     67               );
     68           }

          PersonMonitorTest  >  testFindById()
```

```
  Variables
  ▶  ≡ this = {PersonMonitorTest@3965}
  ▼  ∞ personRepo = {JdbcPersonRepo$$EnhancerBySpringCGLIB$$3b9056a8@3969} "com.apress.cems.re
        f CGLIB$BOUND = false
     ▼  f CGLIB$CALLBACK_0 = {CglibAopProxy$DynamicAdvisedInterceptor@4010}
        ▼  f advised = {ProxyFactory@4017} "org.springframework.aop.framework.ProxyFactory: 0 interfaces
           ▶  f aopProxyFactory = {DefaultAopProxyFactory@4019}
              f listeners = {LinkedList@4020}  size = 0
              f active = true
           ▼  f targetSource = {SingletonTargetSource@4021} "SingletonTargetSource for target object [cor
              ▼  target = {JdbcPersonRepo@4029}
                 ▶  f rowMapper = {PersonRowMapper@4030}
                 ▶  f jdbcTemplate = {JdbcTemplate@4031}
```

Figure 4-7. *Injected bean userRepo structure when proxies are created using CGLIB in the IntelliJ IDEA debugger view*

To use aspects in a Spring application, you need the following.

- spring-aop and aspectjweaver as dependencies

- declare an @Aspect class and declare it as a bean as well (using @Component or @Bean or XML old-school bean declaration element)

- declare an advice method annotated with a typical advice annotation (@Before, @After, etc.) and associate it to a pointcut expression

- enable aspects support by annotating a configuration class with @EnableAspectJAutoProxy or @EnableAspectJAutoProxy(proxy TargetClass = true)

Aspect Support Configuration using XML

Although aspect support configuration has been based on annotations since Spring 3.1, before that version the configuration was done using XML. Since your experience as a developer you might end up working on projects using Spring < 3.1 we find it useful to cover how to configure aspect support using XML.

Obviously, there's a namespace for that, which provides an element definition equivalent to @EnableAspectJAutoProxy.

The specific element is <aop:aspectj-autoproxy../>, which has an <aop:include ../> child element for each aspect defined in the application.

If you want to avoid configuring aspects using annotations (because you are using a Java version less than 5 and annotations are not supported), there is an <aop:config /> element that can declare methods of a bean as advice and associate pointcuts.

```xml
<?xml version="1.0" encoding="UTF-8"?>
<beans xmlns="http://www.springframework.org/schema/beans"
       xmlns:xsi="http://www.w3.org/2001/XMLSchema-instance"
       xmlns:aop="http://www.springframework.org/schema/aop"
       xmlns:context="http://www.springframework.org/schema/context"
       xsi:schemaLocation="http://www.springframework.org/schema/beans
          http://www.springframework.org/schema/beans/spring-beans.xsd
          http://www.springframework.org/schema/aop
          http://www.springframework.org/schema/aop/spring-aop.xsd
          http://www.springframework.org/schema/context
          http://www.springframework.org/schema/context/spring-context.xsd">

   <!-- Configuration for the aspects that apply to the application -->
   <bean id="personRepoMonitor" class="com.apress.cems.aop.
   PersonMonitor"/>

   <context:component-scan base-package="com.apress.cems.aop" />

   <!-- Configure Aspect support -->
   <aop:aspectj-autoproxy>
       <aop:include name="personRepoMonitor"/>
   </aop:aspectj-autoproxy>
```

```xml
<!-- Configure advice -->
<aop:config>
    <aop:aspect ref="personRepoMonitor">
        <aop:before
                pointcut="execution(
            public * com.apress.cems.repos.*.JdbcPersonRepo+.
            findById(..))"
                method="beforeFindById"/>
    </aop:aspect>
</aop:config>

</beans>
```

To configure the use of subclass-based proxies the `<aop:aspectj-autoproxy../>` must have the `proxy-target-class` attribute set to `true`.

Defining Pointcuts

Before advice and the pointcut expression associated with it (which provides the means to identify where to apply the advice) were covered in the Quick Start section, the pointcut expression looked like the following snippet.

```
execution(public * com.apress.cems.repos.*.JdbcPersonRepo+.findById(..))
```

The template that a pointcut expression follows can be defined as follows.

```
execution( [Modifiers] [ReturnType] [FullClassName].[MethodName]
    ([Arguments]) throws [ExceptionType])
```

The expression can contain wildcards like + and * and can be made of multiple expressions concatenated by boolean operators such as &&, ||, and so forth. The * wildcard replaces any group of characters when used to match pieces of package names, classes, and methods, and a single character when used to match method parameters. The + wildcard specifies that the method to advise can also be found in subclasses identified by [FullClassName] criteria. The + wildcard works in a similar way when the criteria used is an interface and the pointcut expression matches the methods in all implementations.

There is also a list of designators that can define the reach of the pointcut, for example the within(...) designator can limit the pointcut to a package, but it works only with AspectJ.

```
execution(public * *.JdbcPersonRepo+.findById(..)) && within(com.apress.*)
```

A pointcut expression can filter only the methods defined in a class annotated with a specific annotation, (e.g., @within(com.apress.cems.aop.ApressService)).

This can also be written as

```
within(@com.apress.cems.aop.ApressService *)
```

Only methods annotated with a specific annotation can be targeted.

```
execution(@com.apress.cems.repos.ApressRepo
        * com.apress.cems.repos.*.*Repo+.*(..))
```

And by using the @annotation designator, the syntax is prettier.

```
@annotation(com.apress.cems.repos.ApressRepo)
```

This is useful when security is involved, because the @annotation can be bound to a method parameter so that the annotation object is available in the advice body.

```
@Around("execution(* *(..)) && @annotation(securedObj)")
public void calculateExecutionTime(ProceedingJoinPoint pjp,
            Secured securedObj) throws Throwable {
// extra security checks using securedObj.allowedRoles()
...
}
```

!   Observations.

- The [ReturnType] is mandatory. If the return type is not a criterion, just use *. If it is missing the application crashes at boot time throwing an java.lang. IllegalArgumentException with a message explaining that the pointcut is not well-formed.

- The [Modifers] is not mandatory and if not specified defaults to public.

- The [MethodName] is not mandatory, meaning no exception will be thrown at boot time. But if unspecified, the join point where to execute the advice won't be identified. It's safe to say that if you want to define a technically useful pointcut expression you need to specify it.

- The [Arguments] is mandatory. If it is missing the application crashes at boot time throwing a java.lang.IllegalArgumentException with a message explaining that the pointcut is not well formed. If the arguments are not a criterion, just use (..) which matches a method with 0 or many arguments. If you want the match to be done on a method with no arguments, use (). If you want the match to be done on a method with a single argument, use (*).

Using pointcut expressions can become tedious when the criterion for determining the method to be advised is complicated. But declaring pointcuts can be made pleasant by breaking down the expressions into several subexpressions that can be combined and reused in other composed expressions. Spring also offers the possibility to externalize expressions in dedicated classes. Yes, even pointcut declarations can be decoupled. In the following code snippets, I'll explain how this can be done.

Let's make things more complicated by declaring a service class that can manage Person instances.

This service class will use the personRepo to interact with the database.

```
package com.apress.cems.aop.service;

...

@Service
public class PersonServiceImpl implements PersonService {
    private PersonRepo personRepo;

    public PersonServiceImpl(PersonRepo personRepo) {
        this.personRepo = personRepo;
    }

    @Override
    public Set<Person> findAll() {
        return  Sets.newHashSet(personRepo.findAll());
    }
```

```java
    @Override
    public long count() {
        return personRepo.count();
    }

    @Override
    public Optional<Person> findById(Long id) {
        return Optional.ofNullable(personRepo.findById(id));
    }

    @Override
    public Person save(Person person) {
        personRepo.save(person);
        return person;
    }

    @Override
    public Optional<Person> findByUsername(String username) {
        return personRepo.findByUsername(username);
    }

    @Override
    public Optional<Person> findByCompleteName(String firstName, String
    lastName) {
        return personRepo.findByCompleteName(firstName,lastName);
    }

    @Override
    public void delete(Person person) {
        personRepo.delete(person);
    }
}
```

We want to write an aspect that will write a message every time an findBy* method is called (in the previous class, three of them were declared) only from a repository or a service class managing Person instances. So the pointcut has to look for a method whose name begins with findBy that has arguments and is found in any of the classes implementing PersonRepo or PersonService.

There are many ways the pointcut expression can be written, and in this section a few of them will be presented. The aspect class and advice look like this:

```
package com.apress.cems.aop;
...

@Aspect
@Component
public class PersonMonitor {
    private static final Logger logger = Logger.getLogger(PersonMonitor.
    class);

    @Before("execution(* com.apress.cems.*.*PersonRepo+.findBy*(..))
        || execution (* com.apress.cems.aop.service.*Service+.findBy*(..)))")
    public void beforeFind(JoinPoint joinPoint) {
        String className = joinPoint.getSignature().getDeclaringTypeName();
        String methodName = joinPoint.getSignature().getName();
        logger.info(" ---> Method " + className + "." + methodName +
            " is about to be called");
    }
}
```

In a small application, when you only have those two classes, the `"execution(` `* findBy*(..))"` pointcut expression will do; but in a big application, this relaxed expression might cause the advice to be applied on methods that you did not intend to be advised. The expression used in the first code snippet is composed of two expressions.

```
@Before("execution(* com.apress.cems.*.*PersonRepo+.findBy*(..))
    || execution (* com.apress.cems.aop.service.*Service+.findBy*(..)))")
```

The two expressions can be split into two pointcut declarations that can be associated to methods. The name of these methods will then be used in a composite expression to identify a pointcut. And that is why these pointcuts are called Named Pointcuts.

```
 package com.apress.cems.aop;
...

@Aspect
@Component
public class PersonMonitor {
    private static final Logger logger = Logger.getLogger(PersonMonitor.
    class);

    @Before("repoFind() || serviceFind()")
    public void beforeFind(JoinPoint joinPoint) {
        String className = joinPoint.getSignature().getDeclaringTypeName();
        String methodName = joinPoint.getSignature().getName();
        logger.info(" ---> Method " + className + "." + methodName
            + " is about to be called");
    }

    @Pointcut ("execution(* com.apress.cems.*.*PersonRepo+.findBy*(..))")
    public void repoFind() {}

    @Pointcut ("execution (* com.apress.cems.aop.service.*Service+.
    findBy*(..)))")
    public void serviceFind() {}
}
```

A dedicated class can be created to group together pointcuts. In this case, the composite expression must be modified to contain the package and classname where the methods are located.

```
 package com.apress.cems.aop;
import org.aspectj.lang.annotation.Pointcut;

public class PointcutContainer {

    @Pointcut("execution(* com.apress.cems.*.*PersonRepo+.findBy*(..))")
    public void repoFind() {}

    @Pointcut ("execution (* com.apress.cems.aop.service.*Service+.
    findBy*(..)))")
    public void serviceFind() {}
}
```

Methods repoFind and serviceFind are moved to the class com.apress.cems. aop.PointcutContainer, so the expression for the beforeFind advice changes to the following.

```
@Before("com.apress.cems.aop.PointcutContainer.repoFind() ||
        com.apress.cems.aop.PointcutContainer.serviceFind()")
    public void beforeFind(JoinPoint joinPoint) throws Throwable {
        ...
    }
```

So, now that the pointcuts are externalized what more can be done? The methods annotated with @Pointcut and associated with pointcut expressions can process data. So far, we have been using the JoinPoint argument (that is, specific to all advice methods except the ones annotated with @Around) to extract context data, like the class name and the method name being called. But context data can be injected by Spring, if told so by using special designators.

The find methods in our example have one or more String arguments that must be processed and an exception must be thrown if the value contains special characters like $, #,&,%. If we do not accept those characters as part of the first name and last name of a person, let's not accept them as part of the search criteria either, just for the sake of creating a more interesting advice. In this scenario, this is only suitable when done in service methods because there is no point in calling a repo method with a bad argument. This means that we need to create a new advice for the save service method only.

```
    package com.apress.cems.aop;
    ...

@Aspect
@Component
public class PersonMonitor {
    private static final Logger logger =
    LoggerFactory.getLogger(PersonMonitor.class);
    private static final String[] SPECIAL_CHARS = new String[]{"$", "#",
    "&", "%"};
```

```
@Before("execution (* com.apress.cems.aop.service.*Service+.
save(..)))")
public void beforeSave(JoinPoint joinPoint) {
    String className = joinPoint.getSignature().getDeclaringTypeName();
    String methodName = joinPoint.getSignature().getName();
    logger.info(" ---> Validating argument of method " + className
        + "." + methodName + ".");

    Object[] args = joinPoint.getArgs();
    Person person = (Person)args[0];
    if (StringUtils.indexOfAny(person.getFirstName(), SPECIAL_CHARS)
    != -1 ||
        StringUtils.indexOfAny(person.getLastName(), SPECIAL_CHARS)
        != -1) {
        throw new IllegalArgumentException("Text contains weird
        characters!");

    }
  }
}
```

Notice how all the information about the context of the advices is extracted from the joinPoint object. The JoinPoint interface provides a couple of methods to access information about the target method, all accessible via the proxy object. A reference to the target object can be obtained by calling: joinPoint.getTarget(). You can convert that to the original type and do whatever you need. In Figure 4-8, a test run was stopped at a breakpoint after calling the joinPoint.getTarget() method and the target object is the focus on the Debugger view in IntelliJ IDEA. You can clearly see its type. The type of the target object can be extracted also by calling joinPoint.getSignature(). getDeclaringTypeName(), the difference is calling this method returns a String value. The joinPoint returns a reference to the actual target object that the AOP proxy is wrapped around.

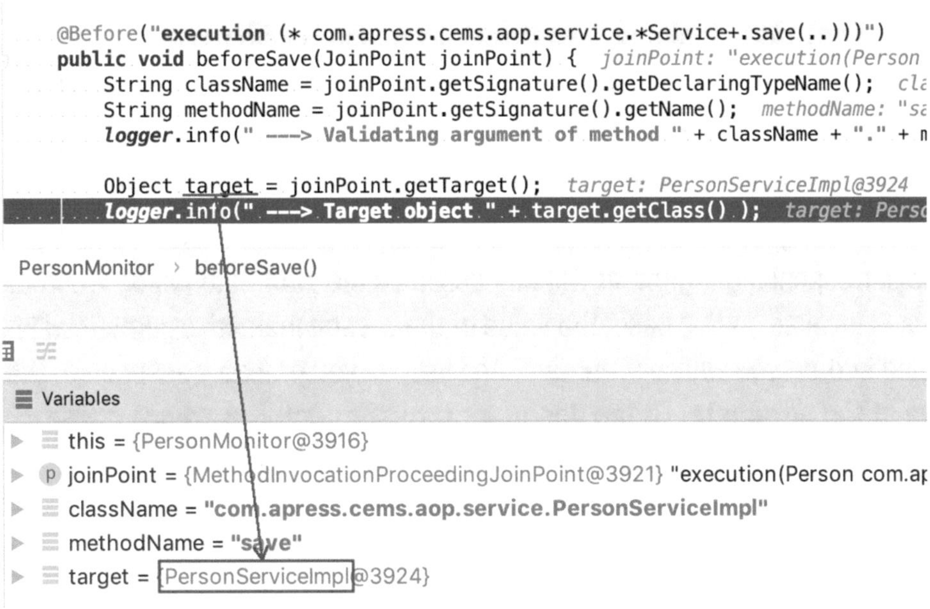

```
@Before("execution (* com.apress.cems.aop.service.*Service+.save(..)))")
public void beforeSave(JoinPoint joinPoint) {   joinPoint: "execution(Person
    String className = joinPoint.getSignature().getDeclaringTypeName();   cla
    String methodName = joinPoint.getSignature().getName();   methodName: "sa
    logger.info(" ---> Validating argument of method " + className + "." + n

    Object target = joinPoint.getTarget();   target: PersonServiceImpl@3924
    logger.info(" ---> Target object " + target.getClass() );   target: Pers

PersonMonitor  ›  beforeSave()
```

Variables
- ▶ ☰ this = {PersonMonitor@3916}
- ▶ ⓟ joinPoint = {MethodInvocationProceedingJoinPoint@3921} "execution(Person com.ap
- ▶ ☰ className = "com.apress.cems.aop.service.PersonServiceImpl"
- ▶ ☰ methodName = "save"
- ▶ ☰ target = {PersonServiceImpl@3924}

Figure 4-8. *The advice target object*

Instead of calling JointPoint methods we'll modify the implementation and use Spring to automatically populate the information we need. The pointcut expression becomes

```
package com.apress.cems.aop;
...

public class PointcutContainer {
...
    @Pointcut("execution (* com.apress.cems.aop.service.*Service+.save(..))
        && args(person) && target(service)")
    public void beforeSavePointcut(Person person, PersonService service){}
}
```

> **!**   The `args()` designator is used to identify methods with a parameter configuration defined by it. It can be used as `args(com.apress.cems.dao.Person)`, when it identifies methods with one parameter of type `Person`. But this designator can make method arguments available in the advice body.
>
> In the preceding code snippet, it is used in its binding form to ensure that the value of the corresponding argument will be passed as the parameter value when the advice is invoked. In this case, the value of the *person* method argument will be injected into *person* advice argument. And yes, as you probably suspected, **the name of the parameter in the designator must match the advice parameter name.**

The advice can now be modified to declare exactly which fields we need to populate, and to use them directly. There is no need to use a `JoinPoint` object to extract them and take care of the conversions in the advice body, because Spring has already done that for us.

```
package com.apress.cems.aop;
...
 import org.apache.commons.lang3.StringUtils;
 ...

@Aspect
@Component
public class PersonMonitor {
    private static final Logger logger =
        LoggerFactory.getLogger(PersonMonitor.class);

    @Before("com.apress.cems.aop.PointcutContainer.
        beforeSavePointcut(person,service)")
    public void beforeSave(Person person, PersonService service) {
        logger.info(" ---> Target object " + service.getClass());

        if (StringUtils.indexOfAny(person.getFirstName(), SPECIAL_CHARS)
        != -1 ||
                StringUtils.indexOfAny(person.getLastName(), SPECIAL_CHARS)
                != -1) {
```

```
        throw new IllegalArgumentException("Text contains weird
        characters!");
      }
   }
}
```

And now that we know how to define pointcuts, it is time to come back and dig deeper into advice types and definitions.

Implementing Advice

In the **Quick Start** section, some technical details about how aspects and advice are implemented in Spring were covered, but the surface was only scratched. The pointcut specifics had to be covered first to make advice declaration easier to understand. This section covers every type of advice that you will most likely need during development of Spring applications.

Before

The Before advice was used in the previous section in the book to test an argument of type Person.

```
import  org.aspectj.lang.annotation.Before;
...

@Before("com.apress.cems.aop.PointcutContainer.
        beforeSavePointcut(person,service)")
public void beforeSave(Person person, PersonService service) {
        logger.info(" ---> Target object " + service.getClass());

        if (StringUtils.indexOfAny(person.getFirstName(), SPECIAL_CHARS)
        != -1 ||
                StringUtils.indexOfAny(person.getLastName(), SPECIAL_CHARS)
                != -1) {
            throw new IllegalArgumentException("Text contains weird
            characters!");
    }
}
```

The UML sequence that describes what happens when `personService.save(..)` is executed is depicted in Figure 4-9.

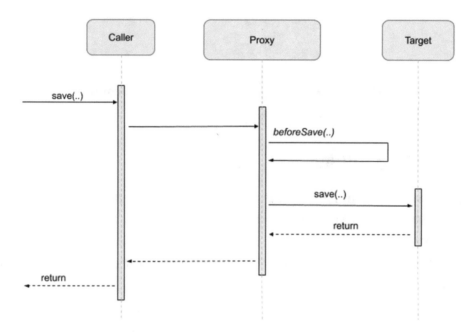

***Figure 4-9.** Before advice UML call diagram*

The proxy object receives the call destined for the target bean and calls first the advice method. If the advice method returns successfully, it then forwards the initial call to the target bean and forwards the result back to the caller. If the advice method throws an exception, the exception is propagated to the caller, and the target method is no longer executed. A test method handling the case in which the advice method throws an exception, should expect an exception of `IllegalArgumentException` type to be thrown. The code is depicted next.

```
package com.apress.cems.aop;
 ...

@ExtendWith(SpringExtension.class)
@ContextConfiguration(classes = {AopConfig.class, TestDbConfig.class})
public class TestPersonMonitor {
```

```
@Test
public void testBadSave() {
    Person person = new Person();
    person.setId(3L);
    person.setUsername("nancy.drew");
    person.setFirstName("Nanc#");
    person.setLastName("&rew");
    person.setPassword("1@#$asta");
    person.setHiringDate(LocalDate.now());
    assertThrows(IllegalArgumentException.class,
        () -> personService.save(person));
    }
}
```

The Before advice is most often used to perform checks and to stop the execution of the target method by throwing an exception when those checks are not passed. Thus, it can validate and correct arguments passed to the target method. The most likely candidate for this is the security concern. In an application that requires users to provide credentials before using it, security rights and roles must be checked every time a method handling sensitive information is called. Including the security check in every method body would be a pain. So an advice that tests the provided credentials is definitely a more practical solution. The Spring Security Framework, which is covered in Chapter 6, makes handling security even easier by providing out of the box security aspects.

After Returning

This type of advice is executed only if the target method executed successfully, and does not end by throwing an exception. An aspect of this type is defined in the following code snippet, for the same save methods in the target bean. This advice will print a message confirming that the save process executed correctly. @AfterReturning has an attribute named returning, which can access the result of the target method execution. The value of this attribute must match the name of the parameter name in the advice method signature because Spring will inject there the result of the execution of the target method.

```
package com.apress.cems.aop;

import  org.aspectj.lang.annotation.AfterReturning;
  ...

@AfterReturning(value="execution (* com.apress.cems.aop.service.*Service+.
save(..))",
     returning = "result")
public void afterServiceSave(JoinPoint joinPoint, Person result) {
       logger.info(" ---> Target object {}",
            joinPoint.getTarget().getClass());
       logger.info(" ---> Was person saved? {}", (result != null));
   }
}
```

The UML sequence diagram that describes what happens when personService.
save(..) is executed is depicted in Figure 4-10.

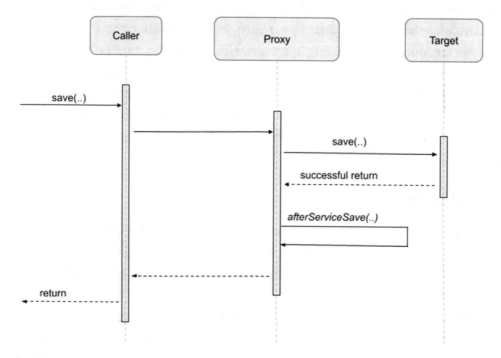

Figure 4-10. *After Returning advice UML sequence diagram*

Because the after returning advice has access to the value returned by the target method, this advice is suitable for use when caching is implemented.

After Throwing

The After Throwing advice is similar to the after returning. The only difference is that its criterion of execution is exactly the opposite. That is, this advice is executed only when the target method ends by throwing an exception. The @AfterThrowing annotation has an attribute named throwing that can access the exception thrown by the target method. The value of this attribute must match the name of the exception parameter of the advice method.

```
package com.apress.cems.aop;
//custom exception type for this example
import com.ps.exception.UnexpectedException;
...
import  org.aspectj.lang.annotation.AfterThrowing;
...
@AfterThrowing(value="execution(public *
    com.apress.cems.repos.*.PersonRepo+.update(..))", throwing = "e")
public void afterBadUpdate(JoinPoint joinPoint, Exception e) {
        String className = joinPoint.getSignature().getDeclaringTypeName();
        String methodName = joinPoint.getSignature().getName();
        if(e instanceof IllegalArgumentException) {
            logger.info("{afterBadUpdate}---> Update method {}.{}
                failed because of bad data.", className, methodName);
        } else {
            throw new UnexpectedException(" Ooops!", e);
        }
    }
}
```

This type of advice does not stop the propagation of the exception, but it can change the type of exception being thrown.

For this example, it is an advice that is executed only after the personRepo.update() is executed. This repository method is executed by the service method and throws a IllegalArgumentException if the new firstName or lastName values contain special characters. This type of exception is expected to be thrown so the advice prints a notification, and the original exception propagates. But if a different type of exception is thrown, then the advice wraps up the original exception into an UnexpectedException to tell the original caller that something wrong has happened that needs to be handled.

This test must pass, and the expected line must be printed in the console.

```
package com.apress.cems.aop;

...

@Test
    void testBadUpdate() {
        personRepo.findById(1L).ifPresentOrElse(
                p -> assertThrows(IllegalArgumentException.class,
                        () -> personService.updateFirstName(p, "Sh$r1oc#")),
                () -> fail("Person not found!")
        );
    }
```

This test must pass, and you can see the expected line printed with a very smart stacktrace in the console.

```
INFO  c.a.c.a.PersonMonitor -  ---> Update method
    com.apress.cems.repos.impl.JdbcPersonRepo.update failed because of bad
    data.
```

The UML sequence diagram that describes what happens when personService.updateFirstname(..) is called is depicted in Figure 4-11. This type of advice can restore the system state after an unexpected failure.

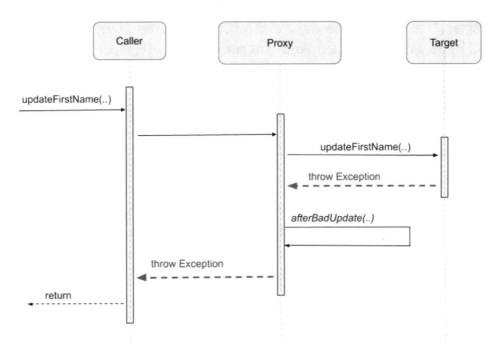

Figure 4-11. *After Throwing advice UML sequence diagram*

After

After advice is executed after the target method regardless of how its execution ended, whether successfully or with an exception and because of this it is suitable to use for auditing or logging.

```
package com.apress.cems.aop;
import  org.aspectj.lang.annotation.After;
 ...
@Aspect
@Component
public class PersonMonitor {

    private static final Logger logger = Logger.getLogger(UserRepoMonitor.
    class);
    private static long findByIdCount = 0;
```

```
@After("com.apress.cems.aop.PointcutContainer.repoFind()
    || com.apress.cems.aop.PointcutContainer.serviceFind()")
public void afterFind(JoinPoint joinPoint) {
    ++findByIdCount;
    String methodName = joinPoint.getSignature().getName();
    logger.info("[afterFind]: ---> Method {}  was called {}  times",
        methodName, findByIdCount);
}
}
```

The UML sequence diagram that describes what happens when any findBy*(..)
method is called is depicted in Figure 4-12.

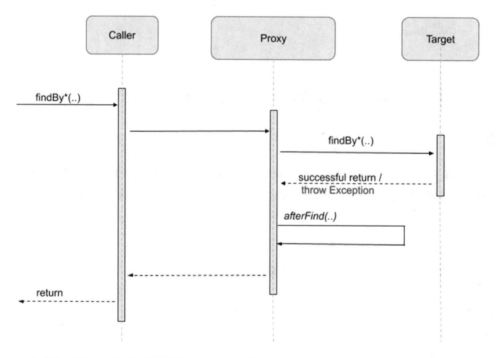

Figure 4-12. *After advice UML sequence diagram*

> **!**   Until now every advice in the default implementation (without using designators
> for binding parameters like `args` or `target`) has as a parameter a reference of
> type `org.aspectj.lang.JoinPoint`. The object that Spring injects at runtime,
> provides access to both the state available at a join point and static information
> about it: type of the target, name of the method target, arguments, reference to the
> target itself. This information can be used for tracing and logging, it does not give
> direct control over the execution of the target method.
>
> The type allowing this is `org.aspectj.lang.ProceedingJoinPoint`
> interface, which is an extension of the `org.aspectj.lang.JoinPoint` interface
> that can be used as a type for the join point parameter only in Around advice.

Around

Around advice is the most powerful type of advice because it encapsulates the target
method and has control over its execution, meaning that the advice decides whether the
target method is called, and if so, when and if the result is to be returned, and **it is the
only one with the power to do this.**[7] For this section, an advice that logs in the duration
of each find operation was created.

```
package com.apress.cems.aop;
 import  org.aspectj.lang.annotation.Around;
 ...
@Around("com.apress.cems.aop.PointcutContainer.repoFind()
    || com.apress.cems.aop.PointcutContainer.serviceFind()")
    public Object aroundFind(ProceedingJoinPoint joinPoint) throws
    Throwable {
        String methodName = joinPoint.getSignature().getName();
        logger.info("[aroundFind]: ---> Intercepting call of {}",
        methodName);
        long t1 = System.currentTimeMillis();
```

---

[7]My technical reviewer considered important to add this affirmation in bold to avoid any doubt
about how powerful the *around* advice is. Yes, he does like this type of advice very much. :)

```
    try {
        //put a pause here so we can register an execution time
        Thread.sleep(1000L);
        Object obj = joinPoint.proceed();
        return obj != null ? obj : Optional.empty();
    } finally {
        long t2 = System.currentTimeMillis();
        logger.info("[aroundFind]: ---> Execution of {} took {} ",
            methodName, (t2 - t1) / 1000 + " ms.");
    }
}
```

The Object type is mandatory as a returned type for this type of advice.

The type ProceedingJoinPoint inherits from JoinPoint and adds the proceed() method that calls the target method. And because in this case the advice method calls the target method directly, exceptions can be caught and treated in the advice method, instead of propagating them. Controlling the exception propagation is part of controlling the execution flow that was mentioned at the beginning of this section. In the previous example, a small artifice was added to prevent the method from returning a null value. This is possible starting with Java 8, when the java.util.Optional class was introduced, and Java developers everywhere rejoiced because NullPointerExceptions could be avoided easily. The UML sequence diagram that describes what happens when any userService.findBy*(..) is called is depicted in Figure 4-13.

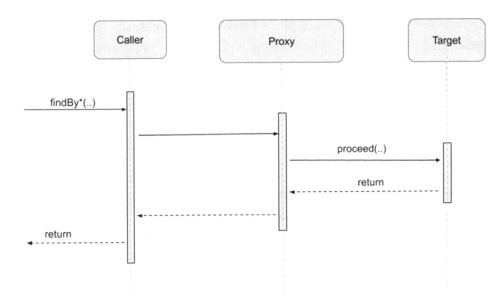

Figure 4-13. *Around advice UML sequence diagram*

Conclusions

Spring AOP and AspectJ provide a very practical way to separate cross-cutting concerns in targeted components. Without AOP, other Spring modules and frameworks would have been much more difficult to develop and to use. Spring transactions, a module that will be covered in the next chapter makes use of Spring AOP to transparently manage transactions. Spring Security, which will be covered in Chapter 6 makes use of AOP to control access to sensitive data.

Spring AOP does have its limitations, and they are listed below.

- Only public Join Points can be advised (you probably suspected that).

- Aspects can be applied only to Spring Beans.

- Even if Spring AOP is not set to use CGLIB proxies, if a Join Point is in a class that does not implement an interface Spring AOP will try to create a CGLIB proxy

- If a method in the proxy calls another method in the proxy, and both match the pointcut expression of an advice, the advice will be executed only for the first method. This is the proxy's nature; it executes the extra behavior only when the caller calls the target method.

Let's consider the following example. We'll create an implementation for StorageService to add a method named saveEvidenceSet() that is supposed to save some records that are linked to the record being saved. The actual body of the method is not important for this scenario.

```
package com.apress.cems.aop.service;
...

@Service
public class StorageServiceImpl implements StorageService {
    private static final Logger logger =
        LoggerFactory.getLogger(StorageServiceImpl.class);
    private StorageRepo storageRepo;

...

    @Override
    public void save(Storage storage) {
        storageRepo.save(storage);
        saveEvidenceSet(storage);
    }

    @Override
    public void saveEvidenceSet(Storage storage){
        //mock method to test the proxy nature
        storage.getEvidenceSet().forEach(ev -> {
            logger.info(" --->
                Pretending to save evidence with number {}" ,
                ev.getNumber());
        });
    }
}
```

Let's consider the following pointcut expression and advice declaration.

```
package com.apress.cems.aop;

// PointcutContainer.java
public class PointcutContainer {
  ...
```

```
    @Pointcut("execution(* com.apress.cems.aop.service.*Service+.
    save*(..))")
    public void proxyBubu(){}
}

// StorageMonitor.java
@Aspect
@Component
public class StorageMonitor {
...

    @Before("com.apress.cems.aop.PointcutContainer.proxyBubu()")
    public void bubuHappens(JoinPoint joinPoint) throws Throwable {
        String methodName = joinPoint.getSignature().getName();
        String className = joinPoint.getSignature().getDeclaringTypeName();
        logger.info("[bubuHappens] ---> BUBU when calling: {}.{}",
            className, methodName);
    }
}
```

To test the previous example, let's use a simple method.

```
package com.apress.cems.aop;
 ...
@ExtendWith(SpringExtension.class)
@ContextConfiguration(classes = {AopConfig.class, TestDbConfig.class})
public class TestStorageMonitor {

    @Autowired
    StorageService storageService;

    @Test
    void testProxyBubu() {
        Storage storage = new Storage();
        storage.setId(1L);
        storage.setName("Edinburgh PD Storage");
        storage.setLocation("EH4 3SD");
```

```
        Evidence ev1 = new Evidence();
        ev1.setNumber("BLOO254");
        ev1.setItemName("Glock 19");
        storage.addEvidence(ev1);

        Evidence ev2 = new Evidence();
        ev2.setNumber("BLOO257");
        ev1.setItemName("Bloody bullet 9mm");
        storage.addEvidence(ev2);

        storageService.save(storage);

        Storage result = storageService.findById(1L);
        assertNotNull(result);
    }
}
```

If the previous test method is executed, the following can be seen in the console.

```
INFO  c.a.c.a.StorageMonitor - [bubuHappens] ---> BUBU when calling:
    com.apress.cems.aop.service.StorageServiceImpl.save
```

The advice method does its thing, and then the target method is called. The target method executes, and it calls the saveEvidenceSet method on the target object. The proxy is not involved in this call in any way, which is why it cannot apply any advice. The UML sequence diagram in Figure 4-14 should make things even clearer.

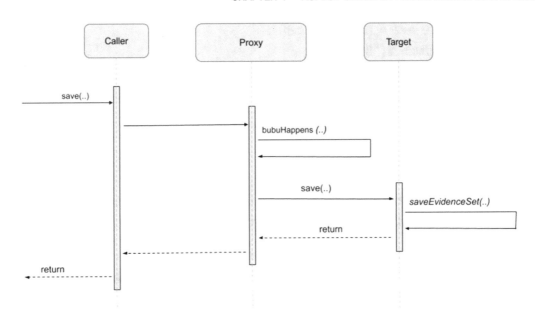

Figure 4-14. *The proxy nature explained via UML sequence diagram*

But how do we know that the saveEvidenceSet matches the joinpoint expression? We create a method in the service bean that calls this method and we write a test for it as well.

```
package com.apress.cems.aop;
...

@ExtendWith(SpringExtension.class)
@ContextConfiguration(classes = {AopConfig.class, TestDbConfig.class})
class TestStorageMonitor {
...
    @Test
    void testSaveEvidenceSet(){
        Storage storage = new Storage();
        storage.setId(1L);
        storage.setName("Edinburgh PD Storage");
        storage.setLocation("EH4 3SD");

        Evidence ev1 = new Evidence();
        ev1.setNumber("BL00254");
        ev1.setItemName("Glock 19");
        storage.addEvidence(ev1);
```

```
        Evidence ev2 = new Evidence();
        ev2.setNumber("BLO0257");
        ev1.setItemName("Bloody bullet 9mm");
        storage.addEvidence(ev2);

        storageService.saveEvidenceSet(storage);
    }
}
```

If the test testSaveEvidenceSet method is executed, we can see the line printed by the advice method and the two log lines that prove that the method was indeed called.

```
INFO  c.a.c.a.StorageMonitor - [bubuHappens] ---> BUBU when calling:
    com.apress.cems.aop.service.StorageServiceImpl.saveEvidenceSet
INFO  c.a.c.a.s.StorageServiceImpl -  --->
    Pretending to save evidence with number BLO0254
INFO  c.a.c.a.s.StorageServiceImpl -  --->
    Pretending to save evidence with number BLO0257
```

Now we can be sure that both methods are matching the pointcut expression, but when the save method calls the saveEvidenceSet directly, the proxy is not involved.

The code snippets used to explain this specific scenario are part of the chapter04/ aop project.

Using Aspects in a Spring Boot Application

Using aspects in a Spring Boot Application is quite simple. To enable aspect discovery the spring-boot-starter-aop must be added a dependency. The aspectjweaver library is a transitive dependency of this boot starter library, so no additional configurations are needed. With the AOP specific configuration, you can immediately start writing your classes and aspects, just like it was done in this chapter.

I know it is hard to believe, but there's nothing more to it. There is nothing more that can be said in this section.

Summary

After reading this chapter, you should possess enough knowledge to write and configure aspects with Spring AOP. Keep in mind the following.

- Cross-cutting concerns cause code scattering and tangling.

- AOP is a programming type that can help reduce code scattering and tangling by modularizing cross-cutting concerns.

- The most common cross-cutting concerns: logging, security, transactions, caching, and so forth.

- AOP concepts: aspect, advice, join point, pointcut, AOP proxy, and so forth.

- The way that aspect support is configured in a Spring application

- The number of advice types

Quick Quiz

Question 1. What does AOP stand for? (Choose one.)

    A. Asynchronous-oriented programming

    B. Aspect object paradigm

    C. Aspect-oriented programming

    D. Abstraction-oriented programming

Question 2. Which options in the following list represents a cross-cutting concern? (Choose all that apply.)

    A. connecting to the database

    B. caching

    C. security

    D. transactions

Question 3. Which annotation declares an advice method? (Choose all that apply.)

A. `@Aspect`

B. `@Before`

C. `@Pointcut`

D. `@AfterReturning`

E. `@Component`

Question 4. What is true about the *After* advice method? (Choose one.)

A. It is not executed if the target method execution ends by throwing an exception.

B. It is executed after the advised method regardless of the outcome.

C. It can catch the target method exception and throw a different exception.

Question 5. Which of the following is true about Spring AOP proxies? (Choose one.)

A. A proxy object implements the interface that the target implements, or is a subclass of the target's type.

B. A proxy object has scope prototype.

C. Spring AOP uses subclass-based proxies by default.

Practical Exercise

In the source code for this book there is a project called `chapter04/aop-practice`. This project can test your understanding of Spring AOP. This project contains part of the implementation depicted in the code snippets. The parts missing are marked with a TODO task and are visible in IntelliJ IDEA in the TODO view. There are six tasks for you to solve to test your acquired knowledge of Spring AOP.

Task TODO 19 requires you to enable aspect support by modifying the `AppConfig` class. If you want to use JDK proxies or CGLIB, it is up to you. The CGLIB dependency is on the classpath and can be used.

Task TODO 20 requires you to declare the `PersonMonitor` as an aspect

Tasks 21–25 require that you configure the methods declared inside the PersonMonitortest class as a different type of advice. Some pointcut expressions are your responsibility as well.

The test methods that can verify your solution are declared in the TestPersonMonitor class. Each test method is commented with the type of advice it tests. Since some of the pointcut expressions might match more than one method, all advices that apply will be executed. To stop that from happening, when working on configuring an advice, comment the annotations on the others.

To run a test case, click anywhere on the class content or on the class name in the project view, and select the Run '{TestClassName'} option. If you want to run a single test, right-click, and select the Run '{TestMethodName}' option from the menu. These instructions were explained to you in the practice section of Chapter 3. You might need to review it.

After you have resolved all the TODOs, you should be able to run the full test suite and you should see something similar to what is depicted in Figure 4-15.

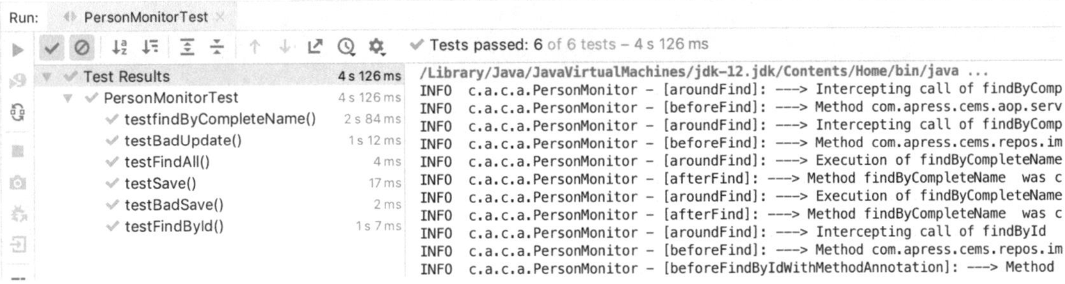

Figure 4-15. *Test suite for the Aspects section with all tests passing*

If you have difficulties solving the TODOs, you can take a peek at chapter04/aop.

!   If you are still hungry for more information, there are two blog entries on the Spring official blog. One is about proxies (see https://spring.io/blog/2012/05/23/transactions-caching-and-aop-understanding-proxy-usage-in-spring) and one is about named pointcuts (see https://spring.io/blog/2007/03/29/aop-context-binding-with-named-pointcuts).

CHAPTER 5

Data Access

Software applications usually handle sets of data that must be stored in an organized manner so they can be easily accessed, managed, and updated. The fact that data can be persisted means that it is available even when the application is down. So storage is decoupled from the rest of the application. The most common way of organizing data for storage is a database. Any storage setup that allows data to be organized in such a way that it can be queried and updated represents a database. The most widely known and used databases nowadays are relational databases (such as MySQL, PostgreSQL, and Oracle) and non-relational databases, also known as NoSQL. XML files can be used as a database as well, but only for small applications, because using XML files for data storage implies that all data must be loaded into memory to be managed.

From an architectural point of view, software applications are multilayered or multitiered, and the database is the base layer, where data is stored. The interface between the base layer (also called the *infrastructure layer*) and the rest of the application is the *data access layer*, also known as the *repository layer*. On top of this, there is the business or *service layer*. This layer transforms user data and prepares it for storage, or transforms database content into data proper for display in the user interface.

On top of the service layer is the *presentation (or interface) layer*, which is responsible for receiving commands and data, and forwarding them for processing to the service layer or to display results. Across all layers are the cross-cutting concerns, as depicted in Figure 5-1.

© Iuliana Cosmina 2020
I. Cosmina, *Pivotal Certified Professional Core Spring 5 Developer Exam*,
https://doi.org/10.1007/978-1-4842-5136-2_5

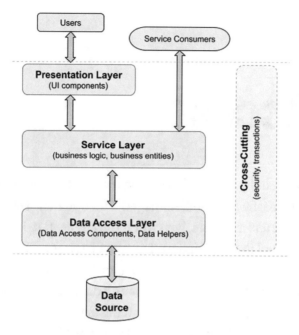

Figure 5-1. *Typical software application architecture*

The database is a central resource in a software application, and thus it can be a source of bottlenecks. That is why accessing a database to perform typical operations like searching for data, creating data, and deleting data need to be managed properly. Spring supports many database implementations, and it can be integrated with most frameworks that provide efficient data access management (Hibernate, EclipseLink, or MyBatis.[1]) This chapter focuses on how Spring manages database access. The code samples cover service, data layers, and transaction-cutting concerns.

Basic Data Access Using JDBC

To perform data operations, a connection to the database is needed. The most basic way to get a connection in Java is to use JDBC. But the basic way is also cumbersome, since the developer has to write the code to open and close the connection and any other stream-based objects used during the processing. Because a connection is not enough, asking for data and receiving it requires additional objects to be created. Any objects

---

[1]MyBatis was previously known as iBatis, before Apache dropped it. More information on the new official site: http://blog.mybatis.org/

that are built on top of a connection, such as a prepared statement and a result set of objects, must be safely discarded; otherwise, the JDBC resources may not be released, and memory leaks and other issues might occur. This leads to ugly cluttered code that is difficult to maintain, difficult to test, and difficult to write. To access a database using JDBC, the following is needed.

- a database driver used to communicate with the database
- a URL connection that is the entry point for the communication
- database credentials (usually user and password)

Using the previous information, a `javax.sql.DataSource` object is created. This is a Java interface that must be implemented by every data source class used to access a database, and each database driver library contains its own implementation.

As an example, the class used to provide access to an oracle database is `oracle.jdbc.pool.OracleDataSource`. To interact with the database using JDBC, the following steps must be implemented.

1. The data source is used to a connection to the database. The connection object is of a type specific to the database that implements `java.sql.Connection`.

2. To extract or save data to the database, a statement instance of type implementing `java.sql.PreparedStatement` is created based on the connection.

3. After the statement has been executed, the results are stored in an object of type implementing `java.sql.ResultSet`.

4. After the communication has ended, the `ResultSet` object must be successfully discarded, and its JDBC resources must be released, so its `close()` method must be called. This is usually done automatically when an application shuts down gracefully, but in case an exception is thrown, a `finally` block must be added where the method is explicitly called.

This goes for the `PreparedStatement` and `Connection` objects as well.

In Chapter 4, the following code sample was provided to depict the code necessary to open and close a database connection with JDBC, code that is replicated every time access to the database is needed.

```
package com.apress.cems.aop.classic;
...
import javax.sql.DataSource;
import java.sql.PreparedStatement;
import java.sql.PreparedStatement;
import java.sql.ResultSet;
import java.sql.SQLException;

public class NativePersonRepo implements PersonRepo {

    @Override
    public Set<Person> findAll() {
        Set<Person> persons;
        String sql = "select p.ID as ID, p.USERNAME as USERNAME," +
                " p.FIRSTNAME as FIRSTNAME, p.LASTNAME as LASTNAME" +
                " from PERSON p ";
        Connection conn = null;
        PreparedStatement ps = null;
        ResultSet rs = null;
        try {
            conn = dataSource.getConnection();
             ps = conn.prepareStatement(sql);
            rs = ps.executeQuery();
            persons = mapPersons(rs);     \\ (*)
        } catch (SQLException e) {
            throw new RuntimeException("Person not found!", e);
        } finally {
            if (rs != null) {
                try {
                    rs.close();
                } catch (SQLException ex) {
                }
            }
            if (ps != null) {
                try {
                    ps.close();
                } catch (SQLException ex) {
```

```
                }
            }
            if (conn != null) {
                try {
                    conn.close();
                } catch (SQLException ex) {
                }
            }
        }
        return persons;
    }
    ...
}
```

The preceding code opens a connection, extracts the data, transforms it into a Set<Person> instance, and then closes the connection.

In an application, each individual SQL statement is treated as a transaction and is automatically committed right after it is executed. Another complication here is that domain objects (entities) that are Java objects corresponding to database records conversion must also be implemented, because JDBC does not know how to do this on its own. In the preceding example, notice the line marked with (*). This is done by the mapPersons, which is depicted in the following code snippet.

```
private Set<Person> mapPersons(ResultSet rs) throws SQLException {
        Set<Person> persons = new HashSet<>();
        Person person;
        while (rs.next()) {
            person = new Person();
            // set internal entity identifier (primary key)
            person.setId(rs.getLong("ID"));
            person.setPersonname(rs.getString("USERNAME"));
            person.setFirstName(rs.getString("FIRSTNAME"));
            person.setLastName(rs.getString("LASTNAME"));
            persons.add(person);
        }
        return persons;
}
```

Basically, the `ResultSet` object is converted to one or more `Person` objects depending on the number of results returned by the statement execution. And as food for thought, imagine how problematic the handling of `Timestamp` and `Date` values becomes with the preceding method.

What happens if a query is not executed correctly? A `java.sql.SQLException` is thrown. The developer has to write the appropriate code to treat it because it is a checked exception. The traditional JDBC usage is redundant, prone to error, poor in exception handling, and cumbersome to use. So, the Spring team decided to provide an alternative.

Spring Data Access

With Spring, there is no need to write basic traditional JDBC code. The Spring framework provides components that were created to remove the necessity of "manually" handling database connections. It doesn't mean that code like the one written to release resources is no longer needed, it's just that developers do not have to write it. It's already written inside the classes that the Spring Framework provides.[2] When writing enterprise applications (using Spring or not), classes called *repositories* (or data access objects) communicate with the database. They are part of the data access layer. In Figure 5-2, you can see the different types of repository classes that can be used and the persistence framework used as a bridge to the database.

---

[2]Take a look at the code of the *JdbcTemplate* class: `https://github.com/spring-projects/spring-framework/blob/master/spring-jdbc/src/main/java/org/springframework/jdbc/core/JdbcTemplate.java`

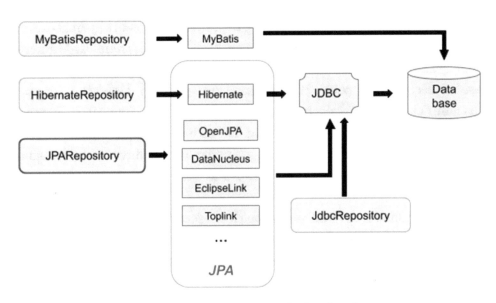

Figure 5-2. *How repository classes interact with the database*

Data storage is a resource. Access to resources has to be managed properly to avoid bottlenecks and memory leaks. In software, the term *bottleneck* refers to a situation in which multiple processes require access to a resource, and if the access to the resource is not managed properly, some processes end up never having access to the resource. A memory leak represents a phenomenon of an object occupying memory after is no longer needed and no longer accessible, having not been released properly. Using pure JDBC access to the resource, the database is handled by the developer explicitly. Spring comes in with persistence frameworks to unburden the developer of this responsibility. So, let's begin with the most basic way of accessing data using Spring: using a JDBC repository class.

Introducing JdbcTemplate

The Spring Framework's JDBC abstraction framework consists of four main packages: core, datasource, object, and support.[3] There is also a small config package containing infrastructure beans and utility classes used in the configuration of embedded databases. Spring simplifies the code that needs to be written in using JDBC

---

[3]More information on the official Spring Reference page: https://docs.spring.io/spring/docs/current/spring-framework-reference/data-access.html#jdbc-packages.

to interact with a database by introducing the `org.springframework.jdbc.core.` `JdbcTemplate` class, which is part of the `core` package. This class hides large amounts of JDBC boilerplate code and unburdens the developer of connection management, since database connections are acquired and released automatically. The `datasource` package contains utility classes for `DataSource` management and a few simple `DataSource` implementations that can be used for testing. The `object` package contains classes that represent RDBMS queries, updates, and stored procedures as thread-safe, reusable objects. The `support` package provides `SQLException` translation functionality and some utility classes.

Exception handling is covered, providing clear exceptions of root causes , using unchecked exceptions so that developers are not forced to write extra boilerplate code to treat them, and making sure that resources are released properly—even in failures. The `JdbcTemplate` class is designed according to the *template method pattern*, which is a behavioral design pattern that defines the skeleton of an algorithm, the effective implementation is defined later or delegated to subclasses.[4]

The simplest example to demonstrate how the `JdbcTemplate` can be used is covered in this section. For this, we need the following.

- **a configuration file containing SQL DDL[5] scripts** for initializing the database structure: *schema.sql* containing SQL code for creating tables

- **a configuration file containing SQL DML[6] test-data.sql** containing insert statements that populate the tables with some initial data. The content of the files is not relevant for this chapter, but they are part of the `chapter05/jdbc` project.

- **a configuration class for the test database**; let's call it `TestDbConfig`. This configuration class contains only two beans: a data source bean named `dataSource` and bean named `jdbcTemplate` of type `org.springframework.jdbc.core.JdbcTemplate`. An in-memory database called H2 is created using the Spring `EmbeddedDatabaseBuilder` class. The `dataSource` bean is of type

---

[4]Other Spring classes to access a different type of resource follow the same pattern: *JmsTemplate*, *RestTemplate*, and so forth.

[5]Data Definition Language

[6]Data Manipulation Language

EmbeddedDatabase, which is a Spring-specific subinterface of `javax.sql.DataSource` that is meant to be used in Spring test environments. This interface exposes a method named `generateUniqueName(..)`. When called with argument `true`, the generated database has a different name in every context where the bean is used. This is quite useful because it avoids collision between tests running in parallel in different application contexts.

Spring supports other two types of in-memory databases: HSQLDB and Derby. To use an external, production specific RDBMS is not that complicated. All is needed is to add a means of providing the connection details (e.g., a properties file) and a new specific data source bean. But more about that later in the chapter. The next code listing depicts the contents of the `TestDbConfig` class.

```
 package com.apress.cems.jdbc;

import org.springframework.context.annotation.Bean;
import org.springframework.context.annotation.Configuration;
import org.springframework.jdbc.core.JdbcTemplate;
import org.springframework.jdbc.datasource.embedded.
EmbeddedDatabase;
import org.springframework.jdbc.datasource.embedded.
EmbeddedDatabaseBuilder;
import org.springframework.jdbc.datasource.embedded.
EmbeddedDatabaseType;

import javax.sql.DataSource;

@Configuration
public class TestDbConfig {

    @Bean
    public JdbcTemplate jdbcTemplate() {
        return new JdbcTemplate(dataSource());
    }
```

```
@Bean
public DataSource dataSource() {
    EmbeddedDatabaseBuilder builder = new
    EmbeddedDatabaseBuilder();
    EmbeddedDatabase db = builder
            .setType(EmbeddedDatabaseType.H2)
            .generateUniqueName(true)
            .addScript("db/schema.sql")
            .addScript("db/test-data.sql")
            .build();
    return db;
}
}
```

! It might not be obvious, but the order of the scrips is important when calling
addScript(..) on a EmbeddedDatabaseBuilder instance. Internally, the
script files are kept in an java.util.ArrayList, and they will be executed by
traversing that list from the first element to the last. So, it's very important to first
call addScript(..) and provide the DDL script as the argument that creates the
database. Then call addScript(..) and provide the DML script as the argument
that populates the database.

The configuration class probably looks familiar to you, since it was
already introduced in Chapter 3.

In the previous edition of the book the test configuration class was
implemented differently. H2 was still used, but the data source
bean was declared to be of type org.springframework.jdbc.
datasource.SimpleDriverDataSource and connection properties
were read from a file (even if an in-memory database was used).
Since connection properties are read from a file, this means
the database name is fixed this time to the value of the db.url
property.

This example is more similar to how a production database would be declared. To create the database schema and populate the tabled a bean of type `org.springframework.jdbc.datasource.init.DatabasePopulator` was used. The previously mentioned types are available in Spring 5, but this approach results in a more complex configuration. The `connection.properties` contents and the configuration class are depicted in the next code listing.

```
#connection.properties
db.driverClassName=org.h2.Driver
db.url=jdbc:h2:sample
db.username=sample
db.password=sample

//TestDbConfig2 configuration class
package com.apress.cems.jdbc;

import org.springframework.beans.factory.annotation.Value;
import org.springframework.context.annotation.Bean;
import org.springframework.context.annotation.Configuration;
import org.springframework.context.annotation.Profile;
import org.springframework.context.annotation.PropertySource;
import org.springframework.context.support.
PropertySourcesPlaceholderConfigurer;
import org.springframework.jdbc.datasource.SimpleDriverDataSource;
...
@Configuration
@PropertySource("classpath:db/connection.properties")
public class TestDbConfig2 {

 @Value("${db.driverClassName}")
    private String driverClassName;
    @Value("${db.url}")
    private String url;
    @Value("${db.username}")
    private String username;
    @Value("${db.password}")
    private String password;
```

```
@Bean
public static PropertySourcesPlaceholderConfigurer
                    propertySourcesPlaceholderConfigurer() {
    return new PropertySourcesPlaceholderConfigurer();
}
@Bean
public DataSource dataSource() {
    try {
        var dataSource = new SimpleDriverDataSource();
        Class<? extends Driver> driver =
                (Class<? extends Driver>) Class.
                forName(driverClassName);
        dataSource.setDriverClass(driver);
        dataSource.setUrl(url);
        dataSource.setUsername(username);
        dataSource.setPassword(password);
        DatabasePopulatorUtils.execute(databasePopulator(),
        dataSource);
        return dataSource;
    } catch (Exception e) {
        return null;
    }
}

@Value("classpath:db/schema.sql")
private Resource schemaScript;

@Value("classpath:db/test-data.sql")
private Resource dataScript;

private DatabasePopulator databasePopulator() {
    final ResourceDatabasePopulator populator =
            new ResourceDatabasePopulator();
    populator.addScript(schemaScript);
    populator.addScript(dataScript);
    return populator;
}
```

```
    @Bean
    public JdbcTemplate jdbcTemplate() {
        return new JdbcTemplate(dataSource());
    }

    @Bean(destroyMethod = "destroy")
    public CleanUp cleanUp() {
        return new CleanUp(jdbcTemplate());
    }

}
// necessary to gracefully shutdown the database
class CleanUp {

    private JdbcTemplate jdbcTemplate;
    CleanUp(JdbcTemplate jdbcTemplate) {
        this.jdbcTemplate = jdbcTemplate;
    }

    private void destroy() {
        jdbcTemplate.execute("DROP ALL OBJECTS DELETE FILES;");
    }
}
```

! The CleanUp class makes sure that any files that were created for your database on your hard drive will be deleted when the application context is shut down. While working with H2 I had the surprise of noticing files were not deleted and subsequent run of tests using the H2 database were failing because the database could not be initialized correctly.

Even now if I look in my home directory, I see a lot of files with the *.mv.db extension. Those are all databases files created when Spring runs H2 embedded.

```
iulianacosmina@Iulianas-MacBook-Pro ~ - $ ls -la | grep db
-rw-r--r--    1 iulianacosmina   staff    20480 30 Jul 14:54 cems.mv.db
-rw-r--r--    1 iulianacosmina   staff    87662 20 Jul 19:53 cems.trace.db
-rw-r-----    1 iulianacosmina   staff    16384 29 Jul 15:46 cems01.mv.db
-rw-r--r--    1 iulianacosmina   staff    16384 30 Jul 14:54 cems_dj.mv.db
```

```
-rw-r-----    1 iulianacosmina   staff    32768 19 Jul 10:05 hamsters.mv.db
-rw-r--r--    1 iulianacosmina   staff   430993  7 Jun 21:39 hamsters.trace.db
-rw-r--r--    1 iulianacosmina   staff    20480 30 Jul 14:53 jupiter.mv.db
-rw-r--r--    1 iulianacosmina   staff    88734 19 Jul 15:58 jupiter.trace.db
-rw-r--r--    1 iulianacosmina   staff    40960  9 Jul 12:18 test.mv.db
```

To overcome issues caused by the database being there when using Spring's
EmbeddedDatabase, all my DDL scripts begin with

```
drop table xxx if exists;.
```

!   An equivalent configuration can be set up using XML and the JDBC namespace.
For an embedded in-memory database with no concern for credentials or
connection URL, the `<jdbc:embedded-database .../>` configuration can be
used.

```
<?xml version="1.0" encoding="UTF-8"?>
<beans xmlns="http://www.springframework.org/schema/beans"
       xmlns:xsi="http://www.w3.org/2001/XMLSchema-instance"
       xmlns:jdbc="http://www.springframework.org/schema/jdbc"
       xmlns:util="http://www.springframework.org/schema/util"
       xsi:schemaLocation="http://www.springframework.org/schema/beans
          http://www.springframework.org/schema/beans/spring-beans.xsd
            http://www.springframework.org/schema/jdbc
            http://www.springframework.org/schema/jdbc/spring-jdbc.xsd">

    <!-- Creates an in-memory "sample" database
        populated with test data for fast testing -->
    <jdbc:embedded-database id="dataSource">
        <jdbc:script location="classpath:db/schema.sql"/>
        <jdbc:script location="classpath:db/test-data.sql"/>
    </jdbc:embedded-database>
</beans>
```

A more complex configuration that allows credentials to be read from an external
configuration file can be set up using the `<jdbc:initialize-database`
`.../>` element and a `SimpleDriverDataSource` bean.

```xml
<?xml version="1.0" encoding="UTF-8"?>
<beans ...>

    <util:properties id="dbProp" location="classpath:db/db.properties"/>

    <bean id="dataSource"
          class="org.springframework.jdbc.datasource.
          SimpleDriverDataSource">
        <property name="driverClass" value="#{dbProp.driverClassName}"/>
        <property name="url" value="#{dbProp.url}"/>
        <property name="username" value="#{dbProp.username}"/>
        <property name="password" value="#{dbProp.password}"/>
    </bean>

    <jdbc:initialize-database data-source="dataSource">
        <jdbc:script location="classpath:db/schema.sql"/>
        <jdbc:script location="classpath:db/test-data.sql"/>
    </jdbc:initialize-database>
</beans>
```

- **an application configuration class** declaring the repository bean to be tested; let's call it JdbcConfig and define it like this:

```java
@Configuration
@ComponentScan(basePackages = {"com.apress.cems.repos.impl"})
public class JdbcConfig {
}
```

- **a repository bean** of JdbcPersonRepo type that uses a bean of type JdbcTemplate to access the database. The code is depicted in the following code listing.

```java
package com.apress.cems.repos.impl;

import com.apress.cems.dao.Person;
import com.apress.cems.repos.PersonRepo;
import com.apress.cems.repos.util.PersonRowMapper;
import org.springframework.jdbc.core.JdbcTemplate;
```

```java
import org.springframework.jdbc.core.RowMapper;
import org.springframework.stereotype.Repository;

import java.util.HashSet;
import java.util.Optional;
import java.util.Set;

@Repository
public class JdbcPersonRepo extends
    JdbcAbstractRepo<Person> implements PersonRepo {
    private RowMapper<Person> rowMapper = new PersonRowMapper();

    public JdbcPersonRepo(JdbcTemplate jdbcTemplate) {
        super(jdbcTemplate);
    }

    @Override
    public Optional<Person> findById(Long id) {
        var sql = "select ID, USERNAME, FIRSTNAME, LASTNAME,
        PASSWORD,
                HIRINGDATE from PERSON where ID= ?";
        return Optional.of(jdbcTemplate.queryForObject(sql,
        rowMapper, id));
    }

    @Override
    public Set<Person> findAll() {
        var sql = "select ID, USERNAME, FIRSTNAME, LASTNAME,
        PASSWORD,
            HIRINGDATE from PERSON";
        return new HashSet<>(jdbcTemplate.query(sql, rowMapper));
    }

    ... // other repository methods
    /**
     * Maps a row returned from a query executed
     * on the PERSON table to a com.apress.cems.dao.Person object.
     */
```

```java
private class PersonRowMapper implements RowMapper<Person> {
    @Override
    public Person mapRow(ResultSet rs, int rowNum) throws
    SQLException {
        var id = rs.getLong("ID");
        var username = rs.getString("USERNAME");
        var firstname = rs.getString("FIRSTNAME");
        var lastname = rs.getString("LASTNAME");
        var password = rs.getString("PASSWORD");
        var hiringDate = rs.getString("HIRINGDATE");

        var person = new Person();
        person.setId(id);
        person.setUsername(username);
        person.setFirstName(firstname);
        person.setLastName(lastname);
        person.setPassword(password);
        person.setHiringDate(toDate(hiringDate));
        return person;
    }
}
}
```

The JdbcAbstractRepo abstract class and the PersonRepo interface were introduced in previous chapters. To keep chapters on point, they won't be depicted in this chapter as well. Also, you can find them on the repository for this book.

In a software application, data is managed as objects that are called *entities* or *domain objects*. The entity classes are written by the developer, and their fields match the columns in a database table. The PersonRowMapper internal class depicted in the previous code snippet does just that. It is covered in more detail later in this section.

- **a test class**: TestJdbcPersonRepo

```
package com.apress.cems.jdbc;

...

import java.util.Set;

@SpringJUnitConfig(classes = {TestDbConfig.class, JdbcConfig.class})
class JdbcPersonRepoTest {

    static final Long PERSON_ID = 1L;

    @Autowired
    PersonRepo personRepo;

    @BeforeEach
    void setUp(){
        assertNotNull(personRepo);
    }

    @Test
    void testFindByIdPositive(){
        personRepo.findById(PERSON_ID).ifPresentOrElse(
                p -> assertEquals("Sherlock", p.getFirstName()),
                Assertions:: fail
        );
    }

    @Test
    void testFindByIdNegative(){
        assertThrows(EmptyResultDataAccessException.class,
            () -> personRepo.findById(99L));
    }

    @Test
    void testFindAll(){
        Set<Person> personSet = personRepo.findAll();
        assertNotNull(personSet);
        assertEquals(2, personSet.size());
    }
}
```

This test class is a simple one that searches for a user object by its ID. The `testFindById` method passes, because there is a `Person` instance with ID=1 found in the database.

The `testFindByIdNegative` test is a negative test, that checks that a record with ID=99 cannot be found. Notice the `org.springframework.dao.EmptyResultDataAccessException` type. The ID is unique in a database, and searching by it should always return a single result. This is a typical Spring data access exception that is thrown when this doesn't really happen.

The central class of Spring JDBC is `org.springframework.jdbc.core.JdbcTemplate` type. It is a Spring specialized class that uses data source implementation to create and release resources, supports statement creation and execution, calling stored procedures and catches JDBC exceptions and translates them to unchecked, precise exceptions declared in the `org.springframework.dao` package. As its name hints, this class was written respecting the template method design pattern in mind. This class exposes a set of methods that can be called on whatever implementation of `DataSource` an object of type `JdbcTemplate` is based on.[7]

Thus, to create a `JdbcTemplate` bean, a bean of `DataSource` type is needed to access database records. Every repository bean will have this bean declared as a dependence, and it will use it to manipulate data when `JdbcTemplate` bean methods are called, as in the following code snippet.

```
String sql = "select ID, USERNAME, FIRSTNAME, LASTNAME, PASSWORD,
    HIRINGDATE from PERSON where ID= ?";
return Optional.of(jdbcTemplate.queryForObject(sql, rowMapper, id));
```

The next sequence of steps is taken by Spring in the background.

1. A database connection is acquired.

2. A transaction is acquired or created so the statement can be executed in its context if in a transactional environment. In the previous case, there is no transaction support, defined declarative using `@Transactional` or programmatic. Both are introduced later in the chapter.

3. The statement is executed.

---

[7]If you want to learn more about the template method behavioral design pattern, here's a useful link: `https://www.oodesign.com/template-method-pattern.html`

4. The ResultSet is processed and transformed into entity object(s) using RowMapper instances.

5. Exceptions are handled.

6. The database connection is released.

What we are interested in when running methods of this test class is what happens in the background, which is because there is no code needed to be developed for connection management. Spring takes care of this, but it would be nice to have proof, right? To see this happen, the logback-test.xml file can be customized to show the Spring JDBC detailed log by adding the following line.

```
<logger name="org.springframework" level="debug"/>
```

Before we look at the log produced when the test class is run, the location of the files must be covered, as shown in Figure 5-3.

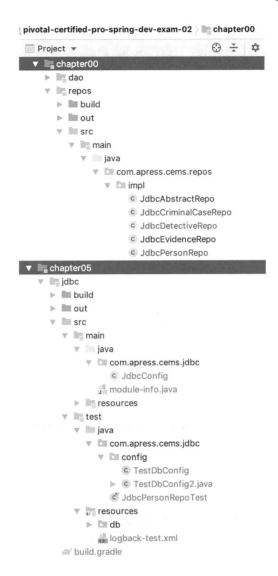

Figure 5-3. *Location of the files in the **chapter05/jdbc** and **chapter00/repos** project*

As you can see, the repository classes are part of the chapter00/repos project. The project is built and added as a dependency to the chapter05/jdbc project. This is useful because the code is kept well organized, in a single place, can be used as a dependency for other projects and code is not duplicated which makes it easier to use and gives you the opportunity to experiment with module configurations.[8]

---

[8]Fortunately, a working module configuration is provided which you can inspect and learn from.

The project has the typical Java project structure consecrated by Maven, and the *sql, *xml, *.properties are resource files, so they are stored in the project in the resources directory from the test or main module. By running the JdbcTemplatePersonRepoTest.testFindByIdPositive() method with the logging setup mentioned previously, if you scan the log, you will find the following lines.

```
#booting up environment
... creating beans ...
DEBUG o.s.j.d.DataSourceUtils - Fetching JDBC Connection from DataSource
DEBUG o.s.j.d.SimpleDriverDataSource - Creating new JDBC Driver Connection
                to [jdbc:h2:~/sample]
DEBUG o.s.j.d.i.ScriptUtils - Executing SQL script from class path
                resource [db/schema.sql]
... listing SQL scripts ...
INFO  o.s.j.d.i.ScriptUtils - Executed SQL script from class path
                resource [db/schema.sql] in 23 ms.
INFO  o.s.j.d.i.ScriptUtils - Executing SQL script from class path
                resource [db/test-data.sql]
... listing SQL scripts ...
INFO  o.s.j.d.i.ScriptUtils - Executed SQL script from class path
                resource [db/test-data.sql] in 5 ms.
DEBUG o.s.j.d.DataSourceUtils - Returning JDBC Connection to DataSource

#executing the test
DEBUG o.s.j.c.JdbcTemplate - Executing prepared SQL query
DEBUG o.s.j.c.JdbcTemplate - Executing prepared SQL statement
                [select id, email, username,password from person where
id= ?]
DEBUG o.s.j.d.DataSourceUtils - Fetching JDBC Connection from DataSource
DEBUG o.s.j.d.SimpleDriverDataSource - Creating new JDBC Driver Connection
                to [jdbc:h2:~/sample]
DEBUG o.s.j.d.DataSourceUtils - Returning JDBC Connection to DataSource
...
```

Basically, every time a JdbcTemplate method is called, a connection is automatically opened for query execution, and then the same connection is released and all the magic is done by the Spring utility class org.springframework.jdbc.datasource. DataSourceUtils. This class is abstract and it is used internally by JdbcTemplate and by transaction manager classes that will be covered in the following sections.

Spring's JdbcTemplate is suitable for small applications designed for academic use. Use it whenever you need to get rid of traditional JDBC. The term *transaction* was mentioned a few times and before moving forward, it needs proper explaining. In software development, a *transaction* is a group of actions that should be performed as if they were a single bulk action. The JDBC default behavior is to treat each individual SQL statement as a transaction. So composing multiple JDBC operations in a single bulk action to execute within a single transaction is not possible. In an enterprise application, transactions will most likely be needed, so more Spring components must be added to the mix. Working with transactions will be covered shortly, but before that, let's see what happens when an unexpected event takes place during communication with a database using a JdbcTemplate bean.

Querying with JdbcTemplate

The JdbcTemplate provides the developer a multitude of methods to query for entities (also called domain objects), generic maps, and lists and simple types (long, int, String). JdbcTemplate methods use queries containing the '?' placeholder for parameters and variables that are bound to it. It takes advantage of varargs and autoboxing to simplify JdbcTemplate. But simple queries, without any bind variables, can be used too. The following example uses a query to count all the persons in the PERSON table and returns the long value.

```
public long count() {
        var sql = "select count(*) from PERSON";
        return jdbcTemplate.queryForObject(sql, Long.class);
}
```

The method queryForObject used here does not need a RowMapper object, since the result is a number of type long. The type of the result is provided as argument to the method as well. This method has replaced in Spring version 3.2.2, specialized methods like queryForInt and queryForLong. Examples of how these methods were used until 3.2.2 (when they became deprecated) can be seen in the following code snippet.

```java
public int count() {
    var sql = "select count(*) from PERSON";
    return jdbcTemplate.queryForInt(sql);
}

public Long findIdByUsername(String username) {
        var sql = "select ID from PERSON where USERNAME = ?";
        return jdbcTemplate.queryForLong(sql, username);
}
```

Sometimes there might be a need to extract a record form a table in a different format from an entity. JdbcTemplate provides a method called queryForMap that extracts a row from the ResultSet as a Map<String,Object>.

```java
public Map<String, Object> findByIdAsMap(Long id) {
        var sql = "select * from PERSON where ID= ?";
        return jdbcTemplate.queryForMap(sql, id);
}
```

The map returned by this method contains pairs of columns [name, column value]. Look at the following example.

```
{
    ID=1,
    USERNAME=sherlock.holmes,
    FIRSTNAME=Sherlock,
    LASTNAME=Holmes,
    PASSWORD=123ss12sh,
    HIRINGDATE=1983-08-18,
    VERSION=1,
    CREATED_AT=1983-08-18,
    MODIFIED_AT=1999-03-18
}
```

The queryForList does the same as the previous methods but for ResultSet instances that contain multiple rows. This method returns a List of Map<String, Object> objects, each map containing a row from the ResultSet.

```
public List<Map<String, Object>> findAllAsMaps() {
        var sql = "select * from PERSON";
        return jdbcTemplate.queryForList(sql);
}
```

The following is sample output.

```
[
    {
            ID=1,
            USERNAME=sherlock.holmes,
            FIRSTNAME=Sherlock,
            LASTNAME=Holmes,
            PASSWORD=123ss12sh,
            HIRINGDATE=1983-08-18,
            VERSION=1,
            CREATED_AT=1983-08-18,
            MODIFIED_AT=1999-03-18
    },
    {
            ID=2,
            USERNAME=irene.adler,
            FIRSTNAME=Irene,
            LASTNAME=Adler,
            PASSWORD=id123ds,
            HIRINGDATE=1990-08-18,
            VERSION=1,
            CREATED_AT=1990-07-18,
            MODIFIED_AT=1998-01-18
    }
]
```

These two methods can be used for testing and auditing.

The first example using JdbcTemplate returns an entity object (also called domain object). To transform a table record into a domain object, Spring provides the org. springframework.jdbc.core.RowMapper<T> interface. This should be implemented for every entity type in an application, because an object of the implementing type is required as a parameter for JdbcTemplate methods that return entities. RowMapper objects are usually stateless, so creating one per repository class and using it as a converter from table records to Java objects is a good practice.

Spring converts contents of a ResultSet into domain objects using a callback approach. The JdbcTemplate instance first executes the query and populates the ResultSet; then the mapRow method of the RowMapper instance used as argument is called. In case the ResultSet contains more than one table row, the method is called for each row.

```java
package com.apress.cems.repos.impl;

import org.springframework.jdbc.core.RowMapper;
...

@Repository
public class JdbcPersonRepo extends
    JdbcAbstractRepo<Person> implements PersonRepo {
    private RowMapper<Person> rowMapper = new PersonRowMapper();

    @Override
    public Set<Person> findAll() {
        var sql = "select ID, USERNAME, FIRSTNAME, LASTNAME, PASSWORD,
            HIRINGDATE from PERSON";
        return new HashSet<>(jdbcTemplate.query(sql, rowMapper));
    }
    ...

    class PersonRowMapper implements RowMapper<Person> {
        @Override
        public Person  mapRow(ResultSet rs, int rowNum) throws SQLException
{
            var id = rs.getLong("ID");
            var username = rs.getString("USERNAME");
            var firstname = rs.getString("FIRSTNAME");
            var lastname = rs.getString("LASTNAME");
            var password = rs.getString("PASSWORD");
            var hiringDate = rs.getString("HIRINGDATE");
```

```
            Person person = new Person();
            person.setId(id);
            person.setUsername(username);
            person.setFirstName(firstname);
            person.setLastName(lastname);
            person.setPassword(password);
            person.setHiringDate(toDate(hiringDate));
            return person;
        }
    }
}
```

The interface is generic. The type of domain object that the repository manages should be used as a parameter. This interface is also a functional interface, so creating the PersonRowMapper is not necessary. Using a lambda expression, the rowMapper field can be initialized directly with the following.

```
protected RowMapper<Person> rowMapper = (rs, rowNum) -> {
        var id = rs.getLong("ID");
        var username = rs.getString("USERNAME");
        var firstname = rs.getString("FIRSTNAME");
        var lastname = rs.getString("LASTNAME");
        var password = rs.getString("PASSWORD");
        var hiringDate = rs.getString("HIRINGDATE");

        var person = new Person();
        person.setId(id);
        person.setUsername(username);
        person.setFirstName(firstname);
        person.setLastName(lastname);
        person.setPassword(password);
        person.setHiringDate(toDate(hiringDate));
        return person;
    };
```

This is possible when the implementation is needed only by the repository class that it is declared in; but when more than one repository manages the same type of domain object, rowMapper is implemented as a top-level class. However, the code to transform a ResultSet into a domain object, or a collection of them, has to be written by the developer. This too will no longer be necessary when ORM (object relational mapping) is used. But more about that later.

So far, only JdbcTemplate methods that return some kind of result have been covered. An example for an execution that does not return a result is appropriate right about now. The most important method in the JdbcTemplate class that executes queries but returns no result is named query. This method is polymorphic,[9] and the method signature differs depending on the purpose of the query result. One of the forms of this method receives as an argument an implementation of org.springframework.jdbc. core.RowCallbackHandler. This is a functional interface declaring a single method that should be implemented to process ResultSet instances returned by the execution of the SQL query provided as argument to the jdbcTemplate.query(..) method. The RowCallbackHandler implementation is called a callback in the software, because its purpose is to be executed at a given time.

The RowCallbackHandler interface, can implemented to stream the rows returned by the query to a file to convert them to XML, or to filter them before adding them to a collection. An instance of this type is provided to the query method along with query parameters if necessary, and the JdbcTemplate will use it accordingly. In the following code snippet, the code of this interface is depicted.[10]

```
package org.springframework.jdbc.core;

import java.sql.ResultSet;
import java.sql.SQLException;

@FunctionalInterface
public interface RowCallbackHandler {
        void processRow(ResultSet rs) throws SQLException;
}
```

---

[9]*Polymorphism* is one of the object-oriented programming principles. The term is of Greek etymology and means one name, many forms. Polymorphism manifests itself in software by having multiple methods all with the same name but slightly different functionalities.

[10]Also publicly available on GitHub: https://github.com/spring-projects/spring-framework/blob/master/spring-jdbc/src/main/java/org/springframework/jdbc/core/RowCallbackHandler.java

The implementation of the method is used by the JdbcTemplate to process the ResultSet row as implemented by the developer. The exceptions are caught and treated by the JdbcTemplate instance. In the following code snippet, the HTMLPersonRowCallbackHandler is used by the JdbcTemplate instance to extract all persons with a username equal to *sherlock.holmes* from the person table, write the resulting rows in HTML, and then print them to the console.

```java
package com.apress.cems.jdbc.repos;
...
import org.springframework.jdbc.core.RowCallbackHandler;

@Repository
public class ExtraJdbcPersonRepo  extends JdbcPersonRepo {

  private class HTMLPersonRowCallbackHandler
                  implements RowCallbackHandler {
        private PrintStream out;

        public HTMLPersonRowCallbackHandler(PrintStream out) {
            this.out = out;
        }

        @Override
        public void processRow(ResultSet rs)
                        throws SQLException {
            out.print("<p>person ID: ".concat(rs.getLong("ID") + "")
                .concat("</p></br>\n")
                .concat("<p>username: ").concat(rs.getString("USERNAME"))
                .concat("</p></br>\n")
                .concat("<p>firstname: ").concat(rs.getString("FIRSTNAME"))
                .concat("</p></br>\n")
                .concat("<p>lastname: ").concat(rs.getString("LASTNAME"))
                .concat("</p></br>"));
        }
    }
```

```
    public void htmlAllByName(String name) {
        String sql = "select * from PERSON where USERNAME= ?";
        jdbcTemplate.query(sql, new HTMLPersonRowCallbackHandler(System.out),
        name );
    }
    ...
}
```

The ExtraJdbcPersonRepo extends the JdbcPersonRepo class and overrides a few default interface methods declared in the PersonRepo interface.

```
package com.apress.cems.repos;

import com.apress.cems.dao.Person;
import java.util.*;

public interface PersonRepo extends AbstractRepo<Person> {
    Optional<Person> findByUsername(String username);

    Optional<Person> findByCompleteName(String firstName, String lastName);

    Set<Person> findAll();

    long count();

    default Map<String, Object> findByIdAsMap(Long id) {
        return new HashMap<>();
    }

    default List<Map<String, Object>> findAllAsMaps() {
        return new ArrayList<>();
    }

    default void htmlAllByName(String name) {}
}
```

This choice was made to avoid polluting the PersonRepo interface and to prevent the need to provide an implementation for these methods in other projects. And because default interface methods were introduced in Java 8, and I wanted the opportunity to use them within this book. 😊

When `personRepo.htmlAllByName("sherlock.holmes")` is called, among all the Spring logs, at the end you should also see the following in the console.

```
<p>person ID: 1</p></br>
<p>username: sherlock.holmes</p></br>
<p>firstname: Sherlock</p></br>
<p>lastname: Holmes</p></br>
```

If the `ResultSet` contains more than one row, the `JdbcTemplate` instance will process each of them using the `HTMLPersonRowCallbackHandler.processRow` method.

Spring also provides the option of processing a full `ResultSet` at once and transforming it into an object, via the `org.springframework.jdbc.core.ResultSetExtractor<T>` functional interface.[11] This feature is very useful when the results are extracted from more than one tables, but must be treated in the application as a single object. The developer is responsible of iterating the `ResultSet` and setting the properties of the object with other objects mapped to entries in the database. This interface is parametrizable by type.

```java
package org.springframework.jdbc.core;

import java.sql.ResultSet;
import java.sql.SQLException;
import org.springframework.dao.DataAccessException;
import org.springframework.lang.Nullable;

@FunctionalInterface
public interface ResultSetExtractor<T> {
    @Nullable
    T extractData(ResultSet rs) throws SQLException, DataAccessException;
}
```

The following code snippet depicts the usage of `DetectiveExtractor` to extract a detective by id from the `DETECTIVE` table with the person details from the `PERSON` table and create an object of type `DETECTIVE` that contains the `person` field populated with the details extracted from the database.

---

[11]Also publicly available on GitHub: `https://github.com/spring-projects/spring-framework/blob/master/spring-jdbc/src/main/java/org/springframework/jdbc/core/ResultSetExtractor.java`

```java
package com.apress.cems.jdbc.repos;
...
import org.springframework.jdbc.core.ResultSetExtractor;

@Repository
public class ExtraJdbcDetectiveRepo extends JdbcDetectiveRepo {

    public ExtraJdbcDetectiveRepo(JdbcTemplate jdbcTemplate) {
        super(jdbcTemplate);
    }

    @Override
    public Optional<Detective> findByIdWithPersonDetails(Long id) {
        String sql = "select d.ID id," +
                " p.ID pid, " +
                " p.USERNAME un," +
                " p.FIRSTNAME fn, " +
                " p.LASTNAME ln, " +
                " p.HIRINGDATE hd," +
                " d.BADGE_NUMBER bno," +
                " d.RANK rank," +
                " d.ARMED armed," +
                " d.STATUS status" +
                " from DETECTIVE d, PERSON p" +
                 "where d.PERSON_ID=p.ID and d.ID=" + id;
        return Optional.of(jdbcTemplate.query(sql, new DetectiveExtractor()));
    }

    private class DetectiveExtractor implements
    ResultSetExtractor<Detective> {
        @Override
        public Detective extractData(ResultSet rs) throws SQLException {
            Detective detective = null;
            while (rs.next()) {
                if (detective == null) {
                    detective = new Detective();
```

```
                    // set internal entity identifier (primary key)
                    detective.setId(rs.getLong("id"));
                    detective.setBadgeNumber(rs.getString("bno"));
                    detective.setRank(Rank.valueOf(rs.getString("rank")));
                    detective.setArmed(rs.getBoolean("armed"));
                    detective.setStatus(
                            EmploymentStatus.valueOf(rs.getString("status")));
                }
                Person p = new Person();
                p.setId(rs.getLong("pid"));
                p.setUsername(rs.getString("un"));
                p.setFirstName(rs.getString("fn"));
                p.setLastName(rs.getString("ln"));
                p.setHiringDate(rs.getDate("hd").toLocalDate());
                detective.setPerson(p);
            }
            return detective;
        }
    }
}
//Test class covering the findByIdWithPersonDetails
package com.apress.cems.jdbc;

@SpringJUnitConfig(classes = {TestDbConfig.class, JdbcConfig.class})
class JdbcDetectiveRepoTest {
    private Logger logger = LoggerFactory.getLogger(JdbcDetectiveRepoTest.
    class);

    static final Long DETECTIVE_ID = 1L;

    @Autowired
    DetectiveRepo detectiveRepo;

    @Test
    void testFindByIdWithDetails(){
        Optional<Detective> detective = detectiveRepo
            .findByIdWithPersonDetails(DETECTIVE_ID);
```

```
        detective.ifPresentOrElse(
                d -> assertNotNull(d.getPerson()),
                Assert::fail
        );
        logger.info("Result: {}", detective);
    }
}
```

This is pretty much all you need to know about JdbcTemplate, so you can use it properly in your code. To summarize,

- JdbcTemplate works with queries that specify parameters using the '?' placeholder.

- use queryForObject when it is expected that execution of the query will return a single result.

- use RowMapper<T> when each row of the ResultSet maps to a domain object.

- use RowCallbackHandler when no value should be returned.

- use ResultSetExtractor<T> when multiple rows, or multiple records from different tables returned in a ResultSet map to a single object.

Querying with NamedParameterJdbcTemplate

Besides the JdbcTemplate class, Spring provides another template class for executing queries with named parameters: org.springframework.jdbc.core.namedparam. NamedParameterJdbcTemplate. This class provides methods analogous to JdbcTemplate that require as a parameter a map containing a pair of named parameters and their values.[12] Once the named parameters have been replaced with the values, the call is delegated behind the scenes to a JdbcTemplate instance. The relationship between the two classes and the interfaces they implement is depicted in Figure 5-4.

---

[12]This approach of providing parameters is used by JPA and Hibernate as well.

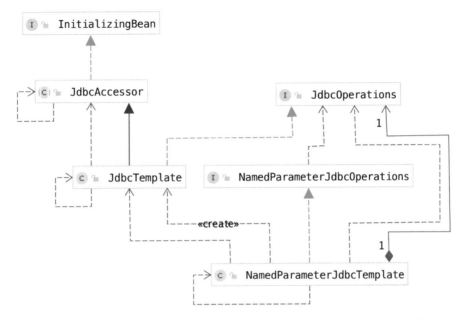

Figure 5-4. *Relationship between JdbcTemplate and NamedParameterJdbcTemplate*

If you look at the code of the NamedParameterJdbcTemplate,[13] you will see the following.

```
package org.springframework.jdbc.core.namedparam;
...

public class NamedParameterJdbcTemplate
    implements NamedParameterJdbcOperations {
    ...
    /** The JdbcTemplate we are wrapping */
    private final JdbcOperations classicJdbcTemplate;
    ...
    /**
```

---

[13]Code accessible on GitHub: https://github.com/spring-projects/spring-framework/blob/master/spring-jdbc/src/main/java/org/springframework/jdbc/core/namedparam/NamedParameterJdbcTemplate.java, or in IntelliJ IDEA, click the class name and press the Control (Command in macOS) key, and the sources will be opened for you.

```
     * Expose the classic Spring JdbcTemplate operations to allow
       invocation of
     * less commonly used methods.
    */
    @Override
     public JdbcOperations getJdbcOperations() {
      return this.classicJdbcTemplate;
     }

     /**
      * Expose the classic Spring {@link JdbcTemplate} itself, if
        available,
      * in particular for passing it on to other {@code JdbcTemplate}
        consumers.
      * <p>If sufficient for the purposes at hand, {@link
        #getJdbcOperations()}
      * is recommended over this variant.
      * @since 5.0.3
      */
     public JdbcTemplate getJdbcTemplate() {
          Assert.state(this.classicJdbcTemplate instanceof JdbcTemplate,
              "No JdbcTemplate available");
          return (JdbcTemplate) this.classicJdbcTemplate;
     }
     ...
}
```

The JdbcTemplate is exposed to the developer via the getJdbcOperations() method or via the getJdbcTemplate() method introduced in Spring 5.0.3, which converts it to the traditional JdbcTemplate.

In the following code snippet, you can compare the findById method written with the two types of JDBC template classes.

```
//using JdbcTemplate
    public Optional<Person> findById(Long id) {
        String sql = "select ID, USERNAME, FIRSTNAME, LASTNAME, PASSWORD,
            HIRINGDATE from PERSON where ID= ?";
```

```
        return Optional.of(jdbcTemplate.queryForObject(sql, rowMapper, id));
    }

//using NamedParameterJdbcTemplate
public Person findById(Long id) {
        String sql = "select ID, USERNAME, FIRSTNAME, LASTNAME, PASSWORD,
            HIRINGDATE from PERSON where ID= :id";
        return Optional.of(jdbcNamedTemplate
            .queryForObject(sql, Map.of("id", entityId) ,rowMapper));
}
```

In writing your application, the decision of using JdbcTemplate or
NamedParameterJdbcTemplate is up to you. But consider this: named queries are
easier to read and safer, since there is little chance to assign the value to the wrong
parameter, or specifying the wrong number of parameters or arguments when
declaring your query. If that would happen an exception of org.springframework.dao.
DataIntegrityViolationException type would be thrown with a concise message. In
the following log snippet, you can see the exception thrown when declaring the wrong
number of parameters for an insert query.

```
org.springframework.dao.DataIntegrityViolationException:
PreparedStatementCallback;
SQL [insert into PERSON(ID, USERNAME,
Parameter "#9" is not set; SQL statement:
insert into PERSON(ID, USERNAME, FIRSTNAME, LASTNAME, PASSWORD, HIRINGDATE,
 CREATED_AT, MODIFIED_AT, VERSION) values(?, ?, ?, ?, ?, ?, ?, ?, ? )
[90012-198];
```

Aside from SELECT queries, JdbcTemplate can execute INSERT, UPDATE, and DELETE
operations using the update method. This method is polymorphic as well[14] and can be
called with or without parameters. It returns an integer representing the number of lines
that were affected. The following are the code snippets for each of them.

---

[14]Its many signatures and recommended uses can be inspected in the official JavaDoc available
   online http://docs.spring.io/spring/docs/current/javadoc-api/org/springframework/
   jdbc/core/JdbcTemplate.html.

- INSERT: The method createPerson inserts a new person.

```
// ExtraJdbcPersonRepo.java
public int createPerson(Long entityId, String username, String
firstName,
        String lastName, String password) {
        return jdbcTemplate.update(
                "insert into PERSON(ID, USERNAME, FIRSTNAME,
                LASTNAME, PASSWORD, HIRINGDATE, CREATED_AT,
                MODIFIED_AT, VERSION) values(?, ?, ?, ?, ?, ?, ?,
                ?, ? )",
                entityId, username,firstName,lastName,password,
                LocalDate.now(),LocalDate.now(),LocalDate.now());
}
...

public Set<Person> findAllByUsernamePart(String part) {
        String sql = "select ID, USERNAME, FIRSTNAME, LASTNAME,
        PASSWORD,
            HIRINGDATE from PERSON where USERNAME like '%' || ? ||
            '%' ";
        return new HashSet<Person>(jdbcTemplate.query(sql,
            new Object[]{part}, rowMapper));
}

// test method in JdbcPersonRepoTest.java
@Test
public void testCreate(){
    int result  = personRepo.createPerson(3L, "chloe.decker",
    "Chloe",
        "Decker", "m0rn1ngstar");
    assertEquals(1, result);
    Optional<Person> personOpt = personRepo.findByUsername("chloe.
    decker");
     personOpt.ifPresentOrElse(p -> assertNotNull(p.getId()),
            Assertions:: fail);
}
```

- UPDATE: The following method updates the password for a person, identifying it by its ID.

```
// JdbcPersonRepo.java
@Override
public int updatePassword(Long personId, String newPass) {
        String sql = "update PERSON set password=? where ID = ?";
        return jdbcTemplate.update(sql, newPass, personId);
}

// test method in JdbcPersonRepoTest.java
@Test
public void testUpdate(){
    int result  = personRepo.updatePassword(1L, "newpass");
    assertEquals(1, result);
}
```

- DELETE: The following method deletes a person identified by its ID.

```
// JdbcPersonRepo.java
public int deleteById(Long userId) {
    return jdbcTemplate.update(
        "delete from PERSON where ID =? ", userId);
}

// test method in JdbcPersonRepoTest.java
@Test
public void testDelete(){
    int result  = personRepo.deleteById(4L);
    assertEquals(1, result);
}
```

DML (Data Manipulation Language) and the database operations presented so far are part of it. The SELECT, INSERT, UPDATE, and DELETE commands are database statements to create, update, or delete data from existing tables.

DDL (Data Definition Language) are database operations that manipulate database objects, such as tables, views, cursors, and so forth. DDL database statements can be executed with JdbcTemplate using the execute method. The following code snippet depicts how to create a table using a JdbcTemplate instance. After creation, a query to count the records in the table is executed. If the table was created, the query will successfully be executed and return 0.[15]

```java
// JdbcAgnosticRepo.java
public int createTable(String name) {
    jdbcTemplate.execute("create table " + name +
            " (id integer, name varchar2)" );
    String sql = "select count(*) from " + name;
    return jdbcTemplate.queryForObject(sql, Integer.class);
}

// test method in JdbcAgnosticRepoTest.java
@Test
void testCreateTable(){
        int result  = agnosticRepo.createTable("new_storage");
        // table exists but is empty
        assertEquals(0, result);
}
```

! Honestly, I'm not sure you would need to do this, but just in case, know that it is possible, but risky. If you look at the previous code, the creation of the SQL query presents some risk for a hacking technique named SQL injection. The reason why the name of the table cannot be provided as a parameter is that SQL parameters are expected to be part of an expression. The table name clearly is not, thus replacing it with an "?" and trying to provide the table name as a parameter will cause a JdbcSQLSyntaxErrorException to be thrown at runtime.

---

[15]This kind of approach leaves an application sensitive to SQL Injection attacks, which is why in enterprise applications, the tables are never created by executing DDL scripts in the code with parameter values provided by the user.

But things do not always go as intended, and sometimes exceptions are thrown. In the next section, what can be done in such unexpected cases and the components involved in treating the situation accordingly are presented.

Spring Data Access Exceptions

When working with data sources, there might be particular cases when things do not go well: sometimes, operations are called on records that no longer exist; sometimes records cannot be created because of database restrictions; sometimes, the database takes too long to respond; and so on. In pure JDBC, the same type of checked exception is always thrown: `java.sql.SQLException`. In the message, there is an SQL code that can be used by the developer to identify the real cause and handle the situation accordingly. As a checked exception, it forces developers to catch it and handle it, or declare it as thrown over the call method call hierarchy. This introduces a form of tight coupling.

In Spring, the data access exceptions are unchecked; they extend `java.lang.RuntimeException`, which is why this class is exhibited in the previous image with a red border and can be thrown up the method call hierarchy to the point where they are most appropriate to handle. This is a more practical way for the developer to handle database access exceptions without knowing the details of the data access API. The Spring data access exceptions hide the technology used to communicate with the database and contain human-readable messages that point exactly to the cause of the problem.

A simplified version of the Spring data access exception hierarchy can be seen in Figure 5-5.

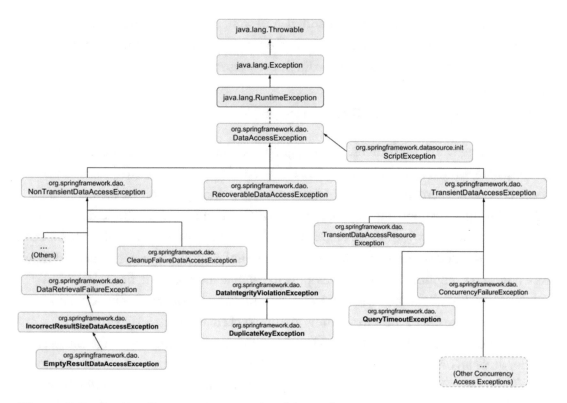

Figure 5-5. *Spring data access exception hierarchy*

The Spring Data Access exceptions are thrown when JdbcTemplate, JPA, Hibernate, and so forth, are used. That is probably why they are part of the `spring-tx` module. Under the hood, there are translator components that can transform any type of data access exceptions into Spring-specific exceptions, which is useful when migrating from one database type to another. For example, the `JdbcTemplate` instance takes care of transforming cryptic `java.sql.SQLExceptions` into clear and concise `org.springframework.dao.DataAccessException` implementations[16] using an infrastructure bean of a type that implements `org.springframework.jdbc.support.SQLExceptionTranslator`.

As you can see in Figure 5-5, the Spring data access exception family has three main branches.

---

[16]Class *org.springframework.dao.DataAccessException* is an abstract class, parent of all the family of Spring Data Access exceptions.

- Exceptions that are considered *non-transient*, which means that retrying the operation will fail unless the originating cause is fixed. The parent class of this hierarchy is the org.springframework.dao. NonTransientDataAccessException abstract class. The most obvious example here is searching for an object that does not exist. Retrying this query will fail until the searched object is found. The following code snippet searches for a person that does not exist. Afterward is a snippet from the console log that depicts the exception type and message.

```
// test method in TJdbcPersonRepoTest.java
@Test
void testFindByIdNeagtive() {
        personRepo.findById(99L).ifPresentOrElse(
                p -> assertEquals("Nancy", p.getFirstName()),
                Assertions:: fail
        );
}
```

```
#log from the console
org.springframework.dao.EmptyResultDataAccessException:
        Incorrect result size: expected 1, actual 0
```

This test will fail until a person with ID equal to 99 and username 'Nancy' is found in the PERSON table.

- org.springframework.dao.RecoverableDataAccessException (which is a concrete type) is thrown when a previously failed operation might succeed if some recovery steps are performed, usually closing the current connection and using a new one. This type of exception is very useful when the database is on a different computer from that of the application and connection to the database fails because of a temporary network hiccup. The exception can be caught and the query retried when the network is up, and the execution will succeed in a new connection.

- Exceptions that are considered *transient*, which extend the abstract class org.springframework.dao.TransientDataAccessException, which means that retrying the operation might succeed without any intervention. These are concurrency or latency exceptions. For example, when the database becomes unavailable because of a bad network connection in the middle of the execution of a query, an exception of type QueryTimeoutException is thrown. The developer can treat this exception by retrying the query.

In addition to these three main branches, there is a less important fourth branch. It contains an exception type used when initialization of a test database with a bean of type DataSourceInitializer fails because of a script error; thus the exception type is named ScriptException. This class is abstract and is the parent of four types of exceptions that can be thrown when executing an SQL script. The branch is not depicted in Figure 5-5 for lack of space. And that is all that can be said about Spring data access exceptions. Sounds pretty simple, right?

!   If you want to test your understanding of Spring JdbcTemplate and related components presented so far, you can open the chapter05/jdbc-practice project and try to complete the TODOs. There are three that you should definitely solve and one that is a bonus in case you really like this section and you enjoy the practice. The parts missing are marked with a TODO task and are visible in IntelliJ IDEA in the TODO view.

Task TODO 26, located in the JdbcPersonRepoTest class, requires you to complete the body of a negative test method that searches for a person that does not exist. The test should pass. To see the user IDs present in the database, inspect the chapter05/jdbc-practice/src/test/resources/db/test-data.sql.

Task TODO 27, located in the JdbcPersonRepoTest class, requires you to complete the body of a test method that counts the persons in the database.

Task TODO 28, located in NamedParameterJdbcPersonRepo, requires you to complete the body of repository methods. You can use either the jdbcNamedTemplate bean or the underlying JdbcTemplate accessed with jdbcNamedTemplate.getJdbcOperations().

The bonus task TODO 29, located in test class
NamedParameterJdbcPersonRepoTest, if you decide to complete it, will help
you test the methods implemented by completing TODO 28.

If you have trouble, you can take a peek at the proposed solution in the
chapter05/jdbc project.

Data Access Configuration in a Transactional Environment

Until now, data access has been covered with Spring in a non-transactional
environment, which means that when a query was executed, a connection was obtained,
the query was executed, then the connection was released. In enterprise applications,
there is a need to group certain SQL operations together so that in case one of them
fails, all the results of previous queries in the same group should be rolled back to avoid
leaving the database in an inconsistent state. The context of execution for a group of SQL
operations is called a *transaction* and has the following properties.

- **A**tomicity is the main attribute of a transaction (and the characteristic
  mentioned earlier). If an operation in a transaction fails, the entire
  transaction fails, and the database is left unchanged. When all operations
  in a transaction succeed, all changes are saved into the database when
  the transaction is committed. Basically, it is "all or nothing."

- **C**onsistency implies that every transaction should bring the database
  from one valid state to another.

- **I**solation implies that when multiple transactions are executed
  in parallel, they won't hinder one another or affect each other in
  any way. The state of the database after a group of transactions is
  executed in parallel should be the same as if the transactions in the
  group had been executed sequentially.

- **D**urability is the property of a transaction that should persist even in
  cases of no power, crashes, and other errors on the underlying system.[17]

---

[17]An exception to this rule would be if the server catches fire or gets really wet.

In a transactional environment, transactions must be managed. In Spring, this is done by an infrastructure bean called the *transaction manager*. The transaction manager bean's configuration is the only thing that has to be changed when the environment changes. There are four basic flavors.

- **JDBC Spring environment**: A local JDBC configuration declaring a basic datasource to be used (even an embedded one will do) and a bean of type `org.springframework.jdbc.datasource.DataSourceTransactionManager`, a Spring-specific implementation. The connections to use can come from a connection pool, and the transaction manager bean will associate connections to transactions according to the configured behavior. Configuring transactional behavior is done declaratively by annotating methods with `@Transactional`. Without an ORM, a component of type `JdbcTemplate` must be used to execute queries at the repository level. How `JdbcTemplate` is used is covered in the previous section. The abstract schema of this configuration is depicted in Figure 5-6.

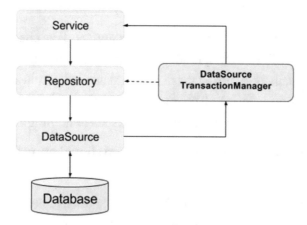

Figure 5-6. *Spring Local JDBC Configuration abstract schema*

- **Hibernate Spring environment**: A local hibernate configuration declaring a basic datasource to be used (even an embedded one will do) and a bean of type `org.springframework.orm.hibernate5.HibernateTransactionManager`, a Spring-specific implementation that uses a hibernate session object created by an

infrastructure bean of type `org.springframework.orm.hibernate5.`
`LocalSessionFactoryBean` to manage entities in a transactional
context. The abstract schema of this configuration is depicted in
Figure 5-7.

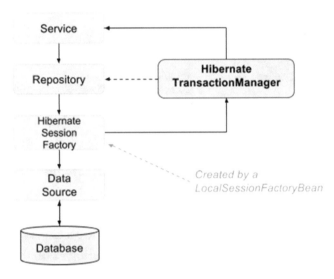

Figure 5-7. *Spring Local Hibernate Configuration abstract schema*

- **JPA Spring environment**: A local configuration declaring a basic
  datasource to be used (even an embedded one will do) and a bean
  of type `org.springframework.orm.jpa.JpaTransactionManager`, a
  Spring-specific implementation that uses an entity manager object
  created by an infrastructure bean of type `org.springframework.`
  `orm.jpa.LocalContainerEntityManagerFactoryBean` to
  manage entities in a transactional context. The abstract schema
  of this configuration is depicted in Figure 5-8. To create the
  `LocalContainerEntityManagerFactoryBean` bean, a persistence
  manager and a JPA adapter bean are needed(the JPA adapter is
  needed to initialize appropriate defaults for the given provider and
  such as persistence provider class and JpaDialect, that is used for
  opening and closing transaction and exception translating). These
  can be provided by Hibernate, Apache OpenJPA, or any other Spring-
  supported persistence framework.

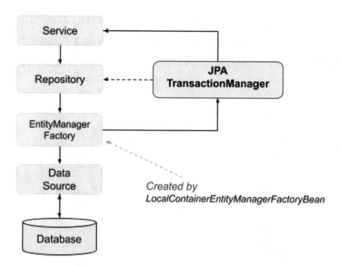

Figure 5-8. *Spring Local JPA configuration abstract schema*

- **Enterprise JTA Spring environment**: This setup requires an application server that will configure and provide a datasource bean using JNDI. JNDI works with other technologies on the Java platform, such as the Enterprise Edition (Java EE), to organize and locate components in a distributed computing environment. Spring loads a bean of type extending `org.springframework.transaction.jta.JtaTransactionManager` specific to the application server used. This transaction manager is appropriate for handling distributed transactions, which are transactions that span multiple resources, and for controlling transactions on application server resources. The abstract schema of this configuration is depicted in Figure 5-9.

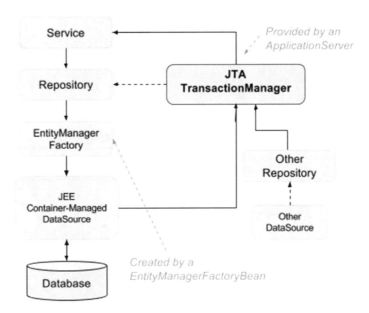

Figure 5-9. *Enterprise JTA Spring environment*

How Transaction Management Works in Spring

In the previous section, a repository class used a JdbcTemplate to execute methods within a connection. To introduce transactions, we need a service class that will call the repository methods in the context of a transaction. Figure 5-10 depicts the abstract UML sequence diagram that describes the examples covered in this section. The diagram mentions only the findById(...) method, but the call sequence for every service method that involves managing database-stored information is the same.

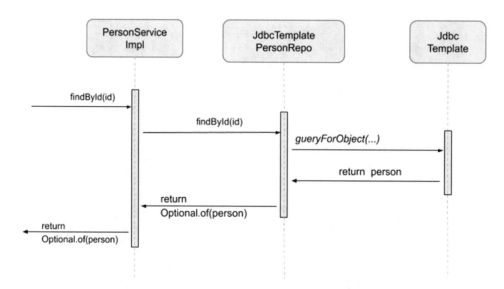

Figure 5-10. *UML call diagram for a service class*

Transaction management is implemented in Spring by making use under the hood of a framework presented in a previous chapter, **AOP**, which is because transactions are a cross-cutting concern. Basically, for every method that must be executed in a transaction, retrieving or opening a transaction before execution and committing it afterward is necessary. For beans that have methods that must be executed in a transactional context, AOP proxies are created that wrap the methods in an `Around` advice that takes care of getting a transaction before calling the method and committing the transaction afterward. The AOP proxies use two infrastructure beans for this: an `org.springframework.transaction.interceptor.TransactionInterceptor` in conjunction with an implementation of `org.springframework.transaction.PlatformTransactionManager`. Spring provides a flexible and powerful abstraction layer for transaction management support. At the core of it is the `PlatformTransactionManager` interface. Any transaction manager provider framework that is supported can be used. JTA providers can as well, which has no impact on the rest of the classes of the application. The following are the most common transaction management providers.

- `DataSourceTransactionManager`, Spring basic transaction management provider class used with JDBC and MyBatis.

- `HibernateTransactionManager`, when Hibernate is used for persistence support.

- `JpaTransactionManager`, when an entity manager is used for persistence support.

- `JtaTransactionManager`, used to delegate transaction management to a Java EE server. It can be used with Atomikos too, removing the need for an application server.[18]

- `WebLogicJtaTransactionManager`, transaction support provided by the WebLogic application server.

Figure 5-11 conceptually shows what happens when a transactional method is called.

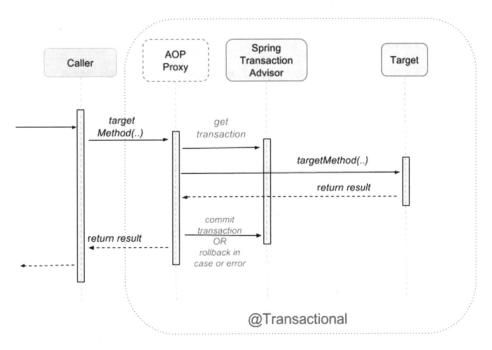

Figure 5-11. *Conceptual UML sequence diagram for a transactional operation*

Methods that need to be executed in a transactional context are annotated with @ `Transactional` Spring annotation. The body of these methods is a functional unit that cannot be subdivided. The official Spring course calls these methods `atomic units of work`. As you probably remember from the AOP chapter, this annotation must be used only on public methods; otherwise, the transactional proxy won't be able to apply the

---

[18]You can find more about Atomikos on their official site: `https://www.atomikos.com/`.

transactional behavior. When the application context is created and support for this annotation is enabled via configuration (this is covered in the following section), under the hood, an internal infrastructure Spring-specific bean of type `org.springframework.aop.framework.autoproxy.InfrastructureAdvisorAutoProxyCreator` is registered and acts as a bean postprocessor that modifies the service or repository bean (whichever is annotated with @Transactional) to add transaction-specific logic. Basically, this is the bean that creates the transactional AOP proxy.

Configure Transactions Support

The simplest way to add transaction management to the application covered in the previous section is to do the following.

- **Configure transaction management support**. Add a declaration of a bean of type `org.springframework.jdbc.datasource.DataSourceTransactionManager` in a configuration class.

```
@Configuration
public class TestTransactionalDbConfig {
...
    @Bean
    public PlatformTransactionManager txManager(){
        return new DataSourceTransactionManager(dataSource());
    }
}
```

And activate it with the @EnableTransactionManagement annotation. Add this annotation on any configuration class for the project.

```
import org.springframework.transaction.annotation.
EnableTransactionManagement;

@Configuration
@EnableTransactionManagement
@ComponentScan(basePackages = {"com.ps.repos.impl", "com.
ps.services.impl"})
public class AppConfig {
}
```

In XML configurations, the transactionManager bean is easily activated using the `<tx:annotation-driven ../>` element (provided by the tx namespace). A sample configuration is depicted in the following code snippet, but XML configuration is not really the object of this book.

```
<beans xmlns="http://www.springframework.org/schema/beans"
        xmlns:xsi="http://www.w3.org/2001/XMLSchema-instance"
        xmlns:tx="http://www.springframework.org/schema/tx"
        xsi:schemaLocation="http://www.springframework.org/schema/
        beans
            http://www.springframework.org/schema/beans/spring-
            beans.xsd
            http://www.springframework.org/schema/tx
            http://www.springframework.org/schema/tx/spring-tx-
            2.0.xsd">

    <bean id="transactionManager"
        class="org.springframework.jdbc.datasource.
        DataSourceTransactionManager">
        <property name="dataSource" ref="dataSource"/>
    </bean>

        <tx:annotation-driven transaction-manager="transactionMana
        ger"/>
</beans>
```

The preceding configuration declares a bean named transactionManager and sets it as the general transaction manager for the application using `<tx:annotation-driven ../>`.

- **Declare transactional methods**. Write a service class containing methods that will call the PersonRepo bean methods in a transaction. A method that is to be executed in a transaction must be annotated with the Spring @Transactional annotation. Because of the proxy based implementation of the transactions in Spring, repository methods called from a transactional service call, do not have to be annotated with @Transactional too.

```
package com.apress.cems.tx.services;

import org.springframework.transaction.annotation.Transactional;
...

@Service
public class PersonServiceImpl implements PersonService {

    private PersonRepo personRepo;

    public PersonServiceImpl(PersonRepo personRepo) {
        this.personRepo = personRepo;
    }

    @Transactional
    @Override
    public Optional<Person> findById(Long id) {
        return personRepo.findById(id);
    }
}
```

CC Both @EnableTransactionManagement and <tx:annotation-driven ../> enable all infrastructure beans necessary for supporting transactional execution. But there is a minor difference between them. The XML configuration element can be used like this: <tx:annotation-driven /> without the transaction-manager attribute. In this case, Spring will look for a bean named transactionManager, and if it is not found, the application won't start. The error message is the typical one displayed when beans are not found.

```
org.springframework.beans.factory.NoSuchBeanDefinitionException:
    No bean named 'transactionManager ' available: No matching
PlatformTransactionManager
        bean found for qualifier 'transactionManager '
```

The @EnableTransactionManagement is more flexible; it looks for a bean of any type that implements the org.springframework.transaction.PlatformTransactionManager, so the name is not important. In case the default transaction manager bean must be established without a doubt, this can be done by making the configuration class

annotated with @EnableTransactionManagement implement the org.springframework.
transaction.annotation.TransactionManagementConfigurer interface and declare
the default transaction manager by providing an implementation for the method
annotationDrivenTransactionManager(..).

```
package com.apress.cems.tx.config;
import org.springframework.transaction.annotation.
TransactionManagementConfigurer;
...
@EnableTransactionManagement
@Configuration
public class TestTransactionalDbConfig2
    implements TransactionManagementConfigurer {

  ...

    @Bean
    public PlatformTransactionManager txManager(){
        return new DataSourceTransactionManager(dataSource());
    }

    @Bean
    public PlatformTransactionManager simpleManager(){
        return new DataSourceTransactionManager(dataSource());
    }

    /* Setting the default transactionManager*/
    @Override
    public TransactionManager annotationDrivenTransactionManager() {
        return txManager();
    }
}
```

This is useful, because in bigger applications requiring more than one datasource,
multiple transaction manager beans need to be declared. If the default to use is not
specified, Spring cannot choose for itself, and the first time a transactional method
is executed the application will fail with an ugly and explicit exception. Look at the
following configuration class.

```
package com.apress.cems.tx.config;

...

@Configuration
public class MultipleTransactionManagersConfig {

    @Bean
    public PlatformTransactionManager txManager(){
        return new DataSourceTransactionManager(dataSource());
    }

    @Bean
    public PlatformTransactionManager simpleManager(){
        return new DataSourceTransactionManager(dataSource());
    }

    @Bean
    public JdbcTemplate jdbcTemplate() {
        return new JdbcTemplate(dataSource());
    }

    @Bean
    public DataSource dataSource() {
        EmbeddedDatabaseBuilder builder = new EmbeddedDatabaseBuilder();
        EmbeddedDatabase db = builder
                .setType(EmbeddedDatabaseType.H2)
                .generateUniqueName(true)
                .addScript("db/schema.sql")
                .addScript("db/test-data.sql")
                .build();
        return db;
    }
}
```

The class in the previous code listing, declares two transaction manager beans named txManager and simpleManager. The rest of the beans and transactions support is enabled by the AppConfig class.

```
package com.apress.cems.tx.config;
...
@Configuration
@ComponentScan(basePackages = {"com.apress.cems.repos"
        ,"com.apress.cems.tx.services"})
@EnableTransactionManagement
public class AppConfig {
}
```

The `MultipleTransactionManagerTest` has a single test method that calls a
transactional method. The reason for this is that a Spring application context can be
created with two transaction manager beans, but the Spring container won't check for a
default one until a transactional method is called.

```
package com.apress.cems.tx;
...

@ExtendWith(SpringExtension.class)
@ContextConfiguration(classes =
      {MultipleTransactionManagersConfig.class, AppConfig.class})
class MultipleTransactionManagerTest {

    @Autowired
    PersonService personService;

    @Test
    void testFindByIdWithTwoTms() {
        personService.findById(1L).ifPresentOrElse(
                p -> assertEquals("Sherlock", p.getFirstName()),
                Assert::fail
        );
    }
}
```

When a transactional method is called a NoUniqueBeanDefinitionException exception is thrown, and at the bottom of the console log, the following error message can be seen.

```
org.springframework.beans.factory.NoUniqueBeanDefinitionException:
 No qualifying bean of type
      [org.springframework.transaction.PlatformTransactionManager]
  is defined: expected single matching bean but found 2
    : txManager, simpleManager
```

The transaction manager to be used when executing a method in a transactional context can be specified by the transactionManager attribute of the @Transactional annotation. In the following code sample, two transaction manager beans are declared: txManager and simpleManager. txManager is configured as the default transaction manager bean by implementing TransactionManagementConfigurer:

```
@ComponentScan(basePackages = "com.apress.cems.tx.one")
@Configuration
@EnableTransactionManagement
public class MultipleTransactionManagersConfig
            implements TransactionManagementConfigurer {

    @Bean
    public PlatformTransactionManager txManager(){
        return new DataSourceTransactionManager(dataSource());
    }

    @Bean
    public PlatformTransactionManager simpleManager(){
        return new DataSourceTransactionManager(dataSource());
    }
        /* Setting the default transactionManagerv*/
    @Override
    public TransactionManager annotationDrivenTransactionManager() {
        return txManager();
    }
    ...
}
```

Then, the following code can be written, and it will work like a charm.[19]

```
package com.apress.cems.tx.services;

...

@Service
public class PersonServiceImpl implements PersonService {
    private PersonRepo personRepo;

    public PersonServiceImpl(PersonRepo personRepo) {
        this.personRepo = personRepo;
    }

    //default txManager is used
    @Transactional
    @Override
    public Optional<Person> findById(Long id) {
        return personRepo.findById(id);
    }

    @Transactional(transactionManager = "simpleManager", readOnly = true)
    @Override
    public Set<Person> findAll() {
        return Set.copyOf(personRepo.findAll());
    }
}
```

Another option for making sure that a default transaction manager bean is used is to annotate one of the transaction manager beans with @Primary. This annotation indicates that a particular bean should be given preference when multiple candidates are qualified to autowire a single-valued dependency. So, the MultipleTransactionManagersConfig class can be also written like this:

```
package com.apress.cems.tx.config;

import org.springframework.context.annotation.Primary;

....
```

---

[19]Well, if you have two databases with person tables that is.

```
@Configuration
public class MultipleTransactionManagersConfig {
...

    @Primary
    @Bean
    public PlatformTransactionManager txManager(){
        return new DataSourceTransactionManager(dataSource());
    }

    @Bean
    public PlatformTransactionManager simpleManager(){
        return new DataSourceTransactionManager(dataSource());
    }
}
```

The txManager bean is used for transactional operations unless another transaction manager is referred explicitly by ID in the @Transactional annotation.

The transactions in the context of which methods are executed in Spring applications are called *declarative transactions* when defined with @Transactional, and this type of declaring transactions is not connected to a JTA (Java Transaction API), which is very practical, because this means that transactions can be used in any environment: local with JDBC, JPA, Hibernate, or JDO (Java Data Objects), or with an application server. Transactional behavior can be added to any method of any bean if the method is public, because declarative transaction behavior is implemented in Spring using AOP. Spring also provides declarative rollback rules and the possibility to customize transactional behavior through attributes of the @Transactional annotation. And at this point, a list of these attributes is appropriate.

- The transactionManager attribute value defines the transaction manager used to manage the transaction in the context of which the annotated method is executed.

- The readOnly attribute should be used for transactions that involve operations that do not modify the database (for example, searching, counting records). The default value is false, and the value of this attribute is just a hint for the transaction manager, which can be ignored depending of the implementation. Although if you tell

Spring that the transaction is supposed only to read data, some performance optimizations will be done for read-only data access. Although it seems useless to use a transaction for reading data, it is recommended to do so to take into account the isolation level configured for the transactions. The isolation attribute will be covered shortly.

- The `propagation` attribute can define behavior of the target methods: if they should be executed in an existing or new transaction, or no transaction at all. The values for this attribute are defined by the Spring `org.springframework.transaction.annotation.Propagation` enum, and they match the ones defined in JEE for EJB transactions. There are seven propagation types.

    - REQUIRED: An existing transaction will be used or a new one will be created to execute the method annotated with `@Transactional(propagation = Propagation.REQUIRED)`.

    - REQUIRES_NEW: A new transaction is created to execute the method annotated with `@Transactional(propagation = Propagation.REQUIRES_NEW)`. If a current transaction exists, it will be suspended.

    - NESTED: An existing nested transaction executes the method annotated with `@Transactional(propagation = Propagation.NESTED)`. If no such transaction exists, it will be created. This approach is quite similar to REQUIRED, so if the datasource supports I think it should be mandatory to use it because it reuses existent resources.

    - MANDATORY: An existing transaction must be used to execute the method annotated with `@Transactional(propagation = MANDATORY)`. If there is no transaction to be used, an exception will be thrown.

    - NEVER: Methods annotated with `@Transactional(propagation = Propagation.NEVER` must not be executed within a transaction. If a transaction exists, an exception will be thrown.

- NOT_SUPPORTED: No transaction executes the method annotated with @Transactional(propagation = Propagation.NOT_SUPPORTED). If a transaction exists, it will be suspended.

- SUPPORTS: An existing transaction executes the method annotated with @Transactional(propagation = Propagation.SUPPORTS). If no transaction exists, the method will be executed anyway, without a transactional context.

In the following code snippet, the findById method is executed in a transaction and the getPersonAsHtml is executed within a nested transaction. Nested transactions work only with transaction managers in an enterprise RDBMS. And as you can see from the log at the end of the code snippet, DataSourceTransactionManager does not support nested transactions working with an in-memory database. This transaction manager supports nested transactions via the JDBC 3.0 "savepoint" mechanism, but it needs a database management system that supports savepoints, such as an enterprise RDBMS like Oracle or SQL Server.[20]

Nested transactions allow complex behavior; a transaction can start before the enclosing transaction is completed. Depending on the application's specifications, a commit in a nested transaction can have no effect, and all changes will be applied to the database when the enclosing transaction is committed. If a nested transaction is rolled back, the enclosing transaction is rolled back to prevent leaving the database in an inconsistent state: partial changes will not be kept. Nested transactions can force atomic execution of multiple methods.[21]

---

[20]Savepoints are used to roll back transactions to a specified point. In the other words, this lets you roll back part of the transaction; in this case, the part corresponding the nested transaction, instead of the entire transaction.

[21]A very good article on nested transactions in case you are curious: http://www.intstrings.com/ramivemula/articles/nested-sql-transactions-explained/

If instead of NESTED, REQUIRED is used, there will be no guarantee
of atomic execution.

```java
//DetectiveServiceImpl.java
package com.apress.cems.tx.services;
...

@Transactional
@Service
public class DetectiveServiceImpl implements DetectiveService {

    private DetectiveRepo detectiveRepo;
    ...
    @Transactional(propagation = Propagation.REQUIRED)
    @Override
    public Detective findById(Long id) {
        return detectiveRepo.findById(id);
    }
}

//PersonServiceImpl.java
@Service
@Transactional
public class PersonServiceImpl implements PersonService {

    ...

    @Transactional(propagation = Propagation.NESTED)
    @Override
    public String getPersonAsHtml(String username) {
        final StringBuilder sb = new StringBuilder();
        personRepo.findByUsername(username).ifPresentOrElse(
                p -> sb.append("<p>First Name: ")
                        .append(p.getFirstName()).append(" </p>")
                        .append("<p>Last Name: ")
                        .append(p.getLastName()).append(" </p>"),
                () -> sb.append("<p>None found with username ")
                        .append(username).append(" </p>")
        );
```

```
            return sb.toString;
        }
    }

    // DetectiveServiceTest.java test class
    @ExtendWith(SpringExtension.class)
    @ContextConfiguration(classes = {TestTransactionalDbConfig.
    class, AppConfig.class})
    class DetectiveServiceTest {

        private Logger logger = LoggerFactory.
        getLogger(DetectiveServiceTest.class);

        @Autowired
        DetectiveService detectiveService;

        @Autowired
        PersonService personService;

        @Test
        void testDetectiveHtml(){
            detectiveService.findById(1L).ifPresent(
                    d -> {
                        Person p = d.getPerson();
                        assertNotNull(p);
                        String html = personService.
                        getPersonAsHtml(p.getUsername());
                        logger.info("Detective personal info: {}",
                        html);
                    }
            );
        }
    }
```

In Figure 5-12, the general behavior of nested transactions is depicted.

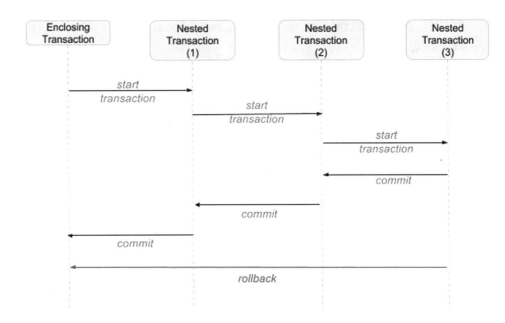

Figure 5-12. *Nested transaction behavior*

When this book was written, the current version of the H2 database does not support nested transactions. It is a capability reserved for a complex enterprise RDBMS like Oracle. The transactional configuration class for the previous example is simple; it declares a single transaction manager named `transactionManager`. When the `testDetectiveHtml()` method is executing, we can see in the logs that Spring is trying to execute the second method in a nested transaction by looking at the transactions created and their attributes.

```
...
DEBUG o.s.b.f.s.DefaultListableBeanFactory - Creating shared instance
    of singleton bean 'transactionManager'
DEBUG o.s.j.d.DataSourceTransactionManager - Creating new transaction with name
    [com.apress.cems.tx.services.DetectiveServiceImpl.findById]:
    PROPAGATION_REQUIRED,ISOLATION_DEFAULT,readOnly
```

```
DEBUG o.s.j.d.SimpleDriverDataSource - Creating new JDBC Driver
Connection to
    [jdbc:h2:mem:6e3f9563-0676-4b3a-a574-031757890980;DB_CLOSE_
    DELAY=-1;
    DB_CLOSE_ON_EXIT=false]
DEBUG o.s.j.d.DataSourceTransactionManager - Acquired Connection
[conn1:
    url=jdbc:h2:mem:6e3f9563-0676-4b3a-a574-031757890980 user=SA]
    for JDBC transaction
DEBUG o.s.j.d.DataSourceUtils - Setting JDBC Connection [conn1:
    url=jdbc:h2:mem:6e3f9563-0676-4b3a-a574-031757890980 user=SA]
    read-only
DEBUG o.s.j.d.DataSourceTransactionManager - Switching JDBC
Connection [conn1:
    url=jdbc:h2:mem:6e3f9563-0676-4b3a-a574-031757890980 user=SA]
    to manual commit
14:31:40.669 [main] DEBUG o.s.j.c.JdbcTemplate - Executing
prepared SQL statement
    [select d.ID, d.BADGE_NUMBER, d.RANK, d.ARMED, d.STATUS,d.
    PERSON_ID,
     p.USERNAME, p.FIRSTNAME, p.LASTNAME, p.HIRINGDATE from DETECTIVE
    d, PERSON p
     where d.ID= ? and d.PERSON_ID=p.ID]
DEBUG o.s.j.d.DataSourceTransactionManager - Initiating
transaction commit
DEBUG o.s.j.d.DataSourceTransactionManager - Committing JDBC
transaction on Connection
    [conn1: url=jdbc:h2:mem:6e3f9563-0676-4b3a-a574-031757890980
user=SA]
DEBUG o.s.j.d.DataSourceTransactionManager - Releasing JDBC
Connection
    [conn1: url=jdbc:h2:mem:6e3f9563-0676-4b3a-a574-031757890980
user=SA] after transaction

    # Not actually nested, because H2 does not support nested
    transactions.
```

DEBUG o.s.j.d.DataSourceTransactionManager - <u>Creating new</u>
<u>transaction with name</u>
  [com.apress.cems.tx.services.PersonServiceImpl.getPersonAsHtml]:
  PROPAGATION_NESTED,ISOLATION_DEFAULT,readOnly
DEBUG o.s.j.d.SimpleDriverDataSource - Creating new JDBC Driver
Connection to
  [jdbc:h2:mem:6e3f9563-0676-4b3a-a574-031757890980;DB_CLOSE_
  DELAY=-1
  ;DB_CLOSE_ON_EXIT=false]
DEBUG o.s.j.d.DataSourceTransactionManager - <u>Acquired Connection</u>
[conn2:
  url=jdbc:h2:mem:6e3f9563-0676-4b3a-a574-031757890980 user=SA]
  <u>for JDBC transaction</u>
DEBUG o.s.j.d.DataSourceUtils - Setting JDBC Connection [conn2:
  url=jdbc:h2:mem:6e3f9563-0676-4b3a-a574-031757890980 user=SA]
  read-only
DEBUG o.s.j.d.DataSourceTransactionManager - Switching JDBC
Connection [conn2:
  url=jdbc:h2:mem:6e3f9563-0676-4b3a-a574-031757890980 user=SA] to
  manual commit
14:31:49.400 [main] DEBUG o.s.j.c.JdbcTemplate - Executing
prepared SQL statement
  [select ID, USERNAME, FIRSTNAME, LASTNAME, PASSWORD, HIRINGDATE
  from PERSON where USERNAME= ?]
DEBUG o.s.j.d.DataSourceTransactionManager - <u>Initiating</u>
<u>transaction commit</u>
DEBUG o.s.j.d.DataSourceTransactionManager - <u>Committing JDBC</u>
<u>transaction on Connection</u>
  [conn2: url=jdbc:h2:mem:6e3f9563-0676-4b3a-a574-031757890980
  user=SA]
DEBUG o.s.j.d.DataSourceTransactionManager - Releasing JDBC
Connection [conn2:

```
url=jdbc:h2:mem:6e3f9563-0676-4b3a-a574-031757890980 user=SA]
after transaction
INFO  c.a.c.t.DetectiveServiceTest - Detective personal info:
            <p> First Name: Sherlock </p>
            <p> Last Name: Holmes </p>
```

1. The `isolation` attribute value defines how data modified in a
   transaction affects other simultaneous transactions. As a general
   idea, transactions should be isolated. A transaction should not be
   able to access changes from another uncommitted transaction.
   There are four levels of isolation at the RDBMS level, and every
   database management system supports them differently. In
   Spring, there are five isolation values that are defined in the `org.
   springframework.transaction.annotation.Isolation` enum.

   - `DEFAULT`: The default isolation level of the DBMS.

   - `READ_UNCOMMITED`: Data changed by a transaction can be read by
     a different transaction while the first one is not yet committed,
     also known as *dirty reads*. Dirty reads are possible at this isolation
     level.

   - `READ_COMMITTED`: Dirty reads are not possible when a transaction
     is used with this isolation level. This is the default strategy for
     most databases. But a different phenomenon could happen here:
     non-repeatable read: when the same query is executed multiple
     times, different results might be obtained. (For example, a person
     is extracted repeatedly within the same transaction. In parallel,
     a different transaction edits the person and commits. If the first
     transaction has this isolation level, it will return the person with
     the new properties after the second transaction is committed.)

   - `REPEATABLE_READ`: This level of isolation does not allow
     dirty reads, and repeatedly querying a table row in the same
     transaction will always return the same result, even if a different
     transaction has changed the data and committed while the
     reading occurs. The process of reading the same row multiple
     times in the context of a transaction and always getting the same

result is called *repeatable read*. But, at this level, *phantom reads* are still possible. A *phantom read* happens when in the course of a transaction, the execution of identical queries leads to different result sets returned.

- SERIALIZABLE: This is the most restrictive isolation level, since transaction are executed in a serialized way. So no dirty reads, no repeatable reads, and no phantom reads are possible.

- timeout: By default, the value of this attribute is defined by the transaction manager provider, but it can be changed by setting a different value in the annotation: @Transactional(timeout=3600). The value represents the number of milliseconds after which a transaction is considered failed, and the default value is 1 which means timeouts are not supported.

- rollbackFor attribute values should be one or more exception classes, subclasses of Throwable. When this type of exception is thrown during the execution of a transactional method, the transaction is rolled back. By default, a transaction is rolled back only when a RuntimeException is thrown. In using this attribute, the rollback can be triggered for checked exceptions as well.

  In the following code snippet, MailSendingException is a checked exception that is thrown when a notification of successful person modification to update the password cannot be sent via email. The normal behavior is that the main operation was performed successfully, and the person data has been updated. It does not make sense to roll back the changes because a notification could not be sent. But, in the next example this is exactly what we are doing: configuring a rollback to happen for this type of exceptions too, so the password is not updated for the person.

```
@Transactional(rollbackFor = MailSendingException.class)
@Override
public Person updatePassword(Person person, String password)
    throws MailSendingException {
        person.setPassword(password);
        Person p =  personRepo.update(person);
```

```
            sendNotification();
            return p;
    }

    private void sendNotification() throws MailSendingException {
            ... // code not relevant here
    }
```

We can check that a rollback occurred by writing a test method for that method and looking in the logs.

```
DEBUG o.s.j.d.DataSourceTransactionManager - Creating new
transaction with name
      [com.apress.cems.tx.services.PersonServiceImpl.
      updatePassword]:
      PROPAGATION_REQUIRED,ISOLATION_DEFAULT,
      -com.apress.cems.aop.exception.MailSendingException
DEBUG o.s.j.d.SimpleDriverDataSource - Creating new JDBC Driver
Connection to [...]
DEBUG o.s.j.d.DataSourceTransactionManager - Acquired
Connection [...]
    for JDBC transaction
DEBUG o.s.j.d.DataSourceTransactionManager - Switching JDBC
Connection [...]
    to manual commit
DEBUG o.s.j.c.JdbcTemplate - Executing prepared SQL update
DEBUG o.s.j.c.JdbcTemplate - Executing prepared SQL statement
      [update PERSON set USERNAME=?, FIRSTNAME=?, LASTNAME=?,
PASSWORD=?,
      MODIFIED_AT=? where ID=?]
DEBUG o.s.j.d.DataSourceTransactionManager - Initiating
transaction rollback
DEBUG o.s.j.d.DataSourceTransactionManager - Rolling back JDBC
transaction
    on Connection [...]
DEBUG o.s.j.d.DataSourceTransactionManager - Releasing JDBC
Connection [...]
```

```
after transaction
```

- noRollbackFor attribute values should be one or more exception
  classes, subclasses of Throwable. When this type of exception
  is thrown during the execution of a transactional method,
  the transaction is not rolled back. By default, a transaction is
  rolled back only when a RuntimeException is thrown. Using
  this attribute, rollback of a transaction can be avoided for a
  RuntimeException as well. Let's take the following example. We
  add an updateUsername(..) method to the PersonServiceImpl
  class. The username is declared to be unique. So updating it with a
  duplicate will throw a DataIntegrityViolationException which is
  a RuntimeException, which causes the rollback of the transaction. If
  the transaction is shared, there is no point to roll it all back because
  the update of the username failed, unless the rest of the operations
  in the transaction involve the new value. But let's assume this will
  never be the case and declare the updateUsername(..) to not cause a
  rollback for DataIntegrityViolationException.

```
package com.apress.cems.tx.services;
...
@Service
@Transactional
public class PersonServiceImpl implements PersonService {
    private PersonRepo personRepo;
    ...

    @Transactional(noRollbackFor = DataIntegrityViolationException.
    class)
    @Override
    public Person updateUsername(Person person, String newUsername) {
        person.setUsername(newUsername);
        return personRepo.update(person);
    }
}
```

And we can check that no rollback occurred by writing a test
method for that method and looking in the logs.

```
DEBUG o.s.j.d.DataSourceTransactionManager - Creating new
transaction with name
    [com.apress.cems.tx.services.PersonServiceImpl.
    updateUsername]:
    PROPAGATION_REQUIRED,ISOLATION_DEFAULT,
    +org.springframework.dao.DataIntegrityViolationException
DEBUG o.s.j.d.SimpleDriverDataSource - Creating new JDBC Driver
Connection to [...]
DEBUG o.s.j.d.DataSourceTransactionManager - Acquired Connection
[...]
    for JDBC transaction
DEBUG o.s.j.d.DataSourceTransactionManager - Switching JDBC
Connection [...]
    to manual commit
DEBUG o.s.j.c.JdbcTemplate - Executing prepared SQL update
DEBUG o.s.j.c.JdbcTemplate - Executing prepared SQL statement
    [update PERSON set USERNAME=?, FIRSTNAME=?, LASTNAME=?,
    PASSWORD=?,
        MODIFIED_AT=? where ID=?]
DEBUG o.s.j.s.SQLErrorCodesFactory - Looking up default
SQLErrorCodes for DataSource
    [o.s.j.d.e.EmbeddedDatabaseFactory$EmbeddedDataSourceProxy@25c
    4de73]
DEBUG o.s.j.s.SQLErrorCodesFactory - SQL error codes for 'H2' found
DEBUG o.s.j.s.SQLErrorCodesFactory - Caching SQL error codes for
DataSource
    [o.s.j.d.e.EmbeddedDatabaseFactory$EmbeddedDataSourceProxy@25c
    4de73]:
        database product name is 'H2'
DEBUG o.s.j.s.SQLErrorCodeSQLExceptionTranslator - Translating
SQLException with
    SQL state '23505', error code '23505', message [Unique index
    or primary key violation:
```

```
"PUBLIC.CONSTRAINT_INDEX_8 ON PUBLIC.PERSON(USERNAME) VALUES
2"; SQL statement:
 update PERSON set USERNAME=?, FIRSTNAME=?, LASTNAME=?,
 PASSWORD=?,
 MODIFIED_AT=? where ID=? [23505-198]]; SQL was [update
 PERSON set USERNAME=?,
 FIRSTNAME=?, LASTNAME=?, PASSWORD=?, MODIFIED_AT=? where
 ID=?]
 for task [PreparedStatementCallback]
DEBUG o.s.j.d.DataSourceTransactionManager - Initiating
transaction commit
DEBUG o.s.j.d.DataSourceTransactionManager - Committing JDBC
transaction on Connection [...]
DEBUG o.s.j.d.DataSourceTransactionManager - Releasing JDBC
Connection [...] after transaction
```

The @Transactional annotation can be used at the class level too. In this case, all the methods in the class become transactional, and all properties defined for the transaction are inherited from the @Transactional class level definition. But they can be overridden by a @Transactional defined at the method level.

```
package com.apress.cems.tx.services;
import org.springframework.transaction.annotation.Propagation;
import org.springframework.transaction.annotation.Transactional;
...

@Service
@Transactional(readOnly = true,
    propagation = Propagation.REQUIRED)
public class PersonServiceImpl implements PersonService {
...
    @Transactional(propagation = Propagation.REQUIRES_NEW)
    @Override
    public Optional<Person> findById(Long id) {
        return personRepo.findById(id);
    }
```

```
@Transactional(propagation = Propagation.SUPPORTS)
@Override
public String getPersonAsHtml(String username) {
... // code not relevant here
}
}
```

From the code samples in the chapter thus far, you see that the `@Transactional` annotation can be used at the class and the method level. A few other things need to be mentioned.

- Transactional behavior is a cross-cutting concern, and the declarative transactional model is supported in Spring using AOP. As expected, interface-based proxies are created, unless specified otherwise by customizing `@EnableTransactionManagement` annotation. This annotation declares a boolean property named `proxyTargetClass` with the default value of `false`. The default behavior is not to create class-based proxies. This can be changed by using `@EnableTrans actionManagement(proxyTargetClass = true)` to annotate the configuration class.

- Thus, you should be very careful where you place the `@Transactional` annotation. The recommendation is to apply the `@Transactional` annotation only to methods with public visibility, this way, regardless of the type of proxy created, you'll always get the transactional behavior where you expect it. Also, keep in mind local calls within the same class cannot be intercepted.

- The `@Transactional` annotation can be used at the class level. In this case, all the public methods inherit the transactional behavior defined by the annotation on the class, but `@Transactional` annotations used at the method level, can override any transactional settings inherited from the class. Therefore, the most derived location takes precedence when evaluating the transactional settings for a method.

- It is recommended and practical to annotate only concrete classes (and methods of concrete classes) with the `@Transactional` annotation.

- The `@Transactional` annotation can be used on an interface (or an interface method), this requires you to use interface-based proxies; otherwise, if class-based proxies are used, the annotations are not inherited from the interface.

- `@Transactional` can also be used on abstract classes as well, and in this case, whether the transactional behavior is applied depends on the type of proxy created.

Although a little repetitive, these affirmations can be summarized as follows: when using declarative transactions in Spring applications, keep it obvious, annotate concrete classes with `@Transactional`, and override the behavior only at the public method level.

Testing Transactional Methods

For test cases involving datasource operations, a few practical annotations were added in Spring 4.1 to the `org.springframework.test.context.jdbc` package. These annotations were introduced in Chapter 3 and are part of the `@Sql` family. In this chapter, they write transactional tests.

- The `@Sql` annotation can specify SQL scripts to be executed against a given database during integration tests. It can be used on classes and on methods. It can be used multiple times when there is more than one SQL file to execute. It can be used as a meta-annotation to create custom composed annotations. The tests specific to this section are integration tests, because they test the communication between a service, a repository, and a database (test database, sure, but still a database). So they are a perfect fit to introduce this annotation.

- The `@SqlGroup` annotation can be used on classes and methods to group `@Sql` annotations. It can be used as a meta-annotation to create custom composed annotations. For example, when more than one datasource is involved, it can be used with `@SqlConfig` to group scripts to be executed to prepare the test environment for a single test case involving both datasources.

```
@SqlGroup({
    @Sql(scripts = "script1.sql", config = @SqlConfig(dataSource =
"dataSource1")),
    @Sql(scripts = "script2.sql", config = @SqlConfig(dataSource =
"dataSource2"))
})
```

As you can see, @SqlGroup is a container annotation, and according to the official documentation,[22] multiple @Sql annotations in the same test class or method causes the equivalent @SqlGroup to be generated. So feel free to use whichever you want.

- The @SqlConfig specifies the configuration of the SQL script.

In the following code snippet, you see how these annotations test your service classes. The first example uses multiple @Sql annotations; the second groups them with @SqlGroup. The example can be tested by running the PersonServiceTest.testCount() method from the 06-ps-tx-practice project.

```
package com.apress.cems.tx;

import org.springframework.test.context.jdbc.Sql;
import org.springframework.test.context.jdbc.SqlConfig;
import org.springframework.test.context.jdbc.SqlGroup;
...
@ExtendWith(SpringExtension.class)
@ContextConfiguration(classes = {TestTransactionalDbConfig.class,
AppConfig.class})
 class PersonServiceTest {

    @Autowired
    PersonService personService;

    @Test
    @Sql(dcripts = "classpath:test/extra-data.sql",
```

---

[22]Official Javadoc: https://docs.spring.io/spring-framework/docs/current/javadoc-api/
index.html?org/springframework/test/context/jdbc/SqlGroup.html

```
    config = @SqlConfig(encoding = "utf-8", separator = ";", commentPrefix
    = "--"))
  @Sql(
        scripts = "classpath:test/delete-test-data.sql",
        config = @SqlConfig(transactionMode =
                SqlConfig.TransactionMode.ISOLATED),
                executionPhase = Sql.ExecutionPhase.AFTER_TEST_METHOD
  )
  void testCount() {
     long count = personService.countPersons();
     assertEquals(4, count);
  }
}
```

Although the syntax is obvious, in case extra clarifications are necessary, here they are.

- The first @Sql annotation specifies a script to be executed to save some data into the test database before executing the test method. The @SqlConfig declares specific SQL syntax details, so Spring can execute the extra-data.sql script correctly.

- The second @Sql annotation executes the script that will clean the test database after the test execution. The attribute that specifies when the script is executed is executionPhase, and in this case, the value used to tell Spring to execute the script after the test method is Sql.ExecutionPhase.AFTER_TEST_METHOD.

The @SqlConfig annotation is quite powerful and provides attributes to declare the isolation level (transactionMode = SqlConfig.TransactionMode.ISOLATED) and a transaction manager to be used. (e.g., transactionManager="txMng").

The following example has the same behavior as the preceding one, but for teaching purposes, the two @Sql annotations have been composed using @SqlGroup.

```
package com.apress.cems.tx;

import org.springframework.test.context.jdbc.Sql;
import org.springframework.test.context.jdbc.SqlConfig;
import org.springframework.test.context.jdbc.SqlGroup;
...
```

```
@ExtendWith(SpringExtension.class)
@ContextConfiguration(classes = {TestTransactionalDbConfig.class,
AppConfig.class})
 class PersonServiceTest {

    @Autowired
    PersonService personService;

    @Test
    @SqlGroup({
            @Sql(value = "classpath:test/extra-data.sql",
      config = @SqlConfig(encoding = "utf-8", separator = ";", commentPrefix
      = "--")),
            @Sql(
                    scripts = "classpath:test/delete-test-data.sql",
                    config = @SqlConfig(transactionMode =
                        SqlConfig.TransactionMode.ISOLATED),
                    executionPhase = Sql.ExecutionPhase.AFTER_TEST_METHOD
            )
    })
    void testCount() {
        long count = personService.countPersons();
        assertEquals(4, count);
    }
}
```

The @Sql annotation has more attributes, but there is one in particular that you will definitely find useful: the statements attribute. This attribute allows you to provide a statement to be executed before or after the test method. This includes DDL statements, which means for testing purposes, when a table is created inside a method can be dropped right after the test method executes. I can imagine a scenario in which some constraints are dropped on a table for the scope of a test, and then put back after the test is done.

```
    @Test
    @Sql(statements = {"drop table NEW_PERSON if exists;"},
      executionPhase = Sql.ExecutionPhase.AFTER_TEST_METHOD)
```

```
void testCreateTable(){
    jdbcTemplate.execute("create table NEW_PERSON(" +
            "  ID BIGINT IDENTITY PRIMARY KEY " +
            ", USERNAME VARCHAR2(50) NOT NULL " +
            ", FIRSTNAME VARCHAR2(50) " +
            ", LASTNAME VARCHAR2(50) " +
            ", UNIQUE(USERNAME)) ");
    long result = jdbcTemplate.queryForObject(
        "select count(*) from NEW_PERSON", Long.class);
    // table exists but is empty
    assertEquals(0, result);
}
```

Repository methods can be tested in a transactional context, decoupled from the service methods. This is useful when the test database must be left unaffected by a test execution. The @Transactional annotation can be used on the test method and configured appropriately. It can be coupled with two other annotations.

- The @Commit annotation can persist data after a test method is executed. This modifies the database and the changes are taken into consideration by the other tests. The default behavior for transactional integration testing is to rollback all changes after the test method execution ends. The @Commit annotation was introduced in Spring 4.2 to modify the default behavior when needed, and has the same effect as @Rollback(true).

- The @Rollback annotation has been part of the Spring test package since version 2.5. As you can probably imagine, you can use one or the other for this purpose, but you should not use them together unless you really want to confuse the Spring IoC Container. The results will be unpredictable.

  ```
  package com.apress.cems.tx;
  import org.springframework.test.annotation.Commit;
  ...
  @ExtendWith(SpringExtension.class)
  @ContextConfiguration(classes = {TestTransactionalDbConfig.class,
  AppConfig.class})
  ```

```
class PersonRepoTest {

    @Autowired
    PersonRepo repo;

     // equivalent to @Rollback(true)
    @Commit
    @Test
    @Transactional
    void testCreatePerson(){
        Person person = new Person();
        person.setId(99L);
        person.setUsername("test.user");
        person.setFirstName("test");
        person.setLastName("user");
        person.setPassword("password");
        person.setHiringDate(LocalDate.now());
        person.setCreatedAt(LocalDate.now());
        person.setModifiedAt(LocalDate.now());
        repo.save(person);
    }

     \\ this might fail
    @Test
    void testCountPersons(){
        long result = repo.count();
        assertEquals(2, result);
    }
}
```

In the previous code sample, we have a test class with two test methods. The testCreatePerson(..) is annotated with @Commit, which means the person record created in its body is persisted to the test database used by the testCountPersons(..) test. If the test methods are executed in parallel, the testCountPersons(..) test method will fail from time to time. This is because aside from the two expected records that the test database seems to be initialized with, when testCountPersons(..) is executed after testCreatePerson(..), the repo.count() takes into account the record created by it.

Both annotations can be used at the class level too. The class level annotation configuration can be overridden by the method level annotation configurations. So, the previous test class can also be written as follows.

```
package com.apress.cems.tx;
import org.springframework.test.annotation.Commit;
import org.springframework.test.annotation.Rollback;
...
@ExtendWith(SpringExtension.class)
@ContextConfiguration(classes = {TestTransactionalDbConfig.class,
AppConfig.class})
@Commit    // equivalent to @Rollback(true)
class PersonRepoTest {

    @Autowired
    PersonRepo repo;

    @Test
    @Transactional
    void testCreatePerson(){
       ...
    }

    @Test
    void testCountPersons(){
        long result = repo.count();
        assertEquals(2, result);
    }
}
```

Up to Spring 4.0, the @TransactionConfiguration could be used on a test class used to define the transactional context for tests. It became deprecated in Spring 4.2, and @Rollback, @Commit at the class level and the transactionManager qualifier in @Transactional are currently recommended to be used. But in case you are interested in an example, here it is.

```
import org.springframework.test.context.transaction.
TransactionConfiguration;
import org.springframework.test.context.junit4.SpringJUnit4ClassRunner;
...
@RunWith(SpringJUnit4ClassRunner.class)
@TransactionConfiguration(defaultRollback = false,
        transactionManager = "txManager")
@Transactional
public class TransactionalJdbcRepoTest {

    @Autowired
    PersonRepo repo;

    @Test
    public void testFindById() {
        long result = repo.count();
        assertEquals(2, result);
    }
    ...
}
```

The default value for the defaultRollback attribute is true, and it was set to false in the previous example to introduce this attribute.

Another useful test annotation is @BeforeTransaction, which can set up or check a test environment before executing the transactional test method. The @BeforeTransaction annotated method is executed in the context of the transaction. The method in the following code snippet checks that the test database was initialized properly.

```
import org.springframework.test.context.transaction.BeforeTransaction;
...
@RunWith(SpringJUnit4ClassRunner.class)
@ContextConfiguration(classes = {TestDataConfig.class, AppConfig.class})
@ActiveProfiles("dev")
public class PersonServiceTest {

...

    @BeforeTransaction
```

```
    public void checkDbInit(){
        int count = personService.countPersons();
        assertEquals(4, count);
    }
}
```

Making Third-Party Components Transactional

For situations in which annotations cannot be used to configure transactional execution
the Spring transaction management configuration can be achieved using XML to declare
a combination of AOP and tx configuration elements. This is the case when a version
earlier than Java 1.5 is used or the service is a third-party implementation that cannot be
changed because it is provided to you as a *.class or part of a *.jar.

```
<beans ..>
  <!-- dataSource bean -->
   <bean id="dataSource"
         class="org.springframework.jdbc.datasource.SimpleDriverDataSource">
        <property name="driverClass" value="org.h2.Driver"/>
        <property name="url" value="jdbc:h2:~/test"/>
        <property name="username" value="test"/>
        <property name="password" value="test"/>
    </bean>

  <!-- target bean -->
  <bean id="detectiveService" class="...DetectiveServiceImpl" />

  <!-- transaction manager bean -->
   <bean id="transactionManager"
      class="org.springframework.jdbc.datasource.DataSourceTransactionManager">
        <property name="dataSource" ref="dataSource"/>
   </bean>

  <!-- AOP pointcut to select target methods -->
  <aop:config>
     <aop:pointcut id="allMethods"
          expression="execution(* com..tx.services.*.Detective
          Service+.*(..))">
```

```
        <aop:advisor pointcut-ref="allMethods"
                advice-ref="transactionalAdvice" />
    </aop:config>

    <!-- Transactional Around advice -->
    <tx:advice id="transactionalAdvice">
        <tx:atributes>
            <tx:method name="find*" read-only="true" timeout="10"/>
            <tx:method name="update*" read-only="false" timeout="30"/>
        </tx:attributes>
    </tx:advice>
</beans>
```

! If you want to test your understanding of Spring transaction management, you can open now the chapter06/transactions-practice project and try to complete the TODOs. There are five tasks for you to solve, numbered from 30 to 34. The parts missing are marked with a TODO task and are visible in IntelliJ IDEA in the TODO view.

Task TODO 30, located in the TestTransactionalDbConfig class, requires you to define a transaction manager bean to manage transactions.

Task TODO 31, located in the AppConfig class, requires you to enable use of declarative transactions. Task TODO 32, located in PersonServiceImpl, requires you to make all the methods transactional.

Task TODO 33, located in class PersonServiceImpl, requires you to complete the transaction definition of the updatePassword(...) method to make the transaction writable, and to roll back for the checked exception thrown by the method.

Task TODO 34, located in test class PersonServiceTest, requires you to complete the body of the method testing the personService.updatePassword(...) method. Implementation recommendation: call personService.findById(..) with IDs 1 or 2, since these are the only ones in the database. If a Person instance is returned, assert that an exception

of `MailSendingException` type is thrown when `personService.`
`updatePassword(..)` is called and the returned instance is provided as an
argument. And use lambda expressions because they are fun.

If you have trouble, you can take a peek at the proposed solution in the
`chapter06/transactions` project.

! Spring Declarative Model Clarification

There was heated argument on the Internet (most of it on StackOverflow[23]) regarding
whether `@Transactional` should be used on repository classes/methods when there
is a service layer involved and service classes/methods are already annotated with
`@Transactional`. To settle this debate, we must consider how declarative transactions
are implemented in Spring. AOP decorates beans with transactional behavior. This
means that when we annotate classes or methods with `@Transactional`, a proxy bean
will be created to provide the transactional behavior, and it is wrapped around the
original bean.

In an application that does not use a service layer, there are no service classes calling
repository classes thus to ensure transactional behavior when interacting with the
database the repository classes/methods must be annotated with `@Transactional`. This
will tell Spring to create transactional proxies for the repository classes. The abstract UML
diagram for this scenario is depicted in Figure 5-11, and the target object is the repository
bean. When a service layer and service classes are added, there are two possibilities:
we annotate the new service classes with `@Transactional` and remove the annotation
from the repository, or we annotate the service classes and keep `@Transactional` on the
repository classes as well. Let's analyze each of these cases in detail.

Case 1.

Only service classes are annotated with `@Transactional`. In this case, the target
object is the service bean, which contains a reference to the repository bean. When a
service method is called, the following happens.

1. The transactional proxy calls the transactional advisor to get a
   transaction.

2. The transactional proxy forwards the initial call to the target
   service bean.

---

[23]The most popular programmers' social network `https://stackoverflow.com`

3. The target service object calls the repository method and returns the result to the proxy.

4. The proxy calls the transactional advisor to commit the transaction.

5. The proxy returns the result to the caller.

The Spring service class has a reference to a repository class, which means that at runtime, the service bean will be created by aggregating the service with the repository bean. Actually, when the Spring application context is created, the following happens.

1. A repository bean declaration is found in the configuration, so a repository bean is created.

2. A service bean declaration is found in the configuration, so a service bean is created. The service bean depends on the previously created repository bean, so the dependency is provided using autowiring. So now the repository is a member of the service bean.

3. Then the `InfrastructureAdvisorAutoProxyCreator` bean creates the proxy object that wraps around the service bean to provide transactional behavior. So the service bean becomes a target object.

To summarize, the service method calls the repository method, and this call is done internally by the target object. The full execution is atomic in the context of the transaction obtained by the proxy from the Spring transactional advisor. This is important, especially when a service method calls more than one repository method, because this approach ensures that all repository methods will be executed within the same transaction. This situation is depicted in the diagram in Figure 5-13.

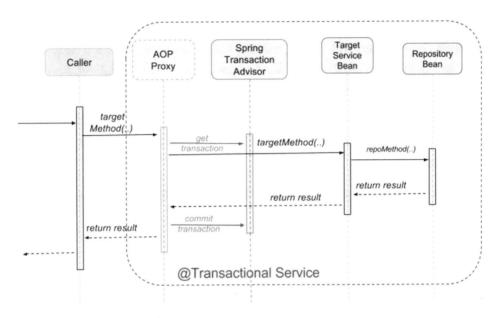

Figure 5-13. *@Transactional annotated service class*

To get a look under the hood, you can execute the DetectiveServiceTest. testFindById() method in debug mode, from project chapter06/transactions in IntelliJ IDEA and take a look at the DetectiveService bean. In the Variables console, you should see what is depicted in Figure 5-14.

Figure 5-14. *IntelliJ IDEA execution of test paused to analyze service transactional bean*

Case 2. Service and repository classes are **both** annotated with @Transactional. This approach is pretty redundant and useless, and this section makes it clear why it makes no sense. In this case, there are two transactional proxies involved, one for service and one for the repository bean. The service bean contains a reference to the repository proxy in this case. When a service method is called, the following happens.

1. The transactional service proxy calls the transactional advisor to get a transaction.

2. The transactional proxy forwards the initial call to the target service bean.

3. The service bean calls the repository method.

4. The transactional repository proxy calls the transactional advisor to get a transaction. The transaction returned depends on the propagation configuration of the @Transactional annotation declared on the repository class.

5. The target repository object method is executed, and the result is returned to the transactional repository proxy.

6. The transactional repository proxy calls the transactional advisor to commit the transaction.

7. The transactional repository proxy returns the result to the caller; in this case, the target service object.

8. The target service object returns the result to the transactional service proxy.

9. The transactional service proxy calls the transactional advisor to commit the transaction.

10. The transactional service proxy returns the result to the caller.

So, to summarize: the service target object calls the repository method on the repository proxy, which takes care of establishing a transactional context for the execution of the repository method. This situation is depicted by the diagram in Figure 5-15.

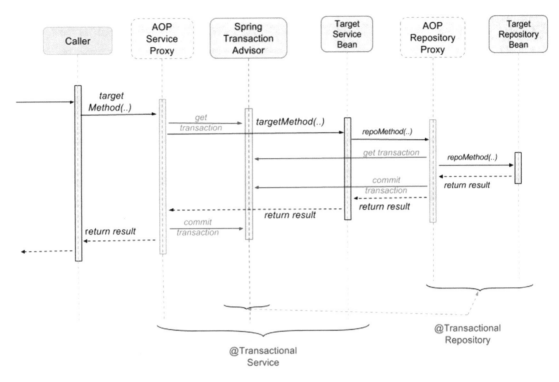

Figure 5-15. *@Transactional annotated service and repository classes*

To get a look under the hood, first uncomment the `@Transactional` annotation from the class `JdbcDetectiveRepo`, which you can find in project `chapter00/repos`.[24] Then execute the `DetectiveServiceTest.testFindById()` method from project `chapter06/transactions` in debug mode in IntelliJ IDEA. Note the `detectiveService` bean. In the `Variables` console, you should see what is depicted in Figure 5-16.

---

[24]You might have noticed that modules of this project depends on each other, code is not duplicated unless there is no choice to do so. This is done for two reasons: reducing code duplication makes the code more easy to navigate and promotes good coding practices and also provides us the opportunity to practice java modules configuration.

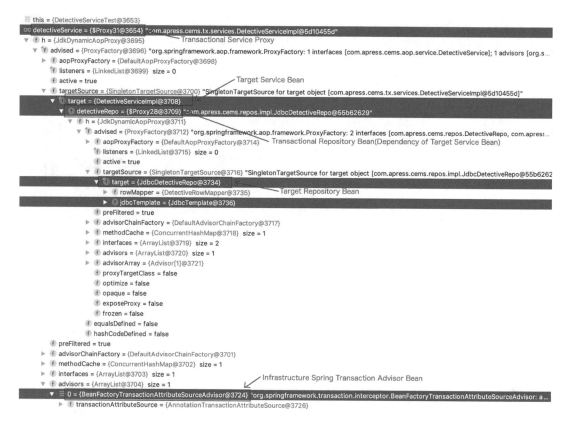

Figure 5-16. *IntelliJ IDEA execution of test paused to analyze service and repository transactional bean*

So there you have it, the end of the debate. Use `@Transactional` in the service layer or the DAO/repository layer, but not both. The service layer is the usual choice, because service methods call multiple repository methods that need to be executed in the same transaction. The only reason to make your repositories transactional is if you do not need a service layer at all, which is usually the case for small educational applications.

Another common discussion point and interview question for jobs that require writing code using Spring is what happens when a method annotated with `@Transactional` calls another method annotated with `@Transactional` on the same object instance? Well, the Spring declarative transaction is implemented using Spring AOP and if you remember this scenario is discussed in Chapter 5, and the conclusion was that when a method of the target object calls another method in the target object, the execution is internal to the target object, so the proxy logic is only executed once. If we were to apply this to a transactional context, when a method annotated with `@Transactional` calls another method annotated with @Transactional on the same object instance, a single transaction is supposed to be created and both methods are should be executed within its context.

Spring Programmatic Transaction Model

With the transaction declarative model, there is the benefit of flexible configuration and clean code, but transaction management is left fully to the transaction management provider. The programmatic model, although a little more tedious to use is practical when some control over transaction management is needed. To have some control over what happens to the transactions, Spring provides the TransactionTemplate class. In the following code snippet, a programmatic transactional service is depicted; it uses an instance of TransactionTemplate to manage transactions.

```
package com.apress.cems.tx.services;

import org.springframework.transaction.PlatformTransactionManager;
import org.springframework.transaction.TransactionStatus;
import org.springframework.transaction.support.TransactionCallback;
import org.springframework.transaction.support.TransactionTemplate;
...
@Service("programaticDetectiveService")
public class ProgramaticDetectiveService implements DetectiveService {
    private DetectiveRepo detectiveRepo;
    private TransactionTemplate txTemplate;

    public ProgramaticDetectiveService(DetectiveRepo detectiveRepo,
        PlatformTransactionManager transactionManager) {
        this.detectiveRepo = detectiveRepo;
        this.txTemplate = new TransactionTemplate(transactionManager);
    }

    @Override
    public Optional<Detective> findById(Long id) {
        return txTemplate.execute(status -> {
            Optional<Detective> opt = null;
```

```
        try {
            opt = detectiveRepo.findById(id);
        } catch (Exception e) {
            status.setRollbackOnly();
        }
        return opt;
    });
  }
}
```

The `status.setRollbackOnly()` method is called to instruct the transaction manager that the only possible outcome of the transaction may be a rollback, and not the throwing of an exception, which would in turn trigger a rollback.[25]

**Distributed Transactions

A distributed transaction is a transaction that involves two or more transactional resources. The most obvious example here is an application that involves JMS and JDBC. Conceptually, what happens when a distributed transaction involving JMS and JDBC resources is executed is depicted in Figure 5-17.

---

[25]The previous code is a simplified version written with lambda expressions. If you are curious about the expanded version, just take a look at this repository `https://github.com/Apress/pivotal-certified-pro-spring-dev-exam` that contains sources for the previous edition of this book.

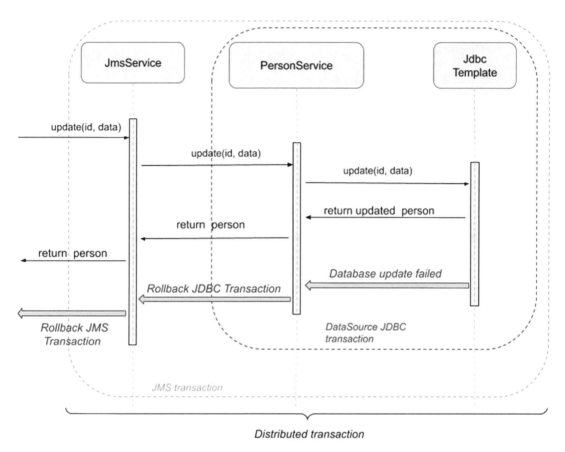

Figure 5-17. *Conceptual UML sequence diagram for a distributed transaction involving JMS and JDBC resources*

!   In this book, distributed transactions are sometimes called *global transactions*. They are also called *XA global transactions* because implementing this kind of behavior requires a JTA and specific XA drivers. So, whenever you see any one of these terms, they mean the same thing: a transaction spanning over multiple transactional resources.

JTA is a general API for managing transactions in Java. The Java Transaction API (JTA) is one of the Java Enterprise Edition (Java EE) APIs that allow distributed transactions to be done across multiple XA resources in a Java environment.

XA is the acronym for e**X**tended **A**rchitecture.

Both JmsService and PersonService are transactional. The sequence or execution steps are as follows.

1. Start messaging transaction.

2. Receive message requesting update of a person record.

3. Start database transaction to edit the person record.

4. Commit the database transaction if database was updated with success; otherwise, roll back the transaction.

5. Commit the messaging transaction if the database transaction was committed with success. If the database transaction was rolled back, roll back the messaging transaction.

Using distributed transactions requires a JTA and specific XA drivers.[26] There are many open source and commercial JTA providers: WildFly, Java Open Transaction Manager (JOTM), and Atomikos.[27] Since distributed transactions are not a topic for the official certification exam, nor part of the Spring Core components, this section will end here, because there are a few interesting topics to cover.

Introducing Hibernate and ORM

JPA (Java Persistence API) is an interface for persistence providers to implement. There are many JPA providers available for Java applications: Hibernate, EclipseLink, Apache OpenJPA, and so forth.

The most popular of them is Hibernate, one of the open source Red Hat projects. Hibernate ORM is an **o**bject **r**elational **m**apping framework that provides support for mapping an object-oriented domain model to a relational database. This framework is open source, and Hibernate has grown over the years into a full-fledged technology that has been split into numerous tools for domain model validation, indexing and searching

---

[26]The most popular article about Spring distributed transactions has since 2009 been David Sayer's https://www.javaworld.com/article/2077963/open-source-tools/distributed-transactions-in-spring--with-and-without-xa.html.

[27]A complete list of steps showing how to configure and use the Atomikos JTA provider is available on the Spring official blog: https://spring.io/blog/2011/08/15/configuring-spring-and-jta-without-full-java-ee/.

a JPA for NoSQL databases (Hibernate OGM),[28] and so on. If you are curious about the Red Hat Hibernate project family, you can find out more on their official site `http://hibernate.org/`. In this section, the basic details for configuring JPA with Hibernate are covered.

Session and Hibernate Configuration

To configure JPA with Hibernate in a Spring application, the following components must be introduced.

- The `org.hibernate.SessionFactory` interface is the core component of Hibernate. An object of this type is thread-safe, shareable, and immutable. Usually, an application has a single `SessionFactory` instance, and threads servicing client requests obtain `Session` instances from this factory. Once a `SessionFactory` instance is created, its internal state is set. This internal state includes all the metadata about *object relational mapping*.

- The `org.hibernate.Session` interface is the hibernate component representing a single functional unit, and it is the main runtime interface between a Java application and Hibernate. The session is a stateful object that manages persistent objects within the functional unit. It acts as a transactional-scoped cache, operations executed in a session are cached, and the changes are persisted to the datasource when the transaction is committed. A `Session` object can be obtained by calling `sessionFactory.getCurrentSession()`.

- `org.springframework.orm.hibernate5.HibernateTransactionManager`: this class is an implementation of `PlatformTransactionManager` for a single `SessionFactory`. Spring 5 currently contains one hibernate package for Hibernate 5[29], and it is expected a package for Hibernate 6 will be added when this version will be released. In this package there is a

---

[28]Hibernate OGM provides Java Persistence (JPA) support for NoSQL solutions. It reuses Hibernate ORM's engine but persists entities into a NoSQL datastore instead of a relational database. Read more about it on the official site: `http://hibernate.org/ogm/`.

[29]Support for Hibernate 3 & 4 has been dropped completely in Spring 5.

class implementing the `PlatformTransactionManager` interface named `HibernateTransactionManager`. To support transactions using Hibernate a bean of this type must be present in the Spring Application context.

```
package com.apress.cems.hib.config;

import org.springframework.orm.hibernate5.
HibernateTransactionManager;
import org.springframework.transaction.PlatformTransactionManager;
...
@Bean
public PlatformTransactionManager transactionManager()  {
    return new HibernateTransactionManager(sessionFactory());
}
```

- `org.springframework.orm.hibernate5.LocalSessionFactoryBuilder`: this is a utility class that can create a `SessionFactory` bean. The session factory bean requires as parameters the datasource used by the application, the package where the entity classes can be found, and the hibernate properties.

```
package com.apress.cems.hib.config;

import org.hibernate.SessionFactory;

import org.springframework.orm.hibernate5.
LocalSessionFactoryBuilder;
...

@Configuration
@PropertySource({"classpath:db/db.properties"})
public class HibernateDbConfig {

    @Value("${db.dialect}")
    private String dialect;
    @Value("${db.hbm2ddl}")
    private String hbm2ddl;
```

```java
@Bean
public static PropertySourcesPlaceholderConfigurer
                        propertySourcesPlaceholder
                        Configurer() {
  return new PropertySourcesPlaceholderConfigurer();
}

  @Bean
  public SessionFactory sessionFactory() {
    return new LocalSessionFactoryBuilder(dataSource())
            .scanPackages("com.apress.cems.dao")
            .addProperties(hibernateProperties())
            .buildSessionFactory();
}

@Bean
public Properties hibernateProperties() {
    Properties hibernateProp = new Properties();
    hibernateProp.put("hibernate.dialect", dialect);
    hibernateProp.put("hibernate.hbm2ddl.auto", hbm2ddl);

    hibernateProp.put("hibernate.format_sql", true);
    hibernateProp.put("hibernate.use_sql_comments", true);
    hibernateProp.put("hibernate.show_sql", false);
    return hibernateProp;
}
}
```

The LocalSessionFactoryBuilder class was introduced in Spring 3.1.
It is used with Hibernate 4 instead of the org.springframework.orm.
hibernate3.annotation.AnnotationSessionFactoryBean class used
with Hibernate 3 and was part of the org.springframework.orm.
hibernate4 package. Another redesign and package change happened
with Hibernate 5. Currently, a single version exists in Spring 5—the one
for Hibernate 5. If you are curious, an XML sample configuration for
Hibernate 3 using the deprecated class is depicted in the following
code snippet.

```xml
<bean id="sessionFactory"
    class="org.springframework.orm.hibernate3.annotation.
                            AnnotationSessionFactoryBean">
        <property name="dataSource" ref="dataSource"/>
        <property name="annotatedClasses">
            <list>
                <value>com.apress.cems.dao.Person</value>
                <value>com.apress.cems.dao.Detective
                </value>
                <value>com.apress.cems.dao.Storage
                </value>
                <!-- other entity classes -->
            </list>
        </property>
        <property name="hibernateProperties">
            <value>
                hibernate.format_sql=true
                hibernate.show_sql=true
            </value>
        </property>
</bean>
```

The "com.apress.cems.dao" is the package in which the entity
classes reside. They represent the metadata that Hibernate needs
so it can map them to database objects. XML configuration of entity
classes and Hibernate were used in previous versions, though
not that much nowadays. In the previous code sample, the class
AnnotationSessionFactoryBean does not have a scanPackages
property, so the entities must be listed in the XML configuration
file as values in a list that is used as argument to set the
annotatedClasses property. The new approach is more practical,
since it removes the necessity of modifying the XML Spring
configuration file when a new entity class is added to the project.

The `hibernateProperties` is a `java.util.Properties` bean that contains specific Hibernate properties. The most useful are listed next.

- `hibernate.dialect`: the value is a dialect class matching the database used in the application (e.g., `org.hibernate.dialect.H2Dialect`).

- `hibernate.hbm2ddl.auto`: the value represents what Hibernate should do when the application starts: update the database to apply changes done in the metadata, re-create the database altogether or do nothing. Possible values: `none` (default value), `create-only`, `drop`, `create`, `create-drop`, `validate`, `update`. This is very practical with embedded test databases, because the developer can focus on the code instead of setting up the test database. If `create-drop` is used, Hibernate will scan all the entities and generate tables and relationships among them according to the specific annotations placed on their fields. The database is destroyed when the application context is destroyed. **So, never, ever use this setting on production!!** Another good practice is to save those values in a properties file, which is exactly what the previous example depicts.

- `hibernate.format_sql`: if true, and the next property is true also, the generated SQL statements are printed to the console in a pretty and readable way.

- `hibernate.show_sql`: if true, all the generated SQL statements are printed to the console.

- `hibernate.use_sql_comments`: if true, Hibernate will put a comment inside the SQL statement to tell the developer what that statement is trying to do.

- Because Hibernate is an advanced tool designed to be used with
  advanced datasource settings, it is time to introduce connection
  pooling. For this section, HikariCP was chosen to create the dataSource
  bean. HikariCP is open source, small, and practical, since only one
  library needs to be added to the project, and it is said to be the fastest
  connection pool in the Java universe.[30] To add the library to the project, it
  must be included in the compile section of the Gradle configuration file.
  The following are configuration sections from the root build.gradle file
  and from the child project chapter05/hibernate build.gradle.

```
// pivotal-certified-pro-spring-dev-exam-02/build..gradle
ext {
        hikariVersion = '3.3.1'
        ...

    misc = [
            hikari    : "com.zaxxer:HikariCP:$hikariVersion",
          ...
    ]
}
// chapter05/hibernate/build.gradle
ext.moduleName = 'com.apress.cems.hib'

dependencies {
    compile project(':chapter04:aop')
    compile spring.jdbc, spring.orm, misc.hikari
    compile hibernate.ehcache, hibernate.em, hibernate.core,
    hibernate.validator
    testCompile testing.api, testing.platformRunner, testing.
    mockito, spring.test
    testImplementation testing.api
    testRuntime testing.engine, testing.platformRunner
}
...
```

---

[30]You can read more about the project on their GitHub page https://github.com/
brettwooldridge/HikariCP.

The database used is still H2, since we want to keep this code stand-alone and running out of the box without needing to install other software.

```
package com.apress.cems.hib.config;

import com.zaxxer.hikari.HikariConfig;
import com.zaxxer.hikari.HikariDataSource;
...
@Configuration
@PropertySource({"classpath:db/db.properties"})
public class HibernateDbConfig {

  @Bean
    public DataSource dataSource() {
        try {
            HikariConfig hikariConfig = new HikariConfig();
            hikariConfig.setDriverClassName(driverClassName);
            hikariConfig.setJdbcUrl(url);
            hikariConfig.setUsername(username);
            hikariConfig.setPassword(password);

            hikariConfig.setMaximumPoolSize(5);
            hikariConfig.setConnectionTestQuery("SELECT 1");
            hikariConfig.setPoolName("hamsterPool");
            return new HikariDataSource(hikariConfig);
        } catch (Exception e) {
            return null;
        }
    }
}
```

The SessionFactory bean is then injected into repositories and creates objects of types implementing org.hibernate.query.Query<R>, which are executed and the result is returned. But more about that after entity classes are covered a little to keep things clear.

Hibernate supports all JPA 2.x annotations in the `javax.persistence.*` package and extends this package to provide behavior not supported by JPA and to perform specific enhancements. The metadata for Hibernate is made of annotations placed on classes, fields, and methods that define how those objects should be treated, what restrictions they have, and so on. The most important annotation is the `@Entity` annotation, which is part of the `javax.persistence.*` and marks classes as templates for domain objects, also called entities. Every entity class must have a unique identifier, also known as a *primary key*. That field is marked with `@Id`.

CC   Classes annotated with `@Entity` are mapped to database tables matching the class name, unless specified otherwise using the `@Table` annotation. Also, be careful with table names; always use uppercase letters to avoid problems.

All the entity classes used in this book have been grouped under the `com.apress.cems.dao` package, which you can find in project `chapter00/dao`. All entity classes used in the book have a few columns in common, which have been grouped under a class named `AbstractEntity`, which is abstract. It is annotated with `@MappedSuperclass` to let Hibernate know that this class is a template for other entity classes.

An architectural decision was made to group all infrastructure-related fields in this class, including the primary key field marked with `@Id` and `@GeneratedValue`, which allow autogeneration of the value; the `LocalDate` fields that are modified when the object is edited; and the `@Version` annotated field that ensures integrity when one is performing the merge operation and for optimistic concurrency control. An entity class can have only one field annotated with `@Version`. This class is depicted in the following code snippet.

```
package com.apress.cems.dao;

import java.io.Serializable;
import java.text.SimpleDateFormat;
import java.time.LocalDate;
import javax.validation.constraints.NotNull;

import javax.persistence.*;
import org.springframework.format.annotation.DateTimeFormat;

@MappedSuperclass
public abstract class AbstractEntity implements Serializable {
```

```
    @Id
    @GeneratedValue(strategy = GenerationType.AUTO)
    @Column(updatable = false)
    protected Long id;

    @Version
    protected int version;

    @NotNull
    @Column(name = "created_at", nullable = false)
    @DateTimeFormat(pattern = "yyyy-MM-dd")
    protected LocalDate createdAt;

    @NotNull
    @Column(name = "modified_at", nullable = false)
    @DateTimeFormat(pattern = "yyyy-MM-dd")
    protected LocalDate modifiedAt;

    ...// setters & getters & other utility methods
}
```

Aside from the fields inherited from AbstractEntity each entity class declares its own fields.

```
 package com.apress.cems.dao;

import javax.persistence.Column;
import javax.persistence.Entity;
 ...
@Entity
public class Person extends AbstractEntity {
    @Column(nullable = false, unique = true)
    private String username;

    @Column(nullable = false)
    @DateTimeFormat(pattern = "yyyy-MM-dd")
    private LocalDate hiringDate;
...
}
```

Entity class members are annotated to specify purpose, column name (if different from the field name), validation rules, relationships with other entities, and many more that you will discover later in the chapter.

By default, all class members are treated as persistent unless annotated with `@Transient`.

The `@Column` annotation is not necessary unless the database column name is required to be different from the field name or restrictions need to be applied for the value of the field (for example, `unique`, `nullable`, `insertable`, `updatable`, `length`, `precision`, or `scale`). Restrictions for the value of the field can also be specified by using validation annotations like `@Size`, `@NotNull`, and so forth.

The `@Id` annotation marks the field as the unique identifier for this entity type and matches the primary-key of the database table. `@Entity` and `@Id` are mandatory for a domain class.

The `@Version` annotation marks a version field or property of an entity class that serves as its optimistic lock value. The version ensures integrity when performing the merge operation and for optimistic concurrency control. To make sure that a record is handled correctly in a transactional and distributed environment, this field is mandatory.

The previously mentioned annotations can be placed on getters as well. This makes the code a little difficult to read, but from a performance and design perspective, using annotations on getters is a better idea than member variables, because it avoids reflection.

`FIELD` is the access type for entity class members annotated with persistence-specific annotations in the previous example. The values are populated by Hibernate using reflection. Even when JPA annotations are placed on fields, using setters and getter to populate entity fields can be forced by using the `@Access` annotation from package `javax.persistence`, but this is not recommended, since it might interfere with other components (for example, listeners and AOP advice).

Relationships between tables are defined by fields annotated with `@OneToMany`, `@ManyToOne`, `@ManyToMany`, `@OneToOne`, and they match the database-equivalent relationship definitions. We are making use of inheritance to avoid writing duplicated code by making all entity classes to extend the `AbstractEntity` class.

In the following code snippet, the `Detective` entity is depicted with most of its fields and annotations. The table that Hibernate will create in the database will be named `DETECTIVE`.

The @OneToMany annotation defines a foreign key in the TRACK_ENTRY table linking detectives with all their activity while on the job and can have attributes defined that specify the behavior of the child entities. In the next code snippet, nothing is defined, because no data should be ever deleted in a criminal management system. But assuming that deleting data should be allowed, using @OneToMany(mappedBy = "detective", cascade = {CascadeType.REMOVE}) would ensure that when a detective record is deleted, its child items in the CRIMINAL_CASE table will be deleted too.

```
package com.apress.cems.dao;

import com.apress.cems.util.CaseStatus;
import com.apress.cems.util.CaseType;
import javax.validation.constraints.NotNull;
import javax.validation.constraints.NotEmpty;

import javax.persistence.*;
import java.util.HashSet;
import java.util.Set;

 @Entity
public class Detective extends AbstractEntity {

    @NotNull
    @OneToOne
    @JoinColumn(name = "PERSON_ID")
    private Person person;

    @NotEmpty
    @Column(unique = true, nullable = false)
    private String badgeNumber;

    @Enumerated(EnumType.STRING)
    private Rank rank;

    private Boolean armed = false;

    @Enumerated(EnumType.STRING)
    private EmploymentStatus status = EmploymentStatus.ACTIVE;
```

```
@ManyToMany
@JoinTable(
        name="working_detective_case",
        joinColumns=@JoinColumn(name="detective_id",
        referencedColumnName="id"),
        inverseJoinColumns=@JoinColumn(name="case_id",
        referencedColumnName="id"))
private Set<CriminalCase> criminalCases;

@OneToMany(mappedBy = "detective")
private Set<TrackEntry> trackEntries;
    ...
}
```

In the `Detective` entity class, the `@OneToOne` links a detective record and a person record and makes sure that when a `Detective` instance is created, the `Person` field is populated with details from the associated record from the database. The `Person` class does not declare a `@OneToOne` relationship to `@Detective` because the relationship is not bi-directional in this case, because from a logical point of view a detective is always a person, but a person is not always a detective.

The `@ManyToMany` annotation is used on collection fields that will be populated with children records from the other side of a relationship declared using an internal table. A detective can work on multiple cases and a case can be worked on by many detectives. Used in combination with the `@JoinTable` annotation on the detective side, we can configure a collection field to be populated with all the cases associated with that detective.[31]

In the `TrackEntry` entity class, the `@ManyToOne` part of the relationship with the `Detective` is declared, and it defines an exact name of the foreign key column using the `@JoinColumn` annotation. The foreign key field will be populated with a reference to the `Detective` entity that is a parent of this domain object. In JPA, the entity declaring the `@OneToMany` relationship is usually called a parent entity, and the one declaring the `@ManyToOne` is called a *child* entity.

---

[31]Since explaining database relationships and JPA is not a topic of this book, if you want a quick tutorial on how many-to-many relationships are configured correctly with Hibernate, take a look at this small repository I created `https://github.com/iuliana/many-to-many`

```
 package com.apress.cems.dao;

import org.hibernate.validator.constraints.NotEmpty;
import javax.persistence.JoinColumn;
import javax.persistence.ManyToOne;
...
@Entity
@Table(name="TRACK_ENTRY")
public class TrackEntry extends AbstractEntity{
...

    @ManyToOne
    @JoinColumn(name = "detective_fk", nullable = false)
    private Detective detective;
}
```

Session and Hibernate Querying

Entities are manipulated by Hibernate `Session` instances that provide methods for search, persist, update, delete. This instance is also in charge of managing transactions and is a good replacement for JPA's `EntityManager`. The current session is obtained from the `SessionFactory` bean by calling

```
sessionFactory.getCurrentSession();
```

The queries for these operations are written in Hibernate Query Language, which allows a more practical way of writing the SQL queries. HQL queries operate on domain objects and are transformed under the hood into matching SQL queries.

Retrieving an object when we know its ID is easy to do with Hibernate, for example. (Hibernate does not use `Optional` yet, but I'm sure it's coming in the next version.)

```
@Override
public Optional<Person> findById(Long entityId) {
    Person person = session().get(Person.class, entityId);
    return person == null? Optional.empty() :Optional.of(person);
}
```

And if we want to see the SQL native query generated by Hibernate, all we must do is look in the log with the two hibernate SQL-specific parameters show_sql and format_sql set to true for the SessionFactory bean.

```
select
        person0_.id as id1_3_0_,
        person0_.created_at as created_2_3_0_,
        person0_.modified_at as modified3_3_0_,
        person0_.version as version4_3_0_,
        person0_.firstName as firstNam5_3_0_,
        person0_.hiringDate as hiringDa6_3_0_,
        person0_.lastName as lastName7_3_0_,
        person0_.password as password8_3_0_,
        person0_.username as username9_3_0_
    from
        Person person0_
    where
        person0_.id=?
Hibernate:
    select
        person0_.id as id1_3_0_,
        person0_.created_at as created_2_3_0_,
        person0_.modified_at as modified3_3_0_,
        person0_.version as version4_3_0_,
        person0_.firstName as firstNam5_3_0_,
        person0_.hiringDate as hiringDa6_3_0_,
        person0_.lastName as lastName7_3_0_,
        person0_.password as password8_3_0_,
        person0_.username as username9_3_0_
    from
        Person person0_
    where
        person0_.id=?
```

HQL supports placeholders and named parameters in queries written by the developer and can return single results or collections and does not need a mapping object. Remember the `RowMapper<T>`? No need for it with Hibernate. This is what ORM is good at. Based on the metadata represented by the annotations in the entity classes, Hibernate can easily transform database records into Java objects and vice versa under the hood. In the following code snippet, you can see a few different HQL queries.

```
//null is returned when no record matches the criterion
Person person = (Person) session()
                .createQuery("from Person p where p.username= ?")
                .setParameter(0, username)
                .uniqueResult();

//the equivalent of the previous query with named parameter
Person person = (Person) session()
                .createQuery("from Person p where p.username= :un")
                .setParameter("un", username).uniqueResult();

//an empty list is returned when no record matches the criterion
List<Person> persons = session().createQuery("FROM Person").list();

//null is returned when no record matches the criterion
Person person = (Person) session()
    .createQuery("from Person p where p.firstName=?1 and p.lastName=?2")
    .setParameter(1, firstName)
    .setParameter(2, lastName)
    .uniqueResult();

// update the person
Person person = session().get(Person.class, entityId);
person.setPassword(password);
session.update(person);

//save a new person in the database
 session.save(person);

// delete a person
session.delete(person);
```

To synchronize domain objects with the database, the `Session` instance provides quite a few methods. The following are the most used.

- `update(entity)` persists changes to an existing database object.

- `persist(entity)` saves a new domain object to the database. If this object has other domain objects associated with it and the association is mapped with `cascade="persist"`, the persist operation will include them as well. This method does not return a value.

- `save(entity)` saves a new domain object to the database. Before saving the object, an identifier is generated. This operation applies to associated instances if the association is mapped with `cascade="save-update"`. This method returns the generated identifier.

- `saveOrUpdate(entity)` saves a domain object to the database. If the object exists, `update` is performed; otherwise, `save` is performed and the operation applies to associated instances if the association is mapped with `cascade="save-update"`.

When Hibernate is used in the application, a repository class will use the `sessionFactory` bean to manipulate data objects. The Hibernate-specific implementation of the `PersonRepo` is depicted in the following code snippet. Notice the `sessionFactory` bean being injected and obtaining the current session.

```
package com.apress.cems.hib.repos;

import org.hibernate.Session;
import org.hibernate.SessionFactory;
import org.springframework.transaction.annotation.Transactional;
...

@Repository("hibernatePersonRepo")
public class HibernateRepo implements PersonRepo {

    private SessionFactory sessionFactory;

    public HibernateRepo(SessionFactory sessionFactory) {
        this.sessionFactory = sessionFactory;
    }
```

```
/**
 * @return the transactional session
 */
protected Session session() {
    return sessionFactory.getCurrentSession();
}

@Override
public Set<Person> findAll() {
    List persons = session().createQuery("FROM Person").list();
    return persons.isEmpty()? Set.of() : new HashSet<>(persons);
}
...
```

The UML sequence diagram when Hibernate is used with Spring is depicted in Figure 5-18.

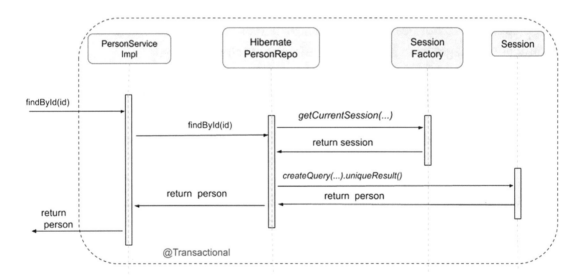

Figure 5-18. *Conceptual UML sequence diagram for operations involving a Hibernate repository class*

Aside from these methods, Hibernate supports the execution of SQL native queries with Session instances.

```
import org.hibernate.query.NativeQuery;
....
    public List<String> findAllUsernames() {
        NativeQuery<String> nq = session()
                .createNativeQuery("select USERNAME from PERSON");
        return nq.getResultList();
    }
```

Exception Mapping

When things go wrong, Hibernate throws its own exceptions, which are equivalent in meaning to the Spring data access exceptions that are already covered in a previous section. Hibernate throws runtime data access exceptions that extend HibernateException, but these exceptions can be translated to Spring exceptions using an exception translator bean. The bean does not require explicit configuration when the transaction manager bean is of HibernateTransactionManager type.

If the configuration does not contain a bean of type HibernateTransactionManager (e.g., when JpaTransactionManager backed up by a HibernateJpaVendorAdapter is used) to enable the exception translation behavior, a postprocessor bean has to be declared to look for all the exception translator beans implementing org. springframework.dao.support.PersistenceExceptionTranslator. It will advise all the repository beans (classes annotated with @Repository) so that the translators can intercept the hibernate exceptions and apply the appropriate translation. In the following code snippet, you can see the postprocessor bean and the Hibernate-specific translator bean being declared in the configuration class.

```
import org.springframework.dao.annotation.
        PersistenceExceptionTranslationPostProcessor;
import org.springframework.orm.hibernate5.
    HibernateExceptionTranslator;
...
```

```
@Bean
public PersistenceExceptionTranslationPostProcessor petpp() {
        return new PersistenceExceptionTranslationPostProcessor();
 }

@Bean
public HibernateExceptionTranslator hibernateExceptionTranslator() {
      return new HibernateExceptionTranslator();
}
```

When exception translation using the
PersistenceExceptionTranslationPostProcessor processor is not possible,
perhaps because the repository classes are part of a third-party library,
XML can define the AOP advice that does the translation using the class
PersistenceExceptionTranslationInterceptor.

```
<bean id="pExInterceptor"
 class="org.springframework.dao.support.
PersistenceExceptionTranslationInterceptor" />
...
<aop:advisor pointcut="execution(* * ..Repo+.*(..))"
      advice-ref="pExInterceptor" />
```

!   Hibernate is not a subject for the official certificate exam, but if you want to
test your understanding of it, there is a project calledchapter06/hibernate-
practice that has four TODO tasks defined, numbered from 35 to 38.

Tasks 35-37 ask you to write some missing HQL queries in the HibernateRepo
that can be tested with classes PersonRepoTest and PersonServiceTest.

Task 38 asks you to complete the HibernateDbConfig class configuration by
declaring a session factory and a transaction manager bean.

The proposed solutions can be found in project chapter06/hibernate.

When executing any of the tests, search in the console log for the words `session` and `transaction`. Note how Hibernate and Spring work together.

```
...
DEBUG o.s.b.f.s.DefaultListableBeanFactory - Creating shared instance of
singleton bean
     'sessionFactory'
DEBUG o.h.i.SessionFactoryImpl - Building session factory
DEBUG o.h.i.SessionFactoryImpl - Instantiated session factory
...
DEBUG o.s.b.f.s.DefaultListableBeanFactory - Autowiring by type from
bean name
  'hibernatePersonRepo'  via constructor to bean named 'sessionFactory'
DEBUG o.s.b.f.s.DefaultListableBeanFactory - Creating shared instance of
singleton
     bean 'transactionManager'
DEBUG o.s.o.h.HibernateTransactionManager - Using DataSource
[HikariDataSource]
    of Hibernate SessionFactory for HibernateTransactionManager
DEBUG o.s.o.h.HibernateTransactionManager - Creating new transaction
with name
   [com.apress.cems.hib.services.PersonServiceImpl.findById]:
   PROPAGATION_REQUIRED,ISOLATION_DEFAULT,readOnly
DEBUG o.s.o.h.HibernateTransactionManager - Opened new Session
     [SessionImpl(1684265526<open>)] for Hibernate transaction
DEBUG o.s.o.h.HibernateTransactionManager - Preparing JDBC Connection of
     Hibernate Session [SessionImpl(1684265526<open>)]
DEBUG o.s.j.d.DataSourceUtils - Setting JDBC Connection
[HikariProxyConnection@1246439562
    wrapping conn0: url=jdbc:h2:~/cems user=SA] read-only
DEBUG o.s.o.h.HibernateTransactionManager - Exposing Hibernate
transaction as JDBC
DEBUG o.h.SQL -
    select
        person0_.id as id1_3_0_,
        person0_.created_at as created_2_3_0_,
```

```
        person0_.modified_at as modified3_3_0_,
        person0_.version as version4_3_0_,
        person0_.firstName as firstNam5_3_0_,
        person0_.hiringDate as hiringDa6_3_0_,
        person0_.lastName as lastName7_3_0_,
        person0_.password as password8_3_0_,
        person0_.username as username9_3_0_
    from
        Person person0_
    where
        person0_.id=?
Hibernate:
    select
        person0_.id as id1_3_0_,
        person0_.created_at as created_2_3_0_,
        person0_.modified_at as modified3_3_0_,
        person0_.version as version4_3_0_,
        person0_.firstName as firstNam5_3_0_,
        person0_.hiringDate as hiringDa6_3_0_,
        person0_.lastName as lastName7_3_0_,
        person0_.password as password8_3_0_,
        person0_.username as username9_3_0_
    from
        Person person0_
    where
        person0_.id=?
...
[main] DEBUG o.s.o.h.HibernateTransactionManager - Initiating
transaction commit
[main] DEBUG o.s.o.h.HibernateTransactionManager - Committing Hibernate
transaction on Session
    [SessionImpl(1684265526<open>)]
DEBUG o.h.e.t.i.TransactionImpl - committing
DEBUG o.s.o.h.HibernateTransactionManager - Closing Hibernate Session
    [SessionImpl(1684265526<open>)] after transaction
```

Hibernate API can be used to implement data access and participate in Spring-managed transactions. It is also completely agnostic regarding the database used. It has no dependency on Spring or the entity classes and provides hooks so Spring can manage transactions in a transparent manner. Implementation and configuration location for Hibernate `sessionFactory` instances, transaction manager, and database can be swapped with other implementations without any changes required in the code. If you use the `LocalSessionFactoryBuilder` Spring class to create the `SessionFactory` bean, it will be wrapped up in a proxy that will make sure that every session opened by this bean will participate in the current transaction. When Hibernate is used, declaring transactions as `readOnly` when they do not perform write operations could lead to considerable performance optimizations, because Hibernate will skip the flushing of the session (after all, there is nothing to flush).

And now that Hibernate has been introduced, some more information about ORM is appropriate before we dive deep into JPA.

Object Relational Mapping

Object Relational Mapping, or ORM, is a method of mapping database objects to application objects and vice versa. This makes for easy handling of data objects. Aside from that, it also provides the possibility of querying the database using an object-oriented approach. Hibernate's full name is Hibernate ORM, because it implements this technique to allow querying and persisting of data objects. A data object is also called a domain object or entity. Whatever its name, this object corresponds to a database object, usually a row from a table. There are more complex objects that can be defined and can encapsulate data from multiple tables, but since this topic is irrelevant for this book, the details will be kept to a minimum. Domain objects are easy to use in the application, because they encapsulate all data related to a table row stored in accessible fields. When a row in a table becomes a domain object, the following correspondences are made.

- The primary key value is stored in an ID field. This field identifies the object in the application. In the database, the identity is a simple topic. In Java, because objects are involved, things are a little different. Two domain objects can be logically equivalent, but only one of them has the ID field set with a primary key value, so the `equals` and `hashcode` methods must be adjusted to take this aspect into consideration.

- One-to-many relationships from the database are mapped to the HAS-A relationship. The domain object has a collection of domain objects as a field. Usually this relationship is bidirectional, and each object in the collection has a field referencing the parent object. This field is mapped in the database to the foreign key column.

- Entries from the same table can be mapped to different types of domain objects in the same hierarchy using a column value as discriminator.

Using an ORM framework introduces the following benefits.

- It provides mapping of database records to application objects.

- No extra code needs to be written.

- It provides a rich object query language that is more intuitive and easier to use than native SQL.

- It speeds up development as eliminates the need for repetitive SQL code, which reduces development time and costs.

- It provides easy navigation through objects using their relationships.

- It provides persistence through reachability. Look at the following code snippet.

```java
public class Detective extends AbstractEntity {
...
@OneToMany(mappedBy = "detective",
    cascade = {CascadeType.PERSIST, CascadeType.REMOVE})
    private Set<TrackEntry> trackEntries = new HashSet<>();
}
```

The cascade attribute defines what happens with child records from the TRACK_ENTRY table, which are mapped to TrackEntry objects, when the parent domain object of type Detective is modified. If the Detective object is created with TrackEntry objects at the same time, only the Detective object must be persisted to the database. The persist operation propagates to the child domain objects because of the CascadeType.PERSIST value. If the Detective object is deleted, child domain objects are deleted as well because of CascadeType.REMOVE.

441

- It provides concurrency support: multiple processes can update the same data in parallel.

- It provides cache management per level.

  - per transaction (first-level cache): when an object is first loaded from the database, the object is stored in this cache, and subsequent requests for it will use the cache instead of going to the database.

  - per datasource (second-level cache at `SessionFactory` level): reduces trips to the database for read-heavy data and is shared by all sessions created by the `SessionFactory` bean. When a domain object is not found in the first-level cache, the next place to look is this cache. If found, the model object is also stored in the first-level cache before it is returned.

- It provides transaction management and isolation.

- It provides key management, since identifiers are automatically propagated and managed. For example: When a `Detective` object and its `TrackEntry` instances are created in the system, the entity ID (primary key) is generated and used automatically to populate the foreign key fields in the `TrackEntry` domain objects as well.

- ORM-specific code can be reused. (In the sample projects for this book, inheritance is used for domain objects, repositories, and services).

- ORM code has already been tested and is maintained by the creators of the framework; thus using an ORM reduces the effort of testing.

Aside from Hibernate, Spring supports integration with all major ORM/persistence providers such as EclipseLink, and Open JPA. ORM introduces a little lag for large amounts of data and support for complex SQL queries is limited, so in these cases, JDBC and native SQL are the better option.

Java Persistence API

The previous example, depicting a Spring repository class using `SessionFactory` directly, ties Spring with Hibernate. Java Persistence API, also called **JPA**, introduces a common interface for object relational mapping and persistence that allows the ORM framework used to be switched easily. JPA is designed for operating on domain objects defined as POJOs. It replaces previous persistence mechanisms: EJB and JDO (Java Data Objects). It was first introduced in 2006 and has overcome initial limitations to successfully provide a set of specific JPA annotations that are supported by all ORM frameworks and persistence frameworks for Java. The annotations introduced in the previous section to configure domain objects are part of the `javax.persistence` package, which contains all JPA components.

The core JPA components are as follows.

- **Persistence Context**: A context containing a set of domain objects/ entities in which for every persistent entity there is a unique entity instance.

- **Entity Manager**: An object that manages entities. It takes care of creation, update, querying, and deletion. Entity Manager classes must implement `javax.persistence.EntityManager`, and instances are associated with a persistence context by annotating them with `@PersistenceContext`. Usually, these instances' life cycles are bound to the transaction in which the method is executed, so they are managed by the container (in our case, the Spring container).

- **Entity Manager Factory**: The naming is very relevant for the purpose of such an object. Entity Manager Factory beans have the responsibility of creating application-managed Entity Manager instances. These factory classes must implement `javax. persistence.EntityManagerFactory`. They are thread-safe, shareable, and they represent a single datasource and persistence context.

- **Persistence Unit**: A group of entity classes defined by the developer to map database records to objects that are managed by an Entity Manager; basically, all classes annotated with @Entity, @MappedSuperclass, and @Embedded in an application. All entity classes must define a primary key, must have a non-arg constructor or not allowed to be final. Keys can be a single field or a combination of fields. This set of entity classes represents data contained in a single datasource. Multiple persistence units can be defined within the same application. Configuration of persistence units can be done using XML. In the official documentation, it is specified that a persistence.xml file must be defined under the META-INF directory, but if Spring and Java configuration are used, that file is no longer necessary because it is replaced by the setPackagesToScan method from the LocalContainerEntityManagerFactoryBean as you will soon see. The following code snippet depicts a persistence.xml sample file.

```
<persistence>
    <persistence-unit name="cemsPU">
        <description>This unit manages persons, detectives, cases
            evidence, storages and track entries.
        </description>
    </persistence-unit>
</persistence>
```

- **JPA Provider**: The framework providing the backend for the JPA, the one that it is actually doing the heavy lifting. The following are the most frequently used frameworks that implement JPA specifications.

  - **Hibernate** provides an implementation for EntityManager, the org.hibernate.jpa.HibernateEntityManager, but starting with Hibernate 5.2, org.hibernate.engine.spi.SessionImplementor is used, because it now extends EntityManager directly. These are internal details, since in the configuration, only the org.springframework.orm.jpa.vendor.HibernateJpaVendorAdapter class is needed.

The class is explained in more detail later in this section. Hibernate is used inside the WildFly (formerly known as JBoss) application server.

– **EclipseLink** is used inside the GlassFish application server.

– **Apache OpenJPA** is used inside WebLogic, WebSphere, and TomEE.

– **Data Nucleus** is used by the Google app engine.

Configure Spring and JPA with Hibernate Support

For the code associated with this section, which you can find under project `chapter06/emf`, Hibernate will be used as a JPA provider. The most recent version of Hibernate is production ready, compliant with JSR-338 for JPA 2 specification, and is still compatible with JPA 2.0. Modifying the application in project `chapter06/hibernate` to support JPA implies the following changes.

- The `SessionFactory` bean declaration is no longer needed, and it will be replaced by a bean declaring an Entity Manager Factory bean. The Spring-specific `LocalContainerEntityManagerFactoryBean` class will be used for this.

```
package com.apress.cems.emf;

import javax.persistence.EntityManagerFactory;
import org.springframework.orm.jpa.
LocalContainerEntityManagerFactoryBean;
import org.springframework.orm.jpa.vendor.
HibernateJpaVendorAdapter;
...
@Configuration
@EnableTransactionManagement
public class JpaDbConfig {

@Bean
    public EntityManagerFactory entityManagerFactory(){
        LocalContainerEntityManagerFactoryBean factoryBean =
                new LocalContainerEntityManagerFactoryBean();
        factoryBean.setPackagesToScan("com.apress.cems.dao");
```

```
        factoryBean.setDataSource(dataSource());
        factoryBean.setJpaVendorAdapter(new
        HibernateJpaVendorAdapter());
        factoryBean.setJpaProperties(hibernateProperties());
        factoryBean.afterPropertiesSet();
        return factoryBean.getNativeEntityManagerFactory();
    }
...
}
```

In the preceding method, `LocalContainerEntityManager`
`FactoryBean` is created by explicit instantiation, and is
not created by Spring. So `afterPropertiesSet()`, which
initializes the factory object must be called explicitly.
The `LocalContainerEntityManagerFactoryBean` object
creates an `EntityManagerFactory` bean as returned by
the `PersistenceProvider` implementation; in this case,
`org.hibernate.jpa.HibernatePersistenceProvider`.
The `EntityManagerFactory` instance created by the
factory bean is retrieved by calling `factoryBean.`
`getNativeEntityManagerFactory()`. The
`HibernatePersistenceProvider` is not visible in the preceding
configuration. The only link to the persistence technology
used under the hood is `HibernateJpaVendorAdapter`. The
`HibernateJpaVendorAdapter` exposes Hibernate's persistence
provider and `EntityManager` extension interface. The locations
where the persistence metadata can be found are set by the
`setPackagesToScan(...)` method, and the datasource bean is
required as well to properly create an `EntityManagerFactory`.

- `HibernateTransactionManager` is replaced by a bean of type
  `JpaTransactionManager` that uses the `EntityManagerFactory`
  implementation to associate Entity Manager operations with
  transactions.

```
package com.apress.cems.emf;

import org.springframework.orm.jpa.JpaTransactionManager;
...
@Configuration
@EnableTransactionManagement
public class JpaDbConfig {

    @Bean
    public PlatformTransactionManager transactionManager()  {
        return new JpaTransactionManager(entityManagerFactory());
    }

...
}
```

- The repository classes will be modified to use an instance of type
  EntityManager mapped to the application persistence context. The
  annotation @PersistenceContext expresses a dependency on a
  container- managed EntityManager and its associated persistence
  context.[32] This field does not need to be autowired, since the
  @PersistenceContext annotation is picked up by an infrastructure
  Spring bean postprocessor bean of type org.springframework.
  orm.jpa.support.PersistenceAnnotationBeanPostProcessor
  class that makes sure to create and inject an EntityManager
  instance. To create this instance, the backend ORM is used; in this
  case, Hibernate 5.x, so the entityManager bean type implements
  the org.hibernate.engine.spi.SessionImplementor interface.
  This interface is internal. You will not notice it unless you are
  looking for it. All that is visible is the type of factory bean that creates
  it, which is org.hibernate.internal.SessionFactoryImpl.

---

[32]The *EntityManager* instance annotated with *@PersistenceContext* cannot be accessed from
a constructor, since it cannot be created and associated with the persistence context in the
constructor. The reason for this is the definition of the *@PersistenceContext*. This annotation has
the following meta-annotation defined: *@Target(value=TYPE,METHOD,FIELD)*. Full JavaDoc
API here: http://docs.oracle.com/javaee/7/api/javax/persistence/PersistenceContext.
html.

```
package com.apress.cems.emf.repos;

import javax.persistence.EntityManager;
import javax.persistence.PersistenceContext;
...
@Repository
public class JpaPersonRepo implements PersonRepo {

    private EntityManager entityManager;

    @PersistenceContext
    void setEntityManager(EntityManager entityManager) {
        this.entityManager = entityManager;
    }
    ...
}
```

In Figure 5-19, the execution of a test was paused in debug mode to depict the type of entity manager being injected into the repository class.

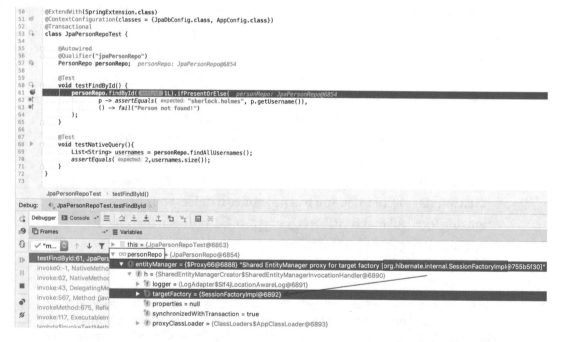

Figure 5-19. *JpaPersonRepoTest.testFindById() execution paused in debug mode to show the type of the entityManager bean that was injected into the JpaPersonRepo class*

The methods of the repository need to be modified to use the `entityManager` bean. The most interesting part of the `EntityManager` API is depicted in Table 5-1.

Table 5-1. *EntityManager JPA Methods*

Method	Action	Comment
<T> T find(Class<T> cl, Object pk);	Find an entity by its primary key	Equivalent to *select from table t where t.pk= PK_VAL*
Query createQuery(String ql);	Create a JPQLquery	Returns a collection if *getResultList()* is called on the JPQL Query object. Returns a single object if *getSingleResult()* is called on the JPQL Query object.
Query createNamedQuery (String name)	Create a JPQL query from a named query in the metadata	Returns a collection if *getResultList()* is called on the JPQL Query object. Returns a single object if *getSingleResult()* is called on the JPQL Query object.
void persist(Object obj)	Adds the entity to the persistence context.	Equivalent to *insert into table...*
<T> T merge(T entity);	Merge the state of the given entity into the current persistence context.	Equivalent to *update table t... where t.pk=PK_VAL*
void flush()	Persist persistence context contents to the database immediately.	Use carefully, because this operation can be used the write all changes to the database before the transaction is committed.
void refresh(Object entity)	Reload a state for an entity from the database.	Changes in the persistence context are discarded, so use carefully.
void remove(Object entity)	Removes the entity from the persistence context.	Equivalent to *delete from table t where t.pk=PK_VAL*

JPQL is an acronym for Java Persistence Query Language.

Comparing with the pure Hibernate implementation with Spring, only the declaration of the transaction manager is changed, the `sessionFactory` bean is replaced with `entityManagerFactory`. The datasource declaration does not change, and the hibernate properties are still needed, since Hibernate is still the backing ORM framework. Also, transactions are still needed, so `@EnableTransactionManagement` remains as well.

Figure 5-20 is a conceptual UML sequence diagram of when JPA searches a person by its ID.

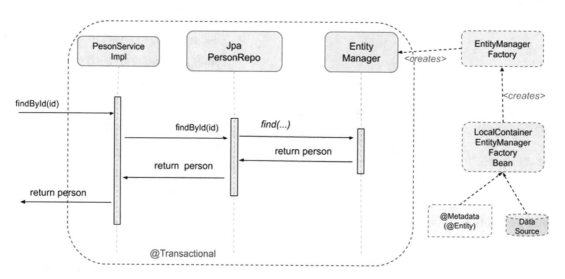

Figure 5-20. *Conceptual UML sequence diagram when Spring is used with JPA*

JPA Querying

The simplest operation with JPA is querying an object by its ID. There is no need to write a query, since `EntityManager` provides a method for this. It returns null when an entity cannot be found. The returned object's type is provided to this method as an argument. There is no need for casting, since under the hood, generics are used, as with pure Hibernate.

```
@Override
public Optional<Person> findById(Long entityId) {
        Person person = entityManager.find(Person.class, entityId);
        return person == null? Optional.empty() :Optional.of(person);
}
```

450

JPQL stands for JPA query language. It writes domain object queries in a manner similar to HQL.

```
@Override
public Optional<Person> findByCompleteName(String firstName, String
lastName) {
        Person person = (Person) entityManager
            .createQuery("from Person p where p.firstName=?1 and
            p.lastName=?2")
            .setParameter(1, firstName)
            .setParameter(2, lastName)
            .getSingleResult();
        return person == null? Optional.empty() :Optional.of(person);
}
```

Named parameters are supported too.

```
@Override
public Optional<Person> findByCompleteName(String firstName, String
lastName) {
    Person person = (Person) entityManager
            .createQuery("from Person p where p.firstName=:fn and
            p.lastName=:ln")
            .setParameter("fn", firstName)
            .setParameter("ln", lastName)
            .getSingleResult();
        return person == null? Optional.empty() :Optional.of(person);
}
```

Named queries are part of the metadata, and are defined with the annotation @NamedQuery, which must be placed on the entity class that the query manages.

The preceding example could be simplified by declaring a named query. The @NamedQueries annotation groups multiple queries together. In the next example, the Person.FIND_BY_LAST_NAME query is included to show how @NamedQueries are used and how a named query can have indexed parameters.

```
//Person.java
package com.apress.cems.dao;

import javax.persistence.NamedQuery;
import javax.persistence.NamedQueries;
...
@Entity
@NamedQueries({
        @NamedQuery(name = Person.FIND_BY_COMPLETE_NAME,
                query = "from Person p where p.firstName=:fn and
                p.lastName=:ln"),
        @NamedQuery(name = Person.FIND_BY_LAST_NAME,
                query = "from Person p where p.lastName= ?1")
})
public class Person extends AbstractEntity {
    public static final String FIND_BY_COMPLETE_NAME =
"findByCompleteName";
    public static final String FIND_BY_LAST_NAME = "findAllByLastName";

    ...// entity fields and methods
}

//JpaPersonRepo.java
package com.apress.cems.emf.repo
...

@Repository("jpaPersonRepo")
public class JpaPersonRepo implements PersonRepo {

@Override
    public Optional<Person> findByCompleteName(String firstName, String
lastName) {
        Person person = (Person) entityManager
                .createNamedQuery(Person.FIND_BY_COMPLETE_NAME)
                .setParameter("fn", firstName)
                .setParameter("ln", lastName)
                .getSingleResult();
```

```
        return person == null? Optional.empty() :Optional.of(person);
    }
  ...
}
```

Named queries support named parameters (e.g. Person.FIND_BY_COMPLETE_NAME), which is the recommended way of writing all queries, because it makes them more readable and prevents errors caused by mistaken parameter indexes.

JPA provides another method for querying entities: by using *criteria queries*. They are a part of the JPA API for creating dynamic queries whose exact structure is only known at runtime. It was introduced in JPA 2. Although it might look complicated, it is useful for dynamic queries. For a simple query like the one implemented in the following code snippet, which only searches for users having a common last name, it looks impractical.

```
import javax.persistence.criteria.*;
...
  @Override
    public List<Person> findAllByLastName(String username) {
        //create the query
        CriteriaBuilder builder= entityManager.getCriteriaBuilder();
        CriteriaQuery<Person> query = builder.createQuery(Person.class);
        Root<Person> personRoot = query.from(Person.class);
        ParameterExpression<String> value = builder.parameter(String.class);
        query.select(personRoot).where(
            builder.equal(personRoot.get("lastName"), value));

        // execute the query
        TypedQuery<Person> tquery = entityManager.createQuery(query);
        tquery.setParameter(value,lastName);
        return tquery.getResultList();
    }
```

JPA also supports the execution of SQL native queries by using the Query createNativeQuery(String sqlString) method, although when not using managed objects, for more control and efficiency, JdbcTemplate is more appropriate.

```
import javax.persistence.Query;
...
@Override
public List<String> findAllUsernames() {
        Query nq = entityManager.createNativeQuery(
            "select USERNAME from PERSON");
        return (List<String>) nq.getResultList();
}
```

Persistence operations that fail throw JPA-specific exceptions. But the Spring exception translator bean takes care of translating these types of exceptions into Spring Data Access as well, thus actually hiding the persistence provider.

Advanced JPA, JTA, JNDI

When JTA and XML configuration are used in a project, the persistence.xml file must be changed to include the datasource and the persistence unit declaration.

```
<persistence>
    <persistence-unit name="cemsPU">
        <description>This unit manages persons, detectives, cases
            evidence, storages and track entries.
        </description>
        <jta-data-source>dataSource</jta-data-source>
        <provider>org.hibernate.jpa.HibernatePersistenceProvider</provider>
        <properties>
                <property name="hibernate.dialect"
          value="org.h2.Driver"/>
          <!-- hibernate properties here -->
        </properties>
    </persistence-unit>
</persistence>
```

When JTA is used and the EntityManagerFactory is provided by an application server, such as JBoss or WebSphere, it can be retrieved using a JNDI lookup.

```
<jee:jndi-lookup id="entityManagerFactory" jndi-name="persistence/
petSitterEMF" />
```

454

! If you want to test your understanding of working with Spring and JPA backed up by Hibernate, take a look at chapter05/emf-practice. It contains only three TODOs, numbered from 39 to 41.

Task 39 is located in the JpaDbConfig class and asks you to declare and configure the entity manager factory and the transaction manager beans.

Task 40 is located in the JpaPersonRepo class and asks you to annotate the setter for the EntityManager instance correctly so the tests in JpaPersonRepoTest and PersonServiceTest can be executed and they pass.

Task 41 is located in the JpaPersonRepo class and asks you to replace the implementation of the findByCompleteName(..) method with a query using named parameters.

As a bonus task, you can enrich the PersonServiceImpl class with new methods that will be tested by the PersonServiceTest class.

Spring Data JPA

Spring Data is a Spring project designed to help defining repository classes in a more practical way. Repository classes have a lot of common functionality, so the Spring team tried to provide the possibility to offer this functionality out of the box. The solution was to introduce abstract repositories that can also be customized by the developer to reduce the boilerplate code required for data access. To use Spring Data components in a JPA project, a dependency on the package spring-data-jpa must be introduced.

The central interface of Spring Data is Repository<T,ID extends Serializable>. The full hierarchy can be seen in Figure 5-21.

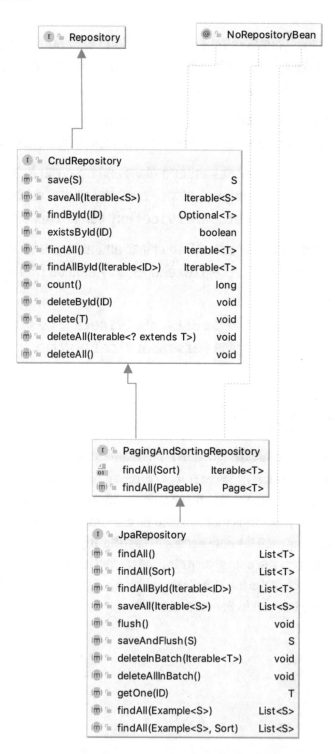

Figure 5-21. *Spring Data JPA Repository hierarchy*

The `NoRepositoryBean` annotation is used to exclude repository interfaces from being picked up, and repository instances are not created for them.

Typically, a repository interface defined by a developer will extend one of the interfaces in the `Repository<T,ID extends Serializable>` hierarchy and a set of methods to manipulate entities will be ready to use. These types of beans are referred to as *instant repositories* because Spring picks up these types of interfaces and implements them at runtime to create the beans. Thus, the types and the beans are created instantly.

In the next code snippet, the `Repository<T,ID extends Serializable>` interface is extended directly.

```
package com.apress.cems.dj.sandbox.repos;

import com.apress.cems.dao.Person;
import org.springframework.data.repository.Repository;

import java.util.List;
import java.util.Optional;

public interface PersonRepo extends Repository<Person, Long> {
    Optional<Person> findById(Long id);

    List<Person> findAll();

    void save(Person person);
}
```

If all that is needed is to extend the `Repository<T,ID extends Serializable>` interface, but you do not like the idea of extending a Spring component, you can avoid that by annotating your repository class with `@RepositoryDefinition`. This will have the same effect as extending the `Repository` interface, since this interface is empty. Since there is no longer the option of using generics to set the type of entity and ID managed, annotation attributes are used. A simple example is depicted next.

```
package com.apress.cems.dj.sandbox.repos;

import com.apress.cems.dao.Detective;
import org.springframework.data.repository.RepositoryDefinition;

import java.util.List;
import java.util.Optional;
```

```
@RepositoryDefinition(domainClass = Detective.class, idClass = Long.class)
public interface DetectiveRepo {
    Optional<Detective> findById(Long id);

    List<Detective> findAll();

    void save(Detective detective);
}
```

The `CrudRepository<T, ID extends Serializable>` is the interfaces that exposes all basic operations for an entity type, even the name makes the purpose obvious. CRUD is an acronym for create, read, update, and delete. When creating your own repository sometimes extending this interface is enough. But, for more advanced operations you might want to go further in the hierarchy, which brings us to the `PagingAndSortingRepository<T, ID extends Serializable>` interfaces that support entity pagination. This interface exposes a special version of the `findAll(..)` method that receives as a parameter an instance of type `Pageable` that is used for pagination information. Extending the interface does not require writing much code, since this is how instant repositories are designed to be used. Right?

```
package com.apress.cems.dj.sandbox.repos;

import com.apress.cems.dao.Storage;
import org.springframework.data.repository.PagingAndSortingRepository;

public interface StorageRepo extends
    PagingAndSortingRepository<Storage, Long> {
}
```

The following code snippet, slices the content of the PERSON table in slices of twos. And the `findAll(..)` can call any of the pages. It's a test method for pagination functionality. As you can probably imagine, the paging functionality is very useful for web applications and REST services.

```
package com.apress.cems.dj.sandbox;

import org.springframework.data.domain.PageRequest;
import org.springframework.test.context.ContextConfiguration;
```

```
@ExtendWith(SpringExtension.class)
@ContextConfiguration(classes = {JpaConfig.class, AppConfig.class})
@Transactional
class StorageRepoTest {
    private Logger logger = LoggerFactory.getLogger(StorageRepoTest.class);

    @Autowired
    StorageRepo storageRepo;

    @Test
    void testFindAllPaginated(){
        int pageNo = 3;
        int pageSize = 2;

        Page<Storage> page = storageRepo.findAll(PageRequest.of(pageNo,
        pageSize));

        assertAll(
                () -> assertEquals(6, page.getTotalPages()),
                () -> assertEquals(12, page.getTotalElements()),
                () -> assertEquals(3, page.getNumber()),
                () -> assertEquals(2, page.getNumberOfElements())
        );

        page.getContent().forEach(s -> logger.info("Storage: {}", s));
    }
}
```

PageRequest implements Pageable. In the previous code sample, it is used to describe the size of a slice (pageSize) of Person records and the number of the slice (pageNo) to be returned by the findAll(..) method. The Page<T> type represents a sublist of objects, that has access to some properties of the full list, such as, number of slices and total number of objects within the list. As a developer you can do a lot of things with this pagination feature, including making sure that you do not take too long to load a web page or kill the browser while doing that. I remember a time when I had to write code to implement pagination from scratch, and it was painful.

Since the project for this section is JPA specific, the repositories used from now on will extend the JpaRepository<T, ID extends Serializable> interface, which is at the top of the hierarchy, and expose a bigger set of methods, sparing the developer quite a lot of work. When a custom repository interface extends JpaRepository, it will automatically be enriched with functionality to save entities, search them by ID, retrieve all of them from the database, delete entities, flush, and so forth. (In Figure 5-21, all the methods are listed.)

Usually, repository classes must perform custom and more complex queries that are not covered by the default methods provided by a Spring Data repository. In this case, the developer must define its own methods for Spring to implement when the repository instance is created. To tell Spring what those methods should do, the @Query annotation is used to annotate them. Inside that annotation should be a query definition that is executed at runtime and the results returned. In the following code snippet, you can see what the PersonRepo component looks like when Spring Data JPA is used.

```java
package com.apress.cems.dj.repos;

import com.apress.cems.dao.Person;
import org.springframework.data.jpa.repository.JpaRepository;
import org.springframework.data.jpa.repository.Query;
import org.springframework.data.repository.query.Param;

import java.util.Optional;

public interface PersonRepo extends JpaRepository<Person, Long> {

    @Query("select p from Person p where p.username like %?1%")
    Optional<Person> findByUsername(String username);

    @Query("select p from Person p where p.firstName=:fn and p.lastName=:ln")
    Optional<Person> findByCompleteName(@Param("fn")String fn,
        @Param("ln")String lastName);
}
```

Every Repository interface must be linked to the type of domain object it handles and the type of the primary key, which is why in the preceding example, the PersonRepo interface extends JpaRepository<Person, Long>. So PersonRepo will manage Person domain objects with a Long primary key value.

For every instant repository, Spring creates a proxy object that is a fully functioning repository bean. Any additional functionality that is not provided is easily implemented by defining a method skeleton and providing the desired functionality using annotations. You can also create your own interfaces and compose them with Spring repository interfaces to develop customized repositories.

When creating a custom implementation for a Spring Data repository, any Spring Data repository interfaces are referred to as *fragments* and the interfaces created by the developer to expose new functionality are named *custom interfaces*. For Spring to recognize the resulting repository as a Spring Data Repository and treat it as such, there are a few implementation rules. In Figure 5-22, the interface in red is the customized Spring Data JPA Repository and the implementation is provided by the only class in the image.

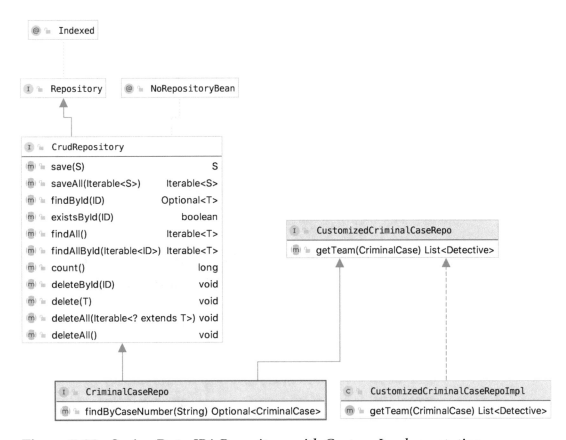

Figure 5-22. *Spring Data JPA Repository with Custom Implementation*

To create a Spring Data JPA Repository with custom implementation the following implementation steps must be taken.

1. Create the customized interface, which exposes the methods representing the custom behavior. In the next code snippet, we declare a special repository method that gathers up all detective assigned to a criminal case.

```
package com.apress.cems.dj.sandbox.repos.cc;

public interface CustomizedCriminalCaseRepo {

    List<Detective> getTeam(CriminalCase criminalCase);
}
```

2. Implement the customized interface to add the customized behavior, and make sure the class name is named as the interface with the Impl suffix. This is important because this is the class Spring will look for to pick up the custom methods.[33]

```
package com.apress.cems.dj.sandbox.repos.cc;
...

public class CustomizedCriminalCaseRepoImpl
        implements CustomizedCriminalCaseRepo {

    private JdbcTemplate jdbcTemplate;

    public CustomizedCriminalCaseRepoImpl(DataSource dataSource) {
        this.jdbcTemplate = new JdbcTemplate(dataSource);
    }

    @Override
    public List<Detective> getTeam(CriminalCase criminalCase) {
        List<Detective> detectiveList = new ArrayList<>();
        detectiveList.add(criminalCase.getLeadInvestigator());
```

---

[33]The implementation is not really optimal and absolutely unnecessary, but bear with it for the sake of the example.

```
        List<Detective> team = jdbcTemplate.query("select d.ID,
        d.BADGENUMBER," +
                " d.RANK, d.ARMED, d.STATUS,d.PERSON_ID, " +
                " p.USERNAME, p.FIRSTNAME, p.LASTNAME,
                p.HIRINGDATE " +
                " from DETECTIVE d, PERSON p, WORKING_DETECTIVE_
                CASE wdc" +
                " where d.PERSON_ID=p.ID" +
                " and d.ID = wdc.DETECTIVE_ID " +
                " and wdc.CASE_ID =?", rowMapper, criminalCase.
                getId());
        if (team != null && !team.isEmpty()) {
            detectiveList.addAll(team);
        }
        return detectiveList;
    }
    private RowMapper<Detective> rowMapper = (rs, i) -> {...};
}
```

The implementation is not Spring Data specific; it can be made of anything. In the previous example an instance of JdbcTemplate was used to execute an SQL native query. Standard dependency injection was used to access the dataSource bean.

3. Write a customized interface that exposes the customized behavior that connects them all. This is the interface outlined in red in Figure 5-22; it extends a Spring Data JPA interface and the customized interface.

```
package com.apress.cems.dj.sandbox.repos.cc;

import com.apress.cems.dao.CriminalCase;
import org.springframework.data.jpa.repository.Query;
import org.springframework.data.repository.CrudRepository;
import org.springframework.data.repository.query.Param;

import java.util.Optional;
```

```
public interface CriminalCaseRepo extends
CrudRepository<CriminalCase, Long>,
                        CustomizedCriminalCaseRepo {

    @Query("select c from CriminalCase c where c.number=:no")
    Optional<CriminalCase> findByCaseNumber(@Param("no") String
    number);

}
```

The CriminalCaseRepo interface is treated as a Spring Data instant repository, and the proxy created at runtime contains the behavior declared in the CustomizedCriminalCaseRepoImpl class.

Custom implementations are not limited to a single interface. Repositories may be composed of multiple custom implementations that are imported in the order of their declaration. They have precedence over Spring Data interfaces, which means customized interfaces can override Spring Data behavior. Also, the same custom interface can be shared among multiple custom implementations, further reducing boilerplate when writing data access code.

To tell Spring that it must create repository instances, a new configuration component must be introduced. The @EnableJpaRepositories tells Spring that it must create repository instances. As an attribute, the base package where the custom repository interfaces have been declared must be provided. In the following code snippet, you can see the most important beans involved in the Spring JPA configuration.

```
package com.apress.cems.dj.config;

import org.springframework.data.jpa.repository.config.
EnableJpaRepositories;
...

@Configuration
@EnableJpaRepositories(basePackages = {"com.apress.cems.dj.repos"})
@EnableTransactionManagement
public class ServiceConfig {

    @Autowired
    DataSource dataSource;
```

```
@Autowired
Properties hibernateProperties;

@Bean
public LocalContainerEntityManagerFactoryBean entityManagerFactory(){
    LocalContainerEntityManagerFactoryBean factoryBean = n
            ew LocalContainerEntityManagerFactoryBean();
    factoryBean.setDataSource(dataSource);
    factoryBean.setPackagesToScan("com.apress.cems.dao");

    JpaVendorAdapter vendorAdapter = new HibernateJpaVendorAdapter();
    factoryBean.setJpaVendorAdapter(vendorAdapter);
    factoryBean.setJpaProperties(hibernateProperties);
    return factoryBean;
}

@Bean
public PlatformTransactionManager transactionManager(EntityManagerFacto
ry emf){
    return new JpaTransactionManager(emf);
}

@Bean
public PersistenceExceptionTranslationPostProcessor
exceptionTranslation(){
    return new PersistenceExceptionTranslationPostProcessor();
}
}
```

The configuration is not different from the JPA backed up by Hibernate, which is used as a persistence tool in this case too.

Because this way of creating repositories is fast and practical, it is currently the preferred way to implement JPA in the Spring application. As this book was written, the current version of the `spring-data-jpa` module was `2.2.0.BUILD-SNAPSHOT`. This module is part of the Spring Data family [34], a project designed to make the creation of

---

[34]Project official page: `https://spring.io/projects/spring-data`

repository components as practical as possible, regardless of the datasource used. In the following section, you will be introduced to Spring Data MongoDB, the library that provides utilities to integrate Spring with the NoSQL database called MongoDB.

!   Before starting the next section, you can play with Spring Data JPA in the `chapter05/data-jpa-practice` project. There is a bonus TODO task numbered with 42, located in the `PersonRepo` Java file, that challenges you to turn that interface into a Spring Data JPA repository so the tests in `PersonServiceTest` class will pass.

Spring Boot JPA

Spring Boot makes everything easier, even writing a Spring application with a transactional context and persistence. In the previous section, we created a Spring JPA application using Spring Data JPA, which made writing the DAO logic very easy. Still, we had to declare a lot of infrastructure beans to use all the benefits. Spring Boot gets rid of that too. By using the `spring-boot-starter-data-jpa` dependency, infrastructure beans don't have to be declared anymore, unless you need to customize the configuration. The hassle of declaring a lot of dependencies for the project is removed as well, as this module declares as dependencies a curated set of libraries that can be used to build a Spring JPA application, as seen in Figure 5-23.

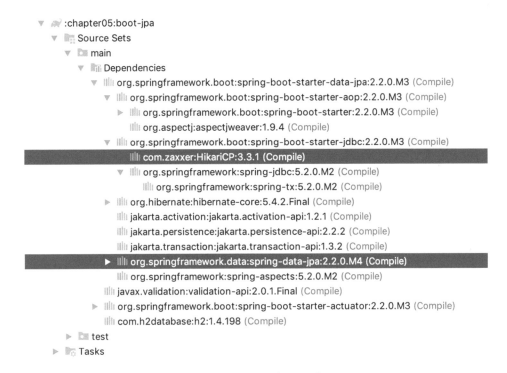

Figure 5-23. *Spring Boot Data JPA Starter dependencies*

All that is needed is to add minimal configuration in the `application.properties` or `application.yml`. Let's take it one by one.

- We need a database, H2 in this case, because we want to keep things simple. We add H2 to the classpath, and then configure the database connection details in the `application.yml`.

```
spring:
  datasource:
    driver-class-name: org.h2.Driver
    url: jdbc:h2:mem:db;DB_CLOSE_DELAY=-1
    username: sa
    password:
```

What else? We want a connection pooling mechanism. In the previous section, we used HikariCP. With Spring Boot 2.x, we do not have to add it as a dependency because it is declared as a transitive dependency for the `spring-boot-starter-data-jpa` module. So the previous configuration must be changed a little.

```
spring:
  datasource:
    hikari:
      driver-class-name: org.h2.Driver
      jdbc-url: jdbc:h2:mem:testdb
      username: sa
      password:
      maximum-pool-size: 5
      connection-test-query: "SELECT 1"
      pool-name: cemsPool
```

- To make things easy, we want to generate the tables based on our entities. So, somehow the value for the `hibernate.hbm2ddl.auto` property must be changed to `create-drop`. We can find out what properties are suitable to do that from the official documentation.[35]

  ```
  spring:
    jpa:
      generate-ddl: true
      hibernate:
        ddl-auto: create-drop
  ```

And that is it. The repositories, service classes are identical to the ones created in the previous section. What is extra in a Spring Boot application is the `Application` class.

```
package com.apress.cems.boot;

import org.slf4j.Logger;
import org.slf4j.LoggerFactory;
import org.springframework.boot.SpringApplication;
import org.springframework.boot.autoconfigure.SpringBootApplication;
import org.springframework.context.ConfigurableApplicationContext;

@SpringBootApplication
public class Application {
```

---

[35]Spring Boot property list: https://docs.spring.io/spring-boot/docs/current/reference/html/common-application-properties.html

```
    private static Logger logger = LoggerFactory.getLogger(Application.class);

    public static void main(String... args) {
        ConfigurableApplicationContext ctx =
            SpringApplication.run(Application.class, args);
        ctx.registerShutdownHook();
        logger.info("Application Started ...");
    }
}
```

Because the spring-boot-starter-data-jpa module is on the classpath, we do not need to add @EnableJpaRepositories or @EnableTransactionManagement on a configuration class. Spring assumes that if this module is used as a dependency, JPA repositories and transactional behavior is required.

What else is left to do? Well, write a Spring Boot test class by using the @SpringBootTest annotation introduced in Chapter 3 and test our PersonServiceImpl to make sure that the Spring Boot JPA application was configured correctly.

```
package com.apress.cems.boot;

import com.apress.cems.boot.services.PersonService;
import com.apress.cems.boot.dao.Person;
import org.junit.jupiter.api.Test;
import org.springframework.beans.factory.annotation.Autowired;
import org.springframework.boot.test.context.SpringBootTest;

import java.time.LocalDate;

import static org.junit.jupiter.api.Assertions.*;

@SpringBootTest
public class ApplicationTest {

    @Autowired
    private PersonService personService;
```

```java
@Test
void testFindById() {
    personService.findById(1L).ifPresentOrElse(
            p -> assertEquals("sherlock.holmes", p.getUsername()),
            () -> fail("Person not found!")
    );
}

@Test
void testfindByCompleteName() {
    personService.findByCompleteName("Sherlock", "Holmes")
            .ifPresent(person ->
                assertEquals("sherlock.holmes", person.getUsername())
    );
}

@Test
void testFindAll() {
    assertNotNull(personService.findAll());
}
}
```

And that's all there is really. If you want to further customize the application, you either add more values for special out-of-the-box Spring Boot properties, or add your own configuration classes. If you are curious about the code, the project in chapter05/boot-jpa makes it pretty clear. Let's see what else is there when it comes to data access.

**Spring and MongoDB

This is a bonus section, and information covered here does not appear in the official exam. But since NoSQL databases are getting used more and more, it was considered appropriate at least to scratch the surface. The NoSQL databases are a product of more and more content being generated and the need to manage it. If you are not familiar with the term Web 2.0, well this is the name given to websites that are based on user-generated content, like Facebook and Reddit. User content is messy and unstructured and relational databases are not good at storing and managing it. Relational databases are robust, designed to store objects and connections between them in a very structured manner, which requires a lot of resourced(think about how Oracle maintains relationships between tables, indexes and views, a lot of disk space and memory is needed for that), and when they get big, they become very slow. Also, since the content is not structured, and the effort to normalize it to be stored in a relational database can become cumbersome and very costly in resources. NoSQL databases provide a mechanism for storage and retrieval of data that is modeled in means other than the tabular relations used in relational databases. Also, many NoSQL databases prioritize availability and speed and make a compromise on consistency.

A more appropriate solution would be to have a database that does not require perfectly structured data, that is cloud friendly and scalable. And thus NoSQL databases were born to support storage and fast access of such amounts of poorly organized, complex, and unpredictable content, also referred to as Big Data. There are currently over 225 NoSQL databases,[36] and depending on their internal organization, they can be categorized as follows.

- **Key-values stores**: A hash table is used with a unique key and a pointer to a particular item of data (e.g., Amazon SimpleDB, Redis). It is the simplest to implement, but it is inefficient when only part of a value must be queried or updated.

- **Column family stores**: Data is organized in columns, keys are still used, but they point to a column family. They were created to store and process very large amounts of data distributed over many machines (e.g., HBase, Cassandra).

- **Document databases**: Similar to key-values stores, but the model is based on versioned documents of collections of key-value pairs. The semistructured documents are stored in formats like JSON. This type of database supports efficient querying (e.g., MongoDB, CouchDB).

- **Graph databases**: To store the data, a flexible graph model is used that can scale across multiple machines (Infinite Graph, Neo4jJ).

---

[36]You can read about them here: `http://nosql-database.org/`.

For the code in this section, MongoDB Community edition[37] was used, because it is lightweight and easy to install on any operating system. The following steps were taken to set up the project 09-ps-mongo-sample.

1. The first step is to install it on your system. Instructions to install on any operating system can be found on their official site at https://docs.mongodb.com/manual/administration/install-community/.

2. The next step is to start MongoDB. On every operating system there is an executable that can do this, but you first need to create a directory where the database files will be saved. In the next case the directory is /home/temp/mongo-db/. The database service will be started on the 27017 port.

```
iuliana.cosmina@home ~ -  $ ./mongod --dbpath /home/temp/mongo-db/
CONTROL  (initandlisten) MongoDB starting : pid=89126 port=27017
        dbpath=/Users/iuliana.cosmina/temp/mongo-db/ 64-bit host=home
CONTROL  (initandlisten) db version v4.0.10
NETWORK  (initandlisten) waiting for connections on port 27017
```

3. Open the mongo shell and test what database is used by executing the db command. The retuned result should be test.

```
iuliana.cosmina@home ~ -  $ mongo
MongoDB shell version v4.0.10
connecting to: mongodb://127.0.0.1:27017/?gssapiServiceName=mongodb
Implicit session: session { "id" : UUID("ca939241-351c-41d9-aab7-
bea8a88317fe") }
MongoDB server version: 4.0.10
Welcome to the MongoDB shell.
For interactive help, type "help".
2019-07-08T01:20:24.802+0100 I CONTROL (initandlisten) ** WARNING:
    soft rlimits too low. Number of files is 256, should be at
    least 1000
```

---

[37]Official site here: https://www.mongodb.com/community.

```
> db
test
>
```

For the purpose of the code sample in this section, there is no need to create a new database, so default database named `test` will do.

4. Create a domain object class that will be mapped to a MongoDB object. You will notice some resemblance when writing code to work MongoDB. Spring is nothing else but consistent, but there are some differences. The class must have an identification field that will be annotated with the Spring Data special annotation @ Id from the package `org.springframework.data.annotation`. Instances of this type will become entries in a collection named the same as the class but lowercased: `person`. The class will be annotated with the @Document annotation from the `org.springframework.data.mongodb.core.mapping` package to mark the instances of this class as domain objects to be persisted to MongoDB. The `Person` instances will be persisted to MongoDB into a collection and the name of this collection can be inferred from the class name or can be explicitly set by using the `collection` attribute.

```
package com.apress.cems.mongo.dao;

import org.springframework.data.annotation.Id;
import org.springframework.data.mongodb.core.mapping.Document;

import java.math.BigInteger;
import java.time.LocalDate;

@Document(collection="person")
public class Person {

    @Id
    private BigInteger id;
    private String username;
    private String password;
```

473

```
        private String firstName;
        private String lastName;
        private LocalDate hiringDate;
        private LocalDate createdAt;
        private LocalDate modifiedAt;

        public Person() {
            createdAt = LocalDate.now();
            modifiedAt = LocalDate.now();
        }

        ... //   setters and getter

        @Override
        public String toString() {
            return "Person{" +
                    "id=" + id +
                    ", username='" + username + '\" +
                    ", firstName='" + firstName + '\" +
                    ", lastName='" + lastName + '\" +
                    '}';
        }
    }
}
```

5. Create a new PersonRepo interface that will extend the Spring
    Data MongoDB-specialized interface

```
package com.apress.cems.mongo.repos;

import com.apress.cems.mongo.dao.Person;
import org.springframework.data.mongodb.repository.
MongoRepository;
import org.springframework.data.mongodb.repository.Query;

import java.util.List;

public interface PersonRepo
                extends MongoRepository<Person, BigInteger> {
```

```
    @Query("{'lastName': { '$regex' : ?0 } }")
    List<Person> findByLastName(String lastName);

    @Query("{ 'username' :   ?0 }")
    Person findByUsername(String username);
}
```

Every MongoRepository interface must be linked to the type of object it handles and the type of unique identifier, which is why in the preceding example, the PersonRepo interface extends MongoRepository<Person, Long>. The personRepo bean manages Person instances with a BigInteger unique identifier.

The @Query annotation is the MongoDB version of the org. springframework.data.mongodb.repository.Query and declares MongoDB queries associated with repository methods.

6. Create a configuration class and annotate it with @EnableMongoRepositories to enable support for MongoDB repository instances. This annotation is similar in functionality to @EnableJpaRepositories, and needs for the package(s) where the Mongo repository interface is declared to be provided as a value for its basePackages attribute. The MongoDB connection details are injected in the configuration class from a properties file that needs to contain at least the database name, the host, and the port where MongoDB is running.

```
#mongo.properties
db.name=test
db.host=127.0.0.1
db.port=27017
```

The previous file contains details specific to a local, typical installation. The configuration class is depicted next.

```
package com.apress.cems.mongo.config;

import com.mongodb.MongoClient;
import org.springframework.data.mongodb.MongoDbFactory;
```

```
import org.springframework.data.mongodb.core.MongoTemplate;
import org.springframework.data.mongodb.core.SimpleMongoDbFactory;
import
  org.springframework.data.mongodb.repository.config.
EnableMongoRepositories;

@Configuration
@EnableMongoRepositories(basePackages = "com.apress.cems.mongo.
repos")
@ComponentScan(basePackages = { "com.apress.cems.mongo.services"})
@PropertySource("classpath:mongo.properties")
public class AppConfig {

    @Value("${db.name}")
    private String dbName;

    @Value("${db.host}")
    private String host;

    @Value("${db.port}")
    private Integer port;

    @Bean
    public MongoDbFactory mongoDb() {
        return new SimpleMongoDbFactory(new MongoClient(host,
        port), dbName);
    }

    @Bean
    public MongoTemplate mongoTemplate() {
        return new MongoTemplate(mongoDb());
    }
}
```

Under the hood, the mongoTemplate bean is used by the repository
instances to manipulate data in the person collection. It can also
be used directly.

7. Just for the fun of it, we create a service class named
PersonServicesImpl that calls a few methods of the PersonRepo
class. There is no need to depict the service class, because aside
from the package name, the code is pretty much the same as the one
managing Person instances for the Spring Data JPA section. If you are
not convinced, the code for this section is available in the chapter05/
mongo-simple project in the GitHub repository for this book.

8. Create a test class to test the PersonServicesImpl class.

```
package com.apress.cems.mongo;

import com.apress.cems.mongo.config.AppConfig;
import com.apress.cems.mongo.dao.Person;
import com.apress.cems.mongo.services.PersonService;
import org.junit.jupiter.api.BeforeEach;
import org.junit.jupiter.api.Test;
import org.junit.jupiter.api.extension.ExtendWith;
import org.springframework.beans.factory.annotation.Autowired;
import org.springframework.test.context.ContextConfiguration;
import org.springframework.test.context.junit.jupiter.
SpringExtension;

import java.util.List;

import static org.junit.jupiter.api.Assertions.assertEquals;
import static org.junit.jupiter.api.Assertions.assertNotNull;

@ExtendWith(SpringExtension.class)
@ContextConfiguration(classes = { AppConfig.class})
class PersonServiceTest {

    @Autowired
    PersonService personService;

    @BeforeEach
    void setUp(){
        assertNotNull(personService);
        init();
    }
```

```
        @AfterEach
        void tearDown(){
            personService.deleteAll();
        }

        @Test
        void testFindByLastName(){
            List<Person> persons = personService.findByLastName("Holmes");
            assertEquals(1, persons.size());
        }

        @Test
        void testFindByUsername(){
            Person person = personService.findByUsername("sherlock.
            holmes");
            assertNotNull(person);
            logger.info("Sherlock {}" , person);
        }

        @Test
        void testFindAll() {
            List<Person> persons = personService.findAll();
            assertEquals(2, persons.size());
        }

         void init() {
            Person person = new Person();
            ...
            personService.save(person);

            person = new Person();
            person.setUsername("jackson.brodie");
            ...
            personService.save(person);
        }
    }
```

The PersonServiceTest class is annotated with @Disabled in this book's code. You must comment this annotation to enable the test class, and you can run it only after you start your local MongoDB instance.

The init(..) method, that is not fully depicted here, creates two Person instances and saves them to the database. This method is executed before every test method is run because it is called from the method annotated with @BeforeEach. The method annotated with @AfterEach deleted the contents of the database so that tests do not hinder each other.

If you want to see the records saved in the database, comment the @AfterEach annotation for a run and then, the mongo shell can inspect the contents of the person collection using the db.person.find() function. The contents of the collection are formatted in JSON form. For a pretty print, use db.person.find().pretty().

```
> db.person.find().pretty()
{
    "_id" : ObjectId("5d228fef12d193b78f10bab2"),
    "username" : "sherlock.holmes",
    "password" : "dudu",
    "firstName" : "Sherlock",
    "lastName" : "Holmes",
    "hiringDate" : ISODate("2019-07-07T23:00:00Z"),
    "createdAt" : ISODate("2019-07-07T23:00:00Z"),
    "modifiedAt" : ISODate("2019-07-07T23:00:00Z"),
    "_class" : "com.apress.cems.mongo.dao.Person"
}
{
    "_id" : ObjectId("5d228fef12d193b78f10bab3"),
    "username" : "jackson.brodie",
    "password" : "bagy",
    "firstName" : "Jackson",
    "lastName" : "Brodie",
    "hiringDate" : ISODate("2019-07-07T23:00:00Z"),
    "createdAt" : ISODate("2019-07-07T23:00:00Z"),
    "modifiedAt" : ISODate("2019-07-07T23:00:00Z"),
    "_class" : "com.apress.cems.mongo.dao.Person"
}
```

Since transactions are supported in MongoDB version 4.0 there is an implementation of Spring's `PlatformTransactionManager` was added for MongoDB, only things get a little complicated. In MongoDB transactions are supported over something called a *replica set*. A *replica set* in MongoDB is a group of `mongod` processes that maintain the same data set. A replica set can be used locally on a single machine, but it is designed to be used across multiple machines connected in a network, something specific to a production environment.

The central class when using MongoDB with transactions is the `MongoTransactionManager` that provides Spring transaction support. This class is part of the `spring-data-mongodb` module.[38] Under the hood, the `MongoTransactionManager` binds a `ClientSession` to the thread. The `MongoTemplate` detects the session and operates on these resources which are associated with the transaction accordingly. The `MongoTemplate` can also participate in other ongoing transactions. Anyway, let get this show on the road, shall we?

To get transactions with MongoDB in a Spring Application, we must make the following changes.

1. We have to start MongoDB database and declare a replica set. A directory to store database file is still needed. In this case, the directory is ~/temp/db-01. The replica set is named rs0. The following command starts the database with a replica set named "rs0". Notice that the `mongod` executable is used.

   ```
   ./mongod --port 27017 --dbpath ~/temp/db-01 --replSet rs0
   ```

2. The next step is to initialize the replica set by running the following command using the mongo shell. Notice that the `mongo` executable is used.

   ```
   ./mongo --eval "rs.initiate()"
   ```

3. Check that everything is alright by looking in the console in which you executed the `mongod` process. You should see something similar to the log entries depicted next (but not as nicely formatted).

---

[38]Javadoc API here: `https://docs.spring.io/spring-data/mongodb/docs/current/api/org/springframework/data/mongodb/MongoTransactionManager.html`

```
2019-07-08T23:23:49.850+0100 I REPL  [replexec-0] New replica set
config in use:
        {
                _id: "rs0",
                version: 1,
                protocolVersion: 1,
                writeConcernMajorityJournalDefault: true,
                members: [ {
                        _id: 0,
                        host: "127.0.0.1:27017",
                        arbiterOnly: false,
                        buildIndexes: true,
                        hidden: false,
                        priority: 1.0,
                        tags: {},
                        slaveDelay: 0,
                        votes: 1
                } ],
                settings: {
                        chainingAllowed: true,
                        heartbeatIntervalMillis: 2000,
                        heartbeatTimeoutSecs: 10,
                        electionTimeoutMillis: 10000,
                        catchUpTimeoutMillis: -1,
                        catchUpTakeoverDelayMillis: 30000,
                        getLastErrorModes: {},
                        getLastErrorDefaults: { w: 1, wtimeout: 0 }, r
                        eplicaSetId: ObjectId('5d23a1c86a65b91682ded4e2')
                }
        }
2019-07-08T23:23:49.850+0100 I REPL  [replexec-0] This node is
127.0.0.1:27017 in the config
```

4. We need a new configuration class. To make things simple
    Spring provides a class to extend to reduce the boiler-plate code
    named `AbstractMongoConfiguration`. This class declares two
    abstract methods `mongoClient()` and `getDatabaseName()` that
    need to be implemented to provide access to the MongoDB
    database. The database name is a text value that has to be
    returned by `getDatabaseName()`, but the client must be told
    that the connections will be made across a replica set and a
    special URL creates it. The `MongoClient` instance is created
    by the `mongoClient()` method. Aside from that a bean of
    `MongoTransactionManager` type must be declared and the class
    must be annotated with `@EnableTransactionManagement`.

The `MongoTransactionManager` bean is backed up by a
bean of type `MongoDbFactory`, which was created under
the hood by Spring. A bean of this type is declared in the
`AbstractMongoConfiguration` class.

```
package com.apress.cems.mongo.config;

import com.mongodb.MongoClient;
import com.mongodb.MongoClientURI;
import org.springframework.beans.factory.annotation.Value;
import org.springframework.context.annotation.Bean;
import org.springframework.context.annotation.ComponentScan;
import org.springframework.context.annotation.Configuration;
import org.springframework.context.annotation.PropertySource;
import org.springframework.data.mongodb.MongoDbFactory;
import org.springframework.data.mongodb.MongoTransactionManager;
import org.springframework.data.mongodb.config.
AbstractMongoConfiguration;

import org.springframework.data.mongodb.repository.config.
EnableMongoRepositories;
import org.springframework.transaction.PlatformTransactionManager;
import org.springframework.transaction.annotation.
EnableTransactionManagement;
```

```
@Configuration
@EnableTransactionManagement
@EnableMongoRepositories(basePackages = "com.apress.cems.mongo.
repos")
@ComponentScan(basePackages = { "com.apress.cems.mongo.services"})
@PropertySource("classpath:mongo.properties")
public class AppConfig extends AbstractMongoConfiguration {

    @Value("${db.name}")
    private String dbName;

    @Value("${db.host}")
    private String host;

    @Value("${db.port}")
    private Integer port;

    @Bean
    PlatformTransactionManager transactionManager
                (MongoDbFactory dbFactory) {
        return new MongoTransactionManager(dbFactory);
    }

    @Override
    public MongoClient mongoClient() {
        return new MongoClient(new MongoClientURI(
            "mongodb://127.0.0.1:27017/?replicaSet=rs0"));
    }
    @Override
    protected String getDatabaseName() {
        return dbName;
    }
}
```

5. Now, we add @Transactional on the PersonServicesImpl and we
    run the PersonServiceTest test. And all should be fine … Only it
    isn't. We get this:

```
INFO  o.m.d.connection - Opened connection
        [connectionId{localValue:3, serverValue:4}] to
        localhost:27017
org.springframework.data.mongodb.MongoTransactionException:
    Command failed with error 263 (OperationNotSupportedInTransaction):
    'Cannot create namespace test.person in multi-document
    transaction.'
        on server localhost:27017.
The full response is {
    "operationTime" : { "$timestamp" : { "t" : 1562628367, "i" : 5
    } },
    "ok" : 0.0,
    "errmsg" : "Cannot create namespace test.person in multi-
    document transaction.",
    "code" : 263,
    "codeName" : "OperationNotSupportedInTransaction",
    "$clusterTime" : { ...};
nested exception is com.mongodb.MongoCommandException:
...
```

The message is obvious. The collection cannot be created, which
is an intended restriction. Operations that affect the database
catalog (such as creating or dropping a collection or an index)
are not allowed in multidocument transactions. For example, a
multi-document transaction cannot include an insert operation
that would result in the creation of a new collection. *See Restricted
Operations in the official documentation.* [39]

---

[39]Documentation reference: https://docs.mongodb.com/manual/core/transactions/

We need to create it manually. To do this, we use the mongo shell to execute the following.

```
db.createCollection("person", { capped : false, size : 5242880,
max : 5000 } )
```

And we try again, and this time the tests pass, because the records can be created in the existing collection. So, we're on the right track. How do we know we have transactions? Well, we look in the logs again.

```
...
DEBUG o.s.d.m.MongoTransactionManager - Creating new transaction
with name
      [com.apress.cems.mongo.services.impl.PersonServicesImpl.
      findByLastName]:
      PROPAGATION_REQUIRED,ISOLATION_DEFAULT
DEBUG o.s.d.m.MongoTransactionManager - About to start transaction
for session
      [ClientSessionImpl@858d8b4 id = {
          "id" : { "$binary" : "6pObfbblSHeOC6tsviGzyA==", "$type" :
          "04" }
      },
      causallyConsistent = true, txActive = false, txNumber = 1,
          error = d != java.lang.Boolean].
DEBUG o.s.d.m.MongoTransactionManager - Started transaction for
session
      [ClientSessionImpl@858d8b4 id = {
          "id" : { "$binary" : "6pObfbblSHeOC6tsviGzyA==", "$type" :
          "04" }
      }, causallyConsistent = true, txActive = true, txNumber = 2,
          error = d != java.lang.Boolean].
DEBUG o.s.d.m.r.q.StringBasedMongoQuery - Created query Document {
      {lastName=Document{{$regex=Holmes}}}} for Document{{}} fields.
```

```
DEBUG o.s.d.m.c.MongoTemplate - find using query:
    {"lastName" : { "$regex" : "Holmes" } } fields: Document{{}}
    for class:
        class com.apress.cems.mongo.dao.Person in collection: person
DEBUG o.s.d.m.MongoTransactionManager - Initiating transaction
commit
DEBUG o.s.d.m.MongoTransactionManager - About to commit
transaction for session
    [ClientSessionImpl@858d8b4 id = {
      "id" : { "$binary" : "6pObfbblSHeOC6tsviGzyA==", "$type" :
      "04" }
    }, causallyConsistent = true, txActive = true, txNumber = 2,
        error = d != java.lang.Boolean].
DEBUG o.s.d.m.MongoTransactionManager - About to release Session
    [ClientSessionImpl@858d8b4 id = {
        "id" : { "$binary" : "6pObfbblSHeOC6tsviGzyA==", "$type" :
        "04" } },
        causallyConsistent = true, txActive = false, txNumber = 2,
        error = d != java.lang.Boolean] after transaction.
    ...
```

Documentation about how to use MongoDB to write Spring applications can be found all over the Internet, but in case you are interested in the evolution of the spring-data-mongodb module, follow the official Spring blog and the repository at https://github.com/spring-projects/spring-data-examples.

The Spring team has set up a public GitHub repository at https://github.com/spring-projects/spring-data-book. It contains an example of a simple Spring application with most of the supported NoSQL databases. If you are curious, feel free to clone it and try the code examples.

There will be no practice section at the end of the chapter, since practice was scattered throughout the chapter after the essential sections.

Spring Boot Application with Embedded MongoDB

After writing configurations from scratch, and installing and configuring databases, here comes Spring Boot to the rescue with the `spring-boot-starter-data-mongodb` module and the possibility to specify the connection details for MongoDB using the `application.yml`. Add in the embedded MongoDB version produced by Flapdoodle[40] and there is a recipe for writing a Spring application to use MongoDb that requires minimum configuration.

The following is Spring Boot application.yml file.

```
logging:
  pattern:
    console: "%d{HH:mm:ss.SSS} [%thread] %-5level %logger{36} - %msg%n"
  level:
    root: INFO
    org.springframework: INFO
    com.apress.cems.mongo: DEBUG

spring:
  data:
    mongodb:
      host: 127.0.0.1
      port: 12345
```

The following is the Spring Boot application class with the declaration of the `MongoTransactionManager` bean.

```
package com.apress.cems.mongo;

import org.springframework.boot.SpringApplication;
import org.springframework.boot.autoconfigure.SpringBootApplication;
import org.springframework.context.annotation.Bean;
import org.springframework.data.mongodb.MongoDbFactory;
import org.springframework.data.mongodb.MongoTransactionManager;
import org.springframework.transaction.PlatformTransactionManager;
```

---

[40]GitHub page for the embedded database library: `https://github.com/flapdoodle-oss/de.flapdoodle.embed.mongo`

```java
@SpringBootApplication
public class Application {
    public static void main(String[] args) {
        SpringApplication.run(Application.class, args);
    }

    @Bean
    PlatformTransactionManager
            transactionManager(MongoDbFactory dbFactory) {
        return new MongoTransactionManager(dbFactory);
    }

}
```

The same test class, `PersonServiceTest`, can be now run as a Spring Boot test class.

```java
package com.apress.cems.mongo;
...

@SpringBootTest
class PersonServiceTest {

    private Logger logger = LoggerFactory.getLogger(PersonServiceTest.class);

    @Autowired
    PersonService personService;

    @BeforeEach
    void setUp(){
        assertNotNull(personService);
        init();
    }

    @AfterEach
    void tearDown(){
        personService.deleteAll();
    }

    @Test
    void testFindByLastName(){
```

```
        List<Person> persons = personService.findByLastName("Holmes");
        assertEquals(1, persons.size());
    }

    @Test
    void testFindByUsername(){
        Person person = personService.findByUsername("sherlock.holmes");
        assertNotNull(person);
        logger.info("Sherlock {}" , person);
    }

    @Test
    void testFindAll() {
        List<Person> persons = personService.findAll();
        assertEquals(2, persons.size());
    }
    void init() {
        logger.info(" -->> Starting database initialization...");
        Person person = new Person();
        person.setUsername("sherlock.holmes");
        person.setFirstName("Sherlock");
        person.setLastName("Holmes");
        person.setPassword("dudu");
        person.setHiringDate(LocalDate.now());
        personService.save(person);

        person = new Person();
        person.setUsername("jackson.brodie");
        person.setFirstName("Jackson");
        person.setLastName("Brodie");
        person.setPassword("bagy");
        person.setHiringDate(LocalDate.now());
        personService.save(person);
        logger.info(" -->> Database initialization finished.");

    }
}
```

And that's about it. MongoDb is cool, Spring Boot is cool, and together they can create awesome applications.

Summary

The following is a list of the core concepts and important details related to Spring Data Access.

- Spring supports data access with a layered architecture; higher layers have no knowledge about data management.

- Spring provides smart unchecked exceptions that are propagated to higher layers if untreated.

- Spring provides consistent transaction management: declarative and programmatic.

- Spring supports most popular persistence and ORM providers, which provide great support for caching, object management, automatic change detection.

- Spring can be used with Hibernate directly, without the JTA API.

- Spring can be used with the JTA API, but must be backed up by a persistence ORM provider.

- Spring Data JPA helps the developer to avoid boilerplate code when creating repository components.

- Spring Data family project also provides support for NoSQL databases.

- Transaction management can be done by Spring-specialized infrastructure beans or by a transaction manager provided by an application server.

- Databases can be defined within the Spring configuration, or they can be provided by an application server via JNDI.

- Support of NoSQL databases has matured over the years; transactions are now supported by MongoDB.

Quiz

Question 1. What is the core class of Spring JDBC? (Choose one.)

    A. `EmbeddedDatabaseBuilder`

    B. `Repository`

    C. `DataSource`

    D. `JdbcTemplate`

Question 2. What are the three `JdbcTemplate` callback interfaces that can be used with queries? (Choose three.)

    A. `RowMapper<T>`

    B. `RowCallbackHandler`

    C. `ResultSetExtractor<T>`

    D. `NamedParameterJdbcTemplate`

Question 3. What is the main interface used to provide access to a database? (Choose one.)

    A. `DataSource`

    B. `Connection`

    C. `JdbcTemplate`

    D. `NamedParameterJdbcTemplate`

Question 4. What kind of SQL statement can be executed with `JdbcTemplate`? (Choose one.)

    A. plain SQL DDL and DML statements

    B. SpEL statements

    C. All of the above

Question 5. How is a transaction defined in software development? (Choose one.)

A. A *transaction* is a group of actions that should be performed as if they were a single bulk action.

B. A transaction represents a contract between two components facilitating data exchange.

C. A transaction is an abstract concept used to describe connections to the database.

Question 6. What happens if a method annotated with @Transactional calls another method annotated with @Transactional on the same object instance? (Choose one.)

A. a transaction is created for each method

B. a single transaction is created and the methods are executed as a single unit of work

C. depends on the configuration for each @Transactional

Question 7. What does ORM stand for? (Choose one.)

A. Object Relational Mapping

B. Object Relations Management

C. Orthogonal Relations Management

Question 8. Analyze the following code snippet.

```
public Set<Person> findAll() {
    String sql = "select id, firstName, lastName, password from person";
    return new HashSet<>(jdbcTemplate.query(sql, rowMapper));
}
```

What can be said about the rowMapper object? (Choose all that apply.)

A. must implement RowMapper<T> interface.

B. Is stateful.

C. Provides a method to transform a ResultSet content into entity objects.

Question 9. When should a transaction be declared as readOnly? (Choose one.)

    A. when it does not include any writing statements execution

    B. when a large set of data is read

    C. when no changes should be allowed to the databases

Question 10. What is a Persistence Context? (Choose one.)

    A. A context containing a set of domain objects/entities in which for every persistent entity there is a unique entity instance.

    B. A Spring application context specific to applications using databases.

    C. A Spring application context specific to applications using transactions.

CHAPTER 6

Spring Web

In the previous chapters, multilayered projects were introduced. On top of the service layer is the presentation layer, or the web layer. This layer is the top layer of an application, and its main function is to translate user actions into commands that lower-level layers can understand and transform the lower-level results into user-understandable data. Web applications can be accessed with clients, such as browsers or specific applications that can correctly interpret the provided interface, such as mobile apps. So far in this book, only Spring components specific to lower-level layers have been introduced. This chapter discusses components specific to the presentation layer that makes the user interface and paves the way for implementing security.

Spring provides support for development of the web layer through frameworks like Spring Web MVC and Spring WebFlow. A typical Java web application architecture is depicted in Figure 6-1.

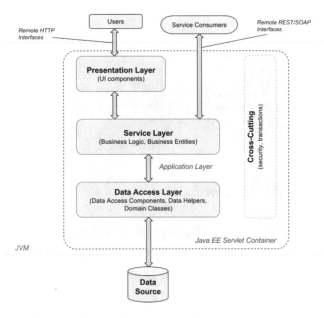

Figure 6-1. *Typical Java web application architecture*

© Iuliana Cosmina 2020
I. Cosmina, *Pivotal Certified Professional Core Spring 5 Developer Exam*,
https://doi.org/10.1007/978-1-4842-5136-2_6

More layers are possible, but web applications usually have at least three.

- **DAO**, where data mapping components (domain objects or entity classes), and repository classes to manage those components, are defined.

- **Service** (also known as **Business**), where all the classes needed to transform the user data to be passed to the DAO layer are located. The business entities are POJOs that help with this conversion. All components specific to this layer implement how data can be created, displayed, stored, and changed.

- **Presentation**, where components that implement and display the user interface and manage user interaction reside.

Spring Web MVC

Spring Web MVC is a popular request-driven framework based on the Model-View-Controller software architectural pattern, which was designed to decouple components that work together to make a fully functional user interface. A typical Model-View-Controller behavior is displayed in Figure 6-2.

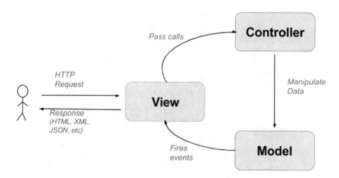

Figure 6-2. *Typical MVC behavior*

The main idea behind MVC is that there are three decoupled components; each of them can be easily swapped with a different implementation, and together they provide the desired functionality. The *view* represents the interface that the user interacts with; it displays data and passes requests to the *controller*. The *controller* calls the business components and sends the data to the *model*, which notifies the view that an actualization is needed. The *model* content is displayed by the *view*.

The central piece of Spring Web MVC is the `DispatcherServlet` class, which is the entry point for any Spring web application. It dispatches requests to handlers with configurable handler mappings, view resolution, locales, time zones, and support for uploading files. The `DispatcherServlet` converts HTTP requests into commands for controller components and manages rendered data as well; it basically acts as a front controller for the whole application. The basic idea of the front controller software design pattern, which implies that there is a centralized point for handling requests, is depicted in Figure 6-3.

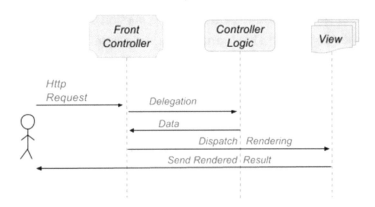

Figure 6-3. *Front controller software design pattern idea*

The Spring Web MVC provides preconfigured beans for the implementation of this behavior, and these beans are contained in two main modules.

- spring-web.jar

- spring-webmvc.jar

A standard servlet listener is used to bootstrap and shutdown the Spring application context. The application context is created and injected into the `DispatcherServlet` before any request is made, and when the application is stopped, the Spring context is closed gracefully. The Spring servlet listener class is `org.springframework.web.context.ContextLoaderListener`.

Spring Web MVC is Spring's web framework, thus Spring's typical configuration style is used and the controller components are beans. Annotation configurations were introduced in Spring 2.5, so the controller components can be declared with a

specialized stereotype annotation: `@Controller`. A Spring application can be deployed
on an application server, run on an embedded server like Jetty, or written using Spring
Boot. It can run on a myriad of embedded servers supported by it. All three flavors are
covered in this chapter.

Spring can be integrated with other frameworks.

- **Struts 2** is an open source framework for building Servlet/JSP
  from Apache based on the Model-View-Controller (MVC) design
  paradigm. More information is on the official site at `https://struts.`
  `apache.org`.

- **Wicket** is an open source Java web framework from Apache that was
  born in 2004 and is still alive and kicking; version 9.x is currently
  under development.[1] This framework was designed with simplicity
  and separation of concerns as its main purposes. More information is
  on the official site at `https://wicket.apache.org`.

- **Tapestry 5.4.4** is a component-oriented framework for creating highly
  scalable web applications in Java, also supported by Apache. More
  information is on the official site at `https://tapestry.apache.org`.

- **Spring WebFlow** is a Spring framework designed for the
  implementation of stateful flows and destined for applications that
  require navigation through sequential steps to execute a business
  task. More information is on the official site at `https://projects.`
  `spring.io/spring-webflow/`.

Spring Web MVC makes writing and running web applications as easy as writing a
simple stand-alone application. Spring provides infrastructure beans for everything that
is needed to boot up a web application. Also, Spring Boot makes it easy to create stand-
alone, production-grade, Spring-based applications by providing infrastructure beans
set up with a default general configuration. So, without further ado, let's get started.

---

[1]Details here: `https://wicket.apache.org/start/wicket-9.x.html`

Spring Web App Configuration

When a user accesses a URL, an HTTP request is sent to a web application hosted on an application server. Based on that request, inside the application context a set of actions must be performed. The result of these actions is returned and needs to be rendered using a view. In a Spring web application, all HTTP requests first reach the DispatcherServlet. Based on configuration, a handler is called, which is a method of a class called *controller*. The result is used to populate a *model* that is returned to the DispatcherServlet, which using another set of configurations, decides the *view* to be used to display the result in.

This abstract representation of this process is depicted in Figure 6-4.

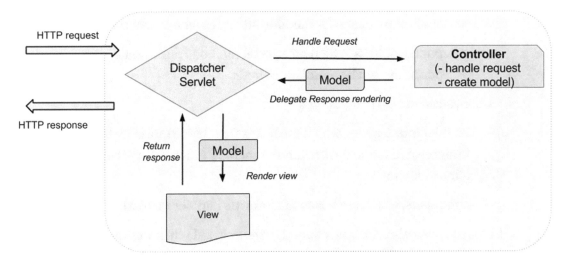

Figure 6-4. *Request processing steps in a Spring web application*

The DispatcherServlet is the entry point of the application, the heart of Spring Web MVC that coordinates all request handling operations. It is equivalent with ActionServlet from Struts and FacesServlet[2] from JEE. It delegates responsibilities to web infrastructure beans, invokes user web components, it is customizable and extensible. In a nutshell, the DispatcherServlet coordinates all request-handling

---

[2]FacesServlet is a servlet that manages the request processing lifecycle for web applications that are utilizing JavaServer Faces to construct the user interface.

operations using other infrastructure components defined in Spring and user defined components and it acts as a Front Controller, an entry point for the web application. The Spring components mentioned earlier can be categorized as follows.

- Spring MVC infrastructure components

  - handler mappings - they map requests to handler methods and a list of interceptors (e.g., to apply a theme to view and internationalization)

  - handler adapters to invoke a handler method mapped to a request

  - view resolvers to identify a view that will be rendered as response

  - personalization beans for theming and internationalization

  - exception resolvers, which are special methods that handle exceptions thrown by handler methods

- User-provided web components

  - handler interceptors, which are beans that define functionality to be applied in tandem with handler method functionality (before, after, or around)

  - controllers, which are beans that provide handler methods

The `DispatcherServlet` must be defined in the `web.xml` when the application is configured using old-style XML configuration. When using configuration without the `web.xml`, a configuration class that extends `AbstractDispatcherServletInitializer` or `AbstractAnnotationConfigDispatcherServletInitializer` must be declared. These are Spring specialized classes from the `org.springframework.web.servlet.support` package that implement `org.springframework.web.WebApplicationInitializer`. Objects of types implementing this interface are detected automatically by `SpringServletContainerInitializer`, which is bootstrapped automatically by any Servlet 3.0+ environment.

More about specialized classes used to bootstrap Spring and configure the `DispatcherServlet` is covered in this chapter.

The `DispatcherServlet` uses Spring for its configuration, so programming using interfaces is a must to allow swapping different implementations.

The `DispatcherServlet` creates a separate "servlet" application context containing all the specific web beans (controller, views, view resolvers). This context is also called the *web application context* or *DispatcherServletContext*. In Chapter 2, I said that all Spring application context classes implement `ApplicationContext`, and instances of this class provide configuration for the application. In a similar way, Spring web application context classes implement `WebApplicationContext`, which is a subinterface of `ApplicationContext`. This interface provides the configuration for a Spring web application and contains a few constants, including the typical web application scopes: `SCOPE_REQUEST`, `SCOPE_SESSION`, and `SCOPE_APPLICATION`, which were mentioned in Chapter 2.

The application context, also called *RootApplicationContext*, contains all non-web beans and is instantiated using a bean of type `org.springframework.web.context.` `ContextLoaderListener`. The relationship between the two contexts is a parent-child relationship, with the application context as the parent. Thus, beans in the web context can access the beans in the parent context, but not vice versa.[3] This separation is useful when there is more than one servlet defined for an application; for example, one that handles web requests and one that handles web services calls, because they can both inherit beans from the root application context. This situation is depicted in Figure 6-5.

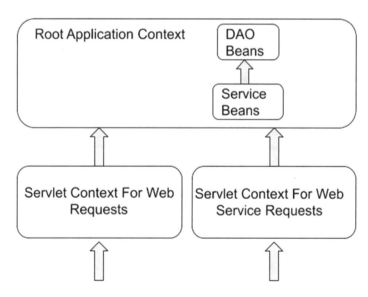

Figure 6-5. *Multiple Spring dispatcher servlets*

---

[3]This resembles classes inheritance, the subclass inherits the parent class and can access its members.

Of course, the beans in the root context can be included in the web context, but most non-trivial Spring applications require separate contexts for the web and the non-web part of the application, as usually the web part of an application is only a small part of the overall application, production applications having many concerns that lie outside the web context.

The configuration of a Spring web application integrates quite a few infrastructure beans. The `DispatcherServlet` looks for implementations of type: `HandlerMapping`, `HandlerAdapter`, `ViewResolver`, `View`, `HandlerExceptionResolver`. Out-of-the-box implementations for the interfaces are provided by Spring. The default configuration is found in `DispatcherServlet.properties`, which is in the `spring-webmvc.jar` in package `org.springframework.web.servlet`.[4]

The `DispatcherServlet` uses these infrastructure beans as depicted in the abstract diagram describing the call sequence shown in Figure 6-6. Handling mappings identify a controller method to call and handler adapters to call it.

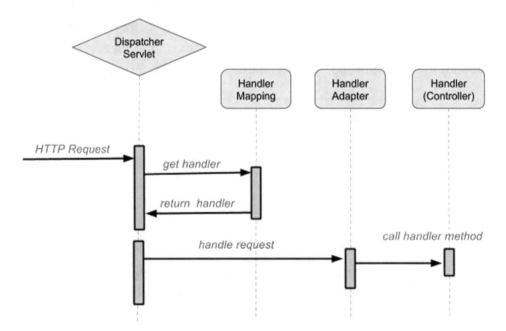

Figure 6-6. *Abstract UML diagram for handling an HTTP request*

---

[4]The contents can be accessed directly on GitHub at `https://github.com/spring-projects/ spring-framework/blob/master/spring-webmvc/src/main/resources/org/springframework/ web/servlet/DispatcherServlet.properties`

In Spring MVC versions prior to 2.5, all configurations were done using XML, and the controller classes had to extend the `org.springframework.web.servlet.mvc.` `AbstractController` Spring class. Support for annotations and the @MVC model were introduced in Spring 2.5. Configuration still relied on XML for MVC infrastructure specific beans, but controller classes no longer need to extend the Spring specialized class, as only annotating them with the stereotype annotation `@Controller` was enough for Spring to know what they are used for. Starting with Spring 3.0 Java configuration was introduced which lead to totally removing XML configuration. Almost, because the `web.xml` typical configuration file for a Java web application was still needed. Starting with Servlet 3.0, `web.xml` is no longer needed either.

The book focuses on applications configured using annotations, which is referred to as @MVC, and Java configuration for web applications, because XML is probably going to be dropped in the future. I scratch the surface of the XML configuration topic, just to give you an idea.

Quick Start

These are the usual steps taken to develop a Spring Web MVC application.

1. Develop back-end application beans (service and repository) and configuration.

2. Develop MVC functional beans, also known as *controllers* that contain methods also known as *handlers*, which handle HTTP requests.

3. Develop views used to display the results returned by handlers (common *.jsp or *.html files).

4. Declare and configure MVC infrastructure beans.

5. Configure the web application.

Controllers

Controllers are classes that define methods used to handle HTTP requests. They are annotated with the stereotype Spring annotation `@Controller`, a specialization of `@Component` which basically marks them as web beans and that are autodetected through classpath scanning. Each handler method is annotated with @RequestMapping (or variations that will be introduced in this chapter) that provides information regarding when this method should be called. In the following code snippet, a controller class is defined, containing one handler method, which is called when the user sends a request with the following URL.

```
http://localhost:8080/mvc-basic/home
```

The URL contains the following elements.

- `http` is HTML protocol definition

- `localhost` is the name/domain/IP of the machine where the application server is installed

- 8080 is the port where the application server can be accessed

- `mvc-basic` is the web application context

- `/home` is the request mapping value

! You might notice that the application context varies throughout the chapter. That is because there is more than one web application provided as example and each of the applications is focused on a specific topic. The context names match the project names and this will help you navigate more efficiently the code provided as example.

Sometimes the port might vary as well. This is because using a different port allows different applications to be run at the same time and tested in parallel to quickly draw some conclusions.

Configuring application context and ports is done using IntelliJ launchers as you will see a little bit further in the chapter.

In the following code snippet, you see a very simple controller class that handles the previous request.

```java
package com.apress.cems.web.controllers;

import org.springframework.stereotype.Controller;
import org.springframework.ui.Model;
import org.springframework.web.bind.annotation.RequestMapping;
import org.springframework.web.bind.annotation.RequestMethod;

import java.time.LocalDateTime;
import java.time.format.DateTimeFormatter;

@Controller
public class HomeController {

    @RequestMapping(value = "/home", method = RequestMethod.GET)
    public String home(Model model) {
        model.addAttribute("message", "Spring MVC JSP Example!!");
        return "home";
    }
}
```

Spring provides a way to specify the type of HTTP request on which the handler method should be called, via the `method` attribute of the `@RequestMapping` annotation.[5] The mapping rules are usually URL based, and they can contain wildcards, regular expressions and can be combined with parameters or path variables declarations.

The `@RequestMapping` can also be used at the class level on controller classes to simplify mappings at the method level when the mappings have common elements. For example, if you have many `@RequestMapping` methods with the common pattern /home, the `HomeController` class can be annotated with `@RequestMapping("/home")`, a situation depicted in the following code snippet.

```java
package com.apress.cems.web.controllers;

...
@Controller
@RequestMapping("/home")
public class HomeController {
```

---

[5]HTTP GET request is used when the user is requesting data from the application. HTTP POST and PUT are requests that send data to the application.

```
    // matches http://localhost:8080/mvc-basic/home/today
    @RequestMapping(value = "/today")
    public String today(Model model){
        LocalDateTime today = LocalDateTime.now();
        DateTimeFormatter formatter = DateTimeFormatter.ofPattern
        ("dd MMM uuuu");
        model.addAttribute("today", today.format(formatter));
        return "home/today";
    }

     // matches http://localhost:8080/mvc-basic/home/hello?name=Bub
    @RequestMapping(value = "/hello")
    public String hello(@RequestParam("name") String name, Model model){
        model.addAttribute("name", name);
        return "home/hello";
    }
}
```

CC   Notice that the HTTP GET method was not specified explicitly in the
@RequestMapping annotation declaration applied to the today() method. This
is because when no HTTP method is specified explicitly, all of them are considered.
Any request to that URL, regardless of the HTTP method will be matched to that
handler method and if the supported by the server the expected view will be
returned; for example, GET and POST requests to http://localhost:8080/
mvc-basic/home/today both return the today.jsp page.

In Spring 4.3, annotations specific to each HTTP method type were introduced, so
we can also write methods in the HomeController, like this:

```
package com.apress.cems.web.controllers;

import org.springframework.web.bind.annotation.GetMapping;
...
@Controller
@RequestMapping("/home")
```

```
public class HomeController {

    @GetMapping(value = "/today")
    public String today(Model model){....}

    @GetMapping(value = "/hello")
    public String hello(@RequestParam("name") String name, Model model)
    {...}
}
```

There is a hierarchy of annotations now all with the responsibility of mapping requests and all of them are grouped under the @Mapping meta-marker annotation (that marks an annotation as a web mapping annotation) in the org.springframework.web. bind.annotation package. The hierarchy is depicted in Figure 6-7.

Figure 6-7. *The @Mapping hierarchy*

The specialization annotations are meta-annotated with @RequestMapping(method = RequestMethod.XXX) where XXX is the name of the HTTP method they are mapping to. They have attributes declared which are used as aliases for the attributes declared in the @RequestMapping, which allow the specializations; for example, let's consider the following annotation.

```
@RequestMapping(value = "/search", method = RequestMethod.
GET,headers="timeout=30")
```

The annotation previously listed is equivalent to

```
@GetMapping(value = "/search", headers="timeout=30")
```

In the next code snippet, you can see the implementation of the @GetMapping annotation.[6]

```java
package org.springframework.web.bind.annotation;

import java.lang.annotation.Documented;
import java.lang.annotation.ElementType;
import java.lang.annotation.Retention;
import java.lang.annotation.RetentionPolicy;
import java.lang.annotation.Target;

import org.springframework.core.annotation.AliasFor;

@Target(ElementType.METHOD)
@Retention(RetentionPolicy.RUNTIME)
@Documented
@RequestMapping(method = RequestMethod.GET)
public @interface GetMapping {

    /**
     * Alias for {@link RequestMapping#name}.
     */
    @AliasFor(annotation = RequestMapping.class)
    String name() default "";

    /**
     * Alias for {@link RequestMapping#value}.
     */
    @AliasFor(annotation = RequestMapping.class)
    String[] value() default {};

    /**
     * Alias for {@link RequestMapping#path}.
     */
```

---

[6]Official source code copied from GitHub: https://github.com/spring-projects/spring-framework/blob/master/spring-web/src/main/java/org/springframework/web/bind/annotation/GetMapping.java

```
@AliasFor(annotation = RequestMapping.class)
String[] path() default {};

/**
 * Alias for {@link RequestMapping#params}.
 */
@AliasFor(annotation = RequestMapping.class)
String[] params() default {};

/**
 * Alias for {@link RequestMapping#headers}.
 */
@AliasFor(annotation = RequestMapping.class)
String[] headers() default {};

/**
 * Alias for {@link RequestMapping#consumes}.
 * @since 4.3.5
 */
@AliasFor(annotation = RequestMapping.class)
String[] consumes() default {};

/**
 * Alias for {@link RequestMapping#produces}.
 */
@AliasFor(annotation = RequestMapping.class)
String[] produces() default {};

}
```

The handler methods have flexible signatures with parameters that can be injected with information about the request context. Spring will transparently provide arguments when the handler methods are called. Depending on the URL type, different annotations can tell Spring what values to use.

- URL (Uniform Resource Locator) http://localhost:8080/mvc-basic/ persons/showPerson?personId=105 is handled by a method that has a parameter annotated with @RequestParam because the request is parametrized, so the parameter value has to be bounded to a method parameter. In the next code listing, the handler method is depicted.

```
import org.springframework.web.bind.annotation.RequestParam;
...
@Controller
@RequestMapping("/persons")
public class PersonController {

    @GetMapping(value = "/showPerson")
    public String show(@RequestParam("personId") Long id, Model
    model) {

        ...
    }
}
```

If the URL parameter has a different name than the handler method parameter, the annotation informs Spring of that.

CC   The convention is that if the name of the parameter is not specified in the @RequestParam annotation, then the request parameter is named the same as the method parameter. In the previous example, the request parameter is named personId and the handler method parameter is named id, so the @RequestParam("personId") Long id binds the two parameters together. But if they already have the same name, the annotation parameter is not necessary. So the previous handler method becomes the following.

```
import org.springframework.web.bind.annotation.RequestParam;
...
@Controller
@RequestMapping("/persons")
public class PersonController {
```

```
@GetMapping(value = "/showPerson")
public String show(@RequestParam Long personId, Model model) {
    ...
}
```
}

- URI (Uniform Resource Identifier) is a cleaner URL that implies cleaner URLs without request parameters. Handling URIs is supported starting from with Spring 3.0.

  ```
  http://localhost:8080/mvc-basic//persons/2
  ```

  The previously mentioned URI is handled by a method that has a parameter annotated with @PathVariable because the request URI contains a piece that is variable and that is where the name of the annotation comes from. In the next code listing, the handler method is depicted.

  ```
  import org.springframework.web.bind.annotation.PathVariable;
  ...
  @Controller
  @RequestMapping("/persons")
  public class PersonController {

      @GetMapping(value = "/{personId}")
      public String show(@PathVariable("personId") Long id, Model
      model) {
          ...
      }
  }
  ```

  If the path parameter has a different name than the method parameter, the annotation informs Spring of that.

CC   The convention is that if the name of the path variable name is not specified in the `PathVariable` annotation, then the path variable is named the same as the method parameter. So the previous handler method becomes the following.

```java
import org.springframework.web.bind.annotation.PathVariable;
...
@Controller
@RequestMapping("/persons")
public class PersonController {

    @GetMapping(value = "/{id}")
    public String show(@PathVariable Long id, Model model) {
        ...
    }
}
```

I've mentioned the flexible signatures of handler methods, but let's get more specific. A handler method can receive as parameter almost any type specific to a web application, and this includes Spring types as well. The following are a few possibilities.

- A handler method can be declared with request headers[7] as parameters, and Spring will provide the proper arguments from the request, if the parameters are annotated with @RequestHeader.

```java
import org.springframework.web.bind.annotation.PathVariable;
...
@Controller
@RequestMapping("/home")
public class HomeController {

    @GetMapping("/headers")
    public String headers(@RequestHeader(value="Host") String host,
```

---

[7]An HTTP request header is a component of a network packet sent by a browser or client to the server to request for a specific page or data on the web server. It is used in Web communications or Internet browsing to transport user requests to the corresponding website's web server.

```
            @RequestHeader(value="User-Agent") String
            userAgent,
             Model model) {
        List<String> dataList = new ArrayList<>();
        dataList.add("These are the headers for this
        request");
        dataList.add("Host: ".concat(host));
        dataList.add("User-Agent:".concat(userAgent));
        model.addAttribute("dataList", dataList);
      return "home/sandbox";
    }
}
```

The sandbox.jsp is a very simple play page used by the examples in this section.

Request headers contain information about the request and the client making the request; for example, the User-Agent header is populated with the name of the browser used to submit the request.

- A handler method can be declared with a parameter of WebRequest, NativeWebRequest, javax.servlet.ServletRequest(or any from the family[8]) type which provide access to request details: headers, request and session attributes. In the next code snippet, the headers and a description of the request containing URI and parameters are extracted from the WebRequest and displayed into the sandbox.jsp page.

```
import org.springframework.web.context.request.WebRequest;
...
@Controller
@RequestMapping("/home")
public class HomeController {

  @GetMapping("/request")
```

---

[8]The Servlet request family: *HttpServletRequest, MultipartRequest*(provided by Spring), *MultipartHttpServletRequest*

513

```
        public String webRequest(WebRequest webRequest, Model model){
            List<String> dataList = new ArrayList<>();
            dataList.add("These are the details of this request: ");
            dataList.add(webRequest.getContextPath());
            webRequest.getHeaderNames().forEachRemaining(dataList:: add);
            dataList.add(webRequest.getDescription(true));
            model.addAttribute("dataList", dataList);
            return "home/sandbox";
        }
    }
```

- a handler method can be declared with a parameter of javax. servlet.ServletResponse(or implementations) type, so the response can be enriched with new headers and attributes before being sent to the user. In the next code sample, we are adding a cookie to the response, just for the fun of it.

```
import org.springframework.web.context.request.WebRequest;
...
@Controller
@RequestMapping("/home")
public class HomeController {

    @GetMapping("/response")
    public String webResponse(HttpServletResponse response, Model
    model){
        List<String> dataList = new ArrayList<>();
        dataList.add("Response was modified. Check the cookies.");
        model.addAttribute("dataList", dataList);
        response.addCookie(new Cookie("SANDBOX_COOKIE",
        "Delicious"));
        return "home/sandbox";
    }
```

- A handler method can be declared with a parameter of javax. servlet.http.HttpSession type, which enforces the presence of a session. This means the session argument is not allowed to be null.

- A handler request can receive as parameter an instance of `javax.servlet.http.PushBuilder` type (Servlet 4.0 push builder API for programmatic HTTP/2 resource pushes).

- A handler method can be declared with a parameter of `java.security.Principal` type when the application is secured and credentials must be checked before performing the action in the handler method. There are other ways to do this, as you will later see in this chapter, but injecting the principal as an argument provides access to the details of the user currently logged in, which could populate an account settings page, for example.

- A handler method can be declared with a parameter of `HttpMethod` type, which can be used for auditing or additional checks.

- A handler method can be declared with a parameter of `Locale` type. What is this useful for? Well, maybe we want to add internationalized messages to the model. Think about international sites like Booking.com, they are available in different languages in different regions of the world. This is done using a `Locale` instance that is initialized with the value specific to the region. Just look at the following code sample, which depicts a handler method that saves a `Person` instance and it also validates it first. The `Locale` instance is used within the `processViolation(..)` method to extract an error message in translated to the message set by the current `Locale`. The code is not really relevant at the moment because it takes away the focus from the handler methods. It is covered later in the section, and more of the involved classes and annotations involved and their purposes will become clear.

```
package com.apress.cems.web.controllers;

import org.springframework.validation.annotation.Validated;
import org.springframework.validation.BindingResult;
import java.util.Locale;

...
@Controller
@RequestMapping("/persons")
public class PersonController {
```

```java
@PostMapping
public String save(@Validated Person person, BindingResult result,
            Locale locale) {
  if (result.hasErrors()) {
        return "persons/edit";
   }
  if(person.getNewPassword() != null) {
        person.setPassword(person.getNewPassword());
  }
  try {
        personService.save(person);
        return "redirect:/persons/" + person.getId();
  } catch (Exception e ) {
        Throwable  cause = e.getCause().getCause();
        if (cause instanceof  ConstraintViolationException) {
            processViolation( (ConstraintViolationException)
            cause, result,
                locale);
        }
        return "persons/edit";
  }
 }
 ...
}
```

In the previous code snippet, a parameter of type BindingResult
and a parameter of type Locale are declared as parameters and the
Sprig IoC container creates and injects the proper objects without
any other hint from the developer. The BindingResult instance
validates and stores validation results. The @Validated annotation is
a Spring provided equivalent of javax.validation.Valid that marks
an object for validation and compared with its counterpart it has
the advantage of supporting validation groups. The BindingResult
instance is being used for validation control (status) and report
(message errors) internally within the method handler and the view.

- A handler method can be declared with a parameter of
  BindingResult, as proven by the previous example.

- The Errors object that is accessed in the previous code sample using
  the BindingResult argument and calling result.hasErrors() can
  be itself provided as an argument for a handler method and used
  directly.

- A handler method can be declared with a parameter of java.
  io.InputStream, java.io.Reader to access the row body of the
  servlet request.

```java
package com.apress.cems.web.controllers;
import java.io.BufferedReader;
import java.io.IOException;
import java.io.Reader;
...
@Controller
@RequestMapping("/home")
public class HomeController {

    @GetMapping("/reader")
    public String readBody(Reader reader, Model model) throws
    IOException {
        List<String> dataList = new ArrayList<>();
        try(BufferedReader br = new BufferedReader(reader)){
            String line = null;
            while ((line = br.readLine()) != null) {
                dataList.add(line);
            }
        }
        model.addAttribute("dataList", dataList);
        return "home/sandbox";
    }
}
```

The previous handler method matches a GET request with a non-empty body. Such a request cannot be performed from a browser, but it can be performed by Postman as depicted in Figure 6-8.

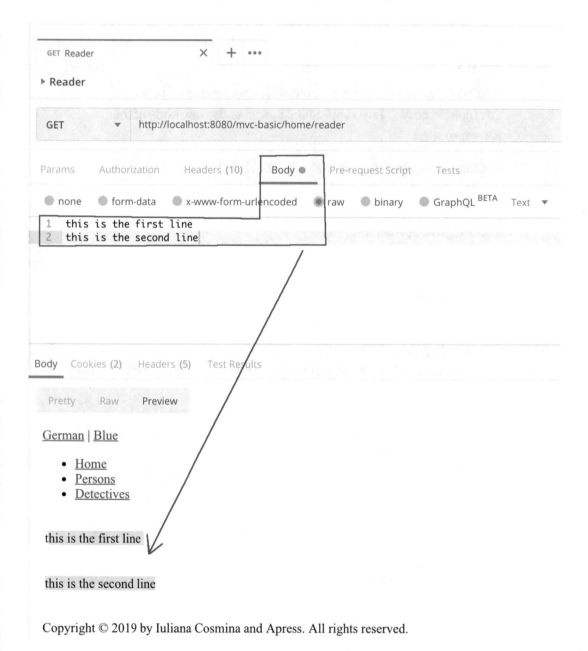

Figure 6-8. GET request with non-empty body in Postman

- A handler method can be declared with a parameter of java.
  io.OutputStream, java.io.Writer to access the row body of the
  servlet response. In this case, since the response is explicitly written,
  view resolving is disabled by annotating the handler method with
  @ResponseBody. You will learn more about this annotation in the
  REST chapter.

```
package com.apress.cems.web.controllers;
import java.io.IOException;

import java.io.Writer;
...
@Controller
@RequestMapping("/home")
public class HomeController {

    @ResponseBody
    @GetMapping("/writer")
    public void writeBody(Reader requestReader, Writer
    reponseWriter)
            throws IOException {
        try(BufferedReader br = new BufferedReader(requestReader)){
            String line = null;
            while ((line = br.readLine()) != null) {
                reponseWriter.append(line).append("\n");
            }
        }
    }
}
```

- A handler method can be declared with a parameter annotated with
  @RequestParam, @PathVariable, or @MatrixVariable. Since the first
  two were mentioned previously, and code samples were provided,
  it is only natural to cover the third one, which provides the mean to
  access name-value pairs in URI path segments.

```
import org.springframework.web.bind.annotation.MatrixVariable;
...
@Controller
@RequestMapping("/home")
public class HomeController {

    //Handles:http://localhost:8080/mvc-basic/home/
    building/75;g=1;u=3
    @GetMapping("/building/{buildingId}")
    public String matrix(@PathVariable String buildingId,
            @MatrixVariable int g, @MatrixVariable int u, Model
            model){
        List<String> dataList = new ArrayList<>();
        dataList.add("building number: ".concat(buildingId));
        dataList.add("ground floor flat number: "+ g);
        dataList.add("upper floor flat number: " + u);
        model.addAttribute("dataList", dataList);
        return "home/sandbox";
    }
```

Also, since we have two matrix variables, we can bind them to a Map<K,V>.

```
import org.springframework.web.bind.annotation.MatrixVariable;
...
@Controller
@RequestMapping("/home")
public class HomeController {

    //Handles:http://localhost:8080/mvc-basic/home/
    building/75;g=1;u=3
    @GetMapping("/building/{buildingId}")
    public String matrix(@PathVariable String buildingId,
                @MatrixVariable Map<String, Integer>
                matrixVars, Model model){
            ...
        return "home/sandbox";
    }
```

Just keep in mind that URLs with matrix parameters are not supported by default in Spring. Extra configuration is needed: a bean of type UrlPathHelper with the removeSemicolonContent property set to false needs to be added to the MVC configuration.[9]

```xml
<!-- XML -->
    <mvc:annotation-driven>
        <mvc:path-matching path-helper="myPathHelper"/>
    </mvc:annotation-driven>

    <bean id="myPathHelper" class="org.springframework.web.util.
    UrlPathHelper">
        <property name="removeSemicolonContent" value="false"/>
    </bean>
```

```java
// Java configuration
import org.springframework.web.util.UrlPathHelper;

...
@Configuration
@EnableWebMvc
@ComponentScan(basePackages = {"com.apress.cems.web.controllers"})
class WebConfig implements WebMvcConfigurer {

    @Override
    public void configurePathMatch(PathMatchConfigurer configurer) {
        UrlPathHelper matrixPathHelper = new UrlPathHelper();
        matrixPathHelper.setRemoveSemicolonContent(false);
        configurer.setUrlPathHelper(matrixPathHelper);
    }
}
```

The @MatrixVariable can be used in ways similar to @RequestParam, @PathVariable to inject the values in handler method arguments with different names, and to specify if the value of the URL parameter is required or not, and so on.

---

[9]More information in the Official Spring Reference documentation: https://docs.spring.io/spring/docs/current/spring-framework-reference/web.html#mvc-ann-matrix-variables

```
import org.springframework.web.bind.annotation.MatrixVariable;
...
@Controller
@RequestMapping("/home")
public class HomeController {

    //Handles:http://localhost:8080/mvc-basic/home/
    building/75;g=1;u=3
    @GetMapping("/building/{buildingId}")
    public String matrix(@PathVariable String buildingId,
            @MatrixVariable("g") int groundFlatNo,
            @MatrixVariable("u")int upperFlatNo, Model model){
        List<String> dataList = new ArrayList<>();
        dataList.add("building number: ".concat(buildingId));
        dataList.add("ground floor flat number: "+ g);
        dataList.add("upper floor flat number: " + u);
        model.addAttribute("dataList", dataList);
        return "home/sandbox";
    }
```

- A handler method can be declared with a parameter annotated with @CookieValue, which provides access to cookies.

- A handler method can be declared with a parameter representing a model that contains data to be rendered in a view. Possible types:java.util.Map, org.springframework.ui.Model, org.springframework.ui.ModelMap.

- A handler method can be declared with a parameter of RedirectAttributes types. This type is a specialization of org.springframework.ui.Model, which selects a set of attributes for a redirection scenario. In the next example, the redirectData(..) handler method does not end with returning a logical view name, but redirects the request to another handler method named listData(..). This method does nothing more than return a logical view name that is populated with data from the model, which is populated behind the scenes with the attribute extracted from the

RedirectAttributes model.[10] Spring knows how to do this, because the parameter of the listData(..) method is annotated with @ModelAttribute and has the same type (List<String> type) as the attribute put in the redirection model by the redirecting method.

```
import org.springframework.web.servlet.mvc.support.
RedirectAttributes;
...
@Controller
@RequestMapping("/home")
public class HomeController {

    @GetMapping("/verifyRedirection")
    public String redirectData(final RedirectAttributes
    redirectAttributes) {
        List<String> dataList = new ArrayList<>();
        dataList.add("Data from HomeController.redirectData");
        redirectAttributes.addFlashAttribute("dataList",
        dataList);
        return "redirect:/home/data-list";
    }

    /**
     * Method which is called via "redirect:"
     *      from the HomeController.redirectData(..)
     */
    @GetMapping(value="/data-list")
    public String listData(@ModelAttribute("dataList")
    ArrayList<String> content) {
        return "home/sandbox";
    }
}
```

---

[10]The method used to store the attribute is named *addFlashAttribute(..)*, that is because these attributes are named *flash attributes* and they provide a way for one request to store attributes that are intended for use in another. You can read more about flash attributes and how they are managed by Spring in the official Spring documentation: https://docs.spring.io/spring/docs/current/spring-framework-reference/web.html#mvc-flash-attributes.

- A handler method can be declared with parameters annotated with
  @SessionAttribute or @RequestAttribute, which bind method
  parameters to session and request attributes. You will learn more
  about session attributes in Chapter 7, because they make more sense
  there. I mean, a session is kinda pointless without a logged-in user to
  attach it to.

It seems handler methods can receive anything as parameter; if none of the previous
cases applies to the parameter, if its type is a primitive, a String or other CharSequence,
a Number, a Date, a Temporal, a URI, a URL, a Locale, or a corresponding array the
parameter will be treated as being annotated with @RequestParam; otherwise, it is treated
like it is annotated with @ModelAttribute, because this annotation is special. This
annotation can be used at the method level to mark a method as being executed before
any other handler method in a controller regardless the HTTP method handled. Why is
this important? Because if there are a lot of handler methods that affect a single object
uniquely identified via its ID, all of these methods can be grouped into a single controller
mapped to a URI including a path variable for the ID. For example, we could create a
controller named SinglePersonController that contains handler methods that manage
a single Person instance, and this instance, does not have to be passed as a parameter to
each handler method.

```
package com.apress.cems.web.controllers;
...
@Controller
@RequestMapping("/persons/{id}")
public class SinglePersonController {
...

    /**
     * Finds the person managed by the methods in
     *    this controller and adds it to the model
     * @param id
     *       the id of the Person instance to retrieve
     * @return person
     */
```

```
@ModelAttribute
protected Person person(@PathVariable Long id) {
    Person person = new Person();
    Optional<Person> personOpt = personService.findById(id);
    return personOpt.orElse(person);
}

/**
 * Handles requests to show detail about one person.
 */
@GetMapping
public String show() {
    return "persons/show";
}

@GetMapping("/edit")
public String edit() {
    return "persons/edit";
}

@PostMapping
public String save(@Validated Person person,
    BindingResult result, Locale locale) {
    ...
        return "persons/show";
}
}
```

As you can see, the base URL for this controller is /persons/{id}, which means handler methods will handle URL's prefixed with that. So making a request to http://localhost:8080/mvc-basic/persons/1/edit will have the following effects. First, person(1) is called to extract the Person with an ID equal to 1 and bind it to the request context. Then, this instance populates the view with the persons/edit logical name, which is returned to the edit() handler method that is the actual handler method of that URL.

An impressive list of handler methods parameter types, and the annotations that can be used on them, was presented, but how about the handler methods, what can they be annotated with? We've already covered the @Mapping family. What else is there? Well, there is an annotation @ResponseStatus that can be used on handler methods to mark the method with the HTTP status code that should be returned for the response. In a web environment HTTP status codes are used as a technique to communicate the type of request that took place and the result. The HTTP status codes are grouped into five categories.[11]

- 1xx: An informational response. The response was received and understood.

- 2xx: The request was received, and the action required was executed successfully.

- 3xx: Redirection. The client needs to take additional action to complete a request, or the browser is instructed to send the request somewhere else automatically. Redirection should take place after a PUT or POST operation to avoid duplication of content.

- 4xx: A client error. The most typical scenario is when a user makes a request to a wrong URL that has no handler method declared. A response consisting in an error page with 404 (Not Found) status code is returned.

- 5xx: A server error. The most typical case is when a request is mapped to a handler method that throws an unexpected exception; in this case, a response results in an error page with a 500 (Internal server error) status code.

The status code is applied to the HTTP response after the invocation of the handler method. It overrides status information set by other means, like returning a customized ResponseEntity<T> (which is used more in Chapter 8) or returning a view logical name containing "redirect:". In a web environment it is recommended to return a response status code appropriate to the HTTP method called. This is useful for debugging the application. In Spring controller classes, annotating handler methods with

---

[11]Read more about HTTP status code here: https://en.wikipedia.org/wiki/
List_of_HTTP_status_codes

@ResponseStatus also makes the code more readable as the purpose of each handler method becomes obvious. Check out the following example code snippet.

```
package com.apress.cems.person;

import org.springframework.web.bind.annotation.ResponseStatus;
...

@Controller
@RequestMapping("/persons/{id}")
public class SinglePersonController2 {

    private PersonService personService;

    public SinglePersonController2(PersonService personService) {
        this.personService = personService;
    }

    @ModelAttribute
    protected Person modelPerson(@PathVariable Long id){

        ...
    }

    @GetMapping
    @ResponseStatus(HttpStatus.OK)
    public String show() {
        return "persons/show";
    }

    @PutMapping
    @ResponseStatus(HttpStatus.NO_CONTENT)
    public String update(@Validated Person person, BindingResult result){
        // do some logic
        return "redirect:/persons/" + person.getId();
    }
```

```
@PostMapping
@ResponseStatus(HttpStatus.CREATED)
public String create(@Validated Person person, BindingResult result){
    //do some logic
    return "redirect:/persons/" + person.getId();
}

@DeleteMapping
@ResponseStatus(HttpStatus.NO_CONTENT)
public String delete(){
    //do some logic
    return "redirect:/persons/list";
}
}
```

Each type of request is specific to an HTTP method, and in some cases, we might want a response status different from the default 200. In the W3's HTTP method definitions glossary,[12] the request for the PUT method implementation should contain a representation of a database entity. A few options for the implementation are defined.

- If an existing resource is modified, either the 200 (OK) or 204 (No Content) response codes should be sent to indicate successful completion of the request. Also, the request should be redirected to a handler that displays the modified entity in a view. As a convention in web development, this is the PUT normal behavior.

- Some applications also support creation of a new resource with the data in a PUT request and returning 201(Created) when an existing record to update cannot be identified. This case also implies a redirection to a handler to display the newly created record.

- Some applications only support an update operation through a PUT method, so if the body references an entity that does exist, and therefore cannot be updated, a 404(Not found) error response is returned.

---

[12]Official page: https://www.w3.org/Protocols/rfc2616/rfc2616-sec9.html

In the previous code sample, for the handler method annotated with @PutMapping the behavior described in the first item in the list is supported. The org.springframework. http.HttpStatus.NO_CONTENT constant has the value of 204 and by annotating the handler method with @ResponseStatus(HttpStatus.NO_CONTENT) we are basically setting this status code on the response in a successful scenario - when a Person instance is updated.

Views and View Resolvers

Handler methods are flexible in regards to what they return as well. In web applications they typically return a string value representing a logical view name and the view is populated with values in the Model object.

CC   By default, the logical view name is interpreted as a path to a JSP page.

Controller methods can also return null or void, and in this case, the default view is selected based on the request URL. A handler method can return void if the response is written explicitly using a ServletResponse object or a response Writer. Handler methods returning void are also specific to REST PUT requests as you will see in Chapter 8.

Controller methods can also return concrete views, but this is usually avoided because it couples the controller with the view implementation.

Controller methods can return concrete objects that are serialized to XML, JSON, or whatever the application making the call requires (also specific to REST controllers).

In the next code snippet, a handler method returning a model instance is depicted. As you will see a little further in the chapter, this kind of handler methods are specific to handling exceptions being thrown during the execution of handler methods.

```
package com.apress.cems.web.controllers;
import org.springframework.web.servlet.ModelAndView;
...
@Controller
@RequestMapping("/persons")
```

```
public class PersonController {

  @RequestMapping(value = "/{personId}", method = RequestMethod.GET)
  public ModelAndView show(@PathVariable("personId") Long id) {
    Person person = ...;// no relevant
    ModelAndView modelAndView = new ModelAndView("person");
    return modelAndView;
  }
}
```

The model contains the data that is used to populate a view. Spring provides view resolvers to avoid ties to a specific view technology. Out of the box, Spring supports JSP, Velocity templates, and XSLT views. The interfaces needed to make this possible are ViewResolver and View. The first provides a mapping between view names and actual views. The second takes care of preparing the request and forwards it to a view technology. The DispatcherServlet delegates to a ViewResolver to map logical view names to view implementations.

Spring comes out of the box with a few *view resolver* implementations. All handler methods must resolve to a logical view name that corresponds to a file, either explicitly by returning a String, View, or ModelAndView instance, or implicitly based on internal conventions. The core view resolver provided by Spring is the InternalResourceViewResolver and is the default view resolver. Inside spring-webmvc.jar there is a file called DispatcherServlet.properties and in it all default infrastructure beans are declared. If you look for the default view resolver, you will find the previously mentioned implementation.

```
org.springframework.web.servlet.ViewResolver=
        org.springframework.web.servlet.view.InternalResourceViewResolver
```

The default implementation can be overridden by registering a ViewResolver bean with the DispatcherServlet through XML or Java configuration. The default view resolver implementation is also customizable, and can be configured to look for view template files in a different location. The previous code snippets returned string values as view names. In Figure 6-9, the configuration and the mechanism of resolving views is depicted.

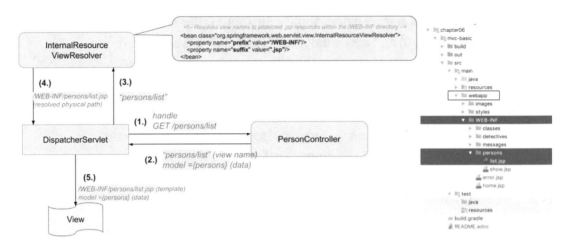

Figure 6-9. *Custom Internal Resource View Resolver Example*

Figure 6-9 depicts how `DispatcherServlet`, `PersonController` and an `InternalResourceViewResolver` bean configured by the developer (using XML configuration; Java configuration is introduced a little bit later) work together to produce a view. Each action has a number, and the following are the corresponding steps.

1. The `DispatcherServlet` identified the handler method for the persons/list GET request and requests the `PersonController` method to handle the request.

2. The handler method is executed, and a logical view named persons/list and a model object containing the collection named persons are returned to the `DispatcherServlet`. The model={persons} is a notation that means the *persons* object is contained by the *model* object.

3. The `DispatcherServlet` asks the `InternalResourceViewResolver` to which view template the persons/list logical view name corresponds.

4. The `InternalResourceViewResolver` that is configured as follows,

```
<bean class="org.springframework.web.servlet.view.
InternalResourceViewResolver">
    <property name="prefix" value="/WEB-INF/"/>
    <property name="suffix" value=".jsp"/>
</bean>
```

takes the logical view name, applies the prefix (`/WEB-INF/`) and the suffix(`.jsp`) and sends the result (`/WEB-INF/persons/list.jsp`), which is the physical path of the view template to the `DispatcherServlet`, which will further use the view template and the model object received from the controller to create a view.

The `View` interface from the `org.springframework.web.servlet` package is the core MVC component for web interactions. Implementations of this interface are responsible for rendering data and exposing model contents. There are various implementations available and the most renown are the ones that are JSP based because of the tag libraries that can make the views dynamic based on the model data. Views are beans instantiated by the `ViewResolver`. The `InternalResourceViewResolver` configured previously is a view resolver for JSP pages and creates beans of type `InternalResourceView` to render JSP pages. If the JSTL tag library is found in the classpath it creates beans of type `JstlView` that expose JSTL-specific request attributes specifying locale. Both view implementations are part of the `org.springframework.web.servlet.view` package.

5. The `DispatcherServlet` will further use the view template provided by the `InternalResourceViewResolver` and the model object received from the `PersonController` to create a view.

But what if we have more than one type of view that we want to render to the user? What if we want to provide the user the possibility to return data in XML, or PDF, or JSON format? There are two ways of doing it, which are introduced next. There is a small section to introduce you to the main configuration elements so that you can recognize them and are able to work with an XML configuration, if the need arises.

View resolvers prioritization. You can declare a priority for the view resolver implementation in our application and the Spring IoC container will use them in the increasing order of their priority to look for a view to render to the user (this approach is also named *resolver chaining*). The following configuration snippet depicts view and view resolver beans, which are part of a bigger Spring Java configuration class, as you will see later in the book.

```
package com.apress.cems.web.config;
import org.springframework.web.servlet.view.BeanNameViewResolver;
...

    @Bean
    public ViewResolver xlsViewResolver(){
        BeanNameViewResolver resolver = new BeanNameViewResolver();
        resolver.setOrder(0);
        return resolver;
    }

    @Bean
    ViewResolver jspViewResolver(){
        InternalResourceViewResolver resolver =
                new InternalResourceViewResolver();
        resolver.setPrefix("/WEB-INF/");
        resolver.setSuffix(".jsp" );
        resolver.setOrder(1);
        return resolver;
    }

    @Bean(name="persons/list.xls")
    public View excelView(){
        return  new PersonsExcelView();
    }
```

In the previous configuration snippet, we've declared two view resolvers:
the InternalResourceViewResolver you already know and a bean of
BeanNameViewResolver type that interprets a view name as a bean name in the current
application context. So a request to the http://localhost:8080/mvc-views/persons/
list.xls URL will cause a response to be rendered to the user containing the view
produced by the persons/list.xls bean. When a view resolver does not result in a
view (usually null is returned - sure, there are view resolvers that throw exceptions, but
let's not consider this right now) Spring examines the application context for other view
resolver beans and inspects each of them until a view is obtained. If this is not possible
a ServletException is thrown. When resolver beans are chained, the inspection is done
based on the value of their order property and the lower the value of the property the
higher the priority when resolving view names.

!   The `InternalResourceViewResolver` resolves the view no matter what view name is returned and throws an exception if it cannot be resolve a view name so this bean always has to be placed the last in the chain; otherwise, Spring will skip looking for other view resolvers beans in the context. Other resolvers that must be last in the chain are XSLT an JSON. Tiles, Thymeleaf, Velocity, and FreeMarker can appear anywhere in the chain.

The downside of prioritizing view resolvers is that it works only when each resource is associated with one view type. But clients might request different content types for the same resource via extension, request header, request parameter, and so forth. In this case, chaining won't work, as the type of view returned depends on some parameters that have to be taken into consideration and then a matching `ViewResolver` must be selected to do the job.

Use content negotiation. This technique was introduced in Spring 3.0. The type of bean used to support this approach is the `ContentNegotiatingViewResolver` type. This bean does not resolve views but delegates the job to the view resolver implementations defined in the application configuration, selecting the view type matching the content type header value in the client request. There are three strategies for a client to request a view from the server.

- Use a distinct URL for each resource by using a different extension in the URL (e.g., `http://localhost:8080/mvc-views/persons/list.xls` requests an Excel view containing a list of persons, while `http://localhost:8080/mvc-views/persons/list.pdf` requests a PDF view containing a list of persons).

- Use the same URL but set the `Accept` HTTP request header to the desired resource type (e.g., a request coming from `http://localhost:8080/mvc-views/persons/list` having the `Accept` header set to `application/pdf` requests a PDF view containing a list of persons.)

- Use a parametrized URL like `http://localhost:8080/mvc-views/persons/list?type="pdf"` and provide the view type as a value for a request parameter.

!   The problem with the `Accept` header is that it cannot be used when the client is a browser, as most browsers force its value to `text/html`. Because of this, web applications are always build to use the first approach, each view type is mapped to its own URL (taking the extension into consideration; for example, /persons/list.html, /persons/list.xls). The `Accept` header approach is most useful for REST web services.

The `ContentNegotiatingViewResolver` implements the `Ordered` interface, so it can be used alongside other resolvers and be part of a view resolver chain, and it has to have the highest priority in the chain. This is due to its behavior, if the `ContentNegotiatingViewResolver` cannot select a `View` (because none of the view resolvers managed by it were able to find a match) it returns null and Spring examines the application context for other view resolver beans and inspects each of them until a view is obtained.

The `ContentNegotiatingViewResolver`bean is very versatile and you can either rely on its default behavior, or you can configure it according to the application's needs. Let's assume that you need this bean to handle a group of view resolvers that export data in various formats in an application, none of them HTML. This means the `ContentNegotiatingViewResolver` would be created, the set of view resolvers managed by it would be explicitly specified, and an HTML view resolver would be configured as a separate view resolver.

Usually, the `ContentNegotiatingViewResolver` is configured to pick up `ViewResolver` implementations automatically from the application context, so it should always resolve to a `View`. The next resolvers in the chain are considered a fallback solution to make sure that a `View` is provided. In the next code snippet, a configuration of a of a `ContentNegotiatingViewResolver` bean is depicted (for the current example the code of the view resolvers and views is not really important).[13]

```
package com.apress.cems.web.config;

import org.springframework.web.accept.ContentNegotiationManagerFactoryBean;
import org.springframework.web.servlet.view.ContentNegotiatingViewResolver;
...
```

----

[13]You can find the entire working project in *chapter06/mvc-views*

```
@Bean
ContentNegotiatingViewResolver viewResolver(){
    ContentNegotiationManagerFactoryBean factory
            = new ContentNegotiationManagerFactoryBean();
    factory.setDefaultContentType(MediaType.TEXT_HTML);
    factory.setIgnoreAcceptHeader(true);
    factory.setFavorParameter(false);
    factory.setFavorPathExtension(true);
    factory.setMediaTypes(
                    Properties.of("html", MediaType.TEXT_HTML_VALUE,
            "xls", "application/vnd.ms-excel",
            "pdf", MediaType.APPLICATION_PDF_VALUE,
            "json", MediaType.APPLICATION_JSON_VALUE));

    ContentNegotiatingViewResolver  resolver
                = new ContentNegotiatingViewResolver();
    resolver.setContentNegotiationManager(factory.getObject());
    resolver.setOrder(-1);
    resolver.setDefaultViews(defaultViewsList());
    resolver.setViewResolvers(resolverList());
    return resolver;
}

private List<View> defaultViewsList(){
    List<View> views = new ArrayList<>();
    views.add(new PersonExcelView());
    views.add(new PersonPdfView());
    views.add(new MappingJackson2JsonView());
    return views;
}

private List<ViewResolver> resolverList(){
    List<ViewResolver> resolvers = new ArrayList<>();
    resolvers.add(new BeanNameViewResolver());
    resolvers.add(thymeViewResolver());
    resolvers.add(new JsonViewResolver());
    return resolvers;
}
```

To manage the `ViewResolver` implementations internally, the `ContentNegotiating ViewResolver` bean makes use of an instance of `ContentNegotiationManager` that is configured using a `ContentNegotiationManagerFactoryBean` instance. After configuring all the details on the factory instance, the object is retrieved by calling `factory. getObject()` and is provided to be used to the `ContentNegotiatingViewResolver`. This approach allows the creation of only one bean of `ContentNegotiatingViewResolver` type and thus less memory is being occupied with beans that are not really necessary, since their only role is a builder role.

The following describes the meaning of each property used in the previous configuration.

- `mediaTypes:` A map containing extension to content-type correspondences. This property is not mandatory and does not have to be set when in the application the Java Activation Framework is used, in which case the types are determine automatically.[14]

- `viewResolvers:` The list of view resolvers to delegate to. This property is not mandatory and when is not set, all view resolver beans in the context will be detected and used, but they have to be ordered.

- `defaultViews:` The default views to use when a more specific view could not be obtained. The property is not mandatory and when not set, if a view cannot be found by any of the view resolvers, nothing will be returned and a debug message letting you know that the view was not resolved is printed in the console. For example, in the previous configuration, if `resolver.setDefaultViews(..)` were removed, requesting `http://localhost:8080/mvc-views/persons/ list.xls` will do nothing in the browser but in the console log the following lines will appear.

---

[14]By default, strategies for checking the extension of the request path and the Accept header are registered. The path extension check will perform lookups through the ServletContext and the Java Activation Framework (if present) unless media types are configured. In order to use the Java Activation Framework, the activation.jar has to be in the classpath of the application.

```
DEBUG o.s.w.s.DispatcherServlet - GET "/mvc-views/persons/list.
xls", parameters={}
DEBUG o.s.w.s.v.ContentNegotiatingViewResolver - View remains
unresolved given
            [application/vnd.ms-excel]
```

- defaultContentType: The type to render in case a match was not found. The property is not mandatory.

- ignoreAcceptHeader: Indicates that the HTTP Accept header should be ignored if true and taken into consideration if false. The property is not mandatory and if not set it defaults to false.

- favorParameter: Indicates if a request parameter named format (the name is configurable by calling setParameterName(..)) should be used to determine the requested content-type. The property is not mandatory and if not set, it defaults to false.

- favorPathExtension: Indicates if the extension of the request URL should be used to determine the requested content-type. The property is not mandatory and if not set it defaults to true.

The Spring application supports not only HTML views, but also JSON, Excel, and PDF. The entire code is found in the chapter06/mvc-views project.

Spring comes out of the box with a set of view resolvers that have specific responsibilities. They are grouped under the org.springframework.web.servlet.view package, which is part of the spring-webmvc module. You can view the relationship between them in Figure 6-10.

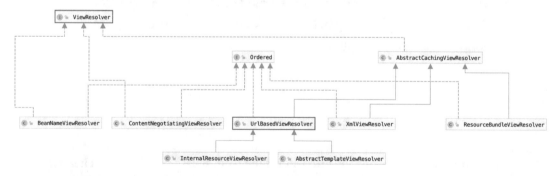

Figure 6-10. *Spring view resolvers hierarchy*

In Figure 6-10, you can see that all Spring view resolvers implement the `org.springframework.core.Ordered` interface, so they can be prioritized. Also, notice the `UrlBasedViewResolver` class, which is the super class of all other implementations. This is the simplest implementation of the `ViewResolver` interface and allows direct resolution of symbolic view names to URLs without explicit mapping definition. A view resolver of the `UrlBasedViewResolver` type can be configured like this, the important information here being the type of view handler methods should be mapped to the following.

```
package com.apress.cems.web.config;

import org.springframework.web.servlet.view.UrlBasedViewResolver;
...

    @Bean
    ViewResolver viewResolver(){
        UrlBasedViewResolver resolver = new UrlBasedViewResolver();
        resolver.setViewClass(JstlView.class);

        return resolver;
    }
```

And it supports returning the full path to a view in the `WEB-INF` directory from a handler method, instead of a logical name.

```
package com.apress.cems.web.config;

@Controller
public class HomeController {

    @RequestMapping(value = "/home", method = RequestMethod.GET)
    public String home(Model model) {
        model.addAttribute("message", "Spring MVC JSP Example!!");
        return "/WEB-INF/home.jsp";
    }
}
```

The `InternalResourceViewResolver` introduced previously is a specialization of this class that supports `InternalResourceView` (i.e., Servlets and JSPs), and subclasses such as `JstlView` and `TilesView` (up to Spring 4.x), without explicitly setting these view types.

The implementation in the `UrlBasedViewResolver` class resolves views for forward and redirect actions. In a previous example, when depicting how `RedirectAttributes` are used, instead of returning a logical view name, a construction like this was returned `redirect:/home/data-list` which had the effect of redirecting the request to be handled by the handler method annotated with `@GetMapping("/data-list")`. The code is depicted again here, for practical reasons, even if it causes some duplication in the book, but the technical editor asked for it, 😊 so here it is.

```
...
@GetMapping("/verifyRedirection")
    public String redirectData(final RedirectAttributes redirectAttributes) {
        List<String> dataList = new ArrayList<>();
        dataList.add("Data from HomeController.redirectData");
        redirectAttributes.addFlashAttribute("dataList", dataList);
        return "redirect:/home/data-list";
    }

    /**
     * Method which is called via "redirect:"
     *      from the HomeController.redirectData(..)
     */
    @GetMapping(value="/data-list")
    public String listData(@ModelAttribute("dataList") ArrayList<String> content) {
        return "home/sandbox";
    }
...
```

The same effect can be obtained with `forward:/home/data-list`, because in the context of a single application there is no difference in behavior.

The forward action sends the request from one JSP to another or from one JSP to a servlet, or from one JSP to another resource in the same web application. The control is passed internally by the container and the browser/client is not involved in this process. The action is handled by the `DispatcherServlet` in a Spring application. The redirect action involves the `sendRedirect(..)` method declared in the `HttpServletResponse` class and is used to redirect the client request to a URL that is available on a different server or context. With a redirect action, the browser redirects the request to a different application altogether.

To summarize everything so far, and to dive completely into the Spring MVC configuration to configure a Spring web application. You must do the following.

1. Define the `DispatcherServlet` as the main servlet of the application, which will handle all requests in the `web.xml` file and link it to the Spring configuration or configure this servlet programmatically by using a class implementing WebApplicationInitializer (only possible in a Servlet 3.0+ environment).

2. Define the application configuration. (In a Spring configuration, a file is named in an obvious way; in `/chapter06/mvc-basic.xml`, the file is named `mvc-config.xml` to make it clear that it contains a configuration specific to an MVC application or a Java configuration class.) It should contain the MVC context used (handler adapter, handler mapping and other infrastructure beans) and a view resolver.

Sounds pretty straightforward, right?

XML Configuration

To define the `DispatcherServlet` as the main servlet of the application, the `web.xml` file located under `webapp/WEB-INF` directory must be modified to include this Spring specialized servlet and the parameters for it. The following configuration snippet is suitable for this scenario.

```
<!-- web.xml -->
<web-app ...>
    <!-- The front controller, the entry point for all requests -->
    <servlet>
        <servlet-name>cems-dispatcher</servlet-name>
        <servlet-class>
            org.springframework.web.servlet.DispatcherServlet
        </servlet-class>
        <init-param>
            <param-name>contextConfigLocation</param-name>
            <param-value>
```

```
            /WEB-INF/spring/mvc-config.xml
        </param-value>
    </init-param>
    <load-on-startup>1</load-on-startup>
</servlet>

<!-- Map all requests to the DispatcherServlet for handling -->
<servlet-mapping>
    <servlet-name>cems-dispatcher</servlet-name>
    <url-pattern>/</url-pattern>
</servlet-mapping>
...
</web-app>
```

The `DispatcherServlet` was named `cems-dispatcher` and the Spring
Web MVC configuration file is referred into the web.xml file as value for the
`contextConfigLocation` parameter. In the preceding case, the `mvc-config.xml` contains
the Spring configuration for the front end (controllers and MVC infrastructure beans),
and the file is loaded by the `DispatcherServlet` and a web execution context for the
application is created.

The `servlet-mapping` element maps all incoming requests to the
`DispatcherServlet` and the `url-pattern` element can even contain a context to further
filter the requests, in case other servlets are used (e.g., security handler server).

The declaration of a view resolver bean should be located in the `mvc-config.xml`
file (that is referred in `web.xml` file) as it is a Spring infrastructure bean. To match the
internal structure of the web application presented earlier the bean is customized like
this:

```
<beans ...>
    <bean class="
        org.springframework.web.servlet.view.
        InternalResourceViewResolver">
        <property name="prefix" value="/WEB-INF/"/>
        <property name="suffix" value=".jsp"/>
    </bean>
    ...
</beans>
```

The `InternalResourceViewResolver` configured like this receives the logical view name from the `DispatcherServlet`, applies the prefix (`/WEB-INF/`) and the suffix (`.jsp`) and sends the result, which will be a something similar to (`/WEB-INF/[template_path/template_name].jsp`). It is the physical path of the view template to the `DispatcherServlet`, which uses the view template and the model object received from the controller to create a view that is displayed to the end user.

The `InternalResourceViewResolver` has more properties, an important one is the `requestContextAttribute` that is the context holder for request-specific state, like current web application context, current locale, current theme, and potential binding errors. Provides easy access to localized messages and Errors instances.

```
<beans ...>
    <bean class="
         org.springframework.web.servlet.view.
         InternalResourceViewResolver">
        <property name="prefix" value="/WEB-INF/"/>
        <property name="suffix" value=".jsp"/>
        <property name="requestContextAttribute" value="requestContext"/>
    </bean>
    ...
</beans>
```

Localization and personalization are advanced subjects that are not needed for the CORE certification exam, but they are pretty easy to set up. The `requestContextAttribute` was mentioned because most developers new to Spring often forget about it and get really confused when changing locale and themes doesn't work even if they declare and configure all the necessary beans. `requestContext` is used in the `*.jsp` files to decide locale and themes. The following JSP snippet depicts how the attribute is used to implement some of the URLs that will set the locale of the application when clicked. Additional taglibs are used: JSTL tglib for conditions and the Spring taglib is used for internationalization. The complete code sample can be found in the code attached to the book.

```
<!-- JSTL taglib import -->
<%@ taglib prefix="c" uri="http://java.sun.com/jsp/jstl/core" %>
<!-- Spring taglib import -->
<%@ taglib prefix="spring" uri="http://www.springframework.org/tags"%>
```

```
...
<c:choose>
    <!-- when locale is English -->
    <c:when test="${requestContext.locale.language eq 'en'}">
        <c:url var="localeUrl" value="/">
                <c:param name="locale" value="de"/>
        </c:url>
        <a href="${localeUrl}"><spring:message code="locale.de"/></a>
        <!-- text: German -->
        <!-- URL: http://localhost:8080/mvc-basic-xml/?locale=de-->
    </c:when>
    <c:otherwise>
    <!-- when locale is German -->
        <c:url var="localeUrl" value="/">
                    <c:param name="locale" value="en"/>
        </c:url>
        <a href="${localeUrl}"><spring:message code="locale.en"/></a>
        <!-- text: English -->
        <!-- URL: http://localhost:8080/mvc-basic-xmml/?locale=en-->
    </c:otherwise>
</c:choose>
```

The next step is to define a controller. The class has been introduced, so the following code snippet only depicts the core element of a controller class. The method covered here handles a request to display a user. The id value is part of the URI and is automatically populated by Spring. The personService is a bean used to extract the data from the database and the persons/show is the logical name of the view, which is resolved by the view resolved to the /WEB-INF/persons/show.jsp view.

```
package com.apress.cems.web.controllers;

//custom exception, implementation not relevant for context
import com.ps.problem.NotFoundException;
...
@Controller
@RequestMapping("/persons")
```

```java
public class PersonController {

    private PersonService personService;

        public PersonController(PersonService personService) {
            this.personService = personService;
        }

    @RequestMapping(value = "/{id}", method = RequestMethod.GET)
    public String show(@PathVariable Long id, Model model) {
        Optional<Person> personOpt = personService.findById(id);
        if(personOpt.isPresent()) {
            model.addAttribute("person", personOpt.get());
        } else {
            throw new NotFoundException(Person.class, id);
        }
        return "persons/show";
    }
}
```

The controller bean has to be identified by component scanning or has to be declared in the mvc-config.xml file.

```xml
<!-- by component scanning -->
<beans ...>
    <context:component-scan base-package="com.apress.cems.web.
    controllers"/>
</beans>

<!--  OR by XML declaration -->
<beans ...>

    <bean id="personController"
        class="com.apress.cems.web.controllers.PersonController>
            <property name="personService" ref="personService" />
    </bean>
```

```
<bean id="personService"
    class=" com.apress.cems.dj.services.PersonServiceImpl" >
... <!-- bean definition -->
</bean>
</beans>
```

The model is populated with the person object by calling the model. addAttribute("person", personOpt.get()) method and therefore assigning to the instance returned by the personOpt.get() the name of person. Now that there are a view resolver and a handler declared, the show.jsp view needs to be defined. The view will reference the model object by its name - person - and display the values of its properties. The following JSP snippet depicts how the person object is used in the code of a JSP page.

```
<!-- Spring taglib import -->
<%@ taglib prefix="spring" uri="http://www.springframework.org/tags"%>
...
<html>
<body>
<!-- other html elements not relevant here -->
    <div class="content">
        <table>
            <tr>
                <th><spring:message code="label.Person.firstname"/></th>
                <td>${person.firstName}</td>
            </tr>
            <tr>
                <th><spring:message code="label.Person.lastname"/></th>
                <td>${person.lastName}</td>
            </tr>
            <tr>
                <th><spring:message code="label.Person.username"/></th>
                <td>${person.username}</td>
            </tr>
```

```
        <tr>
            <th><spring:message code="label.Person.since"/></th>
            <td>${~underline[person].hiringDate}</td>
        </tr>
    </table>
  </div>
</body>
</html>
```

The JSP pages are usually developed using taglibs that extend the collection of JSP elements that can be used in a page and provide a more simple syntax. The Spring taglib declared in the JSP code snippet extracts the text for the table headers according to the locale of the application. For example, when creating the view to be displayed to the end user, the `<spring:message code="label.Person.firstname"/>` will be transformed in *Firstname* if the locale is English and into *Vorname* if the locale is German. The values are retrieved from some special internationalization files located under `WEB-INF` directory and a `MessageSource` and a `LocaleChangeInterceptor` beans retrieve values from them based on the locale. A working example is provided for you in the `/chapter06/mvc-basic`, and since internationalization is not a topic for the exam, no more details will be provided in this chapter.

@MVC

In Spring 3.0 the *@MVC* was introduced as a new configuration model based mostly on annotations. The `@Controller` annotation was introduced in Spring 2.5, booting up the entire Spring MVC mechanism was still a pain. Something was done about it in this version. The main component of an MVC XML configuration was introduced. The `<mvc:annotation-driven/>` element registers all the default infrastructure beans necessary for a web application to work: handler mapping, validation, conversion beans, and many others.

Another component that is important is the `<mvc:default-servlet-handler/>`. Usually in Spring web applications, the default servlet mapping "/" is mapped to the DispatcherServlet. This means that static resources will have to be served by it too, which might introduce a certain lag in providing a response as the DispatcherServlet has to find the resources the request url is mapped to. Think about it like this: a request comes to the DispatcherServlet. The default behavior of DispatcherServlet is to start looking for a controller to handle this request. And when it does not find one, it assumes this a request for a static resource and then asks the static resources handler if it can handle the request. By declaring `<mvc:default-servlet-handler/>` a handler for static resources is defined with the lowest precedence and this handler will be asked first if it can handle the request.

Technically, the `<mvc:default-servlet-handler/>` configures a DefaultServletHttpRequestHandler with a URL mapping of "/*" and the lowest priority relative to all others URL mappings and its sole responsibility is to serve static resources. A common case of explicitly declaring this handler is when the DispatcherServlet is mapped to "/" thus overriding the servlet container's default handling of static resources.

To use the @MVC elements the mvc namespace must be specified.

```
<beans xmlns="http://www.springframework.org/schema/beans"
       xmlns:xsi="http://www.w3.org/2001/XMLSchema-instance"
       xmlns:context="http://www.springframework.org/schema/context"
       xmlns:mvc="http://www.springframework.org/schema/mvc"
       xsi:schemaLocation="http://www.springframework.org/schema/mvc
       http://www.springframework.org/schema/mvc/spring-mvc.xsd
           http://www.springframework.org/schema/beans
           http://www.springframework.org/schema/beans/spring-beans.xsd
           http://www.springframework.org/schema/context
           http://www.springframework.org/schema/context/spring-context.
           xsd">

  <!-- Defines basic MVC defaults (handler mapping, date formatting, etc) -->
    <mvc:annotation-driven/>

    <!-- Configures a handler for serving static resources by forwarding
    to the
        Servlet container's default Servlet.-->
    <mvc:default-servlet-handler/>
</beans>
```

There are a lot of out of the box features that can be used with the @MVC model, but they are out of scope for this book. If you are interested in knowing more, there is a good book that I wrote called *Pivotal Certified Spring Web Application Developer Exam: A Study Guide* (Apress, 2015).[15] It's a little old and it is written for Spring 4, but it should be good enough to introduce you to the Spring Web world.[16]

The `chapter06/mvc-basic-xml` is a working project with a full Spring XML configuration and the configuration snippets from this chapter are taken from there. Feel free to inspect the project structure and run it to confirm it works.

Java Configuration for Spring MVC

In Spring 3.1, the `@EnableWebMvc` annotation was introduced. This annotation, when used on a configuration class, is the equivalent of `<mvc:annotation-driven/>`. Of course, there are a few extra details to take care of to make sure the configuration works as expected, and they are all covered in this section.

The first step is to transform the `mvc-config.xml` into a configuration class. Each bean definition, each scanning element must have a correspondence in the web configuration class. The configuration class has to be annotated with the `@Configuration` and `@EnableWebMvc` annotation and has to either implement `WebMvcConfigurer` or extend an implementation of this interface provided by Spring named `WebMvcConfigurerAdapter`, which gives the developer the option to override only the methods he or she is interested in. Annotating a configuration class with `@EnableWebMvc` has the result of importing the Spring MVC configuration implemented in the `WebMvcConfigurationSupport` class and is equivalent to `<mvc:annotation-driven/>`. This class registers many of the infrastructure Spring components necessary for a web application. Only some of them are covered in this section, since this topic is not needed for the Spring Core certification exam.

---

[15]Official page of the book: `https://www.apress.com/gp/book/9781484208090`

[16]Pivotal no longer provides the Spring Web Developer certification, and the core elements of Spring Web development are now part of the Spring Professional Certification: `https://pivotal.io/training/certification/spring-professional-certification`. The more advanced elements are part of the Pivotal Application Architect Certification: `https://pivotal.io/training/certification/pivotal-application-architect-certification`.

To tell the `DispatcherServlet` that the configuration will be provided by a configuration class instead of a file, the following changes have to be made in `web.xml`.

- An initialization parameter named `contextClass`. Its value is the full class name of the Spring class used to create an annotation-based context.

- An initialization parameter named `contextConfigLocation`. Its value is the full class name of the configuration class written by the developer.

```
<web-app ...>
  <!-- The front controller, the entry point for all requests -->
    <servlet>
        <servlet-name>cems-dispatcher</servlet-name>
        <servlet-class>
            org.springframework.web.servlet.DispatcherServlet
        </servlet-class>
        <init-param>
            <param-name>contextClass</param-name>
            <param-value>
                org.springframework.web.context.
                        support.AnnotationConfigWebApplicationContext
            </param-value>
        </init-param>
        <init-param>
            <param-name>contextConfigLocation</param-name>
            <param-value>
                [com.apress.cems.web.config.WebConfig]
            </param-value>
        </init-param>
        <load-on-startup>1</load-on-startup>
    </servlet>
</web-app>
```

The configuration class for what was configured with XML in the previous section looks like this:

```
package com.apress.cems.web.config;

import org.springframework.context.annotation.Bean;
import org.springframework.context.annotation.ComponentScan;
import org.springframework.context.annotation.Configuration;

import org.springframework.web.servlet.config.annotation.EnableWebMvc;
import org.springframework.web.servlet.config.annotation.WebMvcConfigurer;

import org.springframework.web.servlet.view.InternalResourceViewResolver;

...
@Configuration
@EnableWebMvc // <=><mvc:annotation-driven/>

// <=>   <context:component-scan base-package="com.apress.cems.web.
controllers"/>
@ComponentScan(basePackages = {"com.apress.cems.web.controllers"})
public class WebConfig implements WebMvcConfigurer {

    // <=> <mvc:default-servlet-handler/>
    @Override
    public void configureDefaultServletHandling(
            DefaultServletHandlerConfigurer configurer) {
        configurer.enable();
    }

    @Bean
    InternalResourceViewResolver getViewResolver(){
        InternalResourceViewResolver resolver = new
        InternalResourceViewResolver();
        resolver.setPrefix("/WEB-INF/");
        resolver.setSuffix(".jsp" );
        resolver.setRequestContextAttribute("requestContext");
        return resolver;
    }
... // other beans and method implementations that are not in scope
  }
```

The WebMvcConfigurer can now be used directly as after the adoption of Java 8, all methods have been declared as default, further simplifying the configuration the developer has to provide. This interface replaces class WebMvcConfigurerAdapter class that was extended in the previous version of this book.

Getting Rid of web.xml

Starting with Servlet 3.0+ the web.xml file is no longer necessary to configure a web application. It can be replaced with a class implementing the org.springframework. web.WebApplicationInitializer interface (or a class extending any of the Spring classes that extend this interface). This class will be detected automatically by org. springframework.web.SpringServletContainerInitializer(an internal Spring supported class which is not meant to be used directly or extended), which itself is bootstrapped automatically by any Servlet 3.0+ container.

The SpringServletContainerInitializer[17] extends javax.servlet. ServletContainerInitializer and provides a Spring specific implementation for the onStartup method. This class is loaded and instantiated. The onStartup method is invoked by any Servlet 3.0–compliant container during the container's startup, assuming that the spring-web module JAR is in the classpath. Thus, the web.xml file can be deleted, and XML configuration for Spring MVC is still provided. The class ends up looking like this:

```
package com.apress.cems.web.config;

import org.springframework.web.WebApplicationInitializer;
import org.springframework.web.servlet.DispatcherServlet;

import javax.servlet.ServletContext;
import javax.servlet.ServletException;
import javax.servlet.ServletRegistration;

public class WebInitializer implements WebApplicationInitializer {

    @Override
    public void onStartup(ServletContext servletContext) throws
    ServletException {
```

---

[17]The code of this class can be found here: https://github.com/spring-projects/spring-framework/blob/master/spring-web/src/main/java/org/springframework/web/SpringServletContainerInitializer.java

```
        ServletRegistration.Dynamic registration =
            servletContext.addServlet("cems-dispatcher", new
            DispatcherServlet());
        registration.setLoadOnStartup(1);
        registration.addMapping("/");
        registration.setInitParameter("contextConfigLocation",
            "/WEB-INF/spring/mvc-config.xml");
    }
}
```

There are more ways than one to write the preceding implementation; for example, the application context can be constructed first and then injected into the DispatcherServlet, but they are out of scope for this book.

```
package com.apress.cems.web.config;

import org.springframework.web.WebApplicationInitializer;
import org.springframework.web.servlet.DispatcherServlet;

import javax.servlet.ServletContext;
import javax.servlet.ServletException;
import javax.servlet.ServletRegistration;

public class WebInitializer implements WebApplicationInitializer {

    @Override
    public void onStartup(ServletContext servletContext) throws
    ServletException {
      XmlWebApplicationContext appContext = new XmlWebApplicationContext();
      appContext.setConfigLocation("/WEB-INF/spring/mvc-config.xml");
      ServletRegistration.Dynamic registration =
      servletContext.addServlet("cems-dispatcher", new DispatcherServlet
      (appContext));
      registration.setLoadOnStartup(1);
      registration.addMapping("/");
    }
}
```

If a configuration class annotated with @EnableWebMvc is used, then the implementation of the onStartup(...) method changes to the following.

```
 package com.apress.cems.web.config;

import org.springframework.web.WebApplicationInitializer;
import org.springframework.web.servlet.DispatcherServlet;

import javax.servlet.ServletContext;
import javax.servlet.ServletException;
import javax.servlet.ServletRegistration;

public class WebInitializer implements WebApplicationInitializer {

    @Override
    public void onStartup(ServletContext servletContext) throws
    ServletException {
      ServletRegistration.Dynamic registration =
      servletContext.addServlet("cems-dispatcher", new
      DispatcherServlet());
      registration.setLoadOnStartup(1);
      registration.addMapping("/");
      registration.setInitParameter("contextConfigLocation",
            "com.apress.cems.web.config.WebConfig");
      registration.setInitParameter("contextClass",
            "org.springframework.web.servlet.support
                .AnnotationConfigWebApplicationContext");
    }
}
```

There are many ways to write a configuration using Java configuration classes as well, but only the most common way is depicted here, where the AbstractAnnotationConfigDispatcherServletInitializer class is extended.

```
package com.apress.cems.web.config;

import com.apress.cems.dj.ServiceConfig;
import com.apress.cems.dj.OracleDataSourceConfig;
...
```

```
import org.springframework.web.servlet.support.
    AbstractAnnotationConfigDispatcherServletInitializer;
...
public class WebInitializer extends
    AbstractAnnotationConfigDispatcherServletInitializer {
    @Override
    protected Class<?>[] getRootConfigClasses() {
        return new Class<?>[]{
                OracleDataSourceConfig.class, ServiceConfig.class
        };
    }

    @Override
    protected Class<?>[] getServletConfigClasses() {
        return new Class<?>[]{
                WebConfig.class
        };
    }

    @Override
    protected String[] getServletMappings() {
        return new String[]{"/"};
    }
}
```

This class defines a set of methods that can be overridden by the developer
to provide a complete configuration for a web application without needing any
XML. It is most suitable and easy to use for multimodule applications where the root
context should be separated from web context. In the code depicted previously, the
getRootConfigClasses() is called internally and the configuration classes are used to
create the root application context. The getServletMappings() method sets the context
of DispatcherServlet, and getServletFilters() is used to set an additional filter for
the application.

CC   Classes that replace the `web.xml` configuration file are usually named `WebInitializer` or `WebAppInitializer` to make it obvious that this is what bootstraps the web application.

!   In most examples on the Internet, you will find this class annotated with `@Configuration`. This is useless, because this class is not a Spring configuration class. It really does nothing for the application; it just shows you do not understand how Spring actually works.

Using Spring to create web applications is easy and practical, but it is also a wide subject, which is not covered in this book because only the basic idea is a topic for the certification exam.

Running a Spring Web Application

In the previous edition of this book, all applications were run on a Jetty server using a Gradle Plugin named Gretty.[18] Unfortunately, the plugin was not maintained properly and using it with JDK 11 and a project with a module configuration has proven to be impossible at the moment when this chapter is being written.

Another solution would be to use Tomcat embedded, but embedded Tomcat version 9.0.22, the most recent one when this chapter is being written, was built with JDK 8, so the behavior in combination with a framework as complex as Spring and using JDK 11 is quite unpredictable. So, the most stable option right now is to install Apache Tomcat separately and deploy a Spring application on it. This is done in the context of a small exercise.

!   This exercise is intended to test your understanding of configuring a very simple Spring application. You have to complete the missing pieces, so when deployed, your application will show the page shown in Figure 6-11. Although an Oracle database configuration is available in the `OracleDataSource` (`Config` class, which is part of the `chapter05/data-jpa` project a dependency of all the classic web projects for this chapter) the configuration was replaced with an

---

[18]GitHub repository of this plugin: `https://github.com/gretty-gradle-plugin/gretty`

H2 configuration. The H2DbConfig class spares you the extra work of setting up an Oracle Docker container and the long time it takes hibernate to prepare your database.

There are five TODO tasks for this section numbered from 43 to 47. If you want to test your understanding of Spring Web MVC configuration, you can try solving them.

Task TODO 43, located in the WebConfig class, requires you to complete the configuration of this class to make it usable in creating a web application context.

Task TODO 44, located in the WebConfig class, requires you to provide the configuration for the InternalResourceViewResolver bean.

Task TODO 45 is located in the PersonController class and requires you to configure the controller bean to handle requests (https://localhost:8080/mvc-basic-practice/persons/*).

Task TODO 46 is located in the PersonController class and requires you to configure the list(..) to handle GET requests to https://localhost:8080/mvc-basic-practice/persons/list.

Task TODO 47 is located in the PersonController class and requires you to configure the show(..) to handle GET requests to https://localhost:8080/mvc-basic-practice/persons/show?id=[number].

And if you feel brave, go ahead and solve the TODO 48 which requires you to complete the implementation and configuration of the DetectiveController class. The views have been provided; you just need to turn the class into a controller and configure the handler methods.

If you have trouble, you can take a peek at the proposed solution in the chapter06/mvc-basic project.

Running with Tomcat

Since Apache Tomcat is the server on which the applications will be deployed in this chapter, let's get into that. You can download the latest version of Apache Tomcat from `https://tomcat.apache.org/download-90.cgi`. Get the one matching your OS and install it according to the instructions.

When building a web application, the result is a `*.war` archive named as the project. In the `chapter06/mvc-basic-practice/build.gradle` file, an extra configuration must be added to make sure the war name is `mvc-basic-practice` so that when deploying it on Apache Tomcat the context of the application will be the same.

```
war {
    archivesBaseName = 'mvc-basic-practice'
}
```

After running `gradle build` on the `chapter06/mvc-basic-practice` module, under `mvc-basic-practice/build/libs` the `mvc-basic-practice.war` should be present. Without this configuration the resulting war name will include the version of the project too. So the result will be: `mvc-basic-practice-1.0-SNAPSHOT.war`. Deploying this web application to Tomcat is easy: copy the `mvc-basic-practice.war` under `tomcat/webapps/` and start the server. The application will be deployed and available at `http://localhost:8080/mvc-basic-practice/`. And if all goes well, you should see a page similar to the one depicted in Figure 6-11.

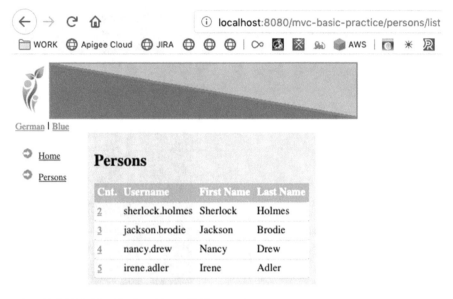

Figure 6-11. *CEMS front page*

The previous method of deployment is the manual way. But because we are using IntelliJ IDEA things can be made easier by creating an application launcher.

There is a section with buttons on the upper right side of the IDE, next to a green triangle. If you click that field, a pop-up menu is opened, as depicted in Figure 6-12.

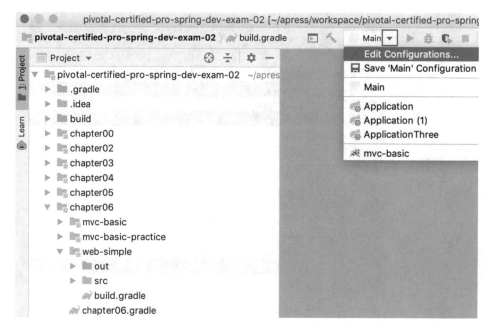

Figure 6-12. *IntelliJ IDEA Launcher Configuration menu*

From the menu, select *Edit Configurations* and a new window will pop up. Click the + (plus sign) in the upper-left corner, and select *Tomcat Server* ➤ *Local* from the menu. On the right side, you can now select the Apache Tomcat information (see Figure 6-13).

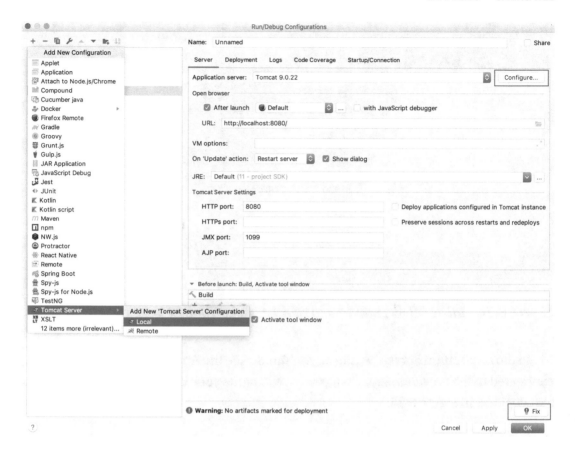

Figure 6-13. *IntelliJ IDEA Tomcat configuration menu*

The Fix button is because no ∗.war was selected yet to be deployed on Tomcat. This is how you know your configuration is still incomplete.

Click the *Configure* button to select the location of your Apache Tomcat server. The window depicted in Figure 6-14 is opened.

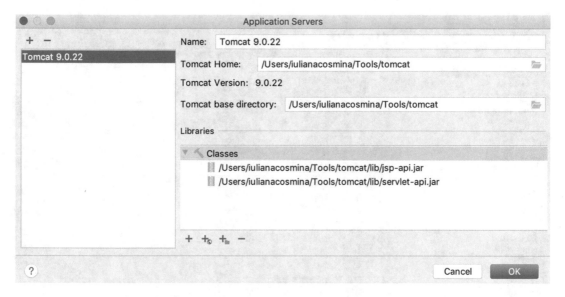

Figure 6-14. *IntelliJ IDEA window to select Apache Tomcat location*

In the Application Servers windows you should see the Apache Tomcat instance configured in the previous step. First, you have to name your launcher. There is a field for that depicted in Figure 6-15.

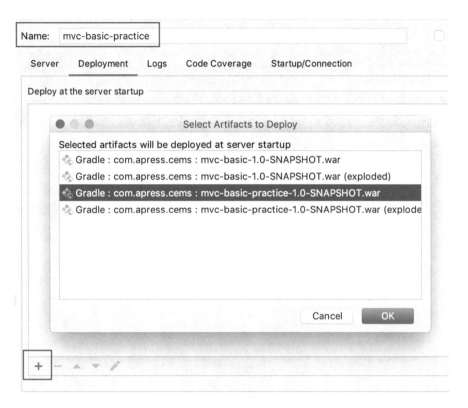

Figure 6-15. *IntelliJ IDEA, the Deployment tab*

It is time to configure what to deploy on this instance. For this, go to the `Deployment` tab and click the + button. IntelliJ IDEA is quite smart and detects the web applications in the project; it will provide you a list to choose from. Choose `mvc-basic-practice` and click the OK button.

- The next step is important. Once you chose the web artifact to deploy, IntelliJ tries to be helpful and generates an application context for you which is not what you want. Just take a look at Figure 6-16.

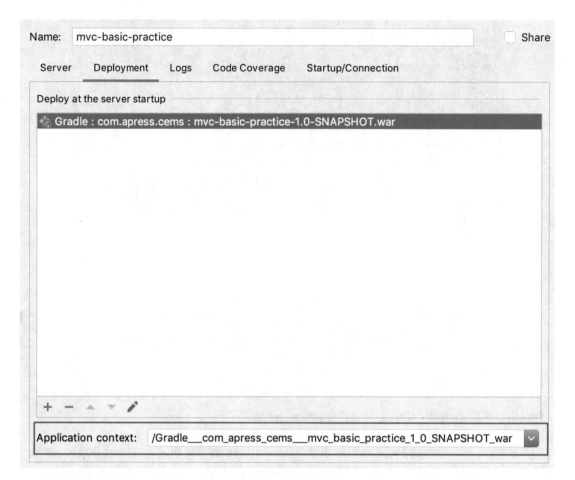

Figure 6-16. *IntelliJ IDEA Launcher configure application context name*

Imagine accessing your application using http://localhost:8080/Gradle__com_apress_cems__mvc_basic_practice_1_0_SNAPSHOT_war/. No, you wouldn't want that for sure. So edit that field and set it to mvc-basic-practice or something even more simple than that. Just make your choice. 😊

And this is how the CEMS application can be run with Apache Tomcat 9. The steps are similar even if a different application server is used, as long as IntelliJ IDEA supports it.

Thymeleaf

In the previous section, the views used were JSP pages. But JSP pages can turn very ugly and convoluted when you have a complex site to build. In the previous edition of the book, there was a section about how to use Spring with Apache Tiles. Since then, the project has been retired.[19] A *new partner* entered the scene: Thymeleaf.[20] Thymeleaf is a modern server-side Java template engine for both web and stand-alone environments. It was created having the idea of perfect integration with Spring to create modern-day HTML5 web applications using elegant natural templates that reduce the effort needed to create a site.

To cover more Spring capabilities for writing Spring applications we therefore need a view technology that is simple, quick to learn and easy to use. Thymeleaf is such a technology. So, how do we integrate Thymeleaf with Spring? Well, the obvious step is to change to a different View resolver bean. So the `InternalResourceViewResolver` used previously must be replaced with `ThymeleafViewResolver` from the `thymeleaf-spring5` library provided by the Thymeleaf team, which must be added to the project classpath.

Thymeleaf supports multiple kinds of templates: HTML, XML, TEXT, JAVASCRPT, CSS, and RAW, but the easiest to use are the HTML templates. And the beauty of it is that it is integrated with Spring controller beans, localization, validation, and messaging beans. The documentation on how the internals of Thymeleaf work is quite good. So let's see what we need to add to a Spring configuration so that we can change our application to use Thymeleaf templates.

```
package com.apress.cems.web.config;

import org.springframework.web.context.ServletContextAware;
import org.thymeleaf.spring5.SpringTemplateEngine;
import org.thymeleaf.spring5.view.ThymeleafViewResolver;
import org.thymeleaf.templateresolver.ServletContextTemplateResolver;

class WebConfig implements WebMvcConfigurer, ServletContextAware {
```

---

[19]Details on the official site: `https://tiles.apache.org/`

[20]Thymeleaf official site: `https://www.thymeleaf.org/`

```java
    private ServletContext servletContext;

    @Override
    public void setServletContext(ServletContext servletContext) {
        this.servletContext = servletContext;
    }

    @Bean
    public ServletContextTemplateResolver templateResolver() {
        ServletContextTemplateResolver resolver =
            new ServletContextTemplateResolver(servletContext);
        resolver.setPrefix("/WEB-INF/");
        resolver.setSuffix(".html");
        resolver.setTemplateMode("HTML5");
        resolver.setCharacterEncoding("UTF-8");
        resolver.setCacheable(false);
        return resolver;
    }

    @Bean
    public SpringTemplateEngine templateEngine() {
        SpringTemplateEngine templateEngine = new SpringTemplateEngine();
        templateEngine.setTemplateResolver(templateResolver());
        templateEngine.setTemplateEngineMessageSource(messageSource());
        return templateEngine;
    }

    @Bean
    public ThymeleafViewResolver viewResolver() {
        ThymeleafViewResolver viewResolver = new ThymeleafViewResolver();
        viewResolver.setTemplateEngine(templateEngine());
        viewResolver.setCharacterEncoding("UTF-8");
        viewResolver.setOrder(1);
        return viewResolver;
    }
    ...
}
```

To keep it short: a `ThymeleafViewResolver` requires a `SpringTemplateEngine` to resolve the templates correctly. The template engine uses Spring infrastructure beans to resolve the templates, replaces Spring-specific elements, and transforms them into views that are rendered to the user. As you can see from the bean declaration method, if a `MessageSource` bean is set (the `messageSource` bean declaration was excluded as it is not relevant for the current topic), internationalized texts will be replaced with the translation from the locale set for the application.

The template engine needs to know where the view template files are located and what type of templates they are. This information is provided to it by the `ServletContextTemplateResolver`. And since we are building a web application the servlet context is injected in this bean so access to the necessary infrastructure beans is ensured.

The `ServletContextTemplateResolver` is a Thymeleaf class and behind the scene, it creates `ServletContextTemplateResource` instances for template resources. For this it needs access to the servlet context of the application. So that is why the `ServletContextAware` interface was implemented in the preceding code sample, so Spring could inject the servlet context to be used by this bean.

The `ServletContextTemplateResolver` class is part of the `org.thymeleaf.templateresolver` package, and its main advantage is that it is not Spring specific, so it can be used in a JEE application as well. Of course, there is a Spring-specific template resolver class that resolves templates using Spring's Resource Resolution mechanism. Honestly, the classes are interchangeable. I haven't noticed any discrepancies when I use one or the other. The only difference between them is that the `SpringResourceTemplateResolver` has access to the Spring application context.

```
package com.apress.cems.web.config;

import org.springframework.context.ApplicationContext;
import org.springframework.context.ApplicationContextAware;
import org.thymeleaf.spring5.SpringTemplateEngine;
import org.thymeleaf.spring5.view.ThymeleafViewResolver;
import org.thymeleaf.spring5.templateresolver.
SpringResourceTemplateResolver;
```

```java
class WebConfig implements WebMvcConfigurer, ApplicationContextAware {

    private ApplicationContext applicationContext;

    @Override
    public void setApplicationContext(ApplicationContext
    applicationContext)
            throws BeansException {
        this.applicationContext = applicationContext;
    }

    @Bean
    public SpringResourceTemplateResolver templateResolver(){
        SpringResourceTemplateResolver springTemplateResolver =
                new SpringResourceTemplateResolver();
        springTemplateResolver.setApplicationContext(this.
        applicationContext);
        springTemplateResolver.setPrefix("/WEB-INF/");
        springTemplateResolver.setSuffix(".html");
        springTemplateResolver.setTemplateMode("HTML5");
        springTemplateResolver.setCharacterEncoding("UTF-8");
        return springTemplateResolver;
    }

    @Bean
    public SpringTemplateEngine templateEngine() {
        SpringTemplateEngine templateEngine = new SpringTemplateEngine();
        templateEngine.setTemplateResolver(templateResolver());
        templateEngine.setTemplateEngineMessageSource(messageSource());
        return templateEngine;
    }

    @Bean
    public ThymeleafViewResolver viewResolver() {
        ThymeleafViewResolver viewResolver = new ThymeleafViewResolver();
        viewResolver.setTemplateEngine(templateEngine());
        viewResolver.setCharacterEncoding("UTF-8");
```

```
        viewResolver.setOrder(1);
        return viewResolver;
    }
    ...
}
```

And now that you know how to configure support for Thymeleaf, let's look at an HTML template. When designing the interface for a web application, there are always common elements, such as a header, a footer, and a navigation menu. The only thing that ever changes is the center of the page that changes based on the option selected from the navigable menu. Each of these parts are called *fragments*, which are declared in special HTML files called *layouts* that reside under the WEB-INF/templates directory. This is a Thymeleaf standard for organizing templates; but as long as the path to fragments is set correctly in the templates that use them, you can name that directory any way you want it.

The following HTML template is called layout.html. For the application specific to this chapter, it is the only template file needed. This file contains a number of fragments, each of them matching a section of the page.

```html
<!DOCTYPE HTML>
<html xmlns:th="http://www.thymeleaf.org">
    <head th:fragment="cemsHead(title)">
        <link rel="icon" type="image/png" th:href="@{/images/favicon.ico}">
        <meta http-equiv="Content-Type" content="text/html; charset=UTF-8" />
        <title th:text="${title}"> Layout Page </title>
        <link type="text/css" rel="stylesheet"
                th:with="cssStyle=${#themes.code('css.style')}"
                th:href="@{(${cssStyle})}" >
        <link type="text/css" rel="stylesheet" th:href="@{/styles/general.
        css}" >
    </head>
    <body>
    <!-- banner, internationalization and theme options  section-->
    <header th:fragment="cemsHeader">
        <div class="banner"></div>
        <div class="themeLocal">
```

```
            <span th:if="${#locale.language eq 'en'}">
                <a th:href="@{/?lang=de}" th:text="#{locale.de}">DE</a>
            </span>
            <span th:unless="${#locale.language eq 'en'}">
                <a th:href="@{/?lang=en}" th:text="#{locale.en}">EN</a>
            </span> |
            <span th:if="${#themes.code('name') eq 'green'}">
                <a th:href="@{/?theme=blue}" th:text="#{theme.Blue}">BLUE
                </a>
            </span>
            <span th:unless="${#themes.code('name') eq 'green'}">
                <a th:href="@{/?theme=green}" th:text="#{theme.
                Green}">GREEN</a>
            </span>
        </div>
    </header>

    <!-- the navigable menu on the left -->
    <section th:fragment="cemsMenu">
        <div class="menu">
            <ul>
                <li><span th:if="${menuTab eq 'home'}">
                        <strong><a th:href="@{/}" th:text="#{menu.
                        home}">HOME</a></strong>
                    </span>
                    <span th:unless="${menuTab eq 'home'}">
                        <a th:href="@{/}" th:text="#{menu.home}">HOME</a>
                    </span>
                </li>
                <li><span th:if="${menuTab eq 'persons'}">
                        <strong><a th:href="@{/persons/list}"
                        th:text="#{menu.persons}">
                            PERSONS
                          </a></strong>
                    </span>
```

```
            <span th:unless="${menuTab eq 'persons'}">
                <a th:href="@{/persons/list}" th:text="#{menu.
                persons}">
                    PERSONS</a>
            </span>
        </li>
        <li><span th:if="${menuTab eq 'detectives'}">
                <strong><a th:href="@{/detectives/list}"
                th:text="#{menu.detectives}">
                    DETECTIVES</a></strong>
            </span>
            <span th:unless="${menuTab eq 'detectives'}">
                <a th:href="@{/detectives/list}" th:text="#{menu.
                detectives}">
                    DETECTIVES</a>
            </span>
        </li>
    </ul>
    </div>
</section>

<!-- the content of the page -->
<section th:fragment="cemsContent">
    <div class="content">
        <p>Page Content</p>
    </div>
</section>

<!-- the footer-->
<footer th:fragment="cemsFooter">
    <div class="footer">
        <p th:text="#{footer.text}"></p>
    </div>
</footer>
</body>
</html>
```

The previous snippet looks like HTML code, only there are a lot of th: elements. Those are elements that are processed by the Thymeleaf template engine and replaced with the proper values. Some of the Thymeleaf elements are underlined and the next list contains explanations for each of them.

- The th:fragment="cemsHead(title)" is a parametrized fragment. It can be used in pages to set a different title in a page using it. To use this element in a page the th:replace element must be used and a value consisting of the location of the file where the fragment is declared, suffixed with :: and the name of the fragment is needed to refer the fragment. The way to read it is: in this page, replace this section with fragment cemsHead from template templates/layout. Yes, the extension is not needed. Because it is a parametrized fragment, a different argument is provided, which sets a relevant title to that page. You can find these templates in project chapter06/mvc-thymeleaf.

  ```
  <!-- persons/list.html -->
  <!DOCTYPE HTML>
  <html xmlns:th="http://www.thymeleaf.org">

  <head th:replace="~{templates/layout :: cemsHead('CEMS List
  Persons Page')}"></head>
  ...
  </html>
  ```

  Non-parametrized fragments are used the same way without specifying an argument.

- The th:href is the element to use to generate contextual URLs. So th:href="@{/images/favicon.ico}", becomes http://localhost:8080/mvc-thymeleaf/images/favicon.ico

- The th:text provides a text value for any HTML element that requires a text value. To check if a Thymeleaf template is a valid HTML document, default values for text values can be used. In the template covered in this section, all text is written with uppercase letters. This is useful because it allows a developer to check its templates by opening them in a browser without the application server being up, because in this case, the templates are opened as a static HTML file. So a template like

```
<a th:href="@{/}" th:text="#{menu.home}">HOME</a>
```

is transformed into

```
<a href="http://localhost:8080/mvc-thymeleaf">Home</a>
```

Also in the previous template, notice the #{menu.home} construct. The # represents a reference to an internationalized code. So the text value is picked up from the properties file specific to the current locale, and in the context of a Spring application with a Thymeleaf engine bean replaces the static HOME text.

The th:with is special because when is processed, the variable within its value is created as a local variable and added to the variables map coming from the context, so that it is as available for evaluation as any other variables declared in the context from the beginning, but only within the bounds of the containing tag.

So the following link

```
<link type="text/css" rel="stylesheet"
      th:with="cssStyle=${#themes.code('css.style')}"
      th:href="@{(${cssStyle})}" >
```

is built into

```
<link type="text/css" rel="stylesheet"
      href="/mvc-thymeleaf/styles/decorator-green.css" >
```

In this case, the cssStyle variable is resolved according to the selected theme.

- The th:if and th:unless are used together as an if-then-else instruction to decide the text of a menu item depending on the current Locale value.

```
<span th:if="${#locale.language eq 'en'}">
            <a th:href="@{/?lang=de}" th:text="#{locale.
            de}">DE</a>
</span>
```

```
<span th:unless="${#locale.language eq 'en'}">
                <a th:href="@{/?lang=en}" th:text="#{locale.
                en}">EN</a>
</span>
```

And this is pretty much it. Thymeleaf was introduced because to further cover Spring Web MVC capabilities more pages have to be created, and creating them using pure JSP was a little too much work.

Another option for creating views that is currently popular is Mustache.[21] Mustache is a logic-less template engine for creating dynamic content like HTML, configuration files, source code, anything really. It is called logic-less because there is no support for statements like `if`, `if-else`, or any kind of loop. The core element of a Mustache template is the `tag`, and tags are indicated by encapsulating them in double curly brackets, sample: `{{person}}`. And because the curly brackets kinda look like moustaches, this is where the name of this template engine name was inspired. This template engine is liked by the Pivotal team, so much so there is a Spring Boot starter module for it: `spring-boot-starter-mustache`. Feel free to try it after traversing the Spring Boot section. Thymeleaf is the preferred template engine for this book, mostly because of the readability of the templates and because of the history it has with Spring.

Exception Handling

When handler methods are executed things can go wrong. Some situations, like trying to access a URL that does not exist might be expected, some might not. In both scenarios, the activity has to be recorded and the end user has to be notified. Spring MVC catches and handles the exceptions using implementations of `HandlerExceptionResolver`. The typical way to treat an MVC exception is to prepare a model and select an error view. Multiple exception resolvers can be used and ordered in a chain to treat different type of exceptions in different ways. Spring MVC supports the following default resolvers (resolvers of these types are created automatically for you in a Spring web application), and they are declared in the `DispatcherServlet.properties` file that is packaged in the `spring-webmvc.jar`.

---

[21]Official page of Mustache: `https://mustache.github.io/`

```
org.springframework.web.servlet.HandlerExceptionResolver=
o.s.w.s.m.a.ExceptionHandlerExceptionResolver,\
o.s.w.s.m.a.ResponseStatusExceptionResolver,\
o.s.w.s.m.s.DefaultHandlerExceptionResolver
```

ExceptionHandlerExceptionResolver resolves exceptions by invoking methods annotated with @ExceptionHandler found within a controller or a class annotated with @ControllerAdvice.

ResponseStatusExceptionResolver resolves methods annotated with @ResponseStatus and maps them to the status code configured using this annotation.

DefaultHandlerExceptionResolver resolves exceptions raised by Spring MVC and maps them to HTTP status codes.[22]

The SimpleMappingExceptionResolver class is not in the previous list, but beans of this type can be declared and configured to map exception classes to view names and it is helpful to render error pages in a browser application. An exception resolver provides information related to the context in which the exception was thrown; that is, the handler method that was executing and the arguments that it was called with.

Let's start with the simplest example: people make mistakes when writing URLs all the time. Let's try to access the following URL: http://localhost:8080/mvc-basic/missing. Since no exception handling is configured, Spring will try to find a view using the InternalResourceViewResolver bean (or whatever other view resolver is found). Since it cannot find one, it assumes it must be a static page and tries to render that. But it fails to provide a proper page, and Apache Tomcat comes to the rescue. It displays its default error page, letting the user know what happened. Just look at Figure 6-17.

---

[22]The equivalent of this class when REST requests are processed is class *ResponseEntityExceptionHandler*

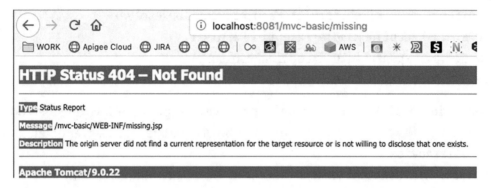

Figure 6-17. *Apache Tomcat default error page for missing view*

The default error message does a good job describing the problem, and it returns the proper HTTP status code for missing resources: 404. But still it's not OK, because this looks like a technical exception or a development problem. The recommended practice is to not let the end user know that. Also, there is no need to give so much details to the end user, because he should not be bothered with the internal problems an application has. So, what can be done? One rule of developing web applications is to keep the look and feel consistent, so instead of the Apache Tomcat page we could display a customized error view. Out of the box, Spring MVC offers no default (fallback) error page when a view or a handler method is not found. It doesn't throw an exception either; it just forwards the responsibility of showing the appropriate message to the server. To override this behavior, we need to make the following changes to a Spring web application configuration.

First, customize the `DispatcherServlet` to throw `org.springframework.web.servlet.NoHandlerFoundException` when a handler method cannot be found. This is done either by overriding the `customizeRegistration(..)` method from the `AbstractDispatcherServletInitializer` class in the `WebInitializer` class.

```
package com.apress.cems.web.config;

import org.springframework.web.servlet.support.
        AbstractAnnotationConfigDispatcherServletInitializer;
import javax.servlet.ServletRegistration;
...
```

```
public class WebInitializer extends
        AbstractAnnotationConfigDispatcherServletInitializer {

...

   @Override
    public void customizeRegistration(ServletRegistration.Dynamic
    registration) {
        registration.setInitParameter("throwExceptionIfNoHandlerFound",
        "true");
    }

}
```

Or, override the createDispatcherServlet(..) method from the AbstractDispatcherServletInitializer class in the WebInitializer class.

```
package com.apress.cems.web.config;

import org.springframework.web.context.WebApplicationContext;
import javax.servlet.ServletRegistration;
...

public class WebInitializer extends
        AbstractAnnotationConfigDispatcherServletInitializer {

...

   @Override
    protected DispatcherServlet createDispatcherServlet
                    (WebApplicationContext servletAppContext) {
        final DispatcherServlet dispatcherServlet =
            (DispatcherServlet) super.createDispatcherServlet(servlet
            AppContext);
        dispatcherServlet.setThrowExceptionIfNoHandlerFound(true);
        return dispatcherServlet;
    }
}
```

Both methods have the same effect: the `throwExceptionIfNoHandlerFound` property is set to true, which causes the `DispatcherServlet` to throw an `org.springframework.web.servlet.NoHandlerFoundException` when a handler method cannot be found. You can use whatever approach you desire, just keep in mind that `createDispatcherServlet(..)` provides more options of customizing the `DispatcherServlet` instance being created.

!   Note that adding this configuration does nothing if `DefaultServletHttpRequestHandler` is used, because requests will always be forwarded to it and a `NoHandlerFoundException` will never be thrown in that case. You can verify this by looking into the logs. If you see something similar to the next output snippet, you still have more steps to go.

```
DEBUG o.s.w.s.DispatcherServlet - GET "/mvc-basic/missing",
parameters={}
DEBUG o.s.w.s.h.SimpleUrlHandlerMapping - Mapped to
org.springframework.web.servlet.resource.DefaultServletHttpRe
questHandler@1eae4902
DEBUG o.s.w.s.DispatcherServlet - Completed 404 NOT_FOUND
```

So if in your configuration you have

```
<mvc:default-servlet-handler/>
```

or

```
@Override
public void configureDefaultServletHandling
    (DefaultServletHandlerConfigurer configurer) {
    configurer.enable();
}
```

just remove them and make do without `DefaultServletHttpRequestHandler` if you want `NoHandlerFoundExceptions` to be thrown.

But this does nothing without a bean of type HandlerExceptionResolver customized to do something else than simply tell the application server what to do. And this brings us to the next change.

Next, implement the HandlerExceptionResolver interface or extend any of the classes that implement it and provide the desired implementation for the doResolveException(...) method that will return the desired view.

```
package com.apress.cems.web.problem;

import org.springframework.http.HttpStatus;
import org.springframework.web.servlet.ModelAndView;
import org.springframework.web.servlet.NoHandlerFoundException;
import org.springframework.web.servlet.handler.
SimpleMappingExceptionResolver;

import javax.servlet.http.HttpServletRequest;
import javax.servlet.http.HttpServletResponse;

public class MissingExceptionResolver extends
        SimpleMappingExceptionResolver {

    @Override
    protected ModelAndView doResolveException(HttpServletRequest request,
            HttpServletResponse response, Object handler, Exception ex) {
        if (ex instanceof NoHandlerFoundException) {
            ModelAndView model = new ModelAndView("error");
            model.addObject("problem","URL not supported : "
                    + request.getRequestURI());
            response.setStatus(HttpStatus.NOT_FOUND.value());
            return model;
        }
        return null;
    }
}
```

> **!**   In the previous code sample, note that the method returns an actual
> `ModelAndView` instance. `HandlerExceptionResolve` implementations are
> designed to make sure an exception is resolved to a view or allowed to bubble up
> to the Servlet container.

- A `HandlerExceptionResolver` can return a `ModelAndView` that points
  to an error view, usually the same one for a related class of problems,
  or for the entire application.

- A `HandlerExceptionResolver` can return an empty `ModelAndView` if
  the exception is handled within the resolver.

- A `HandlerExceptionResolver` can return null if the exception
  remains unresolved, thus allowing other exception resolvers to try to
  handle it. If none of the exception resolvers can handle the exception,
  it is bubbled up to the Servlet container.

- Declare a bean of this type with the lowest priority (highest
  precedence), so that every time something goes wrong within the
  application, this exception resolver will be used first.

  ```
  package com.apress.cems.web.config;

  import com.apress.cems.web.problem.MissingExceptionResolver;
  import org.springframework.web.servlet.HandlerExceptionResolver;
  ...

  @Configuration
  @EnableWebMvc
  @ComponentScan(basePackages = {"com.apress.cems.web.controllers"})
  class WebConfig implements WebMvcConfigurer {
  ...

    @Bean
    HandlerExceptionResolver missingMappingExceptionResolver(){
        SimpleMappingExceptionResolver resolver = new
        MissingExceptionResolver();
  ```

```
        resolver.setOrder(Ordered.HIGHEST_PRECEDENCE);
        return resolver;
    }
}
```

And that is it. Now when a non-exiting URL is accessed, the customized error view will be rendered to the user. So, the new 404 page looks like the one depicted in Figure 6-18. To understand what is going on *under the hood*, we can take a look at the logs.

Figure 6-18. *New customized 404 page*

```
WARN  o.s.w.s.PageNotFound - No mapping for GET /mvc-basic/persons/AA
DEBUG c.a.c.w.p.MissingExceptionResolver - Resolved
    [org.springframework.web.servlet.NoHandlerFoundException:
    No handler found for GET /mvc-basic/persons/AA]
    to ModelAndView [view="error"; model={problem=URL not supported :
    /mvc-basic/persons/AA}]
DEBUG o.s.w.s.DispatcherServlet - Using resolved error view:
    ModelAndView [view="error"; model={problem=URL not supported :
    /mvc-basic/persons/AA}]
```

```
DEBUG o.s.w.s.v.JstlView - View name 'error', model
    {problem=URL not supported : /mvc-basic/persons/AA}
DEBUG o.s.w.s.v.JstlView - Forwarding to [/WEB-INF/error.jsp]
DEBUG o.s.w.s.DispatcherServlet - Completed 404 NOT_FOUND
```

We've solved the issue of error pages displayed when unsupported URLs are accessed. How about treating exceptions that are being thrown during handler method executions? That is even simpler.

A while ago, I introduced the PersonController class, which was used to handle URLs starting with /persons. The method in the next code snippet is mapped to a URL requiring a person id as a path variable and should populate a model to be used to populate a view with that person's details.

```
package com.apress.cems.web.controllers;

...

@Controller
@RequestMapping("/persons")
public class PersonController {

...
    /**
     * Handles requests to show detail about one person.
     */
    @RequestMapping(value = "/{id:[\\d]*}", method = RequestMethod.GET)
    public String show(@PathVariable Long id, Model model) {
        Optional<Person> personOpt = personService.findById(id);
        if(personOpt.isPresent()) {
            model.addAttribute("person", personOpt.get());
        } else {
            throw new NotFoundException(Person.class, id);
        }
        return "persons/show";
    }
}
```

So this method handles URLs like http://localhost:8080/mvc-basic/persons/3, but nothing can stop a user from manually modifying a URL and adding an invalid ID or an ID that does not exist in the database.

The problem caused by a user trying to access a URL like this `http://localhost:8080/mvc-basic/persons/AA`[23] with be handled by the previously declared exception resolver, because the AA does not match the regular expression declared in the `@RequestMapping` so a handler method matching `/persons/AA` is not found.

The other case, where the path variable matches the regular expression, but the id is not found in the database needs to be treated differently. For this scenario, a specific type of exception should be created.

```
package com.apress.cems.web.problem;

public class NotFoundException extends RuntimeException {

    private Long objIdentifier;

    public <T> NotFoundException(Class<T> cls, Long id) {
        super(cls.getSimpleName() + " with id: " + id + " does not exist!");
    }

    public Long getObjIdentifier() {
        return objIdentifier;
    }
}
```

So we have a handler method that might throw a `NotFoundException`. To handle this kind of situation, we have to declare a special controller method annotated with `@ExceptionHandler`. This annotation marks methods for handling exceptions in specific handler classes and/or handler methods.

```
package com.apress.cems.web.controllers;

import com.apress.cems.web.problem.NotFoundException;
import org.springframework.web.bind.annotation.ExceptionHandler;
...
```

---

[23]You might have noticed by now that the application context varies throughout the chapter. That is because there is more than one web application provided as example and each of the application is focused on a specific topic. The context names match the project names and this will help you navigate more efficiently the code provided as example.

```java
@Controller
@RequestMapping("/persons")
public class PersonController {

    ...

    @ExceptionHandler
    public ModelAndView notFound(HttpServletRequest req, NotFoundException
    nfe) {
        ModelAndView mav = new ModelAndView();
        mav.addObject("problem", "Malformed URL: "
            + req.getRequestURI() + "<br/>" + nfe.getMessage());
        mav.setViewName("error");
        return mav;
    }
}
```

This type of method is called an *exception handler method*; and as a handler method, it can have a flexible signature. What is not flexible about it is the return type. Since this method resolves an exception being thrown in a handler method, it must abide to the same rules as the doResolveException(..) exposed by the HandlerExceptionResolver interface. If the exception is generic and the message that is shown to the user is a generic one and it does not require access to the exception message, the previous method can be written like this:

```java
package com.apress.cems.web.controllers;

import com.apress.cems.web.problem.NotFoundException;
import org.springframework.web.bind.annotation.ExceptionHandler;
...

@Controller
@RequestMapping("/persons")
public class PersonController {

    ...
```

```
@ExceptionHandler(NotFoundException.class)
public ModelAndView notFound(HttpServletRequest req) {
    ModelAndView mav = new ModelAndView();
    mav.addObject("problem", "Cannot solve " + req.getRequestURI() );
    mav.setViewName("error");
    return mav;
    }
}
```

And since we are now printing a generic message, we can write an exception handler that handles any type of exception thrown by handler methods in that controller. Not that this would be a good approach, you should always try to have special exception resolver for a set of expected problems. I'm just letting you know that it is possible.

```
package com.apress.cems.web.controllers;

import org.springframework.web.bind.annotation.ExceptionHandler;
...

@Controller
@RequestMapping("/persons")
public class PersonController {

    ...

 @ExceptionHandler(Exception.class)
    public ModelAndView notFound(HttpServletRequest req) {
        ModelAndView mav = new ModelAndView();
        mav.addObject("problem", "The server has a problem resolving your
        request: "
            + req.getRequestURI() );
        mav.setViewName("error");
        return mav;
    }
}
```

To understand what is going on *under the hood* we can take a look at the logs.

```
DEBUG o.s.w.s.m.m.a.ExceptionHandlerExceptionResolver - Using
@ExceptionHandler
    com.apress.cems.web.controllers.PersonController#notFound[HttpServletRe
    quest,
        NotFoundException]
DEBUG o.s.w.s.m.m.a.ExceptionHandlerExceptionResolver -
    Resolved [com.apress.cems.web.problem.NotFoundException:
        Person with id: 99 does not exist!] to ModelAndView
        [view="error";
        model={problem=Malformed URL: /mvc-basic/persons/99 <br/>
            Person with id: 99 does not exist!}]
DEBUG o.s.w.s.DispatcherServlet - Using resolved error view: ModelAndView
    [view="error"; model={problem=Malformed URL: /mvc-basic/persons/99<br/>
        Person with id: 99 does not exist!}]
DEBUG o.s.w.s.v.JstlView - View name 'error', model
    {problem=Malformed URL: /mvc-basic/persons/99<br/>Person with id: 99
    does not exist!}
DEBUG o.s.w.s.v.JstlView - Forwarding to [/WEB-INF/error.jsp]
```

The ExceptionHandlerExceptionResolver is doing its thing, picking up methods annotated with @ExceptionHandler and using them to handle exceptions.

Boom, done. All is well with the Spring Web world. But, there is one thing that should bug any developer a little: having each controller declare its own exception handlers can be viewed like a cross cutting concern, especially when the messages for the end user are generic, as they should be. So from a development point of view, it would be best to have a dedicated component where all exception handler methods are declared, right?

The next configuration sample handles missing records of type Person and Detective by declaring a class named MissingRecordsHandler and annotating it with @ControllerAdvice. (It can be easily extended to do the same for any type of entity class in the application, since they share the common API exposed by AbstractEntity.)

Because this annotation is meta-annotated with @Component a bean of this type is created, which intercepts any handler method exceptions of type NotFoundException and render the error view.

```
package com.apress.cems.web.problem;

import org.springframework.web.bind.annotation.ControllerAdvice;
import org.springframework.web.bind.annotation.ExceptionHandler;
import org.springframework.web.servlet.ModelAndView;

import javax.servlet.http.HttpServletRequest;

@ControllerAdvice
public class MissingRecordsHandler {

    @ExceptionHandler
    public ModelAndView notFound(HttpServletRequest req, NotFoundException
    nfe) {
        ModelAndView mav = new ModelAndView();
        mav.addObject("problem", "Malformed URL: " + req.getRequestURI()
            + "<br/>" + nfe.getMessage());
        mav.setViewName("error");
        return mav;
    }
}
```

To test that this exception handler works as expected, you could try accessing
`http://localhost:8080/mvc-basic/detectives/99` and `http://localhost:8080/`
`mvc-basic/persons/99`. You should view the error page with the proper exception
message. If the response contents are inspected, you will notice that although an error
page is displayed the HTTP status code is still 200. Since the user is trying to access a
resource that does not exist, the HTTP status code should be 404. This can be done
easily by annotating the exception handler method with `@ResponseStatus(HttpStatus.`
`NOT_FOUND)`.

And that's pretty much it when it comes to handling exceptions thrown by the
handler methods. The next step is to write some tests for a Spring web application.

Testing a Spring Web Application

Writing tests for a Spring application is quite easy; for example, if the DAO and service layers were implemented correctly and passed their specific tests, the controller behavior can be isolated and tested using mocks. Let's see how this is done with Mockito. Testing a handler method should cover two aspects: the model was populated as expected and the expected view is returned.

Let's then test the PersonController by mocking the service layer using Mockito.

```
 package com.apress.cems.web.controllers;

import com.apress.cems.dao.Person;
import com.apress.cems.dj.services.PersonService;
import com.apress.cems.web.problem.NotFoundException;
import org.junit.jupiter.api.Test;
import org.junit.jupiter.api.extension.ExtendWith;
import org.mockito.InjectMocks;
import org.mockito.Mock;
import org.mockito.junit.jupiter.MockitoExtension;
import org.springframework.ui.ExtendedModelMap;

import java.util.ArrayList;
import java.util.List;
import java.util.Optional;

import static org.junit.jupiter.api.Assertions.*;
import static org.mockito.ArgumentMatchers.any;
import static org.mockito.Mockito.when;

@ExtendWith(MockitoExtension.class)
class PersonControllerTest {

    @Mock //Creates mock instance of the field it annotates
    private PersonService mockService;

    @InjectMocks // injects mock dependencies
    private PersonController personController;

    @SuppressWarnings("unchecked")
    @Test
```

```java
void testListHandler() {
    List<Person> list = new ArrayList<>();
    Person p = new Person();
    p.setId(1L);
    list.add(p);

    when(mockService.findAll()).thenReturn(list);

    ExtendedModelMap model = new ExtendedModelMap();
    String viewName = personController.list(model);
    List<Person> persons = (List<Person>) model.get("persons");

    assertAll(
            () -> assertNotNull(persons),
            () -> assertEquals(1, persons.size()),
            () -> assertEquals("persons/list", viewName)
    );
}

@Test
void testShowHandler() {
    Person p = new Person();
    p.setId(1L);

    when(mockService.findById(any(Long.class))).thenReturn(Optional.
    of(p));

    ExtendedModelMap model = new ExtendedModelMap();
    String viewName = personController.show(1L, model);
    Person person = (Person) model.get("person");

    assertAll(
            () -> assertNotNull(person),
            () -> assertEquals(1L, person.getId()),
            () -> assertEquals("persons/show", viewName)
    );
}
}
```

Pretty simple, right? Then again, unit tests are pretty elementary.

How about integration tests? Oh well, this is not possible right now. After the introduction of web applications configured without a `web.xml` file, integration tests for controllers using `org.springframework.test.context.web.WebAppConfiguration` and `org.springframework.test.web.servlet.request.MockMvcRequestBuilders`, which requires a mocked servlet container, no longer works. There is an issue on GitHub about testing controllers when using applications configured using `@WebAppConfiguration`. You can read the discussion if you want to, but the most complete list reasons can be found in a comment from Sam Brannen, one of the Spring developers at Pivotal; but it can be summarized as follows.

> *Although Spring does provide mocks for the Servlet API, Spring does not mock a Servlet container and currently has no intention to. Spring has always focused on out of container integration testing. Fully mocking a container is therefore beyond the scope of Spring's testing support.*
>
> `(https://github.com/spring-projects/spring-framework/issues/14` `832#issuecomment-453400355)`

My personal opinion is that since Spring Boot has emerged as the only solution to build and test Spring applications, there is no point in wasting too much time to support old-style development. Nowadays, all applications are built to be stand-alone—and Spring Boot is ideal for this. It is the main requirement so they can be deployed to the cloud and scaled horizontally: start as many instances as necessary and configure a load balancer to distribute the load. Let's look at building a Spring web application using Spring Boot.

Building Web Applications Using Spring Boot

Building web applications using Spring Boot is (as expected) easy, because there's a starter library for that. And to keep things easy, we can add in the mix the `spring-boot-starter-thymeleaf` starter library. The `spring-boot-starter-web` comes with support for embedded Tomcat, because the default dependency is `spring-boot-starter-tomcat`, as depicted in Figure 6-19.

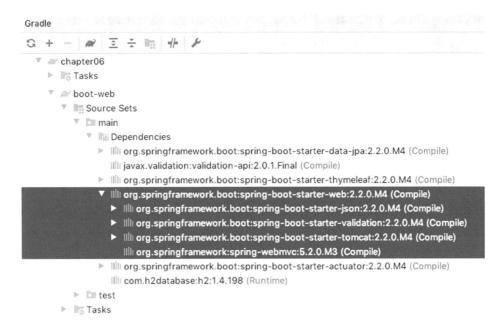

Figure 6-19. *Spring Boot Starter Web dependencies*

But this `spring-boot-starter-tomcat` can be excluded and `spring-boot-starter-jetty` or `spring-boot-starter-undertow` can be used instead. A few server properties can be configured using the `application.yml` file. We can set the port, the application context, HTTP response compression and many more. In the next configuration snippet, you can see server configuration lines from the verb|application.yml| of the `chapter06/boot-web` project.

```
server:
  port: 8081
  servlet:
    context-path: /
  compression:
    enabled: true
  address: 0.0.0.0
```

The server is started on the generic IP address 0.0.0.0 which means the application can be accessed at `http://localhost:8081/` or `http://0.0.0.0:8081/` or `http://127.0.0.1:8081/`, or using any other IP address associated with this computer, because 0.0.0.0 specifies all IP addresses on all interfaces on the system.

A few things in the structure of the project will change. Since this is a stand-alone application, there is no point to have a webapp or WEB-INF directory, since all their content is considered project resources. All static pages, internationalization resources and HTML templates now become resources, so all these will be stored under the resource directory. And since the application that we are building is quite simple and is supposed to be stand-alone, the data access and services are packaged within the same application. So it is time to change the package structure, and we will group classes by feature, which means everything that manages Person instances should be placed under the same package. *Package-by-feature* uses packages to reflect the feature set. So if we were to add support for handling detectives, everything related to this feature would have its own package. The packages resulted from organizing the code this way promote high cohesion and high modularity, and with minimal coupling between packages.[24]

The Spring Boot web application structure is depicted in Figure 6-20.

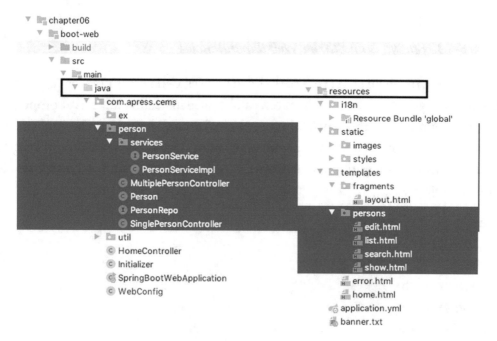

Figure 6-20. *Spring Boot web application structure*

---

[24]If you want to read more about this, I recommend this article: http://www.javapractices.com/ topic/TopicAction.do; jsessionid=0BF4844350780B6F55476E1137FF4893?Id=205

The code for entities, repositories and services is identical to what you would write for a classic Spring Web (or non-web) application. The changes necessary to be made when switching to Spring Boot are listed next.

- First, you need to change the classpath a little. For this application the following dependencies are needed.

  - `spring-boot-starter-data-jpa`, because implementation to access the database is needed

  - `spring-boot-starter-web`, because controllers must be written

  - `spring-boot-starter-thymeleaf`, because this is the template engine that we are using to generate views

  - `spring-boot-starter-test`, because the application must be tested and Spring Boot supports it best

- Create the Spring Boot typical class annotated with `@SpringBootApplication` to run your application.

- All beans that support internationalization and theming should be separated into a separate configuration class. In this case, a class named `WebConfig` was created for them.

- Everything from under `WEB-INF` needs to be moved under `src/main/resources`. The Spring Boot web application structure requires that static resources like images and CSS classes must be stored in a directory named `static` and view templates under a directory named `templates`.

That's pretty much it. Because the `spring-boot-starter-thymeleaf` is on the classpath we do not need to declare and configure the Thymeleaf beans to support views generation. Because `spring-boot-starter-web` is on the classpath, we do not need to declare and configure any Spring web-related infrastructure beans. After doing all the changes listed previously, you should have stand-alone Spring Boot web application that you can start by executing postpone `SpringBootWebApplication`.

And now, it is time for the part that you were expecting probably: testing this application. In the previous chapters, the `@SpringBootTest` annotation was introduced. This is a powerful annotation because when used on a test class it bootstraps the full Spring Boot context for the tests to be run in. This annotation is specific to integration tests. But some mocks can be used to reduce the context the tests run in. There is a useful annotation just for this purpose that was introduced in Spring Boot 1.4.0 named @WebMvcTest. This annotation is meta-annotated with @ExtendWith(SpringExtension. class) and a few other special mocking annotations to provide support for mocking layers of the application that are not needed when writing unit tests.[25]

That said, let's see how this annotation is used to test the web layer. This annotation can receive as parameters the controller name or names that we want to test, and only those controllers will be created. But controllers usually have service dependencies, right? We can mock those dependencies using a Mockito annotation named @MockBean and annotating a test class with @WebMvcTest provides as access to the web application context so these mock beans can be injected instead of the concrete dependencies. This annotation is the one to use when a test focuses only on Spring MVC components because it has the effect of disabling full autoconfiguration and registers configurations only relevant to MVC components: classes annotated with @Controller or @ControllerAdvice and classes implementing WebMvcConfigurer, but not @Service, @Repository, and so forth.

That said, let's introduce the controller class and handler method that will be tested.

```
package com.apress.cems.person;
...

@Controller
@RequestMapping("/persons")
public class MultiplePersonController {
    static Comparator<Person> COMPARATOR_BY_ID =
                Comparator.comparing(Person::getId);

    private Logger logger =
                LoggerFactory.getLogger(MultiplePersonController.class);

    private PersonService personService;
    private MessageSource messageSource;
```

---

[25]Check out its API Documentation here: https://docs.spring.io/spring-boot/docs/current/api/org/springframework/boot/test/autoconfigure/web/servlet/WebMvcTest.html

```java
    public MultiplePersonController(PersonService personService,
            MessageSource messageSource) {
        this.personService = personService;
        this.messageSource = messageSource;
    }

    @GetMapping(value = "/list")
    public String list(Model model) {
        logger.info("Populating model with list...");
        List<Person> persons =  personService.findAll();
        persons.sort(COMPARATOR_BY_ID);
        model.addAttribute("persons", persons);
        return "persons/list";
    }
}
```

If we apply all that was mentioned, the result should be a test class like the one depicted next. When executed, the test should pass.

```java
package com.apress.cems.boot;

import com.apress.cems.person.MultiplePersonController;
import com.apress.cems.person.Person;
import com.apress.cems.person.services.PersonService;
import org.junit.jupiter.api.BeforeEach;
import org.junit.jupiter.api.Test;
import org.springframework.beans.factory.annotation.Autowired;
import org.springframework.boot.test.autoconfigure.web.servlet.WebMvcTest;
import org.springframework.boot.test.mock.mockito.MockBean;
import org.springframework.test.web.servlet.MockMvc;
import org.springframework.test.web.servlet.setup.MockMvcBuilders;
import org.springframework.web.context.WebApplicationContext;

import java.util.ArrayList;
import java.util.List;
import java.util.Optional;
```

```java
import static org.hamcrest.Matchers.*;
import static org.mockito.ArgumentMatchers.anyLong;
import static org.mockito.Mockito.when;
import static org.springframework.test.web.servlet.request.
MockMvcRequestBuilders.get;
import static org.springframework.test.web.servlet.result.
MockMvcResultMatchers.*;

@WebMvcTest(controllers = {MultiplePersonController.class})
class SpringBootWebApplicationTest {

    private MockMvc mockMvc;

    @MockBean
    private PersonService mockService;

    @Autowired
    private WebApplicationContext webApplicationContext;

    @BeforeEach
    void setUp() throws Exception {
        mockMvc = MockMvcBuilders.webAppContextSetup(webApplication
        Context).build();
    }

    @Test
    void testList() throws Exception {
        List<Person> list = new ArrayList<>();
        Person p = new Person();
        p.setId(1L);
        p.setFirstName("Sherlock");
        p.setLastName("Holmes");
        list.add(p);
        when(mockService.findAll()).thenReturn(list);
```

```
mockMvc.perform(get("/persons/list"))
        .andExpect(status().isOk())
        .andExpect(view().name("persons/list"))
        .andExpect(model().attribute("persons", hasSize(1)))
        .andExpect(model().attribute("persons", hasItem(
            anyOf(
                    hasProperty("id", is(1L)),
                    hasProperty("firstName", is("Sherlock")),
                    hasProperty("lastName", is("Holmes"))
            )
        )));
    }
}
```

IntelliJ IDEA detects the Spring Boot application configured with Gradle, so it uses Gradle to execute the test. This leads to a very interesting effect. All the logs of starting up the Boot context the test is executed in are available in a console. So is the fact that the test was executed and it passed. Visually there is not much to look at anymore in IntelliJ IDEA, but a very pretty HTML file is generated with the results of the build, which can be opened in the default browser by clicking the elephant button in the test view. In Figure 6-21, this button is surrounded by a red rectangle. The test passed is mentioned in the console.

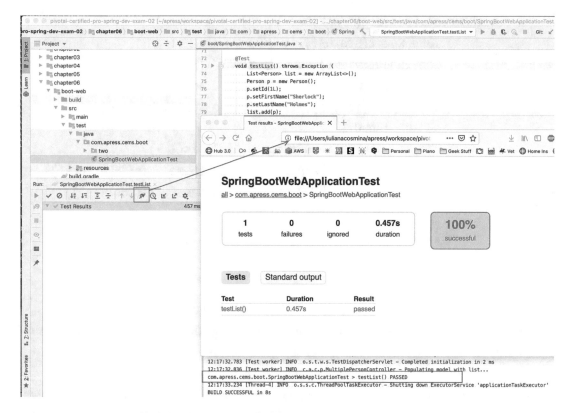

Figure 6-21. *Gradle HTML test result file*

The expectations are checked using a combination of Spring Test and Hamcrest static methods, which work well together and make it readable as well.

The MockMvc class is the core component needed to test Spring MVC applications. The MockMvcBuilders is a utility class used to instantiate the mockMvc object, and provides two methods to create thinned web application contexts used for test execution. In the previous example, the one that receives a WebApplicationContext as argument is used.

If we intend to write an integration test where no mocks are needed, the @AutoConfigureMockMvc can be used with @SpringBootTest to bootstrap the full application context. When this annotation is used, the mockMvc object is created and configured for you automatically. You just need to autowire it in the test class to send requests to the application.

```
package com.apress.cems.boot;

import org.junit.jupiter.api.Test;
import org.springframework.beans.factory.annotation.Autowired;
import org.springframework.boot.test.autoconfigure.web.servlet.
AutoConfigureMockMvc;
import org.springframework.boot.test.context.SpringBootTest;
import org.springframework.test.web.servlet.MockMvc;

import static org.hamcrest.Matchers.*;
import static org.springframework.test.web.servlet.request.
MockMvcRequestBuilders.get;
import static org.springframework.test.web.servlet.result.
MockMvcResultMatchers.*;

@SpringBootTest
@AutoConfigureMockMvc
class SpringBootWebApplicationTest {

    @Autowired
    private MockMvc mockMvc;

    @Test
    void testList() throws Exception {
        mockMvc.perform(get("/persons/list"))
                .andExpect(status().isOk())
                .andExpect(view().name("persons/list"))
                .andExpect(model().attribute("persons", hasSize(4)))
                .andExpect(model().attribute("persons", hasItem(
                        anyOf(
                                hasProperty("id", is(1L)),
                                hasProperty("firstName", is("Sherlock")),
                                hasProperty("lastName", is("Holmes"))
                        )
                )));
    }
}
```

In the previous tests, there was no reference to the port the application was started on, so the assumption is that the default port, 8080 would be used which means multiple Spring Boot tests cannot be executed in parallel. Which is a problem, because running tests in parallel to validate your changes as soon as possible is a very useful feature.

No problem, @SpringBootTest has your back in this case because it supports running the application on a random port by customizing the value of the webEnvironment attribute. The chosen port can be injected into a local variable so it can be used to decide where to send the test requests. The next test class does not use the mockMvc object to make the request to the application, because the web application context is not mocked this time. Instead, the full-blown context of the spring application is created. This means we have to use a different type of object to make the calls. There are a lot of components to choose from, like the TestRestTemplate, but I will postpone using this class until Chapter 8. Instead, I'll introduce a new testing library that I've worked with recently: REST-Assured.[26] REST-Assured was designed with the intent of providing similar syntax to Ruby and Groovy when writing web application tests, and I might say the goal was reached.

The next test class contains two test methods: one testing MultiplePersonController.lis() and one testing SinglePersonController. show(..). The value of the port the application uses is a random value, as configured by the webEnvironment attribute being assigned the SpringBootTest.WebEnvironment. RANDOM_PORT value and is injected in the test context using the @LocalServerPort annotation and added to the URL where the request is being sent to by calling the REST-Assured port(..) method.

```
package com.apress.cems.boot;

import org.junit.jupiter.api.Test;
import org.springframework.boot.test.context.SpringBootTest;
import org.springframework.boot.web.server.LocalServerPort;
import org.springframework.http.HttpStatus;

import static io.restassured.RestAssured.given;
import static org.junit.jupiter.api.Assertions.assertAll;

@SpringBootTest(webEnvironment = SpringBootTest.WebEnvironment.RANDOM_PORT)
```

---

[26]Official site: http://rest-assured.io/

```java
class SpringBootWebApplicationTest3 {

    @LocalServerPort
    private int port;

    @Test
    void testList() throws Exception {
            String responseStr =  given().baseUri("http://localhost")
                .port(port).when().get("/persons/list")
                .then()
                .assertThat().statusCode(HttpStatus.OK.value())
                .extract().body().asString();

            assertAll(
                    () -> responseStr.contains("div class=\"persons\""),
                    () -> responseStr.contains("sherlock.holmes"),
                    () -> responseStr.contains("nancy.drew")
            );
    }

    @Test
    void testShow() throws Exception {
        String responseStr = given().baseUri("http://localhost")
                .port(port).when().get("/persons/1")
                .then()
                .assertThat().statusCode(HttpStatus.OK.value())
                .extract().body().asString();

        assertAll(
                () -> responseStr.contains("sherlock.holmes"),
                () -> responseStr.contains("Employed since ")
        );
    }
```

In conclusion, if Spring Boot is the future, at least it makes it very easy to test applications, so we should expect to enter an age of faultless web applications. Or not, because there is always the human factor. 😊

And since things get complicated from now on, you should practice the simple stuff. The chapter06/boot-web-practice was created so you can practice writing some tests.

Task TODO 48, in class SpringBootWebApplicationTest requires to write a test to check that checks that requesting /persons/1 generates the appropriate response. Look into the code and identify the controller class and method used to handle that request. Then write the method to check that the expected view was returned and that the person model attribute contains Sherlock Holmes' data.

Task TODO 49 in class SpringBootWebApplicationTest requires you to write a test that checks if requesting /persons/99 generates the appropriate response. Look into the code and try to figure out what is going on when a request is performed for a Person that cannot be found in the database. Then write the method to check that the expected view was returned and that the model attribute is not null. Also check that the response code is the expected one. (Hint: Use is4xxClientError().)

Tasks TODO 50 and TODO 51 in class SpringBootWebApplicationTest3 ask you to do the same as the previous two, but using REST-Assured.

Summary

The following is a list of core concepts and important details related to Spring Web MVC, and Spring Boot has been compiled for you.

- Spring Web MVC was built to respect the MVC design pattern.

- The entry point in a Spring web application is the DispatcherServlet that is a front controller for the application.

- The DispatcherServlet assigns HTTP requests to special methods from classes called controllers by using a collection of web-specific infrastructure beans.

- To create a Spring Web MVC application: the DispatcherServlet must be configured as the entry point of the application and the application configuration must contain infrastructure MVC beans and custom controllers and view beans.

- The @EnableWebMvc annotation is used on a configuration class for a classic Spring Web MVC application. This annotation is not necessary in a Spring Boot web application, as its functionality is taken care of by Spring Boot autoconfiguration.

- The MVC configuration class must implement `WebMvcConfigurer` or extend a class implementing this interface to customize the imported configuration. (Although the only class left is `WebMvcConfigurerAdapter`, which is currently deprecated.)

- The @MVC model and an application server supporting Servlet 3.0+ allow an application without any XML configuration.

- Spring Boot is a very good choice when building a Spring web application.

- Spring Boot default configurations can be easily customized.

- Spring Boot provides starter dependencies for a multitude of Spring applications, including secured web applications.

- Spring Boot comes with a wide set of embedded servers, so developers do not have to download, install and configure them on a development environment.

- Spring Boot does not generate code; it dynamically wires up the beans and settings, and applies them to the application context when the application is started according the dependencies and configurations set.

- Spring Boot is awesome, Thymeleaf is awesome, and writing web applications with both is a breeze.

Quiz

Question 1. What does MVC stand for? (Choose one.)

    A. management versus control

    B. model-view-controller

    C. model verbosity clearance

    D. model view conventions

Question 2. Which Spring library is needed in your classpath to write a full-blown Spring web application? (Choose one.)

    A.   spring-core.jar is enough

    B.   spring-core.jar and spring-context.jar are enough

    C.   spring-web.jar is enough

    D.   spring-webmvc.jar is a must because that is where the DispatcherServlet class is

Question 3. What is the purpose of the `@Controller` annotation? (Choose one.)

    A.   to indicate that the bean is to be encapsulated in a special Web Proxy

    B.   to indicate that the class is to be used as a template to create a special type of bean required in a Spring web application to provide handler methods for requests

    C.   to declare a class as the configuration class for a Spring web application

Question 4. Which scopes are web specific? (Choose all that apply.)

    A.   SCOPE_SESSION

    B.   SCOPE_THREAD

    C.   SCOPE_SINGLETON

    D.   SCOPE_FLASH

    E.   SCOPE_REQUEST

    F.   SCOPE_APPLICATION

Question 5. Given the following controller class containing a single handler method, which of the following URLs will be handled by that method? (Choose one.)

```
@Controller
@RequestMapping("/persons")
public class PersonController {
```

```
    @RequestMapping(value = "/showPerson")
    public String show(@RequestParam("personId") Long id, Model model) {
        ...
    }
}
```

A. http://localhost:8080/mvc-basic/persons/
showPerson?personId=aa

B. http://localhost:8080/mvc-basic/persons/showPerson/105

C. http://localhost:8080/mvc-basic/persons/
showPerson?personId=105

D. http://localhost:8080/mvc-basic/persons?showPerson=105

Question 6. Which class in the following list is the default view resolver in Spring: (Choose one.)

A. `JspResourceViewResolver`

B. `ResourceViewResolver`

C. `InternalResourceViewResolver`

Question 7. The main idea of MVC is that there are three decoupled components, each of them can be swapped with a different implementation easily, and together they provide the desired functionality. The *view* represents the interface the user interacts with, it displays data and passes requests to the *controller*. The controller calls the business components and sends the data to the *model* that notifies the view that an actualization is needed. The *model* content is displayed by the *view*.

Does this description fit the MVC design pattern?

A. Yes

B. No

Question 8. What is wrong with the following controller class declaration? (Choose one.)

```
@ControllerAdvice
public class PersonsController {

    @ExceptionHandler(NotFoundException.class)
    @ResponseStatus(HttpStatus.NOT_FOUND)
    public ModelAndView handle(NotFoundException ex) {
        ModelAndView mav = new ModelAndView();
        mav.addObject("problem", ex.getMessage());
        mav.setViewName("error");
        return mav;
    }
}
```

A. Nothing.

B. This is not a controller class declaration, but a special type of bean used for handling exceptions thrown by handler methods.

C. The `handle()` method is not allowed to return an instance of `ModelAndView`

D. The handler method should be annotated with `@RequestMapping` or one of its specializations.

Question 9. Spring Boot Question: Which of the following is true about the `@WebMvcTest` annotation? (Choose all that apply.)

A. This annotation is the one to use when a test focuses only on Spring MVC components.

B. This annotation has the effect of disabling auto-configuration and apply only configuration relevant to MVC tests.

C. This annotation can be applied to a test class to enable and configure auto-configuration of `MockMvc`.

Question 10. Spring Boot Question: When running a Spring Boot MVC test annotated with the following: @SpringBootTest(webEnvironment = SpringBootTest. WebEnvironment.RANDOM_PORT) How can the port value be retrieved? (Choose one.)

  A. Declare a local integer property and annotate it with @LocalServerPort

  B. Declare a local integer property and annotate it with @TestServerPort

  C. Make the test class extend SpringBootWebTest and call the getLocalServerPort()

CHAPTER 7

Spring Security

The web application that we built in an earlier chapter was quite simple. To make things interesting, this section introduces the security layer. This means users will be set up to access the whole application or only parts of it based on their roles. Securing web applications is necessary because they are usually accessed by multiple users in parallel, and each of them needs its own secure session to store its data. Once an application is exposed on the Internet, it is exposed to the risk of being attacked. In the century of Big Data, it is more than true that information is power, and securing applications that are designed to be used on the Internet is well... mandatory.

Imagine the most common necessity nowadays: making online payments. A banking application for making online payments must prove the user's identity beyond any doubt before allowing a payment to be done. And this is what web application security starts with: making sure a user is who he says that he is and giving him access only where he should have it. This chapter covers the basics of securing a web application using Spring Security.

Security Basics

Spring Security is yet another Spring Framework created to make a developer's life easy and the work pleasant, because it secures web applications. It is very easy to use and highly customizable for providing access control over units of an application. When writing secure Spring web applications, this is the default tool developers go for because configuration follows the same standard with all the Spring projects, infrastructure beans are provided out of the box for multiple types of authentication and is obviously compatible with other Spring projects. Spring Security provides a wide set of capabilities that can be grouped in four areas of interest: authentication, authorizing web requests, authorizing methods calls, and authorizing access to individual domain objects.

© Iuliana Cosmina 2020
I. Cosmina, *Pivotal Certified Professional Core Spring 5 Developer Exam*,
https://doi.org/10.1007/978-1-4842-5136-2_7

When talking about securing an application the following concepts are important.

- `Principal` is the term that signifies the user, device, or system that could perform an action within the application

- `Credentials` are identification keys that a principal uses to confirm its identity

- `Authentication` is the process of verifying the validity of the principal's credentials

- `Authorization` is the process of deciding if an authenticated user is allowed to perform a certain action within the application

- `Secured item` is the term used to describe any resource that is being secured.

There are many ways of authentication, and Spring Security supports all of them: Basic, Form, OAuth, X.509, Cookies, Single-Sign-On. When it comes to where and how those credentials are stored, Spring Security is quite versatile, as it supports anything: LDAP, RDBMS, properties file, custom DAOs, and even beans are supported and many others.[1]

Authorization depends on authentication. A user has to be first authenticated, for authorization to take place.

The result of the authentication process is establishing if the user has the rights to access the application and what actions can perform based on roles. The following are the most common user roles within an application.

- ADMIN is a role with full power; this kind of role is specific to users that have the right to access and manipulate any data, including other users.

- MEMBER is a role with limited power; this kind of role is specific to users that can view data and only manipulate their own details.

- GUEST is a role with restricted usage of the application; this kind of role is used for users that can only view limited data.

---

[1]Full list of authentication technologies that Spring Security integrates with can be found here: `http://docs.spring.io/spring-security/site/docs/current/reference/htmlsingle/#what-is-acegi-security`

Spring Security is preferred when developing web applications because it is **flexible** and because of its **portability**. Spring Security does not need a special container to run in, it can be deployed as a secured archive (WAR or EAR) or run in stand-alone environments. A web application secured with Spring Security and archived as a WAR can be deployed on a JBoss, or an Apache Tomcat application server. And as long as the underlying method of storing credentials is configured, the application will run the same way in any of these application servers. Spring Security is very flexible because configuration of authentication and authorization are fully decoupled, thus, the storage system of credentials can change without any action being needed on the authorization configuration to adapt. This makes applications very consistent, because after all the scopes of authentication and authorization are different, so it is only logical to be covered by different, detachable components.

Spring Security is also quite extensible as almost everything related to security can be extended and customized: how a principal is identified, where the credentials are stored, how the authorization decisions are made, where security constraints are stored, etc.

Security is a cross cutting concern, so implementing authorization might lead to code tangling and code scattering. Spring Security is implemented using Spring AOP with separation of concerns in mind. Under the hood, Spring Security uses a few infrastructure beans to implement the two processes. In Figure 7-1, the process of authentication and authorization of a user is depicted in an abstract, but accurate manner.

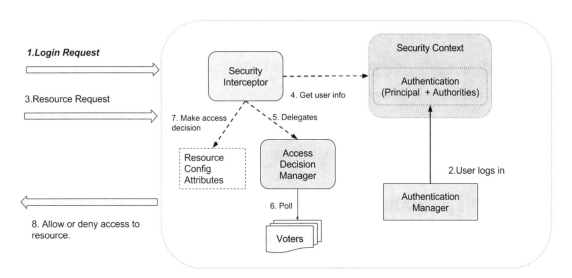

Figure 7-1. *Spring Security under the hood*

The flow depicted in Figure 7-1 can be explained as follows.

1. A user tries to access the application by making a request. The application requires the user to provide the credentials so it can be logged in.

2. The credentials are verified by the `Authentication Manager` and the is granted access to the application. The authorization rights for this user are loaded into the Spring Security context.

3. The user makes a resource request (view, edit, insert, or delete information) and the Security Interceptor intercepts the request before they access a protected/secured resource.

4. The Security Interceptor extracts the user authorization data from the security context and ...

5. ... delegates the decision to the `Access Decision Manager`

6. The Access Decision Manager polls a list of voters to return a decision regarding the rights the authenticated user has on system resources

7. Access is granted or denied to the resource based on the user rights and the resource attributes.

Spring Security Configuration

To configure Spring Security the developer must take care of three things.

- declare the security filter for the application
- define the Spring Security context
- configure authentication and authorization

XML Configuration

To configure Spring Security, `web.xml` must be modified to include the security filter and make the security context the application's root context. The elements that need to be added/modified in the XML configuration of the web application are depicted in the following code snippet.

```
<web-app ...>
<!-- The root web application context is the security context-->
    <context-param>
        <param-name>contextConfigLocation</param-name>
        <param-value>
            /WEB-INF/spring/security-config.xml
        </param-value>
    </context-param>
<!-- Bootstraps the root web application context before servlet
initialization -->
    <listener>
        <listener-class>
            org.springframework.web.context.ContextLoaderListener
        </listener-class>
    </listener>

    <filter>
        <filter-name>springSecurityFilterChain</filter-name>
        <filter-class>
            org.springframework.web.filter.DelegatingFilterProxy
        </filter-class>
    </filter>
    <filter-mapping>
        <filter-name>springSecurityFilterChain</filter-name>
        <url-pattern> /*</url-pattern>
    </filter-mapping>
    ...

    <!-- The front controller, the entry point for all requests -->
    <servlet>
        <servlet-name>pet-dispatcher</servlet-name>
        <servlet-class>
            org.springframework.web.servlet.DispatcherServlet
        </servlet-class>
```

```
    <init-param>
        <param-name>contextConfigLocation</param-name>
        <param-value>
            /WEB-INF/spring/mvc-config.xml
            /WEB-INF/spring/app-config.xml
        </param-value>
    </init-param>
    <load-on-startup>1</load-on-startup>
    </servlet>
</web-app>
```

! The `springSecurityFilterChain` is a mandatory name and it refers
to a bean with the same name in the Spring root application context. The
`delegatingFilterProxy` bean delegates the calls to a list of chained security
filter beans and acts as an interceptor for secured requests. In the preceding case,
as the `<url-pattern .../>` element defines, all requests will be intercepted.
(because of the wildcard being used: /*) Under the hood in a secured web
environment the secured requests are handled by a chain of Spring-managed
beans, which is why the proxy bean is named `springSecurityFilterChain`;
those filters are chained. This chain of filters has the following key responsibilities.

- driving authentication

- enforcing authorization

- managing logout

- maintaining SecurityContext in HttpSession

The Spring Security framework is built upon the foundation of ACEGI Security 1.x.
At the beginning, the security filter beans were manually configured and could be used
individually, but this led to complex XML configurations that were verbose and prone
to errors. Starting with Spring Security 2.0, the filter beans are created and initialized
with default values and manual configuration is not recommended unless the necessity
to change default Spring Security behavior exists. All filter beans implement the
`javax.servlet.Filter` interface. Any bean of type implementing this interface has the

purpose of performing filtering on the request of a resource (a servlet or static content), on the response from a resource, or both. Although these filters work in the background, a little coverage is appropriate. In Table 7-1, the security filters are listed and the purpose of each is presented.

Table 7-1. *Spring Security Chained Filters*

Filter Class	Details
ChannelProcessingFilter	Used if redirection to another protocol is necessary
SecurityContextPersistenceFilter	Used to set up a security context and copy changes from it to HttpSession
ConcurrentSessionFilter	Used for concurrent session handling package
LogoutFilter	Used to log a principal out. After logout a redirect will take place to the configured view.
BasicAuthenticationFilter	Used to store a valid Authentication token in the security context
JaasApiIntegrationFilter	Attempts to obtain a JAAS Subject and continue the FilterChain running as that Subject
RememberMeAuthenticationFilter	Stores a valid Authentication and use it if the security context did not change
AnonymousAuthenticationFilter	Stores an anonymous Authentication and use it if the security context did not change
ExceptionTranslationFilter	Translates Spring Security exceptions in HTTP corresponding error responses
FilterSecurityInterceptor	Protects URIs and raise access denied exceptions

Every time an HTTP request is received by the server, each of the filters performs its action if the situation applies. The fun part is that these filters can be replaced by custom implementations. Their position in the security chain is defined in Spring by a list of enumeration values, and using these values as parameters for the position attribute of the <custom-filter .../> a different filter bean can be specified to use instead of the default one. In the following code snippet, the ConcurrentSessionFilter is replaced by a custom implementation.

```
<beans:beans ...>
    <http>
        <custom-filter position="CONCURRENT_SESSION_FILTER"
                ref="customConcurrencyFilter" />

        <beans:bean id="customConcurrencyFilter"
            class="com.ps.web.session.CustomConcurrentSessionFilter"/>
    </http>
</beans:beans>
```

The list of enumerated values is in `spring-security.xsd`[2] and a match between the filters and the values is depicted in Table 7-2.

Table 7-2. *Spring Security Chained Filters and Their Positions*

Filter Class	Position Enumerated Value
ChannelProcessingFilter	CHANNEL_FILTER
SecurityContextPersistenceFilter	SECURITY_CONTEXT_FILTER
ConcurrentSessionFilter	CONCURRENT_SESSION_FILTER
LogoutFilter	LOGOUT_FILTER
BasicAuthenticationFilter	BASIC_AUTH_FILTER
JaasApiIntegrationFilter	JAAS_API_SUPPORT_FILTER
RememberMeAuthenticationFilter	REMEMBER_ME_FILTER
AnonymousAuthenticationFilter	ANONYMOUS_FILTER
ExceptionTranslationFilter	EXCEPTION_TRANSLATION_FILTER
FilterSecurityInterceptor	FILTER_SECURITY_INTERCEPTOR

The equivalent using Java Configuration, does not use the position enum values, but a set of methods of the HttpSecurity object: addFilterAfter(Filter filter,Class<? extends Filter> afterFilter) and addFilterBefore(Filter filter, Class<? extends Filter> beforeFilter). They receive as a parameter the class of the filter, relative to which the custom implementation should be placed. In the previous example,

---

[2]Available here: http://www.springframework.org/schema/security/spring-security.xsd

the customConcurrencyFilter bean is placed in the chain after the securityContext
PersistenceFilter bean. So the equivalent Java Configuration will look like in the
following code snippet, do not focus on annotations as they will be covered a little bit
later in the section, just pay attention to the custom filter definition and the
http.addFilterAfter(..) call.

```
import com.ps.web.session.CustomConcurrentSessionFilter;
import org.springframework.security.web.context.
SecurityContextPersistenceFilter;
...

@Configuration
@EnableWebSecurity
@EnableGlobalMethodSecurity(jsr250Enabled = true)
public class SecurityConfig extends WebSecurityConfigurerAdapter {
    @Override
    protected void configure(HttpSecurity http) throws Exception {
        http.addFilterAfter(
            customConcurrencyFilter(), SecurityContextPersistenceFilter.
            class);
        http
                .authorizeRequests()
                ...
                .logout()
                .logoutUrl("/logout")
                .logoutSuccessUrl("/");
    }

    ...
    @Bean
    CustomConcurrentSessionFilter customConcurrencyFilter(){
        return new CustomConcurrentSessionFilter();
    }
}
```

The URLs to intercept are defined either in a Spring Security XML file or in a Spring configuration class. The roles that are allowed to access them are defined in the Spring Context, and they are loaded there at authentication time. When using XML, a separate file for security configuration is created; it is named `security-config.xml`. To make configuration easy to set up, Spring provides a special namespace called `spring-security`, which strictly contains security configuration elements. The security configuration file can be written relative to this namespace which removes the necessity to use a prefix for security elements. In the following code snippet, a simple version of a configuration file is depicted. It restricts access to only fully authenticated users. The login form location and logout paths are depicted as well.

```
<beans:beans xmlns="http://www.springframework.org/schema/security"
    xmlns:xsi="http://www.w3.org/2001/XMLSchema-instance"
    xmlns:beans="http://www.springframework.org/schema/beans"
    xsi:schemaLocation="http://www.springframework.org/schema/security
    http://www.springframework.org/schema/security/spring-security.xsd
    http://www.springframework.org/schema/beans
    http://www.springframework.org/schema/beans/spring-beans.xsd">
        <http>
            <intercept-url pattern="/auth*"
                access="IS_AUTHENTICATED_ANONYMOUSLY"/>
            <intercept-url pattern="/persons/**"
                access="IS_AUTHENTICATED_FULLY"/>
            <form-login login-page="/auth" />
            <logout logout-url="/logout" />
        </http>

</beans:beans>
```

The IS_AUTHENTICATED_ANONYMOUSLY value is processed under-the-hood by a bean known as voter, of type `org.springframework.security.access.vote.AuthenticatedVoter`. In this class three values for the access configuration attribute are defined. The voter will process this security configuration attribute and decide if a resource should be available to an anonymous user or not. The anonymous user is used for public access (browsing) a web application, and is the type of user that accesses a site without logging in. The IS_AUTHENTICATED_FULLY configuration attribute is also named in a self-explanatory way: the resource that matches the associated URL can only be accessed by a user that was logged in, his credentials were verified and his identity was confirmed, thus the is user has been fully authenticated. Aside from the two configuration attributes, there is one more: IS_AUTHENTICATED_REMEMBERED. If a resource is protected by such a rule, it can be accessed only if the user is authenticated fully or authenticated using the remember-me method.[3]

The `<form-login ../>` configuration element defines the request URL for the login form where the user can provide his credentials. Using this configuration, when an anonymous user tries to access a secured resource, the application will direct him to the login form page, instead of showing a page that tells him he does not have access to that resource.

The `<logout ../>` configuration element defines the request URL for the logout form. When the user clicks this link, the HTTP session is invalidated, and then a redirect to "/login?success" is done. This behavior can be configured and a different logout success URL can be defined; but most applications redirect the user to the login page and a message such as "You have successfully logged out" is displayed next to the login form, so the user can log in again if needed.

The paths defined as values for the `pattern` attribute are pieces of URLs defined using ANT style paths. The URLs that match them are secured and verified according to rules defined by the `<intercept-url .../>` elements. Wildcards can specify a family of related URLs and apply the same security rule to all of them. The `access` attribute values are typical security token values used to specify what kind of access the user needs to have. Access is linked to user roles, so URLs can be configured to be accessed only by users with certain rights.

```
<beans:beans   ...>
      <http>
            <intercept-url pattern="/persons/newPerson"
                access="ROLE_ADMIN"/>
            <intercept-url pattern="/persons/list"
                access="ROLE_USER"/>
            <intercept-url pattern="/persons/**"
                access="IS_AUTHENTICATED_FULLY"/>
      </http>
   </beans:beans>
```

---

[3]Remember-me or persistent-login authentication refers to web sites being able to remember the identity of a principal between sessions.

!   The order of defining the URL patterns is important, and **the most restrictive must be on top**, otherwise a more relaxed rule will apply and some URL will be accessible to users that should not have access to them.

You might have noticed that writing configuration rules for specific URLs is quite annoying while using token values for security rights, because you have to check the documentation to see what you are allowed to use as a value for the access attribute. Spring Security 3.0 offers the possibility to use Spring EL expressions to declare access rules. So the preceding file can use security-specific methods as values for the access attributes and all that is required is to tell Spring Security that you want to use them by configuring the <http .../> element accordingly, and set the use-expressions attribute value to true.

```
<beans:beans  ...>
        <http use-expressions="true">
                <intercept-url pattern="/auth*" access="permitAll"/>
                <intercept-url pattern="/persons/newPerson"
                    access="hasRole('ROLE_ADMIN')"/>
                <intercept-url pattern="/persons/list"
                    access="hasRole('ROLE_USER')"/>
                <intercept-url pattern="/persons/**"
                    access="hasAnyRole('ROLE_USER, ROLE_ADMIN')"/>
        </http>
    </beans:beans>
```

The expressions have obvious names that reflect their purpose, and can be combined to declare complex rules. The following listing depicts only a few of the possibilities.

- hasRole('AnyRole') checks if the principal has the role given as argument

- hasAnyRole('[RoleList]') checks if the principal has any of the roles in the RoleList

- isAnonymous() allows access for unauthenticated principals

- `isAuthenticated()` allows access for authenticated and remembered principals

- `isAuthenticated()` and `hasIpAddress('192.168.1.0/24')` allows access for authenticated and remembered principals in the network with this IP class: 192.168.1.0/24

- `hasRole('ROLE_ADMIN')` and `hasRole('ROLE_MANAGER')`allows access for principals that have role ROLE_ADMIN **and** ROLE_MANAGER

! Once the support for SpEL expression has been configured using `use-expressions="true"` the previous syntax for access values cannot be used, so roles and configuration attributes cannot be used as values for the `access` attribute directly. So mixing the two ways is not possible.

! Spring Security 4 introduced a simplification that allows access expressions to be specified without the ROLE_prefix in front of them, thus the preceding configuration becomes as follows.

```
<http use-expressions="true">
    <csrf disabled="true"/>
    <intercept-url pattern="/auth*" access="permitAll"/>
    <intercept-url pattern="/persons/newPerson"
        access="hasRole('ADMIN')"/>
    <intercept-url pattern="/persons/list"
        access="hasRole('USER')"/>
    <intercept-url pattern="/persons/**"
        access="hasAnyRole('USER, ADMIN')"/>
</http>
```

! Also in Spring Security 4 the possibility of using CSRF tokens in Spring forms to prevent Cross-site request forgery was introduced.[4] A configuration without a `<csrf />` element configuration is invalid, and any login request will direct you to a 403 error page with the following statement.

```
Invalid CSRF Token 'null' was found on the request parameter
'_csrf' or header 'X-CSRF-TOKEN'.
```

To migrate from Spring Security 3 to version 4, you have to add a configuration for that element, even if all you do is disable using CSRF tokens.

```
<http auto-config="true" use-expressions="true">
      <csrf disabled="true"/>
      <intercept-url pattern="/auth*" access="permitAll"/>
      ...
      <form-login login-page="/auth"
                  authentication-failure-url="/auth?auth_error=1"
                  default-target-url="/"/>
      <logout logout-url="/logout"
              logout-success-url="/"/>
   </http>
```

Or better yet, just add a bean of type `HttpSessionCsrfTokenRepository`, and add it to the configuration as a provided for CSRF tokens.

```
<http auto-config="true" use-expressions="true">
      <csrf token-repository-ref="tokenRepo"/>
      <intercept-url pattern="/auth*" access="permitAll"/>
      ...
      <form-login login-page="/auth"
                  authentication-failure-url="/auth?auth_error=1"
                  default-target-url="/"/>
```

---

[4]This is a type of attack that consists in hacking an existing session to execute unauthorized commands in a web application. You can read more about it here https://en.wikipedia.org/wiki/Cross-site_request_forgery

```
    <logout logout-url="/logout"
            logout-success-url="/"/>
  </http>

<beans:bean id="tokenRepo"
      class="org.springframework.security.web.csrf.
      HttpSessionCsrfTokenRepository">
      <beans:property name="sessionAttributeName" value="_csrf"/>
      <beans:property name="headerName" value="X-CSRF-TOKEN"/>
  </beans:bean>
```

The `authentication-failure-url` attribute defines where the user should be redirected when there is an authentication failure. This can be a special error view that depending on the parameter will show the user a different error message.

The `default-target-url` attribute defines where the user will be redirected after a successful authentication.

! Other critical changes are related to the login form: default Spring resources, like the login URL that indicates an authentication request, and the names of the request parameters (expected keys for generation of an authentication token).[5] These were changed to match JavaConfig. Until Spring 3, the default login URL value is /j_spring_security_check and the default names for the authentication keys are: j_username are j_password, thus the login form in the auth.jsp view, mapped to path /auth until Spring 3 looks like the following.

```
<%@ taglib prefix="c" uri="http://java.sun.com/jsp/jstl/core" %>
 <%@ taglib prefix="spring" uri="http://www.springframework.org/tags" %>
...
    <form action="<c:url value='/j_spring_security_check'/>" method="post">
        <table>
            <tr>
                <td>
```

---

[5]the full list of configuration details changes that were made to match Java Configuration can be found here: https://jira.spring.io/browse/SEC-2783

```
                <label for= "username">
                  <spring:message code="login.username"/>
                </label>
                </td>
            <td>
              <input type='text' id='username' name='j_username'
                  value='<c:out value="${user}"/>'/>
            </td>
        </tr>
        <tr>
            <td>
                <label for="password">
                    <spring:message code="login.password"/>
                </label>
            </td>
            <td><input type='password' id='password'
            name='j_password'/></td>
        </tr>
        <tr>
            <td colspan="2">
                <button type="submit">
                    <spring:message code="login.submit"/>
                </button>
            </td>
        </tr>
    </table>
</form>
```

Starting with Spring 4, the default login URL value is *login* and the default names for the authentication keys are *username* and *password*, thus the login form must be modified as follows.

```jsp
<%@ taglib prefix="c" uri="http://java.sun.com/jsp/jstl/core" %>
<%@ taglib prefix="spring" uri="http://www.springframework.org/tags" %>
...
<form action="<c:url value='/login'/>" method="post">
    <table>
        <tr>
            <td>
                <label for="username">
                    <spring:message code="login.username"/>
                </label>
            </td>
            <td>
                <input type='text' id='username' name='username'
                    value='<c:out value="${user}"/>'/>
            </td>
        </tr>
        <tr>
            <td>
                <label for="password">
                    <spring:message code="login.password"/>
                </label>
            </td>
            <td><input type='password' id='password'
            name='password'/></td>
        </tr>
        <tr>
            <td colspan="2">
                <button type="submit">
                    <spring:message code="login.submit"/>
                </button>
            </td>
        </tr>
    </table>
</form>
```

! All previous examples used default values for login URL and authentication key names: *j_spring_security_check*, *j_username*, *j_password* (in Spring Security 3), *login*, *username*, *password* (in Spring Security 4), but all these values can be redefined using Spring configuration. Just set the following attributes for the `<form-login ../>` element: `login-processing-url`, `username-parameter`, `password-parameter` with the desired values.

```
<form-login login-page="/auth"
    login-processing-url="/my-login"
    username-parameter="my-user"
    password-parameter="my-password"
    ...<!-- other attributes-->
/>
```

Configuring authentication is done in the Spring Security configuration file as well and the default authentication provider is the DAO Authentication provider. A specific `UserDetailsService` implementation provides credentials and authorities. In the examples in the book, the credentials are specified directly in the Spring Security Configuration file.

```
<authentication-manager>
      <authentication-provider>
         <user-service>
            <user name="john" password="doe" authorities="ROLE_USER"/>
            <user name="jane" password="doe" authorities="ROLE_USER,
            ROLE_ADMIN"/>
            <user name="admin" password="admin" authorities=
            "ROLE_ADMIN"/>
         </user-service>
      </authentication-provider>
</authentication-manager>
```

Until Spring 5, it was possible to store passwords in plain text when using in-memory authentication. Starting with Spring 5, configuring Spring Security fails if a password encoder is not set for the authentication provider to use it. For legacy and testing purposes the NoOpPasswordEncoder class is still provided, although it might be removed in the future since it is already marked as deprecated. So the previous configuration, when migrating to Spring 5 needs to become as depicted next for the application to still work.

```
<authentication-manager>
    <authentication-provider>
        <user-service>
            <user name="john" password="doe" authorities="ROLE_USER"/>
            <user name="jane" password="doe" authorities="ROLE_USER,
            ROLE_ADMIN"/>
            <user name="admin" password="admin" authorities=
            "ROLE_ADMIN"/>
        </user-service>
        <password-encoder ref="encoder"/>
    </authentication-provider>
  </authentication-manager>

<beans:bean id="encoder"
    class="org.springframework.security.crypto.password.
    NoOpPasswordEncoder"/>
```

The other option is to use an actual encoder class such as BCryptPasswordEncoder, but this means the values for the password properties must be replaced with their encrypted version. So the previous configuration becomes the following.

```
<authentication-manager>
    <authentication-provider>
        <user-service>
            <user name="john" authorities="ROLE_USER"
                password="$2a$10$bpYnfm/iHOSbiI7Shl835uSDV1G3A7Qtumm
                EqwmARu/NQKbGP97Wy" />
            <user name="jane" authorities="ROLE_USER,ROLE_ADMIN"
                password="$2a$10$bpYnfm/iHOSbiI7Shl835uSDV1G3A7Qtumm
                EqwmARu/NQKbGP97Wy" />
```

```
            <user name="admin" authorities="ROLE_ADMIN"
                password="$2a$10$IzMJqhs2mXd8.9POBvOVbuSlTDlBLy
                PIXOm52XJObZ7TjztaQqsXG" />
        </user-service>
        <password-encoder ref="encoder"/>
    </authentication-provider>
  </authentication-manager>

<beans:bean id="encoder"
    class="org.springframework.security.crypto.bcrypt.BCrypt
    PasswordEncoder"/>
```

In-memory authentication is the go-to for teaching and testing, but it could be used for small-scale applications, designed to be used within a secured institution with no contact to outside networks to prevent security incidents. To increase application security a little more, the credentials could be read from a properties file, where the password is stored in encrypted form and a salt value can be applied using configuration. **Password-salting** is an encryption method used to increase the security passwords by adding a well-known string to them.

```
<!-- security-config.xml -->
<authentication-manager>
    <authentication-provider>
        <password-encoder hash="md5" >
                <salt-source system-wide="SpringSalt"/>
        </password-encoder>
        <user-service properties="/WEB-INF/users.properties" />
    </authentication-provider>
</authentication-manager>

#/WEB-INF/users.properties
john=471540bd22898656564b9c85a18b3e80,ROLE_USER
#password: john

jane=1f533ad8d26c7bec84a291f62668a048,ROLE_USER,ROLE_ADMIN
#password: jane

admin=55c98bea671295de1e020621cc670ac4,ROLE_ADMIN
#password: admin
```

! The passwords presented in the following code snippet were generated by postfixing the password value with the "SpringSalt" text and they applying an MD5 function on the resulting text value. For example,

```
MD5("john" +"SpringSalt") = "471540bd22898656564b9c85a18b3e80"
```

On Windows the MD5 hash can only be generated for files using the FCIV command or the Get-FileHash command in the PowerShell. On macOS there is an md5 command and on Linux systems there is an md5sum command. In the following code snippet, the call to generate the MD5 hash for a password equal to "john" with the salt "SpringSalt" for macOS and Linux are depicted.

```
#MacOS
$ echo "johnSpringSalt" | md5
471540bd22898656564b9c85a18b3e80
#Linux system
$ echo "johnSpringSalt" | md5sum
471540bd22898656564b9c85a18b3e80
```

The credentials were decoupled from the configuration by isolating them in a property file. The file can be edited outside the application and the properties can be reloaded by using a property reader *refreshable bean*.[6]

The credentials property file has a specific syntax.

```
[username] = [password(encrypted)],[role1,role2...]
```

In the previous example, the passwords were added the SpringSalt value then were encrypted using the md5[7] algorithm. But they were all hashed the exact same way and with the same salt. If someone discovered the salt that the server uses, it would still

---

[6]A refreshable bean is a dynamic-language-backed bean that with a small amount of configuration, a dynamic-language-backed bean can monitor changes in its underlying source file resource, and then reload itself when the dynamic language source file is changed (for example when a developer edits and saves changes to the file on the filesystem). Official documentation reference:http://docs.spring.io/spring/docs/current/spring-framework-reference/htmlsingle/#dynamic-language-refreshable-beans

[7]Read more about MD5 here: https://en.wikipedia.org/wiki/MD5

be crackable. That is why the salt should be a random value, different for each user, for example a property unique to that user as its ID.

```
<authentication-manager>
    <authentication-provider>
        <password-encoder hash="md5">
            <!-- id property from class User -->
            <salt-source user-property="id" />
        </password-encoder>
    </authentication-provider>
</authentication-manager>
```

In the preceding examples, only the MD5 algorithm was used, but there are more of them supported in Spring Security and a developer can use one of the supported ones (MD4, Bcrypt, SHA, SHA-256, etc.) or implement his own.

The in-memory, or directly in the configuration file approach is useful for testing and development, but in a production scenario a more secure method of credential storage is usually used. In production environments, credentials are stored in a database or LDAP system. In this case, the service providing the credentials must be changed to a JDBC-based one.

```
<authentication-manager>
    <authentication-provider>
            <jdbc-user-service  data-source-ref="authDataSource" />
    </authentication-provider>
 </authentication-manager>
```

The authentication tables must be accessible using the authDataSource bean and their structure must respect the following rules: one table is named users, one must be named authorities and the following queries must be executed correctly.

```
SELECT username, password, enabled FROM users WHERE username = ?
SELECT username, authority FROM authorities WHERE username = ?
```

The Spring Security reference documentation includes some SQL scripts to create the security tables. The syntax is for HSQLDB, but the scripts can easily be adjusted for any SQL normalized database.[8]

A few details from this section are general and apply in a Java Configuration environment as well, but they were mentioned here to paint a full view of the Spring Security framework. And now it is time to see how Java Configuration can make all these configuration details more practical and quicker to set up.

Spring Security XML Configuration Without web.xml

If `web.xml` disappears what happens with the `springSecurityFilterChain` filter? The security filter is transformed into a class extending a Spring specialized class named `org.springframework.security.web.context.AbstractSecurityWebApplicationInitializer`. And the class that matches the `DispatcherServlet` declaration must be made to extend the `org.springframework.web.servlet.support.AbstractDispatcherServletInitializer` so the root context can be set to be the security context. The following code snippet depicts the situation when Spring Security is configured using XML, and the web application is configured using a web initializer typical class.

```
package com.apress.cems.web.config;
 ....

import org.springframework.security.web.context.
        AbstractSecurityWebApplicationInitializer;
// Empty class needed to register the springSecurityFilterChain bean
public class SecurityInitializer extends
AbstractSecurityWebApplicationInitializer {
}
```

---

[8]Documentation reference for security table DDL scripts: `https://docs.spring.io/`
 `spring-security/site/docs/current/reference/htmlsingle/#appendix-schema`

```java
public class WebInitializer extends AbstractDispatcherServletInitializer {

    @Override
    protected WebApplicationContext createRootApplicationContext() {
        XmlWebApplicationContext ctx = new XmlWebApplicationContext();
        ctx.setConfigLocation("/WEB-INF/spring/security-config.xml");
        return ctx;
    }

    @Override
    protected WebApplicationContext createServletApplicationContext() {
        XmlWebApplicationContext ctx = new XmlWebApplicationContext();
        ctx.setConfigLocations(
            // MVC configuration
            "/WEB-INF/spring/mvc-config.xml",
            // Service configuration
            "/WEB-INF/spring/app-config.xml");
        return ctx;
    }
    ...
}
```

Another version of the same code that does not require you to write the SecurityInitializer class makes use of the onStartup(..) method from WebApplicationInitializer. What is needed is to provide an implementation for this method that configured the DispatcherServlet and adds the security filter explicitly.

```java
package com.apress.cems.web.config;

import org.springframework.web.WebApplicationInitializer;
import org.springframework.web.filter.DelegatingFilterProxy;
import org.springframework.web.servlet.DispatcherServlet;

import javax.servlet.ServletContext;
import javax.servlet.ServletException;
import javax.servlet.ServletRegistration;
```

```
public class WebInitializer implements WebApplicationInitializer {

    @Override
    public void onStartup(ServletContext servletContext) throws
    ServletException {
        ServletRegistration.Dynamic registration =
            servletContext.addServlet("cems-dispatcher", new
            DispatcherServlet());
        registration.setLoadOnStartup(1);
        registration.addMapping("/");
        registration.setInitParameter("contextConfigLocation",
            "/WEB-INF/spring/*.xml");
        servletContext.addFilter("securityFilter",
            new DelegatingFilterProxy("springSecurityFilterChain"))
            .addMappingForUrlPatterns(null, false, "/*");
    }
}
```

So yeah, during your work as a developer, if you ever meet Spring Security being configured using XML, you are now covered. A working example is provided for you in project chapter07/mvc-sec-xml. And now it is time to leave XML behind.

Java Configuration

To develop a working configuration for a Spring Security web application, the XML configuration must be transformed into a security configuration class. The class that replaces the Spring XML configuration should extend WebSecurityConfigurerAdapter so that the amount of code needed to be written for a valid security configuration is minimal. Thus, the example XML configuration becomes the following.

```
package com.apress.cems.web.config;
...
import org.springframework.beans.factory.annotation.Autowired;
import org.springframework.context.annotation.Configuration;
import org.springframework.security.config.annotation
        .authentication.builders.AuthenticationManagerBuilder;
```

```java
import org.springframework.security.config.annotation
        .web.builders.HttpSecurity;
import org.springframework.security.config.annotation]
        .web.configuration.EnableWebSecurity;
import org.springframework.security.config.annotation
        .web.configuration.WebSecurityConfigurerAdapter;

import org.springframework.security.crypto.bcrypt.BCryptPasswordEncoder;
import org.springframework.security.crypto.password.PasswordEncoder;
import org.springframework.security.web.csrf.CsrfTokenRepository;
import org.springframework.security.web.csrf.
HttpSessionCsrfTokenRepository;

@Configuration
@EnableWebSecurity
public class SecurityConfig extends WebSecurityConfigurerAdapter {

    @Autowired
    public void configureGlobal(AuthenticationManagerBuilder auth) {
        try {
            PasswordEncoder passwordEncoder = new BCryptPasswordEncoder();
            auth
                .inMemoryAuthentication()
                .passwordEncoder(passwordEncoder)
                .withUser("john").password(passwordEncoder.encode("doe"))
                    .roles("USER")
                .and()
                        .withUser("jane").password(passwordEncoder.
                        encode("doe"))
                    .roles("USER", "ADMIN")
                .and()
                        .withUser("admin").password(passwordEncoder.
                        encode("admin"))
                    .roles("ADMIN");
        } catch (Exception e) {
```

```
        throw new ConfigurationException(
            "In-Memory authentication was not configured.", e);
    }
}

@Override
protected void configure(HttpSecurity http) throws Exception {
    http
            .authorizeRequests()
            .antMatchers("/resources/**","/images/**","/styles/**").
            permitAll()
            .antMatchers("/persons/newPerson").hasRole("ADMIN")
            .antMatchers("/detectives/**").hasRole("ADMIN")
            .antMatchers("/**").hasAnyRole("ADMIN","USER")
            .anyRequest()
            .authenticated()
            .and()
          .formLogin()
           .usernameParameter("username") // customizable
           .passwordParameter("password") // customizable
           .loginProcessingUrl("/login")  // customizable
            .loginPage("/auth")
            .failureUrl("/auth?auth_error=1")
            .defaultSuccessUrl("/home")
            .permitAll()
            .and()
          .logout()
            .logoutUrl("/logout")
            .logoutSuccessUrl("/")
            .and()
           .csrf().disable();
    }
}
```

The @EnableWebSecurity annotation must be used on Security configuration classes that must also extend org.springframework.security.config.annotation. web.configuration.WebSecurityConfigurerAdapter. Until Spring 4.0, to integrate Spring MVC and Security, the @EnableWebMvcSecurity annotation had to be used on the security configuration class. In Spring 4.0, this annotation became deprecated, and although still present in Spring 5.x, the recommendation is to be replaced by the new @EnableWebSecurity, that you have seen being used in the previous examples, because it will be probably be removed from future versions of Spring.

WebSecurityConfigurerAdapter provides implementation for the configure(HttpSecurity http) method. To simplify the configuration, the configure(WebSecurity web) method can also be overridden to specify resources that Spring Security should be ignoring, like style files and images, for example, thus simplifying the implementation of the configure(HttpSecurity http) method and decoupling unsecured elements from secured ones.

```
package com.pr.config;
...
 import org.springframework.security.config.annotation.web.]
        builders.WebSecurity;

@Configuration
@EnableWebSecurity
public class SecurityConfig extends WebSecurityConfigurerAdapter {

    @Override
    public void configure(WebSecurity web) throws Exception {
        web.ignoring().antMatchers("/resources/**","/images/**","/
        styles/**");
    }

    @Override
    protected void configure(HttpSecurity http) throws Exception {
        http
                .authorizeRequests()
                .antMatchers("/user/edit").hasRole("ADMIN")
                .antMatchers("/**").hasAnyRole("ADMIN","USER")
                .anyRequest()
```

```
                .authenticated()
                .and()
            .formLogin()
                .usernameParameter("username") // customizable
                .passwordParameter("password") // customizable
                .loginProcessingUrl("/login") // customizable
                    .loginPage("/auth")
                .failureUrl("/auth?auth_error=1")
                .defaultSuccessUrl("/home")
                .permitAll()
                .and()
            .logout()
                .logoutUrl("/logout")
                .logoutSuccessUrl("/")
            .and()
            .csrf().disable();
    }
}
```

The antMatcher(...) method is the equivalent of the <intercept-url.../> element from XML. Equivalent methods are available to replace the configuration for the login form, logout URL configuration and CSRF token support. To enable CSRF usage, the preceding configuration must also define a CSRF provider bean and use it in the configuration.

```
package com.apress.cems.web.config;
 ...
import org.springframework.security.web.csrf.CsrfTokenRepository;
import org.springframework.security.web.csrf.
HttpSessionCsrfTokenRepository;

@Configuration
@EnableWebSecurity
public class SecurityConfig extends WebSecurityConfigurerAdapter {
```

```
@Bean
    public CsrfTokenRepository repo() {
        HttpSessionCsrfTokenRepository repo = new
        HttpSessionCsrfTokenRepository();
        repo.setParameterName("_csrf");
        repo.setHeaderName("X-CSRF-TOKEN");
        return repo;
    }

    @Override
    protected void configure(HttpSecurity http) throws Exception {
        http.
        ...
        .and()
        .csrf().csrfTokenRepository(repo());
    }
}
```

Out of the box, Spring provides three CsrfTokenRepository implementations, which are listed and explained in Table 7-3.

Table 7-3. *CsrfTokenRepository Spring Implementations*

Filter Class	Position Enumerated Value
CookieCsrfTokenRepository	Persists the CSRF token in a cookie named "XSRF-TOKEN" and reads from the header "X-XSRF-TOKEN" following the conventions of AngularJS.
HttpSessionCsrfTokenRepository	Persists the CSRF token in the HttpSession in the parameter with the name set by calling method setParameterName() and reads from the header with the name set by calling the setHeaderName()
LazyCsrfTokenRepository	Delays saving new CSRF token until its generated attribute are accessed.

When using CSRF support, logging out needs to be implemented accordingly, and make sure the CSRF token is erased from existence and disabled, so it cannot be used by malevolent requests.[9] So the simple logout link from Spring 3.

```
<%@ taglib prefix="spring" uri="http://www.springframework.org/tags"%>
    ...
    <a href="<spring:url value="/j_spring_security_logout"/>">
        <spring:message code="menu.logout"/>
    </a>
```

In Spring 4, this becomes a full-fledged form that sends the CSRF token to the application, as follows.

```
<%@ taglib prefix="spring" uri="http://www.springframework.org/tags"%>
  ...
  <spring:url value="/logout" var="logoutUrl" />
    <form action="${logoutUrl}" id="logout" method="post">
            <input type="hidden" name="${_csrf.parameterName}"
                value="${_csrf.token}"/>
    </form>
    <a href="#" onclick="document.getElementById('logout').submit();">
        <spring:message code="menu.logout"/>
    </a>
```

The `<spring:message .../>` element is a special Spring tag used for internationalization. The tag library directive must be present in the JSP file and the values for the specific element are taken from properties internationalization files that are located under `WEB-INF`. As internationalization is not a topic for the Spring Core certification exam, we won't go too deep into this here.

And since the configuration section has covered everything needed, it is time to introduce how to use the security context and rules in the code.

---

[9]*Cross-site request forgery* or *session-riding* exploits the trust that a site has in a user's browser. When the CSRF token is stored in the session, it has a specific value for the duration of that session. So even if the session is intercepted and data from is used by an attacker to access the sire by disabling the CSRF token at logout, sensitive requests that require the CSRF token are prohibited.

Using mvcMatchers

In the previous configuration sample, *antMatchers* were used to secure URLs. This means the antMatchers(..) method received as arguments a set of ant patterns (regular expressions) that were used as criteria to filter requests using an instance of AntPathRequestMatcher and secure them if a match was found with any of the patterns. Depending on the Spring MVC configuration, some access to secured handler methods might still be possible by just playing with the URL text and just finding a combination that does not match the ant patterns but does match a URL handled by a handler method. For example, let's assume that we have secured the http://localhost:8080/ mvc-sec/persons URL using http.antMatchers("/persons").hasRole("ADMIN"). But /persons.html and /persons/ might still map to the list(..) handler method, thus escaping security. Sure, we could use wildcards and multiple combinations to make sure any URL containing persons is secured, but there is an easier way.

In Spring 4.1.1 the MvcRequestMatcher implementation was introduced which uses a bean of HandlerMappingIntrospector type to match the path and extract variables. This bean is an MVC infrastructure bean that is created when the application boots up and is populated with information about all the handler methods declared within the application. This means that Spring MVC and Spring Security must share the application context, because HandlerMappingIntrospector is created and registered by the Spring MVC configuration. To use this wonderful new Spring Security feature, we have to modify the SecurityConfig class and replace all antMatchers(..) calls with mvcMatchers(..).

```
package com.apress.cems.web.config;

...

@Configuration
@EnableWebSecurity
public class SecurityConfig2 extends WebSecurityConfigurerAdapter{

    @Override
    public void configure(WebSecurity web) throws Exception {
        web.ignoring().mvcMatchers("/resources/**","/images/**",
        "/styles/**");
    }
```

```
...
@Override
protected void configure(HttpSecurity http) throws Exception {
    http
        .authorizeRequests()
        .mvcMatchers("/resources/**","/images/**","/styles/**")
                        .permitAll()
        .mvcMatchers("/persons/newPerson").hasRole("ADMIN")
        .mvcMatchers("/detectives/**").hasRole("ADMIN")
        .mvcMatchers("/**").hasAnyRole("ADMIN","USER")
        .anyRequest()
        .authenticated()
        .and()
     .formLogin()
        .usernameParameter("username") // customizable
        .passwordParameter("password") // customizable
        .loginProcessingUrl("/login") // customizable
        .loginPage("/auth")
        .failureUrl("/auth?auth_error=1")
        .defaultSuccessUrl("/home")
        .permitAll()
        .and()
     .logout()
        .logoutUrl("/logout")
        .logoutSuccessUrl("/")
        .and()
     .csrf().csrfTokenRepository(repo());
    }
}
```

Next, we have to modify the WebInitializer class to create a single-application context.

```
package com.apress.cems.web.config;

....

import javax.servlet.Filter;

class WebInitializer extends
             AbstractAnnotationConfigDispatcherServletInitializer {

    @Override
    protected Class<?>[] getRootConfigClasses() {
        return new Class[]{};
    }

    @Override
    protected Class<?>[] getServletConfigClasses() {
        return new Class[]{H2DbConfig.class, ServiceConfig.class,
            WebConfig.class, SecurityConfig.class};
    }

    @Override
    protected String[] getServletMappings() {
        return new String[]{"/"};
    }
  ...
}
```

And that's pretty much it. Once the changes are in place, you can restart the application and log in with the *john* to test what he cannot access.

Security Tag Library

When writing JSP pages multiple tag libraries are available to make the work easier, less redundant and provide
    functionality. By adding a tag library reference in the JSP page header, JSP elements defined in that library can be used. Spring Security provides a tag library that can secure JSP elements.

In the configurations examples presented until now, access to certain resources was managed via antMatchers(...) elements or mvcMatchers(...) methods.

```
public class SecurityConfig extends WebSecurityConfigurerAdapter {
...
    @Override
    protected void configure(HttpSecurity http) throws Exception {
        http
                .authorizeRequests()
                .antMatchers("/persons/newPerson")
                .hasRole("ADMIN")
                ...

    }
}
```

The preceding configuration will deny any user with only USER role access to the /person/newPerson URL. In Figure 7-2, the server reply is depicted when a user with USER role, tries to access the /persons/newPerson resource.

Figure 7-2. *Server response when user is not authorized to view resource*

But, does it make sense to display on the page a link to a forbidden resource at all? Of course not. A production application is usually quite big and contains a lot of different URLs, so full configuration using an XML file or a security configuration class can become complex. To simplify this, Spring Security version 2.0 introduced a security tag library that can secure items at the JSP level. In the JSP snippet depicted next, we can choose to display the menu item containing the link to the resource based on the security configuration for the user.

```
// <!-- /persons/list.jsp -->
 <%@ taglib prefix="sec" uri="http://www.springframework.org/security/tags" %>
 <%@ taglib prefix="spring" uri="http://www.springframework.org/tags" %>
 ...
    <div class="menu">
        <ul>
            <li><c:if test="${menuTab eq 'persons'}">
                <strong><a href="<c:url value="/persons/list"/>">
                    <spring:message code="menu.persons"/></a>
                    </strong>
            </c:if>
                <c:if test="${menuTab != 'persons'}">
                    <a href="<c:url value="/persons/list"/>">
                      <spring:message code="menu.persons"/>
                    </a>
                </c:if>
                <sec:authorize access="hasRole('ROLE_ADMIN')">
                    <ul>
                        <li>
                            <c:if test="${navigationTab eq 'newPerson'}">
                                <strong>
                                    <a href="<c:url value="/persons/
                                    newPerson"/>">
                                        <spring:message code="menu.new.
                                        person"/>
                                    </a>
                                </strong>
                            </c:if>
                            <c:if test="${navigationTab != 'newPersons'}">
                                <a href="<c:url value="/persons/
                                newPerson"/>">
                                    <spring:message code="menu.new.person"/>
                                </a>
                            </c:if>
                        </li>
```

```
        </ul>
      </sec:authorize>
    </li>
   ...
  </ul>
</div>
```

The `<spring:url ../>` element is a tag from the Spring tag library that dynamically composes a link based on a parameter. The definition in the previous code snippet resolves to links like the following.

```
http://localhost:8080/mvc-sec/persons/newPerson..
```

With `<sec:authorize ../>`, after a user is authenticated, his roles are loaded into the security context, and when he accesses the `list.jsp` page, the response view takes his roles into account. The security elements in the previous example state that only for users with the ADMIN role the `<td/>` elements containing the `/persons/newPerson` URL should be part of the view. So someone with only the USER role will see a different view than a user with the ADMIN role, as depicted in Figure 7-3.

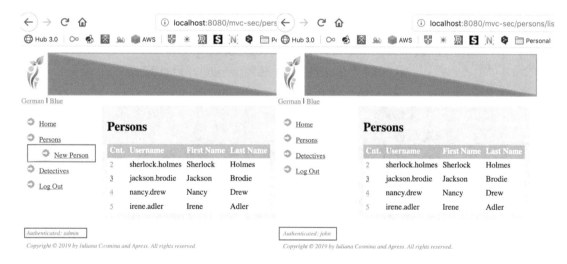

Figure 7-3. */persons/list view for roles ADMIN and USER*

According to what is said before, the link is not displayed, but what happens if the user enters the link manually in the browser? If there is no restriction for that link in the configuration, the view will be shown to the user, regardless of its role. So the restriction from the configuration is needed as well. If the restriction is defined as depicted in the code snippet at the beginning of the section, the security rule can be used in the JSP code to avoid complicated expressions like `'hasRole("ROLE_ADMIN")'`, by replacing the `access` attribute with `url` for the `authorize` element, and replace the `hasRole` expression with the URL defined in the security rule. This will tell Spring to check if the user has access to that URL before displaying the view. And if it does not, the message in Figure 7-2 is displayed. This allows you to link a security rule to a URL pattern that can be used as a security attribute value to secure resources with any URL path. So, the preceding JSP code becomes the following.

```jsp
// <!-- /persons/list.jsp -->
 <%@ taglib prefix="sec" uri="http://www.springframework.org/security/tags" %>
 <%@ taglib prefix="spring" uri="http://www.springframework.org/tags" %>
 ...
    <div class="menu">
        <ul>
            <li><c:if test="${menuTab eq 'persons'}">
                <strong><a href="<c:url value="/persons/list"/>">
                    <spring:message code="menu.persons"/></a>
                    </strong>
            </c:if>
                <c:if test="${menuTab != 'persons'}">
                    <a href="<c:url value="/persons/list"/>">
                      <spring:message code="menu.persons"/>
                    </a>
                </c:if>
                <sec:authorize access="/persons/newPerson">
                    <ul>
                        <li>
                            <c:if test="${navigationTab eq 'newPerson'}">
                                <strong>
                                    <a href="<c:url value="/persons/
                                    newPerson"/>">
                                        <spring:message code="menu.new.
                                        person"/>
                                    </a>
                                </strong>
```

```
                </c:if>
                <c:if test="${navigationTab != 'newPersons'}">
                    <a href="<c:url value="/persons/
                    newPerson"/>">
                        <spring:message code="menu.new.person"/>
                    </a>
                </c:if>
            </li>
        </ul>
    </sec:authorize>
    </li>
    ...
    </ul>
</div>
```

The previous example is pretty simple. We have a page to add new persons and we do not want un-authorized persons to even know it exists. But what if some users should not have access to view data? In the previous configuration samples, the john user should not even be allowed to see the Detectives page. If the application supports web services, how can we prevent a user from calling that method directly and getting the data? Or by using a remote REST call? Because the security is currently defined only in the web layer. The next section is about how Spring Security can secure items on lower levels.

Method Security

To apply security to lower layers of an application, Spring Security uses AOP. The respective bean is wrapped in a proxy that before calling the target method, first checks credentials of the user and only calls the method if the user is authorize to it. There are two alternatives for configuring this.

- Method-level security must be enabled by annotating a configuration class (good practice is to annotate the Security Configuration class to keep all configurations related to security in one place) with @Enable GlobalMethodSecurity(securedEnabled = true). Methods must be secured by annotating them with Spring Security annotation @Secured.

647

```
package com.apress.cems.web.config;
import org.springframework.security.config.annotation
                    .method.configuration.EnableGlobalMethodSecurity;
import org.springframework.security.access.annotation.Secured;
...
@Configuration
@EnableWebSecurity
@EnableGlobalMethodSecurity(securedEnabled = true)
public class SecurityConfig extends WebSecurityConfigurerAdapter {
...
}

//DetectiveServiceImpl.java service class
package com.apress.cems.dj.services.impl;
import org.springframework.security.access.annotation.Secured;
...
@Service
@Transactional
public class DetectiveServiceImpl implements DetectiveService {

    @Secured("ROLE_ADMIN")
    public List<Detective> findAll() {
        return detectiveRepo.findAll();
    }

    ...
}
```

- Method -level security must be enabled by annotating a
  configuration class(good practice is to annotate the Security
  Configuration class to keep all configurations related to security in
  one place) with @EnableGlobalMethodSecurity(jsr250Enabled =
  true). Methods must be secured by annotating them as JSR-250[10]
  annotations.

---

[10]JSR 250: Common Annotations for the Java Platform https://www.jcp.org/en/jsr/
 detail?id=250

```
package com.apress.cems.web.config;
import org.springframework.security.config.annotation
            .method.configuration.EnableGlobalMethodSecurity;
            import javax.annotation.security.RolesAllowed;
...
@Configuration
@EnableWebSecurity
@EnableGlobalMethodSecurity(jsr250Enabled = true)
public class SecurityConfig extends WebSecurityConfigurerAdapter {
...
}

//DetectiveServiceImpl.java service class
import javax.annotation.security.RolesAllowed;
...
@Service
@Transactional
public class DetectiveServiceImpl implements DetectiveService {
    @RolesAllowed("ROLE_ADMIN")
    public List<Detective> findAll() {
        return detectiveRepo.findAll();
    }

    ...
}
```

The JSR 250 are standards-based annotations and allow simple
role-based constraints to be applied but do not have the power
Spring Security's native annotations.

Both approaches will lead to Spring Security wrapping the service class in a secure
proxy. The abstract schema of how a secured method executes and the components
involved is depicted in Figure 7-4.

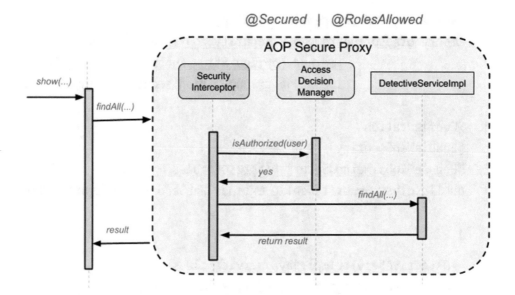

Figure 7-4. *Abstract schema of a secured method execution*

There are four annotations that support expression attributes, which were introduced in Spring 3.0, to allow pre- and post-invocation authorization checks and to support the filtering of submitted collection arguments or return values: @PreAuthorize, @PreFilter, @PostAuthorize and @PostFilter. They are enabled using Java Configuration by the prePostEnabled attribute of the @EnableGlobalMethodSecurity element that must be configured to have the true value.

```
import org.springframework.security.config.annotation
            .method.configuration.EnableGlobalMethodSecurity;
...
@Configuration
@EnableWebSecurity
@EnableGlobalMethodSecurity(prePostEnabled = true)
public class SecurityConfig extends WebSecurityConfigurerAdapter {
...
}
```

The annotation can be used as follows.

```
import org.springframework.security.access.prepost.PreAuthorize;

...
@Service
@Transactional(readOnly = true, propagation = Propagation.REQUIRED)
public class DetectiveServiceImpl implements DetectiveService {

    @PreAuthorize("hasRole('USER')")
    public void create(Detective detective){

      ...

    }
}
```

But the interesting thing about these annotations is that they can access method arguments. In the following snippet, the current logged in user is verified if it has the "admin" permission to delete the detective given as argument. It does this by using Spring ACL (Access Control List) classes.

```
import org.springframework.security.access.prepost.PreAuthorize;
import org.springframework.security.acls.model.Permission;
import org.springframework.security.acls.model.Sid;
...
@Service
@Transactional(readOnly = true, propagation = Propagation.REQUIRED)
public class DetectiveServiceImpl implements DetectiveService {

    @PreAuthorize("hasPermission(#user, 'admin')")
    public void delete(Detective detective, Sid recipient, Permission
    permission){

      ...

    }
}
```

These annotations provide more granularity, as SpEL expressions can restrict the domain that a user is allowed to affect with its actions. In the following example, a user can only affect a detective whose username matches that of the user argument.

```
import org.springframework.security.access.prepost.PreAuthorize;
import org.springframework.security.acls.model.Permission;
import org.springframework.security.acls.model.Sid;
...
@Service
@Transactional(readOnly = true, propagation = Propagation.REQUIRED)
public class DetectiveServiceImpl implements DetectiveService {

    @PreAuthorize("#user.username == authentication.name")
    public void modifyProfile(Detective detective){

    ...

    }
}
```

Spring Security ACL is very powerful and easy to implement when you can stick to the Spring database implementation. So, if a project requires granulated control over resources, it is definitely the way to go.

One more thing and then it's practice time.

Spring Security and Thymeleaf

Since Thymeleaf is used in this book as the favorite view technology, let's see how can we combine it with Spring Security. Configuring Spring Security in a Spring Web Thymeleaf application is simple.

- Add a class extending AbstractSecurityWebApplicationInitializer to register the delegatingFilterProxy to use springSecurityFilterChain before any other registered filter. This that every request is first intercepted by Spring Security.

- Add a Spring security configuration class that extends WebSecurityConfigurerAdapter to configure existing beans and declare any additional beans needed to configure security within the application. In the previous examples, a very complex configuration was used, where the login form was provided as the auth.jsp. This was done so that the login form would match the look and feel of the rest of the application. If no configuration is provided, Spring Security generates a default login form for you.

```
package com.apress.cems.web.config;

@Configuration
@EnableWebSecurity
public class SecurityConfig extends WebSecurityConfigurerAdapter{

    @Override
    public void configure(WebSecurity web) throws Exception {
        web.ignoring().mvcMatchers("/resources/**","/images/**","/
        styles/**");
    }

    @Autowired
    public void configureGlobal(AuthenticationManagerBuilder auth) {
        try {
            PasswordEncoder passwordEncoder = new BCryptPassword
            Encoder();
            auth
             .inMemoryAuthentication()
             .passwordEncoder(passwordEncoder)
             .withUser("john").password(passwordEncoder.encode
             ("doe"))
                        .roles("USER")
             .and().withUser("jane").password(passwordEncoder.
             encode("doe"))
                        .roles("USER", "ADMIN")
             .and().withUser("admin").password(passwordEncoder.
             encode("admin"))
                        .roles("ADMIN");
        } catch (Exception e) {
            throw new ConfigurationException(
                "In-Memory authentication was not configured.", e);
        }
    }

    @Override
    protected void configure(HttpSecurity http) throws Exception {
```

```
http
        .authorizeRequests()
        .mvcMatchers("/resources/**","/images/**","/
        styles/**")
                        .permitAll()
        .mvcMatchers("/persons/*/edit").hasRole("ADMIN")
        .mvcMatchers("/detectives/**").hasRole("ADMIN")
        .mvcMatchers("/**").hasAnyRole("ADMIN","USER")
        .anyRequest()
        .authenticated()
        .and()
    .formLogin()
        .defaultSuccessUrl("/home")
        .permitAll()
        .and()
    .logout()
        .logoutSuccessUrl("/")
        .and()
    .csrf().csrfTokenRepository(repo());
}

@Bean
public CsrfTokenRepository repo() {
    HttpSessionCsrfTokenRepository repo =
            new HttpSessionCsrfTokenRepository();
    repo.setParameterName("_csrf");
    repo.setHeaderName("X-CSRF-TOKEN");
    return repo;
}
}
```

The previous configuration is as default as it can be; the result is that when the
application is accessed, a very simple login form is displayed, like the one in Figure 7-5.

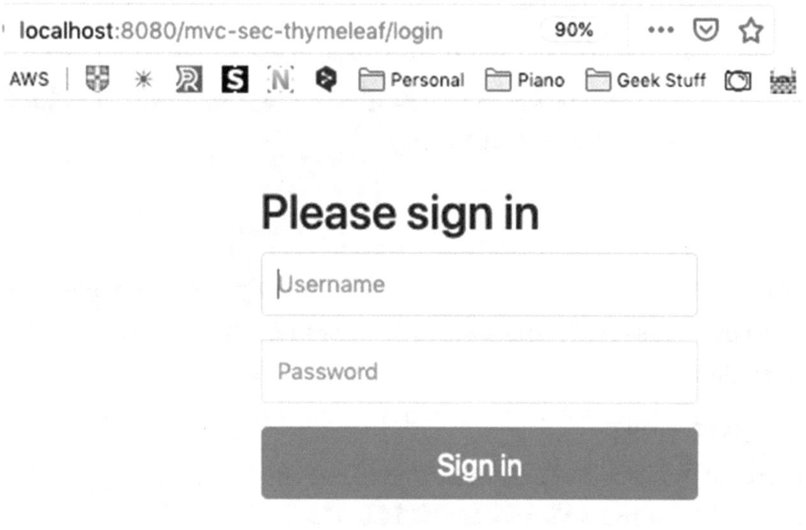

Figure 7-5. *Spring Security default login form*

- To secure parts of the generated views or display user
  information in a similar way, we previously did with Spring
  Security taglibs, the `thymeleaf-extras-springsecurity5` must
  be added to the classpath. This library contains a class named
  `SpringSecurityDialect` that resolves Thymeleaf security elements.
  This dialect class must be added to the template engine bean.

```
package com.apress.cems.web.config;

import org.thymeleaf.extras.springsecurity5.dialect.
SpringSecurityDialect;

@Configuration
@EnableWebMvc
@ComponentScan(basePackages = {"com.apress.cems.web.controllers"}
class WebConfig implements WebMvcConfigurer, ServletContextAware {
...

    @Bean
    @Description("Thymeleaf Template Engine")
    public SpringTemplateEngine templateEngine() {
        SpringTemplateEngine templateEngine = new SpringTemplate
        Engine();
```

```
        templateEngine.setTemplateResolver(templateResolver());
        templateEngine.setTemplateEngineMessageSource(messageSource());
        templateEngine.addDialect(new SpringSecurityDialect());
        return templateEngine;
    }
}
```

- Enrich the Thymeleaf templates using the newly supported elements. In the previous HTML snippet, notice the underlined elements; they are explained later.

```
<!DOCTYPE HTML>
<html xmlns:th="http://www.thymeleaf.org" ...>
<head th:fragment="cemsHead(title)">
...
</head>
<body>
<header th:fragment="cemsHeader">
    <div class="banner"></div>
    <div class="themeLocal">
        <span th:if="${#locale.language eq 'de'}">
            <a th:href="@{/?lang=de}" th:text="#{locale.de}">DE</a>
        </span>
        <span th:unless="${#locale.language eq 'en'}">
            <a th:href="@{/?lang=en}" th:text="#{locale.en}">EN</a>
        </span> |
        <span th:if="${#themes.code('name') eq 'blue'}">
            <a th:href="@{/?theme=blue}" th:text="#{theme.Blue}">
            BLUE</a>
        </span>
        <span th:unless="${#themes.code('name') eq 'green'}">
            <a th:href="@{/?theme=green}" th:text="#{theme.
            Green}">GREEN</a>
        </span> | <span sec:authorize="isAuthenticated()">
            Authenticated: <em sec:authentication="name"></em>
            </span>
    </div>
</header>
```

656

```
<section th:fragment="cemsMenu">
    <div class="menu">
        <ul>
            <li><span th:if="${menuTab eq 'home'}">
                    <strong><a th:href="@{/}" th:text="
                    #{menu.home}">HOME</a></strong>
                </span>
                <span th:unless="${menuTab eq 'home'}">
                    <a th:href="@{/}" th:text="#{menu.home}">
                    HOME</a>
                </span>
            </li>

            ...

            <li sec:authorize="isAuthenticated()">
                <a th:href="@{/logout}" th:text="#{menu.logout}">
                SIGN OUT</a>
            </li>
        </ul>
    </div>
</section>

<footer ../>
</body>
</html>
```

The syntax is quite similar to the Spring Security taglib, right? And
is also quite readable. The sec:authorize attribute can encapsulate a
portion of HTML that is meant to be displayed only when the SPEL
expression given as parameter returns true. The sec:authentication
attribute can access the details of the current authenticated user. The
previous example extracts the name to be displayed in the page, but
it can extract the roles of the authenticated user as well.

```
<span sec:authentication="principal.authorities"></span>.
```

After all the changes are in place, the main interface of our application should look
as depicted in Figure 7-6.

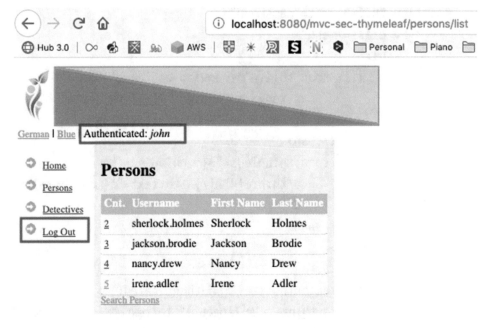

Figure 7-6. *Thymeleaf secured application interface, when user john is logged in*

If you were not using Thymeleaf, and you needed the details of your logged in user to display them in a page, this is where the @AuthenticationPrincipal annotation from package org.springframework.security.core.annotation is useful. This annotation can be placed on a handler method argument of type org.springframework.security. core.userdetails.User to tell Spring to inject the currently logged in principal. The work is performed by a bean of AuthenticationPrincipalArgumentResolver type from the package org.springframework.security.web.method.annotation.

```
package com.apress.cems.web.controllers;

import org.springframework.security.core.annotation.
AuthenticationPrincipal;
import org.springframework.security.core.userdetails.User;
import org.springframework.stereotype.Controller;
import org.springframework.ui.Model;
import org.springframework.web.bind.annotation.RequestMapping;
import org.springframework.web.bind.annotation.RequestMethod;
```

```
@Controller
public class HomeController {

    @RequestMapping(value = "/home", method = RequestMethod.GET)
    public String home(@AuthenticationPrincipal User activeUser,
    Model model) {
        model.addAttribute("currentUser", "Logged in: " +
            activeUser.getUsername() + " with roles: "
                + activeUser.getAuthorities().toString());
        return "home";
    }
}
```

Since the name of the annotation may not make its purpose obvious, you could always create a meta-annotated annotation that is more ... obvious.

```
package com.apress.cems.web.util;

import org.springframework.core.annotation.AliasFor;
import org.springframework.security.core.annotation.
AuthenticationPrincipal;

import java.lang.annotation.*;

@Target({ ElementType.PARAMETER, ElementType.ANNOTATION_TYPE })
@Retention(RetentionPolicy.RUNTIME)
@Documented
@AuthenticationPrincipal
public @interface CurrentUser {

    @AliasFor(annotation = AuthenticationPrincipal.class)
    boolean errorOnInvalidType() default false;

    @AliasFor(annotation = AuthenticationPrincipal.class)
    String expression() default "";
}
```

Spring Security is a vast subject, and entire books have been written about it. You can check out *Pro Spring Security*, the second edition of the book should be out in 2019.[11]

And now, it's time to test your knowledge.

!   This is all that can be said about Spring Security, and before jumping to the next section you can test your knowledge by solving the TODO tasks from project `chapter07/mvc-sec-practice`. There are four TODO tasks numbered from 52 to 55, and if you need inspiration or a confirmation that your solution is correct, you can compare it to the proposed solution in project `chapter07/mvc-sec-thymeleaf`.

Task TODO 52, located in the `SecurityWebApplicationInitializer` class, requires you to complete the configuration of this class to register the `delegatingFilterProxy` bean.

Task TODO 53, located in the `SecurityConfig` class, requires you to complete the configuration of this class to enable support for Spring Security. You can configure the in-memory authentication to support the users in Table 7-4.

Table 7-4. *Application users*

Username	Password	Role
john	doe	USER
jane	doe	USER, ADMIN
admin	admin	ADMIN

Task TODO 54, located in the `WebInitializer` class, requires you to complete the configuration of this class so that the application is secured.

Task TODO 55, located in the `list.html` file, requires you to complete the implementation of this HTML template page to hide the contents of the column with person IDs that contains the URL to the details view using the Thymeleaf `sec:` attribute, if the user is not an administrator. Hint: Use the `hasRole('ROLE_ADMIN')` SpEL expression to secure the `<a ../>` element.

---

[11]Official book page: `https://www.apress.com/gp/book/9781484250518`

Secured Spring Boot Web Applications

Since we've talked about Spring Boot previously, but we've used it only to build a simple unsecured application, now it is time to see what Spring Boot can do when we need to write a secured web application. Since we already have a Spring Boot web application in the chapter07/boot-web module, we'll just copy its contents into a new module named chapter07/boot-sec and add the required libraries on the classpath, and then add security configurations.

Each release of Spring Boot provides a curated list of dependencies that it supports. The versions of the necessary libraries are selected so the API matches perfectly and this is handled by Spring Boot. Therefore, manually configuring the dependency versions is not necessary. Upgrading Spring Boot ensures that those dependencies are upgraded. To write secured applications, the spring-boot-starter-security module must be added to the classpath. This module is configured with transitive dependencies needed to secure a web application. We can take spring-boot-starter-web in IntelliJ IDEA Gradle view, as depicted in Figure 7-7.

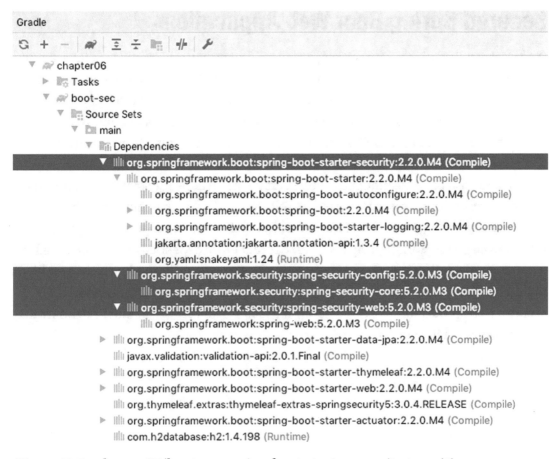

Figure 7-7. *chapter07/boot-sec: spring-boot-starter-security transitive dependencies in IntelliJ IDEA Gradle view*

The version of Spring Boot and the project version are inherited from the `pivotal-certified-pro-spring-dev-exam-02` project. To have this project built and running, one class annotated with `@SpringBootApplication` is needed. But since security is involved, we need to provide the desired settings. A configuration class that extends `WebSecurityConfigurerAdapter` needs to be created because there are two things that need configured that Spring Boot cannot guess for us: users that will access the application and their credentials and the customized security settings for application URLs. Let's configure the users first, and let's use a different approach. Instead of overriding the `configureGlobal(..)` method, we'll just declare a `UserDetailsService` and a `PasswordEncoder` bean.

```
package com.apress.cems;

import org.springframework.security.core.userdetails.User;
import org.springframework.security.core.userdetails.UserDetails;
import org.springframework.security.core.userdetails.UserDetailsService;
import org.springframework.security.crypto.bcrypt.BCryptPasswordEncoder;
import org.springframework.security.crypto.password.PasswordEncoder;
import org.springframework.security.provisioning.
InMemoryUserDetailsManager;
...

@Configuration
@EnableWebSecurity
public class SecurityConfig extends WebSecurityConfigurerAdapter {

    @Bean
    @Override
    public UserDetailsService userDetailsService() {
        UserDetails john = User.withUsername("john").password(encoder()
            .encode("doe")).roles("USER").build();
        UserDetails jane = User.withUsername("jane").password(encoder()
            .encode("doe")).roles("USER", "ADMIN").build();
        UserDetails admin = User.withUsername("admin").password(encoder()
            .encode("admin")).roles("ADMIN").build();
        return new InMemoryUserDetailsManager(john,jane,admin);
    }

    @Bean
    PasswordEncoder encoder(){
        return new BCryptPasswordEncoder();
    }
...
}
```

We need the PasswordEncoder bean, because Spring Boot will use it to encrypt passwords provided by the users to compare them with the credentials stored in memory.

The rest of the configuration is nothing special, but we'll list it anyway and add some new features.

```
package com.apress.cems;

import org.springframework.context.annotation.Bean;
import org.springframework.context.annotation.Configuration;
import org.springframework.security.config.annotation.web.builders.
HttpSecurity;
import org.springframework.security.config.annotation.web.builders.
WebSecurity;
import org.springframework.security.config.annotation.web.configuration.
          EnableWebSecurity;
import org.springframework.security.config.annotation.web.configuration.
          WebSecurityConfigurerAdapter;
import org.springframework.security.web.csrf.CsrfTokenRepository;
import org.springframework.security.web.csrf.
HttpSessionCsrfTokenRepository;
...

@Configuration
@EnableWebSecurity
public class SecurityConfig extends WebSecurityConfigurerAdapter {
    @Override
    public void configure(WebSecurity web) throws Exception {
        web.ignoring().mvcMatchers("/resources/**","/images/**",
        "/styles/**");
    }
    ...

    @Override
    protected void configure(HttpSecurity http) throws Exception {
        http
                .authorizeRequests()
                .mvcMatchers("/persons/*/edit").hasRole("ADMIN")
                .mvcMatchers("/**").hasAnyRole("ADMIN", "USER")
                .anyRequest()
```

```
                .authenticated()
                .and()
                .formLogin()
                .defaultSuccessUrl("/home")
                .permitAll()
                .and()
                .logout()
                .logoutSuccessUrl("/")
                .invalidateHttpSession(true)
                .clearAuthentication(true)
                .and()
                .csrf().csrfTokenRepository(repo());
    }

    @Bean
    public CsrfTokenRepository repo() {
        HttpSessionCsrfTokenRepository repo = new
        HttpSessionCsrfTokenRepository();
        repo.setParameterName("_csrf");
        repo.setHeaderName("X-CSRF-TOKEN");
        return repo;
    }
}
```

clearAuthentication(true) is called to configure the clearing of the Authentication object at logout time, which is kinda important from a security point of view.

invalidateHttpSession(true) is called to configure the invalidation of the HTTP session at logout time. Once we have security, we can configure a few details regarding the user session. Let's take internationalization into consideration. Until now in the chapter, a cookie was used to hold the desired locale of the application. So as long as the cookie is saved in the browser memory, the application will be displayed in the language decided by the cookie value. This means that even if the user logs out, when logging in the application will be displayed in the language decided by the cookie. Of course, this is valid only for the duration of the cookie's lifespan. Also, if the current user logs out and another log is after him, the new user would get the locale of the previous user, because the cookie is in the browser memory still. But, if we were to replace

CookieLocaleResolver with SessionLocaleResolver, the locale would be saved within the HTTP session. And because of the previous configuration, the locale value would be reset to the default value at logout time.

Beans can have session scopes as well, which could keep track of the user's actions in an application while being logged in. Let's create a class named PersonAudit and declare a bean of this type with the scope session. We will then inject this bean in all the controllers managing Person instances and log every URI accessed by the current logged in user.

```
package com.apress.cems.person.services;

import org.slf4j.Logger;
import org.slf4j.LoggerFactory;
import org.springframework.context.annotation.Scope;
import org.springframework.context.annotation.ScopedProxyMode;
import org.springframework.stereotype.Service;
import org.springframework.web.context.WebApplicationContext;

import java.time.LocalDateTime;
import java.util.*;

@Service
@Scope(value = WebApplicationContext.SCOPE_SESSION,
     proxyMode = ScopedProxyMode.TARGET_CLASS)
public class PersonAudit {
    private static Logger logger = LoggerFactory.getLogger(PersonAudit.
    class);

    private Map<LocalDateTime, String> auditMessages;

    public PersonAudit() {
        logger.debug(" ->> Creating  the PersonAudit for this session ...");
        auditMessages = new HashMap<>();
    }

    public void recordAction(String action) {
        auditMessages.put(LocalDateTime.now(),action);
    }
```

```
    public Map<LocalDateTime, String> getAuditMessages() {
        return auditMessages;
    }
}
```

The implementation is naive, and instead of injecting this bean everywhere, an aspect would be more suitable, but this is not the focus of this section. This bean is injected in the HomeController, and when the home page is accessed, a textarea component is populated with all the audit messages.

```
package com.apress.cems;

import com.apress.cems.person.services.PersonAudit;
import org.springframework.stereotype.Controller;
import org.springframework.ui.Model;
import org.springframework.web.bind.annotation.RequestMapping;
import org.springframework.web.bind.annotation.RequestMethod;

@Controller
public class HomeController {

    private PersonAudit audit;

    public HomeController(PersonAudit audit) {
        this.audit = audit;
    }

    @RequestMapping(value = {"/","/home"}, method = RequestMethod.GET)
    public String home(Model model) {
        StringBuilder sb = new StringBuilder();
        audit.getAuditMessages().forEach((k,v) ->
            sb.append(k).append(": ").append(v).append("\n"));
        model.addAttribute("logs", sb.toString());
        return "home";
    }
}
```

If the user logs in and accesses a few /persons/ URLs, when it goes back to the home page, the whole activity should be listed in the text area. A sample of how the page should look is seen in Figure 7-8.

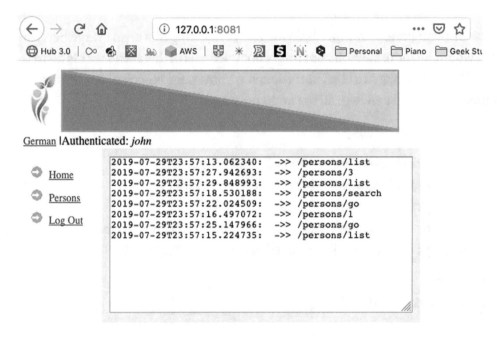

Figure 7-8. *Audit messages recorded by a session bean*

If the user logs out, the next time is logged in, the audit text area is empty, because this application was configured to clear the session at logout. So here it is, an example on how to use a session bean. Beans created with the session scope are bound to the HTTP session, and they store data that doesn't change between user requests. Since the session is specific to a user, even if there is more than one user logged at the same time, their data will not collide (as it happens with cookies). And that's pretty much it about the session scope.

Testing Spring Boot–Secured Applications

Unfortunately, a classic Spring web-secured application is still a web application, so testing it using @WebMvcTest or org.springframework.test.context.web. WebAppConfiguration does not really work because of a bug that was mentioned in Chapter 6. But Spring Boot web applications can be tested just fine.

When developing Spring secured applications, we might want to write tests to check the security configurations without starting up the entire application. In the previous chapter, an instance of MockMvc type was used to send requests to the application and check that results matched expectation. To run the same tests but include the security layer we need two things: we need to initialize the MockMvc with a security context and we need a method to provide some users to authenticate the requests.

The first uses the @WebMvcTest, which is familiar to you from the previous chapter. To configure it, the MockMvc instance should be created with a security context a Spring utility test class named SecurityMockMvcConfigurers. This class works with MockMvcConfigurer to provide security-related mock implementations. The SecurityMockMvcConfigurers.springSecurity() method configures the verb|MockMvcConfigurer| to use Spring security by providing the security bean named springSecurityFilterChain as a filter that is applied on all the requests.

To emulate a user that makes a request, the test method is annotated with the @WithMockUser annotation, which is part of the spring-security-test module. This annotation supports declaring the user by name or by providing full information: password, roles, and authorities. The default role is USER.

Let's see what the test method to check access for user *john* in the persons/list URI looks like.

```
package com.apress.cems;

import com.apress.cems.person.Person;
import com.apress.cems.person.services.PersonService;
import org.junit.jupiter.api.BeforeEach;
import org.junit.jupiter.api.Test;
import org.springframework.beans.factory.annotation.Autowired;
import org.springframework.boot.test.autoconfigure.web.servlet.WebMvcTest;
import org.springframework.boot.test.mock.mockito.MockBean;
import org.springframework.security.test.context.support.WithMockUser;
import org.springframework.test.web.servlet.MockMvc;
import org.springframework.test.web.servlet.setup.MockMvcBuilders;
import org.springframework.web.context.WebApplicationContext;

import java.util.ArrayList;
import java.util.List;
import java.util.Optional;
```

```
import static org.mockito.ArgumentMatchers.anyLong;
import static org.mockito.Mockito.when;
import static  org.springframework.security.test.web.servlet
      .setup.SecurityMockMvcConfigurers.springSecurity;
import static org.springframework.test.web.servlet.request.
MockMvcRequestBuilders.get;
import static org.springframework.test.web.servlet.result.
MockMvcResultMatchers.*;

@WebMvcTest
class BootSecureAppMockTest {

    @Autowired
    private MockMvc mockMvc;

    @MockBean
    private PersonService mockService;

    @Autowired
    private WebApplicationContext webApplicationContext;

    @BeforeEach
    void setUp() {
        mockMvc = MockMvcBuilders.webAppContextSetup(webApplicationContext)
                .apply(springSecurity()).build();
    }

    @WithMockUser(value="john")
    @Test
     void johnShouldHaveAccessToPersons() throws Exception {
        List<Person> list = new ArrayList<>();
        Person p = new Person();
        p.setId(1L);
        p.setFirstName("Sherlock");
        p.setLastName("Holmes");
        list.add(p);
        when(mockService.findAll()).thenReturn(list);
```

```
        mockMvc.perform(get("/persons/list")).andExpect(status().isOk());
    }
}
```

As you can see in this test, the `PersonService` bean was mocked to keep things quick and simple, since the focus of the test is the access to the URI, and not the actual response. The fact that the *john* user has access to this URI is represented here just by the `status().isOk()` construct. The preceding test doesn't tell us much. I mean, if the security context would not be there the test would still pass. Let's write another test method to check that indeed the security context is valid and the security configurations do their job. This can be easily done by testing that the user *john* does not have access to the page to edit persons.

```
package com.apress.cems;
...

@WebMvcTest
class BootSecureAppMockTest {

  ...

    @WithMockUser(value="john")
    @Test
    void johnShouldNotBeAllowedToEditPersons() throws Exception {
        Person p = new Person();
        p.setId(1L);
        p.setFirstName("Sherlock");
        p.setLastName("Holmes");
        when(mockService.findById(anyLong())).thenReturn(Optional.of(p));
        mockMvc.perform(get("/persons/1/edit")).andExpect(status().
        isForbidden());
    }
}
```

If the class is run again, both tests should pass. If the test is run in IntelliJ IDEA as a Gradle test, there should be a file named `com.apress.cems.BootSecureAppMockTest.html` located under `fchapter07/boot-sec/build/reports/tests/` that shows the status of your build. This file can be opened automatically in the default browser by clicking the Gradle button from your Run view, as depicted in Figure 7-9.

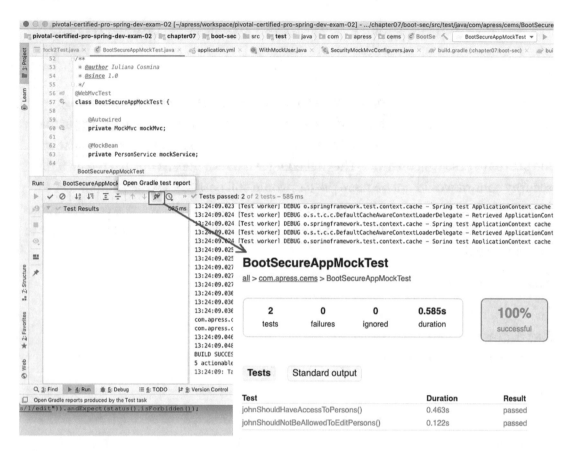

Figure 7-9. *Gradle test run results file*

The other alternative is to use @AutoConfigureMockMvc in combination with
@SpringBootTest(webEnvironment = SpringBootTest.WebEnvironment.MOCK). The
first annotation enables the auto-configuration of the MockMvc object so that it can send
requests to the application. The second annotation is typically used on Spring Boot
tests. But when the WebEnvironment.MOCK is provided as an argument, the test web
application context is created with a mock servlet environment if the servlet APIs are on
the classpath, which tends to speed up execution tests.

```
package com.apress.cems;

import org.junit.jupiter.api.Test;
import org.springframework.beans.factory.annotation.Autowired;
import org.springframework.boot.test.autoconfigure.web.servlet.
AutoConfigureMockMvc;
```

```
import org.springframework.boot.test.context.SpringBootTest;
import org.springframework.security.test.context.support.WithMockUser;
import org.springframework.test.web.servlet.MockMvc;

import static org.hamcrest.Matchers.*;
import static org.springframework.test.web.servlet.request.
MockMvcRequestBuilders.get;
import static org.springframework.test.web.servlet.result.
MockMvcResultMatchers.*;
import static org.springframework.test.web.servlet.result.
MockMvcResultMatchers.model;

@SpringBootTest(webEnvironment = SpringBootTest.WebEnvironment.MOCK)
@AutoConfigureMockMvc
class BootSecureAppMock2Test {

    @Autowired
    private MockMvc mockMvc;

    @WithMockUser(value="john")
    @Test
    void johnShouldHaveAccessToPersons() throws Exception {
        mockMvc.perform(get("/persons/list")).andExpect(status().isOk());
    }

    @WithMockUser(value="john")
    @Test
    void johnShouldHaveAccessToThisPerson() throws Exception {
        mockMvc.perform(get("/persons/1")).andExpect(status().isOk());
    }

    @WithMockUser(value="john")
    @Test
    void johnShouldBeAllowedToEditThisPerson() throws Exception {
        mockMvc.perform(get("/persons/1/edit")).andExpect(status().
        is4xxClientError());
    }

}
```

As you can see, as usual, there is a huge benefit in using Spring Boot to write Spring applications. That's it, we are doomed to never build an application from scratch again. 😄

This is it for this chapter. Since configuring security in a Spring Boot application is not different than in a classic Spring application, there is no need to add a practice exercise, so this chapter ends here. Have fun doing the quiz!

Summary

- Spring Security allows authentication to be fully decoupled from authorization.

- URLs can be protected using security rules, JSP elements can be protected using security taglibs.

- Method security is implemented using AOP using Spring Security Specific and JSR 250 annotations: `@Secured`, `@RolesAllowed`, `@PreAuthorized`, and so forth.

- Encrypting and salting passwords are supported.

- `@EnableWebSecurity` is the annotation used on a configuration class to have Spring Security enabled.

- This class must also implement `WebSecurityConfigurer` or extend a class implementing it to customize the imported configuration.

- `@WebMvcTest` can be used in combination with `@WithMockUse` to test security configurations.

Quiz

Question 1. What is authentication? (Choose one.)

    A.   the process of securing resources

    B.   the process of deciding whether a user should be allowed to access a resource

    C.   the process of verifying the validity of the principal's credentials

Question 2. What is authorization? (Choose one.)

A.   is the process of verifying the validity of the principal's credentials

B.   the process of deciding if an authenticated user is allowed to perform a certain action within the application

C.   the process of generating credentials for a user

Question 3. What can be said about application security? (Choose one.)

A.   it is unnecessary

B.   it should be provided by third-party frameworks

C.   it is a cross-cutting concern

Question 4. Using ant matchers to secure URLs is more secure than using taglibs. True or false?

A.   True

B.   False

Question 5. What is the default name of the spring security filter that is applied to all requests in a secured Spring web application? (Choose one.)

A.   `springSecurityFilter`

B.   `springSecurityFilterChain`

C.   `delegatingFilterProxy`

Question 6. What is the effect of annotating a method with `@Secured("ROLE_ADMIN")`? (Choose one.)

A.   a list of security configuration attributes for the method is defined

B.   in a Spring secured application with method security enabled, access to call that method is restricted to users with the `ROLE_ADMIN` role

C.   in a Spring secured application, where `@EnableGlobalMethodSecu rity(securedEnabled = true)` is used on a configuration class, it causes the class containing the method to be wrapped in a secure proxy to restrict access only to users with the `ROLE_ADMIN`

CHAPTER 8

Spring REST

In Chapters 6 and 7, the objects handled by Spring were created on a JVM and were accessed and manipulated indirectly by the user using the HTTP protocol. In this case, all the end user needs to access the objects in the JVM is the web interface of the application. The end user sends commands by using HTTP methods and sends data by using request parameters, HTTP headers, or the request body content. The results of these commands include retrieving objects, creating a new object, or modifying or deleting an existing object. There are other types of applications that support remote access, which should be mentioned first.

Remoting and web services are ways to communicate between applications. The applications can run on the same computer, on different computers, or on different networks, and can be written in different languages (a Python application can consume a web service provided by a Java application, for example). In remoting, the applications communicating know about each other. There is a server application and a client application, and to ensure security, each one is configured with the location and other data to identify the other. Because of this, it supports state management options, can correlate multiple calls from the same client, and support callbacks.

On the client application, a proxy of the server target object is created and used to access the object on the server. Remoting can be used across any protocol, but it does not do well with firewalls. Remoting relies on the existence of the common language runtime assemblies that contain information about data types. The client and server instance handle the same data types. This limits the information that must be passed about an object, and allows objects to be passed by value or by reference. The communication is done using a binary, XML, or JSON format. These limitations made remoting deprecated when this book was written. Spring remoting is not a part of the certification exam and was replaced by web services.

© Iuliana Cosmina 2020
I. Cosmina, *Pivotal Certified Professional Core Spring 5 Developer Exam*,
https://doi.org/10.1007/978-1-4842-5136-2_8

Web services are cross-platform interprocess communication methods that use common standards and work through firewalls. They work with messages, not objects. Basically, the client sends a message, and a reply message is returned. Web services work in a stateless environment where each message results in a new object created to service the request. Web services support interoperability across platforms and are good for heterogeneous environments. They expose their own arbitrary sets of operations, such as via WSDL[1] and SOAP.[2]

REST, or **RE**presentational **S**tate **T**ransfer, is an HTTP-based web service for communication between applications. REST is currently the most popular way applications communicate with each other. RESTful services and how can they be implemented using Spring is the focus of this chapter. Why? Because Spring Boot is very suitable for building microservices[3] and REST facilitates microservices working together, thus being able to understand REST is practical. And is also necessary for the certification exam, just in case, you needed more arguments. REST services allow access and manipulation of textual representations of web resources using a uniform and predefined set of stateless operations.

The most common protocol used with REST services is HTTP so the HTTP methods map on REST operations such as GET, POST, PUT, DELETE, and so forth. Initially, web resources were documents or files accessed using a URL,[4] but at some point in the past, a web resource became anything (object, entity) that can be accessed via web and is identified by a URI.[5] Since REST maps perfectly on all CRUD operations is the most practical way to expose an application's API. Because of its simplicity and the fact that applications can communicate with each other using HTTP and no other infrastructure is required, REST has become the de facto standard for building microservices.

---

[1]Web Services Description Language

[2]Simple Object Access Protocol

[3]A microservice is a small software application that is independently developed, deployed and updated. Each microservice is focused on a single functionality. Multiple microservices can be coupled together via a common API and used to provide a complex service.

[4]Uniform Resource Locator, also known as a web address

[5]Uniform Resource Identifier

What Is REST?

REST was introduced and defined in 2000 by Roy Fielding in his doctoral dissertation. REST is a lightweight alternative to mechanisms like RPC (Remote Procedure Call) and Web Services (SOAP, WSDL, etc.). REST is an architecture style for designing networked (distributed) applications. The idea is that, rather than using complex mechanisms such as CORBA, RPC, or SOAP to connect between machines, simple HTTP is used to make calls between machines. RESTful applications use HTTP requests to post data (create and/or update), read data (e.g., make queries), and delete data. Thus, REST uses HTTP for all four CRUD (Create/Read/Update/Delete) operations.

Web applications are not only used by browser clients, but programmatic clients can connect using HTTP (e.g., mobile applications and basically any application that was developed to request and receive data using HTTP as communication protocol). The REST architectural style describes best practices to expose web services over HTTP that is used not only as a transport but as an application protocol. The following HTTP specifications are used.

- HTTP verbs are used as actions to execute on the resources (GET, PUT, PATCH, POST, DELETE, HEAD, and OPTIONS).[6] The main REST HTTP methods with their actions are presented in Table 8-1.

Table 8-1. *Most Used HTTP Methods*

HTTP method	Purpose	Observation
GET	Read	Reads a resource, does not change it. It is considered **safe**. Reading the same resource always returns the same result. It is considered **idempotent.** This does not apply when the resource is not cached and modified by a parallel operation on the server that it is being retrieved from.
POST	Create	Used to create a new resource. **Neither safe nor idempotent**. Two identical POST requests will result in two identical resources being created or errors at the application level.

(continued)

---

[6]Although REST seems strongly connected to HTTP, REST principles can be followed using other protocols too, for example, POP, IMAP and any protocol that uses URL-like paths and supports GET and POST methods.

Table 8-1. (*continued*)

HTTP method	Purpose	Observation
PUT	Update	Most often used for update capabilities. **It is not safe**, as it modifies the state on the server, **but is idempotent** (unless subsequent calls of the same PUT request increments a counter within the resource for example).
DELETE	Delete	Used to delete resources. **Not safe, but can be considered idempotent**. Because requests to delete a resource that no longer exists will always return a 404 (not found).

- URIs[7] identify resources. The resources are conceptually separate from representations. Representations of the resources are returned from the server to the client, after a client request(typically JSON or XML).[8] Representations contain metadata information that can be used by the client to modify or delete the resource on the server, provided it has permission to do so. In this book, the focus will be on JSON, because its structure makes it quite easy to read.

- With an HTTP response, the response body, codes, and headers deliver state to clients. The clients deliver state using request body contents, request headers, and the URI.

A RESTful architecture is a stateless client-server architecture, so the system is disconnected (loosely coupled). Server might not be available all the time, so operations are asynchronous. Thus, clients cannot assume direct connection to the server. Sometimes requested resources can be cached and some other unknown software and hardware layers can be interposed between client and server.

Intermediary servers may improve system scalability and/or security by enabling load-balancing and providing shared caches and enforcing security policies.

In REST communication, the objects handled are representation of resources. Representations can link to other resources thus providing the opportunity of extension and discovery. HTTP headers and status codes are used to communicate results to

---

[7]Uniform Resource Identifier

[8]REST uses various representation to represent a resource like text, JSON, XML. JSON is the most popular one.

clients. When working with a specific container, a session is used to preserve state across multiple HTTP requests. Using REST there is no need for this, because REST communication is stateless, which increases the scalability as the server does not have to maintain, update, or communicate the session state. As HTTP is supported by every platform/language this means REST communication can be done between a wide range of different systems, thus it is very scalable and definitely interoperable.

To analyze contents of the REST requests and responses the Postman application is recommended. To download the application, go to `www.getpostman.com/downloads/`. When you start the application, there is an orange button in the upper-left corner labeled New. This button can be used to either create a collection of Postman requests or a single request. For the purpose of this chapter, all requests are grouped under a collection named `00Pivotal_Spring_Exam`. Postman supports exporting and importing collections of requests in JSON format. Along with the sources for this chapter, you are provided with a collection of Postman requests to test your solutions.

Figure 8-1 shows how Postman can be used to create a REST request.

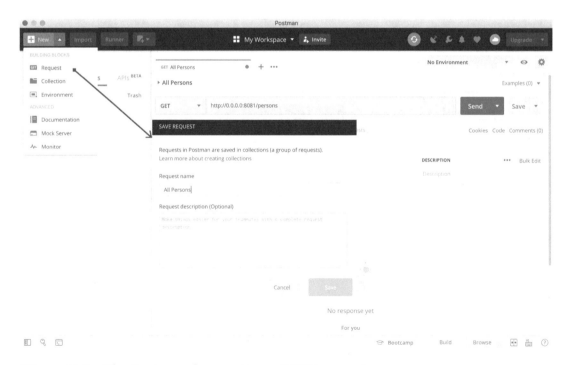

Figure 8-1.   *The Postman for creating a REST request*

Spring Support for REST

On the server side, the core component for REST support is Spring MVC. A controller that was designed to handle web requests can handle REST requests as well with a few small modifications. If you skipped Chapter 6, you might want to give it a look, because the base code for this section is a Spring unsecured web application. In this section, a basic classic Spring web application (not using Boot) will be modified to support REST requests. After covering all the configuration details needed to support REST communication, the rest of the projects for this chapter will be developed using Spring Boot, because the configuration is provided out of the box by the starter library.

The classic Spring web application is developed in module `chapter08/rest-classic`. In this project we have two controllers that manage `Person` instances. One of them is named `MultiplePersonController` because its handler methods populate models with multiple `Person` instances and the other is named `SinglePersonController` because it populates a model with a single `Person` instance.

This is the initial `MultiplePersonController.list()` method body.

```
package com.apress.cems.rest.controllers;
...
@Controller
@RequestMapping("/persons")
public class MultiplePersonController {
    ...
    @RequestMapping(path = "/list", method = RequestMethod.GET)
    public String list(Model model) {
        List<Person> persons =  personService.findAll();
        persons.sort(COMPARATOR_BY_ID);
        model.addAttribute("persons", persons);
        return "persons/list";
    }
}
```

Composed annotations were introduced Spring 4.3. They replace the `@RequestMapping` annotation with a certain HTTP method. They are grouped in the `org.springframework.web.bind.annotation` package. Spring annotations and their equivalents are listed in Table 8-2.

Table 8-2. *Spring HTTP Methods Annotations*

HTTP Method	@RequestMapping	Spring 4.3 Annotation
GET	@RequestMapping(method=RequestMethod.GET)	@GetMapping
POST	@RequestMapping(method=RequestMethod.POST)	@PostMapping
DELETE	@RequestMapping(method=RequestMethod.DELETE)	@DeleteMapping
PUT	@RequestMapping(method=RequestMethod.PUT)	@PutMapping

The previous method can also be written like this:

```
package com.apress.cems.rest.controllers;
import org.springframework.web.bind.annotation.GetMapping;
...
@Controller
@RequestMapping("/persons")
public class MultiplePersonController {

    ...
    @GetMapping (path = "/list")
    public String list(Model model) {
        List<Person> persons =  personService.findAll();
        persons.sort(COMPARATOR_BY_ID);
        model.addAttribute("persons", persons);
        return "persons/list";
    }

}
```

To make the `MultiplePersonController` support REST requests, first we have to make sure that data is no longer put in models, but converted to JSON and returned as response body. We have to tell the `DispatcherServlet` that the result of the execution of a controller method does not have to be mapped to a view, but return a REST representation of the requested resource. One way to do this is to use the `@ResponseBody` on handler methods or at the class level. This annotation indicates that the value returned by the method needs to be bind to the response body. Having a controller/ or handler method annotated with `@ResponseBody` will stop the `DispatcherServlet` from trying to find a view to render, thus handler methods that return void, will return a response with an empty body (the methods that return an empty body are usually the delete and update methods). The previous method should be annotated with it.

```
package com.apress.cems.rest.controllers;
import org.springframework.web.bind.annotation.ResponseBody;
...
@Controller
@RequestMapping("/persons")
public class MultiplePersonController {
    ...
    @GetMapping(value = "/list")
     @ResponseBody
    public String list(Model model) {
        List<Person> persons =  personService.findAll();
        persons.sort(COMPARATOR_BY_ID);
        model.addAttribute("persons", persons);
        return "persons/list";
    }

}
```

So, theoretically, we have a handler method for a REST GET request. But since the application has more than one controller, all controllers that handle REST requests must be annotated with @ResponseBody. But wait, what if they return no data, what's the @ResponseBody good for then? We'll get there. There is an alternative to writing REST specific controller methods, so you don't have to sprinkle ResponseBody everywhere.

@ResponseBody is useful at the method level, when in a project a controller handles Web requests mapped to views as well. But when you have a controller that handles only REST requests (none of the handler methods is resolves to a view), you can annotate that controller class with @RestController.

```
package com.apress.cems.rest.controllers;
import org.springframework.web.bind.annotation.RestController;
...
@RestController
@RequestMapping("/persons")
```

```
public class MultiplePersonController {

    ...
    @GetMapping(value = "/list")
    public String list(Model model) {
        List<Person> persons =  personService.findAll();
        persons.sort(COMPARATOR_BY_ID);
        model.addAttribute("persons", persons);
        return "persons/list";
    }

}
```

This annotation was added in Spring 4 and is a meta-annotation of @Controller. It is also annotated with @ResponseBody and designed to be used for marking controllers that contain only methods that handle REST requests, so methods that do not return results mapped to a view, but to a REST representation.

! You might think at this point, since @RestController is a specialization of @Controller, this makes it a stereotype annotation, right? Wrong. First, there are five stereotype annotations in Spring: @Component, @Repository, @Service, @Indexed and @Controller and they are grouped under the org. springframework.stereotype package. All of them, except @Indexed are meta-annotated with a single Spring annotation, which means that the meta-annotated annotation can be treated the same as the annotation it is annotated with. They are part of the stereotype package and have a fundamental role in declaring beans. @Indexed is a special case because it was added in Spring 5 to indicate that the annotated element represents a stereotype for the index. This is useful when classpath scanning is replaced with reading a metadata file generated at compile time for identifying bean types.

Anyway, @RestController is different because it is a composed annotation that is meta-annotated with @Controller and @ResponseBody. Because of that @RestController cannot be treated the same way as @Controller and thus it cannot be a stereotype annotation if it cannot be treated the same as one.

But is this enough? Will the preceding handler method actually do the job? Of course not. All we did was modify the handler method to support REST requests, but the returned value is a String, so a request to http://localhost:8080/rest-classic/persons/list will be resolved to the persons/list text value.

It is expected the request to return a list of Person instances serialized to JSON, so the returned type must be changed as well. For now, let's return the List<Person> and remove the Model parameter, because it useless for a REST handling method.

```
package com.apress.cems.rest.controllers;
import org.springframework.web.bind.annotation.RestController;
...
@RestController
@RequestMapping("/persons")
public class MultiplePersonController {
    ...
    @GetMapping(value = "/list")
    public  List<Person> list() {
        List<Person> persons =  personService.findAll();
        persons.sort(COMPARATOR_BY_ID);
        return persons;
    }
}
```

But this is not enough either, because Spring does not know how to convert the output before sending it as response. So, something about needs to be done as well.

HTTP Message Converters

The @ResponseBody introduced earlier is also used to facilitate the understanding of the REST message format between client and server. The resource representation can have different formats: XML, JSON, HTML, and so forth. The client must know the format to use, or request a resource with a representation it understands form the server. Representations are converted to HTTP requests and from HTTP responses by implementations of the org.springframework.http.converter.HttpMessageConverter<T> interface. Message converters are automatically detected and used by Spring in applications configured with @EnableWebMvc. In the code sample for this chapter, the representations are in JSON format, so MappingJackson2HttpMessageConverter is used.

In an MVC environment, implementations of `HttpMessageConverter<T>` are used to negotiate content conversion in an HTTP communication. By default a list of implementations of the `HttpMessageConverter<T>` interface are enabled and the list can be customized by providing an implementation for the `configureMessageConverters(..)` method in `WebMvcConfigurer` interface. In Table 8-3, you can see a few of the most used message converters and the datatype handled.

Table 8-3. *Message Converters Table*

Message Converter	Data Type	Observation
StringHttpMessageConverter	text/plain	
MappingJackson2HttpMessageConverter	application/*+json	Only if Jackson 2 is present on the classpath
AtomFeedHttpMessageConverter	application/atom+xml	Only if Rome is present on the classpath
RssChannelHttpMessageConverter	application/rss+xml	Only if Rome is present on the classpath
MappingJackson2XmlHttpMessageConverter	application/*+xml	Only if Jackson 2 is present on the classpath

Implementations are picked up automatically when libraries containing `HttpMessageConverter<T>` implementations are added to the classpath. So, this means the last step in making sure the response is converted to JSON is to provide an implementation of `HttpMessageConverter<T>` to be used. In a previous project, the Jackson library was used to render a JSON view. The same library can be used to provide Spring with a converter to use.

```
ext {
    jacksonVersion = '2.9.9'

    misc = [
        ...
```

```
    jacksonDatabind : "com.fasterxml.jackson.core:jackson-
    databind:$jacksonVersion"
]
...
}
```

In earlier versions of Spring the converter bean had to be explicitly declared, because it was not picked up and registered automatically just because the library was on the classpath. In the previous version of this book, in the WebConfig class these two beans were declared.

```
package com.apress.cems.rest.config;

import com.fasterxml.jackson.annotation.JsonInclude;
import com.fasterxml.jackson.databind.ObjectMapper;
import com.fasterxml.jackson.databind.SerializationFeature;
import org.springframework.http.converter.HttpMessageConverter;
import org.springframework.http.converter.json.
MappingJackson2HttpMessageConverter;

...

@Configuration
@EnableWebMvc
@ComponentScan(basePackages = {"com.apress.cems.rest.controllers"})
class WebConfig implements WebMvcConfigurer

    @Bean
    public MappingJackson2HttpMessageConverter
            mappingJackson2HttpMessageConverter() {
        MappingJackson2HttpMessageConverter
            mappingJackson2HttpMessageConverter =
                new MappingJackson2HttpMessageConverter();
        mappingJackson2HttpMessageConverter.setObjectMapper(objectMapper());
        return mappingJackson2HttpMessageConverter;
    }
```

```
    @Bean
    public ObjectMapper objectMapper() {
        ObjectMapper objMapper = new ObjectMapper();
        objMapper.enable(SerializationFeature.INDENT_OUTPUT);
        objMapper.setSerializationInclusion(JsonInclude.Include.NON_NULL);
        return objMapper;
    }
    ...
}
```

The mappingJackson2HttpMessageConverter is the converter bean, and this bean had to be declared and configured to use a bean of type ObjectMapper that is used to write the JSON text according to the provided options. Depending on the serialization/deserialization specifics, the bean of ObjectMapper may be needed.

Once the library is on the classpath, when the application is restarted, accessing the http://localhost:8080/ rest-classic/persons/list should display all Person instances in JSON format. If you want to use Postman to test your REST requests, you can create a simple GET request to call the recently mentioned URL. When sending the request, the received response should be a valid JSON text. If you inspect it closely, you will notice something that is ... not right.

```
[
    {
        "id": 2,
        "createdAt": {
            "year": 2019,
            "month": "AUGUST",
            "dayOfWeek": "MONDAY",
            "dayOfYear": 217,
            "monthValue": 8,
            "dayOfMonth": 5,
            "chronology": {
                "id": "ISO",
                "calendarType": "iso8601"
            },
```

```
        "era": "CE",
        "leapYear": false
    },
    "modifiedAt": {
        "year": 2019,
        "month": "AUGUST",
        "dayOfWeek": "MONDAY",
        "dayOfYear": 217,
        "monthValue": 8,
        "dayOfMonth": 5,
        "chronology": {
            "id": "ISO",
            "calendarType": "iso8601"
        },
        "era": "CE",
        "leapYear": false
    },
    "username": "sherlock.holmes",
    "firstName": "Sherlock",
    "lastName": "Holmes",
    "password": "dudu",
    "hiringDate": {
        "year": 1983,
        "month": "AUGUST",
        "dayOfWeek": "MONDAY",
        "dayOfYear": 227,
        "monthValue": 8,
        "dayOfMonth": 15,
        "chronology": {
            "id": "ISO",
            "calendarType": "iso8601"
        },
        "era": "CE",
        "leapYear": false
    },
```

```
      "newPassword": null
   },
   ...
]
```

Converting a `Person` instance to JSON format, referred to as JSON serialization, goes as expected for numbers and text values, but for calendar dates not so much. Although the value is still readable it is a little inconvenient. So, it would be nice if we could tell Spring how we want the date values to be serialized, right? That is possible using the `@JsonFormat` Jackson annotation. This annotation must be placed on every calendar date field in entity classes. And this annotation can be used to specify the type the date must be parsed to in the JSON and the format used to convert the date. To work with the calendar types introduced in Java 8, like the `LocalDate` and `LocalDateTime` fields, an extra dependency named `jackson-datatype-jsr310`[9] must be added to the classpath. The module that does this job must be configured to be used by an `ObjectMapper` bean.

```
ext {
    jacksonVersion = '2.9.9'

    misc = [
        ...
        jacksonJava8 :
            "com.fasterxml.jackson.datatype:jackson-datatype-
            jsr310:$jacksonVersion",
    ]
    ...
}
```

Once this library is on the classpath, this library is registered automatically and will be used to convert annotated `LocalDateTime` instances to the appropriate JSON representation if configuration is in place for that. In the `WebConfig` class, a bean of `ObjectMapper` type must be added and configured to support modules that provide special converters.

---

[9]Official repository: `https://github.com/FasterXML/jackson-modules-java8`

```
package com.apress.cems.rest.config;

import com.fasterxml.jackson.annotation.JsonInclude;
import com.fasterxml.jackson.databind.ObjectMapper;
import com.fasterxml.jackson.databind.SerializationFeature;
import org.springframework.http.converter.HttpMessageConverter;
import org.springframework.http.converter.json.
MappingJackson2HttpMessageConverter;
...

@Configuration
@EnableWebMvc
@ComponentScan(basePackages = {"com.apress.cems.rest.controllers"})
class WebConfig implements WebMvcConfigurer

    @Bean
    public ObjectMapper objectMapper() {
        ObjectMapper objMapper = new ObjectMapper();
        objMapper.enable(SerializationFeature.INDENT_OUTPUT);
        objMapper.setSerializationInclusion(JsonInclude.Include.NON_NULL);
        objMapper.findAndRegisterModules();
        return objMapper;
    }
...
}
```

In the previous configuration the objMapper.findAndRegisterModules() method was called, that is a convenience method that scans and registers all modules in the classpath. When more control is needed and only specific modules must be registered the objMapper.registerModule(..) can be called explicitly and provided as argument an object of the module type needed. For example, in the previous scenario, only the module for converting LocalDateTime instances was needed. The objMapper.findAndRegisterModules() can be replaced with objMapper.registerModule(new JavaTimeModule()).

Once the configuration is in place, the entity fields must be annotated with @JsonFormat, so they can be identified at serialization time and converted as configured.

```
package com.apress.cems.dao;

import com.apress.cems.util.DateProcessor;
import com.fasterxml.jackson.annotation.JsonFormat;
import org.springframework.format.annotation.DateTimeFormat;
...
@MappedSuperclass
public abstract class AbstractEntity implements Serializable {

    @JsonFormat(shape = JsonFormat.Shape.STRING,
              pattern = DateProcessor.DATE_FORMAT)
    @Column(name = "created_at", nullable = false)
    @DateTimeFormat(pattern = DateProcessor.DATE_FORMAT)
    protected LocalDateTime createdAt;

    @JsonFormat(shape = JsonFormat.Shape.STRING,
          pattern = DateProcessor.DATE_FORMAT)
    @Column(name = "modified_at", nullable = false)
    @DateTimeFormat(pattern = DateProcessor.DATE_FORMAT")
    protected LocalDateTime modifiedAt;

...
}
```

In the previous code sample, the `shape` attribute was initialized with `JsonFormat.Shape.STRING` to tell the Jackson converter bean that the value of the field should become a text value in the JSON object and the `pattern` attribute was initialized with the template value declared in the `DateProcessor` class (`yyyy-MM-dd HH:mm`), which is the custom value used everywhere in the project.[10]And now, if we restart the server and make the same call again, we see an improvement.

```
[
    {
        "id": 2,
        "createdAt": "2019-08-05",
        "modifiedAt": "2019-08-05",
```

---

[10]The *@DateTimeFormat* is a validation annotation, which was introduced in the previous chapter.

```
      "username": "sherlock.holmes",
      "firstName": "Sherlock",
      "lastName": "Holmes",
      "password": "dudu",
      "hiringDate": "1983-08-15",
      "newPassword": null
    },
    ...
]
```

But still, something is not OK. The `password` field is written in the JSON response. This is bad due to security reasons. The `newPassword` field is a transient field that is written too, which is just ... useless, because it is always null when retrieving data from the server. How can this be fixed? Easily, as you probably imagine. There is a Jackson annotation for that, and its name is self-explanatory: `@JsonIgnore`.

```
package com.apress.cems.dao;

import com.fasterxml.jackson.annotation.JsonIgnore;
...
@MappedSuperclass
public class Person extends AbstractEntity {

    @JsonIgnore
    @NotNull
    @Size(min = 4, max = 50)
    @Column(nullable = false)
    private String password;

    @JsonIgnore
    @Transient
    private String newPassword;
...
}
```

OK, this is more like it. Now in the response there is only the appropriate information.

```
[
    {
        "id": 2,
        "createdAt": "2019-08-05 15:08",
        "modifiedAt": "2019-08-05 15:08",
        "username": "sherlock.holmes",
        "firstName": "Sherlock",
        "lastName": "Holmes",
        "hiringDate": "1983-08-15 00:20"
    },
    ...
]
```

Since more than one representation can be supported, the type of representation for the response can be narrowed by using the produces attribute. This attribute is declared by the @RequestMapping annotation, but all of its specializations have aliases declared (even if the only annotation that really makes sense is @GetMapping). To limit the type of representation produced to JSON, the method can be annotated with @GetMapping(value = "/list", produces = MediaType.APPLICATION_JSON_VALUE).[11]where MediaType is part of the org.springframework.http package and contains a selection of constants and utility methods that add support for quality parameters as defined in the HTTP specification.[12]

```
package com.apress.cems.rest.controllers;
import org.springframework.web.bind.annotation.RestController;
...
@RestController
@RequestMapping("/persons")
public class MultiplePersonController {
    ...
```

---

[11]Developers writing handling methods that could return content containing special characters also use *APPLICATION_JSON_UTF8_VALUE*. This media type is now deprecated and while RFC7159 clearly states that "no charset parameter is defined for this registration", some browsers require it for interpreting correctly UTF-8 special characters.

[12]HTTP specification https://tools.ietf.org/html/rfc7231#section-3.1.1.1

```
@GetMapping(path = "/list", produces = MediaType.APPLICATION_JSON_VALUE)
public  List<Person> list() {
   List<Person> persons =  personService.findAll();
   persons.sort(COMPARATOR_BY_ID);
   return persons;
   }
}
```

The produces attribute defines the producible media types of the mapped request, narrowing the primary mapping and the value of the Accept header(on the client side) must match at least one of the values of this property for a method to handle a specific REST request.

The same goes for requests that contain a JSON body. The primary type consumed by the handler method can be limited using the consumes attribute. The consumes attribute defines the consumable media types of the mapped request (defined on the server) and the value of the Content-Type header (defined on the client side) must match at least one of the values of this property for a method to handle a specific REST request.

The two situations are depicted in Figure 8-2 .

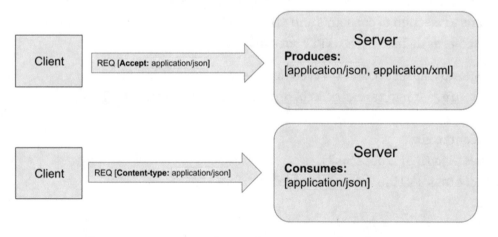

Figure 8-2. *Produces, consumes and matching request headers*

The following method receives a CriteriaDto representation from the client, which must be converted to a CriteriaDto instance before extracting the Person instances that will be returned as a JSON response body.

```
package com.apress.cems.rest.controllers;
import org.springframework.web.bind.annotation.RestController;
...
@RestController
@RequestMapping("/persons")
public class MultiplePersonController {
    ...
    @ResponseStatus(HttpStatus.OK)
    @GetMapping(value = "/search", consumes = MediaType.APPLICATION_JSON_
    VALUE,
            produces = MediaType.APPLICATION_JSON_VALUE)
    public List<Person> processSubmit(@Validated @RequestBody CriteriaDto
    criteria) {
        return personService.getByCriteriaDto(criteria);
    }
}
```

This is the CriteriaDto class introduced in the previous chapter.

```
package com.apress.cems.dto;
...
public class CriteriaDto {

    private String fieldName;

    @NotEmpty
    private String fieldValue;

    private Boolean exactMatch;
    ...
}
```

The REST request samples discussed so far are simple GET requests, with no parameters, no path variables, pretty simple examples to get things warmed up. Request parameters are rarely used when REST APIs are designed. They are used for sorting or pagination, because request parameters are incompatible with the URI.

Everything introduced in Chapter 6 (in regards to supported URLs) is valid for REST requests too. But the preferred way of making REST requests is to use URIs, which is an acronym for Uniform Resource Identifier, because REST is used for managing resources. A REST Server simply provides access to resources and REST clients access and modify those resources.

In a previous example, `http://localhost:8080/rest-classic/persons/list` was introduced to provide access to a list of `Person` instances. The typical way of writing a REST controller is to have the same URI mapped to multiple handlers using the HTTP method as criteria and use URIs as simply as possible. If what we are handling is `Person` instances, the URL to retrieve them all should be `http://localhost:8080/rest-classic/persons`. Also, it is best practice to use plurals as the root, and then further customize the URIs using path variables (e.g., `\persons`, `\persons\1`, `\persons\1\children`, etc.). Starting from this base URI, we can define others and narrow the scope by keeping URIs as simple as possible.

Table 8-4 lists the combination of URIs and HTTP methods that should be handled by the `PersonsController`.

Table 8-4. *Typical REST URIs and HTTP Methods*

URI	HTTP Method	Return type	Observation
/persons	GET	List<Person>	
/persons/ search	GET	List<Person>	Parameters provided in the request body.
/persons	POST	created Person instance or Location header	Depending on the implementation, the serialized created instance is returned or the location header pointing to the created instance.
/persons/[id]	GET	Person instance identified by id	@PathVariable argument needed.
/persons/[id]	PUT	nothing	@PathVariable argument and request body needed.
/persons/[id]	DELETE	nothing	@PathVariable argument needed.

Before moving forward, this controller configuration needs a little more explaining. If all that the application must expose are REST services practically there is no need for the spring-webmvc module, because there is no need for views and view resolvers. Also, since REST is all about data, the application is not concerned with internationalization or theming either. Internationalization may be useful for returning validation messages, but it could be circumvented by returning typical error codes that can be explained separately in an error dictionary. Unfortunately, what is needed is the DispatcherServlet and this class is part of the spring-webmvc module, so using this module as a dependency cannot be avoided at the moment. This does make for a simple WebConfig class; so much so that the configuration in this class can be combined with the WebApplicationInitializer implementation.

```
package com.apress.cems.rest.config;

import com.apress.cems.dj.ServiceConfig;
import com.fasterxml.jackson.annotation.JsonInclude;
import com.fasterxml.jackson.databind.ObjectMapper;
import com.fasterxml.jackson.databind.SerializationFeature;
import org.springframework.context.annotation.Bean;
import org.springframework.context.annotation.ComponentScan;
import org.springframework.context.annotation.Configuration;
import org.springframework.web.WebApplicationInitializer;
import org.springframework.web.context.ContextLoaderListener;
import org.springframework.web.context.support.
    AnnotationConfigWebApplicationContext;
import org.springframework.web.servlet.DispatcherServlet;
import org.springframework.web.servlet.config.annotation.EnableWebMvc;
import org.springframework.web.servlet.config.annotation.WebMvcConfigurer;

import javax.servlet.ServletContext;
import javax.servlet.ServletException;
import javax.servlet.ServletRegistration;

@Configuration
@EnableWebMvc
@ComponentScan(basePackages = {"com.apress.cems.rest.controllers"})
class WebConfig implements WebMvcConfigurer, WebApplicationInitializer {
```

```java
@Bean
public ObjectMapper objectMapper() {
    ObjectMapper objMapper = new ObjectMapper();
    objMapper.enable(SerializationFeature.INDENT_OUTPUT);
    objMapper.setSerializationInclusion(JsonInclude.Include.NON_NULL);
    objMapper.findAndRegisterModules();
    return objMapper;
}

@Override
public void onStartup(ServletContext servletContext) {
    var rootContext = new AnnotationConfigWebApplicationContext();
    rootContext.register(H2DbConfig.class, ServiceConfig.class);
    servletContext.addListener(new ContextLoaderListener(rootContext));

    var dispatcherContext =
            new AnnotationConfigWebApplicationContext();
    dispatcherContext.register(WebConfig.class);

    var dispatcher =
            servletContext.addServlet("cems-dispatcher",
                new DispatcherServlet(dispatcherContext));
    dispatcher.setLoadOnStartup(1);
    dispatcher.addMapping("/");
    }
}
```

But easier than this is to use Spring Boot, which requires no explicit configuration and the next section will introduce the Spring Boot configuration for a Spring Boot Web application exposing REST services.

Using Spring Boot to Expose REST Services

For REST applications Spring Boot is the perfect solution, because all the configuration needed is already set up under the bonnet. (Any customization would be part of a classic configuration.) From this point on in this chapter, everything applies to both types of applications. If there is anything specific to one of them, it will be pointed out.

Configuring a Spring Boot application to expose REST services is quite simple. The most important dependency is the `spring-boot-starter-web`, because the `DispatcherServlet` is needed. But this module has a lot of useful dependencies for writing a REST application. In Figure 8-3, you can see the transitive dependencies of the `spring-boot-starter-web` module.

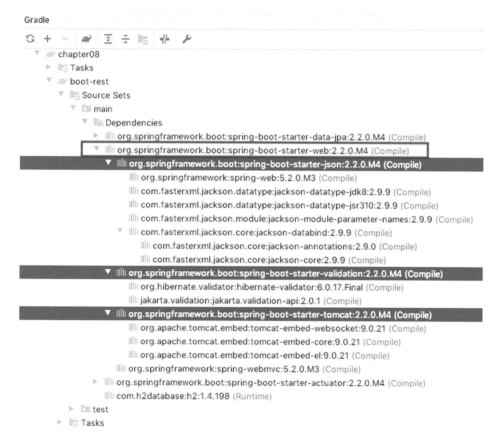

Figure 8-3. *Spring Boot setup for a REST application*

One of the dependencies of `spring-boot-starter-json` is the Jackson library, and because it is found on the classpath an automatically configured `ObjectMapper` bean is part of the configuration.

The `spring-boot-starter-validation` is used for Java bean validation with a Hibernate validator. And the `spring-boot-starter-tomcat` is used for Tomcat as *the embedded servlet container. This is the default embedded server* implementation and if a different one is preferred; it has to be excluded first. The next configuration snippet,

Tomcat is replaced by Jetty. The `spring-boot-starter-jetty` is declared in the project root configuration and used in the `chapter08/boot-rest-jetty` configuration where it is referred by its alias, `starterJetty`.

The first snippet is part of the root project configuration. `pivotal-certified-pro-spring-dev-exam-02` is the parent of all `chapterXX\...` projects.

```
//pivotal-certified-pro-spring-dev-exam-02/build.gradle
ext {

    springBootVersion = '2.2.0.M5'

    ..

    //we group libraries by their purpose so we can import them easier in
    the modules
    boot = [
            starterWeb  :
                "org.springframework.boot:spring-boot-starter-
                web:$springBootVersion",
            (starterJetty)  :
                "org.springframework.boot:spring-boot-starter-
                jetty:$springBootVersion",

            ...

    ]
...
}

//chapter08/boot-rest-jetty/build.gradle
...
dependencies {
    compile boot.starterJpa, boot.starterJetty
    compile (boot.starterWeb){
        exclude group: "org.springframework.boot", module: "spring-boot-
        starter-tomcat"
    }
    runtimeOnly misc.h2
    implementation boot.actuator
```

```
    testImplementation testing.restAssured, testing.restAssuredAll
    testImplementation (boot.starterTest) {
        exclude group: "org.junit.vintage", module: "junit-vintage-engine"
        exclude group: "junit", module: "junit"
    }
}
```

> **!** The H2 dependency is declared as `runtimeOnly` because its API is not used directly in the code, so there is no need for it at compile time.
>
> The `Spring Boot Actuator` dependency, which is the Spring Boot monitoring module, is declared as a dependency using `implementation` because it is used only for monitoring and is not a dependency of the project. Gradle allows declaring dependencies in various ways, according to their scope.

Now that this is covered let's continue our voyage into the world of REST services.

REST Operations

In the previous code sample, an HTTP GET handling method was introduced as an example of how Spring can handle REST requests. But more HTTP methods are supported and a URI can be mapped to multiple handler methods and the HTTP method is used as a filtering criteria. The `/persons` URI was mapped previously to a handler method specific to the GET method that was retrieving all `Person` instances, but the same URI can be used with a POST method and mapped to a handler method creating a `Person` instance. In the next code snippet, you can see the two handlers together. The differences are analyzed after the snippet.

```
package com.apress.cems.person;

import org.springframework.validation.BindingResult;
import org.springframework.validation.annotation.Validated;
import org.springframework.web.bind.annotation.GetMapping;
import org.springframework.web.bind.annotation.PostMapping;

...
```

```java
@RestController
@RequestMapping("/persons")
public class PersonsController {

    private PersonService personService;
    static Comparator<Person> COMPARATOR_BY_ID = Comparator.
    comparing(Person::getId);

    public PersonsController(PersonService personService) {
        this.personService = personService;
    }

    @ResponseStatus(HttpStatus.OK)
    @GetMapping
    public List<Person> list() {
        List<Person> persons =  personService.findAll();
        persons.sort(COMPARATOR_BY_ID);
        model.addAttribute("persons", persons);
        return persons;
    }

    @ResponseStatus(HttpStatus.CREATED)
    @PostMapping(consumes = MediaType.APPLICATION_JSON_VALUE)
    public Person create(@Validated(Person.BasicValidation.class)
       @RequestBody Person person, BindingResult result) {
         if (result.hasErrors()) {
             throw new IllegalOperation("Cannot save entry!");
         }
         person.setPassword(NumberGenerator.getPassword());
         return personService.save(person);
    }
...
}
```

If you want a better example, the /persons/{id} URI can be mapped to handler methods that can return, update, or delete the Person instance with the ID provided as a path variable.

```
package com.apress.cems.person;

import org.springframework.validation.BindingResult;
import org.springframework.validation.annotation.Validated;
import org.springframework.web.bind.annotation.GetMapping;
import org.springframework.web.bind.annotation.PostMapping;

@RestController
@RequestMapping("/persons")
public class PersonsController {

    private PersonService personService;
    static Comparator<Person> COMPARATOR_BY_ID = Comparator.
    comparing(Person::getId);

    public PersonsController(PersonService personService) {
        this.personService = personService;
    }

    /**
     * Returns the {@code Person} instance with id {@code id}
     */
    @ResponseStatus(HttpStatus.OK)
    @GetMapping(path = "/{id}", produces = MediaType.APPLICATION_JSON_VALUE)
    public Person show(@PathVariable Long id) {
        Optional<Person> personOpt = personService.findById(id);
        if(personOpt.isPresent()) {
            return personOpt.get();
        } else {
            throw new NotFoundException(Person.class, id);
        }
    }

    /**
     * Updates the {@code Person} instance with id {@code id}
     */
    @ResponseStatus(HttpStatus.NO_CONTENT)
    @PutMapping(path = "/{id}",
        consumes = MediaType.APPLICATION_JSON_VALUE,
```

```
         produces = MediaType.APPLICATION_JSON_VALUE)
public Person update(@RequestBody Person updatedPerson, @PathVariable
Long id) {
    Optional<Person> personOpt = personService.findById(id);
    if(personOpt.isPresent()) {
        Person person = personOpt.get();
        person.setUsername(updatedPerson.getUsername());
        person.setFirstName(updatedPerson.getFirstName());
        person.setLastName(updatedPerson.getLastName());
        return personService.save(person);
    } else {
        throw new NotFoundException(Person.class, id);
    }
}

/**
 * Delete the {@code Person} instance with id {@code id}
 */
@ResponseStatus(HttpStatus.NO_CONTENT)
@DeleteMapping("/{id}")
public void delete(@PathVariable Long id) {
    Optional<Person> personOpt = personService.findById(id);
    personOpt.ifPresent(value -> personService.delete(value));
}
...
}
```

Web applications use a collection of status codes to let the client know what happened to a request, it if was successfully processed or not and the state of the resource. The most familiar to you is probably the 404 Not Found status code that is returned to you when a requested resource cannot be found. A full list of HTTP status codes can be found on Wikipedia.[13] You should look at it if you are unfamiliar with HTTP status codes. If you want to read about these status codes in the context of a REST application, I recommend that you go to www.restapitutorial.com/httpstatuscodes.html.

---

[13]http://en.wikipedia.org/wiki/List_of_HTTP_status_codes

In Spring MVC, the status code of a response is easily set by using the @ResponseStatus annotation on controller methods. This annotation can receive as a value any of the constants defined in Spring enum HttpStatus. Table 8-5 lists the most common response statuses used in RESTful applications.

Table 8-5. *HTTP Status Codes*

HTTP Status	HttpStatus constant	Observation
200	OK	Successful GET with returned content
201	CREATED	Successful PUT or POST (when PUT introduces data that was not recorded previously in the database, PUT can be implemented to behave as a POST), should return a location header that contains the URI of new resource or response containing new resource.
204	NO_CONTENT	Empty response, after successful PUT or DELETE
404	NOT_FOUND	Resource was not found.
403	FORBIDDEN	Server is refusing to respond to the request, because the request is not authorized.
405	METHOD_NOT_ALLOWED	Http method is not supported for the resource identified by the Request-URI. Web servers can be configured to allow or disallow any method. Also, a handler method might not be declared for the HTTP method requested.
409	CONFLICT	Problems when making changes, when PUT or POST try to save data that already exists and is marked as unique.
415	UNSUPPORTED_MEDIA_TYPE	The server is refusing to service the request because the entity of the request is in a format not supported by the requested resource for the requested method.

In the previous examples, the @ResponseStatus annotation was used to set an explicit HTTP status code to be returned; otherwise, any request that is successful will cause the response to have the default HTTP status code of 200. Why would we want to have different status codes? HTTP status codes are important for identifying the type of request that was handled and its effect, because this can help with testing and debugging the application.

What is noticeable in the @PostMapping example is the customized @Validated(Person.BasicValidation.class) annotation. The client sends a JSON representation of a Person instance. Because of the @Validated annotation the Person instance is validated after being deserialized, and values for fields that have validation annotations on them will be tested against the validation rules defined for them. BasicValidation is an empty marker interface that is provided as an argument for the groups attribute in validation annotations (e.g., @NotNull, @Size, @NotEmpty) to group fields that should be validated. Validation annotations that are not in this group are ignored. This is helpful when some fields are not actually needed for an operation, or when there are fields that should be validated in a secondary step. For the Person entity, the validation for the password field was left out, because we do not intend to create a person by sending the password in text. To simplify things, we will generate a password for them. In the next code listing, you can see the fields that are part of the BasicValidation group.

```java
package com.apress.cems.person;

 import com.fasterxml.jackson.annotation.JsonProperty;

 ...
 @Entity
public class Person  extends AbstractEntity {
    interface BasicValidation{}

    @NotNull(groups = BasicValidation.class)
    @Size(min = 3, max = 30, groups = BasicValidation.class)
    @Column(nullable = false, unique = true)
    private String username;

    @NotNull(groups = BasicValidation.class)
    @Size(min = 3, max = 30,  groups = BasicValidation.class)
    @Column(nullable = false)
    private String firstName;

    @NotNull(groups = BasicValidation.class)
    @Size(min = 3, max = 30, groups = BasicValidation.class)
    @Column(nullable = false)
    private String lastName;
```

```
@JsonProperty(access = JsonProperty.Access.WRITE_ONLY)
@NotNull
@Size(min = 4, max = 50)
@Column(nullable = false)
private String password;

@JsonFormat(shape = JsonFormat.Shape.STRING,
            pattern = DateProcessor.DATE_FORMAT)
@NotNull(groups = BasicValidation.class)
@Column(nullable = false)
@DateTimeFormat(pattern = DateProcessor.DATE_FORMAT)
private LocalDateTime hiringDate;

@JsonIgnore
@Transient
private String newPassword;

... // setters and getters

}
```

In the previous code snippet, the interface was created within the Person class because of its scope—to group fields of class Person. But it can be declared within its own file, or in a package grouping validation interfaces for the whole application.

The @JsonProperty annotation can be used on a field or a non-static method (setter or getter) to specify when the field should be used (serialization, deserialization) as a logical property.[14] So, if we would actually intend to create a new Person instance and set the password for it, using this annotation and configuring its access attribute to Access.WRITE_ONLY we can specify that this property is to be set only when de-serializing an object.[15] In this case, a POST request could send an object like this:

---

[14]For the full list of cases where *@JsonProperty* can be used check the Javadoc here: http://fasterxml.github.io/jackson-annotations/javadoc/2.9/index.html?com/fasterxml/jackson/annotation/JsonFormat.html

[15]If the value *Access.WRITE_ONLY* seems confusing, according to the documentation, the direction of read and write is from perspective of the property, not from external data format: this may be confusing in some contexts. Just try to see it like this: READ = property can be accessed during serialization, WRITE = property can be accessed during deserialization.

```
{
    "username": "gigi.pedala",
    "firstName":  "Gigi",
    "password": "gpiegd"
    "lastName": "Pedala",
    "hiringDate": "1987-08-12 00:20"
}
```

And that JSON body would be transformed into a `Person` instance with the `password` field set with the value the client sent. And because this field is not part of the `BasicValidation` group, it can be validated separately, some extra logic can be applied to it or it can be skipped altogether, so different execution flows can be set up for these two different scenarios.

Without this annotation, the `password` field will be available at serialization and deserialization. With this annotation, but no access value specified, it defaults to `Access.AUTO`, which means visibility rules automatically determine read and/or write-access of this property, and since in the previous example there are no visibility rules defined, the file will be available at serialization and deserialization.

Handling Errors

Sometimes REST requests cannot be resolved successfully; maybe the client requested a resource no longer available, or some action requested by the client generated an error on the server. In this case, the `@ResponseStatus` can be used on controller exceptions handler methods to give the client a basic idea of why the request was not processed correctly.

```
package com.apress.cems.person;
...

@RestController
@RequestMapping("/persons")
public class PersonsController {
...
    @ResponseStatus(HttpStatus.NOT_FOUND)
    @ExceptionHandler({NotFoundException.class})
    public void handleNotFound() {
        // just return empty 404
    }
```

```
    @ResponseStatus(HttpStatus.BAD_REQUEST)
    @ExceptionHandler({IllegalOperation.class})
    public void handleIllegalOperation() {
        // just return empty 400
    }
...
}
```

Let's take the following two handler methods, which resolve a POST and a PUT request.

```
package com.apress.cems.person;
...

@RestController
@RequestMapping("/persons")
public class PersonsController {
....
    @ResponseStatus(HttpStatus.CREATED)
    @PostMapping(consumes = MediaType.APPLICATION_JSON_VALUE)
    public Person create(@Validated(Person.BasicValidation.class)
            @RequestBody Person person, BindingResult result) {
        if (result.hasErrors()) {
            String errString = createErrorString(result);
            throw new IllegalOperation("Cannot save entry because:"
            + errString);
        }
        if(StringUtils.isEmpty(person.getPassword())){
            person.setPassword(NumberGenerator.getPassword());
        }
        return personService.save(person);
    }

    @ResponseStatus(HttpStatus.NO_CONTENT)
    @PutMapping(path = "/{id}", consumes = MediaType.APPLICATION_JSON_VALUE,
        produces = MediaType.APPLICATION_JSON_VALUE)
    public Person update(@RequestBody Person updatedPerson, @PathVariable
    Long id) {
```

```
        Optional<Person> personOpt = personService.findById(id);
        if(personOpt.isPresent()) {
            ...
            return personService.save(person);
        } else {
            throw new NotFoundException(Person.class, id);
        }
    }

    private String createErrorString(BindingResult result) {
        ... // code not relevant for the context
        return errString;
    }

}
```

The results of the validation in the method annotated with @PostMapping are stored in the BindingResult object, but since there is no model to show them a JSON error string is returned as a response body that contains the error message. The IllegalOperation class is a custom exception class that does not give much information.

```
package com.apress.cems.ex;

public class IllegalOperation extends RuntimeException {
    public IllegalOperation(String message) {
        super(message);
    }

    public IllegalOperation(String message, Throwable cause) {
        super(message, cause);
    }
}
```

For example, the following POST request body, will cause a @Size error for the firstName field, since the field is annotated with @Size(min = 3, max = 30, groups = BasicValidation.class) which requires for the field value to be at least 3 characters long.

```
{
    "username": "gigi.pedala",
    "firstName":  "Gi",
    "password": "gpiegd"
    "lastName": "Pedala",
    "hiringDate": "1987-08-12 00:20"
}
```

The response received from the server is depicted in the next code listing.

```
{
    "timestamp": "2019-08-08T23:00:38.293+0000",
    "status": 500,
    "error": "Internal Server Error",
    "message": "org.springframework.web.util.NestedServletException:
     Request processing failed; nested exception is com.apress.cems.
     ex.IllegalOperation:
          Cannot save entry!",
    "path": "/persons"
}
```

The error is telling the user that there is a problem with the request body, but the returned response is too technical, which is useless to the user unless he/she is a hacker willing to learn about the internals of your application. The exception handlers declared previously do nothing more than return an empty body with the proper HTTP status code that lets the user know something went wrong. It would be nice to use the information in the exception message to deliver a more readable message. Right?

Another method to process REST request related exception is to define a specialized exception class for a REST controller and a specialized component to intercept those types of exceptions and treat them in a certain way. For example, considering a class called PersonsException that is thrown every time a method in the PersonsController is not executed correctly, we could design this exception class to store the HTTP response status code too, which differs depending on the situation when the exception was thrown.

```java
package com.apress.cems.person;

import org.springframework.http.HttpStatus;

public class PersonsException extends RuntimeException{
    private HttpStatus status;

    public PersonsException(String message) {
        super(message);
    }

    public PersonsException(HttpStatus status, String message) {
        super(message);
        this.status = status;
    }

    public PersonsException(HttpStatus status,Throwable cause) {
        super(cause);
        this.status = status;
    }

    public PersonsException(String message, Throwable cause) {
        super(message, cause);
    }

    public String errorMessage(){
        return status.value() + ":".concat(getMessage());
    }

    public HttpStatus getStatus() {
        return status;
    }
}
```

This is very practical because it leads to the need for a single exception handler method for all the REST APIs managing Person instances. To use this exception, the handler methods must be updated.

```
package com.apress.cems.person;

...

@RestController
@RequestMapping("/persons")
public class PersonsController {
....
    @ResponseStatus(HttpStatus.CREATED)
    @PostMapping](consumes = MediaType.APPLICATION_JSON_VALUE)
    public Person create(@Validated(Person.BasicValidation.class)
            @RequestBody Person person, BindingResult result) {
        if (result.hasErrors()) {
            String errString = createErrorString(result);
            throw new PersonsException(HttpStatus.BAD_REQUEST,
                "Cannot save entry because: "+ errString);
        }
        if(StringUtils.isEmpty(person.getPassword())){
            person.setPassword(NumberGenerator.getPassword());
        }
        return personService.save(person);
    }

    @ResponseStatus(HttpStatus.NO_CONTENT)
    @PutMapping(path = "/{id}", consumes = MediaType.APPLICATION_JSON_VALUE,
            produces = MediaType.APPLICATION_JSON_VALUE)
    public Person update(@RequestBody Person updatedPerson, @PathVariable
    Long id) {
        Optional<Person> personOpt = personService.findById(id);
        if(personOpt.isPresent()) {
            ...
            return personService.save(person);
        } else {
            PersonsException(HttpStatus.NOT_FOUND,
                "Unable to find entry with id " + id );
        }
    }
```

```
    private String createErrorString(BindingResult result) {
      ... // code not relevant for the context
      return errString;
    }

}
```

And assuming more than one controller is declared in the application, all exceptions handlers for different types of objects can be grouped in a class annotated with the @ControllerAdvice annotation.

```
package com.apress.cems;

import com.apress.cems.person.PersonsException;
import org.springframework.http.HttpStatus;
import org.springframework.http.ResponseEntity;
import org.springframework.web.bind.annotation.ControllerAdvice;
import org.springframework.web.bind.annotation.ExceptionHandler;
import org.springframework.web.bind.annotation.ResponseBody;

@ControllerAdvice
public class RestExceptionsHandler {

    @ExceptionHandler
    @ResponseBody
    public ResponseEntity<String> handleException(PersonsException pe) {
            return new ResponseEntity<>(pe.errorMessage(), pe.getStatus());
    }
}
```

The ResponseEntity<T> class is a specialized Spring class to construct a response object with the body, status code, and headers. By returning this type of instance, we can customize the response status from inside the method body, instead of using the @ResponseStatus annotation. This is useful because we can reduce the number of exception handler methods to be created, thus reducing boilerplate code.

In the previous code sample, the exception type is used as a parameter in the handler method so that all exceptions of that type are handled by this method. Even more restrictions can be implemented also by configuring the @ControllerAdvice annotation. The scope for a controller advice can be limited to exceptions thrown by methods of controllers declared in a specific set of packages (or subpackages) by setting the basePackages attribute.

```
package com.apress.cems;
...

@ControllerAdvice(basePackages = {"com.apress.cems.person"})
public class RestExceptionsHandler {

    @ExceptionHandler
    @ResponseBody
    public ResponseEntity<String> handleException(Exception e) {
        if(e instanceof PersonsException) {
            PersonsException pe = (PersonsException) e;
            return new ResponseEntity<>(pe.errorMessage(), pe.getStatus());
        }
        return new ResponseEntity<>("Unexpected Exception: " + e.getMessage(),
            HttpStatus.INTERNAL_SERVER_ERROR);
    }
}
```

In the previous code listing, the handler method takes into account that other types of exceptions can be thrown, aside the expected ones of PersonsException type. And if we want to narrow the scope even more, the controller advice can be limited to a class or hierarchy of classes by setting the basePackageClasses attribute.

```
...

@ControllerAdvice(basePackageClasses = PersonsController.class)
public class RestExceptionsHandler {

    @ExceptionHandler
    @ResponseBody
     public ResponseEntity<String> handleException(Exception e) {
        if(e instanceof PersonsException) {
            PersonsException pe = (PersonsException) e;
            return new ResponseEntity<>(pe.errorMessage(), pe.getStatus());
        }
```

```
        return new ResponseEntity<>("Unexpected Exception: " + e.getMessage(),
            HttpStatus.INTERNAL_SERVER_ERROR);
    }
}
```

In the previous example, the type provided as a parameter when creating the ResponseEntity<T> is String. This means that when a PersonsException is thrown, the exception is treated and resolved to a String. But, a special type of class can be created to display more structured messages. The following JsonError is a simple implementation.

```
package com.apress.cems;
...

public class JsonError {
    private String url;
    private String message;

    public JsonError(String url, String message) {
        this.url = url;
        this.message = message;
    }

    ...//getters and setters
}
```

And the exception handler method can be modified to add to the response body instances of this class.

```
package com.apress.cems;
...

@ControllerAdvice(basePackageClasses = PersonsController.class)
public class RestExceptionsHandler {

    @ExceptionHandler
    @ResponseBody
    public ResponseEntity<JsonError> handleException(HttpServletRequest req,
                Exception e) {
```

```
        String errorURL = req.getRequestURL().toString();
        if(e instanceof PersonsException) {
            PersonsException pe = (PersonsException) e;
            return new ResponseEntity<>(new JsonError(errorURL,
                    pe.getMessage()), pe.getStatus());
        }
        return new ResponseEntity<>(new  JsonError(errorURL,
            "Unexpected Exception: " + e.getMessage()),
            HttpStatus.INTERNAL_SERVER_ERROR);
    }
}
```

Using RestTemplate to Test RESTful Applications

A RESTful application can be accessed by any type of client that supports creating the type of request supported by the application (HTTP requests in the current case). These clients include browsers, mobile applications, desktop applications, and so forth. A RESTful service can be tested using a browser, because the browser knows how to render representations. If complex requests need to be set up, Postman is resourceful. Consider the following POST request method handler, which is in charge of validating and creating a Person instance.

```
package com.apress.cems.person;

...

@RestController
@RequestMapping("/persons")
public class PersonsController {

    @ResponseStatus(HttpStatus.CREATED)
    @PostMapping(consumes = MediaType.APPLICATION_JSON_VALUE)
    public Person create(@Validated(Person.BasicValidation.class)
            @RequestBody Person person, BindingResult result) {
        if (result.hasErrors()) {
            String errString = createErrorString(result);
            throw new PersonsException(HttpStatus.BAD_REQUEST,
                    "Cannot save entry because: "+ errString);
```

```
            }
            if(StringUtils.isEmpty(person.getPassword())){
                person.setPassword(NumberGenerator.getPassword());
            }
            try {
                return personService.save(person);
            } catch (Exception e) {
                throw  new PersonsException(HttpStatus.UNPROCESSABLE_ENTITY, e);
            }
        }
    }
}
```

To test the handler method depicted in the previous code listing, a POST request can be created in Postman. Figure 8-4 offers recommendations on how to do so.

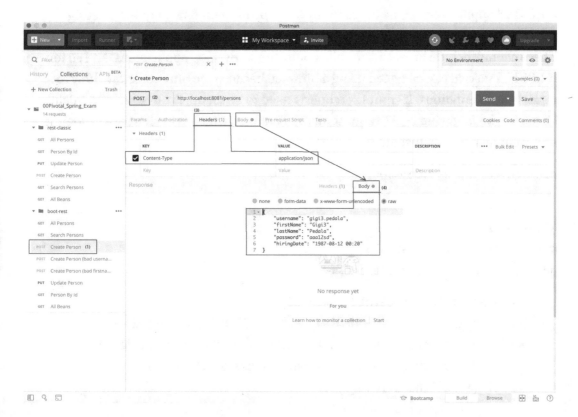

Figure 8-4. Postman test request

The numbers in the previous figure mark the following.

1. Marks the name of the Postman request, (in this case, Create Person).

2. Marks the type of request, which in this case is POST.

3. Marks the Headers tab, where headers can be added. In this case, the Content-Type header must be added with an application/json value to tell the REST application that the body of the request is in JSON format, so the application knows what converter to use for deserialization. Without explicitly setting this header, the default value is considered `text/plain;charset=UTF-8` and a 500 Server Error will be received, since in `PersonsController` we kept things simple and only declared that the handler method expects a body with the `MediaType.APPLICATION_JSON_VALUE` type.

4. Marks the Body tab, where the request body can be added. In this case, the body is of type raw in JSON format and represents a `Person` instance to be saved.

Postman requests can be run by an automated job on a continuous improvement tool such as Jenkins. But there is also a programmatic approach to test REST handler methods using a class provided by Spring named `RestTemplate`. This class can be instantiated to create a synchronous client to perform HTTP requests, which exposes a simple API for testing various request scenarios.

In Spring 4.0, the class `AsyncRestTemplate` was introduced to support the same API in an asynchronous manner. The class is now deprecated; in the future, both `RestTemplate` and `AsyncRestTemplate` will be replaced by the non-blocking reactive `org.springframework.web.reactive.client.WebClient` implementations (depending on the server used), which offer a modern alternative for testing REST handler methods in a synchronous and asynchronous manner. More information about the reactive `WebClient` is available in Chapter 12. The `RestTemplate`[16] is the Spring's central class for synchronous client-side HTTP access. This class provides a wide set of methods for each HTTP method that can access RESTful services.

---

[16]Javadoc for this class can be found here: `http://docs.spring.io/spring/docs/current/javadoc-api/org/springframework/web/client/RestTemplate.html`

A correspondence between HTTP methods and RestTemplate methods that can access REST Services is depicted in Figure 8-5.

The execute and exchange methods can be used for any type of REST calls as long as the HTTP method is given as a parameter for the methods. I prefer using exchange because it returns ResponseEntity<T>, which allows me to test the response status as well. The execute method returns an object, and the tests check if the object returned is the expected one.

All methods are polymorphic,[17] many of them based on varargs, and using one or the other depends on the requirements and the developer's preferences. RestTemplate methods support making calls using URI templates and concrete URIs. The following two calls are identical.

```
//using URI Template
String url = "http://localhost:8081/persons/{id}";
Person person = restTemplate.getForObject(url, Person.class, 1);
```

```
// using URI
String url = "http://localhost:8081/persons/1";
Person person= restTemplate.getForObject(url, Persons.class);
```

The execute method can also be given a org.springframework.web.client. RequestCallback implementation as a parameter that tells the RestTemplate object what to do with the request before sending it to the server. Considering this, a GET Request for a Person instance with id=1 could be written with the exchange method like this:

```
package com.apress.cems;

import org.springframework.web.client.HttpMessageConverterExtractor;
import org.springframework.http.client.ClientHttpRequest;
import org.springframework.web.client.RequestCallback;
import org.springframework.web.client.RestTemplate;
...

@SpringBootTest(webEnvironment =
            SpringBootTest.WebEnvironment.RANDOM_PORT)
class RestTemplateTest {
```

---

[17]Multiple methods with the same name, but different signatures are provided. Just check out the Spring API for **RestTemplate** http://docs.spring.io/spring/docs/current/javadoc-api/ org/springframework/web/client/RestTemplate.html

```java
@LocalServerPort
private int port;

private String baseUrl = "http://localhost";

private static RestTemplate restTemplate = null;

@BeforeAll
static void init() {
    restTemplate = new RestTemplate();
}

@BeforeEach
void setUp(){
    baseUrl = baseUrl.concat(":").concat(port +"").concat("/persons");
}

@Test
void shouldReturnAPersonWithCallback(){
    String url = baseUrl + "/{id}"; // http://localhost:XXXX/persons/1
    Person person  = restTemplate.execute(url, HttpMethod.GET,
            new RequestCallback() {
                @Override
                public void doWithRequest(ClientHttpRequest request) {
                    HttpHeaders headers = request.getHeaders();
                    headers.add("Accept", MediaType.APPLICATION_JSON_
                    VALUE);
                    System.out.println("Request headers = " + headers);
                }
            }, new HttpMessageConverterExtractor<>(Person.class,
                    restTemplate.getMessageConverters())
            , new HashMap<String, Long>() {{
                put("id", 1L);  // ->  http://localhost:XXXX/persons/1
            }});
}
```

```
    assertAll(
            () -> assertNotNull(person),
            () -> assertEquals("sherlock.holmes", person.getUsername())
    );
  }
}
```

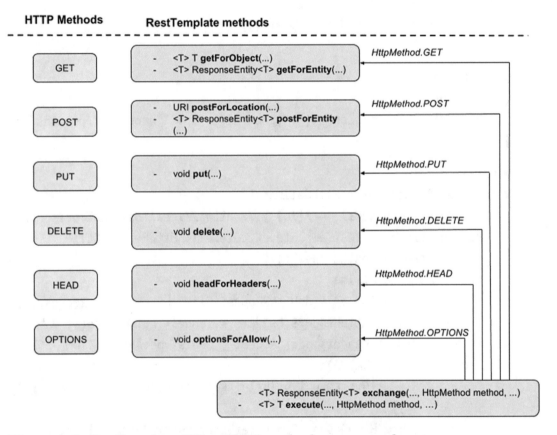

Figure 8-5. *RestTemplate API to HTTP methods correspondence*

! For a classic Spring web application that exposes REST services, the test is
identical. The only differences are that you have to start the application using a
launcher, the request URI must be hardcoded (in our case, the port value must be
manually set to be the same the application was started on) and the tests cannot
be automated. They must be run manually after the application is up.

Objects handled by the getForObject(), postForLocation(), and put() methods are converted to HTTP requests, and from HTTP responses by HttpMessageConverter<T> implementations.

The exchange method uses an HttpEntity<T> object to encapsulate request headers and use it as a parameter. The method returns a ResponseEntity<T> object containing the result of a REST request, and its body is automatically converted using the registered HttpMessageConverter<T> implementation.

```java
package com.apress.cems;

import org.springframework.http.ResponseEntity;
...

@SpringBootTest(webEnvironment =
            SpringBootTest.WebEnvironment.RANDOM_PORT)
class RestTemplateTest {
...

    @Test
    void shouldCreateAPersonUsingExchange() {
        Person person = buildPerson("gigi.pedala", "Gigi", "Pedala", "1dooh2" );

        HttpHeaders headers = new HttpHeaders();
        headers.setContentType(MediaType.APPLICATION_JSON);

        HttpEntity<Person> postRequest = new HttpEntity<>(person, headers);
        ResponseEntity<Person> responseEntity = restTemplate.exchange(baseUrl,
                HttpMethod.POST, postRequest, Person.class);

        Person newPerson = responseEntity.getBody();

        assertAll(
                () -> assertEquals(HttpStatus.CREATED, responseEntity.
                    getStatusCode()),
                () -> assertNotNull(newPerson),
                () -> assertEquals(person.getUsername(), newPerson.
                    getUsername()),
                () -> assertNotNull(newPerson.getId())
        );
    }
}
```

The application contained in the chapter08/boot-rest-practice is a Spring Boot Web RESTful application that can test your understanding of Spring support components for REST applications. The PersonsController class provides handler methods that resolve REST requests managing Person instances. The client is the RestTemplate instance from the PersonsControllerTest class. The RestTemplate instance in this class can be used to test all REST operations with persons exposed by the PersonsController controller. The class is a typical Spring Boot test class that bootstraps the full context and exposes the services on a random port that is accessed by using @LocalServerPort. The REST Services exposed by the controller are available using URIs like http://localhost:xxxx/persons/*. The PersonsControllerTest class contains methods to test REST requests using the four main HTTP methods.

- **GET**: A method to retrieve a representation of a resource and might have length restrictions depending on server settings and client used.[18] When a resource is not found, a **404 (Not found)** status code is returned; otherwise, it is **200(OK)**. In Figure 8-6, the GET request and response contents are depicted.

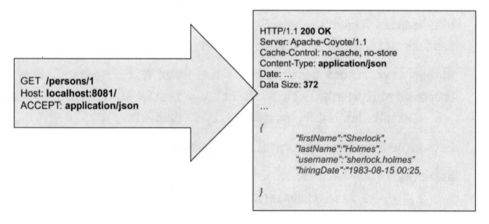

Figure 8-6. GET request and response example

---

[18]Most web servers have a limit of 8192 bytes (8KB), which is usually configurable in the server configuration. As for the client, the HTTP 1.1 specification warns about URIs lengths bigger than 255 bytes, because older client or proxies implementations might not properly support them.

A REST GET request can be sent with a `RestTemplate` instance; all that is needed is the REST URI, an ID to identify the resource, and a converter (or more, depending on the application). The path variable was named `id` to keep things obvious. The following code snippet depicts the test method performing a GET request for a person resource that has the ID equal to 1;

```
package com.apress.cems.practice;
...

@SpringBootTest(webEnvironment =
        SpringBootTest.WebEnvironment.RANDOM_PORT)
public class PersonsControllerTest {

    @LocalServerPort
    private int port;

    private String baseUrl = "http://localhost";

    @BeforeAll
    static void init() {
        restTemplate = new RestTemplate();
    }

    @BeforeEach
    void setUp(){
        baseUrl = baseUrl.concat(":").concat(port +"").concat("/persons");
    }

    @Test
    void shouldReturnAPerson(){
        Person person = restTemplate.getForObject(
                baseUrl.concat("/{id}"), Person.class, 1);
        assertAll(
                () -> assertNotNull(person),
                () -> assertEquals("sherlock.holmes", person.getUsername())
        );
    }
}
```

But, taking into consideration the actual code of the handler method, what happens when the resource is not found?

```
package com.apress.cems.person;
...
@RestController
@RequestMapping("/persons")
public class PersonsController {

    @ResponseStatus(HttpStatus.OK)
    @GetMapping(path = "/{id}", produces = MediaType.APPLICATION_JSON_VALUE)
    public Person show(@PathVariable Long id) {
        Optional<Person> personOpt = personService.findById(id);
        if(personOpt.isPresent()) {
            return personOpt.get();
        } else {
            throw new PersonsException(HttpStatus.NOT_FOUND,
                "Unable to find entry with id " + id );
        }
    }
}
```

A PersonsException exception is thrown and the HTTP response status code is set to 404. But what is actually returned is decided by the error handler method.

```
package com.apress.cems.practice;
....
@ControllerAdvice(basePackageClasses = PersonsController.class)
public class RestExceptionsHandler {

    @ExceptionHandler
    @ResponseBody
    public ResponseEntity<String> handleException(Exception e) {
        if(e instanceof PersonsException) {
            PersonsException pe = (PersonsException) e;
            return new ResponseEntity<>(pe.errorMessage(), pe.getStatus());
        }
```

```
    return new ResponseEntity<>("Unexpected Exception: " + e.getMessage(),
        HttpStatus.INTERNAL_SERVER_ERROR);
  }
}
```

This means that when restTemplate.getForObject(baseUrl.concat("/{id}"), Person.class, 99) is called, an empty response with the HTTP 404 error status code is returned. The test fails. If you run the previous positive test but replace the ID path variable with 99, the following is shown in the log.

```
404 Not Found
org.springframework.web.client.HttpClientErrorException$NotFound: 404
Not Found
  at org.springframework.web.client.HttpClientErrorException
      .create(HttpClientErrorException.java:85)
  at org.springframework.web.client.DefaultResponseErrorHandler
      .handleError(DefaultResponseErrorHandler.java:123)
  at org.springframework.web.client.ResponseErrorHandler
      .handleError(ResponseErrorHandler.java:63)
  at org.springframework.web.client.RestTemplate.
      handleResponse(RestTemplate.java:785)
  at org.springframework.web.client.RestTemplate.doExecute(RestTemplate.
      java:743)
  at org.springframework.web.client.RestTemplate.execute(RestTemplate.
      java:677)
  at org.springframework.web.client.RestTemplate.getForObject(RestTemplate.
      java:318)
  at com.apress.cems.practice.PersonsControllerTest
      .shoulReturnAPerson(PersonsControllerTest.java:96)
...
```

Also the error handler method returns a ResponseEntity<String>, this means a negative test must expect this type of object to be returned, and the restTemplate. getForObject(..) is not suited for this situation. Also, the 404 is an error status code, so we have to make sure the RestTemplate instance does not consider this an actual server error. We have to trick it, plain and simple, so we can test an expected erroneous situation. This is done by setting an error handler for the `RestTemplate` instance that, regardless of the HTTP status code, always consider that the response has no errors. This allows the test method to access the `ResponseEntity<T>` and test the expected negative behavior. The next code snippet includes all of these changes.

```java
package com.apress.cems.practice;
import org.springframework.http.ResponseEntity;
...

@SpringBootTest(webEnvironment =
        SpringBootTest.WebEnvironment.RANDOM_PORT)
public class PersonsControllerTest {

    @LocalServerPort
    private int port;

    private String baseUrl = "http://localhost";

    @BeforeAll
    static void init() {
        restTemplate = new RestTemplate();
        restTemplate.setErrorHandler(new DefaultResponseErrorHandler() {
            @Override
            public boolean hasError(HttpStatus statusCode) {
                return false;
            }
        });
    }

    @BeforeEach
    void setUp(){
        baseUrl = baseUrl.concat(":").concat(port +"").concat("/persons");
    }

    @Test
    void shouldReturn404(){
        ResponseEntity<String> err = restTemplate.getForEntity
                (baseUrl.concat("/{id}"), String.class, 99);
        assertAll(
```

```
            () -> assertNotNull(err),
            () -> assertEquals(HttpStatus.NOT_FOUND, err.getStatusCode()),
            () -> assertTrue(err.getBody().contains("Unable to find entry
                with id 99"))
        );
    }
}
```

- **POST**: A method to create a new resource. When the resource created requires a parent that does not exist, a **404 (Not found)** status code is returned.[19]

! In our code, we are handling Person instances. Imagine that a Person instance required a Parent instance to be created. When a POST request is made, the ID of that Parent instance is sent. If a Parent with that id is not found, the Person instance cannot be created. The reason is because its parent was not found, so returning a 404 status code fits the situation perfectly.

When an identical resource already exists, a **409 (Conflict)** status code is returned. When the resource was created correctly a **201 (Created)** status code is returned. In Figure 8-7, the POST request and response contents are depicted.

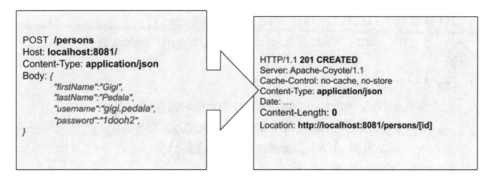

Figure 8-7. *POST request and response example*

---

[19]For example, a POST request to create a detective contains the ID of the person, which make the person to be in a parent-to-child relationship with detective. If a person with the specified id does not exist in the database, a 404 should be used to notify the client of the failure.

When executing a POST request, there are two possible outcomes: either the recently created entity is returned, or a response header named Location is set with the URI to access the recently created entity. The next test scenario matches a handler method that implements the second scenario, which happens to be the recommended practice when writing REST APIs; but returning a Person instance allowed more testing approaches to be shown in this book.

```
package com.apress.cems.person;
...
@RestController
@RequestMapping("/persons")
public class PersonsController {

    @ResponseStatus(HttpStatus.CREATED)
    @PostMapping(consumes = MediaType.APPLICATION_JSON_VALUE)
    public void create(@Validated(Person.BasicValidation.class)
        @RequestBody Person person, BindingResult result,
          @Value("#{request.requestURL}")
            StringBuffer originalUrl, HttpServletResponse response) {
        if (result.hasErrors()) {
            String errString = createErrorString(result);
            throw new PersonsException(HttpStatus.BAD_REQUEST,
                "Cannot save entry because: "+ errString);
        }
        if(StringUtils.isEmpty(person.getPassword())){
            person.setPassword(NumberGenerator.getPassword());
        }
        try {
            Person newPerson = personService.save(person);
            response.setHeader("Location", getLocationForUser(
                    originalUrl, newPerson.getId()));
        } catch (Exception e) {
            throw  new PersonsException(HttpStatus.UNPROCESSABLE_ENTITY, e);
        }
    }
}
```

```
    static String getLocationForUser(StringBuffer url,
        Object childIdentifier) {
      UriTemplate template = new UriTemplate(url.toString() + "/{id}");
      return template.expand(childIdentifier).toASCIIString();
    }
}
```

A REST POST request can be sent with a `RestTemplate` instance; all that is needed is the REST URI and a person object. The URI is identical to the one used to retrieve all person resources, but the HTTP method is different.

```
package com.apress.cems.practice;
import org.springframework.http.ResponseEntity;
...

@SpringBootTest(webEnvironment =
        SpringBootTest.WebEnvironment.RANDOM_PORT)
public class PersonsControllerTest {

    @LocalServerPort
    private int port;

    private String baseUrl = "http://localhost";

    @BeforeEach
    void setUp(){
        baseUrl = baseUrl.concat(":").concat(port +"").concat("/persons");
    }
    ...

    @Test
    void shouldCreateAPerson() {
      Person person = buildPerson("gigi.pedala", "Gigi", "Pedala", "1dooh2" );

      HttpHeaders headers = new HttpHeaders();
      headers.setContentType(MediaType.APPLICATION_JSON);

      HttpEntity<Person> postRequest = new HttpEntity<>(person, headers);
      URI uri = restTemplate.postForLocation(baseUrl, postRequest, Person.
      class);
```

```
        assertNotNull(uri);
        Person newPerson = restTemplate.getForObject(uri, Person.class);
        assertAll(
                () -> assertNotNull(newPerson),
                () -> assertEquals(person.getUsername(), newPerson.getUsername()),
                () -> assertNotNull(newPerson.getId())
        );
    }
}
```

The `postForLocation` method is used, and the successful creation of the resource is tested after making the POST request, which is done by making a GET request with the returned location. The `HttpHeaders` object sets the headers of the request, like the media type of the message, so that Spring knows which message converter to use to convert the JSON representation into the user instance that needs to be saved.

- **PUT**: Updates an existing resource or creates it with a known destination URI (normally). The URI of a resource contains an identifier for that resource. In our case, when a PUT request refers to an existing resource, the resource is updated; otherwise, an exception is thrown, because the generation of a database primary key is not something an end user is allowed to do. That is why the choice was made to throw an exception that is intercepted by the exception handler method, and a response containing an error message and the 404 status code is returned.

When the resource being updated requires a parent that does not exist (remember the same situation forms POST),[20] or the resource requested to be updated does not exist, a **404 (Not found)** status code is returned. When the resource is updated correctly and nothing is returned as a response body, **204 (No content)** response status is returned.

In Figure 8-8, the PUT request and response contents are depicted.

---

[20]In the CEMS project, the detectives cannot be created without specifying a person is. The person is the parent in this case, because a detective cannot be created without it. A REST service that allows you to change the detective linked to a person needs the id of that person. If an id that is not present in the database is provided a 404 HTTP response code is returned.

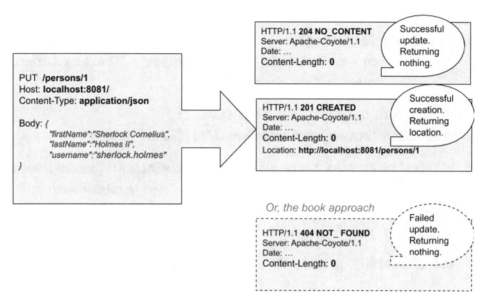

Figure 8-8. *PUT request and response example*

A REST PUT request can be sent with a `RestTemplate` instance: all that is needed is the REST URI, a `Person` object, and a converter. The URI is identical to the one used to retrieve a user resource, but the HTTP method is different.

```
package com.apress.cems.practice;
import org.springframework.http.ResponseEntity;
...

@SpringBootTest(webEnvironment =
        SpringBootTest.WebEnvironment.RANDOM_PORT)
public class PersonsControllerTest {

    @LocalServerPort
    private int port;

    private String baseUrl = "http://localhost";

    @BeforeEach
    void setUp(){
        baseUrl = baseUrl.concat(":").concat(port +"").concat("/persons");
    }
    ...
```

```
@Test
void shouldUpdateAPerson() {
    Person person = buildPerson("sherlock.holmes", "Sherlock Cornelius",
            "Holmes", "complicated");

    HttpHeaders headers = new HttpHeaders();
    headers.setContentType(MediaType.APPLICATION_JSON);

    HttpEntity<Person> postRequest = new HttpEntity<>(person, headers);
    ResponseEntity<Person> responseEntity = restTemplate.exchange
        (baseUrl.concat("/{id}"), HttpMethod.PUT, postRequest, Person.
        class, 1);

    assertEquals(HttpStatus.NO_CONTENT, responseEntity.getStatusCode());
}
}
```

The exchange method was used here for teaching purposes, but RestTemplate provides put methods with various signatures, which are much easier to use.

- **DELETE**: Deletes a resource. There are two possible approaches here: when the resource being deleted does not exist, a **404 (Not found)** status code should be returned, but since there is nothing to do, there shouldn't be any reason for a **200 (OK)** status code to be returned, right? Just make the decision depending on the sensibility of the operation in your project. When the resource was deleted correctly, a **200 (OK)** status code is returned. In Figure 8-9, the DELETE request and response contents are depicted.

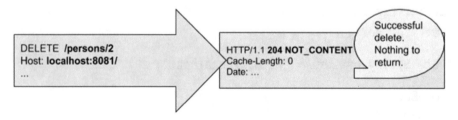

Figure 8-9. *DELETE request and response example*

A REST DELETE request can be sent with a `RestTemplate` instance; all that is needed is the REST URI, the ID, and a converter. The URI is identical to the one used to retrieve a user resource, but the HTTP method is different.

```
package com.apress.cems.practice;
import org.springframework.http.ResponseEntity;
...

@SpringBootTest(webEnvironment =
        SpringBootTest.WebEnvironment.RANDOM_PORT)
public class PersonsControllerTest {

    @LocalServerPort
    private int port;

    private String baseUrl = "http://localhost";

    @BeforeEach
    void setUp(){
        baseUrl = baseUrl.concat(":").concat(port +"").concat("/persons");
    }
    ...

    @Test
    void shouldDeleteAPerson(){
        restTemplate.delete(baseUrl.concat("/2"));

        ResponseEntity<String> err = restTemplate.getForEntity(
            baseUrl + "/{id}", String.class, 2);
        assertAll(
            () -> assertNotNull(err),
            () -> assertEquals(HttpStatus.NOT_FOUND, err.getStatusCode()),
            () -> assertTrue(err.getBody().contains(
                    "Unable to find entry with id 2"))
        );
    }
}
```

The delete response has an empty body if the operation succeeds. The only way to test the success of a deletion is to request the resource with URI equal to: `http://localhost:8081/persons/2` and expect a failure or a response with 404 (Not Found) status to be returned, because the resource has already been deleted.

This testing scenario does not test the 204 being returned because the `restTemplate.delete(..)` method returns void. So, if we really want to test the response status code returned when a DELETE request is done, we have to use `exchange(..)`.

```java
package com.apress.cems.practice;
import org.springframework.http.ResponseEntity;

...

@SpringBootTest(webEnvironment =
        SpringBootTest.WebEnvironment.RANDOM_PORT)
public class PersonsControllerTest {

    @LocalServerPort
    private int port;

    private String baseUrl = "http://localhost";

    @BeforeEach
    void setUp(){
        baseUrl = baseUrl.concat(":").concat(port +"").concat("/persons");
    }
    ...

    @Test
    void shouldDeleteAPerson(){
        final HttpHeaders headers = new HttpHeaders();

        final HttpEntity<Person> deleteRequest = new HttpEntity<>(headers);
        ResponseEntity<Void> responseEntity = restTemplate
            .exchange(baseUrl.concat("/{id}"), HttpMethod.DELETE,
                deleteRequest, Void.class, 3);

        assertEquals(HttpStatus.NO_CONTENT, responseEntity.getStatusCode());
    }
}
```

The only case that we are missing is the one where there is nothing to delete. In this book's code, I wanted to use the ifPresent() optional method; thus, an exception is not thrown and a 404 is never returned. In the following code snippet, you can see the handler method body.

```
@ResponseStatus(HttpStatus.NO_CONTENT)
@DeleteMapping("/{id}")
public void delete(@PathVariable Long id) {
    Optional<Person> personOpt = personService.findById(id);
    personOpt. ifPresent(value -> personService.delete(value));
}
```

You are welcome to change the provided implementation, and write a test for it. An exception class named NotFoundException and an exception handler that sets the response status code to 404 are already provided. for you

The Advantages of REST

- REST is simple.

- REST is widely supported.

- Resources can be represented in a wide variety of data formats. (JSON, XML, etc.)

- You can make good use of HTTP cache and proxy server to help you handle high load and improve performance.

- It reduces client/server coupling.

- Browsers can interpret representations if no security is in place.

- A REST service can be consumed by applications written in different languages.

- It makes it easy for new clients to use a RESTful Application, even if the application was not designed it specifically for them.

- Because of statelessness of REST systems, multiple servers can be behind a load-balancer and provide services transparently, which means increased scalability.

- Because of the uniform interface, little or no documentation of the resources and basic operations API is necessary.[21]

- Using REST does not imply specific libraries at the client level to communicate with the server. With REST all that is needed is a network connection.

Practice Section

The chapter08/boot-rest-practice application is a Spring Boot MVC application exposing REST services. This project is incomplete, there are annotations and method bodies missing. To test your understanding of implementing Spring RESTful applications and testing them you can try completing it. There are seven TODO tasks numbered from 56 to 62 and if you need inspiration or a confirmation that your solution is correct you can compare it with the proposed solution that you can find in project chapter08/boot-rest

Task TODO 56 located in the PersonsController class, requires you to complete the configuration of this class to register this class as a controller that handles REST requests with the root URI of /persons.

Task TODO 57 located in the PersonsController class, requires you to complete the configuration of the create(..) method, so that it can handle an HTTP POST request and create a Person instance. If you want to test the method right away, enable the PersonsControllerTest by commenting the @Disabled annotation and solve task TODO 58 in the PersonsControllerTest class to use a RestTemplate object to send an HTTP POST request.

Task TODO 59 located in the PersonsController class, requires you to complete the configuration of the update(..) method so that it can handle an HTTP PUT request and update a Person instance. If you want to test the method right away, enable the PersonsControllerTest by commenting the @Disabled annotation and solve TODO 60 in the PersonsControllerTest class to use a RestTemplate object to send an HTTP PUT request.

Task TODO 61 located in the PersonsControllerTest class, requires you to complete the test method body to make a REST call using a RestTemplate object to request a person instance with id equal to 1.

Task TODO 62 located in the PersonsControllerTest class, requires you to complete the test method body to make a REST call using a RestTemplate object to request deletion of the person instance with ID equal to 1.

---

[21]Most companies now use Swagger: https://swagger.io/

Securing RESTful Spring Applications with Spring Boot

Accessing resources exposed by a web application using URIs is practical, but it is also dangerous without the proper security measurements in place. In previous chapters you were introduced to security as relying on form authentication. Applications exposing REST services do not provide a form for you to use to insert username and password so they rely on different methods of authentication. There are a few methods for securing your REST APIs, which are only superficially discussed in this chapter since it is not a topic for the exam. Useful links to more advanced resources are provided, however.

Basic Authentication

The most basic way of authentication when accessing REST APIs is, well ... *basic API authentication.* This is the simplest technique and the most used as well. The basic authentication scheme is best explained here: `https://tools.ietf.org/html/rfc7617` It involves sending your credentials (username and password) as part of the request. The credentials are combined using a colon (username:password) and encoded using the Base64 algorithm. Encoding the username and password with the Base64 algorithm typically makes them unreadable to the human eye; they are as easily decoded as they are encoded. Security is not the intent of the encoding step. Rather, the intent of the encoding is to encode non-HTTP-compatible characters in the username or password into those that are HTTP compatible. The main problem of this security technique is that the credentials are propagated in plain text over the Internet. They can be intercepted and used by not so well intended parties. The encoding doesn't offer much protection since there are ways to decode the text, either programmatically or by using specialized sites like `www.base64encode.org`. That is why basic authentication is typically used over HTTPS, which involves encrypting the entire server communication, thus making it impossible to discern from the outside that authentication is taking place.

Since this is the simplest way to authenticate in this section, the chapter08/boot-rest application will be modified to support basic authentication with HTTPS. This means that we need an SSL certificate to configure with Spring Boot so that we can make HTTPS requests. In production, an SSL certification generated by a trusted authority is used. For the purpose of this example, a self-signed certification is used. To transform chapter08/boot-rest into chapter08/boot-rest-secured, we have to do the following.

1. Configure security to support basic authentication for REST requests.

    •   Declaring an authentication entry point: in a secured web
        application the authentication entry point is the login form, but for
        REST applications that is not suitable. A bean of type `Authentication`
        `EntryPoint` (provided by the Spring Security module) must
        be declared as the starting point for authentication. The
        `AuthenticationEntryPoint` is an interface that is implemented by
        the form specific `BasicAuthenticationEntryPoint`, but a REST
        application has no login form. To provide a REST authentication
        entry point, the interface must be implemented. Since the interface
        has a single method named `commence` that represents the starting
        point of the authentication process, there is no need for a bean to be
        declared. Yes, we can switch to a functional configuration for this one.
        A simple lambda expression can declare a property of this type in the
        Spring Security configuration class. The `AuthenticationEntryPoint`
        instance declared in the next code snippet returns the 401 HTTP
        status error code without setting any headers to the response.

```
package com.apress.cems.secured.config;
...
import org.springframework.security.web.
AuthenticationEntryPoint;
import javax.servlet.http.HttpServletResponse;

@Configuration
@EnableWebSecurity
@EnableGlobalMethodSecurity(prePostEnabled = true)
@ComponentScan("com.apress.cems.secured")
public class SecurityConfig extends
WebSecurityConfigurerAdapter {

    AuthenticationEntryPoint restAuthenticationEntryPoint =
        (request, response, authException) -> response
        .sendError(HttpServletResponse.SC_UNAUTHORIZED,
        "Unauthorized");
}
```

- The typical web login form works because of an authentication
  processing filter of type `org.springframework.security.web.`
  `authentication. UsernamePasswordAuthenticationFilter.`
  Form authentication is configured by calling the `formLogin()`
  method on the `HttpSecurity` instance configured in the Spring
  Security configuration class. Calling this method also configures
  default success and failure to authenticate handlers, but because
  REST is stateless it is mandatory to send the username/password
  for each interaction with the server, so custom success and failure
  of authentication handlers must be provided. In case of failure, the
  default `SimpleUrlAuthenticationFailureHandler` implementation
  works as intended. But for authentication success, we need
  different behavior in a REST application. When using a form to
  log in, in a successful authentication, the user is redirected to a
  home page; thus, the HTTP response status code is 301 MOVED_
  PERMANENTLY (a permanent redirect that prohibits the user
  from accessing the login form again), which is not the behavior
  desired for authentication using a REST request (because there is
  no login form in the first place). For authentication using a REST
  request, we need to return 200. So, a class extending the default
  `SimpleUrlAuthenticationSuccessHandler` must be added and the
  security configuration class must make use of it.

```
// RestAuthenticationSuccessHandler.java
package com.apress.cems.secured.config;

import org.springframework.security.core.Authentication;
import org.springframework.security.web.authentication.
    SimpleUrlAuthenticationSuccessHandler;
import org.springframework.security.web.savedrequest.
HttpSessionRequestCache;
import org.springframework.security.web.savedrequest.RequestCache;
import org.springframework.security.web.savedrequest.SavedRequest;
import org.springframework.stereotype.Component;
import org.springframework.util.StringUtils;
```

```java
import javax.servlet.http.HttpServletRequest;
import javax.servlet.http.HttpServletResponse;

@Component
public class RestAuthenticationSuccessHandler
            extends SimpleUrlAuthenticationSuccessHandler {

    private RequestCache requestCache = new
    HttpSessionRequestCache();

    @Override
    public void onAuthenticationSuccess(HttpServletRequest request,
        HttpServletResponse response,
            Authentication authentication) {

        SavedRequest savedRequest =
            requestCache.getRequest(request, response);

        if (savedRequest == null) {
            clearAuthenticationAttributes(request); // (1)
            return;
        }
        String targetUrlParam = getTargetUrlParameter();  // (2)
        if (isAlwaysUseDefaultTargetUrl()   // (3)
                || (targetUrlParam != null
                && StringUtils.hasText(request.getParameter
                (targetUrlParam)))) {
            requestCache.removeRequest(request, response);
            clearAuthenticationAttributes(request);
            return;
        }
        clearAuthenticationAttributes(request);
    }

    public void setRequestCache(RequestCache requestCache) {
        this.requestCache = requestCache;
    }
}
```

A more detailed explanation is needed since there are
a lot of methods being called that seem to come from
nowhere. In Figure 8-10, the full class hierarchy for the
RestAuthenticationSuccessHandler is depicted. The methods
called in the code snippet are marked with the numbers from
the comments.

Figure 8-10. *RestAuthenticationSuccessHandler class hierarchy*

The HttpSessionRequestCache saves the last URL requested
by the client in a user session. This is used by Spring Security,
when it redirects you to a login page to restore the URL after
a successful login. But, for REST authentication, this is not
needed, so we make sure that this cache is always empty.

The clearAuthenticationAttributes(..) is provided by the
SimpleUrlAuthenticationSuccessHandler class and is used
to clear temporary authentication-related data was stored in
the request session during the authentication process. Since
REST is stateless, authentication information is not needed
after the user was authenticated so we remove it.

The getTargetUrlParameter() method is provided by the abstract class AbstractAuthenticationTarget UrlRequestHandler that provides logic to handle redirection and is one of the core classes involved in redirecting the user after a successful form authentication. If the alwaysUseDefaultTargetUrl property is set to true, the defaultTargetUrl property will be used for the destination. If a special functionality is enabled that allows to get the destination from the targetUrlParameter set on the request, extra care must be taken to ensure security, because an attacker can modify the request and redirect to a malicious site. In the previous code snippet, we make sure to disregard both redirection strategies, because they are not needed for REST authentication. So, now that we no longer have redirection logic, it is time to put all the parts together in a Spring Security configuration class.

```
package com.apress.cems.secured.config;
...
import org.springframework.security.web.authentication.
        SimpleUrlAuthenticationFailureHandler;
import javax.servlet.http.HttpServletResponse;

@Configuration
@EnableWebSecurity
@EnableGlobalMethodSecurity(prePostEnabled = true)
@ComponentScan("com.apress.cems.secured")
public class SecurityConfig extends
WebSecurityConfigurerAdapter {

    SimpleUrlAuthenticationFailureHandler authenticationFailure
    Handler =
            new SimpleUrlAuthenticationFailureHandler();

    @Autowired
    RestAuthenticationSuccessHandler authenticationSuccess
    Handler;
```

```
@Override
protected void configure(final HttpSecurity http) throws
Exception {
    http.exceptionHandling()
            .accessDeniedHandler(accessDeniedHandler)
            .authenticationEntryPoint(restAuthenticationEntry
            Point)
            .and()
        .authorizeRequests()
            .mvcMatchers("/persons/**").hasRole("ADMIN")
            .mvcMatchers("/**").hasAnyRole("ADMIN", "USER")
            .and()
        .formLogin()
            .successHandler(authenticationSuccessHandler)
            .failureHandler(authenticationFailureHandler)
            .and()
            .httpBasic()
            .and()
            .logout();

    }
}
```

- Although optional, a customized access denied handler should
  be provided, because when a user tries to access a resource he
  is not authorized to, he should be notified. The class should
  implement the AccessDeniedHandler functional interface that
  declares a single method named handle(..). So, yep, you can use
  lambda expressions again.

```
package com.apress.cems.secured.config;
...
import org.springframework.security.web.access.
AccessDeniedHandler;
import javax.servlet.http.HttpServletResponse;
```

```
@Configuration
@EnableWebSecurity
@EnableGlobalMethodSecurity(prePostEnabled = true)
@ComponentScan("com.apress.cems.secured")
public class SecurityConfig extends
WebSecurityConfigurerAdapter {

    AccessDeniedHandler accessDeniedHandler = (request, response,
       accessDeniedException) -> {
          response.getOutputStream().print("You shall not pass!");
          response.setStatus(403);
    };

    @Override
    protected void configure(final HttpSecurity http) throws
    Exception {
          http.
             ...
              .accessDeniedHandler(accessDeniedHandler)
             ...

    }
}
```

To put all this together, all we need to do is to provide a
UserDetailsService, a PasswordEncoder and to disable CSRF
support to make testing easier.

```
package com.apress.cems.secured.config;
...

@Configuration
@EnableWebSecurity
@EnableGlobalMethodSecurity(prePostEnabled = true)
@ComponentScan("com.apress.cems.secured")
class SecurityConfig extends WebSecurityConfigurerAdapter {

    @Bean
    @Override
```

```
public UserDetailsService userDetailsService() {
    UserDetails john = User.withUsername("john").
    password(encoder()
        .encode("doe")).roles("USER").build();
    UserDetails jane = User.withUsername("jane").
    password(encoder()
        .encode("doe")).roles("USER", "ADMIN").build();
    UserDetails admin = User.withUsername("admin").
    password(encoder()
        .encode("admin")).roles("ADMIN").build();
    return new InMemoryUserDetailsManager(john,jane,admin);
}

@Bean
PasswordEncoder encoder(){
    return new BCryptPasswordEncoder();
}

AccessDeniedHandler accessDeniedHandler = (request, response,
  accessDeniedException) -> {
    response.getOutputStream().print("You shall not pass!");
    response.setStatus(403);
};

AuthenticationEntryPoint restAuthenticationEntryPoint =
    (request, response, authException) -> response.sendError(
        HttpServletResponse.SC_UNAUTHORIZED, "Unauthorized");
SimpleUrlAuthenticationFailureHandler authentication
FailureHandler =
    new SimpleUrlAuthenticationFailureHandler();

@Autowired
RestAuthenticationSuccessHandler authenticationSuccessHandler;

@Override
protected void configure(final HttpSecurity http) throws Exception {
    http.csrf().disable()
            .exceptionHandling()
            .accessDeniedHandler(accessDeniedHandler)
```

```
                    .authenticationEntryPoint(restAuthenticationEntryPoint)
                    .and()
                    .authorizeRequests()
                    .mvcMatchers("/persons/**").hasRole("ADMIN")
                    .mvcMatchers("/**").hasAnyRole("ADMIN", "USER")
                    .and()
                    .formLogin()
                    .successHandler(authenticationSuccessHandler)
                    .failureHandler(authenticationFailureHandler)
                    .and()
                    .httpBasic()
                    .and()
                    .logout();
        }
    }
```

2. To test the secured REST requests, `TestRestTemplate` must be used. It is a special Spring Boot REST client that exposes the same API as `RestTemplate` and supports authentication. There is two ways this class can be used. The credentials - username and password - are either provided as arguments at instantiation time, or they can be provided later calling the `withBasicAuth(..)`. This method is useful when we want to test restrictions that are in place for some users or roles. A security role defines how different users access different types of records.[22]

```
import org.springframework.boot.test.web.client.TestRestTemplate;
...
TestRestTemplate testRestTemplate = new TestRestTemplate("jane",
"doe");
// or
testRestTemplate = new TestRestTemplate();
testRestTemplate.withBasicAuth("jane", "doe");
```

---

[22]In Chapter 7, you were introduced to the two roles used in this book: ADMIN (users with this role are allowed to do anything) and USER (users with this role are restricted to viewing data).

The TestRestTemplate class exposes almost the same API as RestTemplate, so as long as we make sure the TestRestTemplate is initialized with the proper credentials, the tests written previously in the section should still work after switching RestTemplate with TestRestTemplate.

```
package com.apress.cems.secured;
import org.springframework.boot.test.web.client.TestRestTemplate;
...

@SpringBootTest(webEnvironment = SpringBootTest.WebEnvironment.
RANDOM_PORT)
class SecuredRestApplicationTest {
    @LocalServerPort
    private int port;

    private String baseUrl = "http://localhost";

    private static  TestRestTemplate testRestTemplate = null;

    @BeforeAll
    static void init() {
        testRestTemplate = new TestRestTemplate("jane", "doe");
    }

    @BeforeEach
    void setUp(){
        baseUrl = baseUrl.concat(":").concat(port +"").concat
        ("/persons");
    }

    @Test
    void shouldReturnAListOfPersons(){
        ResponseEntity<Person[]> response = testRestTemplate.
            getForEntity](baseUrl, Person[].class);

        Person[] persons = response.getBody();
        assertAll(
                () -> assertEquals(HttpStatus.OK, response.
                getStatusCode()),
```

```
                            () -> assertNotNull(persons),
                            () -> assertTrue(persons.length >= 4)
            );
        }
        @Test
        void shouldCreateAPerson() {
            Person person = buildPerson("gigi.pedala", "Gigi", "Pedala",
            "1dooh2" );

            HttpHeaders headers = new HttpHeaders();
            headers.setContentType(MediaType.APPLICATION_JSON);

            HttpEntity<Person> postRequest = new HttpEntity<>(person,
            headers);
            URI uri = testRestTemplate.postForLocation(baseUrl,
                postRequest, Person.class);

            assertNotNull(uri);
            Person newPerson = testRestTemplate.getForObject
            (uri, Person.class);
            assertAll(
                    () -> assertNotNull(newPerson),
                    () -> assertEquals(person.getUsername(),
                        newPerson.getUsername()),
                    () -> assertNotNull(newPerson.getId())
            );
         }

    @Test
     void shouldUpdateAPerson() {
            Person person = buildPerson("sherlock.holmes", "Sherlock
            Tiberius",
                    "Holmes", "complicated");

            final HttpHeaders headers = new HttpHeaders();
            headers.setContentType(MediaType.APPLICATION_JSON);

            final HttpEntity<Person> putRequest = new
            HttpEntity<>(person, headers);
            ResponseEntity<Void> responseEntity = testRestTemplate
```

```
            .exchange(baseUrl.concat("/1"), HttpMethod.PUT,
                    putRequest, Void.class);

    assertEquals(HttpStatus.NO_CONTENT, responseEntity.
    getStatusCode());
}

@Test
void shouldNotUpdateAPerson403(){
    Person person = buildPerson("sherlock.holmes", "Sherlock
    Cornelius",
            "Holmes", "complicated");
    final HttpHeaders headers = new HttpHeaders();
    headers.setContentType(MediaType.APPLICATION_JSON);

    final HttpEntity<Person> putRequest = new
    HttpEntity<>(person, headers);
    ResponseEntity<Void> responseEntity = testRestTemplate
            .withBasicAuth("john", "doe"). // USER role
            .exchange(baseUrl.concat("/1"), HttpMethod.PUT,
                    putRequest, Void.class);
    assertEquals(HttpStatus.FORBIDDEN, responseEntity.
    getStatusCode());
}
}
```

! TestRestTemplate could be used to test a classic Spring web application that exposes only secured REST services; but since it is a Spring Boot–specific component, I want to show you a different way.[23] It involves using a practical library called REST Assured.[24] REST Assured can make secured REST calls that require basic authentication. This means that an authentication call is done before the effective call, with the credentials provided. Usually, tests for classic Spring web applications require the application to be started with a launcher and the port is exposed on is known and hard-coded in the tests.

---

[23]Postman can also be used for this as well.
[24]Official site: http://rest-assured.io/

A small Spring web application exposing secured REST calls is
provided to you in the project chapter08/rest-classic-secured.
Do not worry yourself with the configuration of this application.
The security configurations are the same for Boot and classic style,
so the SpringSecurity class and additional classes needed to
build it are plugged in to set up the configuration for classic too.
Assuming a launcher was created to expose the application on
http://localhost:8080/rest-classic-secured/, the following
shows how some REST Assured tests are written to test it.

```java
package com.apress.cems.sec;
import static io.restassured.RestAssured.given;
import static org.hamcrest.CoreMatchers.*;
import static org.hamcrest.Matchers.*;
...

class RestAssuredSecuredTest {

    @BeforeEach
    void setupURL() {
        // setup the default URL and API base path to use throughout
        the tests
        RestAssured.baseURI = "http://localhost";
        RestAssured.port = 8080;
        RestAssured.basePath = "/rest-classic-secured/persons";
    }

    @Test
    void shouldReturnAListOfPersons() {
        List<Person> personList =
                given()
                .auth().preemptive() .basic("jane", "doe")
                .when().get("/")
                .then()
                .assertThat().statusCode(HttpStatus.OK.value())
                .and()
                .contentType(ContentType.JSON)
                .and()
```

```
                .statusCode(HttpStatus.OK.value())
                .and()
                .extract().response().body().jsonPath().getList("$");
        assertNotNull(personList);
        assertTrue(personList.size() >= 4);
    }

    @Test
    void shouldUpdateAPerson() {
        Person person = buildPerson("sherlock.holmes",
                    "Sherlock Cornelius", "Holmes", "complicated");

        given()
                .auth().preemptive() .basic("jane", "doe")
                .contentType(ContentType.JSON)
                .body(person)
                .log().all()
                .when().put("/2")
                .then()
                .log().all()
                .assertThat().statusCode(HttpStatus.NO_CONTENT.value());

    }

    @Test
    void shouldNotUpdateAPerson403() {
        Person person = buildPerson("sherlock.holmes",
                "Sherlock Cornelius", "Holmes", "complicated");

        given()
                .auth().preemptive().basic("john", "doe")
                .contentType(ContentType.JSON)
                .body(person)
                .when().put("/2")
                .then()
                .log().all()
                .assertThat().statusCode(HttpStatus.FORBIDDEN.value());

    }
```

```
        private Person buildPerson(final String username, final String
        firstName,
            final String lastName, final String password) {
            Person person = new Person();
            ...  // set all the fields
            return person;
        }
    }
```

The preemptive() call is needed because Tomcat sends a challenge-response mechanism[25] to tell the client it needs to authenticate to access the resource. REST Assured needs to send the credentials without waiting for an *Unauthorized* response from the server. If everything goes well, calls like get(..), post(..), put(..), and delete(..) can then be made to the server.

Imagine it like this: it's like you are entering a secured building and show the access card to the guard before he can say to you require a card to enter.

3. For testing purposes, HTTP is fine, but if you want a bit more security with basic authentication, you need to get an SSL certificate and set up HTTPS. Most computers have a tool named keytool that can generate a PKCS12 keystore. To do this, the following command must be executed.

```
keytool -genkeypair -alias tomcat -keyalg RSA -keysize 2048
-storetype PKCS12 \
    -keystore keystore.p12 -validity 3650
```

After this you will receive a set of questions and the reply is saved within the generated file.

```
Enter keystore password:
springboot     // masked with '*'
```

---

[25]Read about it here: https://tools.ietf.org/html/rfc2617#section-1.2

```
What is your first and last name?
  [Iuliana Cosmina]:  Iuliana Cosmina
What is the name of your organizational unit?
  [Apress]:  Apress
What is the name of your organization?
  [Apress]:  Apress
What is the name of your City or Locality?
  [Edinburgh]:  Edinburgh
What is the name of your State or Province?
  [Midlothian]:  Midlothian
What is the two-letter country code for this unit?
  [UK]:  UK
Is CN=Iuliana Cosmina, OU=Apress, O=Apress, L=Edinburgh,
ST=Midlothian, C=UK correct?
  [no]:  yes
```

At the end of the process a file named keystore.jks should appear in the location where the command was executed. This file contains the certificate inside of it.

4. Enable HTTPS in Spring Boot. Save the previously generated file into the src/main/resources/ in your Spring Boot project and modify the application.yml according to the documentation[26] to enable HTTPS support in Spring Boot.

```
server:
  port: 8443
  servlet:
    context-path: /
  compression:
    enabled: true
  address: 0.0.0.0
  ssl:
```

---

[26]Configure SSL support in Spring Boot https://docs.spring.io/spring-boot/docs/current/reference/htmlsingle/#howto-configure-ssl

```
enabled: true
key-store-type: PKCS12
key-store: classpath:keystore.jks
key-store-password: springboot
```

5. Redirect HTTP requests to HTTPS - Spring Boot 2.x does
    not support HTTP and HTTPS simultaneously, so no extra
    configuration needs to be added.

6. Distribute the SSL certificate to clients -this application uses a self-
    signed SSL certificate, so the browser won't trust the application
    and will warn that it's not secure. It's possible to make a client
    trust your application by providing the certificate, but first it must
    be taken out of the keystore file. `keytool` supports this as well.

    ```
    keytool -export -keystore keystore.jks -alias tomcat -file rest.crt
    ```

    Now the `rest.crt` file can import the certificate into your
    client, most likely a browser, and start accessing your APIs using
    `https://locahost:8443/persons`.

For a classic Spring web application, the SSL certificate must be installed on the
Apache Tomcat server. It requires more steps than a Spring Boot application. And since,
installing an SSL certificate on an external Apache Tomcat server is not really a Spring-
related topic, I'll provide a link to very good reading material on the official Apache
Tomcat site: `https://tomcat.apache.org/tomcat-7.0-doc/ssl-howto.html`

DIGEST Authentication

This type of authentication uses a hashing algorithm like MD5, SHA-1, or BCrypt[27] to
encrypt the password sent by the user before sending it to the server. This makes it
safer, because even if intercepted, the password is useless since hashing algorithms
can't be reverse engineered. The only problem is that once the password hash is saved
in the database, if the user forgets the password, the only solution is to generate a new
password and a new password hash. The HTTP Digest Access Authentication process is
explained at `https://tools.ietf.org/html/rfc7616`.

---

[27]More on hashing algorithms can be read here: `https://howtodoinjava.com/security/`
`how-to-generate-secure-password-hash-md5-sha-pbkdf2-bcrypt-examples/`

Client CERT Authentication

This is a more complex form of authentication that involves a trust agreement between the client end the server through certificates. The certificates are special files with binary content (also known as gibberish) and are signed by an agency established to ensure that the certificate presented for authentication is legitimate, which is known as CA. When communicating with the server the client presents the certificate. The certificate contains information that identifies the user through the legitimate CA. Certificates often contain authorization information as well. To avoid the certificate from being intercepted and stolen, this authentication techniques should always be used in conjunction with HTTPS (Secure HTTP).

OAUTH2 API Keys

The OAUTH 2.0 is a protocol specific to communication between applications in the cloud. Identification is done by providing an API key and secret. The API key and secret are some random encoded strings which is impossible to guess. The API key and secret are handled by a *resource server* which is service designed to handle domain-logic requests and does not have any kind of login workflow or complex authentication mechanism.

The API key and secret are turned into an access token by an *authorization server*. The resource server receives the access token that guarantees a user has grant permission to access the server and delivers the expected response. The OAUTH 2.0 protocol flow is explained pretty neatly at `https://tools.ietf.org/html/rfc6749`. You should take a look at it because this is the protocol that you will use when communicating with GitHub, Twitter, or Facebook.

Security is very important; the data that you send on the Internet can and will be used against you, if given the chance. Read about security on the Internet and secure your applications like the most motived hacker is out to get you. Because he probably is.

That is pretty much it for writing Spring RESTful applications. I hope you enjoyed this chapter.

Summary

The following is a simple list of topics that you should keep handy when reviewing the acquired knowledge to prepare for the exam.

- What is REST?

- What type of clients can access a web application?

- How are resources exposed to the client?

- How many types of representations are supported?

- What is the difference between @Controller and @RestController?

- Make sure you can describe Spring MVC support for RESTful applications.

- Understand how to access Request/Response Data.

- What are @ResponseBody and @RequestBody used for.

- Use message converters.

- Is Spring MVC needed in the classpath in the configuration of a RESTful application?

- `RestTemplate` is the core Spring class for creating clients for REST applications, but REST Assured is good too.

- How do you secure Spring RESTful applications?

- What is `TestRestTemplate` good for?

Quick Quiz

Question 1. Which of the following methods are HTTP methods? (Choose all that apply.)

A. PUT

B. GET

C. SUBMIT

D. OPTIONS

Question 2. What does CRUD mean? (Choose one.)

A. Create, Read, Update, Delete

B. Create, Remove, Update, Deploy

C. Configure, Release, Upload, Deploy

Question 3. Which of the following HTTP methods are or can be considered idempotent? (Choose all that apply.)

A. PUT

B. POST

C. GET

D. DELETE

Question 4. What can be said about the `@RestController` annotation? (Choose all that apply.)

A. It is used to declare a controller providing REST Services.

B. It is annotated with @Controller and @ResponseBody.

C. Controllers methods annotated with this annotation assume `@ResponseStatus` semantics by default.

Question 5. Which of the following `RestTemplate` methods can be used to make a GET REST call? (Choose all that apply.)

A. restTemplate.getForObject(...)

B. optionsForAllow(...)

C. getForEntity(...)

D. exchange(..., HttpMethod.GET,...)

Question 6. Spring Boot question: Which of the following affirmations is true about `RestTemplate` and `TestRestTemplate`? (Choose all that apply.)

    A.   Both implementations can be used for integration tests.

    B.   `TestRestTemplate` is a convenient alternative for `RestTemplate` provided by Spring Boot.

    C.   `TestRestTemplate` class extends the `RestTemplate` class.

    D.   `TestRestTemplate` exposes the same API as `RestTemplate` and can carry basic authentication headers.

CHAPTER 9

Monitoring Spring Applications

So far in this book, a wide range of applications have been built using Spring with or without a user interface. Application monitoring is a process that ensures that a software application processes and performs in an expected manner and scope. To check that an application works as intended, the only techniques used so far in the book are logging and test executions. Logging is the most basic way of monitoring and helps developers identify problems in the application during development and after deploying it into production. After an application is deployed into production, it's the job of an operations team to monitor logs, identify problems, and forward them to the development team doing the maintenance on the application. To monitor a running application, operation engineers use a myriad of tools to perform the following tasks.

- monitoring application log data

- monitoring application errors

- monitoring basic server metrics like memory and CPU usage

- monitoring network performance

- performance monitoring individual web requests or transactions

- monitoring usage and performance of all dependencies (databases, caches, web services, etc.)

- trace transactions in detail (down to specific lines of codes)

- performance profiling

© Iuliana Cosmina 2020
I. Cosmina, *Pivotal Certified Professional Core Spring 5 Developer Exam*,
https://doi.org/10.1007/978-1-4842-5136-2_9

- monitoring custom framework metrics, like counters and JMX beans

- monitoring custom application metrics created by the dev team or business

and more.

A simple Google search can recommend the best tools for the job. In the past, I've used App Dynamics,[1] New Relic,[2] DynaTrace,[3] and Apache JMeter (which is open source, so no license needed).[4] They are enterprise tools, and licenses to use them are expensive. If you are curious, you can sign up for limited trials; but to fully understand the capabilities of these tools, you also need a complex application.

In the course of this book, the applications built are of small or medium complexity. Any of the previous tools for application management would be considered overkill. The purpose of this chapter is to introduce you to the monitoring capabilities of Spring Boot. But before jumping to that, let's look at how basic monitoring for a classic Spring web application is done.

Simple Monitoring of a Spring Application

In this section, we use a very small Spring web application that exposes the REST services that manage `Person` and `Detective` instances. To make things simple, the application is organized using the package by feature model. The root context is declared using a single configuration class named `RootConfig`. This class contains all bean declarations except web beans; that configuration is provided by the `WebConfig` class. The structure of the application is depicted in Figure 9-1.

---

[1]App Dynamics official site: `https://www.appdynamics.com/`

[2]New Relic official site: `https://newrelic.com/`

[3]DynaTrace official site: `https://www.dynatrace.com/`

[4]JMeter official site: `https://jmeter.apache.org/`

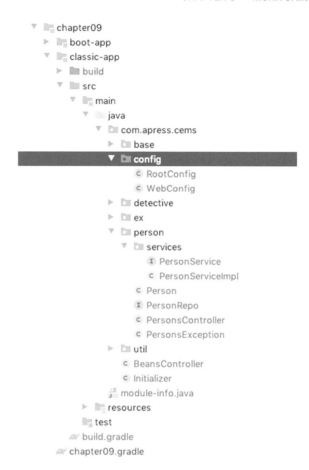

Figure 9-1. *Classic Spring web application to be monitored structure*

To run this application, an IntelliJ IDEA launcher can be created, as explained in Chapter 6. The `BeansController` in Figure 9-1 is a special REST controller that returns a map with all the beans declared within the application context. The map is populated with their names and their types.

```
package com.apress.cems;

import org.springframework.beans.BeansException;
import org.springframework.context.ApplicationContext;
import org.springframework.context.ApplicationContextAware;
import org.springframework.web.bind.annotation.GetMapping;
import org.springframework.web.bind.annotation.RestController;
```

```java
import java.util.Arrays;
import java.util.HashMap;
import java.util.Map;

@RestController
class BeansController implements ApplicationContextAware {
    private ApplicationContext ctx;

    @Override
    public void setApplicationContext(ApplicationContext
    applicationContext)
       throws BeansException {
         this.ctx = applicationContext;
    }

    @GetMapping(path = {"/", "/beans"}, produces = MediaType.APPLICATION_
    JSON_VALUE)
    Map<String,String> allBeans() {
        Map<String,String> map = new HashMap<>();
        Arrays.stream(ctx.getBeanDefinitionNames()).forEach(beanName -> {
            map.put(beanName, ctx.getBean(beanName).getClass().toString());
        });
        return map;
    }
}
```

This controller is useful because if the `http://localhost:8080/classic-app/` can be accessed, it means the application started correctly. In Figure 9-2, you can see the response returned by the `allBeans()` handler method.

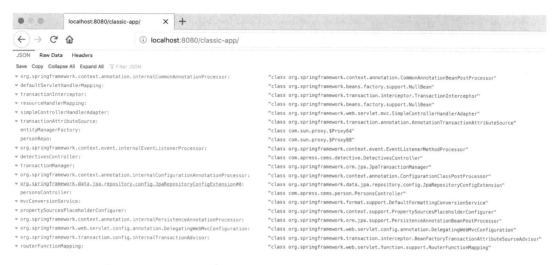

Figure 9-2. *Classic Spring web application beans*

The second reason why it is useful is because it lists all the beans making up the application context: infrastructure and specific to the business logic. Viewing all the beans can lead to optimizations because you might discover beans that are not needed in your application, or beans that are necessary only for specific functions and do not need to occupy memory all the time. All beans displayed by the controller are managed by the servlet container which is provided in this case by the Apache Tomcat server. This means that monitoring the application actually means monitoring the behavior of Apache Tomcat. The simplest way to see how the server behaves is to try to overwhelm it with requests. This is easy, because there is a JUnit 5 annotation that is very helpful with that. It's called @RepeatedTest(no). It is a specialization of @TestTemplate, which is used to mark a test method as a test template method. A test template is not a test case but rather a template for test cases. To try to overwhelm the server let's write a test class that executes 3000 POST requests to create Person instances and 3000 GET requests, that retrieve the full list of Person instances. A RestTemplate instance is used to make these calls. And because we are using JUnit Jupiter, the calls will be made in parallel, so this should do the job we are interested in.

```
package com.apress.cems;

import com.apress.cems.person.Person;
import org.junit.jupiter.api.BeforeAll;
import org.junit.jupiter.api.RepeatedTest;
import org.springframework.http.*;
```

```java
import org.springframework.web.client.DefaultResponseErrorHandler;
import org.springframework.web.client.RestTemplate;

import java.net.URI;
import java.time.LocalDateTime;

import static com.apress.cems.util.NumberGenerator.randomCharacter;
import static org.junit.jupiter.api.Assertions.*;

class PersonsControllerTest {

    private static String BASE_URL = "http://localhost:8080/classic-app/";

    private static RestTemplate restTemplate = null;

    @BeforeAll
    static void init() {
        restTemplate = new RestTemplate();
        restTemplate.setErrorHandler(new DefaultResponseErrorHandler() {
            @Override
            public boolean hasError(HttpStatus statusCode) {
                return false;
            }
        });
    }

    @RepeatedTest(3000)
    void shouldReturnAListOfPersons(){
        Person[] persons = restTemplate.getForObject(BASE_URL.concat("/
        persons"),
            Person[].class);
        assertAll(
                () -> assertNotNull(persons),
                () -> assertTrue(persons.length >= 4)
        );
    }

    @RepeatedTest(3000)
        void shouldCreateAPerson() {
            Person person = buildPerson();
```

```
    HttpHeaders headers = new HttpHeaders();
    headers.setContentType(MediaType.APPLICATION_JSON);

    HttpEntity<Person> postRequest = new HttpEntity<>(person, headers);
    URI uri = restTemplate.postForLocation(BASE_URL.concat("/persons"),
        postRequest, Person.class);

    assertNotNull(uri);
    Person newPerson = restTemplate.getForObject(uri, Person.class);
    assertAll(
            () -> assertNotNull(newPerson),
            () -> assertEquals(person.getUsername(), newPerson.
                getUsername()),
            () -> assertNotNull(newPerson.getId())
    );
}

private Person buildPerson() {
    Person person = new Person();
      ...
    return person;
}
}
```

Now we have the test class, how do we monitor Apache Server while the application is running? Simple, we use the simplest tool the JDK provides: JConsole.[5] In previous versions, Java Management Console was also part of JDK and it was started by executing the jmc executable. This is an advanced management tool as it is also able to record application activity. Now it is available as a separate download.[6] The JConsole executable can be found under JAVA_HOME/bin directory. So, after starting the IntelliJ IDEA launcher for the classic-app, open a terminal and run jconsole. In Figure 9-3, you can see the initial JConsole dialog window.

---

[5]In the previous version, VisualVM was part of the JDK monitoring tools, but it has become an independent project. Check it out if you are interested: https://visualvm.github.io/

[6]Download JMC from here: https://www.oracle.com/technetwork/java/javase/downloads/amc-download-2255283.html

Figure 9-3. JConsole initial dialog window

All local Java processes currently executing are listed in the text box. In the left column, the name of the main class is seen. On the right, there is the process identifier, which is a number used by the operating system to uniquely identify the process. The process specific to the Apache Tomcat instance can be easily identified after the name of the main class org.apache.catalina.startup.Bootstrap. Select that process and click the Connect button. The next dialog window asks the user to choose the type of connection to connect to the process; since HTTP is used, the Insecure connection button should be clicked, as depicted in Figure 9-4.

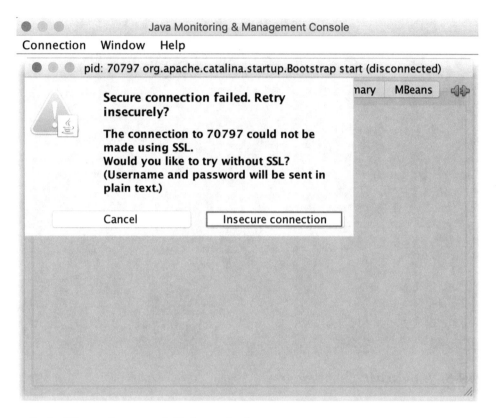

Figure 9-4. *JConsole second dialog window*

After this step, the main JConsole window is displayed. You must wait for a few seconds for the graphs to stabilize. The window is depicted in Figure 9-5.

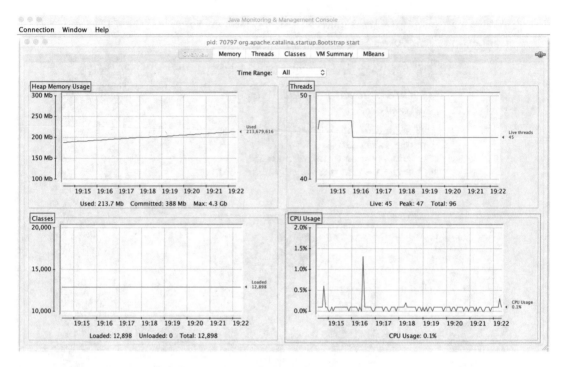

Figure 9-5.   JConsole main window

Notice the four main sections.

- **Heap Memory Usage**: Situated in the upper-left corner, it reflects the memory used by Apache Tomcat while running the `classic-app` application

- **Threads**: Situated in the upper-right corner, it reflects the number of threads created by Apache Tomcat to respond to requests to the `classic-app` application

- **Classes**: Situated in the lower-left corner, it reflects the number of classes loaded by the JDK class loader

- **CPU Usage**: Situated in the lower-right corner, it reflects the percentage of the CPU used by Apache Tomcat while running the `classic-app` application

As you start the tests, the graphs change a little, as depicted in in Figure 9-6.

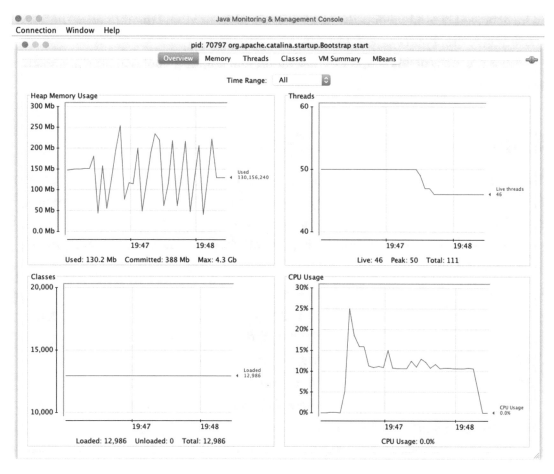

Figure 9-6. *JConsole graphs changes when tests are run*

The number of classes that are loaded won't change much, because all Spring classes are loaded at boot time. The number of threads won't change much either, since the Spring Framework is very fond of singletons. The only values that will fluctuate are the CPU percentage and the amount of memory used. The CPU consumption increases because the server needs it to resolve the parallel requests. The memory consumption spikes every time a GET request is executed, since the list of Person instances becomes bigger and drops when the Garbage Collector does its job.

By using JConsole and other such tests, the load supported by the server and the amount of CPU and memory needed to host an application can be tested. These values should be increased when the application is more complex and requires more resources. Still, the metrics that I explained previously are basic; for applications that are meant to be deployed in production, advanced tools like the ones that I mentioned at the beginning of the chapter should be used.[7]

Since the focus of this chapter is the wonder that is Spring Boot Actuator, this section will end here.

Simple Monitoring of a Spring Boot Application

The Spring Boot application built in this section has a structure identical to the classic Spring web application built previously. The only difference is that the configuration is provided by Spring Boot and customized using the `application.yml` file. The server and database are configured as introduced in previous chapters. The actuator configuration is relevant to this chapter.

! In case it wasn't obvious and to avoid any confusion, all throughout this book Spring Boot 2.x is used. There are significant differences between Spring Boot Actuator version 1.x and Spring Boot Actuator 2.x in the number of endpoints exposed, the location where they are exposed, number of metrics supported and how to configure them using properties/YAML files. So everything in this chapter only applies to Spring Boot Actuator 2.x.

The Spring Boot Actuator module provides endpoints and infrastructure beans useful for monitoring and managing a Spring Boot application. It provides production-ready features, including the following.

- health check-up: The `/health` endpoint exposes basic or detailed info, depending on the configuration.

- auditing: A flexible audit framework is provided that publishes events, security events by default, but components can be written to publish `AuditApplicationEvents`; all event information is exposed via the `/auditevents` endpoint.

---

[7]A very good article about monitoring Apache Tomcat: `https://www.comparitech.com/net-admin/tomcat-monitoring-guide-tools/`

- metrics gathering: The /metrics endpoint is provided that can be used diagnostically to examine the metrics collected by an application;[8] default dependency management and auto-configuration are provided for Micrometer, a metric facade that supports multiple monitoring systems. Read more about it at https://micrometer.io/.

- HTTP tracing: Enabled automatically for all requests, using the / httptrace endpoint.

The Spring Boot Actuator documentation is pretty good, and although it feels a little useless to repeat a lot of details in this book,[9] the most used configuration techniques are going to be depicted and working code is provided to test them. Spring exposes all this information about your application using HTTP or JMX, depending on your needs. In the next sections, all configurations cover web-specific properties, but equivalent configuration properties exist for JMX too.

Default Endpoints

Let's start with configuring the actuator. To do this, the spring-boot-starter-actuator module must be added to the classpath of the project.

```
//pivotal-certified-pro-spring-dev-exam-02/build.gradle
ext {
    springBootVersion = '2.2.0.M5',
    ...
    boot = [
        actuator :
            "org.springframework.boot:spring-boot-starter-
            actuator:$springBootVersion",
        ...
    ]
}
```

---

[8]It integrates with monitoring systems introduced at the beginning of the chapter like New Relic, but also others like Prometheus, Influx and graphing solutions like Graphana

[9]Since the documentation is public and can be accessed here: https://docs.spring.io/spring-boot/docs/current/reference/html/howto-actuator.html

```
//chapter09/boot-app/build.gradle
dependencies {
    implementation boot.starterJpa, boot.starterWeb
    runtimeOnly misc.h2
    implementation boot.actuator
    ...
}
```

After adding the dependency without any other configuration, two actuator endpoints are provided out of the box (/health and /info) under the /actuator prefix. They can be viewed by accessing http://localhost:8081/actuator. In Figure 9-7, you can see the main actuator page.

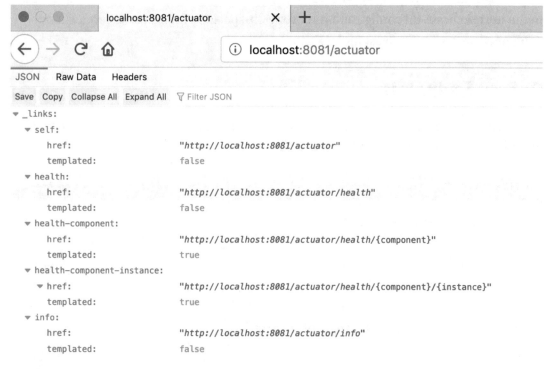

Figure 9-7. *Spring Boot actuator default exposed endpoints. To do this, the* spring-boot

For example, the /health endpoint exposes basic information about the application's health. By default, it just returns {"status":"UP"} - yes, really basic. To view more details the property management.endpoint.health.show-details must be set to always in the application.yml file.

```
management:
  endpoint:
    health:
      show-details: always
```

With this setting in place, details about the database used and its status are provided, along with the details about the disk space.

```
{
  "status": "UP",
  "details": {
    "db": {
      "status": "UP",
      "details": {
        "database": "H2",
        "result": 1,
        "validationQuery": "SELECT 1"
      }
    },
    "diskSpace": {
      "status": "UP",
      "details": {
        "total": 499963170816,
        "free": 324985479168,
        "threshold": 10485760
      }
    }
  }
}
```

Most endpoints are sensitive (they are not public by default), so if the application is secured, most information exposed by them will be omitted. The grouping of all endpoints under /actuator, was introduced in Spring Boot 2.x. In the previous version,

each available endpoint was exposed directly under the application context, so the /
health endpoint was exposed under http://localhost:8081/health.

Customizing the endpoints' root path is possible if you do not like the actuator
name or if you want to use it for something else. (I'm not sure anybody would need to
do that, but it's nice to know you have the freedom to do it.) by setting the management.
endpoints.web.base-path property with a different value in the application.yml file.
For example, the next configuration exposes all actuator endpoints under /monitoring.

```
management:
  endpoints:
    web:
      base-path: /monitoring
```

Also, existing endpoints can be mapped to different paths by setting the management.
endpoints.web.path-mapping.[ID] property to the new path. The following
configuration exposes the health endpoint on /actuator/salud.

```
management:
  endpoints:
    web:
      path-mapping:
        health: salud
```

Customizing the port on which the actuator endpoints are exposed can be done by
setting the management.server.port property with a chosen value in the application.
yml file. This helps isolate this feature from the actual API of the application.

```
management:
  server:
    port: 9091
```

And, if for security reasons, we want these endpoints to be accessible only internally,
the IP address can be configured by setting the management.server.address property
with a specific value in the application.yml. In the following configuration, the IP the
application can be accessed on is the general one 0.0.0.0, but access to the endpoints is
restricted only to 127.0.0.1.

```
server:
  port: 8081
  address: 0.0.0.0
management:
  server:
    port: 9091
    address: 127.0.0.1
```

Another simple endpoint is the /info endpoint. This endpoint displays general information about the project that is being read from META-INF/build-info.properties or Git files like git.properties, or through any environment property under the info key. The information exposed by this endpoint can be configured using the application.yml file. By default, as expected, accessing this endpoint displays the JSON equivalent of nothing ({}). Adding the following properties in the application.yml file, makes this endpoint a little most useful.

```
info:
    app:
      name: Spring Actuator Application
      description: This is a very simple Spring Boot Application
      version: 1.0-SNAPSHOT
```

When accessing the /info endpoint, the following text is returned:

```
{
  "app": {
    "name": "Spring Actuator Application",
    "description": "This is a very simple Spring Boot Application",
    "version": "1.0-SNAPSHOT"
  }
}
```

Customized endpoints can be tested just like any REST service using the Spring Boot test module. The only difference is that the management port must be injected instead of the application port when testing, which is done by using the @Value annotation to inject the value of the local.management.port custom key into a local test field to construct the test URLs. The following codes snippet depicts a test class containing a test method that verifies the contents of the response returned by accessing the /info endpoint.

```java
package com.apress.cems;
...
@ActiveProfiles("one")
@SpringBootTest(webEnvironment = SpringBootTest.WebEnvironment.RANDOM_PORT)
class RestApplicationOneTest {
    @Value("${local.management.port}")
    private int mgt;

    private String mgtUrl = "http://localhost";

    private static RestTemplate restTemplate = null;

    @BeforeAll
    static void init() {
        restTemplate = new RestTemplate();
    }

    @BeforeEach
    void setUp(){
        mgtUrl = mgtUrl.concat(":").concat(mgt + "").concat("/monitoring");
    }

    @Test
    void shouldReturn200WhenSendingRequestToInfoEndpoint() {
        @SuppressWarnings("rawtypes")
        ResponseEntity<Map> entity = restTemplate.getForEntity(
                mgtUrl.concat("/info"), Map.class);

        @SuppressWarnings("unchecked")
        Map<String, String> content = (Map<String, String>) entity
            .getBody().get("app");

        assertAll(
                () -> assertEquals(HttpStatus.OK, entity.getStatusCode()),
                () -> assertEquals(3, content.size()),
```

```
        () -> assertEquals("Spring Actuator Application",
            content.get("name")),
        () -> assertEquals("1.0-SNAPSHOT", content.get("version"))
    );
  }
}
```

The configurations provided in this chapter are not always compatible with each other, so they have been split in YAML files named `application-one.yml`, `application-two.yml` and so on, and the `@ActivateProfiles` activates the property file specific to the profile received as argument. This makes it easier for you to test and customize the source code without affecting the application too much.

Customizing the `/info` endpoint seems easy to do, but can we customize any other endpoints? Sure, we are still talking about a Spring project here, so everything is customizable. For example, customizing the output of the `/health` endpoint can be done by declaring a bean of a type implementing the `org.springframework.boot.actuate.health.HealthIndicator` functional interface. Any type implementing that interface is used to provide an indicator of the application's health. Spring Boot Actuator contains quite a few auto-configured `HealthIndicator` implementations for all databases and services supported.(For example, `CassandraHealthIndicator` checks that a Cassandra database is up, `JmsHealthIndicator` checks that a JMS broker is up, etc.)[10]

Just for the fun of it, let's create an implementation that communicates that the database population was successful.

```
package com.apress.cems.mine;

import org.springframework.beans.BeansException;
import org.springframework.boot.actuate.health.Health;
import org.springframework.boot.actuate.health.HealthIndicator;
import org.springframework.context.ApplicationContext;
import org.springframework.context.ApplicationContextAware;
import org.springframework.context.annotation.Profile;
...
```

---

[10]Full list available here: `https://docs.spring.io/spring-boot/docs/current/reference/html/production-ready-endpoints.html#_auto_configured_healthindicators`

```java
@Profile("two")
@Component
public class HealthChecker implements HealthIndicator,
    ApplicationContextAware {
    private ApplicationContext ctx;

    @Override
    public void setApplicationContext(ApplicationContext
    applicationContext)
        throws BeansException {
        this.ctx = applicationContext;
    }

    @Override
    public Health health() {
        // check initialization of Person table by counting the records
        Map<String,String> inits = new HashMap<>();
        if(personCheck(ctx.getBean(PersonRepo.class))) {
            inits.put("personInit","SUCCESSFUL");
        } else {
            return Health.down().withDetail("personInit", "FAILED").
            build();
        }
        if(detectiveCheck(ctx.getBean(DetectiveRepo.class))) {
            inits.put("detectiveInit","SUCCESSFUL");
        } else {
            return Health.down().withDetail("detectiveInit", "FAILED").
            build();
        }
        return Health.up().withDetails(inits).build();
    }

    private boolean personCheck(PersonRepo personRepo){
        return personRepo.findAll().size() == 4;
    }
```

```
    private boolean detectiveCheck(DetectiveRepo detectiveRepo){
        return detectiveRepo.findAll().size() == 4;
    }
}
```

The `Health.Builder` static class is a builder class used to construct a `Health` instance, with the details of the application that are being checked. The properties of this instance are added to the existing set of details exposed by the actuator `/health` endpoint. If everything is OK, the builder should create a `Health` instance using the `up()` method, that sets the status property to `"UP"` on this instance and adds the details specific to each inspected component. If not, a `Health` instance should be created with the `down()` method that sets the status property to `"DOWN"` on this instance and adds the details telling which component failed. The final system state is derived by an implementation of the `HealthAggregator` functional interface, which sorts the statuses from each `HealthIndicator` based on an ordered list of statuses. If a `HealthIndicator` is found with a of the `"DOWN"` status the HTTP response status is also set to 503 (Service Unavailable).

There are four health status values declared in the `org.springframework.boot.actuate.health.Status` final class. They are mapped to HTTP status codes by the `HealthStatusHttpMapper` class (from the same package).

- UP is mapped to HTTP status 200 (OK)

- DOWN is mapped to HTTP status 503 (Service Unavailable)

- OUT_OF_SERVICE means no explicit mapping; defaults to HTTP status 200 (ok)

- UNKNOWN means no explicit mapping; defaults to HTTP status 200 (OK)

New statuses can be declared and mapped to HTTP status code using YAML (properties) configuration. For example, the next snippet declares a status named FATAL, and maps it to HTTP status code 501. And since we've added a new status instance, we are customizing the severity order too.

```
management:
  health:
    status:
      http-mapping:
```

```
      FATAL: 501
      order: FATAL, DOWN, OUT_OF_SERVICE, UNKNOWN, UP
```

We declared it; now we must use it. It is quite simple. In the previous implementation, rather than calling Health.down(), we'll call Health.status(FATAL) after creating the new status instance.

```
...
@Component
public class HealthChecker implements HealthIndicator,
ApplicationContextAware {

    private final static Status FATAL = new Status("FATAL", "All Systems
    Down!");
    ...

    @Override
    public Health health() {
        // check initialization of Person table by counting the records

        Map<String,String> inits = new HashMap<>();
        if(personCheck(ctx.getBean(PersonRepo.class))) {
            inits.put("personInit","SUCCESSFUL");
        } else {
            return Health.status(FATAL).withDetail("personInit", "FAILED").
            build();
        }
        if(detectiveCheck(ctx.getBean(DetectiveRepo.class))) {
            inits.put("detectiveInit","SUCCESSFUL");
        } else {
            return Health.status(FATAL).withDetail("detectiveInit",
            "FAILED").build();
        }
        return Health.up().withDetails(inits).build();
    }
    ...
}
```

The bean of HealthChecker type has been annotated with the @Profile("two") meaning it will be part of the context only when this profile is enabled. This is also done, so it doesn't clash with other configurations that will be introduced in this chapter. To test the effect of this bean on the output produced by accessing the /health endpoint, we can write another test and activate the two profile for it.

```
package com.apress.cems;
...

@ActiveProfiles("two")
@SpringBootTest(webEnvironment = SpringBootTest.WebEnvironment.RANDOM_PORT)
class RestApplicationTwoTest {
    ...
    @Test
    void shouldReturn200WhenSendingRequestToHealthEndpoint() {
        @SuppressWarnings("rawtypes")
        ResponseEntity<Map> entity = restTemplate.getForEntity(
                mgtUrl.concat("/health"), Map.class);

        @SuppressWarnings("unchecked")
        Map<String,String> content = (Map<String, String>) ((Map)
            ((Map) Objects.requireNonNull(entity.getBody()).get("details"))
            .get("healthChecker")).get("details");

        assertAll(
                () -> assertEquals(HttpStatus.OK, entity.getStatusCode()),
                () -> assertTrue(content.containsKey("personInit")),
                () -> assertTrue(content.containsKey("detectiveInit"))
        );
    }
}
```

Extracting the map with the properties added by our bean is doable. It is also unnecessary, because checking the response status is enough, considering that if any HealthIndicator implementation returns a Health instance with the status property on anything but UP, the response status code is set to 503. If inspecting the response contents is necessary, the test can be run in debug and the execution paused to do so, as depicted in Figure 9-8.

```
    @Test
    void shouldReturn200WhenSendingRequestToHealthEndpoint() {
        /rawtypes/
        ResponseEntity<Map> entity = restTemplate.getForEntity(  entity: "<200,{stat
            mgtUrl.concat("/health"), Map.class);

        assertEquals(HttpStatus.OK, entity.getStatusCode());  entity: "<200,{status=
    }
```

RestApplicationTwoTest > shouldReturn200WhenSendingRequestToHealthEndpoint()

)9:boot-app:test ×

Variables

▶ ≡ this = {RestApplicationTwoTest@12612}
▼ ≡ entity = {ResponseEntity@12613} "<200,{status=UP, details={healthChecker={status=UP,
    ▶ ⓕ status = {Integer@12681} 200
    ▶ ⓕ headers = {ReadOnlyHttpHeaders@12682} size = 4
    ▼ ⓕ body = {LinkedHashMap@12614} size = 2
        ▶ ≡ "status" -> "UP"
        ▼ ≡ "details" -> {LinkedHashMap@12705} size = 3
            ▶ ≡ key = "details"
            ▼ ≡ value = {LinkedHashMap@12705} size = 3
                ▼ ≡ "healthChecker" -> {LinkedHashMap@12712} size = 2
                    ▶ ≡ key = "healthChecker"
                    ▼ ≡ value = {LinkedHashMap@12712} size = 2
                        ▶ ≡ "status" -> "UP"
                        ▼ ≡ "details" -> {LinkedHashMap@12722} size = 2
                            ▶ ≡ key = "details"
                            ▼ ≡ value = {LinkedHashMap@12722} size = 2
                                ▶ ≡ "personInit" -> "SUCCESSFUL"
                                ▶ ≡ "detectiveInit" -> "SUCCESSFUL"
                ▶ ≡ "db" -> {LinkedHashMap@12714} size = 2
                ▶ ≡ "diskSpace" -> {LinkedHashMap@12716} size = 2
```

*Figure 9-8.* Inspecting contents of the response received from a customized /health endpoint

Spring Boot Actuator provides a big collection of endpoints exposing data (usually in JSON format) that can be interpreted by more advanced monitoring systems. The full list of endpoints can be seen in the official documentation: `https://docs.spring.io/spring-boot/docs/current/reference/html/production-ready-endpoints.html#production-ready-endpoints`, and a few of them will be listed and explained in the next section after you will be taught how to enable, disable, expose or hide some of them.
```

Exposing/Enabling and Hiding/Disabling Actuator Endpoints

Almost all actuator endpoints are enabled when the Spring Boot Actuator starter library is on the classpath, except the /shutdown endpoint that allows the application to be gracefully shut down. You can imagine why this endpoint shouldn't be that easily accessible, right? Also, there are some endpoints specific only to web applications, so there would be no point to enable those for a non-web application, right?

Most endpoints are enabled, but only a few are exposed by default, as shown in Figure 9-7. In this section, a few configurations covering exposing/hiding and enabling/disabling endpoints are presented.

Let's start by exposing them all. This can be easily done by setting the management.endpoints.web.exposure.include property to "*". Since we are using YAML format for our configuration, the following snippet does just what is needed, but using YAML syntax.

```
management:
  endpoints:
    web:
      exposure:
        include: "*"
```

If we start the application now and access http://localhost:8081/actuator/, the output has become increasingly bigger, a lot more endpoints are exposed. The following are descriptions of the most important ones.

- /beans - do you remember the BeansController that was written for a classic Spring web application? Well, this endpoint is the advanced version of that, because it exposes all the beans in the context and their properties such as, aliases, scope, and dependencies. If you access this endpoint for a Spring Boot web application, the first thing you will notice is that there are a lot more infrastructure beans than compared to a classic Spring web application. This is the drawback of Spring Boot applications, the infrastructure is much more complex, some beans are part of the context although you might not use them, there are the beans that make up the embedded server and as expected beans that make up the actuator.

- `/auditevents`: Exposes audit events information (by default, only events regarding security, failed and successful login/logout operations, but it can be extended with customized audit events)

- `/caches`: Exposes available caches and when suffixed with `/{cacheName}` exposes that cache's details (supports filtering)

- `/conditions`: Exposes information about conditions and auto-configuration

- `/health`: Exposes basic application health information (supports filtering)

- `/info`: Exposes arbitrary application info

- `/configprops`: Exposes all properties (including those declared with `@ConfigurationProperties`) used to configure the application (if you access `http://localhost:8081/actuator/configprops` you can easily find the properties read from the `application.yml` file)

- `/env`: Exposes environment details, including the application classpath. This endpoint supports filtering, so accessing `http://localhost:8081/actuator/env/java.class.path` will expose only the application classpath.

- `/loggers`: Exposes information about application logging, can customize logging while the application is running and supports filtering

- `/heapdump` and `/threadump`: Performs a heapdump[11] and a threadump.[12]

- `/mappings`: Exposes information about all `@RequestMapping` paths (including information about the actuator endpoint mappings)

- `/metrics`: Exposes metrics for the application. This endpoint supports filtering. Just access `http://localhost:8081/actuator/`

---

[11]Contents of a heapdump file can be inspected using the *JMC* `https://www.oracle.com/technetwork/java/javase/downloads/amc-download-2255283.html` utility or the Eclipse Memory Analyzer `https://www.eclipse.org/mat/`

[12]A very good article on how to read and interpret the contents of a thread dump `https://dzone.com/articles/how-to-read-a-thread-dump`

metrics, pick a metric name, and then access the `http://localhost:8081/actuator/metrics/{metricName}` to view current values for it

We've exposed all the endpoints. How do we hide them all? The `management.endpoints.web.exposure.exclude` property to cut HTTP access to all actuator endpoints the must be set to "*".

```
management:
  endpoints:
    web:
      exposure:
        exclude: "*"
```

This is fine, but there are certainly situations where *all or none* does not apply, right? Well, to expose only some of the endpoints, a combination of the two property names, wildcards and endpoint names can be used.

The `management.endpoints.web.exposure.exclude` property lists the IDs of the endpoints that should not be exposed.

The `management.endpoints.web.exposure.include` property lists the IDs of the endpoints that are exposed

The next configuration exposes all endpoints, except the ones specified as value for the `management.endpoints.web.exposure.exclude` property.

```
management:
  endpoints:
    web:
      exposure:
        include: "*"
        exclude: env,beans,mapping,configprops
```

Accessing an endpoint that is not exposed (or does not exist) results in an empty response with HTTP status error code of 404 (Not Found). It was mentioned at the beginning of this section that the `/shutdown` is disabled. If we write a test to check access to it, the observation is that the response is the same as if the endpoint were not exposed.

```
package com.apress.cems;
...

@ActiveProfiles("three")
@SpringBootTest(webEnvironment = SpringBootTest.WebEnvironment.RANDOM_PORT)
class RestApplicationThreeTest {
    ...
    @Test
    void shouldReturn404WhenSendingRequestToShutdownEndpoint() {
        ResponseEntity<Map> entity = restTemplate.getForEntity(
                mgtUrl.concat("/shutdown"), Map.class);

        assertEquals(HttpStatus.NOT_FOUND, entity.getStatusCode());
    }
}
```

So, let's enable it, shall we? To enable any endpoint Spring Boot provides the management.endpoint.<endpointID>.enabled, where endpointID is the name of the endpoint. So enabling the /shutdown endpoint requires the management.endpoint. shutdown.enabled to be set on true in the YAML file (or properties, whichever you prefer).

```
management:
  endpoint:
    shutdown:
      enabled: true
```

Now the endpoint is enabled and exposed. How do we test it? To shut down the application, a POST request should be sent to this endpoint. So we write another test, and we use restTemplate.exchange(...) to send the request. If successful, the response HTTP status code should be 200 (OK), so we test this assumption. The response is 200, because 201 makes no sense in this context; nothing is created. The application is receiving a request to shut down. The 200 is the confirmation that the request was received, and it will be resolved accordingly.

```
package com.apress.cems;
...

@ActiveProfiles("four")
@SpringBootTest(webEnvironment = SpringBootTest.WebEnvironment.RANDOM_PORT)
```

```
class RestApplicationFourTest {
    ...
 @Test
    void shouldReturn200WhenSendingRequestToShutdownEndpoint() {
        final HttpHeaders headers = new HttpHeaders();
        headers.setContentType(MediaType.APPLICATION_JSON);

        final HttpEntity postRequest = new HttpEntity(headers);
        ResponseEntity<Map>  entity = restTemplate.exchange(mgtUrl.
        concat("/shutdown"),
            HttpMethod.POST, postRequest, Map.class);

        assertEquals(HttpStatus.OK, entity.getStatusCode());
    }
}
```

Spring Boot Actuator also supports the management.endpoints.enabled-by-default that can be set to false to disable all endpoints by default. This means, that endpoints can then be specifically enabled by setting management.endpoint.<endpointID>.enabled to true. Although more granular, this method provides a readable list of actuators that are enabled.

Another endpoint that you might find useful is the /loggers endpoint, because it allows you to configure log levels while the application is running. You can access the entire list of loggers and configurations by accessing http://localhost:8081/actuator/loggers. From that list you can choose one and submit a POST request to the http://localhost:8081/actuator/loggers/[ID] containing a map with the logging property you want to set and its value.

For example, when we access the http://0.0.0.0:8081/actuator/loggers/com.apress.cems.Initializer we get this:

```
{
      "configuredLevel":null,
      "effectiveLevel":"INFO"
}
```

The POST request body is a part of the previous map containing only the property we want to set and the new value for it. You can use Postman for this, or you can write a test. The next code snippet contains a test method that sends a POST request to `http://0.0.0.0:8081/actuator/loggers/com.apress.cems.Initializer` and then makes a GET request to the same URL and checks if the property was set.

```
@Test
  void shouldReturn200WhenSendingRequestToLoggerEndpoint() {
      @SuppressWarnings("rawtypes")

      final HttpHeaders headers = new HttpHeaders();
      headers.setContentType(MediaType.APPLICATION_JSON);

      var levelCfg = Map.of("configuredLevel", "DEBUG");
      HttpEntity<Map<String,String>> postRequest =
          new HttpEntity<>(levelCfg, headers);
      ResponseEntity<Map>  entity = restTemplate.exchange(
              mgtUrl.concat("/loggers/com.apress.cems.Initializer"),
              HttpMethod.POST, postRequest, Map.class);

      assertEquals(HttpStatus.NO_CONTENT, entity.getStatusCode());

      ResponseEntity<Map>  response = restTemplate.exchange(
              mgtUrl.concat("/loggers/com.apress.cems.Initializer"),
              HttpMethod.GET, postRequest, Map.class);
      assertEquals("DEBUG",
          Objects.requireNonNull(response.getBody()).
          get("configuredLevel"));
  }
```

‼   Some endpoints support filtering and the data they display can be reduced by adding component names as suffixes to their URIs. Depending on the endpoint in question, those values can be bean names, fully qualified class names, property names, and so forth. You might think of them as path variables or filters, but the Pivotal team prefers to call them **tags**. So, if you see tag referenced with actuators in the certification exam, know that this is what they are referring to.

Securing Actuator Endpoints

Some actuator endpoints expose sensitive data that should not be exposed publicly. Sure, we can configure actuator endpoints to be available only on an internal IP, but the best way to secure sensitive information is to set up an authentication and authorization process. As shown in Chapter 7, securing an application using Spring Boot is simple. Well, securing actuator endpoints is not hard either, since Spring Boot provides a class named EndpointRequest that can be used in combination with the requestMatcher(..) method to configure who should have access to the actuator endpoints. The configuration is depicted in the following code snippet.

```
package com.apress.cems.sec.config;
import org.springframework.boot.actuate.autoconfigure.security.servlet.
EndpointRequest;

...

@Configuration
@EnableWebSecurity
@ComponentScan("com.apress.cems.sec")
class SecurityConfig extends WebSecurityConfigurerAdapter {

    ...
    @Override
    protected void configure(final HttpSecurity http) throws Exception {
        http.csrf().disable()
                .exceptionHandling()
                .accessDeniedHandler(accessDeniedHandler)
                .authenticationEntryPoint(restAuthenticationEntryPoint)
                .and()
                .authorizeRequests()
                .mvcMatchers("/persons/**").hasRole("USER")
                .mvcMatchers("/detectives/**").hasRole("ADMIN")
                .mvcMatchers("/**").hasAnyRole("ADMIN", "USER")
```

```
                    .and()
                    .formLogin()
                    .successHandler(authenticationSuccessHandler)
                    .failureHandler(authenticationFailureHandler)
                    .and()
                    .requestMatcher(EndpointRequest.toAnyEndpoint()).
                    authorizeRequests()
                    .anyRequest().hasRole("ADMIN")
                    .and()
                    .httpBasic()
                    .and()
                    .logout();
    }
}
```

In the previous configuration, only authenticated users with the ADMIN role have access to the /actuator endpoint.

Now that an actuator requires basic authentication, accessing http://0.0.0.0:8081/actuator/[13] in a browser no longer works for a user that is not authenticated. Sure, we can write tests using a TestRestTemplate instance, but the quickest way to test the configuration is to create a Postman GET request with Basic Authentication, like the one depicted in Figure 9-9.

---

[13]The *server.address* property is set to the generic 0.0.0.0 IP address in the configuration for this application. http://localhost:8081/actuator/ and http://127.0.0.01:8081/actuator/ can be used as well.

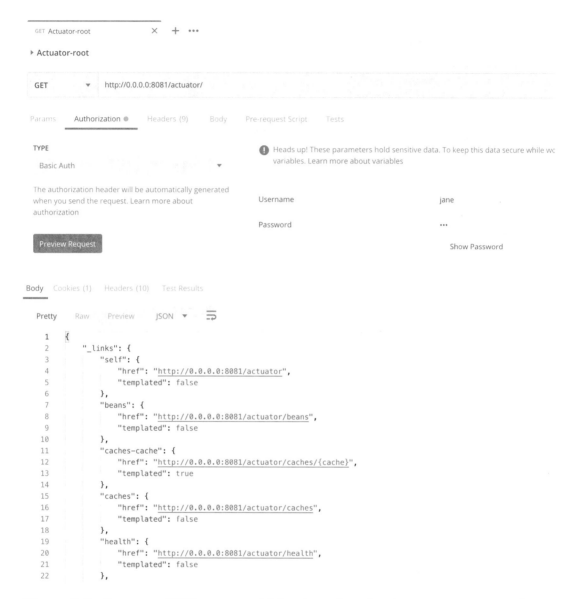

Figure 9-9. *Postman GET request with basic authentication to test access to the Actuator main page*

If you want to filter the exposed endpoints based on roles, there is the possibility to customize, because the EndpointRequest provides a method named to(..) that receives as arguments a list of endpoints to apply the security rules to. In the next code snippet, access to the /health and /info is configured for users with role USER.

```
package com.apress.cems.sec.config;
import org.springframework.boot.actuate.autoconfigure.security.servlet.
EndpointRequest;
...

@Configuration
@EnableWebSecurity
@ComponentScan("com.apress.cems.sec")
class SecurityConfig extends WebSecurityConfigurerAdapter {
    ...
    @Override
    protected void configure(final HttpSecurity http) throws Exception {
        http.csrf().disable()
                .exceptionHandling()
                .accessDeniedHandler(accessDeniedHandler)
                .authenticationEntryPoint(restAuthenticationEntryPoint)
                .and()
                .authorizeRequests()
                .mvcMatchers("/persons/**").hasRole("USER")
                .mvcMatchers("/detectives/**").hasRole("ADMIN")
                .mvcMatchers("/**").hasAnyRole("ADMIN", "USER")
                .and()
                .formLogin()
                .successHandler(authenticationSuccessHandler)
                .failureHandler(authenticationFailureHandler)
                .and()
                .requestMatcher(EndpointRequest.to("health", "info"))
                    .authorizeRequests()
                .anyRequest().hasRole("USER")
                .and()
                .httpBasic()
                .and()
                .logout();
    }
}
```

When configuring access to an endpoint, we use its name—health, info, beans, and so forth. When discussing the information that the endpoint exposes, we use the URL where it can be accessed—\health, \info, \beans, and so forth.

And that's all there is really. Now we can test actuator endpoints access in the same way depicted until now, by using the TestRestTemplate instance so that authentication can be performed, or Postman. If you are feeling adventurous, you can try REST Assured.

Custom Endpoints

As expected, Spring Boot Actuator provides the option to create your own endpoints. This is done by annotating a bean with @Endpoint. Annotating its methods with @ReadOperation (handling GET requests), @WriteOperation (handling POST requests)[14] and @DeleteOperation (handling DELETE requests) exposes them over JMX and HTTP both. If only JMX access is desired then the @Endpoint annotation should be replaced with its specialization for JMX: @JmxEndpoint. If only HTTP access is required then the @Endpoint annotation should be replaced with its specialization for HTTP: @WebEndpoint. All the annotations mentioned here are in the org.springframework.boot.actuate.endpoint subpackages. Anyway, let's get practical and try to create an HTTP endpoint that exposes if the population of tables in the database succeeded.

@Endpoint, @JmxEndpoint, and @WebEndpoint declare two attributes: id, which is the identifier of the endpoint (this is mandatory), and enableByDefault, which is true by default. It can enable or disable an endpoint. With this information at hand, let's look at the endpoint implementation.

```
package com.apress.cems.sec.mine;

import com.apress.cems.sec.detective.DetectiveRepo;
import com.apress.cems.sec.person.PersonRepo;
import org.springframework.beans.BeansException;
import org.springframework.boot.actuate.endpoint.annotation.
DeleteOperation;
import org.springframework.boot.actuate.endpoint.annotation.ReadOperation;
import org.springframework.boot.actuate.endpoint.annotation.Selector;
import org.springframework.boot.actuate.endpoint.annotation.WriteOperation;
```

---

[14]PUT operations are not supported, also there's really no point for them either. Why would you want to change any kind of information about the system anyway?

```java
import org.springframework.boot.actuate.endpoint.web.annotation.
WebEndpoint;
import org.springframework.context.ApplicationContext;
import org.springframework.context.ApplicationContextAware;
import org.springframework.data.jpa.repository.JpaRepository;
import org.springframework.stereotype.Component;

import java.util.LinkedHashMap;
import java.util.Map;

@Component
@WebEndpoint(id = "dao")
public class DaoEndpoint implements ApplicationContextAware {
    private ApplicationContext ctx;

    @Override
    public void setApplicationContext(ApplicationContext
    applicationContext)
        throws BeansException {
        this.ctx = applicationContext;
    }

    @ReadOperation
    public DaoHealth daoHealth(){
        Map<String, Object> details = new LinkedHashMap<>();
        if(personCheck(ctx.getBean(PersonRepo.class))) {
            details.put("personInit","SUCCESSFUL");
        }
        if(detectiveCheck(ctx.getBean(DetectiveRepo.class))) {
            details.put("detectiveInit","SUCCESSFUL");
        }
        DaoHealth daoHealth = new DaoHealth();
        daoHealth.setDaoDetails(details);
        return daoHealth;
    }

    @ReadOperation
    public DaoHealth repoHealth(@Selector String name){
```

```
    JpaRepository repo = (JpaRepository) ctx.getBean(name);
    Map<String, Object> details = new LinkedHashMap<>();
    if(repo instanceof PersonRepo && personCheck((PersonRepo) repo)) {
        details.put("personInit","SUCCESSFUL");
    } else if(repo instanceof DetectiveRepo &&
        detectiveCheck((DetectiveRepo) repo)) {
        details.put("detectiveInit","SUCCESSFUL");
    } else {
        details.put("repoInit", "N/A");
    }
    DaoHealth daoHealth = new DaoHealth();
    daoHealth.setDaoDetails(details);
    return daoHealth;
}

@WriteOperation
public void writeOperation(@Selector String name) {
    ...
}

@DeleteOperation
public void deleteOperation(@Selector String name){
    ...
}

private boolean personCheck(PersonRepo personRepo){
    return personRepo.findAll().size() == 4;
}

private boolean detectiveCheck(DetectiveRepo detectiveRepo){
    return detectiveRepo.findAll().size() == 4;
}
}
```

The @Selector annotation that you see as a prefix for all the operation methods indicates that a parameter can be used to select a subset of the endpoint's data.

The methods exposed by the endpoint need to return an instance that can be serialized to JSON. For this purpose, the class DaoHealth was created.

```
package com.apress.cems.sec.mine;

import com.fasterxml.jackson.annotation.JsonAnyGetter;
import com.fasterxml.jackson.annotation.JsonInclude;

import java.util.Map;

@JsonInclude(JsonInclude.Include.NON_EMPTY)
public class DaoHealth {
    private Map<String, Object> daoDetails;

    @JsonAnyGetter
    public Map<String, Object> getDaoDetails() {
        return this.daoDetails;
    }

    public void setDaoDetails(Map<String, Object> daoDetails) {
        this.daoDetails = daoDetails;
    }
}
```

The annotations used in this class customize how the values will be serialized. The @JsonInclude(JsonInclude.Include.NON_EMPTY) makes sure that if the daoDetails is an empty map, an empty JSON object ({}) is returned. The @JsonAnyGetter is a special annotation. When used on key-value pairs it allows the flexibility of using a Map<K,V> field as a standard property.

Now let's get back to the endpoint class. The @WebEndpoint(id = "dao") annotation sets the id of the endpoint to dao. This means that to access this endpoint the base URL is http://0.0.0.0:8081/actuator/dao. Two methods annotated with @ReadOperation are provided, because the endpoint was designed to support filtering.

So sending a GET request to http://0.0.0.0:8081/actuator/dao without a path variable endpoint returns the following.

```
{
    "personInit": "SUCCESSFUL",
    "detectiveInit": "SUCCESSFUL"
}
```

The daoHealth() method is called when accessing the URL mentioned above, because it is annotated with @ReadOperation. And since there is no parameter annotated with @Selector, it does not support filtering.

And sending a GET request to http://0.0.0.0:8081/actuator/dao/personRepo endpoint returns:

```
{
    "personInit": "SUCCESSFUL"
}
```

The repoHealth(..) method is called when accessing the URL mentioned above, because it is annotated with @ReadOperation. And since there is a parameter annotated with @Selector, it supports filtering. The personRepo value is injected into the parameter annotated with @Selector.

The methods annotated with @WriteOperation and @DeleteOperation have empty bodies and are added to the example just for teaching purposes, since, a POST and DELETE request have no sense for an endpoint that exposes application health information.

Enough about endpoints. It is time to see how the data exposed by them is actually used.

Using Spring Boot Actuator with Micrometer

If you expand the dependency tree in the Gradle view in IntelliJ IDEA, you will notice that one of the dependencies of the spring-boot-starter-actuator is the micrometer-core dependency. You should see something similar to what is depicted in Figure 9-10.

Figure 9-10. *Gradle view in IntelliJ IDEA showing the micrometer-core dependency*

This dependency is used for gathering metrics that are exposed by the /metrics endpoint. Micrometer is an open source metrics facade that provides a vendor-neutral metrics collection API (the parent abstract class of all these metric implementations is io.micrometer.core.instrument.MeterRegistry[15]). The implementations for a variety of monitoring systems were mentioned at the beginning of this chapter. It can be used with Spring Boot Actuator, but it is an independent platform that can be used by itself. If it's hard to wrap your head around it, think of SLF4J. SLF4J is a facade or abstraction for various logging frameworks. This means the developer can use SLF4J to write log messages that are gathered and written to the desired support by the framework configured by the application. In this book SLF4J is used together with Logback Classic, but if we were to change our mind, we could easily swap Logback Classic with Log4j2, without any need of changes in the code.

You could have the same for metrics starting with Spring Boot Actuator 2.x. Micrometer can gather metrics and expose them in a format that any (almost) advanced monitoring system can interpret.

---

[15]Source code here: https://github.com/micrometer-metrics/micrometer/blob/master/ micrometer-core/src/main/java/io/micrometer/core/instrument/MeterRegistry.java

Spring Boot 2 autoconfigures a long list of metrics out of the box. This list is returned by a GET request to the `http://0.0.0.0:8081/actuator/metrics` endpoint. The next code listing depicts the names of these metrics.

```
{
    "names": [
        "jvm.threads.states",
        "jdbc.connections.active",
        "process.files.max",
        "jvm.gc.memory.promoted",
        "hikaricp.connections.idle",
        "jvm.memory.max",
        "hikaricp.connections.pending",
        "jvm.memory.used",
        "system.load.average.1m",
        "jvm.gc.max.data.size",
        "jdbc.connections.max",
        "jdbc.connections.min",
        "jvm.memory.committed",
        "hikaricp.connections",
        "system.cpu.count",
        "logback.events",
        "http.server.requests",
        "hikaricp.connections.active",
        "hikaricp.connections.creation",
        "jvm.gc.pause",
        "jvm.buffer.memory.used",
        "tomcat.sessions.created",
        "jvm.threads.daemon",
        "system.cpu.usage",
        "jvm.gc.memory.allocated",
        "jdbc.connections.idle",
        "hikaricp.connections.max",
        "hikaricp.connections.min",
        "tomcat.sessions.expired",
        "jvm.threads.live",
```

```
        "jvm.threads.peak",
        "process.uptime",
        "hikaricp.connections.usage",
        "tomcat.sessions.rejected",
        "process.cpu.usage",
        "hikaricp.connections.timeout",
        "jvm.classes.loaded",
        "hikaricp.connections.acquire",
        "jvm.classes.unloaded",
        "tomcat.sessions.active.current",
        "tomcat.sessions.alive.max",
        "jvm.gc.live.data.size",
        "process.files.open",
        "jvm.buffer.count",
        "jvm.buffer.total.capacity",
        "tomcat.sessions.active.max",
        "process.start.time"
    ]
}
```

The metrics can be grouped into a few categories.

- JVM, Garbage Collector activity, memory consumption, thread utilization, number of classes, and so forth (seems a lot like what we've seen in JConsole, right?)

- CPU usage

- Spring-specific components activity

- Cache activity

- Datasource and HikariCP activity

- Uptime

- Tomcat usage

- Spring MVC and WebFlux request latencies (available only for Spring Boot MVC and WebFlux applications)

- Other custom components activity: RestTemplate latencies, file descriptor usage, event logging, RabbitMQ or ApacheMQ (if used) connection factories

We have a lot of data about our application that is collected while the application is running. What can we do with it? We must compose it into reports and graphs that can be viewed with the naked eye. Micrometer cannot help with this, but there's a tool that easily does the trick and integrates perfectly with Spring Boot Actuator and Micrometer: Prometheus.[16] Prometheus is an open source systems monitoring and alerting toolkit built by SoundCloud.[17] It was released in 2012, and since then, it has become a stand-alone open source project with large and active developer and user communities. Seriously, go to the site, read about it and you can even go through the `Hello World!` tutorial where you are taught how to install Prometheus and make it monitor itself. This monitoring tool is really awesome.

Anyway, let's look at how we can make it monitor `chapter09/prometheus-boot-app`. This application is a simple Spring Boot web application exposing `Person` and `Detective` managing services. It's identical to the `secured-boot-app` only it's missing the security module. This application is not secured because of practical reasons: skipping the step of configuring Prometheus to use basic authentication to access the actuator metrics.

Let's start with the configuration. To integrate our Spring Boot application with Prometheus, a dependency of the `micrometer-registry-prometheus` must be added. In the next configuration snippet, the Prometheus de- pendency is declared in the root project `pivotal-certified-pro-spring-dev-exam-02` configuration file and used in the `chapter09/prometheus-boot-app` project.

```
//pivotal-certified-pro-spring-dev-exam-02/build.gradle
ext {
    micrometerPrometheusVersion = '1.2.0',
    ...
```

---

[16]Official site: `https://prometheus.io`

[17]Yes, the music sharing platform SoundCloud: `https://soundcloud.com/`

```
boot = [
    micrometerPrometheus :
        "io.micrometer:micrometer-registry-prometheus:$micrometerProm
        etheusVersion",
        ...
]
}
//chapter09/prometheus-boot-app/build.gradle
dependencies {
    implementation boot.starterJpa, boot.starterWeb, boot.actuator
    runtimeOnly misc.h2
    implementation micrometerPrometheus
    ...
}
```

After adding this dependency, if you check the IntelliJ IDEA Gradle view, the dependency should be there, as depicted in Figure 9-11.

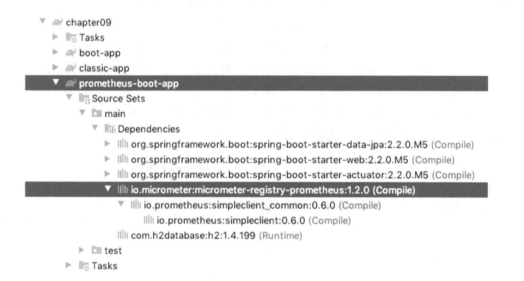

Figure 9-11. *Gradle view in IntelliJ IDEA showing the Prometheus dependency*

After adding this dependency if you start the application and go to http://0.0.0.0:8081/actuator, you will see that there is an extra endpoint available, as depicted in Figure 9-12.

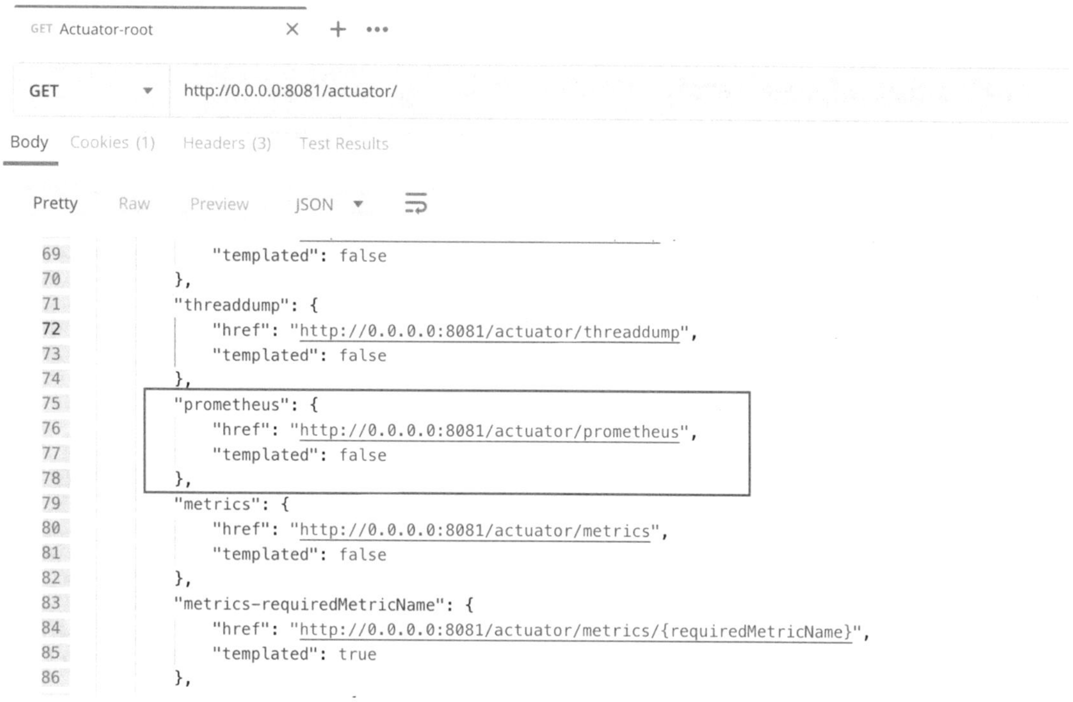

```
69              "templated": false
70          },
71          "threaddump": {
72              "href": "http://0.0.0.0:8081/actuator/threaddump",
73              "templated": false
74          },
75          "prometheus": {
76              "href": "http://0.0.0.0:8081/actuator/prometheus",
77              "templated": false
78          },
79          "metrics": {
80              "href": "http://0.0.0.0:8081/actuator/metrics",
81              "templated": false
82          },
83          "metrics-requiredMetricName": {
84              "href": "http://0.0.0.0:8081/actuator/metrics/{requiredMetricName}",
85              "templated": true
86          },
```

Figure 9-12.   *The Prometheus endpoint*

This endpoint is provided by the PrometheusScrapeEndpoint class, from package org.springframework.boot.actuate.metrics.export.prometheus, which is part of the Spring Actuator project, It translates the metrics provided by Micrometer into a format that can be scrapped by the Prometheus server. You can see the exposed metrics by accessing the Prometheus endpoint at http://0.0.0.0:8081/actuator/prometheus.

```
# HELP hikaricp_connections_max Max connections
# TYPE hikaricp_connections_max gauge
hikaricp_connections_max{pool="cemsPool",} 5.0
# HELP http_server_requests_seconds
# TYPE http_server_requests_seconds summary
http_server_requests_seconds_count{exception="None",method="GET",outcome=
"SUCCESS",status="200",
    uri="/persons/{id}",} 3000.0
http_server_requests_seconds_sum{exception="None",method="GET",outcome=
"SUCCESS",status="200",
  uri="/persons/{id}",} 4.199754747
```

```
http_server_requests_seconds_count{exception="None",method="GET",outcome=
"SUCCESS",status="200",
  uri="/actuator/prometheus",} 580.0
http_server_requests_seconds_count{exception="None",method="GET",outcome=
"SUCCESS",status="200",
  uri="/persons",} 6000.0
http_server_requests_seconds_sum{exception="None",method="GET",outcome=
"SUCCESS",status="200",
  uri="/persons",} 452.607297541
```

Or if you prefer the Postman view, see Figure 9-13.

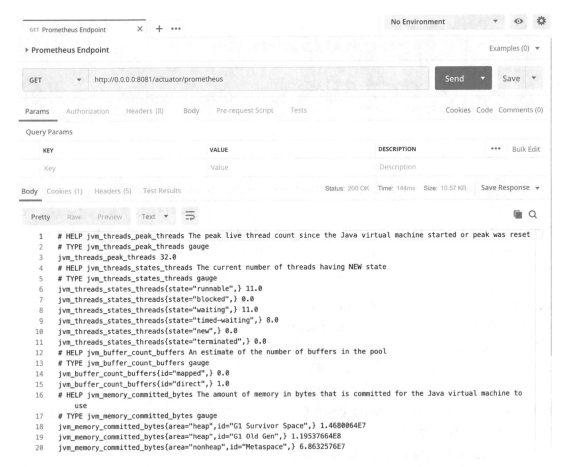

Figure 9-13. *The Prometheus endpoint information depicted in Postman*

The next step is to install Prometheus locally. There are two ways to do this, as explained on the official site[18] or by setting up a Docker container. In `chapter09/prometheus-boot-app`, you will find a `README.adoc` document explaining how to set up Prometheus in a Docker container; these steps are skipped here since they tend to derail the focus of the chapter.

Assuming that you have Prometheus running in a Docker container or locally, we need to tell it where to get the metrics from, which is done via a configuration file named `prometheus.yml`. The name is not mandatory, but it does make its purpose obvious. According to the official documentation, we must define a *job* that tells Prometheus how often to query the metrics and from where. The syntax is YAML and the most important properties are underlined in the next configuration snippet.

```
global:
  scrape_interval:     15s # get metrics from every target every 15 seconds

scrape_configs:
  # Prometheus itself self-monitoring configuration
  - job_name: 'prometheus'

    # Override the global default and scrape targets from this job every 5
    seconds.
    scrape_interval: 5s

    static_configs:
      - targets: ['0.0.0.0:9090']
  # Job to get metric from the prometheus-boot-app
  - job_name: 'prometheus-boot-app'
    metrics_path: '/actuator/prometheus'
    # Override the global default and scrape targets from this job every 5
    seconds.
    scrape_interval: 5s

    static_configs:
    # When Prometheus is run in a Docker container the real IP within the
    network must be used
      - targets: ['192.168.0.24:8081']
```

---

[18]Take a look if you are interested: `https://prometheus.io/docs/introduction/first_steps/`

We now have a property file that tells Prometheus where to get the metrics from. How do we check that everything is fine?

First, you have to start the prometheus-boot-app, which is done by executing the PrometheusApplication main class. After the application is up, we start Prometheus. If not configured, the Prometheus server web interface can be accessed at http:// localhost:9090; it is simplistic. You can see it in Figure 9-14.

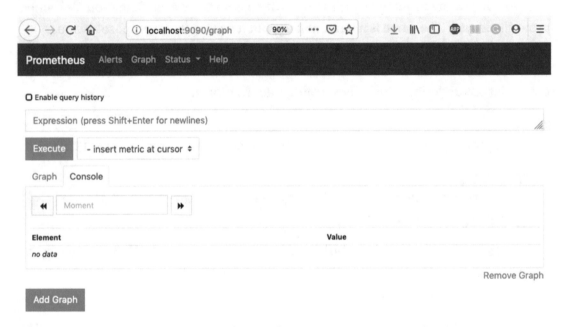

Figure 9-14. *The Prometheus web interface*

Prometheus is up, and the prometheus-boot-app is up. How do we know they can actually communicate? Under the Status menu there is a menu item named Targets. When clicked, it opens a page with all the monitored targets, and the prometheus-boot-app should be there and in the State column, you should see the text UP highlighted in green, as depicted in Figure 9-15.

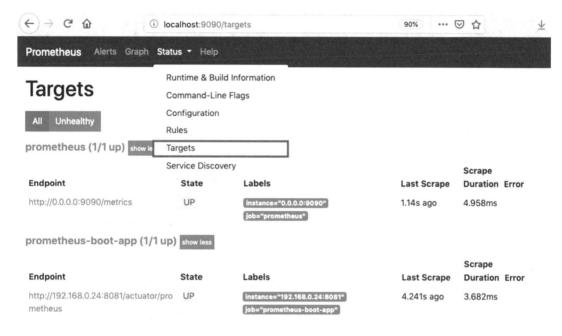

Figure 9-15. *The Prometheus targets page*

If the text is DOWN and highlighted in red, the application is either not started or the static_configs.targets was not set properly.

If all is fine, we can go back to the main page and start analyzing some metrics. But to have something to analyze, we have to give the application something to do. The PersonsControllerTest class can help with this. It contains three test methods: one creates Person instances, one retrieves a single Person instance, and one retrieves them all. Each is repeated 6000 times. This should provide enough metric data for some graphs to be plotted.

In the http://localhost:9090/graph page, there is a text field where metrics are selected. The text field shows you several metric names to select from. One of the most visible metrics is the system_cpu_usage, so select that. Now, still the information is not really visible in the Graph tab until we reduce the interval for the metrics analysis by setting the value in the textfield on the left corner. The graph should be interesting, similar to what is depicted in Figure 9-16.

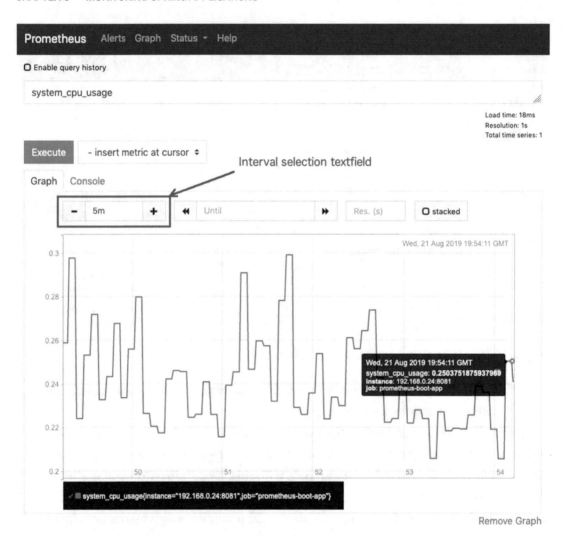

Figure 9-16. *The Prometheus graph for the system_cpu_usage metric*

Let's make a small modification and introduce a different delay for each of the
Person instances returned when http://localhost:8081/persons/{id} is called. It is
called by adding Thread.sleep() in the handler method for the following URI.

```
package com.apress.cems.person;
...
@RestController
@RequestMapping("/persons")
public class PersonsController {
    private PersonService personService;
```

```
public PersonsController(PersonService personService) {
    this.personService = personService;
}

@ResponseStatus(HttpStatus.OK)
@GetMapping("/{id}")
public Person show(@PathVariable Long id) {
    Optional<Person> personOpt = personService.findById(id);
    if(personOpt.isPresent()) {
        int msec = 1000;
        try {
            Thread.sleep(msec * id);
        } catch (InterruptedException e) {
            e.printStackTrace();
        }
        return personOpt.get();
    } else {
        throw new NotFoundException(Person.class, id );
    }
}

}
```

After adding this small modification, metric like http_server_requests_seconds_
count (a metric that records how much time is takes the application to resolve an HTTP
request) become a little bit more useful. This metric has been plotted on a graph while
running the test, and you can see the result in Figure 9-17.

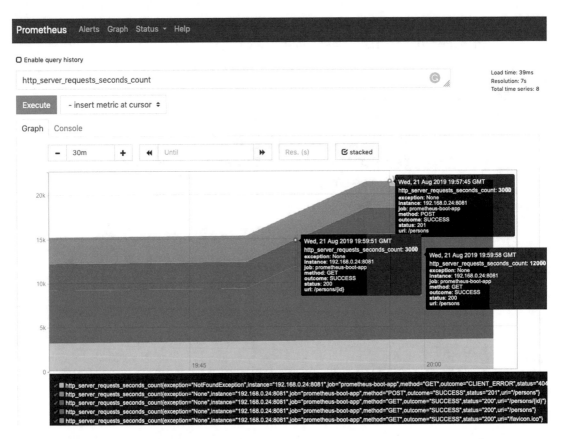

Figure 9-17. *The Prometheus graph for the http_server_requests_seconds_count metric*

Notice the different time values representing the duration of each type of request. The requests to `http://localhost:8081/persons` increase in duration because the PERSON table gets bigger and bigger due to the POST requests creating records.

The Prometheus graphs are simple. The default Micrometer metrics are basic too. In a production application, teams can define their own metrics depending on the services the application provides. For example, in a banking application, login failures coupled with certain originating IPs might reveal a hacking attempt, so a metric that groups failed logins and a class of IPs in which requests are generated from is a must-have.

The leading solution in visualizing metrics seems to be Grafana.[19] The good news is that it knows how to interpret Prometheus metrics. The Prometheus metrics can be forwarded to Grafana and *high-definition* graphs can be plotted.

---

[19]Grafana official site: `https://grafana.com/`

Summary

Monitoring applications in production is important, because the happiness of the clients depends on the application being up and performing the tasks in the expected amount of time. Aside from availability, monitoring an application can provide information regarding hacking attempts, periods of peak loading, memory leaks, and so forth. Usually, there is an Ops or a DevOps team monitoring applications and setting alarms based on metrics values. Spring Boot Actuator, together with projects like Prometheus and Grafana provide a way for developers to configure and monitor applications themselves. Also, in a world where every application is deployed on the cloud, the lines between OPS/DevOps/developers have become blurred. That is why recently, from what I observed, there are a lot of job offers for full stack developers. And apparently Pivotal has seen the importance of monitoring done by developers too because Spring Boot Actuator is now part of the certification exam.

After reading this chapter, you should be able to answer the following questions.

- What is Spring Boot Actuator good for?
- What are the two protocols that Actuator endpoints can be accessed on?
- Which are the endpoints provided out of the box?
- What is the /health endpoint good for? How can it be configured to show more details?
- What is the /info endpoint good for?
- Can you provide your own endpoints? How?
- What is a health indicator?
- What is the purpose of the /metrics endpoint?
- What tools do you know that can interpret Actuator metrics?

Quick Quiz

Question 1. Spring Boot Actuator helps you manage and monitor your applications by providing endpoints accessible on which protocols? (Choose all that apply.)

- A. SFTP
- B. HTTP
- C. JMX
- D. TCP/IP

Question 2. Which endpoints are provided out of the box when Spring Boot Actuator is on the classpath? (Choose all that apply.)

- A. `/actuator`
- B. `/beans`
- C. `/info`
- D. `/health`

Question 3. How can data exposed by the `/info` endpoint be customized? (Choose one.)

- A. by declaring a bean of type `InfoIndicator`
- B. by setting `info.*` properties into the `application.yml` or `application.properties` file

Question 4. What is the purpose of the `HealthIndicator` interface? (Choose one.)

- A. Spring beans of types that implement it provide custom health information
- B. If a Spring endpoint is declared that implements this interface, it will override the `/health` endpoint.

Question 5. You have a Spring Boot application using Actuator. The following configuration is part of the `application.yml` file. What is its effect? (Choose one.)

```
management:
  endpoints:
    web:
      base-path: /monitoring
```

    A.   All Actuator endpoints are available under the `/actuator/monitoring` prefix

    B.   All Actuator endpoints are available under the `/monitoring` prefix

Question 6. The Developer can provide its own status values to be used by a `HealthIndicator`. Is this true? (Choose one.)

    A.   No

    B.   Yes

CHAPTER 10

Spring and Kotlin

Until this chapter in the book, Spring applications were written using Java. This chapter teaches you how to write Spring applications using Kotlin. Kotlin is a JVM programming language that my favorite software company, JetBrains (the same company that develops IntelliJ IDEA), started working on in 2011. As an IntelliJ IDEA fan since 2005, I cannot imagine JetBrains producing something that is not absolutely great. So, clearly, Kotlin had to be another awesome product. After seeing Josh Long's "Bootiful Kotlin[1]" presentation at the Spring IO conference in Barcelona, I decided that this was a programming language that I needed to learn.

Kotlin is designed to be practical, modern, and functional. Kotlin is the missing link between Java and Scala. Scala is a programming language providing support for functional programming and a strong static type system. But being so concise, the Scala learning curve tends to be steep. If you are a programmer that has worked for years with a language as readable as Java, you might have some difficulties moving to Scala, no matter how praised Scala is for being a cleaner and more organized language. Also, support from the IDE is important, and while working with Scala in IntelliJ, I encountered a few bugs that did not make my Scala coding experience too pleasant.

Enter Kotlin, the missing link. Figure 10-1 is a funny image that came into my mind when I realized learning Kotlin helped me better understand Scala.

---

[1]View it on YouTube: `https://youtu.be/SlBRce-aBOc`

© Iuliana Cosmina 2020
I. Cosmina, *Pivotal Certified Professional Core Spring 5 Developer Exam*,
https://doi.org/10.1007/978-1-4842-5136-2_10

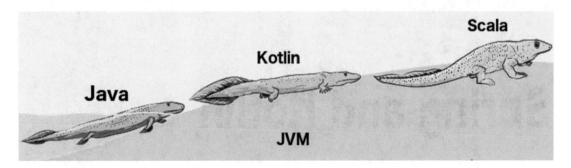

Figure 10-1. *Kotlin, the missing link*

Kotlin brings the elegance and conciseness of Scala while managing to remain readable and approachable. And in some cases, Kotlin is more concise. Just look at Figure 10-2, which depicts the same class with a `main()` method calling a `sum(..)` method that adds to integers in the three languages.

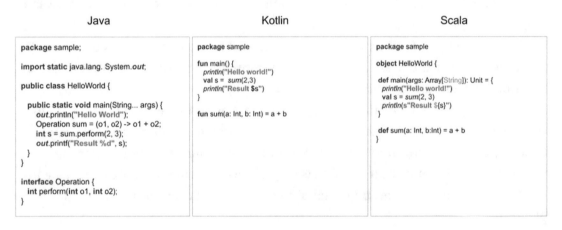

Figure 10-2. *Three flavors of HelloWorld with a main method*

Sure, in Figure 10-2, the Java version could be simplified by using `Integer.sum(..)`, but still, somehow the Kotlin code seems more elegant, doesn't it?

Anyway, the next section will quickly list why Kotlin is so great and after that, the rest of the chapter will be spent on migrating a very simple Spring Boot web application (`chapter06/boot-web`) to Kotlin.

Why Is Kotlin So Great?

Aside from being more concise and providing a faster way of writing software solutions,[2] Kotlin is safe and interoperable. A wide range of problems are eliminated by assuming that objects are immutable and are not nullable. With Google pitching in, Kotlin is currently widely used in tandem with Gradle to build Android applications. And since Gradle was mentioned, for Kotlin projects, the Gradle configuration files can be written in Kotlin. And if that is not enough, Kotlin can be compiled to JavaScript, so Kotlin code can run in the browser. There is a project that aims to compile Kotlin code to native binaries that can run without a virtual machine.

One of the strengths of Kotlin is that it is statically typed, which means types are determined at compile time. Coming from a language like Java that is dynamically typed, you might see this as a nuisance, but having the compiler know the exact type of an object does help IDEs enforce coding rules that lead to safer code. Being statically typed, it restricts the code a developer can write. Just look at the following depiction of a class named CollectionPlay.

```
package sample;

import java.util.ArrayList;
import java.util.List;

public class CollectionPlay {

    public static void main(String... args) {
        List<String> list = List.of("1", "2");
        List<String> list2 =  new ArrayList<>();
        list2.add("1"); list2.add("2");
        list2 = list;
        list2.add("3");
    }
}
```

---

[2]Just for fun, have you ever tried processing files in a hierarchy of directories using Java? Try writing code like that in Kotlin, you will see how easy it is because of functions like *File(..).walkBottomUp()* or *File(..).walkTopDown()*

Code like that can still be written in Java, it compiles and it crashes at runtime, because starting with the marked line `list2` references an immutable list. The solution for that problem came in JDK 11 with the introduction of the `var` keyword, which was borrowed from statically typed languages. It allows the compiler to make a decision about the type of variable and fail at compile time. In Figure 10-3, you can see the compile-time error in the IDE when using the `var` keyword.

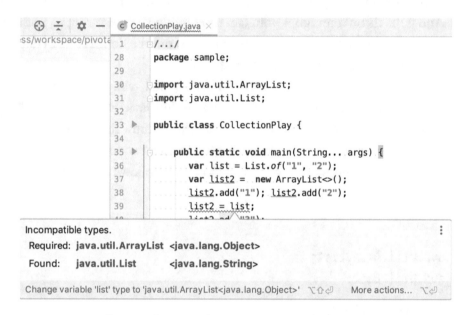

Figure 10-3. *Statically typed example in Java using the var keyword*

Kotlin is a little bit restrictive, but at the same time, it is all for the greater good of preventing erroneous code from being written. In Figure 10-4, you can see the compile-time error in the IDE when writing the same code using Kotlin.

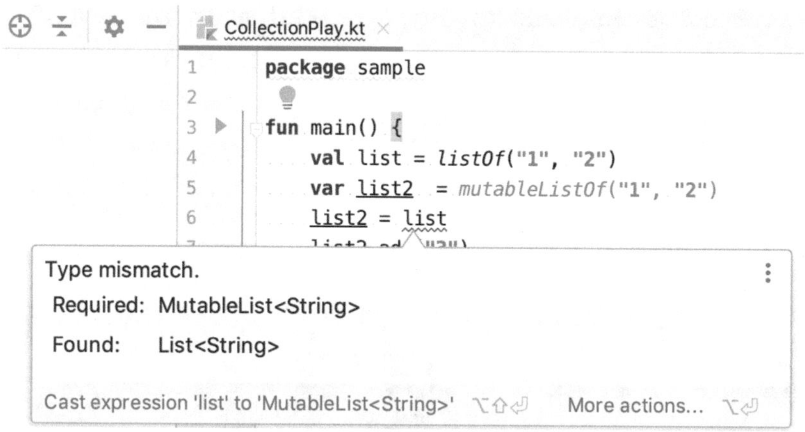

Figure 10-4. *Statically typed example in Kotlin*

There are two keywords: the var keyword, which has the same responsibility as the one in Java, but also the val keyword, which declares a constant reference; that is, it cannot be reassigned with a different value after being initialized.

Look at the different errors thrown by the compiler. In the Java example, the compiler cannot figure out the types of elements in list2 because of generics. In the Kotlin example, all types are known, including the collections and elements in them. And that's what it means for a language to be truly statically typed.

Another reason why Kotlin is great is that it supports both object-oriented and functional programming styles. Of course, under the hood, you cannot have functions just hanging about everywhere in the code, since you are running this code on a JVM. Let's take the following piece of code.

```kotlin
//in file CollectionPlay.kt
package sample

fun main() {
    val list = listOf("1", "2")
    var list2  = mutableListOf("1", "2")
    //list2 = list
    //list2.add("3")
}
```

This piece of code is compiled into some bytecode that can run on a JVM. If that code is decompiled, we can see a class named CollectionPlayKt that has a method named main() containing the code listed previously, but also a static main(String[] args) that represents the entry point of that class, so it can be executed. You can do the decompiling yourself in IntelliJ IDEA. Go to the Tools menu, select Kotlin, and then Show Kotlin Bytecode, as depicted in Figure 10-5.

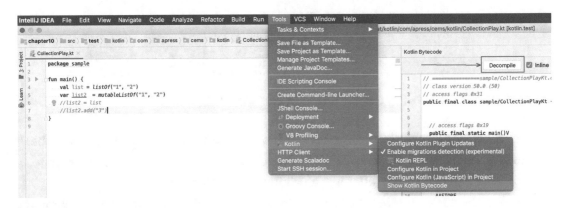

Figure 10-5. *View Kotlin Bytecode in IntelliJ IDEA*

On the right side of your Kotlin code, a window will pop-up with the bytecode text representation in it and it should look half-Java, half-Gibberish. On top of it there's a button named Decompile. When clicked, IntelliJ IDEA, takes that bytecode and tries to turn it back into Java code. The results are … uncanny and depicted in the following code listing.

```
package sample;

import java.util.List;
import kotlin.Metadata;
import kotlin.collections.CollectionsKt;

@Metadata(
    mv = {1, 1, 15},
    bv = {1, 0, 3},
    k = 2,
    d1 = {"\u0000\b\n\u0000\n\u0002\u0010\u0002\n\u0000
        \u001a\u0006\u0010\u0000\u001a\u00020\u0001Â¨\u0006\u0002"},
    d2 = {"main", "", "kotlin.test"}
)
```

```
public final class CollectionPlayKt {
   public static final void main() {
      List list = CollectionsKt.listOf(new String[]{"1", "2"});
      List list2 = CollectionsKt.mutableListOf(new String[]{"1", "2"});
   }

   // $FF: synthetic method
   public static void main(String[] var0) {
      main();
   }
}
```

But it does look a lot like a Java class, right?

Kotlin runs on a JVM, which means that it can interoperate with other JVM languages and tools, and execute on any platform that supports a JVM. Java types can be used, but the implementation must abide by the Kotlin compiler rules.

From a syntax point of view, the following is the short list of things you need to know to find your way in Kotlin code.

- Does not use semicolons. Really. Unless you really want to write more statements on the same line, but why would you need to do that?

- Has a reduced number of brackets.

- Uses var to declare references that can be reassigned in the code.

- Uses val to declare references that should not be reassigned. (you can see val like a combination of var + final from java)

- Prints messages with println(..); includes variables in the output by prefixing them with $:

  ```
  val str = "World!"
   println("Hello $str")
   // results in "Hello World!"
  ```

  If you want to include properties of an object, or call a method within the text printed by println, include the entire statement in ${..}.

```
val str = "World!"
println("Hello ${str.length}")
println("Hello ${str.toUpperCase()}")
```

Placeholders are so cool. And most of all, useful.

- Everything is immutable. When you declare a variable, you must initialize it.

- Default non-nullability. When you declare a variable and initialize it, you cannot initialize it with null. Unless you do an artifice. In Figure 10-6, I tried initializing a String variable with null and the Kotlin compiler is not having it.

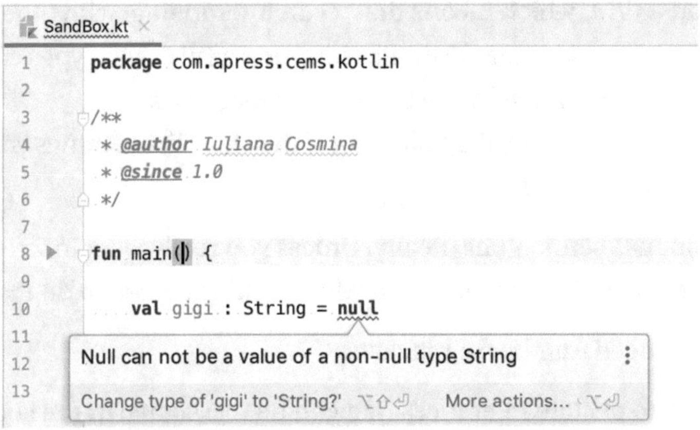

Figure 10-6. Kotlin default non-nullability paradigm

IntelliJ IDEA is supportive by stating exactly what I have to do to make that work: add a question mark when specifying the type of the variable. Yup, val gigi : String? = null will compile just fine.

- Kotlin supports multiline strings. The following compiles just fine, and the text is printed exactly as you see it.

This makes logging details very practical.

```
val gigi : String = """
        gigi
        nu
        stie
        sa
        zica
        rau
        ratusca
        randunica
    """
        println(gigi)
```

- Simple syntax, and no getters, setters, or constructors are needed (unless you really need them). Also, the new operator is not needed either.

- Awesome type casting and type inference.

- Ranges

- Inline functions

- The when expression

- Inheritance without keywords (just the plain old ":". whether you implement interfaces or extend classes)

- Data classes (compact classes that can be used as entity classes, you'll learn about them later in the chapter)

I am just scratching the surface, but I am in love with this language, and if you are at least curious, you can start learning Kotlin using the official documentation.[3]

And because it is so awesome, Kotlin was quickly adopted in the industry and now companies like Google, Gradle, Evernote, Atlassian, Gradle, and Pivotal are using it and supporting its growth. So, without further ado, let's see how a Spring application is written using Kotlin and discover the benefits.

---

[3]Official Kotlin site: https://kotlinlang.org

Migrating a Spring Boot Application to Kotlin

First, we need to figure out the dependencies, which is not easily done without Spring Initializr. I mentioned the plan to migrate chapter06/boot-web to Kotlin, so looking at the dependencies of this project, it is clear what we need to select at https://start. spring.io/. The specifications are as follows.

- The project will have a Gradle setup.

- It will be written in Kotlin.

- The most recent version of Spring Boot is available at https:// start.spring.io/, 2.2.0.M6.

- The group name is the same one used all throughout the book: com. apress.cems.

- The artifact name is kotlin to make it obvious what the project is.

- The packaging can be jar; I don't really care.

- The JDK version is 12.

- When it comes to Spring Boot dependencies, since we are building a web application, Web needs to be selected. We've used Thymeleaf until now, so this dependency is needed too. It's a bit late in the book to switch the templating engine, and I'm not good at building user interfaces. To keep it simple, let's skip security.

- We have entities and repositories so JPA is a must; so is H2, the in-memory database.

- We can add Actuator, and since we are writing code in a new language let's add DevTools too, so the application restarts automatically every time we change classes.

After selecting everything, your Spring Initializr window should look similar to the one depicted in Figure 10-7.

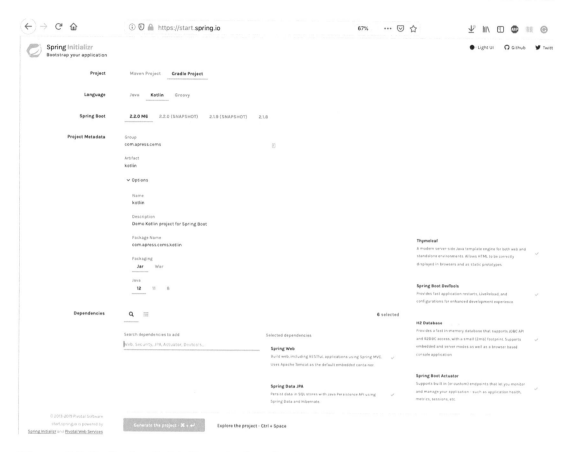

Figure 10-7. *Spring Initializr window for Spring Boot Kotlin project*

You can click the `Explore the project` button if you want to see what Spring Initializr will generate for you. You should see something similar to the contents depicted in Figure 10-8.

Figure 10-8. *Contents of Spring Boot Kotlin project generated by Spring Initializr*

The reason I insisted on putting the screenshot shown Figure 10-8 in this book is because the current situation with Kotlin and the required JVM version was a little confusing when this chapter was written. Although the Java 12 version was selected in the Spring Initializr interface, as you can see in Figure 10-8, the Java version used is 8, so this project cannot be included in the big multi-module `pivotal-certified-pro-spring-dev-exam-02`. It has to be developed and run independently from it, because to write Kotlin code we need the Kotlin Standard Library JDK extension and there is no extension for JDK 12.

So, if you click `Generate Project` and download the results, after unpacking it, you will notice a few things. Each of them is explained in the following list. If I missed anything, feel free to send me an email.

- There are no `settings.gradle` and `build.gradle` files. Why have these types of configuration files written in Groovy when you can have Gradle configuration files written in Kotlin DSL? Gradle's Kotlin DSL provides an alternative syntax to the traditional Groovy DSL with an enhanced editing experience in supported IDEs, with superior content assist, refactoring, documentation, and more.[4] And it can be used for Java projects too if you are looking for an alternative to the Groovy syntax.

  The new files are named `settings.gradle.kts` and `build.gradle.kts` and the `kts` is the extension of a Kotlin script.

- When using Spring Initializr, the `settings.gradle.kts` is generated to contain the `pluginManagement` block, which manages the plugin repositories. Itis very useful for a Spring Boot project using a milestone version that is only available on a Spring milestone repository. It has the same syntax as `settings.gradle`.

- The `build.gradle.kts` is the core configuration file of the project and each section is explained next.

  – The file starts with this line:

  ```
  import org.jetbrains.kotlin.gradle.tasks.KotlinCompile
  ```

    The `KotlinCompile` is a special Kotlin task implementation that can enable support for JSR-305 annotations.[5] Why is this important? Kotlin is fond of keeping everything non-nullable and enforcing it at compile time. This is a little bit difficult with Java APIs. The Spring Framework provides null-safety of the whole Spring Framework API via tooling-friendly annotations declared in the `org.springframework.lang` package. This Kotlin task is configured at the end of the configuration file to support JSR-305 annotations, which ensures non-nullability for Java platform types at compile time

---

[4]Official documentation here: `https://docs.gradle.org/current/userguide/kotlin_dsl.html`

[5]JSR-305 covers development of standard annotations (such as *@NonNull*) that can be applied to Java programs to assist tools that detect software defects. `https://jcp.org/en/jsr/detail?id=305`

by configuring the-Xjsr305 flag with the strict value. The same task is configured to tell the Kotlin compile to generate Java 8 bytecode.

```
tasks.withType<KotlinCompile> {
  kotlinOptions {
    freeCompilerArgs = listOf("-Xjsr305=strict")
    jvmTarget = "1.8"
  }
}
```

– The next section is the plugin section:

```
plugins {
        id("org.springframework.boot") version "2.2.0.M5"
        id("io.spring.dependency-management") version
        "1.0.8.RELEASE"
        kotlin("jvm") version "1.3.50"
        kotlin("plugin.spring") version "1.3.50"
        kotlin("plugin.jpa") version "1.3.50"
}
```

When writing this chapter, the latest version of Kotlin is 1.3.50, and thus all Kotlin-related plugins share this version. I'll skip explaining the Spring Boot plugin and the Spring Dependency Management plugin because their purposes are obvious by names. Let's jump directly to the Kotlin specific plugins.

– kotlin("jvm") is the Kotlin Gradle plugin and is needed to build a Kotlin project with Gradle.[6]

– kotlin("plugin.spring") is the Kotlin Gradle plugin that is needed to compile a Spring project with Gradle.[7] This plugin automatically opens classes and methods annotated with

---

[6]Reference: https://kotlinlang.org/docs/reference/using-gradle.html

[7]Reference: https://kotlinlang.org/docs/reference/compiler-plugins. html#spring-support

Spring annotations making creation of proxies possible, thus allowing Kotlin support for `@Transactional` or `@Secured` annotations.

- `kotlin("plugin.jpa")` allows using JPA annotations on Kotlin data classes. It also allows no-argument constructors to be generated for entity classes.

- Next is the informational section, which contains the project's groupId, version, and the source compatibility indicator, which cannot be anything but Java 8.

```
group = "com.apress.cems"
version = "0.0.1-SNAPSHOT"
java.sourceCompatibility = JavaVersion.VERSION_1_8
```

The value for the `java.sourceCompatibility` property is selected from the `JavaVersion` enum, as depicted in Figure 10-9. It has a lot more values in it. Although there are values for Java 9+, neither of them would have any effect in a Kotlin project.

```
11    group = "com.apress.cems"
12    version = "0.0.1-SNAPSHOT"
13    java.sourceCompatibility = JavaVersion.VERSION_1_8
14                                        f VERSION_1_8 (org.gradle.api.JavaVersion)
15    val developmentOnly by configuratio f VERSION_11 (org.gradle.api.JavaVersion)
16    configurations { this: NamedDomainObje f VERSION_12 (org.gradle.api.JavaVersion)
17        runtimeClasspath { this: Configurati f VERSION_1_1 (org.gradle.api.JavaVersion)
18            extendsFrom(developmentOnly f VERSION_1_10 (org.gradle.api.JavaVersion)
19        }                                f VERSION_1_2 (org.gradle.api.JavaVersion)
20    }                                    f VERSION_1_3 (org.gradle.api.JavaVersion)
21                                         f VERSION_1_4 (org.gradle.api.JavaVersion)
22    repositories { this: RepositoryHandler f VERSION_1_5 (org.gradle.api.JavaVersion)
23        mavenCentral()                   f VERSION_1_6 (org.gradle.api.JavaVersion)
24        maven { url = uri( path: "https:, f VERSION_1_7 (org.gradle.api.JavaVersion)
25    }                                    f VERSION_1_9 (org.gradle.api.JavaVersion)
26                                         f VERSION_HIGHER (org.gradle.api.JavaVersion)
```

Figure 10-9. *Gradle JavaVersion enum values*

- The next section declares a special type of dependency for the project. This dependency qualifier is only needed for the `devtools` dependency, which is designed to facilitate development by automatically restarting the Spring Boot application when changes happen on the classpath, so feedback is received as soon as possible.

```
val developmentOnly by configurations.creating
configurations {
        runtimeClasspath {
                extendsFrom(developmentOnly)
        }
}
```

- The next section is the one configuring the repositories where the dependencies of the project will be downloaded from.

```
repositories {
        mavenCentral()
        maven { url = uri("https://repo.spring.io/milestone") }
}
```

A milestone version of Spring Boot was used, so the milestone Spring repositories need to be configured.

And here we are, the dependency section.

```
dependencies {
    implementation("org.springframework.boot:spring-boot-starter-actuator")
    implementation("org.springframework.boot:spring-boot-starter-data-jpa")
    implementation("org.springframework.boot:spring-boot-starter-web")
    implementation("org.springframework.boot:spring-boot-starter-
    thymeleaf")

    implementation("org.jetbrains.kotlin: kotlin-stdlib-jdk8")
    implementation("org.jetbrains.kotlin: kotlin-reflect")
    implementation("com.fasterxml.jackson.module:jackson-module-kotlin")

    developmentOnly("org.springframework.boot:spring-boot-devtools")
    runtimeOnly("com.h2database:h2")
```

```
testImplementation("org.springframework.boot:spring-boot-starter-
test") {
    exclude(group = "org.junit.vintage", module = "junit-vintage-
    engine")
}
}
```

Aside from the typical Spring Boot starter dependencies, it is important to note that there are Kotlin-specific dependencies.

- `kotlin-stdlib-jdk8` is the Java 8 variant of Kotlin standard library (as previously mentioned, there is no Java 11 variant yet)

  - `kotlin-reflect` is the Kotlin reflection library. Although we do not like to hear it mentioned because reflection is associated with low performance, Spring does use reflection to identify proxying candidates and beans to be created by using component scanning. To do the same for Kotlin, this library needs to be in the classpath.

- `jackson-module-kotlin` is a library that adds support for serialization/deserialization of Kotlin classes and data classes. On the official web page (`www.kotlinresources.com/library/jackson-module-kotlin/`), only JSON examples are provided. XML is not mentioned anywhere.

• The `src` file contains the default project structure and the Spring Boot main Kotlin class and a default Kotlin test class designed to check that your context loads correctly. The structure of the project is depicted in Figure 10-8. In Figure 10-10, you can see the structure of the project after all development was done.

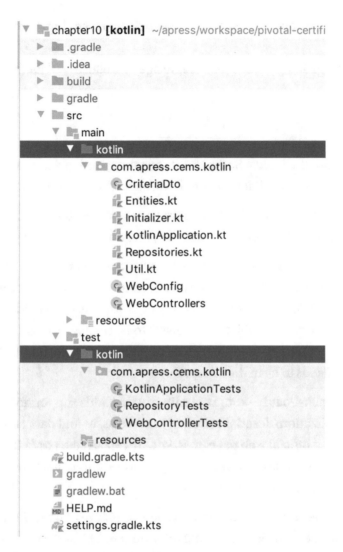

Figure 10-10. *Chapter10 project structure*

The sources and test sourced of the project are grouped under a directory named kotlin. The class name is made from the artifact name you provided to Spring Initializr by adding `Application` to it. The following are the contents of the main class.

```kotlin
package com.apress.cems.kotlin

import org.springframework.boot.autoconfigure.SpringBootApplication
import org.springframework.boot.runApplication
```

```
@SpringBootApplication
class KotlinApplication

fun main(args: Array<String>) {
        runApplication<KotlinApplication>(*args)
}
```

The test class is named KotlinApplicationTests. Its contents are pretty basic as well.

```
package com.apress.cems.kotlin

import org.springframework.boot.test.context.SpringBootTest
import org.junit.jupiter.api.Test

@SpringBootTest
class KotlinApplicationTests{

        @Test
        fun `Context Loads`() {}

}
```

Kotlin supports spaces in method names if they are wrapped in grave accents.

That pretty much it, now let's start with all the changes needed to migrate our Spring Boot web application to Kotlin.

Migrating the Web Interface

The web interface of the project represents in this case the Thymeleaf templates, CSS files, images, and internationalization files. Since they are agnostic to the programming language used to manage them, migrating the web interface is as simple as copying the contents of the boot-web/src/main/resources directory into chapter10/src/main/resources, as depicted in Figure 10-11 .

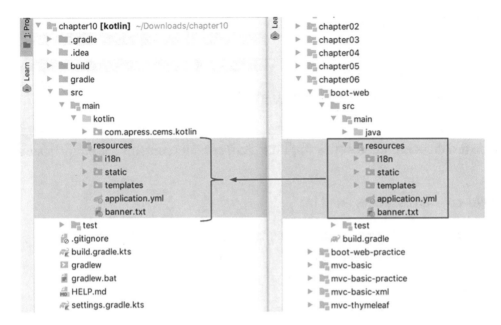

Figure 10-11. *Migrating the web static components to the Spring Boot Kotlin application*

Creating the Entity Classes

In typical a Spring application using a database, classes named *entities* model the structure of database tables, and each instance matches a record from a table. These classes are annotated with the JPA `@Entity` annotations, and their fields or methods are annotated with other JPA-specific annotations; rules state that the values of the fields must abide to or mark the field for a specific purpose (`@Id`, `@Version`). More information about this is in Chapter 5.

In Kotlin, entity classes can be easily implemented by using *data classes.* In Kotlin, data classes are classes designed to hold data. Which is what an entity class is if you think about it. Each class with this purpose follows a template and provides some standard functionality as methods to store the data (setters), methods to access that data (getters) and methods to compare that data (`hashCode`, `equals` methods). In Kotlin data classes are declared by adding the `data` in front of the class declaration. The compiler generates the following methods for these types of classes.

- `hashCode()`/`equals()` functions

- `toString()` function, which returns a `String` value generated following this template: `ClassName(property=value,...)`

- componentN() functions, which are special Kotlin functions replacing getters and setters[8]

- copy(), which is equivalent to the Java clone() method (sort of). The copy() method can copy an object, which alters some of its properties, but keeps the rest unchanged.

Since Kotlin classes are a lot more compact than Java classes, there's no point in creating a file for each data class. For the purpose of this project, a single file named Entities.kt is created that contains all the data classes.

We have a hierarchy of entities and all of them extend AbstractEntity. In Java, this is an abstract class that is inherited by all other entity classes and its purpose is to group common field declarations such as id, version, createdAt, and modifiedAt. In Java, the AbstractEntity class looks like the following.

```
package com.apress.cems.base;

import com.apress.cems.util.DateProcessor;
import com.fasterxml.jackson.annotation.JsonFormat;
import org.springframework.format.annotation.DateTimeFormat;

import javax.persistence.*;
import java.io.Serializable;
import java.time.LocalDateTime;
import java.util.Comparator;
import java.util.Objects;

@MappedSuperclass
public abstract class AbstractEntity implements Serializable {

    @Id
    @GeneratedValue(strategy = GenerationType.AUTO)
    @Column(updatable = false)
    protected Long id;

    @Version
    protected int version;
```

```java
@Column(name = "created_at", nullable = false)
@DateTimeFormat(pattern = DateProcessor.DATE_FORMAT)
protected LocalDateTime createdAt;

@Column(name = "modified_at", nullable = false)
@DateTimeFormat(pattern = DateProcessor.DATE_FORMAT)
protected LocalDateTime modifiedAt;

/**
 * This constructor is required by JPA.
   All subclasses of this class will inherit this constructor.
 */
protected AbstractEntity() {
    createdAt = LocalDateTime.now();
    modifiedAt = LocalDateTime.now();
}

public Long getId() {
    return id;
}

public void setId(Long id) {
    this.id = id;
}

public LocalDateTime getCreatedAt() {
    return createdAt;
}

public void setCreatedAt(LocalDateTime createdAt) {
    this.createdAt = createdAt;
}

public LocalDateTime getModifiedAt() {
    return modifiedAt;
}

public void setModifiedAt(LocalDateTime modifiedAt) {
    this.modifiedAt = modifiedAt;
}
```

```java
    // IDE generated methods
    @Override
    public boolean equals(Object o) {
        if (this == o) return true;
        if (o == null || getClass() != o.getClass()) return false;

        AbstractEntity that = (AbstractEntity) o;
        if (!Objects.equals(id, that.id)) return false;
        return true;
    }

    @Override
    public int hashCode() {
        return id != null ? id.hashCode() : 0;
    }

    @Override
    public String toString() {
        return String.format("AbstractEntity[id='%d%n', createdAt='%s',
                DateProcessor.toString(createdAt),
                DateProcessor.toString(modifiedAt), version);
    }
}
```

I must confess, I intentionally added the full code of this class here to emphasize how compact Kotlin actually is. Ready to see how the same class can be written in Kotlin? OK, here it is.

```kotlin
//Entities.kt file
package com.apress.cems.kotlin

import org.springframework.format.annotation.DateTimeFormat
import java.io.Serializable
import java.time.LocalDateTime
import javax.persistence.*
import javax.validation.constraints.NotEmpty
import javax.validation.constraints.NotNull
import javax.validation.constraints.Size
```

```kotlin
@MappedSuperclass
open class AbstractEntity(@Id @GeneratedValue(strategy = GenerationType.AUTO)
         @Column(updatable = false) var id: Long? = null,
         @Version var version: Int = 0,
       @DateTimeFormat(pattern = DateProcessor.DATE_FORMAT)
         val createdAt: LocalDateTime = LocalDateTime.now(),
       @DateTimeFormat(pattern = DateProcessor.DATE_FORMAT)
         var modifiedAt: LocalDateTime = LocalDateTime.now())
  : Serializable
```

This class is a template, and it needs to be extended. To allow a class to be inherited, its declaration is prefixed with the open keyword. Since it is a template for our data classes, this is not a data class.

At this point, I should mention that since all data classes are compact, I put all of them in a file named Entities.kt. The import set that you see in the previous code snippet is the complete set of import statements for the file; it won't be repeated in the following code snippets.

The declaration might look weird, there is no class body after all. That is because all members are declared and initialized at the same time. Notice how the createdAt field is declared with val so that its initial value can never be changed.

Note how this class implements the Serializable interface by adding : Serializable at the end of its declaration.

Before moving forward to data classes, let's take a look at the implementation of DateProcessor that was referenced in the previous code snippet. Its implementation is part of the Util.kt file. Since Kotlin is so compact, the contents of the com.apress. cems.util package from the java implementation have all been added to the same Kotlin file.

```kotlin
//Util.kt file
object DateProcessor {
    const val DATE_FORMAT: String = "yyyy-MM-dd HH:mm"
    val formatter: DateTimeFormatter = DateTimeFormatter.ofPattern(DATE_
    FORMAT)

    fun toDate (date: String) : LocalDateTime {
        return LocalDateTime.parse(date,formatter)
    }
```

```
    fun toString(date: LocalDateTime):String {
        return date.format(formatter)
    }
}
```

Since this class declares methods, its body must be contained within {}. The AbstractEntity class declared previously does not declare any custom methods, so it can be declared without a body enclosed in {}. The declaration of the class serves as a constructor declaration as well (the same is true for most data classes). In Java, the class DateProcessor was a final class exposing only two static methods used to convert String values to LocalDateTime and vice versa. In Kotlin, when we need a class to exist simply to provide static functions, and there is never any interest to extend or instantiate the class, instead of creating a class, an object can be created. The object keyword declares the construct in the previous code listing as a singleton. Just like a variable declaration, an object declaration is not an expression, and cannot be used on the right-hand side of an assignment statement. An object declaration's initialization is thread-safe. You could say that the declaration of an object is at the same time a declaration and instantiation. Because the compiler will create a single object of that type that is referred using the type name directly, as you have seen in the code of the AbstractEntity class.[9]

Time to introduce a data class, the Person class.

```
//Entities.kt file
package com.apress.cems.kotlin

...

@Entity
data class Person(@Size(min = 3, max = 30) @NotEmpty @Column(unique = true)
        var firstName: String? = null,
    @Size(min = 3, max = 30) @NotEmpty @Column(unique = true)
        var lastName:String? = null,
    @Size(min = 3, max = 60) @NotEmpty @Column(unique = true)
        var username: String? = null,
```

---

[9]More about Kotlin objects here: https://kotlinlang.org/docs/reference/object-declarations.html

```
    @Size(min = 4, max = 50) @NotEmpty var password: String? = null,
    @DateTimeFormat(pattern = DateProcessor.DATE_FORMAT)
        var hiringDate: LocalDateTime = LocalDateTime.now())
  : AbstractEntity()
```

This class is pretty simple, it has its own fields an no relationship to another entity class. The annotations are the same JPA and validation annotations you've seen used all throughout the book.

What is interesting here is how the extending the class AbstractEntity is actually done. At the end of the class declaration, you see : AbstractEntity(), which tells the compiler that it is extending the class but the base class can (and must) be initialized right there by using the parameters of the primary constructor. The AbstractEntity class has none, so that makes things easy.

Let's see what the Detective class looks like; maybe it is more interesting.

```
//Entities.kt file
package com.apress.cems.kotlin

...

@Entity
data class Detective(@NotNull @OneToOne val person: Person,
        @NotEmpty @Column(unique = true, nullable = false)
            var badgeNumber:String? = null,
        @NotNull @Enumerated(EnumType.STRING) var rank: Rank,
            var armed: Boolean  = false,
        @NotNull @Enumerated(EnumType.STRING)
            var status: EmploymentStatus = EmploymentStatus.ACTIVE)
    : AbstractEntity()
```

The novelty in this class are the enum fields. Kotlin supports enums, which are easier to declare since no private constructors nor getters are needed. For example, the two enums (Rank and EmploymentStatus) in the previous snippet look like this:

```
//Util.kt file
enum class Rank(val code: Int){
    TRAINEE(1),
    JUNIOR(2),
    SENIOR(3),
```

```kotlin
    INSPECTOR(4),
    CHIEF_INSPECTOR(5)
}

enum class EmploymentStatus {
    ACTIVE,
    SUSPENDED,
    VACATION,
    UNDER_INVESTIGATION,
    RETIRED
}
```

There is one little more thing I want to show you, in which the CriminalCase entity is needed.

```kotlin
//Entities.kt file
package com.apress.cems.kotlin

...

@Entity
data class CriminalCase(
        @NotEmpty @Column(name = "case_number", unique = true, nullable =
        false)
            var number: String? = null,
        @NotNull @Column(name = "case_type") @Enumerated(EnumType.STRING)
            var type : CaseType = CaseType.UNCATEGORIZED,
        @NotEmpty @Column(name = "short_description")
            var shortDescription: String? = null,
            var detailedDescription: String? = null,
        @NotEmpty @Enumerated(EnumType.STRING)
            var status: CaseStatus = CaseStatus.SUBMITTED,
                        var notes: String? = null,
        @ManyToOne @JoinColumn(name = "LEAD_INVESTIGATOR", nullable = false)
            var leadInvestigator: Detective? = null,
        @ManyToMany @JoinTable(name = "working_detective_case",
                joinColumns = [JoinColumn(name = "case_id",
                    referencedColumnName = "id")],
```

```
        inverseJoinColumns = [JoinColumn(name = "detective_id",
            referencedColumnName = "id")])
        val assigned: MutableSet<Detective> = mutableSetOf())
 : AbstractEntity()
```

In the Java version, the `assigned` field was declared like this:

```
private Set<Detective> assigned = new HashSet<>();
```

In Kotlin, this is no longer possible. `mutableSetOf()` returns `MutableSet`, which is exactly the type that we must use to prevent problems later in the code.

That's it for the entity classes. As you can see, Kotlin is more compact and reduces a lot of the boilerplate code that a developer needs to write. Sure, in Java, tools like Lombok[10] can do the same thing, but it all depends on how IDEs and plugins support it. You might have your code working fine, and after an IDE or plugin update, all your code becomes red, and your build is broken and complaining about missing getters, setters, constructors, and so on.[11]

Creating and Testing the Repositories

Creating Kotlin JPA repositories is easy, but we cannot really credit Kotlin for this. Using Spring Data JPA removes a lot of the hassle in Java too. So, as we did earlier, a file named `Repositories.kt` contains all repository declarations.

```
//Repositories.kt
package com.apress.cems.kotlin

import org.springframework.data.jpa.repository.JpaRepository
import org.springframework.data.jpa.repository.Query
import org.springframework.data.repository.query.Param
import java.time.LocalDateTime
import java.util.*

interface DetectiveRepo : JpaRepository<Detective, Long>

interface CriminalCaseRepo : JpaRepository<CriminalCase, Long>
```

---

[10]Official site:https://projectlombok.org/

[11]There are other disadvantages; just take a peek at this discussion on StackOverflow: https:// stackoverflow.com/questions/3852091/is-it-safe-to-use-project-lombok

```kotlin
interface PersonRepo : JpaRepository<Person, Long> {
    @Query("select p from Person p where p.username like %?1%")
    fun findByUsername(username: String): Optional<Person>

    @Query("select p from Person p where p.firstName=:fn and p.lastName=:ln")
    fun findByCompleteName(@Param("fn") fn: String,
            @Param("ln") lastName: String): Optional<Person>

    @Query("select p from Person p where p.username like %?1%")
    fun findByUsernameLike(username: String): List<Person>

    // etc; you get the point
}
```

Java method declarations annotated with custom queries are replaced by function declarations with the same characteristics.

Up until now we have a Spring JPA application. Before writing the controllers, we could test it and make sure that our repositories and entities actually work together. For this, a very smart annotation for testing repositories provided by the Spring Boot Test module can be used: @DataJpaTest. When used on a test class, in a Spring Boot application, this annotation will disable full auto-configuration and instead apply only configuration relevant to JPA tests. This means tests will be transactional and will run on an in-memory embedded database. This annotation also enables the creation of a bean of type TestEntityManager that exposes a slimmed down collection of methods of an EntityManager and can set up a test environment.

The RepositoryTests class contains two test methods, one tests that the personRepo bean can save a Person instance and one that tests that the findByCompleteName(..) custom repository method works as expected.

```kotlin
// RepositoryTests.kt
package com.apress.cems.kotlin

import org.junit.jupiter.api.Test
import org.assertj.core.api.Assertions.assertThat
import org.springframework.beans.factory.annotation.Autowired
import org.springframework.boot.test.autoconfigure.orm.jpa.DataJpaTest
import org.springframework.boot.test.autoconfigure.orm.jpa.
TestEntityManager
```

```kotlin
@DataJpaTest
class RepositoryTests @Autowired constructor(
        val entityManager: TestEntityManager,
        val personRepo: PersonRepo) {

    @Test
    fun `Person save`(){
        val person  =  Person("test", "person", "test.person","test",
                DateProcessor.toDate("1983-08-15 00:23"))
        val savedPerson = personRepo.save(person)

        assertThat(savedPerson.id).isNotEqualTo(0)
        assertThat(savedPerson).isEqualTo(person)
    }

    @Test
    fun `Person findByCompleteName`() {
        val person = Person("test", "person", "test.person", "test",
                DateProcessor.toDate("1983-08-15 00:23"))
        entityManager.persist(person)
        entityManager.flush()

        val found  = personRepo.findByCompleteName("test", "person");
        assertThat(found.get()).isEqualTo(person)
    }
}
```

Since Spring 4.3, the @Autowired annotation is no longer needed if the bean class has a single constructor. This is only valid for Java applications, however. Kotlin requires @ Autowired in the constructor of the RepositoryTests class; otherwise, it cannot inject the required dependencies.

In the `Person save` test method, we are testing that the equals method generated by the Kotlin compiler works as expected. The test should pass, and the Gradle report should look as it is shown in Figure 10-12.

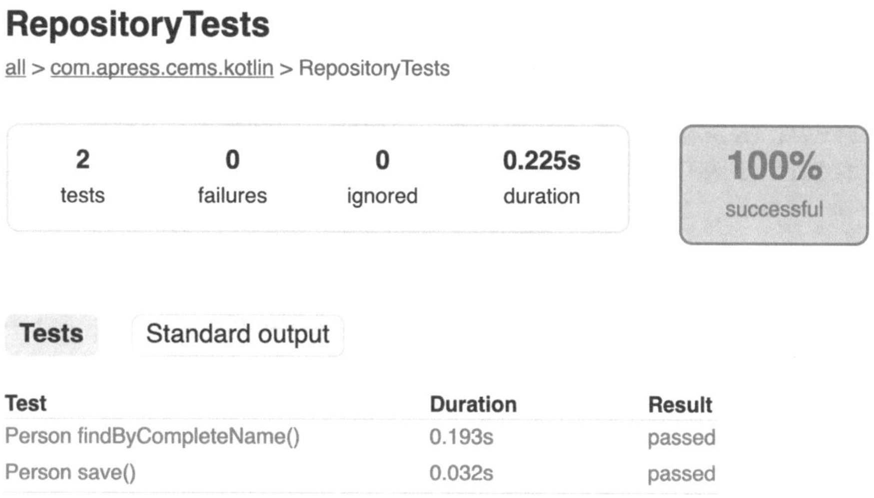

RepositoryTests

all > com.apress.cems.kotlin > RepositoryTests

2	0	0	0.225s	100%
tests	failures	ignored	duration	successful

Tests   Standard output

Test	Duration	Result
Person findByCompleteName()	0.193s	passed
Person save()	0.032s	passed

Figure 10-12. *Gradle report showing passing tests*

Since the application we are building has no complex logic between the repositories and the controller, we can skip implementing the service layer, so the controllers will reference the repositories directly. You won't be able to do that in a production application.

Creating the Controllers and Testing Them

So, the data access has now been verified, it is time to migrate the controllers. As you can assume by now, a single file is needed and it is named `WebControllers.kt`. To start things slowly let's first write the controller as a simple class that populates the home page with a message.

```kotlin
// WebControllers.kt
package com.apress.cems.kotlin

import org.springframework.stereotype.Controller
import org.springframework.web.bind.annotation.GetMapping
import org.springframework.ui.Model
import org.springframework.ui.set

@Controller
class WebControllers {
```

```kotlin
    @GetMapping(value = ["/", "/home"])
    fun home(model: Model): String {

        model["message"] = "Spring MVC Kotlin Example!"
        return "home"
    }
}
```

To set a property in Kotlin, you do not have to call a method. To set the message attribute in Java, you have to write something like this:

```java
model.addAttribute("message", "Spring MVC Kotlin Example!");
```

Start the application. If you see the homepage depicted in Figure 10-13, you're on the right track.

Figure 10-13. *Spring Boot Kotlin application frontpage*

To add the rest of controller methods, like the ones that populate models with Person instances the personRepo bean must be injected as a dependency. So the WebControllers becomes the following.

```kotlin
// WebControllers.kt
package com.apress.cems.kotlin

package com.apress.cems.kotlin
```

```kotlin
import org.springframework.context.MessageSource
import org.springframework.stereotype.Controller
import org.springframework.web.bind.annotation.GetMapping
import org.springframework.ui.Model
import org.springframework.ui.set
import org.springframework.validation.BindingResult
import org.springframework.validation.FieldError
import org.springframework.validation.annotation.Validated
import org.springframework.web.bind.annotation.ModelAttribute
import org.springframework.web.bind.annotation.PathVariable
import java.time.LocalDateTime
import java.time.format.DateTimeParseException
import java.util.*

@Controller
class WebControllers(private val personRepo: PersonRepo,
     private val messageSource: MessageSource) {

    @GetMapping(value = ["/", "/home"])
    fun home(model: Model): String {
        model["message"] = "Spring MVC Kotlin Example!"
        return "home"
    }

    @GetMapping("/persons")
    fun persons(model:Model) : String {

        model["persons"] = personRepo.findAll()
        return "persons/list"
    }
    @GetMapping("/persons/{id}")
    fun person(@PathVariable id: Long, model:Model) : String {
        personRepo.findById(id).ifPresent { p ->

            model["person"] = p
        }
        return "persons/show"
    }
```

```kotlin
    @GetMapping("/persons/form")
    fun getSearchForm(criteria: CriteriaDto): String {
        return "persons/search"
    }

    @GetMapping("persons/search")
    fun performSearch(@Validated @ModelAttribute("criteriaDto")criteria:
    CriteriaDto,
        result: BindingResult , model: Model, locale: Locale) :String {
    if (result.hasErrors()) return "persons/search"

        return try {
            val persons = getByCriteriaDto(criteria)
            if (persons.isEmpty()) {
                result.addError(FieldError("criteriaDto", "noResults",
                    messageSource.getMessage("NotEmpty.criteriaDto.noResults",
                    null, locale)))
                "persons/search"
            } else if (persons.size == 1) {
                "redirect:/persons/" + persons[0].id
            } else {
                model["persons"] =  persons
                "persons/list"
            }
        } catch (ice: InvalidCriteriaException) {
            result.addError(FieldError("criteriaDto", ice.fieldName,
            messageSource.getMessage(ice.messageKey, null, locale)))
            "persons/search"
        }
    }

    @Throws(InvalidCriteriaException::class)
    fun getByCriteriaDto(criteria: CriteriaDto): List<Person> {
    ... // code not relevant for the example
    }
}
```

So, you can see a lot of familiar elements in the previous code, such as the typical Spring Web–specific annotations, like @Controller on the class, @GetMapping on functions handling URIs, and so on. The novelty here is the @Throws(InvalidCriteriaException::class). The exception class is declared in the Util.kt class and extends RuntimeException.

```
class InvalidCriteriaException(var fieldName: String = "",
    var messageKey: String = "") : RuntimeException()
```

The @Throws(InvalidCriteriaException::class) annotation is a hint for the Kotlin compiler that this exception should be declared by a function when compiled to a JVM method. But since the type is RuntimeException, the Kotlin compiler is smart enough to ignore it. So if you decompile the WebControllers class as shown to you in a previous section, you will see that the getByCriteriaDto(..) method does not throw InvalidCriteriaException. If the declaration of the class changes to extend Exception, decompiling the class will reveal the method declared with InvalidCriteriaException.

The IDE recommended putting that annotation there. After reading about it, I decided to keep it because it makes the code easier to read and offers information about the function, such as it might throw a InvalidCriteriaException. This supports the proper development of functions calling it, because the possibility of this exception being thrown can be taken into account and handled properly.

Conclusion

Kotlin is awesome for building Spring applications, because it reduces the need for writing boilerplate, but still manages to remain readable. Kotlin is widely supported in the IT industry and its promise of efficient coding and increasing development productivity makes it an interesting candidate for startups and companies that are trying to improve their codebase.

This chapter was added to the book because the relationship between Pivotal and Kotlin seems to be getting stronger. I can totally see the next edition of this book containing even more Kotlin-based examples.

This chapter was designed to be a step-by-step guide to migrate an existing Spring Boot Java project to Kotlin. A working codebase is provided to you in the chapter10 directory under the pivotal-certified-pro-spring-dev-exam-02 project root. Try to follow the steps to migrate chapter06/boot-web yourself. Use the sources in chapter10 for verification purposes.

CHAPTER 11

Microservices with Spring Cloud

Microservices[1] are a specialization and implementation approach for service-oriented architectures (SOA). They are used to build flexible, independently deployable services. Although not part of the exam, the topic of microservices is covered in an optional session because they are widely used nowadays, which has had an effect on Spring Cloud. The number of projects that can be used to create microservices and integrate them with existing technologies has grown considerably since the previous edition of this book. Just take a look at the official page at `https://spring.io/projects/spring-cloud/#samples`.

The microservices paradigm requires services to be broken down into highly specialized instances of functionality and interconnected through agnostic communication protocols (like REST) that work together to accomplish a common business goal. Each microservice is a small unit of stateless functionality, a process that does not care where the input is coming from and does not know where its output is going to. It has no idea what the big picture is. By being this specialized and decoupled, each problem can be identified; the cause localized and fixed; and the implementation redeployed without affecting other microservices. This means that microservices systems have a high cohesion of responsibilities and really low coupling. These qualities allow the architecture of an individual service to evolve through continuous refactoring, reduces the necessity of a big up-front design, and allows software to be released earlier and continuously. Splitting up a large complex application into smaller detached applications allows the rapid, frequent, and reliable delivery of features, but also facilitates the evolution of the technology stack used by a company.

---

[1] A good site to keep up to date with the innovations in the industry: `https://microservices.io/`

© Iuliana Cosmina 2020

I. Cosmina, *Pivotal Certified Professional Core Spring 5 Developer Exam*,
https://doi.org/10.1007/978-1-4842-5136-2_11

Microservices have grown in popularity in recent years, and their small granularity and lightweight communication protocols have become the preferred way to build enterprise applications. Microservices' modular architectural style seems particularly well suited to cloud-based environments. This architectural method is scalable and considered ideal when multiple platforms and devices must be supported. Consider the biggest players, including Twitter, Netflix, Amazon, PayPal, and SoundCloud. They have large-scale websites and applications that have evolved from monolithic architectures to microservices so that they can be accessible from any kind of device.

Amazon and Google are currently the biggest in the business providing a suite of cloud computing services that are ideal for building complex applications made up of numerous microservices working together. Businesses that provide software and services for banks, retailers, restaurants, small businesses, telecom and technology have no choice but to rely on AWS or GCP to keep their services available to their clients at all times by building their microservices using Apigee[2] or the Amazon API Gateway.[3]

Amazon and Google provide the infrastructure for the microservices to communicate, and even some tools to build them; but writing the code for these services is still the responsibility of the developers. Spring Boot is a good tool to build a small, niched application that represents a microservice in a more complex application.

Classic application development is characterized by multiple types of services being developed as a single unit—a monolithic autonomous unit deployed on a server for clients to access. Usually, these applications are multilayered, and each layer corresponds to different functional areas of the application. The monolith application handles HTTP/HTTPS requests, executes business logic, and handles database operations.

In a monolithic infrastructure, the services that make the system are organized logically within the same code base and unit of deployment. The disadvantage of monolithic applications is that changes end up being tied to another and sometimes problems are harder to identify when there are multiple layers involved. A modification made to a small section of an application might require building and deploying an entirely new version. Regression tests verify that code previously developed and tested

---

[2]Apigee, part of Google Cloud, helps leading companies design, secure, and scale application programming interfaces (APIs). Read more about it here: `https://cloud.google.com/apigee/`

[3]Amazon API Gateway is a fully managed service that makes it easy for developers to create, publish, maintain, monitor, and secure APIs at any scale. Read more about it here: `https://aws.amazon.com/api-gateway/`

performs correctly after it was changed; these are mandatory. Thus, underlining advantages and disadvantages of microservices can only be done by comparing them to old-style monolithic architecture.

What are the main advantages of using microservices? The following is praised in the IT industry.

- increased granularity

- increased scalability

- easy-to-automate deployment and testing, because microservices are characterized by well-defined interfaces that facilitate communication (JSON/ WSDL/JMS/AMQP) (depends on the context, because if transactions are involved, things start to become difficult)

- increased decoupling, since microservices do not share state of the service[4]

- enhanced cohesion

- suitable for continuous refactoring, integration and delivery

- increased module independence

- specialized: organized around capabilities; each microservice is designed for one specific capability

- improved agility and velocity, because when a system is correctly decomposed into microservices, each service can be developed and deployed independently and in parallel with the others

- each service is elastic[5], resilient, composable, minimal, and complete.

- improvement of fault isolation

- elimination of long-term commitment to a single technology stack, because micro services can be written in different programming languages

- makes it easier to integrate new developers in a team

---

[4]When sharing state is necessary it can be done using a database.
[5]A microservice must be able to scale, up or down, independently of other services in the same application.

Microservices seem cool, but there must be some disadvantages, right? Yup, here's a few of them.

- Microservices introduce additional complexity and the necessity of carefully handling of requests between services.

- Handling shared resources like entity classes can cause problems.

- Handling multiple databases and transactions (distributed transactions) can be painful.

- Testing microservices can be cumbersome, as each dependency of a microservice must be confirmed valid, before the service can be tested.

- Deployment can become complex as well, requiring coordination among services.

The new-age titan applications that need to support multiple clients and platforms are very good candidates for microservices. Microservices help break up monolith applications into individual units of deployment, which are able to evolve their own scaling requirements, irrespective of the other subsystems. Let's see if Spring can make development of microservices based applications as practical as it has made monolith applications development.

Microservices with Spring

Microservices architecture idea is similar do how beans are managed by the Spring container and communicate in a Spring application context. Imagine it like this: if a Spring application context is a forest, then each bean is a tree. Microservices are the full-blown ecosystem. This example was given to you because programming is nothing else than modeling the real world using software components, and might make the idea of microservices more approachable. The demo application built in this book is basically a site that is an interface for a complex system managing information about police personnel and their work on criminal cases. It is obviously not realistic enough to be used, but it does provide interesting development challenges.

If it is built with microservices (as it should, because this application should be distributed and accessed by police personnel in a certain region), separate microservices would have to be developed for persons (people in the system that do not do police work, but need to be registered and kept track of because of their access), detectives, criminal cases, evidence, and storage management. This also means that a few moving components are needed to set up such a system, because communication between microservices must be covered too. Figure 11-1 depicts the classic monolith architecture and the microservices architecture side by side. (The representations are not complete and do not list all components since that would make the diagrams too complex.)

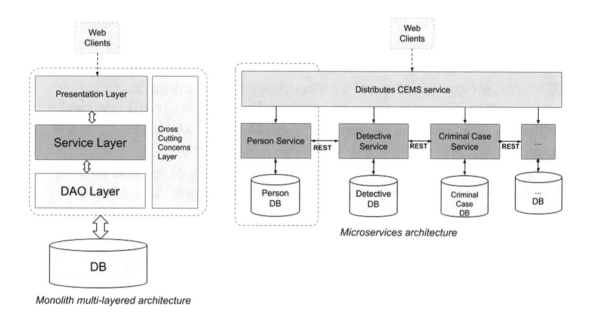

Monolith multi-layered architecture

Figure 11-1. *Monolith and microservices architecture*

Figure 11-1 is generic, and it might lead to the idea that each microservice has its own database, which is correct, but there is not actually a need to provision a database server for each service. It really depends on the type of application you are building. The database used in development can be relational (SQL based) or non-relational (NoSQL). If a relational database is used, there are three options of database implementation strategies.

- **private-tables-per-service**: each service owns a set of tables that must only be accessed by that service

- **schema-per-service**: each service has a database schema that's private to that service

- **database-server-per-service**: each service has its own database server

The chosen microservice database strategy implementation influences the type of database that is most suitable for the application. Private-tables-per-service and schema-per-service have the lowest overhead. Using a schema per service is appealing since it makes ownership clearer. Also, if there is one database server that is shared among microservices, a relational database is suitable as all the data is in one place and organized properly by following normalization standards, even if this might cause problems with concurrent access to it and network traffic. Having a different database for each service might make sharing data among services difficult and introduce data redundancy. NoSQL databases are more suitable for this type of implementation as they are better am handling redundant data. Also, keep in mind that a downside of not sharing databases is that maintaining data consistency and implementing queries is more challenging. Also, when it comes to entity classes, how should they be implemented and shared among services? A possible answer will be provided later in the chapter.

Spring Boot is the only tool for Java development of advanced applications as those based on the microservices architecture, because of the following characteristics.

- dependency injection and integration

- super practical configuration and service creation

- straightforward service discovery registry

To develop a microservices application with Spring components good knowledge of the following Spring technologies is needed.

- a service registration and discovery technology like Netflix's OSS Eureka

- Spring Cloud projects like Eureka or Consul

- REST concepts

Spring Boot is designed for developer heightened productivity by making common concepts, like RESTful HTTP and embedded web application runtimes easy to wire up and use. It is flexible and allows developer to pick only modules they want to use, removing the overwhelming or bulky configurations and runtime dependencies.

Spring Cloud[6] is a big umbrella project that provides development tools designed to ease the development of distributed applications and contains components designed to build common patterns in distributed systems.

- configuration management (Spring Cloud Config provides centralized external configuration backed by a Git repository)

- service discovery (Eureka is a service registry for resilient mid-tier load balancing and failover and is supported by Spring Cloud)

- circuit breakers (Spring Cloud supports Netflix's Hystrix is a library that provides components that stop calling services when a response is not received in a predefined threshold)

- intelligent routing (Zuul forwards and distributes calls to services)

- micro-proxy (client-side proxies to mid-tier services)

- control bus (a messaging system can be used for monitoring and managing the components within the framework as is used for "application-level" messaging)

- one-time tokens (used for data access only once with Spring Vault[7])

- global locks (used to coordinate, prioritize, or restrict access to resources)

- leadership election (the process of designating a single process as the organizer of some task distributed among several nodes)

- distributed messaging (Spring Cloud Bus links the nodes of a distributed system with a lightweight message broker)

- cluster state (cluster state request is routed to the master node to ensure that the latest cluster state is returned)

- client-side load balancing

If you are interested in building microservices applications with Spring Cloud, the official Spring documentation covers all the basics.

---

[6]Official project page: https://spring.io/projects/spring-cloud
[7]Official page of Spring Vault: https://projects.spring.io/spring-vault/

Coordinating distributed systems is not easy and can lead to boilerplate code. Spring Cloud just makes it easier for developers to write this type of management code and the result works in any distributed environment including a development station, data centers or managed platforms as Cloud Foundry.[8] Spring Cloud builds on Spring Boot and it comes with the typical Spring Boot advantages: preconfigured infrastructure beans that can be further configured or extended to create a custom solution. It follows the same Spring declarative approach, relying on annotations and property files.

Spring Cloud Netflix provides integration with Netflix OSS (Netflix Open Source Software; `https://netflix.github.io/`). It is a collection of open source libraries that the developers wrote to solve distributed-systems problems at scale. Written in Java, it became the most used software for writing microservices applications in Java.

Registration and Discovery Server

The microservices architecture ensures on the fact that a set of processes will work together toward a common goal: providing the end user a competent and reliable service. For this to work, the processes must communicate efficiently. To communicate with each other, first have to know of each other. This is where Netflix Eureka registration server comes in. And because it is open source, it was incorporated in Spring Cloud and the simplicity principles of Spring now apply.

In the previous edition of this book, there was a single project that contained the microservices implementations and each of them was started from a main class based on command line arguments. In this version of the book, there are separate projects to respect the microservices architecture even more. All the projects are declared in the Chapter 11 module, and you can see them listed in Figure 11-2.

---

[8]Spring Cloud projects are publicly available on GitHub: `https://github.com/spring-cloud`

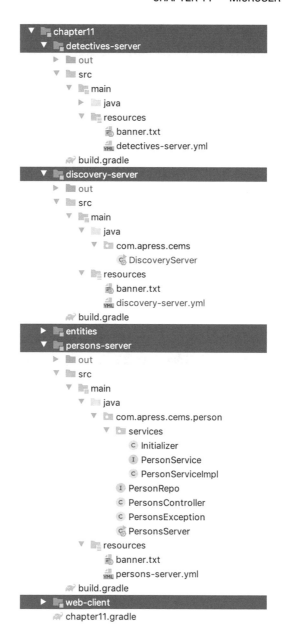

Figure 11-2. *Microservices project structure*

The discovery-server project implements a registration or discovery server that is used by our microservices to register and discover each other.

The configuration of the project is nothing special, it is just a simple Spring Boot web application with the Eureka server dependency on the classpath. The next configuration snippet contains the Gradle configuration for this project.

As usually, the first snippet is the declaration of the dependencies in the pivotal-certified-pro-spring-dev-exam-02/build.gradle and the second is the configuration of the chapter11/discovery-server/build.gradle. The new thing here is the dependency on the BOM special spring cloud version. The dependency on this file ensures that dependency management loads the proper dependencies for the project.

```
//pivotal-certified-pro-spring-dev-exam-02/build.gradle
ext {

    springBootVersion = '2.2.0.M5'
    springDataCommonsVersion = '2.1.10.RELEASE'
    springCloudVersion = '2.1.2.RELEASE'
    cloudReleaseTrainVersion ='Hoxton.M2'

        cloud = [
            cloudStarter :
                "org.springframework.cloud:spring-cloud-starter-
                config:$springCloudVersion",
            eurekaServer :
  "org.springframework.cloud:spring-cloud-starter-netflix-eureka-
  server:$springCloudVersion",
            eurekaClient :
   "org.springframework.cloud:spring-cloud-starter-netflix-eureka-
   client:$springCloudVersion",
            bom :
                "org.springframework.cloud:spring-cloud-dependencies:$cloud
                ReleaseTrainVersion"
    ]

    boot = [
            starterWeb :
                "org.springframework.boot:spring-boot-starter-
                web:$springBootVersion",
            actuator :
                "org.springframework.boot:spring-boot-starter-
                actuator:$springBootVersion",
            ...
```

```
    ]
...
}
//chapter11/discovery-server/build.gradle
apply plugin: 'java-library'
apply plugin: 'org.springframework.boot'
apply plugin: 'io.spring.dependency-management'

dependencies {
    implementation  `[cloud.cloudStarter], [cloud.eurekaServer], spring.jdbc,
            boot.starterWeb,  boot.actuator
}

dependencyManagement {
    imports {
        mavenBom cloud.bom
    }
}
```

The persons-server and detectives-server are standalone Spring Boot applications that manage Person and Detective instances through beans of type PersonServices and DetectiveServices. They each work with their own database (just because it was easier to set them up with an in-memory H2 database, instead of using an Oracle database in a Docker container).

The entities project contains entity and utility classes that are used by persons-server and detectives-server projects. This project is not a microservice in itself; it is just a module that groups together classes used by multiple micro-services for compilation purpose.

The web-client project is a special type of microservice that will be introduced later.

Each of the projects has been customized to read the application configuration from a configuration file named as the project instead of the typical application.yml file. This makes for better visibility when navigating the project.

And now that the project structure was covered let's dig into each of them separately.

The discovery-server project implements a registration or discovery server, which coordinates communication between the microservices. The application stores all the information about all the microservices. The service is named Eureka and is a dynamic service discovery and every microservice will be registered in the server so that Eureka will know all the client applications running on each port and IP address. Eureka comes with a server and a client-side component. The discovery server application uses the Eureka server component, while all the other microservices use the client-side component. The server component will be the registry in which all the microservices register their availability. Each microservice will be configured with the location of the Eureka server and after booting up will connect to the Eureka server to register.

The discover server application can be declared like in the following snippet.

```
package com.apress.cems;

import org.slf4j.Logger;
import org.slf4j.LoggerFactory;
import org.springframework.boot.SpringApplication;
import org.springframework.boot.autoconfigure.SpringBootApplication;
import org.springframework.cloud.netflix.eureka.server.EnableEurekaServer;

import java.io.IOException;

@SpringBootApplication
@EnableEurekaServer
public class DiscoveryServer {

    private static Logger logger = LoggerFactory.getLogger(DiscoveryServer.
    class);

    public static void main(String... args) throws IOException {
        // Look for configuration in discovery.properties or discovery-
        server.yml
        System.setProperty("spring.config.name", "discovery");

        var ctx = SpringApplication.run(DiscoveryServer.class, args);
        assert (ctx != null);
        logger.info("Started ...");
        System.in.read();
        ctx.close();
    }
}
```

✱✱ The System.in.read(); call is used so you can stop the application gracefully by pressing the <ENTER> key.

To use the Eureka Server in a project, the spring-cloud-starter-netflix-eureka-server[9] starter project must be included as a dependency of the project. Notice the @EnableEurekaServer annotation. This annotation is very important since it activates Eureka Server related configuration. That annotation is responsible for providing a Eureka server instance for the project. The server has a home page with a UI and HTTP API endpoints per the normal Eureka functionality all accessible from the pain page at http://localhost:[port]/.

The discovery.yml file contains settings for this server. By default, Spring Boot looks for a file named application to read configuration from. To specify that configuration should be read from a different file, the name of the file must be added as a value for the system property spring.config.name by calling System.setProperty("spring.config.name", "discovery-server"); before creating the Spring context.

```
spring:
  application:
    name: discovery-service
# Configure this Discovery Server
eureka:
  instance:
    hostname: localhost
  client:
    registerWithEureka: false # do not auto-register as client
    fetchRegistry: false

server:
  port: 3000    # where this discovery server is accessible
  waitTimeInMsWhenSyncEmpty: 0
  address: 0.0.0.0
```

! If the port value is not specified, the default value for the port is implicitly set to 8761. (In the preceding example, the port is set to 3000.)

---

[9]There are considerable differences between Spring Cloud 1.x and Spring Cloud 2.x. In the previous edition of the book, since Spring Cloud 1.x was used the dependency was *spring-cloud-starter-eureka-server*.

The server will be available on the 3000 port and when the preceding class is run, the server interface depicting a few stats and registered microservices becomes accessible from the browser at location `http://localhost:3000/` or `http://127.0.0.1:3000/` or `http://0.0.0.0:3000/` depending on how the Spring Boot application is configured. In the previous configuration, the server is available on all IPs of the machine.

Figure 11-3 depicts the interface of a naked Eureka Server, with no microservices registered yet.

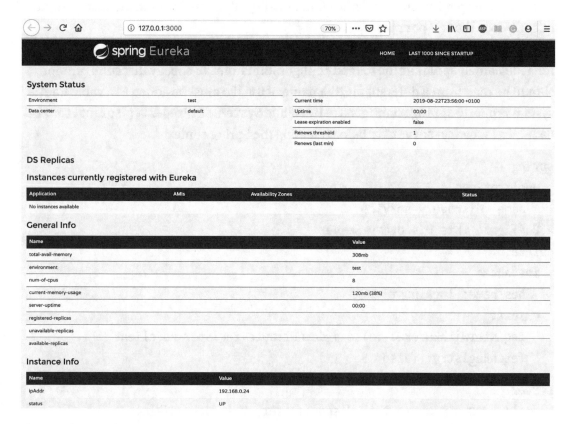

Figure 11-3. *Spring Eureka web interface with no microservices registered yet*

Netflix's original version of the Eureka server avoids answering clients for a configurable period of time if it starts with an empty registry. The `waitTimeInMsWhenSyncEmpty` property controls this behavior. It was designed so that clients would not get partial/empty registry information until the server had enough time to build the registry. In the previous example, it is set to zero to start answering clients as soon as possible.

! If not set, the default value for the `server.waitTimeInMsWhenSyncEmpty` is **5 minutes**.

! The `eureka.client.registerWithEureka` property has "true" as a default value and registers Eureka clients. As the application registers a server, it must be explicitly set to "false" to stop the server from trying to register itself.

The Spring Eureka interface provides also monitoring information about the machine the microservices run on. And now that we have the registration server, the microservices can be developed, but before getting into that there is another thing worth mentioning.

In the code for the book, all projects share a complex Gradle configuration that ensures the stability of the full build, when versions are upgraded. When writing microservices applications using Spring Boot, if you are not interested in a Gradle configuration, you can use Spring Initializr (available at `https://start.spring.io/`) to generate the configuration for your discovery project. Figure 11-4 depicts the dependencies that you need to select.

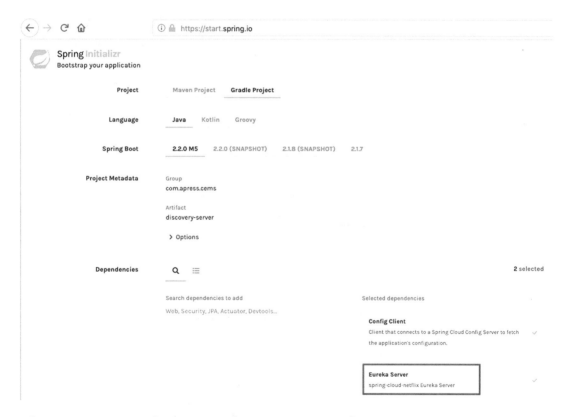

Figure 11-4. *Using Spring Initializr to generate a discovery server Spring Boot project*

Microservices Development

To create a microservice, a service implementation and a class that will interact with the registration and discovery server to register itself as client are needed. The implementation of the service is a typical Spring service and in our example, we'll have three microservices: one that will handle persons, one that will handle detectives and one that will connect the functionality of the two of them. Figure 11-5 is a schema of how these microservices interact.

The web service aggregates information from the other two services to compose views and render them to the end user. It communicates with the other microservices using a dynamic routing and load balancer called Ribbon.

A microservice is a stand-alone process that handles a well-defined requirement. When creating a distributed application that is based on microservices, each microservice components should be wrapped up together in packages based on their purpose and the overall implementation should be very loosely coupled, but very cohesive. In this scenario, all the components making up the microservice application managing Person instances are grouped under the com.apress.cems.person package. And this goes for the Person entity as well, but this entity is in a different project.

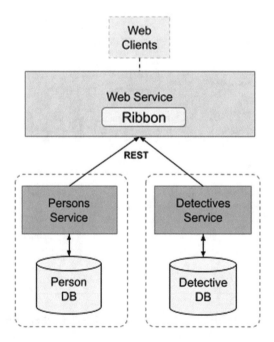

Figure 11-5. *Microservices interaction: abstract depiction*

In Figure 11-6, the `persons-server` and `entities` projects structure is depicted.

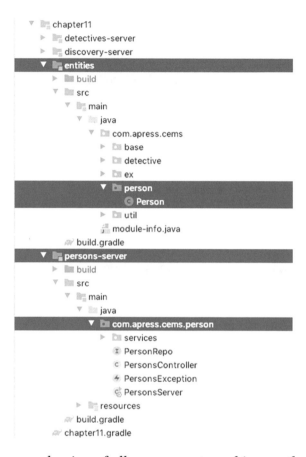

Figure 11-6. *Proper packaging of all components making up the microservice application managing Person instances*

The structure of the microservice application managing `Detective` instances is pretty similar, the only difference is that the last package in the hierarchy is named `detective` instead of `person`.

Now, both `persons-server` and `detectives-server` projects contain the code of a Spring REST web application that expose REST services APIs for managing `Person`, respectively `Detective` instances. Wouldn't it be nice to have another microservice that has a web interface and communicates with these two to retrieve information from them and display it in a pretty web interface? I mean a web service that manages `Person` and `Detective` instances. Yes, it would be nice, and although rarely mentioned until now, this special microservice application is part of the code for this book.

In Figure 11-7, all the beans making up the microservices and their interactions are depicted.

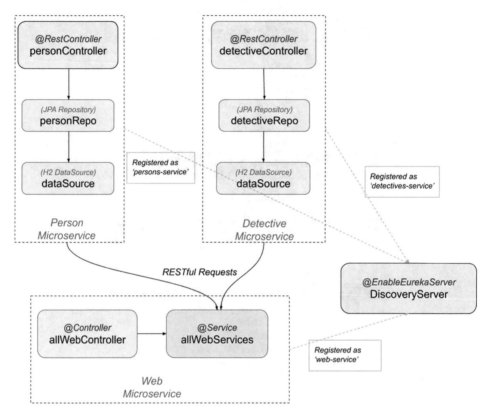

Figure 11-7. *Chapter 11 project architecture*

The persons-service and detectives-service microservices implementations are similar, each of them uses a Spring Data JPA repository bean (JpaRepository<T,ID> implementation) and a Spring REST controller to provide a RESTful interface to expose their data.

```
package com.apress.cems.person;
 ...

@RestController
@RequestMapping("/persons")
public class PersonsController {
```

```
@ResponseStatus(HttpStatus.OK)
@GetMapping(produces = MediaType.APPLICATION_JSON_VALUE)
public List<Person> list() {
    List<Person> persons =  personService.findAll();
    persons.sort(COMPARATOR_BY_ID);
    return persons;
}

@ResponseStatus(HttpStatus.OK)
@GetMapping(value ="/{id}", produces = MediaType.APPLICATION_JSON_VALUE)
public Person show(@PathVariable Long id) {
    var personOpt = personService.findById(id);
    if(personOpt.isPresent()) {
        return personOpt.get();
    } else {
        throw new NotFoundException(Person.class, id );
    }
}
...
}
```

The PersonsServer class is a Spring Boot special class that registers with the Eureka discovery and registration server configured. This application registers itself as a client. To use the Eureka client in a project, the spring-cloud-starter-netflix-eureka-client project must be included as a dependency of the project.[10]

```
package com.apress.cems.person;

import org.slf4j.Logger;
import org.slf4j.LoggerFactory;
import org.springframework.boot.SpringApplication;
import org.springframework.boot.autoconfigure.SpringBootApplication;
import org.springframework.boot.autoconfigure.domain.EntityScan;
import org.springframework.cloud.netflix.eureka.EnableEurekaClient;
```

[10]In the previous edition of the book, using Spring Cloud 1.x, both the Eureka server and client were part of the *spring-cloud-starter-eureka-server* module. In Spring Cloud 2.x the two have been separated each in its own module.

```java
import java.io.IOException;

@EntityScan(basePackages = "com.apress.cems.person")
@SpringBootApplication
@EnableEurekaClient
public class PersonsServer {

    private static Logger logger = LoggerFactory.getLogger(PersonsServer.
    class);

    public static void main(String... args) throws IOException {
        // Look for configuration in persons-server.properties or persons-
        server.yml
        System.setProperty("spring.config.name", "persons-server");

        var ctx = SpringApplication.run(PersonsServer.class, args);
        assert (ctx != null);
        logger.info("Started ...");
        System.in.read();
        ctx.close();
    }
}
```

Two things need to be mentioned here.

- Since the entity classes come from an external project, Spring Boot
  has to be told where those entities can be found. This is where the
  @EntityScan annotation comes in handy.

- The @EnableEurekaClient annotation is the key component that
  transforms this application into a microservice, because it enables
  service registration and discovery. The process registers itself with
  the application named persons-service and specifies that it is
  available on port 4001 in the persons-server.yml configuration file.

The contents of the persons-server.yml relevant for the Eureka configuration are
depicted in the following configuration snippet.

```
# Spring properties
spring:
  application:
    name: persons-service # Service registers under this name

# HTTP Server
server:
  port: 4001    # HTTP (Tomcat) port

# Discovery Server Access
eureka:
  client:
    registerWithEureka: true
    fetchRegistry: false
    serviceUrl:
      defaultZone: http://localhost:3000/eureka/

  instance:
    leaseRenewalIntervalInSeconds: 5
    preferIpAddress: false
```

The previous configuration snippet contains three sections.

- The **Spring section** defines the application name as persons-service. The microservice will register itself with this name in the Eureka server.

- The **Server section** defines the custom port to listen on. All the microservice processes in the application are using Tomcat by default, because it is the implicit dependency of the spring-boot-starter-web and will try to use the 8080 port, and only one process can listen on a port at one time. So each microservice will have a different port assigned via configuration. persons-service has 4001, detectives-service has 4002 and web-service has 4000.

- The **Eureka section** defines the URL where the server to register to is located using the eureka.client.serviceUrl.defaultZone. Other properties can be set to customize the interaction with the Eureka server.

! The eureka.client.registerWithEureka property has true as a default value and registers Eureka clients. It is used here explicitly, for teaching purposes, to make it more obvious that the persons-service microservice is a client.

Eureka clients fetch the registry information from the server and cache it locally. After that, the clients use that information to find other services. As the persons-service does not need to communicate with other microservice it has no use for the registry information. So the eureka.client.fetchRegistry is set to false to not waste time and resources with a useless operation.

Eureka clients need to tell the server they are still active by sending a signal called heartbeat. By default, the interval is 30 seconds. But it can be set to smaller intervals by customizing the value of the eureka.instance.leaseRenewalIntervalInSeconds property. During development it can be set to a smaller value, which will speed up registration, but on production this will generate extra communication with the server that might cause service lag. For production the default value should not be modified.

The eureka.instance.preferIpAddress tells the Eureka server if it should use the domain name or an IP. In our case, because everything is working on the same machine, we prefer the domain name (localhost); so that is why the property is set to false.

All these details and much more are available on the Netflix GitHub page https://github.com/Netflix/ eureka/wiki/Understanding-eureka-client-server-communication. Only the ones important for the implementation given as example were quoted and explained here.

In the code for the book, all projects share a Gradle configuration (a small snippet was depicted earlier) that ensures the stability of the full build, when versions are upgraded. When writing microservices applications using Spring Boot, if you are not interested in a Gradle configuration, you can use Spring Initializr (available at https://start.spring.io/) to generate the configuration for your microservices projects. In Figure 11-8, the dependencies you need to select when doing so are depicted.

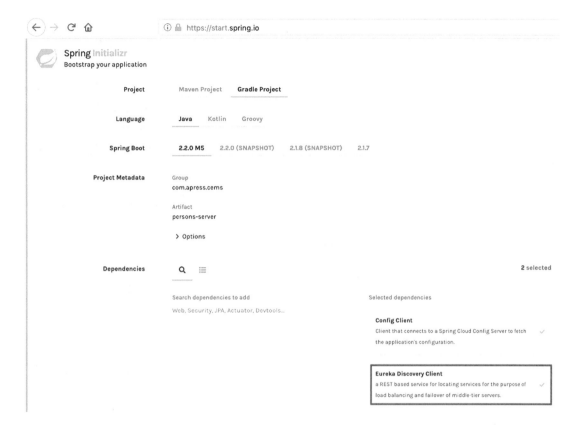

Figure 11-8. *Using Spring Initializr to generate a microservice Spring Boot project*

Before introducing the `web-service` project we should start the microservices we have and ensure everything is working properly. I am assuming at this point that your `discovery-server` project is still running, if not, this one must be started first because this exposes the server that the rest of the microservices will register with.

To start the `persons-service` application, the `PersonsServer` main class should be run. To start the `detectives-service` application, the `DetectivesServer` main class should be run. Both should be run after the `PersonsServer` main class and after confirming that the Eureka server is up.

When a microservice application is started, registration takes up to 30 seconds, if not set; otherwise, through a smaller value for the eureka.instance. leaseRenewalIntervalInSeconds property, so be patient and watch the console log of the registration server. All the main classes end with the Started ... text being displayed. If this text is displayed and no exceptions can be seen in any of the console, this means all instances were started correctly. You can also check the console for the console of the DiscoveryServer class. The registration should be completed for both of the microservices when you see the following output.

```
DEBUG o.s.c.n.e.server.InstanceRegistry - register PERSONS-SERVICE, vip
persons-server,
    leaseDuration 90, isReplication false
INFO  c.n.e.r.AbstractInstanceRegistry - Registered instance
        PERSONS-SERVICE/192.168.0.24:persons-server:4001 with status UP
        (replication=false)
DEBUG o.s.c.n.e.server.InstanceRegistry - renew PERSONS-SERVICE serverId
    192.168.0.24:persons-server:4001, isReplication {}false
INFO  c.n.e.r.PeerAwareInstanceRegistryImpl - Current renewal threshold is : 3
INFO  c.n.e.r.AbstractInstanceRegistry - Running the evict task with
compensationTime 2ms
DEBUG o.s.c.n.e.server.InstanceRegistry - register DETECTIVES-SERVICE, vip
detectives-server,
    leaseDuration 90, isReplication false
INFO  c.n.e.r.AbstractInstanceRegistry - Registered instance
    DETECTIVES-SERVICE/192.168.0.24:detectives-server:4002 with status UP
    (replication=false)
```

After registration, when accessing the http://localhost:3000/ interface for the Eureka server, you should see all the client services that were registered in the instances section, as depicted in Figure 11-9.

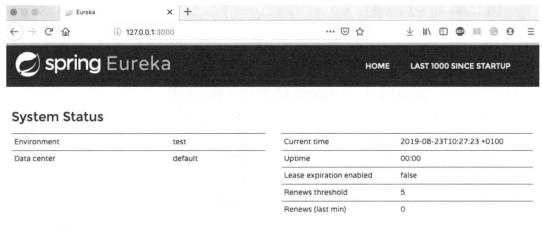

Figure 11-9. *Client microservices registered with the Eureka server*

More information about the registered microservices is at `http://localhost:3000/eureka/apps/`.

```
<applications>
  <versions__delta>1</versions__delta>
  <!-- how many instances are up: 2 -->
  <apps__hashcode>UP_2_</apps__hashcode>

  <application>
    <name>DETECTIVES-SERVICE</name>
    <instance>
        <instanceId>192.168.0.24:detectives-server:4002</instanceId>
        <hostName>192.168.0.24</hostName>
        <app>DETECTIVES-SERVICE</app>
        <ipAddr>192.168.0.24</ipAddr>
```

```
    <status>UP</status>
    <overriddenstatus>UNKNOWN</overriddenstatus>
    <port enabled="true">4002</port>
    <metadata>
            <management.port>4002</management.port>
    </metadata>
    <homePageUrl>http://192.168.0.24:4002/</homePageUrl>
    <statusPageUrl>http://192.168.0.24:4002/actuator/info</statusPageUrl>
    <healthCheckUrl>http://192.168.0.24:4002/actuator/health</healthCheckUrl>
    <vipAddress>detectives-server</vipAddress>
    ...
  </application>
  <!-- the others persons-service and web-service -->
  ...
</applications>
```

The same information is available at http://192.168.56.1:3000/eureka/apps/ DETECTIVES-SERVICE if the service was started correctly; otherwise, a 404 error will be displayed. If your services started on 0.0.0.0, they are available at any IP associated with the machine that they are running on. I preferred to use the real IP of my machine within the network to mimic a production situation. In an actual production environment you will either use real IPs from different machines or dedicated hostnames (like the ones provided by AWS).

At registration time, each microservice gets a unique registration identifier from the server, which you can see in the <instanceId> element in the previous output snippet. If another process registers with the same id, the server treats it as a restart, so the first process is discarded. To run multiple instances of the same process, for reasons of load balancing and resilience and because after all it is a distributed application and it should be possible to do this, we have to make sure the server generates a different registration ID. The simplest way this can be done is by providing the option of specifying a different port for the microservice. The registration ID (in the <instanceId> element) generated based on this template:

${ipAddress}:${spring.application.name:${server.port}}

The registration ID generation template can be set using Eureka property configurations.

```
eureka:
  instance:
    metadataMap:
      instanceId:
      ${spring.application.name}:${spring.application.instance_id:${server.
      port}}
```

If the `spring.application.instance_id` is not defined, it falls back to the default format.

When running a microservices application locally (as I imagine you are doing while going through this book), the main method for a microservice can be parametrized to take the port as an argument. This will allow you to start as many instances of that service as you wish.

```
// in the PersonsServer.main(...) method
 ...
    public static void main(String... args) throws IOException {
        if (args.length == 1) {
            System.setProperty("server.port", args[0]);
        }
        // Look for configuration in persons-server.properties or persons-
        server.yml
        System.setProperty("spring.config.name", "persons-server");
        ...
    }
...
```

In Figure 11-10, you can see that two `persons-service` instances were started and registered: the default on port 4001 and a second one on port 4003.

DS Replicas

Instances currently registered with Eureka

Application	AMIs	Availability Zones	Status
DETECTIVES-SERVICE	n/a (1)	(1)	UP (1) - 192.168.0.24:detectives-service:4002
PERSONS-SERVICE	n/a (2)	(2)	UP (2) - 192.168.0.24:persons-service:4001 , 192.168.0.24:persons-service:4003

Figure 11-10. *Two different PERSONS-SERVICE microservices registered with the Eureka Server*

Microservices Communication

Microservices communicate using agnostic protocols such as REST. The persons-service and detectives-service both expose RESTful interfaces over HTTP (although different protocols can be set up as well: JMS or AMQP, for example). In the next example, another service called web-service is introduced that uses REST to access their data. This service also exposes a web interface, where an end user can request data. To consume RESTful services, Spring provides the RestTemplate class, which can send HTTP requests to a RESTful server and fetch data in a number of formats such as XML or JSON. For simplicity, we'll use the JSON format for the data, because it is readable. The web-service microservice client uses a special RestTemplate to connect and request data from the other two registered microservices while being agnostic of their location and the exact URL as Spring will automatically configure the locations for it.

This project was depicted in Figure 11-2 and is named web-client to make it obvious that it contains the implementation of a microservice consuming the services provided by the other two.

The implementation of the web-client is a little different as a web interface is configured for it. The Eureka server uses FreeMarker templates by default, so if a different implementation is desired, these have to be first ignored via configuration by setting the spring.application.freemarker.enabled to false. The configuration file is named web-client.yml and its contents are depicted in the following configuration listing.

```
# Spring properties
spring:
  application:
    name: web-service
  freemarker:
    enabled: false      # Ignore Eureka dashboard FreeMarker templates
  thymeleaf:
    cache: false
    prefix: classpath:/templates/

# HTTP Server
server:
  port: 4000    # HTTP (Tomcat) port
  servlet:
    context-path: /
  compression:
    enabled: true

# Discovery Server Access
eureka:
  client:
    registerWithEureka: true
    fetchRegistry: true
    serviceUrl:
      defaultZone: http://localhost:3000/eureka/

  instance:
    leaseRenewalIntervalInSeconds: 5
    preferIpAddress: false
```

Aside from the freemarker.enabled property being set to false, to allow our application to use Thymeleaf templates, the most important property in the previous configuration is eureka.client.fetchRegistry that is set to true for this service. For the persons-service and detectives-service this property is set to false, because these two microservices do not care what other microservices are registered with the Eureka server. They were designed to be independent and stand-alone; they do not need other microservices to their job. So there is no need when they register themselves with the Eureka server, to ask it about other registered services.

The web-client microservice needs two microservices, persons-service and detectives-service, to do its job. After registering with the Eureka server, it needs to know if those two are registered as well, and setting this property to true makes this happen.

Communication with these two microservices is facilitated by a load balancer called Ribbon, but it made no sense earlier in the chapter to delve into it since it was not relevant for the context. Ribbon is a client-side load balancer that provides control over the behavior of HTTP and TCP clients. Ribbon's Client component offers a good set of configuration options such as connection timeouts, retries, retry algorithm (exponential, bounded back off), and so forth. Ribbon comes built in with a pluggable and customizable load-balancing component. Since we are using Spring Boot, there is no need to tweak the default configurations much.

Ribbon is added as a dependency to the project when spring-cloud-starter-netflix-eureka-client is on the classpath, and is part of the spring-cloud-netflix-ribbon module.[11] Ribbon is used under the hood by a special RestTemplate instance annotated with @LoadBalanced to identify existing microservices and direct calls to them or by LoadBalancerClient beans.

Since the web-client is actually a Spring Boot web application, with internationalized Thymeleaf templates extra configuration must be added. In the example for this book, internationalization configurations are added in a class named WebConfig. This class implements the WebMvcConfigurer as shown in Chapter 6, but it is not annotated with @EnableWebMvc. Since this is a Spring Boot web project, that has the spring-boot-starter-web on the classpath, this has been taken care of by Spring Boot. Using that annotation explicitly negatively affects the Spring Boot autoconfiguration mechanism. The following shows the contents of the WebConfig class, and they should be familiar to you by now.

```
package com.apress.cems.web;

...

@Configuration
class WebConfig implements WebMvcConfigurer {
```

---

[11]If you are interested in more advanced usage of Ribbon as a load balancer, here is a good tutorial: https://dzone.com/articles/
microservices-tutorial-ribbon-as-a-load-balancer-1

```java
@Override
public void addInterceptors(InterceptorRegistry registry) {
    registry.addInterceptor(localeChangeInterceptor());
}

@Bean
MessageSource messageSource() {
    ReloadableResourceBundleMessageSource messageResource =
            new ReloadableResourceBundleMessageSource();
    messageResource.setBasename("classpath:i18n/global");
    messageResource.setDefaultEncoding("UTF-8");
    messageResource.setUseCodeAsDefaultMessage(true);
    //messageResource.setCacheSeconds(0);
    return messageResource;
}

@Bean
LocaleChangeInterceptor localeChangeInterceptor() {
    LocaleChangeInterceptor localeChangeInterceptor =
        new LocaleChangeInterceptor();
    localeChangeInterceptor.setParamName("lang");
    return localeChangeInterceptor;
}

@Bean
CookieLocaleResolver localeResolver() {
    CookieLocaleResolver cookieLocaleResolver = new
    CookieLocaleResolver();
    cookieLocaleResolver.setDefaultLocale(Locale.ENGLISH);
    cookieLocaleResolver.setCookieMaxAge(3600);
    cookieLocaleResolver.setCookieName("locale");
    return cookieLocaleResolver;
}
}
```

In the previous configuration, a CookieLocaleResolver is used for convenience. Because our services are not secured, a SessionLocaleResolver wouldn't make much sense. The special RestTemplate bean annotated with @LoadBalanced must be declared in the Spring Boot main class. It is named WebClient and injected in the AllWebServices bean using constructor injection. This leads to a class that looks like the one depicted in the following code snippet.

```
package com.apress.cems.web;

import org.slf4j.Logger;
import org.slf4j.LoggerFactory;
import org.springframework.beans.factory.annotation.Autowired;
import org.springframework.boot.SpringApplication;
import org.springframework.boot.autoconfigure.SpringBootApplication;
import org.springframework.cloud.client.ServiceInstance;
import org.springframework.cloud.netflix.eureka.EnableEurekaClient;
import org.springframework.cloud.client.loadbalancer.LoadBalanced;
import org.springframework.cloud.client.loadbalancer.LoadBalancerClient;
import org.springframework.context.annotation.Bean;
import org.springframework.context.annotation.ComponentScan;
import org.springframework.stereotype.Controller;
import org.springframework.ui.Model;
import org.springframework.web.bind.annotation.GetMapping;
import org.springframework.web.client.RestTemplate;

import java.io.IOException;
import java.net.URI;

@Controller
@SpringBootApplication
@EnableEurekaClient
public class WebClient  {

    private static Logger logger = LoggerFactory.getLogger(WebClient.class);

    public static void main(String... args) throws IOException {
        // Look for configuration in  web-client.properties or web-client.yml
        System.setProperty("spring.config.name", "web-client");
```

```java
    var ctx = SpringApplication.run(WebClient.class, args);
    assert (ctx != null);
    logger.info("Started ...");
    System.in.read();
    ctx.close();
}

@Bean
@LoadBalanced
RestTemplate restTemplate() {
    return new RestTemplate();
}

@Autowired
LoadBalancerClient loadBalancer;

@GetMapping(value = {"/","/home"})
 String home(Model model) {
    StringBuilder sb = new StringBuilder();
    URI uri = null;
    try {
        ServiceInstance instance = loadBalancer.choose("persons-service");
        uri = instance.getUri();
        sb.append("Found microservice: ").append(uri.toString()).
        append("; ");
    } catch (RuntimeException e) {
        sb.append("Not Found microservice ")
            .append("persons-service").append("; ");
    }

    try {
        ServiceInstance instance = loadBalancer.choose("detectives-service");

        uri = instance.getUri();
        sb.append("Found microservice: ").append(uri.toString()).
        append("; ");
```

```
    } catch (RuntimeException e) {
        sb.append("Not Found microservice ")
            .append("detectives-service").append("; ");
    }

    model.addAttribute("message", sb.toString());
    return "home";
    }
}
```

Whoa, that's a big class! Well, it's not as bad as it looks. Let me explain what I did there.

The class is annotated with @Controller because it contains a method annotated with @GetMapping that populates the home page of this application with some interesting details. It's a convenience and a lazy implementation; if you ever need code like this, make sure you put it in its own controller. Before jumping to writing the AllWebController and AllWebServices classes, you might want to know if your service can reach the other microservices, right? Because spring-cloud-netflix-ribbon is on the classpath a bean of RibbonLoadBalancerClient type (that implements the Spring Cloud LoadBalancerClient interface) is automatically configured. This bean can look for a microservice instance if you know the name of the service and query some of its details, such as the URI of this service.

The home(..) handler method uses this bean to access the ServiceInstance bean matching each of the microservices registered with the Eureka server. It uses them to extract the URIs of the two microservices that we are interested in, and prints them on the homepage of this application. So without configuring anything else, we can log into http://localhost:4000/ (or any other local IP, depends on the local configuration) and if we see the home page populated correctly, we can continue the development. For the scenario covered in this chapter the homepage for the web-client should look similar to the one depicted in Figure 11-11. (Don't be bothered by the fact that in the image my real IP appears, it works the same with localhost as well.)

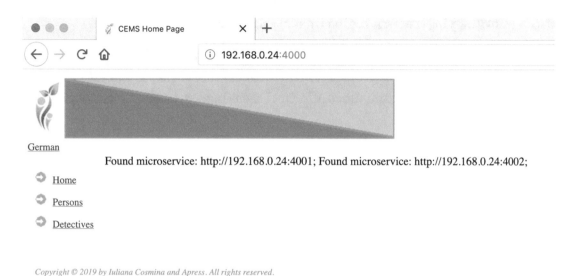

Figure 11-11. *Home page of the web-service microservice*

The WebClient class is annotated with @EnableEurekaClient, because it does configure a microservice application that is a client for the Eureka server.

The @LoadBalanced annotation is used on the RestTemplate bean declaration to tell Spring to configure this bean to use the LoadBalancerClient. This ensures that the REST calls will be send to the appropriate microservices, and to the appropriate instance (one with the less work to do). What happens is that the RestTemplate bean will be intercepted and auto-configured by Spring Cloud to use a custom ClientHttpRequest, that uses Netflix Ribbon[12] to do the microservice lookup and to facilitate inter-process communication in the cloud (or on a single machine as in this scenario).

The RibbonLoadBalancerClient implementation is the one that takes the logical service-name (as registered with the discovery-server) and converts it to the actual hostname of the chosen microservice. The method that does this is called reconstructURI and the code is depicted in the following code snippet.[13]

---

[12]Ribbon is yet another Netflix OSS. It provides client-side software load-balancing algorithms. More about it here: https://github.com/Netflix/ribbon/wiki

[13]Full code is publicly available on GitHub: https://github.com/spring-cloud/spring-cloud-netflix/blob/master/spring-cloud-netflix-ribbon/src/main/java/org/springframework/cloud/netflix/ribbon/RibbonLoadBalancerClient.java

```java
package org.springframework.cloud.netflix.ribbon;

import org.springframework.cloud.client.ServiceInstance;
import org.springframework.cloud.client.loadbalancer.LoadBalancerClient;
import org.springframework.cloud.client.loadbalancer.LoadBalancerRequest;
...

public class RibbonLoadBalancerClient implements LoadBalancerClient {

    private SpringClientFactory clientFactory;

    public RibbonLoadBalancerClient(SpringClientFactory clientFactory) {
        this.clientFactory = clientFactory;
    }

    @Override
    public URI reconstructURI(ServiceInstance instance, URI original) {
        Assert.notNull(instance, "instance can not be null");
        String serviceId = instance.getServiceId();
        RibbonLoadBalancerContext context = this.clientFactory
                .getLoadBalancerContext(serviceId);

        URI uri;
        Server server;
        if (instance instanceof RibbonServer) {
            RibbonServer ribbonServer = (RibbonServer) instance;
            server = ribbonServer.getServer();
            uri = updateToSecureConnectionIfNeeded(original, ribbonServer);
        } else {
            server = new Server(instance.getScheme(), instance.getHost(),
                instance.getPort());
            IClientConfig clientConfig = clientFactory.
            getClientConfig(serviceId);
            ServerIntrospector serverIntrospector =
            serverIntrospector(serviceId);
            uri = updateToSecureConnectionIfNeeded(original, clientConfig,
                serverIntrospector, server);
        }
```

```
        return context.reconstructURIWithServer(server, uri);
    }

    @Override
    public ServiceInstance choose(String serviceId) {
        return choose(serviceId, null);
    }

    public ServiceInstance choose(String serviceId, Object hint) {
        Server server = getServer(getLoadBalancer(serviceId), hint);
        if (server == null) {
            return null;
        }

        return new RibbonServer(serviceId, server, isSecure(server,
        serviceId),
            serverIntrospector(serviceId).getMetadata(server));
    }
...
}
```

Ribbon can select from multiple instances of the same service the proper one to use, meaning the one to respond the quicker, and this is usually done in ClientHttpRequestFactory by first calling the choose(...) method also depicted in the preceding code snippet.[14]

The AllWebServices bean is a service bean that uses the balanced RestTemplate bean to retrieve data from the persons-service and detectives-service microservices, and to wrap it up nicely for the AllWebController to use. In the next snippet, the content of this class is depicted, covering only the two main methods used to retrieve all persons and all detective instances.

```
package com.apress.cems.web;

import com.apress.cems.detective.Detective;
import com.apress.cems.ex.InvalidCriteriaException;
```

[14]You can take a look at the code of RibbonLoadBalancerClient available at: https://github.com/spring-cloud/spring-cloud-netflix/blob/master/spring-cloud-netflix-ribbon/src/main/java/org/springframework/cloud/netflix/ribbon/RibbonLoadBalancerClient.java

```java
import com.apress.cems.person.Person;
import com.apress.cems.util.CriteriaDto;
import org.springframework.http.*;
import org.springframework.web.client.RestTemplate;

import java.util.Arrays;
import java.util.List;

import static com.apress.cems.base.AbstractEntity.COMPARATOR_BY_ID;

@Service
public class AllWebServices {

    private RestTemplate restTemplate;

    private static final String PERSONS_SERVICE_URL = "http://persons-service";

    private static final String DETECTIVES_SERVICE_URL = "http://
    detectives-service";

    public AllWebServices(RestTemplate restTemplate) {
        this.restTemplate = restTemplate;
    }
    List<Person> getAllPersons(){
        Person[] persons = restTemplate.getForObject(PERSONS_SERVICE_URL
            .concat("/persons"), Person[].class);
        assert persons != null;
        List<Person> personsList = Arrays.asList(persons);
        personsList.sort(COMPARATOR_BY_ID);
        return personsList;
    }

     List<Detective> getAllDetectives(){
        Detective[] detectives = restTemplate.getForObject(DETECTIVES_
        SERVICE_URL.
            concat("/detectives"), Detective[].class);
        assert detectives != null;
        List<Detective> detectiveList = Arrays.asList(detectives);
```

```
        detectiveList.forEach(d ->
            d.setPerson(restTemplate.getForObject(PERSONS_SERVICE_URL
                .concat("/persons/" + d.getPersonId()), Person.class))
        );
        detectiveList.sort(COMPARATOR_BY_ID);
        return detectiveList;
    }
    ...
}
```

The previous implementation is a normal Spring service class, annotated with the @Service stereotype annotation. It is a wrapper for the balanced RestTemplate instance that sends requests to the two microservices using the URLs constructed using the names they were registered with the Eureka Server. These URLs are references to microservices persons-service and detectives-service.

As you probably remember from the REST chapter, the RestTemplate is thread-safe so it can access any number of services in different parts of an application. In this example two microservices are accessed by the same RestTemplate bean.

! In case you are confused why the term URL is used everywhere, although we are working with REST, here is the explanation: The two microservices URLs, http://persons-service and http://detectives-services, are resolved to http:/localhost:4001 and http:/localhost:4002 by the LoadBalancerClient bean used by the RestTemplate bean, so they are URLs (locations). They become URIs (resources) when concatenated with /persons{id} and /detectives/{id}.

The AllWebController is just a normal controller class that uses the AllWebServices class, which is the central class of this application, that requests information from the persons-service and the detectives-service microservices. It wraps it up in objects that can be rendered in Thymeleaf views. The code for the AllWebController is nothing special, just a typical Spring controller class using a service instance to access data.

```
package com.apress.cems.web;

...

@Controller
```

```java
public class AllWebController {

    private static Logger logger = LoggerFactory
        .getLogger(AllWebController.class);

    private AllWebServices allWebServices;
    private MessageSource messageSource;

    public AllWebController(AllWebServices allWebServices, MessageSource
    messageSource) {
        this.allWebServices = allWebServices;
        this.messageSource = messageSource;
    }

    @GetMapping(value = "/persons")
    public String listPersons(Model model) {
        logger.info("Populating model with person list...");
        List<Person> persons =  allWebServices.getAllPersons();
        model.addAttribute("persons", persons);
        return "persons/list";
    }

    @GetMapping(value = "/detectives")
    public String listDetectives(Model model) {
        logger.info("Populating model with detective list...");
        List<Detective> detectives =  allWebServices.getAllDetectives();
        model.addAttribute("detectives", detectives);
        return "detectives/list";
    }
...
}
```

The MessageSource dependency is used in a method that is not depicted in this code sample, but it is available in the book code.

Things Worth Mentioning

Writing a microservices based distributed application requires advanced knowledge of Spring Boot and Spring Cloud. The chapter11 encapsulates all modules making up such an application. Some artifices were made to keep things simple. For example, the persons-server and detectives-server projects each has its own in-memory database and the Detective entity class has been modified so it can be detached from the Person entity. The @OneToOne annotation was removed from the person field (of type Person) and a Long field was introduced to store the Person entity ID. The person field has become transient and optional, so it can stay empty when is not needed.

```
@Entity
public class Detective extends AbstractEntity {

    @NotNull
    @JoinColumn(name = "PERSON_ID")
    private Long personId;

    @Transient
    private Person person;
    ...
}
```

You've probably noticed the body of the getAllDetectives() method in the AllWebServices class.

```
List<Detective> getAllDetectives(){
        Detective[] detectives = restTemplate.getForObject(DETECTIVES_
        SERVICE_URL
            .concat("/detectives"), Detective[].class);
        assert detectives != null;
        List<Detective> detectiveList =  Arrays.asList(detectives);
                detectiveList.forEach(d ->
                        d.setPerson(restTemplate.
                        getForObject(PERSONS_SERVICE_URL
                            .concat("/persons/" + d.getPersonId()),
                            Person.class))
        );
```

```
        detectiveList.sort(COMPARATOR_BY_ID);
        return detectiveList;
    }
```

This method, extracts the `Person` entity with the ID matching the `personId` field in the `Detective` instance using the `persons-service` microservice and sets it as a value for the `person` field, so that that all the data relevant for a `Detective` instance can be added to a view. So the link between the two entities is now a little more relaxed, and another microservice could be created to synchronize the two databases. Sure, for production it might not be a great idea; database replication might be preferred.

After all the microservices instances are in place you can start playing with them. Try to access `http://localhost:4001/actuator/info`. You should see the application information set up for you in the `persons-server.yml` file.

```
{
  "app": {
    "name": "persons-server",
    "description": "Spring Cloud Application Managing Person Instances",
    "version": "1.0-SNAPSHOT"
  }
}
```

The same goes for all other microservices. In Figure 11-12, you can see the `actuator/info` contents for each of the microservices running, and since there are two `persons-services` started, one on port 4001 and one on 4003, the information displayed is the same.

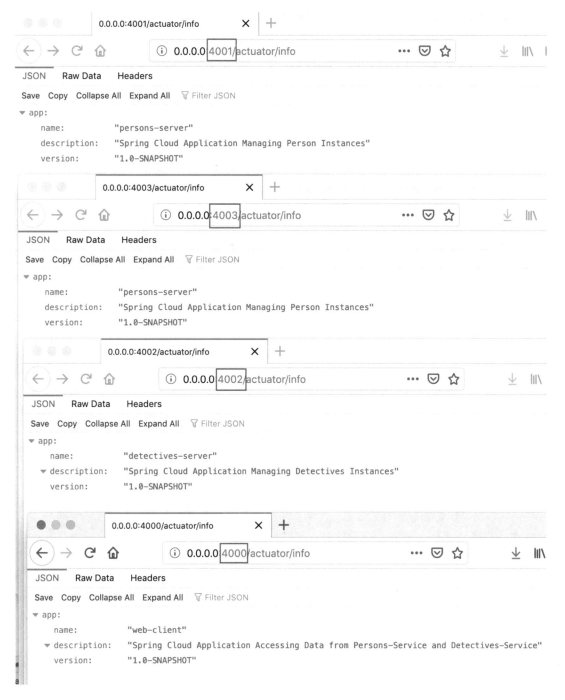

Figure 11-12. *Actuator/info contents for all microservices*

- `http://localhost:4001/persons` - displays all person instances in JSON format

- `http://localhost:4001/persons/1` - displays information about person with id=1 in JSON format

- `http://localhost:4002/detectives` - displays all detectives in JSON format

- `http://localhost:4002/detectives/1` - displays information about detective with id=1 in JSON format

In Figure 11-13, you can see the contents of the response returned when accessing `http://localhost: 4001/persons/1`, `http://localhost:4002/detectives/1` and the page displayed when accessing `http://localhost:4000/detectives/1` that displays information from both previous requests.

Figure 11-13. *Person and Detective information in all microservices*

- `http://localhost:4000/` - it should display the page in Figure 11-11

Another thing worth mentioning is that all microservices main classes were annotated with `@EnableEurekaClient`, except the `discovery-server` main class. This annotation enables Eureka discovery configuration when we know for sure that the registration server is a Eureka server. Spring Cloud provides its own annotation: `@EnableDiscoveryClient`. This annotation is part of the `org.springframework.cloud.client.discovery` package and is generic. It can enable a discovery client implementation, regardless of the discovery and registration server used. This introduces a bit of flexibility, since it allows for a registration and discovery server to be swapped with a different one without affecting the entire application.[15]

Summary

After reading this chapter, you should have a proper understanding of how Spring can develop distributed applications based on the microservices architecture. The following is a simple list of topics that you should keep in handy when reviewing the acquired knowledge.

- Describe the microservices architecture
- Spring Cloud is built upon Spring Boot
- What are typical Spring cloud annotations used when developing microservices applications
- Netflix has developed and outsourced numerous projects designed to support development and running of distributed applications
- How Service Discovery is set up
- How is a microservice RESTful interface accessed
- What Eureka is
- What Ribbon is

---

[15]Eureka Server alternatives: Consul.io, JetNexus, Azure Traffic Manager, Google Cloud load balancer, and so forth.

Even if microservices are not a topic for the exam, you are invited to test your knowledge by solving the following quiz.

Quick Quiz

Question 1. Which of the following affirmations describe the microservices architecture? (Choose all that apply.)

    A.   In a microservices architecture, services should have a small granularity and the communications protocols should be lightweight.

    B.   In a microservices architecture the inter-processes communication can only be done using RESTful interfaces.

    C.   In a microservices architecture the design is unified and components are interconnected and interdependent.

Question 2. Which of the following are advantages of the microservices architecture? (Choose all that apply.)

    A.   microservices based applications are highly scalable

    B.   improvement of fault isolation

    C.   transaction management is not needed

    D.   deploying microservices based application is painless

Question 3. Which of the following is the core component of a microservices based distributed application? (Choose one.)

    A.   a service implementation

    B.   a database

    C.   a registry and discovery server

Question 4. What can be said about Spring Cloud? (Choose all that apply.)

A.   it is built upon Spring Boot

B.   it is an umbrella project that provides tools for developers to quickly build some of the common patterns in distributed systems

C.   it is a proprietary Pivotal service for building distributed applications available only by paid subscription

Question 5. Which of the following annotations declares an instance of a Eureka server? (Choose one.)

A.   @EnableNetflixEureka

B.   @EurekaAutoConfiguration

C.   @EnableEurekaServer

Question 6. Which of the following annotations is used for service registration and discovery with a discovery server? (Choose all that apply.)

A.   @EnableDiscoveryClient

B.   @EnableEurekaClient

C.   @EnableSeviceRegistration

Building Reactive Applications Using Spring

Reactive programming, as defined by Wikipedia, *is a declarative programming paradigm concerned with data streams and the propagation of change. With this paradigm it is possible to express static (e.g., arrays) or dynamic (e.g., event emitters) data streams with ease, and also communicate that an inferred dependency within the associated execution model exists, which facilitates the automatic propagation of the changed data flow.*[1]

Reactive programming is viewed lately as the panacea to solve all development problems regarding resilience, responsiveness, and scalability of an application. As its name says, reactive programming is oriented to reaction. A component does something, and another component that is observing it is triggered to do its own thing, which might make you think of the observer pattern;[2] and you would be right, but reactive programming is much more than that. Reactive programming implies smart routing and the consumption of events.

One of the best analogies to help understand the paradigm of reactive programming comes from a user on StackOverflow. I can't rephrase it any better. Imagine your program is a spreadsheet and all of your variables are cells. If any of the cells in a spreadsheet change, any cells that refer to that cell change as well. It's the same with FRP. Now imagine that some of the cells change on their own (or rather, are taken from the outside world). In a GUI situation, the position of a mouse would be a good example.[3]

---

[1]Exact quote from here: `https://en.wikipedia.org/wiki/Reactive_programming`

[2]The Observer Pattern is one of the four most important patterns in programming `https://en.wikipedia.org/wiki/Observer_pattern`

[3]Direct quote from `https://stackoverflow.com/questions/1028250/what-is-functional-reactive-programming`

I. Cosmina, *Pivotal Certified Professional Core Spring 5 Developer Exam*,
https://doi.org/10.1007/978-1-4842-5136-2_12

Reactive programming is a very good approach for developing non-blocking applications that are asynchronous and event-driven and require a small number of threads to scale internally within the JVM (rather than creating multiple instances of the application to deal with an unexpected load). This is especially efficient for applications hosted on private clouds like AWS, Azure, and GCP, which bill their clients by the number of instances spanned, because it helps reduce the number of instances needed to deal with load and thus reduces costs.

That is why its adoption is on the rise, with existing frameworks being redesigned according to the reactive paradigm and new frameworks appearing seemingly every other day. But, take it with a grain of salt, because this panacea for developing high-performance, concurrent, asynchronous, non-blocking, responsive, resilient, and so forth, applications is only limited by the developers' understanding of it.

One of the most notable features introduced in Spring 5 (first milestone June 2016) is the support for reactive programming using Project Reactor.[4] Project Reactor is a Java framework from the Pivotal open source team (the same one that created Spring). Project Reactor is a very practical reactive library for building non-blocking applications on the JVM that builds directly on Reactive Streams.[5] What this means is that this project was among the first to provide an implementation abiding by the rules of the Reactive Manifesto that was first made public in 2014[6] and it made a request for software to be developed in such a way that applications are Responsive, Resilient, Elastic and Message Driven, in short they should be reactive. The following briefly explains each of the four terms.

- **Responsive**: Provides fast and consistent response times

- **Resilient**: Remains responsive during failure and is to recover

- **Elastic**: Remains responsive and is able to handle various workloads

- **Message Driven**: Communicates using asynchronous messages, avoids blocking and applying back-pressure to make sure that producers do not overwhelm consumers

---

[4]Official site: https://projectreactor.io/
[5]Read about Reactive Streams here: http://www.reactive-streams.org/
[6]Read it here: https://www.reactivemanifesto.org/

Applications designed this way are supposed to be more flexible, loosely coupled, and scalable, but at the same time, they should be easier to develop, amendable to change, and more tolerant of failure. But to accomplish all that, a common API for communication is needed.

JDK introduced support for building this type of applications in JDK 9 via their Publish-Subscribe Framework,[7] but Spring was already there in version 5 with reactive support from Project Reactor. Project Reactor ended up being the backbone of the Spring WebFlux, the functional and reactive web framework designed to provide reactive programming support for web applications in Spring Framework 5, because Oracle postponed the release of JDK 9 a little bit too much.

Project Reactor is one of the first libraries for reactive programming and its classes provide a non-blocking stable foundation with efficient demand management for building reactive applications. It works with Java 8, but does provide adapter classes for JDK9 reactive streams classes, that fortunately can be used within a JDK 11 project as well. Project Reactor is suitable for microservices applications and provides a lot more classes designed to make development of reactive applications more practical than the JDK does. Project Reactor provides two main publisher implementations: `reactor.core.publisher.Mono<T>` which is a reactive stream publisher representing zero or one element and `reactor.core.publisher.Flux<T>` which is a reactive stream publisher representing an asynchronous sequence of 0 to N emitted items with basic flow operators. The reason that I mention these two publisher implementations is because it seems the Project Reactor team did not like the terminology used by Oracle, so they introduced their own.

In the JDK, there is a single `java.util.concurrent.Flow` class that contains all interrelated interfaces and static methods for establishing flow-controlled components, in which `Publishers` produce items consumed by one or more `Subscribers` each managed by a `Subscription`. There is also an interface named `Processor` that acts both as a `Publisher` and `Subscriber`.

In Figure 12-1, you can see an abstract representation of the Reactive Streams implementation in JDK and Project Reactor side by side.

---

[7]Read more about it online `https://openjdk.java.net/jeps/266` or read about it in my book *Java for Absolute Beginners, the Java 9+ way* published in 2018 `https://www.apress.com/in/book/9781484237779`

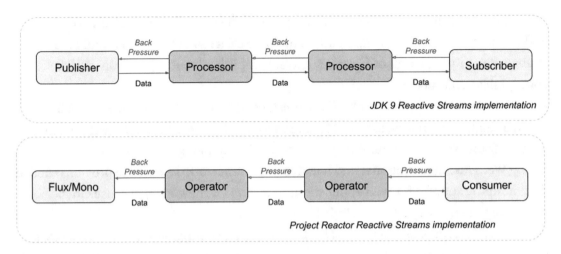

Figure 12-1. *Reactive Streams implementation in JDK and Project Reactor*

You will see Flux<T> and Mono<T> used often in this chapter, so a small introduction is required. If you want to read more about them, the official documentation is quite helpful.[8]

If you look in the official documentation, you will most likely encounter the schema in Figure 12-2.[9]

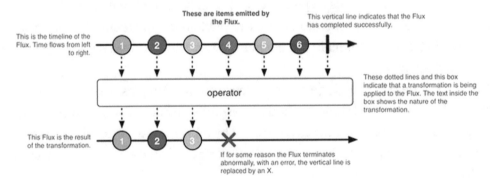

Figure 12-2. *Project Reactor Flux Publisher implementation*

[8]The Project Reactor official documentation: `https://projectreactor.io/docs/core/release/reference/ #core-features`

[9]Image source: Project Reactor Public API JavaDoc `http://projectreactor.io/docs/core/release/api/reactor/core/publisher/Flux.html`

This is an abstract schema of how the `Flux<T>` publisher works. The `Flux<T>` emits elements, can throw exceptions and can complete when there are no more elements to publish, and the Project Reactor team just found a pretty way to draw it.

The drawing for the `Mono<T>` implementation is similar to `http://projectreactor.io/docs/core/release/api/reactor/core/publisher/Mono.html`.

The full hierarchy of classes is depicted in Figure 12-3.

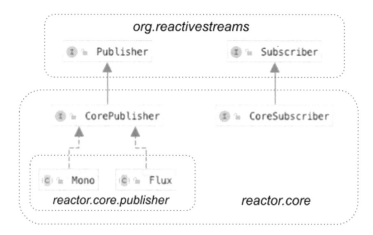

Figure 12-3. *Project Reactor Flux and Mono Publisher implementations hierarchy*

The `CorePublisher<T>` and `CoreSubscriber<T>` interfaces were introduced in `reactor.core` version 3.3.0. `Flux<T>` and `Mono<T>` were modified in this version to implement `CorePublisher<T>` instead of `org.reactivestreams.Publisher<T>` directly so that support for the context-aware and more resilient `CoreSubscriber<T>` could be added.[10] Previous to this change only `org.reactivestreams.Subscriber<T>` implementations were supported.

`CorePublisher<T>`'s code is simple. You can view it easily in IntelliJ IDEA or check it put on GitHub: `https://github.com/reactor/reactor-core/blob/master/reactor-core/src/main/ java/reactor/core/CorePublisher.java`.

---

[10]In the JavaDoc of *CoreSubscriber<T>* it is mentioned that this implementation has relaxed rules for §1.3 and §3.9 compared to the original *org.reactivestreams.Subscriber* from Reactive Streams. You can find the rules here: `https://github.com/reactive-streams/reactive-streams-jvm/blob/v1.0.3/README.md`

```
package reactor.core;

import org.reactivestreams.Publisher;
import org.reactivestreams.Subscriber;

public interface CorePublisher<T> extends Publisher<T> {

        void subscribe(CoreSubscriber<? super T> subscriber);

}
```

And since Flux<T> and Mono<T> have been introduced, I think a small section of playing with them is in order.

Getting Familiar with *Flux<T>* and *Mono<T>*

Reactive programming can be explained in the simplest way as "programming with reactive (asynchronous) streams." Streams are central to the reactive programming model, and they are used to support asynchronous processing of anything. In a nutshell, reactive libraries offer the possibility for anything to be used as a stream (variables, user inputs, caches, data structures, etc.), and thus support stream-specific operations, such as filtering a stream to create another, merging streams, mapping values from one stream to another, and so on. The word *reactive* in reactive programming means that a stream is an observable object that is observed by a component and reacts to it according to the objects emitted.

A stream can emit three types of events: values, errors, and "completed" signals. These events are captured asynchronously by defining a function to be executed when a value is emitted, when an error is emitted, and when "completed" is emitted.

To turn a normal application into a reactive application, the first logical step is to modify components to produce and handle data streams. There are two types of data streams provided by Project Reactor.

- reactor.core.publisher.Flux[11] - a stream of [0..n] elements. The following is the easiest way to create a Flux.

```
Flux simple = Flux.just("1", "2", "3");
//or from an existing list: List<Person>
Flux<Person> fromList = Flux.fromIterable(list);
```

- reactor.core.publisher.Mono[12] - stream of [0..1] elements. The easiest way to create a Mono is as follows.

```
Mono simple = Mono.just("1");
//or from an existing object of type Person
Mono<Person> fromObject = Mono.justOrEmpty(Person);
```

Both interfaces extend org.reactivestreams.Publisher<T> augmented with a lot of operators that can generate, transform, and orchestrate Flux/Mono sequences. You might wonder if the Mono<T> implementation is actually needed. The answer is yes due to practical reasons; depending on the type of operation done with the values a stream is emitting, it is always useful to know the cardinality. Imagine a reactive repository class; for example, would it make sense for the findOne method to return a Flux<T>? Obviously not.

In the previous code samples, the data streams were just created from readily available data and they are not emitting data yet (the data doesn't flow). To start emitting data, one of the subscribe() methods must be called (the Flux<T> declares a bunch of them).

A stream can emit three types of events. Project Reactor provides practical ways to capture those events and react to them. But first, let's use the log() method to observe reactive stream signals and trace them (displaying a log entry for each type of signal being emitted) and the subscribe() method to start emitting them.

```
Flux.just("0", "1", "2", "3", "4", "5", "6", "7")
       .log()
       .subscribe();
```

---

[11]Detailed explanation here: https://projectreactor.io/docs/core/release/ reference/#flux

[12]Detailed explanation here: https://projectreactor.io/docs/core/release/ reference/#mono

When executing the previous code, you should see the following in the console.

```
INFO reactor.Flux.Array.1 - | onSubscribe([Synchronous Fuseable] FluxArray.
                                ArraySubscription)
INFO reactor.Flux.Array.1 - | request(unbounded)
INFO reactor.Flux.Array.1 - | onNext(0)
INFO reactor.Flux.Array.1 - | onNext(1)
INFO reactor.Flux.Array.1 - | onNext(2)
INFO reactor.Flux.Array.1 - | onNext(3)
INFO reactor.Flux.Array.1 - | onNext(4)
INFO reactor.Flux.Array.1 - | onNext(5)
INFO reactor.Flux.Array.1 - | onNext(6)
INFO reactor.Flux.Array.1 - | onNext(7)
INFO reactor.Flux.Array.1 - | onComplete()
```

The previous log listing tells you a lot about how a stream data is handled under the hood. The following list explains the contents of the console log in detail.

- the log() function prints a message for each event captured and the log category is decided by the following template:

  - reactor because we are using Project Reactor.

  - Flux is the type of stream emitting the events.

  - Array is the source for this stream; in this case, an Array instance. The following code snippet produces the same output as before, but the log category is reactor.Flux.Iterable.1, because the source of the stream is a List<T> instance, and List<T> extends Iterable<T>.

    ```
    Flux.fromIterable(List.of("0", "1", "2", "3", "4", "5",
    "6", "7"))
    .log()
    .subscribe();
    ```

  - 1 is a numeric identifier generated by an AtomicLong instance for this thread. The SignalLogger intercepts all reactive calls and traces them, so it must identify each data stream uniquely.

- onSubscribe()writes a log entry to notify that subscribe() was
  called. Calling the log() method on a Flux<T> instance only
  enables logging. Until a subscriber is registered, the elements will
  not be emitted and traced. By providing a custom Subscriber<T>
  implementation that prints a message every time any type of
  event is emitted, the log() method can be skipped. A very simple
  implementation of Subscriber<T> is depicted next.

```
package com.apress.reactive;

import org.reactivestreams.Subscriber;
import org.reactivestreams.Subscription;
import org.slf4j.Logger;
import org.slf4j.LoggerFactory;

public class SimpleSubscriber implements Subscriber<String> {

    private Logger logger =
        LoggerFactory.getLogger(SimpleSubscriber.class);

    @Override
    public void onSubscribe(Subscription subscription) {
        logger.info("onSubscribe() -> {}", Long.MAX_VALUE);
        subscription.request(Long.MAX_VALUE);
    }

    @Override
    public void onNext(String item) {
        logger.info("onNext() -> {}", item);
    }

    @Override
    public void onError(Throwable throwable) {
        logger.error("onError()", throwable);
    }

    @Override
    public void onComplete() {
        logger.info("onComplete -> All Done.");
    }
}
```

To inspect the elements of this stream, now we only have to register a subscriber instance with it by calling:

```
Flux.just("0", "1", "2", "3", "4", "5", "6", "7")
                .subscribe(new SimpleSubscriber());
```

Project Reactor provides a big hierarchy of subscribers that can be used directly or customized further. Instead of implementing Subscriber<T>, we might as well extend the BaseSubscriber<T> class and provide a custom implementation for the method handling events that we are interested in, such as values.

```
package com.apress.reactive;

import reactor.core.publisher.BaseSubscriber;
import org.slf4j.Logger;
import org.slf4j.LoggerFactory;

public class GenericSubscriber<T> extends BaseSubscriber<T> {
    private static final Logger log =
            LoggerFactory.getLogger(GenericSubscriber.class);

    @Override
    protected void hookOnNext(T value) {
        log.info("consumed {} ", value);
        super.hookOnNext(value);
    }
}
```

- onNext() is a log entry written when data is emitted successfully.

- onComplete() is not used here, but can be overridden; for example, to write a log entry to notify that the stream has emitted a "completed" signal.

- onError() is not used here, but can be overridden to write a log entry to notify that the stream has emitted an "error" signal.

Now that we have data stream representations, where does that functional part of the programming come in? Well, Project Reactor provides an amazing toolbox to combine, create and filter these streams. Streams can be used as inputs to processing streams, also known as operators, even multiple streams can be used as inputs to another stream. Values from a stream can be mapped to another stream. Here's another example, we are taking a stream of `Strings`, using it to create a stream of `Integers` and then adding them all together into a `Mono<Integer>`.

```
Flux<Integer> ints =  Flux.just("0", "1", "2", "3", "4", "5", "6", "7")
                               .map(Integer::parseInt);

ints.reduce(0, Integer::sum) // Mono<Integer>
                .subscribe(s -> logger.info("Sum: {}", s));
```

Streams can be merged, and *merging* is called *zipping* in Project Reactor because of the method involved, which is named `zip(..)`. In the following code sample, the `persons` stream that emits `Person` instances is zipped with the `periodFlux` stream, which contains a list of timestamp values emitted two seconds apart from each other.

```
import reactor.core.publisher.Flux;
import reactor.core.publisher.Mono;
import reactor.util.function.Tuple2;
...
 public Flux<Person> persons() {
        Flux<Person> persons = reactiveRepo.findAll();
        Flux<Long> periodFlux = Flux.interval(Duration.ofSeconds(2));
        return Flux.zip(persons, periodFlux).map(Tuple2::getT1);
}
```

The `zip` operation is a special reactive stream operation that waits for all the sources to emit one element and combine these elements once into a `Tuple2` instance. This means that the resulting stream will emit `Person` instances every two seconds. And because these instances are wrapped in `Tuple2` instances another `map(...)` call is necessary to extract the initial `Person` instance.

If some methods seem familiar is because some of them are very similar to stream methods introduced in JDK 8. But these are reactive streams, and a myriad of classes and methods to work with them is provided by Project Reactor; but without the context of an application, we can only go so far. Hopefully, my short introduction was enough for you to grasp the basics of reactive programming and understand the functionality that `spring-webflux` brings to the table.[13] But before introducing the star of this chapter, let's try to transform a normal Spring Boot web application into a reactive application, because after all, Tomcat does support reactive components.

Spring Boot Reactive (Hybrid) Application

To modify a Spring Boot web application and transform it into a reactive application, we have to take a few steps. But, before modifying the dependencies, let's see which components can be modified to be implemented as reactive. H2 is the database used to store information, and this is an in-memory relational database and it is not reactive. Reactive implementations are quite useless with implementations that are not reactive, but since we are making the change gradually, the project specific to this section is going to be a hybrid. Since the H2 database is not reactive, building a reactive repository is tedious. We have to write JDBC statements and wrap the results of their executions in `Flux<T>` and `Mono<T>` instances. So, we'll use Spring Data instant non-reactive repositories and implement the service layer in a reactive manner.

Assuming that we have a typical non-reactive `PersonRepo` interface, the `PersonService` interface can be redesigned like in the following code listing. It will be renamed `PersonReactiveService` to make it obvious that the methods exposed are reactive.

```
package com.apress.cems.reactive.person;

import com.apress.cems.person.Person;
import reactor.core.publisher.Flux;
import reactor.core.publisher.Mono;

public interface PersonReactiveService {

    Mono<Person> findById(Long id);

    Flux<Person> findAll();

    Mono<Person> save(Mono<Person> personMono);
```

---

[13]If you need more resources about the reactive programming model and programming with reactive streams you might want to try the reference documentation, code samples, and Javadoc of Project Reactor `https://projectreactor.io/docs` or this really great introduction to Reactive Programming: `https://gist.github.com/staltz/868e7e9bc2a7b8c1f754`

```
    Mono<Void> update(Long id, Mono<Person> personMono);

    Mono<Void> delete(Long id);
}
```

Notice how all methods return either a `Flux<T>` or a `Mono<T>` instance, even methods that usually return void. Also, parameters are declared as reactive streams where possible. The reason for this is so that an instance of this type can be used as a dependency in a reactive controller. The implementation of the previous interface should be similar to the one depicted in the next code listing.[14]

```
package com.apress.cems.reactive.person;

import com.apress.cems.person.Person;
import com.apress.cems.util.NumberGenerator;
import org.springframework.stereotype.Service;
import org.springframework.util.StringUtils;
import reactor.core.publisher.Flux;
import reactor.core.publisher.Mono;

import java.util.Optional;

@Service
public class PersonReactiveServiceImpl implements PersonReactiveService {

    private PersonRepo personRepo;

    public PersonReactiveServiceImpl(PersonRepo personRepo) {
        this.personRepo = personRepo;
    }

    @Override
    public Mono<Person> findById(Long id) {
        return Mono.justOrEmpty(personRepo.findById(id));
    }
}
```

---

[14]In the code snippet, there is a comment mentioning a workaround for a Jackson bug; basically, the password field value is lost during deserialization. This is an issue already on GitHub: `https://github.com/FasterXML/jackson-databind/issues/935#issuecomment-520070413`. It is closed, but the bug is still there in version 2.9.9 when I asked about it, I was told to create a new issue, which I will, as soon as this book is published.

```java
@Override
public Flux<Person> findAll() {
    return Flux.fromIterable(personRepo.findAll());
}

@Override
 public Mono<Person> save(Mono<Person> personMono) {
    return personMono.doOnNext(person ->  {
        //work around for Jackson issue
        if(StringUtils.isEmpty(person.getPassword())){
            person.setPassword(NumberGenerator.getPassword());
        }
        Mono.just(personRepo.save(person));
    });
}

@Override
 public Mono<Void> update(Long id, Mono<Person> personMono) {
    Optional<Person> personOpt = personRepo.findById(id);
    if(personOpt.isPresent()) {
        Person original = personOpt.get();
        return personMono.doOnNext(
                updatedPerson -> {
                    original.setUsername(updatedPerson.getUsername());
                    original.setFirstName(updatedPerson.getFirstName());
                    original.setLastName(updatedPerson.getLastName());
                    personRepo.save(original);
                }
        ).thenEmpty(Mono.empty());
    }
    return Mono.empty();
}

@Override
public Mono<Void> delete(Long id) {
    personRepo.findById(id).ifPresent(person -> personRepo.
    delete(person));
```

```
        return Mono.empty();
    }
}
```

Ok... we now have a reactive service implementation. Writing a reactive controller is easy, we just provide a bean of this type as dependency and we make sure every controller method returns a Flux<T> or a Mono<T> instance.

```
package com.apress.cems.reactive.person;

import com.apress.cems.person.Person;
import org.springframework.http.HttpStatus;
import org.springframework.http.MediaType;
import org.springframework.web.bind.annotation.*;
import reactor.core.publisher.Flux;
import reactor.core.publisher.Mono;
import reactor.util.function.Tuple2;

import java.time.Duration;

@RestController
@RequestMapping("/persons")
public class PersonController {

    final PersonReactiveService reactiveService;

    public PersonController(PersonReactiveService reactiveService) {
        this.reactiveService = reactiveService;
    }

    @GetMapping(path = "/", produces = MediaType.TEXT_EVENT_STREAM_VALUE)
    Public Flux<Person> persons() {
        Flux<Person> persons = reactiveService.findAll();
        Flux<Long> periodFlux = Flux.interval(Duration.ofSeconds(2));
        return Flux.zip(persons, periodFlux).map(Tuple2::getT1);
    }
```

```java
@ResponseStatus(HttpStatus.OK)
@GetMapping(path="/{id}", produces = MediaType.APPLICATION_JSON_VALUE)
public Mono<Person> show(@PathVariable Long id) {
    return reactiveService.findById(id);
}

@ResponseStatus(HttpStatus.CREATED)
@PostMapping(consumes = MediaType.APPLICATION_JSON_VALUE,
        produces = MediaType.APPLICATION_JSON_VALUE)
public Mono<Person> save(@RequestBody Person person){
    return reactiveService.save(Mono.just(person));
}

@ResponseStatus(HttpStatus.NO_CONTENT)
@PutMapping(path="/{id}", consumes = MediaType.APPLICATION_JSON_VALUE)
public Mono<Void> update(@PathVariable Long id, Mono<Person> personMono) {
    return reactiveService.update(id, personMono).then();
}

@ResponseStatus(HttpStatus.NO_CONTENT)
@DeleteMapping("/{id}")
public Mono<Void> delete(@PathVariable Long id) {
    return reactiveService.delete(id);
}}
```

Notice how all handler methods return either a Flux<T> or a Mono<T> instance. Also, the handler methods receive reactive streams as arguments where they fit. MediaType. TEXT_EVENT_STREAM_VALUE is a special mime type introduced in Spring 4.3.6 to be used with controllers that return a reactive stream of data. Flux<T> is a reactive representation of a stream of events, so W3C Specifications require it to be designated as *text/event-stream*.[15] Still, how do we know this controller is reactive? We test it. You might have noticed that aside from Flux<T> or a Mono<T> instance used everywhere, there's nothing special about the implementation so far. There is nothing new that might lead you to think that we are using the Spring WebFlux anywhere. And that is because this is a hybrid application. It is not fully reactive. So, there is no need for Spring WebFlux.

---

[15]W3C event streaming specifications: https://www.w3.org/TR/eventsource/

If we want to test this application, a reactive HTTP client is needed, which is part of the Spring WebFlux module. That is why the Glade configuration for this project will just use the Spring WebFlux module as a test dependency, a small artifice to make testing easier. The Gradle configuration for the project is depicted next. The first section is part of the root parent project where versions and dependencies are declared, and the second section is the configuration where they are used of the reactive-boot-hybrid.

```
//pivotal-certified-pro-spring-dev-exam-02/build.gradle
ext {

  springBootVersion = '2.2.0.M6'
  reactorVersion = '3.3.0.M3'

  boot = [
            starterWeb :
                "org.springframework.boot:spring-boot-starter-
                web:$springBootVersion",
            starterWebflux :
                "org.springframework.boot:spring-boot-starter-
                webflux:$springBootVersion",
            starterJpa :
                "org.springframework.boot:spring-boot-starter-data-
                jpa:$springBootVersion",
            actuator :
                "org.springframework.boot:spring-boot-starter-
                actuator:$springBootVersion",
            starterTest :
                "org.springframework.boot:spring-boot-starter-
                test:$springBootVersion",
            ...
  ]

  misc = [
            projectReactor : "io.projectreactor:reactor-
            core:$reactorVersion",
            ...
  ]
```

```
testing = [
         reactorTest : "io.projectreactor:reactor-test:$reactorVersion",
         ...
  ]
}

//reactive-boot-hybrid/build.gradle
dependencies {
    implementation project(':chapter11:entities')
    implementation boot.starterJpa, boot.starterWeb, boot.actuator, misc.
    projectReactor

    runtimeOnly misc.h2

    testImplementation testing.reactorTest, boot.starterWebflux
    testImplementation (boot.starterTest) {
        exclude group: "org.junit.vintage", module: "junit-vintage-engine"
        exclude group: "junit", module: "junit"
    }
}
```

Spring WebFlux is not used, the controller is reactive because its methods return reactive streams. Because of this little change in the implementation, under the hood, HandlerMapping and HandlerAdapter are still used because they are non-blocking, but they operate on the reactive ServerHttpRequest and ServerHttpResponse (added to the spring-web module in version 5, these two interfaces are part of the org. springframework.http.server.reactive package) rather than on HttpServletRequest and HttpServletResponse. For hosting this application, the Tomcat server is used because it supports reactive components starting in version 9.

Notice how the persons() handler method uses the zip() method to slow down the generation of the Person instances.

** This might be funny, but this is how I like to see the Flux<T> instance in comparison to List<T> instances. Imagine having a bucket full of plastic balls. When a controller returns a list, is like somebody just pours the full contents of the bucket in another location. In the case of a flux, the source is still a bucket, but when a controller returns a flux, it's like somebody just throws the balls one by one to the new location.

Testing the reactive controller's methods is easy. You can do it by making the calls directly in a browser. Modern browsers know how to handle reactive data. If you access http://localhost:8081/persons/ in a browser, the request is sent to the application, and the response is returned with a little delay because the Persons instances are emitted every two seconds. The browser knows that the response body contains a stream because of the response Content-Type header value which is text/event-stream. So the browser waits until the stream emits the complete event and then it returns the response to the user as a downloadable file. The contents of the file are the Person instances serialized as JSON. If you have a Linux or Unix system, you can test that URL by executing the following command in a terminal.

```
curl -H "text/event-stream" http://localhost:8081/persons/
```

In the terminal, you see each Person instance returned every two seconds.

Postman can test the handler methods in a reactive controller as well. If you create a GET request in Postman with http://localhost:8081/persons/, and then send it, it will take at least eight seconds, but that data will be loaded.

There is also the programmatic version. Writing a test class for this controller is possible using reactive clients like WebTestClient from module spring-test, WebClient and ExchangeFunction from module spring-webflux.

The next test uses WebTestClient because it provides the same API as WebClient, but in addition to those it provides methods to check response status, header, and body.

In the next code sample, the controller method returning a Flux<Person> instance emitting Person instances and the controller method returning a Mono<Person> instance are tested. Since we know the persons() handler method uses zip to slow down the emission of elements, we increase the timeout of the WebTestClient instance used to test the request.

```java
package com.apress.cems.reactive;

import com.apress.cems.person.Person;
import org.junit.jupiter.api.*;
import org.springframework.boot.test.context.SpringBootTest;
import org.springframework.boot.web.server.LocalServerPort;
import org.springframework.http.MediaType;
import org.springframework.test.web.reactive.server.WebTestClient;

import java.time.Duration;

import static org.junit.jupiter.api.Assertions.*;
@SpringBootTest(webEnvironment = SpringBootTest.WebEnvironment.RANDOM_PORT)
class ReactiveHybridTest {

    @LocalServerPort
    private Integer port;

    private String baseUrl = "http://localhost";

    private WebTestClient webTestClient = null;

    @BeforeEach
    void setUp(){
        baseUrl = baseUrl.concat(":").concat(port .toString()).concat("/
        persons");
        webTestClient = WebTestClient
                .bindToServer()
                .baseUrl(baseUrl)
                .responseTimeout(Duration.ofSeconds(3600))
                .build();
    }

    @Test
    void shouldReturnAListOfPersons(){
        webTestClient.get().uri("/").accept(MediaType.TEXT_EVENT_STREAM)
                .exchange()
                .expectStatus().isOk()
                .expectHeader().contentType("text/event-stream;charset=UTF-8")
```

```
            .expectBodyList(Person.class).consumeWith(Assertions::asser
            tNotNull);
    }

    @Test
    void shouldReturnAPerson() {
        webTestClient.get().uri("/1")
                .exchange()
                .expectStatus().isOk()
                .expectHeader().contentType(MediaType.APPLICATION_JSON)
                .expectBody(Person.class).consumeWith(responseEntity -> {
            Person person = responseEntity.getResponseBody();
            assertAll("person", () ->
            {
                assertNotNull(person);
                assertAll("person",
                        () -> assertEquals("Sherlock", person.
                            getFirstName()),
                        () -> assertEquals("Holmes", person.
                            getLastName()));
            });

        });
    }
}
```

The base URL for WebTestClient is set by calling baseUrl(..). All requests to be tested have to specify only the URI part the handler methods are mapped to in the controller class being tested, which is quite practical.

If you run the tests in IntelliJ using a Gradle launcher, a report should be generated with the results, which should confirm that all tests passed. The report is located at reactive-boot-hybrid/build/reports/tests/test/index.html. If you open it in a browser, you should see something similar to what is depicted in Figure 12-4.

ReactiveHybridTest

underlineall > com.apress.cems.reactive > ReactiveHybridTest

2	0	0	9.065s	100%
tests	failures	ignored	duration	successful

Tests   Standard output

Test	Duration	Result
shouldReturnAListOfPersons()	8.055s	passed
shouldReturnAPerson()	1.010s	passed

Figure 12-4. *ReactiveHybridTest execution report*

The ExchangeFunction functional interface can exchange ClientRequest for a delayed ClientResponse.

These interfaces are part of the org.springframework.web.reactive.function. client package. Together with test classes from Project Reactor, can be used to write tests for reactive methods. Depending on your preference, you can use this approach instead of WebTestClient. In the following code snippet, a GET call to /persons is tested using ExchangeFunction and the reactor.test.StepVerifier interface.

```
package com.apress.cems.reactive;

import com.apress.cems.person.Person;
import org.junit.jupiter.api.*;
import org.slf4j.Logger;
import org.slf4j.LoggerFactory;
import org.springframework.boot.test.context.SpringBootTest;
import org.springframework.boot.web.server.LocalServerPort;
import org.springframework.http.HttpMethod;
import org.springframework.http.client.reactive.ReactorClientHttpConnector;
import org.springframework.web.reactive.function.client.ClientRequest;
import org.springframework.web.reactive.function.client.ExchangeFunction;
import org.springframework.web.reactive.function.client.ExchangeFunctions;
import reactor.test.StepVerifier;
```

```java
import java.net.URI;

@TestMethodOrder(MethodOrderer.OrderAnnotation.class)
@SpringBootTest(webEnvironment = SpringBootTest.WebEnvironment.RANDOM_PORT)
class ExchangeFunctionTest {

    private static Logger logger = LoggerFactory.
    getLogger(ExchangeFunctionTest.class);

    @LocalServerPort
    private Integer port;

    private String baseUrl = "http://localhost";

    private static ExchangeFunction exchange;

    @BeforeAll
    static void init(){
        exchange = ExchangeFunctions.create(new
        ReactorClientHttpConnector());
    }

    @BeforeEach
    void setUp(){
        baseUrl = baseUrl.concat(":").concat(port.toString()).concat
        ("/persons");
    }

    @Order(1)
    @Test
    void shouldReturnAListOfPersons(){
        URI uri = URI.create(baseUrl);
        logger.debug("GET REQ: "+ uri.toString());
        ClientRequest request = ClientRequest.create(HttpMethod.GET, uri).
        build();

        exchange.exchange(request).flatMapMany(
            response -> response.bodyToFlux(Person.class))
                .as(StepVerifier::create)
```

```
                .expectNextCount(4)
                .verifyComplete();

    }
}
```

This was mentioned before but it needs underlining: reactive implementations are useless with implementations that are not reactive. There is not much advantage in the previous implementation since the repository and the database are not reactive, because they block the whole data flow, until they can provide that requested data. So, what can be done? Use a database that is reactive.

Getting Comfortable with Spring WebFlux

The Spring WebFlux module was introduced in Spring 5 as an alternative module to build Spring Web Reactive applications. This module is also known as the Spring functional module because its design is very functional. In Figure 12-5, the main components of this framework are depicted in parallel with their non-reactive analogous Spring Web equivalents.

In Figure 12-5, a few components are placed at the intersection of the two frameworks. The `@RestController` and the `@RequestMapping` annotation family can be used to write reactive applications that can be hosted on Tomcat and Jetty. The module contains support for reactive HTTP and WebSocket clients as well as for reactive server web applications, including REST, an HTML browser, and WebSocket-style interactions.

As you saw in the previous section, there are Spring web components—such as `@RestController` and `@RequestMapping` (and specializations)—that can be used to build a reactive application. This is also possible because servers like Tomcat and Jetty support reactive requests when used with Servlet 3.1.

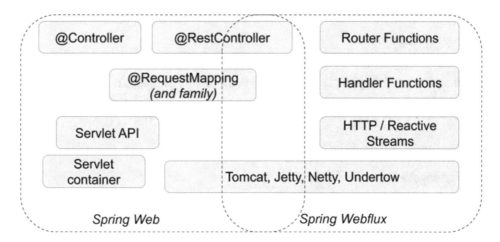

Figure 12-5. Spring Web and Spring WebFlux comparison

Aside from the classic annotation-based model, this module provides components to build Spring Web Reactive applications by writing functional code using Java 8 lambda style for routing and handling . Mapping requests to handler functions is done using an instance of type `RouterFunction<T extends ServerResponse>`.

This is a functional interface declared in the `org.springframework.web.reactive. function.server` package. It can be implemented to link URIs to `HandlerFunction<Ser verResponse>` functions, which are used to resolve `ServerRequest` into `ServerResponse`. This functional interface is part of the same package and simplifies the configuration to map handlers to URIs in reactive applications.

Now that the surface has been scratched on how incoming HTTP requests are mapped to reactive handler functions, let's switch again to the *bottom-up* style of development and build a reactive application starting from the database. To build a fully reactive application, we need a reactive database. Since most applications use relational databases to store their data, the key to creating a fully reactive application is to switch to a NoSQL database. Several NoSQL database vendors provide reactive database clients for their databases and MongoDB[16] is one of them, which makes things really easy because MongoDB was used in this book before.

To build an application using reactive MongoDB, the easiest way is to create a Spring Boot project that has the `spring-boot-starter-data-mongodb-reactive` on the classpath. Adding this module as a dependency will make sure everything needed

---

[16]The others are Cassandra, Couchbase, and Redis, as mentioned on their official sites. Also, code samples with Spring Data and Reactive databases can be found here: `https://github.com/ spring-projects/spring-data-examples`

to communicate with MongoDB reactively is brought over using the Spring Boot smart dependency solving system.

In the following configuration snippet, the Gradle dependencies and the configuration for the /chapter12/reactive-boot-mongo project are depicted.

```
//pivotal-certified-pro-spring-dev-exam-02/build.gradle
 ext {
    springBootVersion = '2.2.0.M5'
    springMongoVersion = '2.1.9.RELEASE'
    reactorVersion = '3.3.0.M3'
    ...

    boot = [
      starterWebflux :
          "org.springframework.boot:spring-boot-starter-
          webflux:$springBootVersion",
      starterMongoReactive :
  "org.springframework.boot:spring-boot-starter-data-mongodb-
  reactive:$springBootVersion",
      actuator :
          "org.springframework.boot:spring-boot-starter-
          actuator:$springBootVersion",
      ...
    ]

    testing = [
      mongo           : "de.flapdoodle.embed:de.flapdoodle.embed.
                        mongo:$mongoVersion",
      reactorTest    : "io.projectreactor:reactor-test:$reactorVersion",
      ...
    ]
}

// chapter12/reactive-boot-mongo/build.gradle
 dependencies {
    implementation boot.starterMongoReactive, boot.starterWebflux, boot.
    actuator
```

```
testImplementation testing.reactorTest, testing.mongo
testImplementation (boot.starterTest) {
    exclude group: "org.junit.vintage", module: "junit-vintage-engine"
    exclude group: "junit", module: "junit"
}
}
```

In Figure 12-6, you can see all the libraries that the `spring-boot-starter-data-mongodb-reactive` declares as dependencies.

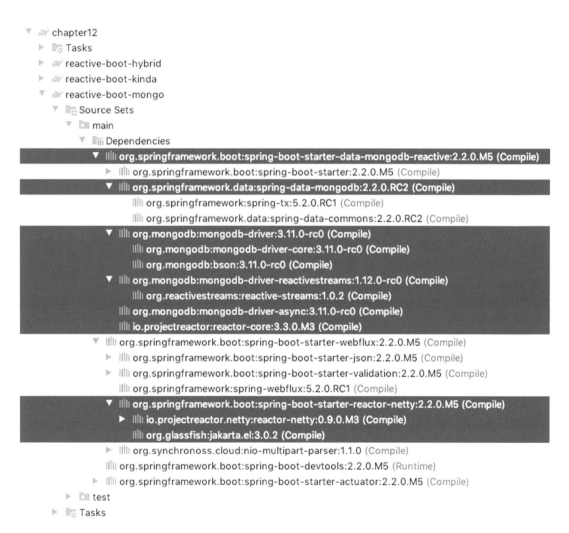

Figure 12-6. *Spring Boot reactive MongoDB starter dependencies*

The `mongodb-driver-reactivestreams` module is the one containing the implementation of the reactive driver that provides asynchronous stream processing with non-blocking back pressure for MongoDB.

The `spring-data-mongodb` module contains the `ReactiveMongoRepository<T,ID>` interface, that is designed to be extended so that Spring knows to provide instant reactive repositories. The code that needs to be developed to create a reactive repository looks similar to the one needed to be written for a normal reactive repository. The MongoDB queries have the same syntax that was introduced in Chapter 5.

```
package com.apress.reactive.person;

import org.springframework.data.mongodb.repository.Query;
import org.springframework.data.mongodb.repository.
ReactiveMongo  Repository;
import reactor.core.publisher.Flux;
import reactor.core.publisher.Mono;

public interface PersonReactiveRepo extends
             ReactiveMongoRepository<Person, String> {

    @Query("{'lastName': { '$regex' : ?0 } }")
    Flux<Person> findByLastName(String lastName);

    @Query("{ 'username' :  ?0 }")
    Mono<Person> findByUsername(String username);
}
```

If we weren't using Spring Boot, `@EnableReactiveMongoRepositories` from package `org.springframework.data.mongodb.repository.config` would need to be placed on a configuration class to enable Spring Mongo Reactive repositories.

The `Person` instance is not going to be depicted again, because the implementation is the same one that was used for the non-reactive MongoDB example specific to Chapter 5.

Now that we have a reactive repository, a reactive service can be created as well. The interface in the next code snippet describes a reactive service implementation.

```
package com.apress.reactive.person.services;

import com.apress.reactive.person.Person;
import reactor.core.publisher.Flux;
import reactor.core.publisher.Mono;
```

```
public interface PersonReactiveService {

    Mono<Person> findById(String id);

    Flux<Person> findAll();

    Mono<Person> save(Person person);

    Mono<Void> update(String id, Mono<Person> personMono);

    Mono<Void> delete(String id);
}
```

The implementation is quite simple.

```
package com.apress.reactive.person.services;

import com.apress.reactive.person.Person;
import com.apress.reactive.person.PersonReactiveRepo;
import org.slf4j.Logger;
import org.slf4j.LoggerFactory;
import org.springframework.stereotype.Service;
import reactor.core.publisher.Flux;
import reactor.core.publisher.Mono;

@Service
public class PersonReactiveServiceImpl implements PersonReactiveService {

    private static Logger logger = LoggerFactory
        .getLogger(PersonReactiveServiceImpl.class);

    private final PersonReactiveRepo personRepository;
    public PersonReactiveServiceImpl(PersonReactiveRepo personRepository) {
        this.personRepository = personRepository;
    }

    //added the subscriber just to make sure our service works
    @Override
    public Mono<Person> findById(String id) {
        return personRepository.findById(id);
    }
```

```java
    @Override
    public Flux<Person> findAll() {
        return personRepository.findAll();
}

    @Override
    public Mono<Person> save(Person person) {
        return personRepository.save(person);
    }

    @Override
    public Mono<Void> update(String id, Mono<Person> personMono) {
        return personRepository.findById(id).doOnNext(original ->
            personMono.doOnNext(
                    updatedPerson -> {
                        original.setUsername(updatedPerson.getUsername());
                        original.setFirstName(updatedPerson.getFirstName());
                        original.setLastName(updatedPerson.getLastName());
                        personRepository.save(original);
                    })
        ).then(Mono.empty());
    }

    @Override
    public Mono<Void> delete(String id) {
        return personRepository.findById(id).doOnNext(personRepository::
        delete)
            .then(Mono.empty());
    }
}
```

So far, even if reactive, a repository and a service were easy to implement and the code looks pretty familiar, as it resembles the non-reactive one a lot. Since we can assume that the repository works as intended, we can go ahead and test the service. A Spring Boot test will be written to start the application with a mock web environment that is not used within the test context, as you learned in Chapter 3. To test the reactive service, we have to call its methods and use utility methods from the `reactor-test` to check the behavior. The most important methods to test reactive behavior are grouped in the `reactor.test.StepVerifier` interface. This interface provides a declarative way of specifying verification code for an asynchronous `org.reactivestreams.Publisher<T>` (which `Flux<T>` and `Mono<T>`) sequence. The verification is triggered by calling one of the `verify*()` methods, declared in a separate interface declared inside `StepVerifier` named `LastStep`, and the name says it all, since these methods are to be called last in the chain to test a reactive stream. There's a bunch of them declared for each stream signal and consumers can be provided as arguments. In the next code snippet, only `verifyComplete()` is depicted. This interface also exposes a set of `assert*(..)` methods specific for checking assertions on streams.[17] Let's see it in action, shall we?

```java
package com.apress.reactive;

import com.apress.reactive.person.Person;
import com.apress.reactive.person.services.PersonReactiveService;
import org.junit.jupiter.api.Test;
import org.springframework.beans.factory.annotation.Autowired;
import org.springframework.boot.test.context.SpringBootTest;
import reactor.test.StepVerifier;

@SpringBootTest(webEnvironment = SpringBootTest.WebEnvironment.MOCK)
class MongoReactiveServiceTest {

    @Autowired
    PersonReactiveService personService;

    @Test
    void shouldReadAllPersons() {
        personService.findAll()
                .as(StepVerifier::create)
                .expectNextCount(3)
                .verifyComplete();
    }
```

---

[17]You can find the full API here: `https://projectreactor.io/docs/test/release/api/reactor/test/StepVerifier.html`

```
    @Test
    void shouldReturnSherlockById() {
        Person gigi = createPerson( "gigi.pedala", "Gigi", "Pedala", "12345");
        personService.findById("gigipedala43")
                .as(StepVerifier::create)
                .assertNext(gigi::equals)
                .verifyComplete();
    }

    Person createPerson( String username, String fn, String ln, String
    password) {
        Person person = new Person();
        // call setters
        return person;
    }
}
```

How does the StepVerifier work? Well, to quote the official documentation, it "is a verifiable, blocking script usually produced by terminal expectations of the said script." StepIdentifier is created by calling StepVerifier::create, and the result of this call is a <T> StepVerifier.FirstStep<T> function that wraps around the reactive stream returned by the personService.findAll() and allows assertions to be configured for the stream. The verify*() calls are those that control all the actions and test the assertions. This is because of the declarative style of reactive operations. Things no longer happen when specific methods are called, but they are declared to happen to a certain point in the future, when a special method is called that starts the whole stream processing.

Now that the service is tested and works fine, it is time to develop the web layer. On the web layer is where the significant differences begin. At the beginning of this chapter it was mentioned that requests are handled by HandlerFunctions. It is good practice to group handler functions for each entity type in a single class, in the same way you would group all handler methods in a controller. In this case, a class named PersonHandler will be created. This class will also be configured as a bean using @Component, and this bean is used by the routing function, so requests can be mapped to handler functions. For each of the methods in the PersonReactiveService a handler function will be declared. The following code snippet uses a lot of lambda expressions. The methods must be public since they are to be mapped to URIs in the routing function.

```java
package com.apress.reactive.person;

import com.apress.reactive.person.services.PersonReactiveService;
import org.springframework.http.MediaType;
import org.springframework.stereotype.Component;
import org.springframework.web.reactive.function.server.HandlerFunction;
import org.springframework.web.reactive.function.server.ServerRequest;
import org.springframework.web.reactive.function.server.ServerResponse;
import reactor.core.publisher.Mono;

import java.net.URI;

import static org.springframework.web.reactive.function.BodyInserters.
fromObject;

@Component
public class PersonHandler {
    private PersonReactiveService personService;

    public PersonHandler(PersonReactiveService personService) {
        this.personService = personService;
    }

    public HandlerFunction<ServerResponse> list =
            serverRequest -> ServerResponse.ok()
            .contentType(MediaType.APPLICATION_JSON)
            .body(personService.findAll(), Person.class);

    Public Mono<ServerResponse> show(ServerRequest serverRequest) {
        Mono<Person> personMono = personService.findById(serverRequest
                    .pathVariable("id"));
        return personMono
                .flatMap(person -> ServerResponse.ok()
                .contentType(MediaType.APPLICATION_JSON).
                body(fromObject(person)))
                .switchIfEmpty(ServerResponse.notFound().build());
    }
```

```
public Mono<ServerResponse> save(ServerRequest serverRequest) {
    Mono<Person> personMono =  serverRequest.bodyToMono(Person.class)
                .doOnNext(personService::save);
    return personMono
            .flatMap(person -> ServerResponse
            .created(URI.create("/persons/" + person.getId()))
            .contentType(MediaType.APPLICATION_JSON).
            body(fromObject(person)))
            .switchIfEmpty(ServerResponse.notFound().build());
}

public HandlerFunction<ServerResponse> update =
        serverRequest -> ServerResponse.noContent()
        .build(personService.update(serverRequest.pathVariable("id"),
                serverRequest.bodyToMono(Person.class)));

public HandlerFunction<ServerResponse> delete =
        serverRequest -> ServerResponse.noContent()
        .build(personService.delete(serverRequest.pathVariable("id")));
}
```

The next step is to create a bean of type RouterFunction<ServerResponse> and map URIs to these HandlerFunction<ServerResponse> instances. Since this is a Spring Boot application, and its main class is also a configuration class, the bean can be declared in it.

```
package com.apress.reactive;

import org.springframework.web.reactive.function.server.RouterFunction;
import org.springframework.web.reactive.function.server.ServerResponse;

import static org.springframework.web.reactive.function.BodyInserters.
fromObject;
import static org.springframework.web.reactive.function.server.
RequestPredicates.GET;
import static org.springframework.web.reactive.function.server.
RequestPredicates.POST;
```

```java
import static org.springframework.web.reactive.function.server.
RequestPredicates.PUT;
import static org.springframework.web.reactive.function.server.
RequestPredicates.DELETE;
import static org.springframework.web.reactive.function.server.
RouterFunctions.route;
import static org.springframework.web.reactive.function.server.
ServerResponse.ok;
...

@SpringBootApplication
public class MongoReactiveApplication {

    private static Logger logger =
        LoggerFactory.getLogger(MongoReactiveApplication.class);

    private final PersonHandler personHandler;

    public MongoReactiveApplication(PersonHandler personHandler) {
        this.personHandler = personHandler;
    }

    @Bean
    RouterFunction<ServerResponse> routingFunction() {
        return route(GET("/home"), serverRequest -> ok().
        body(fromObject("works!")))
                .andRoute(GET("/persons"), personHandler.list)
                .andRoute(GET("/persons/{id}"), personHandler::show)h
                .andRoute(PUT("/persons/{id}"), personHandler.update)
                .andRoute(POST("/persons"), personHandler::save)
                .andRoute(DELETE("/persons/{id}"), personHandler.delete)
                .filter((request, next) -> {
                    logger.info("Before handler invocation: " + request.
                    path());
                    return next.handle(request);
        });
    }
```

```
public static void main(String... args) {
    ConfigurableApplicationContext ctx = SpringApplication.run(
            MongoReactiveApplication.class, args);
    ctx.registerShutdownHook();
    logger.info("Application Started ...");
}
}
```

The RouterFunction<ServerResponse> instance is created by calling the RouterFunctions.route(..) method. This method receives as arguments a RequestPredicate instance that contains the type of request supported for a URI and a reference to a HandlerFunction<ServerResponse>. Additional mappings named routes in this context, can be added by calling andRoute(..) on the RouterFunction<ServerResponse> instance. This method requires the same argument types as the route(..) and returns the modified RouterFunction<ServerResponse> which is practical because it allows chaining of multiple calls or chaining with other methods declared in RouterFunction<ServerResponse>, like the filter(...) method that is used to declare HandlerFilterFunction<T,S>[18] instances to be called before and after the execution of the handler functions. In Spring Web this was done by declaring interceptors.

When the MongoReactiveApplication class runs, a web application starts. As you saw in Figure 12-6, spring-webflux uses the Netty server. Netty is a NIO client/server framework that enables the quick and easy development of network applications, such as protocol servers and clients.[19]

To configure the port and location where the MongoDB is accessible, and the port used by the Netty Server, the following properties must be added to the application. yml file.

```
spring:
  data:
    mongodb:
      host: localhost
      port: 27017
server:
  port: 8081
```

---

[18]*HandlerFilterFunction<T,S>* is also a functional interface.
[19]Official Netty site: https://netty.io/

```
servlet:
  context-path: /
compression:
  enabled: true
address: localhost
```

MongoDB must be started before the Spring application is started.[20]

When testing the application, there is no need for an external database, since an in-memory MongoDB (the one provided by FlapDoodle) can be used to keep things simple. To test this application the WebTestClient is used. The following test class is similar to what was written for the previous section. A WebTestClient is a reactive client, which can test reactive applications. The next class covers all routes declared by the RouterFunction<ServerResponse> bean

```
package com.apress.reactive;

import com.apress.reactive.person.Person;
import org.junit.jupiter.api.*;
import org.slf4j.Logger;
import org.slf4j.LoggerFactory;
import org.springframework.boot.test.context.SpringBootTest;
import org.springframework.boot.web.server.LocalServerPort;
import org.springframework.http.MediaType;
import org.springframework.test.web.reactive.server.WebTestClient;
import reactor.core.publisher.Mono;

import java.time.LocalDateTime;
import java.time.format.DateTimeFormatter;
import java.util.UUID;

import static org.junit.jupiter.api.Assertions.*;

@SpringBootTest(webEnvironment = SpringBootTest.WebEnvironment.RANDOM_PORT)
class MongoReactiveApplicationTests {
    private static Logger logger =
        LoggerFactory.getLogger(MongoReactiveApplicationTests.class);
```

---

[20]Instructions on how to do so are provided in a README.adoc document in the project sources.

```
@LocalServerPort
private Integer port;

private String baseUrl = "http://localhost";

private WebTestClient webTestClient = null;

@BeforeEach
void setUp(){
    baseUrl = baseUrl.concat(":").concat(port.toString()).concat("/
    persons");
    webTestClient = WebTestClient
            .bindToServer()
            .baseUrl(baseUrl)
            .build();
}

@Test
void shouldReturnAListOfPersons(){
    webTestClient.get().uri("/").accept(MediaType.TEXT_EVENT_STREAM)
        .exchange()
        .expectStatus().isOk()
        .expectHeader().contentType(MediaType.APPLICATION_JSON)
        .expectBodyList(Person.class).consumeWith(
            listEntityExchangeResult ->
              {
                    assertEquals(3,
                        listEntityExchangeResult.getResponseBody().
                        size());
                    listEntityExchangeResult.getResponseBody()
                        .forEach(p -> logger.info("All: {}",p));
              }
    );
}

@Test
void shouldReturnNoPerson(){
    webTestClient.get().uri("/99sdsd").accept(MediaType.TEXT_EVENT_STREAM)
```

```java
        .exchange()
        .expectStatus().isNotFound();
}

@Test
void shouldCreateAPerson(){
    Person person = new Person();
    person.setId(UUID.randomUUID().toString());
    person.setUsername("catherine.cawood");
    person.setFirstName("Catherine");
    person.setLastName("Cawood");
    person.setPassword("ccwoo");
    person.setHiringDate(DateProcessor.toDate("1986-05-27 00:38"));

    webTestClient.post().uri("/").body(Mono.just(person),
        Person.class).exchange().expectStatus().isCreated();
}

@Test
void shouldReturnAPerson() {
    webTestClient.get().uri("/gigipedala43").accept(MediaType.TEXT_
    EVENT_STREAM)
            .exchange()
            .expectStatus().isOk()
            .expectHeader().contentType(MediaType.APPLICATION_JSON)
            .expectBody(Person.class).consumeWith(responseEntity -> {
        Person person = responseEntity.getResponseBody();
        assertAll("person", () ->
        {
            assertNotNull(person);
            assertAll("person",
                    () -> assertEquals("Gigi", person.getFirstName()),
                    () -> assertEquals("Pedala", person.getLastName()));
        });
    });
}
```

```
    @Test
    void shouldUpdateAPerson() {
        webTestClient.get().uri("/gigipedala43").accept(MediaType.TEXT_
        EVENT_STREAM)
                .exchange()
                .expectStatus().isOk()
                .expectHeader().contentType(MediaType.APPLICATION_JSON)
                .expectBody(Person.class).consumeWith(responseEntity -> {
            Person person = responseEntity.getResponseBody();
            person.setFirstName("Gigi Lopata");
            webTestClient.put().uri("/1").body(Mono.just(person),
                Person.class).exchange().expectStatus().isNoContent();
        });
    }

    @Test
    void shouldDeleteAPerson() {
        webTestClient.delete().uri("/gigipedala43").exchange()
                .expectStatus().isNoContent();
    }
}

class DateProcessor {
    private static final String DATE_FORMAT = "yyyy-MM-dd HH:mm";
    private static DateTimeFormatter formatter =
        DateTimeFormatter.ofPattern(DATE_FORMAT);

    public static LocalDateTime toDate(final String date) {
        return LocalDateTime.parse(date, formatter);
    }
}
```

If the test is run in IntelliJ IDEA using a Gradle launcher (and in the newer versions it seems to do this automatically for Gradle projects), a test report is generated for you, which is located at reactive-boot-mongo/build/reports/tests/test/index.html. If you open this file in a browser, you should see something similar to what is depicted in Figure 12-7.

MongoReactiveApplicationTests

all > com.apress.reactive > MongoReactiveApplicationTests

6	0	0	0.678s	100%
tests	failures	ignored	duration	successful

Tests   Standard output

Test	Duration	Result
shouldCreateAPerson()	0.018s	passed
shouldDeleteAPerson()	0.014s	passed
shouldReturnAListOfPersons()	0.042s	passed
shouldReturnAPerson()	0.105s	passed
shouldReturnNoPerson()	0.480s	passed
shouldUpdateAPerson()	0.019s	passed

Figure 12-7. *MongoReactiveApplicationTests execution report*

A few log messages have been printed to give you a better idea of what is going on when tests are running. If you are curious, you can look in the console log. Clear log messages inform about the application starting on the Netty server on a random port, the embedded database starting on port 12345, the handler methods called, the URIs where the requests were sent, the Person instances returned as a reactive stream, and at the end, log messages informing that the tests have passed and the application is shutting down.

```
...
INFO  o.s.b.a.mongo.embedded.EmbeddedMongo - 2019-09-19T23:23:42.037+0100 I
CONTROL
    [initandlisten] MongoDB starting : pid=27046 port=12345
...
[Test worker] INFO  o.s.b.w.e.netty.NettyWebServer - Netty started on
port[s]: 62749
[Test worker] INFO  c.a.r.MongoReactiveApplicationTests -
    Started MongoReactiveApplicationTests in 3.524200879 seconds [JVM
    running for 4.526]
```

```
[reactor-http-nio-3] INFO  c.a.r.MongoReactiveApplication -
     Before handler invocation: /persons/99sdsd
[reactor-http-nio-3] INFO  c.a.r.MongoReactiveApplication -
     Before handler invocation: /persons/gigipedala43
[nioEventLoopGroup-2-4] INFO  c.a.r.p.s.PersonReactiveServiceImpl - Found
person: Person {
        id=gigipedala43
        , username='gigi.pedala'
        , firstName='Gigi'
        , lastName='Pedala'
}
[reactor-http-nio-3] INFO  c.a.r.MongoReactiveApplication -
     Before handler invocation: /persons/
[reactor-http-nio-3] INFO  c.a.r.MongoReactiveApplication -
     Before handler invocation: /persons/gigipedala43
[nioEventLoopGroup-2-4] INFO  c.a.r.p.s.PersonReactiveServiceImpl - Found
person: Person {
        id=gigipedala43
        , username='gigi.pedala'
        , firstName='Gigi'
        , lastName='Pedala'
}
[reactor-http-nio-3] INFO  c.a.r.MongoReactiveApplication -
     Before handler invocation: /persons/1
[reactor-http-nio-3] INFO  c.a.r.MongoReactiveApplication -
     Before handler invocation: /persons/
[Test worker] INFO  c.a.r.MongoReactiveApplicationTests - All: Person {
        id=696d1f2c-4ec5-4085-8f11-a2ece1b62cee
        , username='sherlock.holmes'
        , firstName='Sherlock'
        , lastName='Holmes'
}
```

```
[Test worker] INFO  c.a.r.MongoReactiveApplicationTests - All: Person {
  id=c95fbce1-b05f-4539-825f-197e28774ebf
        , username='jackson.brodie'
        , firstName='Jackson'
        , lastName='Brodie'
}
[Test worker] INFO  c.a.r.MongoReactiveApplicationTests - All: Person {
        id=gigipedala43
        , username='gigi.pedala'
        , firstName='Gigi'
        , lastName='Pedala'
}
[reactor-http-nio-3] INFO  c.a.r.MongoReactiveApplication -
        Before handler invocation: /persons/gigipedala43

com.apress.reactive.MongoReactiveApplicationTests > shouldReturnNoPerson() PASSED
com.apress.reactive.MongoReactiveApplicationTests > shouldReturnAPerson() PASSED
com.apress.reactive.MongoReactiveApplicationTests > shouldCreateAPerson() PASSED
com.apress.reactive.MongoReactiveApplicationTests > shouldUpdateAPerson() PASSED
com.apress.reactive.MongoReactiveApplicationTests > shouldReturnAListOf
Persons() PASSED
com.apress.reactive.MongoReactiveApplicationTests > shouldDeleteAPerson() PASSED
...
EmbeddedMongo - 2019-09-19T23:23:46.743+0100 I CONTROL (conn6) now exiting
EmbeddedMongo - 2019-09-19T23:23:46.743+0100 I CONTROL (conn6) shutting
down with code:0
```

Another topic must be discussed. In the test methods, reactive data is transformed from Flux<T> and Mono<T> bytes into objects, and vice versa. This is done by the Decoder<T> and Encoder<T> interfaces from package org.springframework.core. codec added to the spring-core module. The spring-boot-starter-webflux adds also support for JSON (Jackson) and XML (JAXB) by declaring spring-boot-starter-json as a dependency. This means the request body can be either an instance of an object, Person in this case, or any reactive stream implementation that emits Person instances, like Flux<Person>, Mono<Person>.

Building reactive applications with Spring Boot is easy, especially using Spring Initializr that generates a full working configuration is pretty practical. It is possible to build reactive applications using classic style of development, without using Spring Boot, but extra care must be taken when declaring dependencies. You can use the annotation model, but when using Spring WebFlux the routing model should be used, because currently the two are not compatible (the cannot be used in the same application).

Although Spring uses Project Reactor as a core dependency for most of its internal APIs, it also supports RxJava[21] at the application level.

Using Spring Data R2DBC

To access a relational database from a Java application the JDBC driver is needed. The problem with the old generation JDBC drivers is that their design does not support reactive access. To write reactive applications that work with relational databases, JDBC must be replaced by a reactive API that reactive drivers can implement.

Enter R2DBC,[22] the Reactive Relational Database Connectivity API created by the Pivotal team. It can be implemented by driver vendors to provide reactive access to relational databases.

Since most existing application are still based on relational databases, R2DBC is needed for migrating existing applications, or transforming them into reactive applications, non-blocking applications that can handle concurrency with a small number of threads and scale with fewer hardware resources since migrating data from a relational database to a NoSQL database is most times not an option. Migrating SQL data to a NoSQL database is a pain because maintaining relationships between tables can become cumbersome.

R2DBC was announced at Spring One in 2018, but is still in the experimental phase, and thus unstable. However, since there are drivers built on it for MySQL, PostgreSQL, and H2, it deserves being mention in this chapter.

The application introduced in the previous section should be easily modified to use a reactive H2 instead of a reactive MongoDB, but because R2DBC is still experimental, the Spring Boot starter for it is only available on the Snapshot repository and Spring Initializr

---

[21]RxJava is a Java VM implementation of Reactive Extensions (http://reactivex.io/), a library for composing asynchronous and event-based programs by using observable sequences. Official code and documentation can be found on GitHub: https://github.com/ ReactiveX/RxJava

[22]R2DBC official site: https://r2dbc.io/

cannot be used to generate a working configuration. Also, for resolving the dependencies a specific BOM version must be specified in the Gradle configuration to make sure Spring Data for

R2DBC is used and the proper dependencies are added to the classpath. The following configuration snippet covers the Gradle configuration needed to make project chapter12/reactive-boot-r2dbc work.

```
//pivotal-certified-pro-spring-dev-exam-02/build.gradle
 ext {
    springBootR2dbcVersion = '0.1.0.BUILD-SNAPSHOT'
    reactorVersion = '3.3.0.M3'
    bootR2dbcReleaseTrainVersion = 'Moore-BUILD-SNAPSHOT'
    ...

    spring = [
                dataBom:
      "org.springframework.data:spring-data-releasetrain:
      $bootR2dbcReleaseTrainVersion",
                        ...
    ]

    boot = [
            starterR2dbc :
    "org.springframework.boot.experimental:spring-boot-starter-data-r2dbc:
    $springBootR2dbcVersion",
            starterR2dbcH2 :
    "org.springframework.boot.experimental:spring-boot-starter-r2dbc-h2:
    $springBootR2dbcVersion"
     ]

     testing = [
        reactorTest   : "io.projectreactor:reactor-test: $reactorVersion",
        ...
     ]
}
```

```
//chapter12/reactive-boot-r2dbc/build.gradle
buildscript {
    def springRepo = 'http://repo.spring.io'

    repositories {
        mavenLocal()
        mavenCentral()

        maven { url "$springRepo/release" }
        maven { url "$springRepo/snapshot" }
        maven { url "$springRepo/milestone" }
        maven { url "$springRepo/libs-milestone" }
    }
    dependencies {
        classpath boot.springBootPlugin
    }
}
apply plugin: 'java-library'
apply plugin: 'org.springframework.boot'
apply plugin: 'io.spring.dependency-management'

dependencies {
    implementation boot.starterR2dbc, boot.starterR2dbcH2, boot.
    starterWebflux, boot.actuator

    testImplementation testing.reactorTest
    testImplementation boot.starterTest {
        exclude group: "org.junit.vintage", module: "junit-vintage-engine"
        exclude group: "junit", module: "junit"
    }
}
dependencyManagement {
    imports {
        mavenBom spring.dataBom
    }
}
...
```

With that configuration, when the project is built, a set of dependencies are added to the classpath, as shown in Figure 12-8.

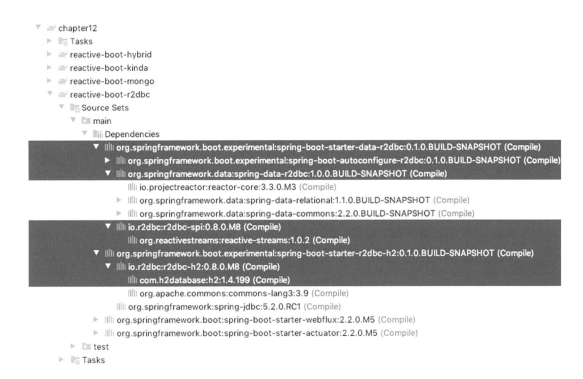

Figure 12-8. *Spring Boot R2DBC Starter dependencies*

Notice that two Spring Boot starters are needed to it R2DBC and the reactive H2 driver: `spring-boot-starter-data-r2dbc` and `spring-boot-starter-r2dbc-h2`. In the typical Spring Boot approach we would expect that `spring-boot-starter-r2dbc-h2` would declare `spring-boot-starter-data-r2dbc` as a transitive dependency, but it is not so for the version currently available.

Now that the configuration was introduced, let's get to the code. The `spring-boot-starter-data-r2dbc` provides a way to create instant reactive repositories for relational databases but a database connection is required. The database can be accessed through a bean of type `io.r2dbc.spi.ConnectionFactory`. An instance of this type can be created by specifying a number of properties specific to a database connection like: protocol, database name, port, user password, and so on, or by providing a connection URL. This is the simplest approach so this is what we're going to use. An instance of type `io.r2dbc.spi.ConnectionFactory` is created by calling the `get(..)` method of the `io.r2dbc.spi.ConnectionFactories` class and providing the connection URL as argument.

```
package com.apress.cems;

import io.r2dbc.spi.ConnectionFactories;
import io.r2dbc.spi.ConnectionFactory;
import org.springframework.context.annotation.Bean;
import org.springframework.context.annotation.Configuration;
import org.springframework.data.r2dbc.config.AbstractR2dbcConfiguration;

@Configuration
public class ReactiveH2Config  extends AbstractR2dbcConfiguration {

    @Override
    @Bean
    public ConnectionFactory connectionFactory() {
        return ConnectionFactories.get("
        r2dbc:h2:mem:///test?options=DB_CLOSE_DELAY=-1;DB_CLOSE_ON_
        EXIT=FALSE");
    }
}
```

AbstractR2dbcConfiguration is useful because it declares the other infrastructure beans necessary for R2DBC to work, including an ExceptionTranslator bean that translates R2DBC exceptions into exceptions in Spring's practical DataAccessException hierarchy. It also declares the DatabaseClient bean that we will use later in this section.

In the previous configuration class, the protocol must be r2dbc; otherwise, the application will not start because the ConnectionFactory instance cannot be used with a non-reactive driver.

Now that there is a connection, reactive repositories can be created. Since we are using Spring Data, an instant repository to manage Person instances can be created just by declaring a type that extends the ReactiveCrudRepository<T, ID> interface.

```
package com.apress.cems.person;

import org.springframework.data.r2dbc.repository.query.Query;
import org.springframework.data.repository.query.Param;
import org.springframework.data.repository.reactive.ReactiveCrudRepository;
import reactor.core.publisher.Flux;
import reactor.core.publisher.Mono;
```

```
public interface PersonRepo extends ReactiveCrudRepository<Person, Long> {

    @Query("select * from Person p where p.firstName=:fn")
    Flux<Person> findByFirstName(@Param("fn") String firstName);

    @Query("select * from Person p where p.username like '%' || ?1 || '%'")
    Mono<Person> findByUsername(String username);
}
```

At runtime, Spring creates a full repository implementation with all the basic CRUD operations needed to work with a database, and a full implementation for the two methods declared in the previous code snippet will be provided too. Notice how there is also a special type of Query for execution of reactive queries.

The PersonReactiveServiceImpl class is almost identical to the one written for the MongoDB version, the only change here is the type of the Id, which is Long (for MongoDB, it was String). The same goes for the PersonHandler class that contains the HandlerFunction<ServerResponse> for each of CRUD operations.

Same goes for the application class, the one annotated with @SpringBootApplication, inside it a RouterFunction<ServerResponse> bean will be declared to map URIs to HandlerFunction<ServerResponse> instances.

Because the Spring Boot specific starter is used, there is no need to add a configurations annotation like @EnableR2dbcRepositories to enable reactive repositories, or @EnableTransactionManagement to enable support for transactions. If you are curious to know how Spring supports transactions in reactive applications; here is the short explanation: a reactive transaction manager implementation was introduced named ReactiveTransactionManager. This transaction manager is an abstraction for reactive and non-blocking integrations that use transactional resources. It is a foundation for reactive @Transactional methods that return data as a reactive stream. If you want to know more, there is a very good article at https://spring.io/blog/2019/05/16/reactive-transactions-with-spring.

Testing is done using the WebTestClient, and since the PersonHandler and the RouterFunction<ServerResponse> beans are very similar to the ones in the MongoDB application introduced in the previous section, the test is very similar too. The only real difference is the database initialization. When this chapter was written, with the versions available for the reactive H2 driver, the Spring Boot application seems unable to initialize the reactive H2 instance with data, unless the application is run in a test context. This means the content of the database must be initialized before executing the test methods. I've isolated the initialization in a class TestBase that is depicted next.

```
package com.apress.cems;

import com.apress.cems.person.Person;
import org.springframework.beans.factory.annotation.Autowired;
import org.springframework.data.r2dbc.core.DatabaseClient;
import reactor.test.StepVerifier;

import java.time.LocalDateTime;
import java.util.Arrays;
import java.util.List;

public abstract class TestBase {

    @Autowired
    protected DatabaseClient databaseClient;

    protected void init(){
        List<String> statements = Arrays.asList(
                "drop table PERSON if exists;",
                "create table PERSON\n" +
                        "(\n" +
                        "  ID BIGINT IDENTITY PRIMARY KEY\n" +
                        ", USERNAME VARCHAR2(50) NOT NULL\n" +
                        ", FIRSTNAME VARCHAR2(50)\n" +
                        ", LASTNAME VARCHAR2(50)\n" +
                        ", PASSWORD VARCHAR2(50) NOT NULL\n" +
                        ", HIRINGDATE TIMESTAMP\n" +
                        ", VERSION INT\n" +
                        ", CREATEDAT TIMESTAMP NOT NULL\n" +
                        ", MODIFIEDAT TIMESTAMP NOT NULL\n" +
                        ", UNIQUE(USERNAME)\n" +
                        ");");
```

```
    statements.forEach(it -> databaseClient.execute(it)
            .fetch()
            .rowsUpdated()
            .as(StepVerifier::create)
            .expectNextCount(1)
            .verifyComplete());

    databaseClient.insert()
            .into(Person.class)
            .using(createPerson(
                1L, "sherlock.holmes", "Sherlock", "Holmes", "dudu"))
            .then()
            .as(StepVerifier::create)
            .verifyComplete();

    databaseClient.insert()
            .into(Person.class)
            .using(createPerson(
                2L, "jackson.brodie", "Jackson", "Brodie", "bagy"))
            .then()
            .as(StepVerifier::create)
            .verifyComplete();

    databaseClient.insert()
            .into(Person.class)
            .using(createPerson(
                3L, "gigi.pedala", "Gigi", "Pedala", "dooooh"))
            .then()
            .as(StepVerifier::create)
            .verifyComplete();
}

protected Person createPerson(
    Long id, String username, String fn, String ln, String password) {
    Person person = new Person();
    person.setId(id);
    person.setUsername(username);
    person.setFirstname(fn);
```

```
        person.setLastname(ln);
        person.setPassword(password);
        person.setHiringdate(LocalDateTime.now());
        return person;
    }
}
```

The table is also created in this method and `StepVerifier` is used to check that the creation succeeded. The same goes for each record created. The `PersonRepository` could have been used to insert these records, but since there was an opportunity to use the `org.springframework.data.r2dbc.core.DatabaseClient` interface, which is a high-level abstraction for storing and querying rows, why waste it?

When this section was written, R2DBC and drivers written based on it seems to have quite a few bugs and are not usable in production. But they do show great potential for building reactive applications with relational databases in the future. And since this project was begun by the Pivotal team, I have no doubt it will grow into something magnificent. If you want to read more about R2DBC and its usage in Spring reactive applications, the official documentation is good. Go to `https://docs.spring.io/spring-data/r2dbc/docs/1.0.0.M2/reference/html/#r2dbc.getting-started`. What it is lacking (at the time this section was written) is a Gradle configuration, but you were provided one in this project.

Summary

Reactive programming is not an easy topic, but it does seem to be the future of programming. Keep in mind that reactive implementations are quite useless with implementations that are not reactive. I mean, there is no use to design and use reactive components with non-reactive components, because you might accidentally introduce failure points and slow things down. For example, if you are using an Oracle database, there is no point in defining a repository class that returns elements using reactive streams, because an Oracle database does not support reactive access at the moment (remember the bucket of balls analogy?). So you will just be adding a reactive layer, that just adds extra implementation and development costs will increase, because there are no real benefits in this case. But if your database of choice is MongoDB, you can use reactive programming confidently, because MongoDB supports reactive access. Also, if you are building a web application with a ReactJS or Angular interface, you can design your controller classes to provide data reactively to be displayed by the interface.

This chapter

- explained what reactive programming is

- explained why Spring chose Project Reactor for its reactive support

- demonstrated how to build reactive applications using the Spring Web MVC annotation model and Tomcat

- demonstrated how to build a fully reactive application with a reactive MongoDB and Netty server

- demonstrated how to use the R2DBC driver to write reactive applications using relational databases

Appendix A

The purpose of this Appendix is to help you set up the development environment that you will use to write, compile, and execute the Spring applications specific to this book and to provide detailed responses for the questions in the quiz attached to each chapter.

Study Guide Projects

The appendix for this book is quite small because it was written in such a way that you are guided through the normal sequence of steps that you would have to follow every time you start development of an application.

- Choose your tools

- Install your tools

- Verify installation

- Design the application

- Develop & test

At the end of Chapter 1, the tools were presented to you and you were instructed how to install them and how to verify the correct installation. The code samples for the book were written on an Apple Mac computer. One of the strong points of Java is that it is multi-platform, so the code can be run in any operating system. The tools recommended are Java based and versions for any operating system are available on their official sites. The installation instructions are almost identical for any operating system, the only difference is in how an environment variable is set. Information about doing this on different operating systems is widely available on the internet, and considering this book is for developers with a little experience, this should not be a problem for you.

© Iuliana Cosmina 2020
I. Cosmina, *Pivotal Certified Professional Core Spring 5 Developer Exam*,
https://doi.org/10.1007/978-1-4842-5136-2

In the book, IntelliJ IDEA is the recommended editor. When installing it the first time, a number of plugins will be recommended for you. Make sure you select the Gradle plugin and if you choose to use the Ultimate version (30-day trial), select every Spring plugin listed. This will save you headaches later. All plugins are compatible and I have rarely needed to do anything extra to get a project working. Theoretically, the project can be built in Eclipse as well, if you know how to configure Eclipse properly. So make sure you know what you're doing if you stray from the recommended path.

The code for this book is organised in a single Gradle multi-module project named `pivotal-certified-pro-spring-dev-exam-02`. Every module is named as the chapter sources are specific to and each module contains a series of projects, some of them with working code samples, some of them with missing code samples for you to complete. The ones suffixed with `-practice` are missing pieces of code that the reader should provide to test his or her understanding of the chapter. All modules, except `chapter10`, inherit configurations from the global `build.gradle` file under the `pivotal-certified-pro-spring-dev-exam-02` directory. The Spring Boot projects, come with a predefined set of dependencies, thus these projects cannot inherit too much configuration from the `pivotal-certified-pro-spring-dev-exam-02` project. The overall project grows gradually from simple toy implementations to a complete web application, with persistence and security. Using this study guide, you will not only learn how to build Spring applications, you will learn how to design a workflow for you and your team and how to design a multi-layered application from scratch.

The project structure is depicted in Figure A-1

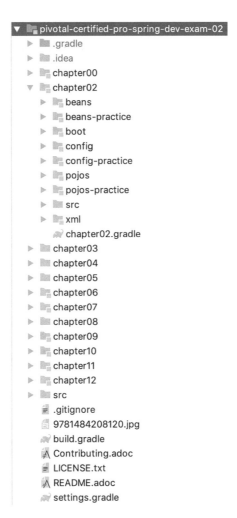

Figure A-1. *pivotal-certified-pro-spring-dev-exam-02 project structures in Intellij IDEA side by side*

Gradle Configuration Explained

`pivotal-certified-pro-spring-dev-exam-02` is the parent project that defines a set of libraries available for the children modules to use. The parent project has the Gradle configuration in a file typically named `build.gradle`. All the chapter modules utilize the naming convention, `[chapter[number]].gradle`, for example *chapter02.gradle*, so the user can quickly find the configuration file. Also, there's a closure element in `pivotal-certified-pro-spring-dev-exam-02/settings.gradle` that verifies at build time if all chapter modules have their configuration file present. This is important, because all projects in a chapter share the same dependencies and that means we can ensure that the file is present and valid.

```
rootProject.children.each { project ->
    project.buildFileName = "${chapternumber}.gradle"
    assert project.projectDir.isDirectory()
    assert project.buildFile.exists()
    assert project.buildFile.isFile()
}
```

If a Gradle build file is not named the same as the module, when executing any Gradle task an error will be thrown. The error is similar to the one depicted in the following code snippet, where the chapter02.gradle file was renamed to chapter14.gradle.

```
 $ gradle clean
Starting a Gradle Daemon subsequent builds will be faster

FAILURE: Build failed with an exception.

* Where:
Settings file '~/pivotal-certified-pro-spring-dev-exam-02/settings.gradle'
line: 34

* What went wrong:
A problem occurred evaluating settings 'pivotal-certified-pro-spring-dev-
exam-02'.
> assert project.buildFile.exists
             |       |        |
             |       |        false
             |       ~/pivotal-certified-pro-spring-dev-exam-02/chapter02/
             |       chapter02.gradle
          :chapter02

* Try:
Run with --stacktrace option to get the stack trace. Run with --info or
--debug option
    to get more log output. Run with --scan to get full insights.
```

```
* Get more help at https://help.gradle.org BUILD
FAILED in 3s
```

chapter14.gradle is not mentioned in the previous error because Gradle doesn't know about the existence of this file. Because of the configuration above, what Gradle can tell you is that it expects the module chapter02 to be configured using a file named chapter02.gradle, and no such file can be found.

This was a development choice; the configuration file of a module is also more visible in an editor this way. Another approach for a multi-modular project would have been to have only one build.gradle file for the whole project, and use Gradle-specific closures to customise configurations for each module. But in the spirit of good development practices, it was decided to keep configurations for the modules as decoupled as possible and in the same location with the module contents.

Building and troubleshooting

After you download the sources, you need to import the project in the IntelliJ IDEA editor. To do this, these steps must be followed:

[Step 1] Select from the Intellij IDEA menu File ➤ New ➤ Project from Existing Sources. (Menu options are depicted in Figure A-2)

Figure A-2. *Project import menu options in Intellij IDEA*

After selecting the proper option, a popup window will appear requesting the location of the project.(Figure A-3)

APPENDIX A

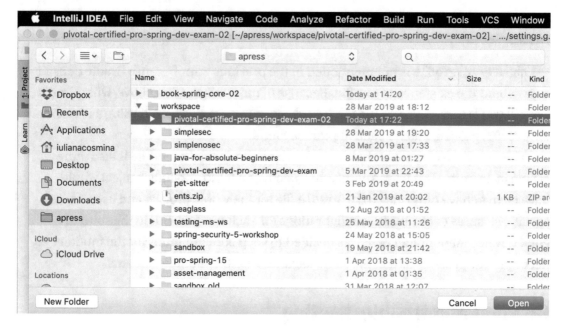

Figure A-3. *Select project root directory popup in Intellij IDEA*

[Step 2] Select the `pivotal-certified-pro-spring-dev-exam-02` directory. The following popup will ask for the project type. Intellij IDEA can create its own type of project from the selected sources and build it with its internal Java builder, but this option is not useful here as `pivotal-certified-pro-spring-dev-exam-02` is a Gradle project.

[Step 3] Check the `Import project from external model` radio button and select `Gradle` from the menu as depicted in Figure A-4:

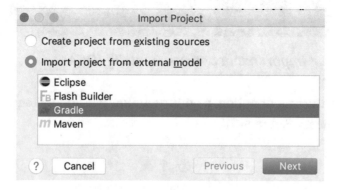

Figure A-4. *Selecting the project type Intellij IDEA*

[Step 4] The last popup will appear and ask for the location of the `build.gradle` file and the Gradle executable. The options will be already populated for you, with whatever IntelliJ IDEA was able to find installed in your system. If you have Gradle installed in the system, you might want to use it. (Figure A-5)

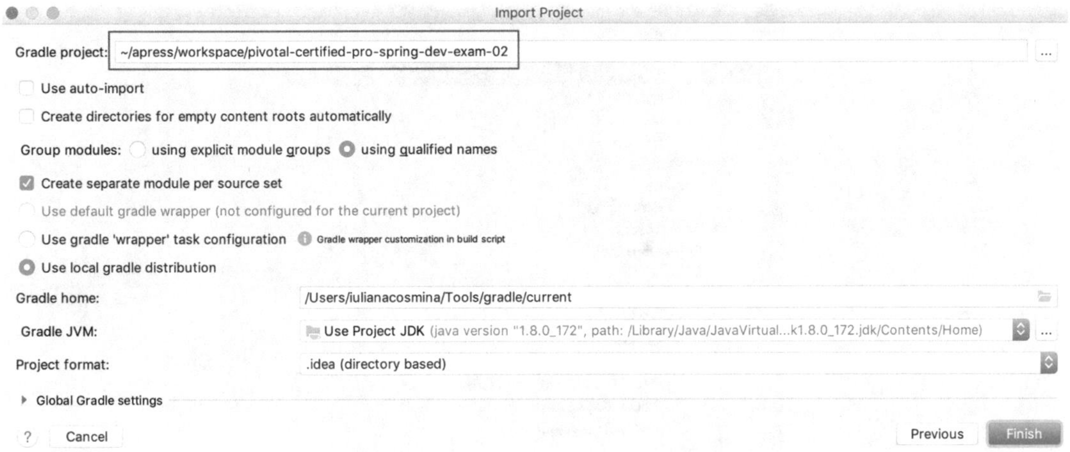

Figure A-5. *Last popup for project import in Intellij IDEA*

Also, make sure you select the right JDK. In the previous image IntelliJ IDEA found JDK 8 on my system, but for `pivotal-certified-pro-spring-dev-exam-02`, you need at least JDK 11.

Before getting to work, you should build the project. This can be done in Intellij IDEA by clicking the Gradle view `Refresh` button, marked with (1) in in Figure A-6. Clicking this button will cause IntelliJ IDEA to: scan configuration of the project, resolve dependencies, download any missing libraries, and do an internal light build of the project – just enough to remove compile time errors cause by missing dependencies.

The Gradle `build` task executes a full build of the project. It Can be used in the command line `.../workspace/pivotal-certified-pro-spring-dev-exam-02 $ gradle build` or from Intellij IDEA as depicted in Figure A-6, where the task is marked with (2).

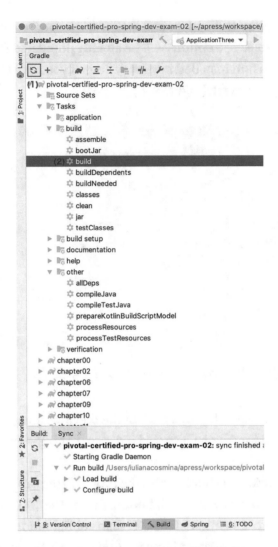

Figure A-6. Last popup for project import in Intellij IDEA

The Gradle build task compiles, assembles and tests the project. It does not run the clean task, so you need to make sure to run this task manually when building a project multiple times, to make sure the most recent versions of the classes are used.

The Gradle build task also executes the tests, so building the project the first time might take a while.

```
$ gradle clean build
This project is a Criminal Evidence Management System proof of concept
application.
```

It is meant to be used together with the "Pivotal Certified Professional
Spring
Developer Exam, 2nd Edition" published by Apress in order to learn and
practice Spring 5.x.

```
<=============-> 97% CONFIGURING [5s]
> :chapter12:reactive-boot-r2dbc > Resolve dependencies of
    :chapter12:reactive-boot-r2dbc:compile
...
com.apress.cems.jdbc.JdbcPersonRepoTest > testCreatePerson() SKIPPED
com.apress.cems.jdbc.JdbcPersonRepoTest > testFindAll() SKIPPED
...
com.apress.cems.R2dbcApplicationTests > shouldUpdateAPerson() PASSED
com.apress.cems.R2dbcApplicationTests > shouldDeleteAPerson() PASSED
...
BUILD SUCCESSFUL in 5m 10s
410 actionable tasks: 338 executed, 72 up-to-date
```

To prevent failures, the test classes in *-practice projects were annotated with
@Disabled. When solving the practice exercises and providing your own solutions,
this annotation must be either put in a comment or deleted altogether, so the tests
can be run.

If you want a quicker build, you can just comment all include statements you are not
interested in from the settings.gradle file.

Also starting with Gradle version 5, cached builds were introduced, which means
Gradle can store build results in a local cache and thus drastically reduce the duration of
your builds. The command to run is:

```
gradle --build-cache clean build assemble
```

Another option available, in case you need it, is to execute the Gradle build task, but
to skip the tests with the following argument:

```
.../workspace/pet-sitter $ gradle build -x test
```

Deploy on Apache Tomcat

There are a few web applications under `pivotal-certified-pro-spring-dev-exam-02` developed in the classic style, without Spring Boot. These web applications are intended to be run on Apache Tomcat. There are certain advantages in using an external container like an Apache Tomcat server. Starting the server in debug mode and using breakpoints to debug an application is easy and multiple applications can be run at the same time, using different contexts, without the need to stop the server.

Embedded servers are quite suitable for testing and educational purposes, and in tandem with Spring Boot, for development of applications suitable for being run in a cloud environment.

Here is what you have to do if you are interested in doing this. First download the latest version of Apache Tomcat from their official site[1]. You can get the latest version - 9.x will work with the sources of this book, and unpack it somewhere on your system. Then configure an IntelliJ IDEA launcher to start the server and deploy the chosen application. This is quite easy to do, but there are a number of steps to be executed. They are as follows:

[Step 1] From the runnable configuration menu, choose `Edit Configurations...(1)`. A popup window will appear listing a set of Launchers. Click on the + and select the `Tomcat Server` option. The menu will expand; select `Local(2)` because you are using a server installed on your computer. Figure A-7 depicts these menu options.

---

[1]Apache Tomcat official site `http://tomcat.apache.org/`

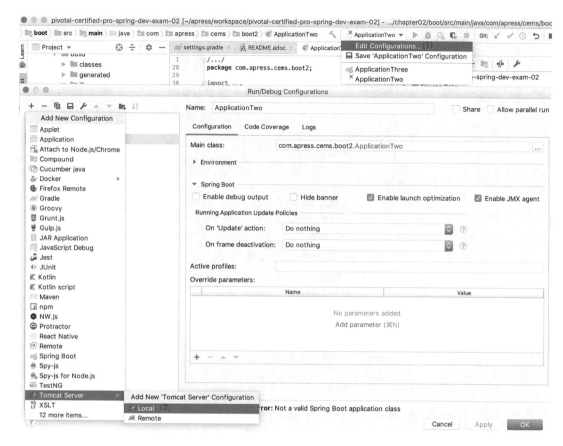

Figure A-7. *Menu options to create a Tomcat launcher in Intellij IDEA*

[Step 2] A popup window like the one in Figure A-8 will appear and will request some information.

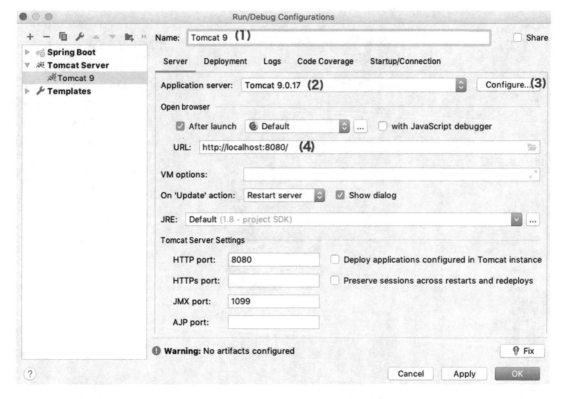

Figure A-8. *Popup to create a Tomcat launcher in Intellij IDEA*

In the previous figure, some items are numbered and their meaning is explained in following list:

1. The launcher name.

2. The Tomcat version being used.

3. The button that will open the popup window to insert the Tomcat instance location. The popup is depicted in Figure A-9.

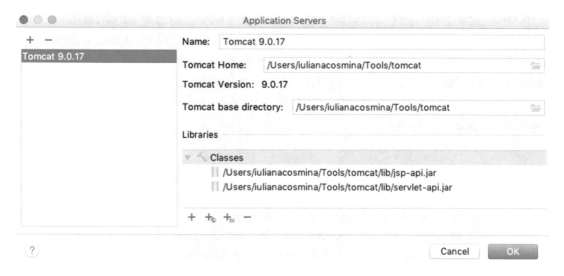

Figure A-9. *Configure Tomcat instance in Intellij IDEA*

4. The URL where the application can be accessed(in Figure A-8).

5. The Fix button shown in Figure A-8 button is used to choose an artifact to deploy on the Tomcat instance. If there is no web archive set to be deployed to Tomcat, this button will be displayed with a red lightbulb icon on it.

[Step 3] Click the Fix button marked with (5) in Figure A-8 and select an artifact. IntelliJ IDEA will detect all artifacts available (Figure A-10) and present them to you in a list. If you intend to open the server in debug mode and use breakpoints in the code, select an artifact with a name postfixed with (exploded); this way Intellij IDEA manages the contents of the exploded .war file and can link the actions in the browser with the breakpoints in the code.

[Step 4] Complete the configuration by clicking the Ok button. You can specify a different application context by inserting a new value in the Application context field. Choosing a different application context will tell Tomcat to deploy the application under the given name and the application will be accessible via this URL: http://localhost:8080/[app_context_name]/. In Figure A-11, you can see the the Application context field. The application configured like the one shown in the image will be accessible via this URL: http://localhost:8080/rest-classic-secured/.

Other application servers can be used in a similar way as long as IntelliJ IDEA provides support for them. Launcher configurations can be duplicated and multiple Tomcat instances can be started at the same time as long as they function on different ports, all for faster testing and comparisons between implementations. IntelliJ IDEA is really flexible and practical and that's why it was recommended for practicing the exercises in this study guide.

```
Gradle : com.apress.cems : classic-app-1.0-SNAPSHOT.war
Gradle : com.apress.cems : classic-app-1.0-SNAPSHOT.war (exploded)
Gradle : com.apress.cems : mvc-basic-1.0-SNAPSHOT.war
Gradle : com.apress.cems : mvc-basic-1.0-SNAPSHOT.war (exploded)
Gradle : com.apress.cems : mvc-basic-practice-1.0-SNAPSHOT.war
Gradle : com.apress.cems : mvc-basic-practice-1.0-SNAPSHOT.war (exploded)
Gradle : com.apress.cems : mvc-basic-xml-1.0-SNAPSHOT.war
Gradle : com.apress.cems : mvc-basic-xml-1.0-SNAPSHOT.war (exploded)
Gradle : com.apress.cems : mvc-sec-1.0-SNAPSHOT.war
Gradle : com.apress.cems : mvc-sec-1.0-SNAPSHOT.war (exploded)
Gradle : com.apress.cems : mvc-sec-practice-1.0-SNAPSHOT.war
Gradle : com.apress.cems : mvc-sec-practice-1.0-SNAPSHOT.war (exploded)
Gradle : com.apress.cems : mvc-sec-thymeleaf-1.0-SNAPSHOT.war
Gradle : com.apress.cems : mvc-sec-thymeleaf-1.0-SNAPSHOT.war (exploded)
Gradle : com.apress.cems : mvc-sec-xml-1.0-SNAPSHOT.war
Gradle : com.apress.cems : mvc-sec-xml-1.0-SNAPSHOT.war (exploded)
Gradle : com.apress.cems : mvc-thymeleaf-1.0-SNAPSHOT.war
Gradle : com.apress.cems : mvc-thymeleaf-1.0-SNAPSHOT.war (exploded)
Gradle : com.apress.cems : mvc-views-1.0-SNAPSHOT.war
Gradle : com.apress.cems : mvc-views-1.0-SNAPSHOT.war (exploded)
Gradle : com.apress.cems : rest-classic-1.0-SNAPSHOT.war
Gradle : com.apress.cems : rest-classic-1.0-SNAPSHOT.war (exploded)
Gradle : com.apress.cems : rest-classic-secured-1.0-SNAPSHOT.war (exploded)
```

Figure A-10. *Deployable artifact list in Intellij IDEA*

Quiz answers

The following sections contains answers to the Quiz questions for all chapters. Answers to questions that are simple enough, will not be detailed here. Extra details will be provided only for questions that could be considered tricky.

Quiz Solutions for Chapter 2

1. **Answer**: E

2. **Answer**: B, C

3. **Answer**: A, C

4. **Answer**: A, C

5. **Answer**: C

6. **Answer**: C

7. **Answer**: A, B, D

8. **Answer**: A

9. **Answer**: A

10. **Answer**: A

11. **Answer**: A, E, F

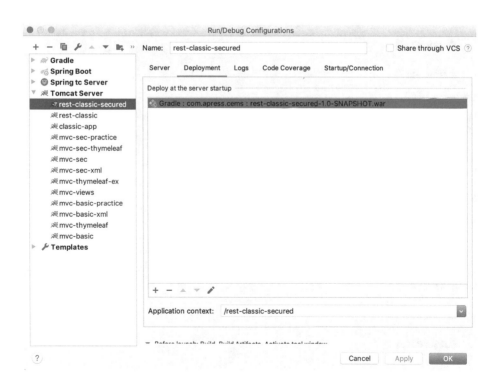

Figure A-11. *Insert new application context in Intellij IDEA*

Quiz Solutions for Chapter 3

1. **Answer**: A

2. **Answer**: A, C

3. **Answer**: A

4. **Answer**: B

5. **Answer**: A (To write unit tests for a Java application, even a Spring application, JUnit is mandatory.)

6. **Answer**: C

Quiz Solutions for Chapter 4

1. **Answer**: C

2. **Answer**: A, B, C, D

3. **Answer**: B,D

4. **Answer**: B

5. **Answer**: A

Quiz Solutions for Chapter 5

1. **Answer**: D

2. **Answer**: A, B, C

3. **Answer**: A

4. **Answer**: A

5. **Answer**: A

6. **Answer**: B

7. **Answer**: A

8. **Answer**: A, C

9. **Answer**: A

10. **Answer**: A

Quiz Solutions for Chapter 6

1. **Answer**: B

2. **Answer**: D

3. **Answer**: B

4. **Answer**: A,E,F

5. **Answer**: C

6. **Answer**: C

7. **Answer**: A

8. **Answer**: B

9. **Answer**: A, B, C

10. **Answer**: A

Quiz Solutions for Chapter 7

1. **Answer**: C

2. **Answer**: B

3. **Answer**: C

4. **Answer**: A

5. **Answer**: B

6. **Answer**: C (this is the most complete answer, leaving nothing to interpretation)

Quiz Solutions for Chapter 8

1. **Answer**: A, B, D

2. **Answer**: A

3. **Answer**: A, C, D

4. **Answer**: A, B

5. **Answer**: A, C, D

6. **Answer**: A, B, D

Quiz Solutions for Chapter 9

1. **Answer**: B, C

2. **Answer**: C, D (When Actuator is on the classpath without any configuration, the only enabled endpoints are /info and /health. actuator is not an endpoint.)

3. **Answer**: B

4. **Answer**: A (B is not a correct answer, because you can choose to override the /health endpoint, but just implementing the HealthIndicator will not suffice to do so.)

5. **Answer**: B

6. **Answer**: B

Exam sample

Question 1: The main idea of MVC is that there are three decoupled components, each of them can be swapped with a different implementation easily, and together they provide the desired functionality. The *view* represents the interface the user interacts with and it displays data and passes requests to the *controller*. The controller calls the business components and sends the data to the *model* that notifies the view that an actualization is needed. The *model* content is displayed by the *view*.

Does this description fit the MVC design pattern?

A. Yes.

B. No.

Question 2: Where can the @Profile annotation be used? (Choose one)

A. on a bean declared with @Component or its specializations

B. on a bean declared with @Bean

C. on a @Configuration class

D. all of the above

Question 3: Analyze the following code snippet:

```
public interface PersonRepo extends JpaRepository<Person, Long> {

    @Query("select p from Person p where p.username like %?1%")
    List<Person> findAllByUsername(String username);
}
```

What can be said about the findAllByUserName() method? (choose one)

A. it is not a valid Spring Data JPA repository method

B. the argument for @Query is a JPQL query

C. the interface is not a repository, because it is not annotated with @Repository

D. this code will not compile

Question 4: What is the @Value annotation used for ? (choose one)

A. to inject a scalar/literal value to be injected in a field

B. to read the value of a field

C. to inject a static value

Question 5: Spring Security provides means to prevent CSRF attacks. True or false?

A. False.

B. True.

Question 6: Which of the following is a type of proxy supported in Spring? (Choose two)

A.   CGLIB-based class proxy

B.   JDK-interface based proxy

C.   native Spring proxy

Question 7: What is REST? (choose one)

A.   a software design pattern

B.   a framework

C.   architecture style

Question 8: What is not true about Spring Boot?

A.   Spring Boot simplifies configuration, but complicates deployment

B.   Each release of Spring Boot provides a curated list of
     dependencies it supports

C.   Spring Boot is a collection of pre-configured sets of frameworks/
     technologies designed to reduce boilerplate configuration

Question 9: Spring does not support programatic transactions. Is this true?

A.   no

B.   yes

Question 10: Which of the following affirmations about @SpringBootTest are not
true? (choose two)

A.   @SpringBootTest enables usage of SpringBootContextLoader for
     creating the test context.

B.   enables automatic search for a class annotated with
     @SpringBootConfiguration to use as a configuration class
     for the test context.

C.   disables usage of nested configuration classes.

D.   does not provide support for starting a web server in a test context.

Question 11: Your application contains join points, pointcuts and advice. What are you using? (choose one)

A. Spring Data JPA

B. pring MVC

C. Spring AOP

Question 12: What is the purpose of the `HealthIndicator` interface? (choose one)

A. Spring beans of types that implement it provide custom health information

B. If a Spring endpoint is declared that implements this interface, it will override the `/health` endpoint.

Question 13: What can be done to declare an instant repository with Spring Data JPA? (choose all that apply)

A. extend the `Repository` interface

B. no need to extend an interface; just annotate the interface with @ `RepositoryDefinition`

C. for multiple methods out of the box extend `JpaRepository`

D. implement the `Repository` interface

Question 14: Which of the following annotations enables auto-configuration of the Spring Application Context, guessing the beans needed to build a Spring Boot application? (choose one)

A. `@SpringBootConfiguration`

B. `@ConfigurationPropertiesScan`

C. `@EnableAutoConfiguration`

Question 15: Which of the following affirmations is true about the `DispatcherServlet`? (choose one)

A. The `DispatcherServlet` is the front controller of a Spring Web application acting like a central point where URIs are received and matched to handlers.

B. The `DispatcherServlet` is the type of servlet Spring uses to handle static resources.

C. The `DispatcherServlet` is in charge of view rendering.

Question 16: What does REST stand for? (choose one)

A. Reliant Stable Transfer

B. Representational State Transfer

C. Reactive Stable Transfer

Question 17: We have the following bean declaration. What is the ID of the created bean? (choose one)

```
@Component
public class SimpleServiceImpl implements SimpleService {
}
```

A. `simpleServiceImpl`

B. `simpleService`

C. `SimpleServiceImpl`

Question 18: Why should a transaction be declared as `readOnly`? (choose all that apply)

A. Because this is mandatory with Hibernate.

B. Might provide some optimizations when a large set of data is read.

C. Because it may improve performance with Hibernate.

Question 19: In the `application.yml` configuration file of your Spring Boot application you find the following configuration snippet:

```
management:
 endpoint:
  health:
   show-details: always
```

What is the effect of this configuration? (choose one)

A. The /health endpoint is always exposed, regardless of security settings.

B. The /health endpoint exposes detailed content.

C. The /health endpoint exposes detailed content, regardless of security settings.

Question 20: What is an aspect in the context of a Spring application?(choose one)

A. a special type of bean

B. a class annotated with @Aspect containing advice methods

C. a special class saved in a file with the *.aj extension containing advice methods

Question 21: @SpringBootApplication is meta-annotated with ... (choose all that apply)

A. @Component

B. @ComponentScan

C. @SpringBootConfiguration

D. @EnableAutoConfiguration

E. @Controller

Question 22: Which of the following statements about declarative transactions is true? (choose all that apply)

A. @Transaction can be placed only at method level

B. @Transactional should be used on interfaces

C. @Transactional configurations at method level override @ Transactional configurations at the enclosing class level.

D. @Transactional is taken into consideration only when configured via @EnableTransactionManagement or <tx:annotation-driven ../>

Question 23: Given the following controller class containing a single handler method, which of the following URLs will be handled by that method?

```
@Controller
@RequestMapping("/persons")
public class PersonController {

    @GetMapping(value = "/{id:\\d*} ")
    public String show(@PathVariable(Long id, Model model) {
    ...
    }
}
```

    A. `http://localhost:8080/mvc-basic/persons/aa`

    B. `http://localhost:8080/mvc-basic/persons/105`

    C. `http://localhost:8080/mvc-basic/persons/?id=105`

    D. `http://localhost:8080/mvc-basic/persons?id=aa`

Question 24: When executing a query, `RowMapper` should be used when ... (choose one)

    A. ... the execution of the query is expected to return a single result.

    B. ... each row of the `ResultSet` maps to a domain object.

    C. ... when the `ResultSet` contains a single row with results from multiple tables.

Question 25: What is a bean factory post processor bean? (Choose two)

    A. an infrastructure bean that allows for custom modification of bean definitions

    B. an infrastructure bean of a type that implements `BeanFactoryPostProcessor`

    C. an infrastructure bean that allows for custom modification of beans

Question 26: To provide configuration for a Spring Boot application, you can use ... (choose one)

    A.   properties files

    B.   YAML files

    C.   environment variables

    D.   command-line arguments

    E.   all of the above

Question 27: What is the purpose of a `HttpMessageConverter<T>` (choose two)

    A.   `HttpMessageConverter<T>` implementations are used to negotiate content conversion in a HTTP communication in an MVC environment

    B.   `HttpMessageConverter<T>` implementations are used to transform representations into resources in a Spring application.

    C.   `HttpMessageConverter<T>` is a MVC infrastructure bean responsible for content negotiation.

Question 28: The following test class is designed to test handler methods in the `PersonController` using a mock web environment.

```
@SpringBootTest(webEnvironment =
    SpringBootTest.WebEnvironment.NONE)
class ApplicationWebTest {

    @Autowired
    PersonController personController;

    private MockMvc mockMvc;

    @BeforeEach
    void setup() {
        // ...
    }
...
}
```

Which of the following statements can be used to build a suitable MockMvc instance? (choose one)

A. `this.mockMvc = MockMvcBuilders.build();`

B. `this.mockMvc = MockMvcBuilders.webAppContextSetup().build();`

C. `this.mockMvc = MockMvcBuilders.standaloneSetup(this.personController).build();`

Question 29: Which of the following annotations can be used on a handler method? (choose all that apply)

A. `@RequestMapping`

B. `@Controller`

C. `@GetMapping`

D. `@ControllerAdvice`

E. `@DeleteMapping`

Question 30: What is the `@ContextConfiguration` used for? (choose one)

A. to load and configure a `TestApplicationContext` instance

B. to load and configure an `ApplicationContext` for integration testing

C. to inject beans used in unit testing

Question 31: What is the correct annotation to use on a test-managed transactional method for its results to be committed? (choose all that apply)

A. `@Rollback(false)`

B. `@NoRollback`

C. `@Commit`

Question 32: Which of the following is the default bean scope? (Choose one)

A. A.unique

B. single

C. singleton

D. prototype

Question 33: Choose one true affirmation about component scanning in the context of a Spring Boot application from the list below.

A. If no attribute is set relating to component scanning, by default the package where the class annotated with `@SpringBootApplication` is and its sub-packages will be scanned for bean annotations.

B. If no attribute is set relating to component scanning, by default the package where the class annotated with `@SpringBootApplication` is will be scanned for bean annotations.

C. To enable component scanning, the `basePackages` attribute must be set with the value of the desired packages.

Question 34: Spring Boot can auto-configure embedded H2, HSQL, and Derby databases. What do you need to provide to make this happen? (choose one)

A. You need to provide a connection URL.

B. You need only to include a build dependency to the embedded database that you want to use.

C. You need both listed previously.

Question 35: Which advice types can be used to try and catch exceptions? (choose two)

A. `after`

B. `after throwing`

C. `around`

D. `after returning`

Question 36: In a Spring Boot Web application, an embedded server is autoconfigured by default. Choose it from the list below.

A. Apache Tomcat

B. Jetty

C. Undertow

Question 37: What is the default rollback policy in transaction management?

A. Rollback for any Exception

B. Rollback for RuntimeException

C. Rollback for checked exceptions

D. Always commit

Question 38: In the `application.yml` configuration file of your Spring Boot application you find the following configuration snippet:

```
management:
server:
    port: 9091
```

What is the effect of this configuration? (choose one)

A. Actuator endpoints are accessible on port 9091.

B. The application is accessible on port 9091.

Question 39: When declaring URLs to intercept in a Spring security configuration class, does the order matter ? (choose one)

A. Yes, the most restrictive URL must be configured first, otherwise a more relaxed rule will apply and some URLs will be accessible to users that should not have access to them.

B. Yes, the most restrictive URL must be configured last, otherwise a more restrictive rule will apply and some URLs will be inaccessible to users that should have access to them.

C. No.

Question 40: What is component scanning? (choose one)

A. the container's search for classes annotated with `@Component`

B. a process of discovering beans in a Spring application

C. a process of bean discovery that is configured by default in Spring

Question 41: Spring Boot Actuator provides endpoints and infrastructure beans for ...? (choose all that apply)

    A.   monitoring Spring Boot Applications

    B.   monitoring both Spring Boot and Spring classic applications

    C.   managing Spring Boot Applications

    D.   auditing and metrics gathering for Spring Boot applications

Question 42: Does `JdbcTemplate` support execution of SQL native queries? (choose one)

    A.   yes

    B.   no

    C.   only if configured so

Question 43: Which annotation can be used to inject the Spring Boot Actuator port value in a field used in a Spring Boot class? (choose all that apply)

    A.   `@LocalServerPort`

    B.   `@Value("${local.management.port}")`

    C.   `@ActuatorPort`

Question 44: What is an application container? (choose one)

    A.   a driver used to read application configuration

    B.   any instance of a class that implements `ApplicationContainer`

    C.   any instance of type `ApplicationContext` that passes a dependency to a dependent object that will use it

Question 45: What is the default name of the spring security filter bean that gets applied to all requests in a Secured Spring web application? (choose one)

    A.   `springSecurityFilter`

    B.   `springSecurityFilterChain`

    C.   `delegatingFilterProxy`

Question 46: When should setter injection be used? (choose two)

  A.   when the created bean must support further reconfiguration

  B.   when creating an immutable bean that depends on another bean

  C.   when the type of bean being created does not support other types
       of injection (e.g.: legacy or third party code)

Question 47: Which of the following is true about the @WebMvcTest? (choose two)

  A.   It can be used together with @MockBean to mock dependencies
       required by controllers being tested.

  B.   It can be used together with @WithMockUser to test controllers that
       are part of an application secured with basic authentication.

  C.   It loads the full application context and configures MockMvc.

Question 48: The following configuration snippet is part of an application.yml file
used to configure a Spring Boot application.

```
server:
  port: 8081
  servlet:
    context-path: /boot
spring:
  datasource:
    url: jdbc:oracle:thin:@localhost:1521:xe
    username: sample
    password: sample
    driver-class-name: oracle.jdbc.OracleDriver
  jpa:
    generate-ddl: true
    hibernate:
      ddl-auto: create-drop
```

What are the effects of the previous configuration snippet? (choose all that apply)

  A.   a DataSource bean is declared of type OracleDataSource

  B.   the contents of the database are created when the application
       boots up and dropped when it shuts down

C. an embedded Tomcat instance will be started on port 8081

D. an embedded Jetty instance will be started on port 8081

E. the Spring Boot application will be accessible at `http://locahost:8081/boot`

Question 49: What is a pointcut?(choose all that apply)

A. a predicate used to identify join points

B. a parameter that every advice method must specify in its signature that provides access to the execution context

C. an expression to identify methods to which the advice applies to

Question 50: Which of the following statements is true about Inversion of Control? (choose one)

A. Inversion of control is a software design pattern related to Dependency Injection

B. Inversion of control is just another name for Dependency Injection

C. Inversion of control is a common characteristic of frameworks that facilitate injection of dependencies

Answers

1. A
2. D
3. B
4. A
5. B
6. A, B
7. C
8. A

9. A

10. C, D

11. C

12. A

13. A, B, C

14. C

15. A

16. B

17. A

18. B, C

19. B

20. B

21. B, C, D

22. C, D

23. B

24. B

25. A, B

26. E

27. A, B

28. C

29. A, C, E

30. A

31. A, C

32. C

33. A

34. B

35. B, C

36. A

37. B

38. A

39. A

40. B (A is not correct because it is incomplete, C is not correct because component scanning is not configured by default in Spring applications. The only valid answer is B, because it mentions exactly what component scanning is without touching other details about how it is configured or how ti is being done.)

41. A, C, D

42. A

43. A, B (When the Actuator port is not configured to be different then the application port @LocalServerPort can be used too.)

44. C

45. B

46. A, C (Using setter injection allows for the setter to be called explicitly later within the execution of the application, which allows for further customisation of the bean. That is why A is correct. B is not correct for the same reason, if a setter exists, it can be called later within the execution of the application and a different dependency can be injected, thus the dependant bean is not immutable. C is correct because if you are using classes from a third party library, that cannot be modified in any way and that declare only setters to provide dependencies, you have no choice but to declare your beans using setter-injection.)

47. A, B (Answer B is correct, tests with `@WithMockUser` and `@WebMvCTest` can be found in module `chapter07/boot-sec`. Answer C is not correct; the part that makes this answer incorrect is the *loads the full application context* that contradicts the Javadoc: *Using this annotation will disable full auto-configuration and instead apply only configuration relevant to MVC tests.*)

48. A, B, C, E

49. A, C

50. C (Inversion of control is not a design pattern. It is a design principle implemented by writing code according to dependency injection pattern, observer pattern, and the template method pattern. Thus A is not considered correct.)

Footnote

Here are a bunch of links that you might find useful while you are learning Spring.

- Apache Tomcat official site: `http://tomcat.apache.org/`

- MongoDB official site: `https://www.mongodb.com/`

- Gradle official manual: `https://docs.gradle.org/current/userguide/userguide.html`

- IntelliJ IDEA download page: `https://www.jetbrains.com/idea/download`

- Spring Projects Reference: `https://spring.io/docs/reference`

- Spring R2DBC Reference: `https://docs.spring.io/spring-data/r2dbc/docs/current-SNAPSHOT/reference/html/#reference`

- Docker official site: `https://www.docker.com/`

Also, keep your eyes on the official study guide contents that you can find on the official page of the exam: `https://pivotal.io/training/certification/spring-professional-certification`, because they tend to change at least once a year.

Index

A

AbstractR2dbcConfiguration, 950
AbstractRepo interface, 25
Abstract UML diagram, 502
AccessDeniedHandler, 747
@ActivateProfiles, 781
@After annotation, 215
After advice, 311, 312
afterProperties method, 120
@AfterReturning, 307
@AfterThrowing annotation, 309
After Throwing advice, 309, 310
@AliasFor annotation, 103, 104
Annotation-based configuration, 44
annotationDrivenTransactionManager(..)
    method, 379
AnotherComplexBean, 122
antMatcher(...) method, 637
AppApplicationTests class, 194
AppConvertersCfgTest class, 145
Application monitoring, 763, 764
application.properties file, 187
Around advice, 313, 315
aspectjweaver library, 320
Aspect-oriented programming (AOP)
    advice, 284
    AOP proxy, 285
    aspect, 278, 284
    class org.springframework.jdbc.core.
      JdbcTemplate, 281

code scattering, 279
code tangling and scattering, 282
conceptual schema, findById()
    method, 281
connection pooling, 281
cross-cutting concern, 277–281
JDBC repository method, 278, 279
join point, 284
pointcut, 285
Spring (*see* Spring AOP)
target method, 284
target object, 284
UML call diagram, JDBC method, 280
weaving, 284
Aspects, Spring Boot Application, 320
assertThrows(..) method, 218
AuthenticationEntryPoint, 742
Authentication-failure-url attribute, 623
Authorization server, 759
@Autowired annotation, 61, 67, 72, 157, 848
Autowiring/initialization
    annotations, 45, 161

B

basePackages attribute, 717
BasicAuthenticationEntryPoint, 742
BasicUserSettings interface, 92
@Bean annotation, 54, 59, 64, 120, 128,
    149, 165, 260
@Bean declarations, 100

991

K